Fortnite

The Ultimate Fortnite Battle Royale Guide
Including Tips, Tricks, and Strategies

Contents

Introduction

It's dangerous to go alone! Take this guide. It has all the hottest tricks and coolest tips from the world's best *Fortnite* players and streamers, such as Ninja, Dakotaz and TSM_Myth. Learn how to ramp rush and defend against it, discover how bloom, a secret targeting variable, makes hand cannon and hunting rifle miss in crucial moments, use the Claw Grip technique for seamless looting, learn how to shave off an extra ½ second when building on console, find out where the Supply Llamas drop and how to use C4 without blowing yourself up. Having read this guide, you'll gain the wisdom of the entire *Fortnite* community accumulated over thousands of hours of game time. How pumped are you?

Keep in mind that *Fortnite* is still a game under construction. Although the fundamentals are pretty much set in stone, there might be some tweaks to items and mechanics as they are removed or added without prior notice. In fact, as of this guide being written (March 2018) *Fortnite* devs released patch 3.3 that temporarily removed boogie bombs until an exploit that allowed a player to pick up infinite equipment was fixed, added Supply Llamas, replaced smoke bombs with C4 and apparently disabled "double shot" mechanic that allowed players to avoid reloading by quickly switching between weapons in their inventory. Despite this being a free-to-play video game, it's possible to sink in a significant amount of money on largely cosmetic upgrades, which you might regret later on in Early Access if developers decide to change one or all the things you liked at the start. With that out of the way, let's skydive right into the game.

Chapter 1 – Landing

As the match starts, the players are on Spawn Island where they are invulnerable and can test out all sorts of weapons and building designs until 100 players have joined the game. This is when the match starts, not when you land or when you find a weapon or when you start shooting at someone. You need to get focused and stay sharp throughout the entire game, not letting anything distract or upset you. The Spawn Island is where you warm up, get all cozy and find out if things are just the way they're supposed to be, including your settings and controls.

Up in the air, the Bus is then launched and flies in a straight line across the map with all the players inside, who can jump out after 10 seconds of flight. The flight path of the Bus is always determined randomly and here's where you have to decide on your landing spot and stick to your decision, since panicking at any point is a sure way to die in the most miserable way possible. A dozen *Fortnite* players will give you a dozen contradictory advice on where to land, but the best way for a newbie to start is on the outskirts of the map, learning the spot and becoming comfortable with the terrain, looting, building and movement.

First time, eh? As you jump you'll start skydiving and the glider will automatically open once you reach 50 height units above the ground, so try aiming for valleys, ocean, ravines and canyons to skydive as long as possible and land as soon as possible – landing quickly means finding a weapon quickly. The maximum distance a glider can go is the length of a single grid square on the map. If you still find yourself lagging behind everyone else and can't figure out why, write down your flight time in each match and just focus on trimming it down until you've nailed it. If you can record and review your in-game footage, that's even better.

Where should I land?

Skipping all over the map works, but you'll want to learn a couple of landing spots close together really well until you can navigate them blindfolded. If the final circle ends up being at one of those spots, you'll essentially have home field advantage compared to players that simply land wherever every single match. Once you've mastered an area, land a bit closer to the center areas and again explore the zone to your heart's content. Have in mind that most players will jump out during the first half of the flight, land somewhere close to the Bus trail, and move towards the circle. Take that into account to figure out where the danger lies. Places with many buildings between the final circle and the Bus' flight path tend to become bottlenecks with intense firefights.

The best strategy is aiming to land in the square adjacent to the one you jumped in, so look downwards when gliding to accelerate and point up to go longer distances. Swing the camera around to look through windows for chests and loot as you're gliding past buildings. Some *Fortnite* pros argue that the best way to learn the game is by jumping straight into one of the center areas of the map (Pleasant Park or Tilted Towers) to go through trial by fire but that can lead to a very frustrating and disheartening experience as a wild pro appears, mows you down alongside a dozen other newbies, sweeps up the loot and just skips off into the distance. The choice is ultimately up to you.

Chapter 2 – Storm

About 100 seconds after the Bus is launched the Storm begins to gather on the edges of the map, but it won't be closing in just yet. You have exactly 3 minutes and 20 seconds before the Storm starts to shrink, so hoard as much loot as you can and head towards the safe zone at your own pace. You should start eyeing the highest ground possible within the safe circle and prepare yourself for the end game, during which you should have a fort on the high ground, assault rifle (AR) with at least 300 ammo, a shotgun, heavy weapon (sniper, rocket or grenade launcher),and at least 200 wood and healing items. Each of these gives you a little bit of an advantage, so try to get them all. The map will show a white circle as the safe zone before the Storm starts shrinking again, a blue line to the Storm front and a white line showing a direct route to the safe zone.

You can't outrun the storm. If you get caught in it you will take constant damage and, as the match goes on and the Storm closes in, it will do more and more damage, but don't be afraid of it. Knowing how long it takes you to traverse any amount of terrain is crucial and if you can find a launchpad, put it to good use by gliding towards the safe zone from a high spot. In any case, the Storm will shrink seven times total and during the Storm shrinking for the first time it will do 1 damage per second to your HP. It takes about 45 seconds to travel across a single square on the map and about 60 seconds to cross it diagonally. Practice moving as fast as you can with as few resources spent and gradually add in looting, shooting and building until it's all one smooth motion.

Not the Storm, aaargh, not the STORM!

It's essential that you remain calm and don't panic when the Storm starts to chip away at your HP because you can recover as long as you have healing items. Remember, it's only the last HP that matters. Even staying behind in the Storm has its benefits, but it's mostly a risk-reward type of calculation that you should be doing on the fly. Do you have solid weapons or should you try going for one more chest? Can you farm one last tree before the Storm gets you? Can you reach that medkit you dropped way back there?

Try to understand how a typical *Fortnite* player thinks and anticipate their moves: they will usually underestimate Storm's speed, panic when the purple daze engulfs them and dash along the white line straight to the safe zone, so make an ambush on high ground and greet stragglers with several well placed shots to get some easy kills and juicy loot. Of course, this means getting to the safe zone well before others and knowing from which way they'll come, which leads us to another big area where skill matters: movement.

Chapter 3 – Movement

A skip, a hop and you're already at the Supply Drop! Wait, you're standing right beneath it? SPLAT! Dying is a surefire way to improve in *Fortnite,* but only if you adopt an attitude of a curious explorer, one that never gets tired and that wants to be pushed to his absolute limits every step of the way. There are three goals whenever you make any kind of movement in *Fortnite*: to scout the surroundings, to get yourself in a more advantageous position and to avoid being shot. These three key skills sound so easy and straightforward, but they are actually so complicated that you should seriously consider dedicating as many matches as it takes to just hone each of them to perfection. Scouting the surroundings is done by using what's known as "shoulder peek." Because the camera in *Fortnite* is constantly looking over the right shoulder of your character, you can take a peek around a right corner without being seen or exposing yourself to enemy shots, but not around a left corner. If you decide to engage using "peek shots,"; you have the upper hand and can simply do a few steps to the right, shoot and do a few steps to the left to get back in the cover. You always want to position yourself to be the one who decides when the fight starts and ends. If you can do that, the firefight is pretty much already over.

Scouting also includes being able to constantly scan the environment even while on the move and mid-jump. Practice jumping, swinging your camera and turning 180 degrees mid-air without stopping and while switching weapons, as this will be used in the later portions of this guide. You want to be in total control of your camera and make it work for you.

Getting yourself in a more advantageous position means learning the environment and how characters move through it to the point where you can "read" your opponent and know exactly where he's going and what he's about to do. Thanks to this gut instinct you'll be able to counteract your opponent *before* they've done what they plan on doing. For example, once you've been through the same building enough times, you'll learn the most common hiding/ambush spots and if an enemy runs inside you'll pretty much know where they are and where they're heading. Once you get it going it'll feel like you're hacking and your enemies might actually accuse you of hacking. When that happens, you've completed this lesson.

Finally, you want to learn how to avoid firefights and being shot. There is no dishonor in running away from a fight you're disadvantaged in and if that's what it takes to survive – do it. You never want to engage in a fight you're not likely to win or allow the enemy to take free shots at you. As you become more and more experienced (meaning, as you die more and more) you'll develop your own movement patterns based on deaths you had that will look like quirks to everyone else watching you. As you play around, you'll notice that you can jump off of stacks of tires to get launched about one wall section height up into the air, but if you run into the tires and press JUMP at the moment you touch them, you'll be launched twice as high. Fire hydrants can be used to jump off of, too, but only when shot.

These are not only normal but are actually a great way to have this kind of erratic, unpredictable movement pattern that makes life miserable for enemy snipers. For example, one pro player might constantly do squats with their character while drinking shield potions to minimize the chances of getting a random headshot out of nowhere, even behind cover. This isn't a skill that can be learned through reading, only through playing, and even if any particular dodging advice would get popular it would be easily exploited by players looking for free kills and easy loot from your hapless body.

Chapter 4 – Looting

Everything you've learned in the "Movement" section gets translated to your looting speed, which determines how much loot you'll get and how soon you can use it. Seconds shaved off of scouring through chests and grabbing floor loot on the fly mean you'll always get the chance to fire sooner, engage in a firefight under favorable conditions and get more free shots off in a situation where you all started off without a weapon. The perfect looting technique accomplishes three goals: finds loot quickly, loots in relative safety and gets the needed items quickly.

To find loot quickly, learn the chest spawn points and optimize your route through the area. If nobody disturbs you within the first 5 minutes it's very likely you'll find game-ending gear right then and there and get to choose the terms of engagement heading towards the safe zone. Each zone in the *Fortnite* world has a certain number of predetermined chest spawn points while floor loot only spawns inside and on top of buildings. When you're near a chest it will give out a blingy call with the direction you're facing, determining how loud you'll hear the sound. So if you hear a chest, try looking around and the volume of its call will point you to where it's at, even through walls and obstacles. You can also find inconspicuous ammo boxes, which come in two varieties: small and large.

To loot safely, always try to stay in cover when picking up loot. If loot is found out in the open, try to build cover around yourself before looting. In general, you shouldn't rush to grab the loot that just dropped from an enemy you killed, even though it acts like a physical object and slides down hills, ramps and inclines. It can be really hard to ignore juicy loot slipping through your fingers and beckoning you from yonder, but be patient and bide your time until it's safe to come out. Once you do, pick up whatever you determine is better than your current gear and move on. You can even turn this kind of situation into an ambush by killing an opponent in the open and waiting for someone you just heard to come and start picking it up.

Finally, to get the things you want into your hands quickly, always hold your pickaxe to avoid losing a weapon to something you don't want on the ground and walk over certain items to automatically pick them up. Bring up the inventory screen (hold ALT on PC) and drop items you don't need to share them with your friends. You will be expected to make snap judgments until you've mastered the skill of looting to the point where you instinctively know what you'll need without dwelling on it. You should always have the same setup in your inventory and reserve each slot for a specific item so you develop a muscle memory and instantly reach for what you need in and between firefights.

Which zones have the best loot?

Each zone has its own advantages, varying in chest numbers, floor loot, building material and safety. For example, Moisty Mire can have three chests, trees give a lot of wood and you'll get a good choice of weapons. In more active areas around the center of the map (Tilted Towers, Pleasant Park, Loot Lake) you want to be shooting people as a way to loot the place but landing in one of the fringe locations (Moisty Mire, Lonely Lodge) generally means having to go through the entire area yourself.

In Tilted Towers, go for the roofs (such as the one on the big red building) to grab a weapon quickly, get an overview of the entire area and decide on your next move. It's generally a hectic place so take it easy and don't rush unless you're going for some kind of world record. There's not a lot of materials there except pallets so if you play defensively you'll burn through them and die miserably to aggressive players who will run over you. Keep in mind that chests don't take into account where you find them, so even the ones at the very edge of the map can have the best stuff. The reverse is true as well and not even cleaning the place up guarantees the best loot, as seen in the screenshot below.

Chests and ammo boxes will take damage and can be destroyed, with the former having 200 and the latter 120 HP, and will also get annihilated if they're up in the air and their supporting structure section gets taken out underneath them. Use your world awareness skills and constantly pay attention: if there's a weapon on the ground but no ammo around it, a player has already been through the loot and gotten the best items. Also, if you see someone about to loot a chest right in front of you but you haven't got a weapon, wait until they've opened it and grab the loot before they do.

Claw Grip looting technique

Being able to loot quickly and efficiently for console players means using the Claw Grip technique. Using the example of a Sony controller, you will normally hold it with your thumbs on the left and right stick, index fingers on L1 and R1 and your middle fingers on L2 and R2. If you come to the point where you have to loot something, the most intuitive way of looting would be to let go of the right stick and use your right thumb to press SQUARE to pick up the loot. This would mean losing control of your camera and briefly staring at the same spot while who knows what happens behind your back. If you consider that you'll be looting at least 20 times per match and lose camera control for 1-2 seconds each time you're not using Claw Grip; that means at least 20-40 seconds of time when you're blind to the world around you. With the Claw Grip technique, you would keep your right thumb on the right stick while using your right index finger to tap SQUARE and TRIANGLE if need be without losing sight of your surroundings. It looks and feels like your finger became a claw, hence the name.

Chest loot drop chances

All of the following drop rates are current as of 23 March 2018. All golden chests will always drop a weapon, some ammo for that weapon type, a consumable and some resources. Though they look identical, they can drop any weapon in the game except handguns, pump and tactical shotguns, which have to be found as floor loot. Drop chances for consumables and resources stay the same regardless of what weapon is in the chest; it's only the weapon type and rarity that changes.

31.7% of all golden chests will drop an Assault Rifle (AR), with the subtypes being as follows:

- 51.8% for common
- 25.9% for uncommon
- 10.4% for rare
- 5.2% for scoped rare
- 3.9% for epic SCAR
- 1.9% for scoped epic
- 1% for legendary SCAR

21.2% of all golden chests will drop a Burst AR, with the following subtype chances:

- 64.5% for common
- 25.8% for uncommon
- 9.7% for rare

19% of all golden chests will drop an SMG, with the rarities distributed:

- 48% for suppressed common
- 24% for tactical uncommon
- 12.8% for suppressed uncommon
- 8% for tactical rare
- 4% for tactical epic
- 3.2% for suppressed rare

8.5% of all golden chests will have a sniper, with distributions:

- 39.4% for hunting rifle uncommon
- 24.6% for bolt action rare
- 14.8% for hunting rifle rare
- 13.8% for semi-auto epic
- 4.9% for bolt action epic
- 1.5% for semi-auto legendary

- 1% for bolt action legendary

4.2% of all golden chests will have a suppressed handgun, with rarities:

- 83.3% for epic
- 16.7% for legendary

4.2% of all golden chests will have a crossbow, which can be:

- 80% for rare
- 20% for epic

3.4% of all golden chests will have a hand cannon, which can spawn as:

- 80% for epic
- 20% for legendary

3.2% of all golden chests will have a rocket launcher (grenade launcher spawns from the same chest), with rarity chances:

- 57.1% for grenade launcher rare
- 28.6% for rocket launcher rare
- 7.6% for grenade launcher epic
- 3.8% for rocker launcher epic
- 1.9% for grenade launcher legendary
- 1% for rocket launcher legendary

2.4% of all golden chests will spawn a minigun, which comes in two types:

- 66.7% for epic
- 33.3% for legendary

Finally, 2.1% of all golden chests will drop a slug shotgun (aka heavy shotgun), with subtypes:

- 75.2% for epic
- 24.8% for legendary

Now that you know the weapon drop rates from golden chests, let's take a step back and analyze them. 71.9% of all golden chests will drop an AR, burst AR or SMG. These weapons are ideal for short to medium range combat, which tells us this is how the *Fortnite* devs intended the combat to unfold.

The ammo dropped from a chest is always for the weapon that dropped, and can come as: 12 light bullets (SMG, suppressed handgun, minigun); 10 medium bullets (assault auto, assault); 6 heavy bullets (sniper, hand cannon) or 2 rockets. Consumables have the following drop rarities and quantities:

- 21.2% for 1x shield potion
- 17.7% for 5x bandage
- 14.1% for 3x grenade
- 14.1% for 3x small shield potion
- 7.1% for 1x med kit
- 7.1% for 4x remote explosives
- 5.7% for 1x slurp juice
- 4.2% for 1x boogie bomb
- 4.2% for 3x impulse grenade
- 2.4% for 1x chug jug
- 2.1% for 1x bush

Note that there is a combined 68.2% chance to get some sort of healing item (shields or HP) from a golden chest, meaning it's always worth it to look for one nearby if you're in need of a medic. When it comes to resources, they always drop as a single stack of 30, and can be:

- 47.6% for wood
- 35.7% for stone
- 16.7% for metal

83.3% of resources will be wood or stone, meaning that only 1-in-7 golden chests will provide metal. To find out your chances of several things happening at once, multiply the chances. For example, there is a 0.324% (32.4 divided by 100) chance you'll get a legendary SCAR from any given golden chest, or roughly 1-in-310.

Floor loot drop chances

Now let's examine drop rates for floor loot:

- 21% for nothing to spawn
- 14.2% for ammo, one stack (28.6% for light bullets, 28.6% for medium bullets, 22.9% for 5x shells, 14.3% for heavy bullets, 5.7% for rockets)
- 11.4% for consumables, one stack (28.7% for bandage, 20.5% for shield potion, 16.4% for grenade, 16.4% for small shield potion, 8.2% for med kit, 6.6% for slurp juice, 3.3% for smoke grenade)
- 8.5% for resources, one stack (47.6% for wood, 35.7% for stone, 16.7% for metal)
- 7.4% for handgun (70.7% for common pistol, 17.7% for uncommon pistol, 7.1% for rare pistol, 3.5 for epic suppressed pistol, 1.1% for legendary suppressed pistol)
- 7.1% for shotgun (71.4% for uncommon tactical shotgun, 21.4% for rare tactical shotgun, 7.1% for epic tactical shotgun)
- 7.1% for pump shotgun (75.2% for common pump shotgun, 24.8% for uncommon pump shotgun)
- 5.7% for assault auto rifle (same rarities as for the AR chest)
- 5.1% for SMG (same rarities as for the SMG chest)
- 4% for revolver (71.4% for common revolver, 21.4% for rare revolver, 7.1% for rare revolver)
- 3.4% for trap (81.8% for damage trap, 9.1% for campfire and 9.1% for launch pad)
- 2.8% for assault rifle (same rarities as for the burst AR chest)
- 1.1% for sniper (same rarities as for the sniper chest)
- 0.6% for crossbow (same rarities as for the crossbow chest)
- 0.3% for hand cannon (same rarities as for the hand cannon chest)

As you can see, there's about a 55% chance that any given floor loot spawn will be non-combat (not be a weapon or a trap). Any of these rarities is subject to further tweaking sometime in the future, but seeing how consistently they've been present in the game up to this point, it's safe to say they are pretty much what you can expect throughout the game's lifetime.

Ammo boxes

Small ammo boxes come in two varieties that are visually different but drop the exact same loot:,

- 27.3% for 5x shells
- 27.3% for 12x light bullets
- 22.7% for 10x medium bullets
- 13.6% for 6x heavy bullets
- 9.1% for 2x rockets

Large ammo boxes drop the following:

- 28.6% for 10x medium bullets
- 21.4% for 6x heavy bullets
- 21.4% for 2x rockets
- 14.3% for 5x shells
- 14.3% for 12x light bullets

Note how the large ammo boxes have nearly double the chance of dropping rockets, but almost half the chance of dropping shells.

Supply Drops

Supply Drops contain a weapon, two stacks of ammo for it, two consumables, two stacks of resources and a single trap. Consumables, resources and traps have the same rarity distribution as the chest/floor loot, but weapons have the following drop rates:

- 28.6% for rocket (50% legendary rocket launcher, 50% legendary grenade launcher)
- 28.6% for sniper (50% for bolt action legendary sniper, 50% for semi-auto legendary sniper)
- 14.3% for legendary SCAR
- 14.3% for legendary minigun

- 7.1% for legendary hand cannon
- 7.1% for legendary heavy shotgun

Shooting Supply Drops a couple of times marks them and lets you know if they're popped and where they are. However, you can pop them completely to make them go down faster. If you see a player rushing to get to it, make an ambush. Supply Drops spawn every 180 seconds, give or take 30 seconds. That's not an approximation – before every match a random number between 150-210 is chosen and that's the number of seconds a Supply Drops appears during that game, but it will always take 60 seconds to come down.

Supply Llamas

Patch 3.3 added Supply Llamas, which are essentially Supply Drops on steroids. Their bright pink, teal, blue and purple coloring makes them stand out against the game's mostly green backdrop, so you should be able to spot one from a mile away. However, they're extremely rare and only 3 spawn each match on random locations anywhere on the map. The drops from a Supply Llama are always the same and absolutely bonkers: 500 of each building material, 10 stacks of each ammo category, 3 traps and 3 consumables, but no weapon. Llamas can spawn in weird locations, such as on top of trees and fences, but they are sadly opened like a chest rather than smashed with a pickaxe.

There's a lot of speculation on whether Llamas really appear at random or in certain spots around the map, such as near the 2nd Storm's safe circle. The official confirmation is that the spawn spots are truly random so don't fret about going Llama hunting, just play as you normally do, and when you spot one make a 1x1 fort around it before looting for extra protection.

Chapter 5 – Building

Though *Fortnite* shares so many things with *PUBG* to the point where players have jokingly dubbed it *FUBG*, the building mechanic is unique in the first person shooter genre, in the video game market and probably even in the history of gaming. Looking at *Fortnite* players' amazing building skills is probably what got you impressed in the first place and made you try out the game, isn't it? Go on, you can admit it. The possibility of building awesome forts to shoot out from is the exact reason why so many people have flocked to *Fortnite*, which makes it all the more tragic that they suck at it.

The most common mistake a newbie does in *Fortnite* is getting swept up in highfaluting looting and shooting to the point where he doesn't even build. Being able to create cover out of nowhere will save your skin, so you need to build fast and you need to build correctly. 1x1 base (four walls immediately around you and a ramp below you) is the most effective building method in the game, so practice how fast you can build it to gain a height advantage on everyone around and adjust whatever it takes to shave off every fraction of a second. Examine the screenshot below to see Dakotaz building a 1x1 and doing peek shots to keep himself in cover while shooting down the enemy structure as it's being built.

Use everything you know and have to put yourself in an advantageous position and keep your enemies from doing the same. If you're playing on PC and your mouse has extra buttons, assign them to different building sections and practice laying them all down as needed until you get that smooth, flawless motion of building while jumping, running and looking around. Keep in mind, things that are in the process of being built take extra damage from enemy fire, so shoot them as you see them coming up. Of course, this depends on how many materials your opponent has and how his stack compares to your ammo reserves, so the building process itself becomes this subtle measuring of risk and reward compared to what the situation is.

Just like cat and mouse

Note that enemies will try to anticipate your movement based on the shape of the fort you've built, so if you make a 1x1 they will expect you to do peek shots, which will make your head pop up at the top of the ramp and they'll happily snipe it off your shoulders. Instead of that you might edit a side of the 1x1, sneak out without using a door, since it produces a sound, and flank them. Because the most common tactic against a 1x1 base is to build a ramp outside it and jump in with a shotgun, you should also consider building a roof on top if you estimate there's a danger of being rushed. When you're happy with your progress and how quickly you can build, test out different locations, for example by landing and building on top of trees or in midair.

Combine all the things you've learned in previous sections and practice landing, moving quickly while scouting the surroundings, looting and building a 1x1 together. When you get stuck or frustrated simply trace your steps back to the point where your game plan falls apart and fortify it (pun intended). It's really all about the practice until you can do things smoothly, precisely and with ease, no matter your platform and play experience. If you want to get good at something in *Fortnite*, get good at building.

Wood vs brick vs metal

Each building material has up and downsides, but structure sections cost 10 material no matter what they're built out of. Metal builds the slowest but also has the most HP (400), wood builds the fastest but has the least HP (200), while brick is somewhere in the middle both with regards to HP (300) and building speed. Wood is hands down the most valuable material in combat and you can expect to constantly use it both defensively and offensively simply because it's found everywhere, builds super quickly and always blocks at least one shot from a shotgun. Frankly speaking, wood HP is probably a little too much and it's a surprise *Fortnite* devs still haven't nerfed it by at least 20%, so exploit it like there's no tomorrow.

Brick is an OK material, used mostly out of combat, when you lack wood or near end game when you're out of metal but not for much else. Metal is the most valuable for late game when you can expect everyone to be wielding explosives since it can survive one rocket or grenade hit, so try to shield your metal sections with wood and take down enemy metal sections as they're being built

Building cover

The potential of the building mechanic to provide you cover at any given moment is what equalizes all weapons, allowing you to win, or at the very least have a fighting chance when you can't find a strong weapon. Speaking of cover, consider making multiple layers if you have the mats for it, especially when you're healing up. Over time and as you're flexing your building muscle you will discover the nifty little tricks that help your structure sections stay up more than expected. For example, when you're building stairs beneath you and want to quickly change direction, build a wall to the desired side and keep building. It's simpler, more flexible and provides cover compared to building a floor in the same spot.

Ramps can be built so a portion of them is inside the terrain, so if you have to climb a mountain don't make a gigantic ramp that spans the entire map, is visible from outer space and makes you vulnerable

to having the ground knocked out from beneath you, but approach the mountain as much as you can and you'll spare material, keep the ramp less visible and have a safer landing spot if someone shoots at you and hits the ramp. Keep in mind that a building section placed inside terrain becomes impossible to edit. You can also build inside houses and use all sorts of tricks to funnel enemies to a kill zone, such as blocking a stairwell to corner the enemy.

Editing

Editing is an extremely useful skill that can help you easily outplay your opponents and does not cost resources. You can edit your own structure as it's being built or after and even if you don't want to confirm the edit you'll be able to see through the section, giving you a sort of wallhack. Doors edited into the wall are always closed and have to be opened, so avoid making them whenever possible. A nonsensical edit will make the remaining tiles in the layout glow red and, if you confirm it, will destroy the building section, so you can use it instead of a pickaxe.

If you're in a squad and your teammates suddenly decide to mess with you and block you in, remember that you can edit your teammates' buildings without wasting time or ammo. Try to always have control of the building you're fighting in and avoid stepping inside the enemy fort since you can be easily blindsided. Instead, destroy it with explosives, build an even bigger fort, or just back away and snipe from afar. The roof section is rarely used, though it does have its purposes, namely to stop grenades from being lobbed down your throat when you're in 1x1. You can also build a roof section on a flat surface to strafe onto and then drop a wall in front to give yourself a peek shot possibility when sniping. One rarely mentioned capability of the roofs is to build them over downed teammates that need cover or over items you plan on picking up later on. No matter what your preferred edits are, strive to make them as efficient as possible out of combat, but when in combat don't spare anything and think about making multiple layers of protection and editing for maximum mobility and cover.

Ramp rushing

Ramp rushing is the bread and butter of aggressive building strategies. The idea is that high ground gives you a greater chance to score headshots, your structure (the ramp) gives you cover and you get to close in on an opponent, controlling when and how you'll engage. Ramp rushing works in solo, duo and squad modes, making it the best overall strategy in *Fortnite*. It's really simple: move towards your opponent and build a ramp, climb over it, jump towards him with your weapon out and shoot. Now, the best case scenario is when the opponent stays on ground level, either because he doesn't know how to build or because he doesn't have mats. Versus a skilled opponent, you'll have to break a sweat and soften him up with a couple of peek shots from the top of the ramp before you can descend like a hawk with a shotgun,

Once you've done some damage, he'll go into panic mode and try to run away to patch up, so that's when you want to get into kiss range and pump his face full of lead for quick and easy kills and loot. When ramp rushing became the most popular strategy in the game, players quickly came up with a counter to it: just shoot down the ramp before it's built.

Countering ramp rushes

As said previously, wood structure sections are incredibly strong and can withstand one full point blank shotgun blast as they're being built, making shotgun a poor weapon of choice against ramp rushers. Instead, you can try using an SMG, which does tons of damage, has a solid fire rate and a hefty clip to take down the ramps as they're being put down. Remember, you don't have to necessarily kill the opponent right away – if you can make him waste his resources more than you waste yours that's as good as scoring a headshot. So, avoid conflict, take a favorable position and just annoy the living daylights out of him, at least until late game when you can afford to just spray and pray.

Ramp rushers eventually evolved and came up with an even more aggressive strategy: build two ramps next to one another and rush. In this way even if one ramp gets shot down the ramp rushers count on being quick enough to just hop onto the adjacent one and carry on. You see the problem with this strat? *It burns through wood twice as fast as the normal ramp rushing.* Another favorite strategy of ramp rushers is to do a normal ramp rush and build a wall in front of it to shield it from incoming fire. Again, twice the wood spent. If you see that, just disengage and don't fire a single shot while moving into cover. Since structures can't be reclaimed, the rusher just wasted at least 20 wood on nothing.

When you're being ramp rushed, it's essential that you don't panic, don't freeze and don't just run in a straight line. Avoid the firefight whenever you're disadvantaged, frustrate your opponent, let him run out of resources and when he finally loses control of his emotions because ramp rushing didn't work, then you set up a trap and strike back. If you're trying to run away and there's no cover to be found, don't backpedal while building walls - it's too slow and doesn't offer any protection. Instead, start running away from the opponent, jump, turn 180 degrees, place a wall (or roof) between you, then turn another 180 before you land and keep running in the same direction. Remember when we talked about this exact maneuver in the "Movement" section? Practice it until you start dreaming it and that's when you'll know you've mastered the art of defense against ramp rushing.

Building faster on console

If you're playing *Fortnite* on console, there's no doubt that you'll be handicapped when it comes to building. A pro player playing on PC, such as Ninja, can place 11 building sections in 5 seconds flat during a live gunfight, while even the fastest console player takes at least a second more to do the same. There are two reasons why console players are having trouble, the first being that the two most used structure sections (wall and stairs) are actually not placed next to one another, meaning that a console player has to constantly tap shoulder buttons to switch from one to the other if he's using the Combat Pro button layout. You did switch the layout to Combat Pro, didn't you?

The second problem is that the game spazzes out if the shoulder buttons are tapped too quickly, causing a bit of jerkiness and input lag that are an absolute nightmare for anyone trying to play competitively. PC players don't have the same problem because they can hotkey each section and place it instantly but console players have to learn a brand new set of skills. Recording and slowing down the footage can reveal the console input lag with the previous section still being displayed for up to 4 frames, sometimes causing you to get stuck on the wrong section and build that instead. The screenshot below shows exactly what's going on, with the outline showing stairs while the selection box is still on the wall section.

The workaround for this issue is a bit clunky and has to be done before each match, preferably on the Spawn Island. Bring up the roof section and place the blueprint to a spot near you. Edit the two tiles of the roof section closest to you and you'll get a custom piece that will actually be identical in stats, build speed and material cost to stairs, except that it's rotated away from you so confirm the edit and rotate it twice. Now instead of going over the floor section to reach the stairs each time, you can simply move the selection to the left and access the "stairs" immediately. This method saves you a shoulder tap, which comes out to about 0.5 a second per tap. *Fortnite* patch 3.0.0 smoothened out the interface jerkiness and it shouldn't be as obvious right now, but this little workaround still has its uses and is worth getting used to. In any case, building different structures efficiently comes down to having a lot of practice and a strong muscle memory, where you can build whatever is needed without consciously thinking about it.

Edit patterns for all sections

The following will list edit patterns for all four structure sections, showing you what can be built out of them. To make things easier to read and remember, we'll number the tiles in a section with 1-4 (1-9 for walls) starting from the top left tile and going left to right, top to bottom and tell you which ones to edit (remove) to get a certain structure. For example, "window" asks you to just remove "5," which is the center tile. Some of these patterns can be shifted and/or flipped and/or rotated across the wall section, but that's best left for you to discover.

Wall section can be edited into the following shapes:

- Window (5)
- Side windows (4, 6)
- Door (5, 8)
- Window door (4, 6, 9)
- Half-wall door (1, 2, 3, 6, 9)
- Arch (5, 7, 8, 9)
- Half-arch (5, 6, 8, 9)
- Triangle (2, 3, 6)
- Half-wall (1, 2, 3)
- Low wall (1, 2, 3, 4, 5, 6)
- Partial low wall (1, 2, 3, 4, 5, 6, 7)
- Partial half-wall (1, 2, 3, 4, 5, 7, 8)
- Column (1, 2, 4, 5, 7, 8)

A floor section has only four tiles and can be edited into:

- Corner floor (2)
- Half-floor (1, 3)
- Corner balcony (1, 2, 3)
- Bridge (1, 4)

Roof section has four tiles as well, giving us the following shapes:

- One-quarter pyramid (1)
- Inverted one-quarter pyramid (1, 2, 3)
- Tent (1, 4)
- Ramp (1, 2)

Stairs are the trickiest to edit since they have eight tiles going around the center one, which you can't edit. In simplest terms, editing stairs means tracing a path you want the stairs to take, starting from a corner. There are three stairs variations:

- Half-stairs (9, 6, 3)
- L-stairs (7, 8, 9, 6, 3)
- U-stairs (7, 8, 9, 6, 3, 2, 1)

Knocking down enemy forts

Most weapons in the game have a different amount of damage they do to buildings for balancing reasons, except crossbow, boogie bomb and impulse grenade that do 0 to buildings. For example, pickaxe always does 10 damage to player, 50 to environment and 25 to player buildings (double if you hit the critical hit marker). The three best castle crushers are the grenade and rocket launcher (all rarities), which do 375 damage flat to any building section they hit, and hand grenades with a whopping 393 damage. Since metal walls have 400 HP, they're the only ones that can take the full brunt of the explosion of these three and still remain standing, wood and brick get annihilated on contact. A pistol is also slightly better at knocking down player structures than an AR, as is a suppressed SMG compared to a tactical SMG. Keep in mind that grenades from the grenade launcher can be bounced off of structures you've built, so experiment with building a ramp and testing angles to become a pinball master that leaves salty *Fortnite* players in his wake. When you get accused of hacking is when you're doing it right.

Unlike *Minecraft*, a structure in *Fortnite* can be knocked down if the supporting sections are destroyed. This means that as long as the fort has at least some contact with the ground it will stay up, no matter how large, but as soon as that's gone it will start crumbling apart, with the sections disappearing in the same order in which they were built. Good players won't allow their fort to have a single point of impact; everyone else can get taken out by a single brick of C4.

Chapter 6 – Weapons

There is no ultimate weapon in *Fortnite* and that's by design. Even if it levels enemy forts with a single shot, a weapon such as a rocket launcher performs poorly in kiss range and you can often find yourself missing 6-7 shots without doing a single point of damage. For each situation and encounter, there is a specific weapon that performs better than all the others and it's actually your job to test them all and see which one fits your playstyle best. Hitting enemies from angles they don't expect using weapons they never saw coming is the hallmark of a pro player and any attempt you make at mastering all weapons alongside your other skills brings you closer to becoming a player to be respected and feared.

To become a good *Fortnite* player you'll merely have to avoid making mistakes, such as the situation with using rocket launcher in melee range described above, but becoming a master *Fortnite* player means developing a killer instinct, a way to instinctively react at any given moment and to always make the right choice, no matter which weapons you happen to have. We talked about this with regards to landing, Storm, movement, looting and building, so apply your experiences from those areas on weapons and toy with them, because some *Fortnite* weapons really do hit with the ferocious intensity of a squeaky toy and make you wonder, "Why is this in the game?"

Assault rifle

27-36 body damage per bullet. Everyone keeps an AR on them at all times and you should too. Perfect for medium range firefights, your AR is the butter that you spread all over the wooden walls, which kind of do look like slices of bread. Keep an AR in the same inventory slot every game to develop a reflex of switching to it whenever you're in a squeeze. Your long range weapon might go in slot 1, AR in 2 and your close range weapon in slot 3. This way you can be holding your AR at all times and be only 1 click/tap/flick away from a close- or long-range weapon depending on what you need. For example, explosives go in slot 4, and meds go in slot 5 so you don't accidentally start healing yourself when you wanted to shoot. When using ARs, don't hold down fire, but rather tap it for better accuracy.

Shotguns

67-74 body damage per blast for tactical shotgun, 90-95 for pump shotgun, 147-154 for heavy shotgun. Tactical shotgun is the undisputed king of kiss-range combat, being able to do 100 body damage per second (DPS) and down a full HP opponent in one second flat. For comparison, pump shotgun has 33% less DPS (66) but is still a formidable weapon. True, shotguns are the only weapons in the game that have damage falloff, meaning that you'll do less damage after a certain distance between you and the target, but they are just too good to pass up.

SMG

14-19 body damage per bullet. An SMG is great due to its large magazine size. The large spread makes it less useful in combat but good for knocking down enemy structures.

Minigun

17 body damage per bullet. Fires 12 bullets per second. Minigun is great for destroying structures and pressuring enemies while your squadmates push, so give it to a support role in your squad. Appearing in epic and legendary rarities, a minigun requires no reload and can fire as many bullets as you are currently carrying as one enormous hail of metal.

Bolt action sniper rifle

105-116 body damage. Has 3 seconds reload time, decreasing slightly with better quality.

Hunting rifle

86-90 body damage. Poor man's version of bolt action sniper rifle.

Handguns

23-78 body damage. Handguns (hand cannon, pistol, revolver, suppressed pistol) are a varied bunch and have something to suit everyone's taste. Be warned when using the hand cannon, its short range and unpredictable bloom (check the "Shooting" chapter) make it a typical noob trap: you fall in love with it and keep using it even though it's inferior to other, plainer options.

Crossbow

75-79 body damage. Does not produce noise and has unlimited bolts. Slow reload time and inability to damage cover make it a poor weapon of choice in the late stages of the match.

Semi-auto sniper rifle

63-66 body damage. Solid clip size but avoid spraying your shots without having a clear line of sight.

Grenade launcher

100-110 body damage. Great for destroying forts, poor in direct combat.

Rocket launcher

110-121 body damage. An exploit that still hasn't been patched allows teammates to jump on your rockets and ride them until they explode.

Impulse grenade

Impulse grenade is one of those weapons that seem like a placeholder or an inside joke. Usually too situational to waste an inventory slot on beyond the early stages of the match, you'll sometimes find yourself pinned down behind cover as the Storm steadily bites at your heels. You take a deep breath and the world slows down around you. In a brief moment of lucidity, your mind goes over a thousand scenarios in the span of a single second and your hands sift through what's left in your inventory. You notice impulse grenades and things finally snap into place – that's it!

So, you throw one beneath your own feet, since they do no damage you're not immediately hurt, but the shockwave sends you flying up sky-high. You misjudge the landing point and end up flying off a cliff to your death as everyone else points and laughs. Well, next time try having your opponent do the same. It will take you a lot of patience and dying to finally get to the point where you can sneak up on people and catapult them into the stratosphere, but boy is it satisfying. Look at him go, weeee!

On a serious note, an impulse grenade under your feet with a shotgun equipped gives a great opportunity for juicy headshots from an angle nobody expects, but that's about it with regards to its utility. Be careful with tossing impulse grenades around your teammates, as they too can be launched in the air and killed if landing in the wrong spot. You do not want to wield impulse grenades against armed enemies, so just shoot them in the head rather than going for the meme kill that might work once in 50 tries.

Boogie bomb

Well, it's come to this, we're fighting back using the power of disco. When thrown, boogie bomb explodes almost immediately in a brilliant flash of color that makes anyone hit by its explosion, including you and your teammates, dance uncontrollably for 5 seconds. A large disco ball appears on top of the screen of the player that's been affected and the character model starts flailing his arms around. The radius on boogie bomb is quite difficult to determine, meaning you'll hit yourself constantly, and its effects wear off after the target has taken any sort of damage. You can't build or shoot when hit by a boogie bomb, but you can jump, crouch and move albeit at a speed slower than walking. If you want to toy with people using boogie bombs, box them in a roofed 1x1 after you've hit them with it to make their lives miserable, and then set a trap inside. Other than that, you really shouldn't expect to see one except when thrown by accident, where it can lose you the game if you are in the final stages.

A more interesting use for boogie bomb was being able to pick unlimited equipment, ignoring the inventory slot limitation. The trick was to hit yourself with a boogie bomb and pick whatever you wanted during the dance animation. The item wouldn't show up in your inventory but it was still there, just like anything else you picked up afterward. As you cycled through items you could access and normally use or throw out the glitched items, with weapons being able to kill just like any other. When the glitch went viral on Reddit, the *Fortnite* devs promptly removed the boogie bomb from the game until further notice.

Bush

A deeply rooted thought sprouts in your head, it branches out and becomes an idea, "Can I win a match without a single kill?" Oh, yes you can and with style. Bushes can be found in chests, they are meme-tier legendaries that can still win you the game if you simply sneak around and, well, pretend to be a bush until everyone else has died. Try not to hold a pickaxe while hidden in a bush, that thing is so huge that it's like a "SHOOT ME I AM HERE" billboard in your hands. Since the bush texture is attached to the torso of your character model, crouch for best camouflage but also try to think and act like a bush and blend in by hanging out with your bushy friends. Bush wins have led to a good deal of paranoia amongst players, who are starting to frantically shoot down every single bush within their sight simply to deny Bush Wookies the chance to win a match.

Bushes are one-time use only and destroyed the instant they take any damage, which includes Storm and fall damage, so keep moving and stay nimble. You can shoot while wearing a bush but if you ADS your scope will be blocked by a little bit of green to remind you what's going on. Regarding natural bushes that spawn around the map, you can still hide in them except that they have different sizes and some may expose your head more than is healthy. Bushes are tons of fun for those who want something different and have to challenge themselves at every single turn. The best weapon for it is the crossbow as you're perfectly silent.

Smoke grenades

Smoke grenades were utility items removed with the 3.3 patch that also added C4 to the game. They were useful in certain situations, except that they were plagued by the same problem boogie bombs and impulse grenades have – you had to drop actual gear that helps you kill people and survive their shots for something that kind of works at times. When they were in the game, smoke grenades were extremely popular in teams where you wanted to grief your teammate, such as luring them in a room, throwing a smoke inside and closing the doors. Some more tactically inclined players wish for them to make a speedy return, but unless we get a special slot for grenades it's no use having them around as visual clutter on our screens.

Spike trap

If you go back and read every second letter in the first word of each paragraph in the "Landing" chapter, you'll discover a secret message – SPIKE! Just like that, you've fallen for my trap card, Kaiba. There's a lesson to be learned here, as we're all driven by incredibly powerful curiosity to find out what's going to happen, just like you flipped all the way back to the start of this guide to find out the secret message without knowing what to expect. Use this curiosity against people as you trap the bejesus out of the *Fortnite* world and score easy kills. A trap does 125 damage and triggers as soon as an enemy enters the floor cell it's targeting, but can miss if set on a wall. As seen in the screenshot below, a player entering a corner to recover shields was almost impaled by a trap but was luckily just out of range as he swerved out of the trigger cell and into a nearby safe one.

Spike traps can't hit you or your teammates and take about 3 seconds after placement to activate, so again you shouldn't use them in immediate combat. Drop an item or a weapon (especially a high rarity one) you don't plan to use in the middle of a room and drop some ammo for it nearby so it looks like a legitimate floor loot spawn point. Set up a spike trap, preferably at an angle that can't be seen from the direction you expect the enemy to come from, such as beneath a window that you expect an enemy to drop down from. It's hard to see, can't be avoided, and guarantees a kill. You should also use traps in your forts late game due to how many people ramp rush and jump into other people's forts without looking. You can shoot enemy traps down but keep in mind they replace the structure section where they're built and taking them out also means taking out the wall, ceiling or floor they were on.

Launchpad

Launchpads have to be placed on a floor you built. They give you some altitude so you can glide further, can be used as long as the match lasts or until they're destroyed by anyone and can't be moved once placed. If you try jumping off of a launchpad while shooting at it or destroying its supporting floor section, the game will glitch out and you'll die a hilarious death. They can be used both offensively, to reach a better position, and defensively, to get you out of a tricky situation, so use them wisely. Though they do no damage they do belong to the trap category, which technically makes them weapons.

Cozy campfire

Cozy Campfire is a floor trap that heals about 2 HP per second for a total of 50 HP over its lifetime to each of the players around it, including enemies. A campfire will heal through your structure sections if within range, so you can make a 1x1 fort with a ramp inside and place the campfire underneath so it heals you as you're peeking over the top of the ramp. Another great use for it is being able to heal your downed squadmate(s) as you're fighting off the enemies. Campfire must be placed on a flat floor surface.

Using a Cozy Campfire on Spawn Island used to glitch out your character, causing him to have a bugged HP bar. This should have been patched by now but if it happens to you try falling from a height to take some fall damage and/or drink a slurp juice.

C4

As the old saying goes, "Give a man fire and he'll stay warm for the rest of the day but place C4 beneath him to set him on fire and he'll stay toasty for the rest of his life." C4 is a little explosive surprise meant for the sneaky ones among us who just love pranking people. Found as a stack of 4, each C4 brick does 70 damage to players in a small blast radius and destroys any player-built structure section immediately around. C4 is tossed in a very low arc with the fire button, though you can hold it to get the grenade arc, and triggered with the ADS one. You need 3 in a tight cluster to kill someone with full HP and shields but the blast from just one has been known to take out multiple people at once.

C4 is not a weapon for direct confrontation or anti-ramp rushing because there's a slight delay before a brick can be detonated, but the funny part is you can actually use it when *you* are ramp rushing someone: simply drop a couple down enemy forts and kablamo! C4 doesn't produce noise when it's set but it does blink with a blue light every couple seconds and the ones thrown by your opponent blink red. They will stick to the surface they're thrown at.

The blast radius is quite modest: if you set it on the floor in the middle of a tile it will take out 1x1 wood, brick or metal fort around it, they will destroy trees but won't damage the default buildings. Note how the player in the screenshot above accidentally threw a C4 in front of him instead of triggering the one in the distance because he confused the fire and ADS buttons, so pay attention or that can happen to you as well. Throwing C4 on wavy terrain might not blow up or even damage nearby player walls, since it seems the C4 brick needs to have an unobstructed line of sight to an entire structure section to affect it. C4 bricks can be shot by you or the enemy; they will explode and might even kill you. You can detonate the ones you placed from anywhere on the map, you can place as many as you can find, and they are detonated in the order placed, with a small delay between each detonation. Ready for some *Bomberman* action? That's right, indulge in some evil cackling. Setting them up close together will create a chain reaction as they will blow one another up, so watch out. 10 is the carry limit.

Chapter 7 – Shooting

You've come a long way to become a master of landing, moving, building and weapons. Now it's time to steady your hands, clear out your mind and visualize the bullet hitting the enemy right between the eyes. Your very first firefight is where you'll realize just how *Fortnite* devs intended combat to develop, allowing things such as instakills on players through brutal headshots. This simply means that you always go for the headshot and you always go for the instakill. Anything else is a suboptimal play. As a counter to the fast metagame and the overpowering presence of shotguns you want to shield up, heal up and cover up.

Double shot

The exploit that was present for quite some time in *Fortnite* is the "double shot." The idea is that by carrying two weapons of the single-shot variety in your inventory (shotguns in particular but works with sniper rifles as well), shooting with one of them and then quickly switching over to the other and shooting with that as well, switching back to the first and shooting etc., you get a faster fire rate than if you had just shot normally with either one. Other competitive shooters (such as *Quake Live*) won't allow the player to switch over to another weapon until the first one has finished its firing cooldown, so whether the double shot mechanic is intended by the *Fortnite* devs is unknown. The current status of this exploit is unclear, as it can be seen used on present streams but some players report that they're unable to perform it

Snipers, bullet drops and leading tricks

If shotguns are kings in *Fortnite*, then snipers are gods. With perfect accuracy and extreme damage values, a typical sniper will reach over the valley and touch your enemy right where it hurts the most. The drawback of sniper rifles is that they have bullet travel and bullet drop, meaning a moving target becomes a hassle to hit. There are two types of snipers: bolt action and semi-auto. Bolt action sniper rifles come in rare, epic and legendary quality, while semi-autos come only as epic and legendary. Higher quality sniper rifles deal slightly more damage, reload slightly faster and have a bit more impact.

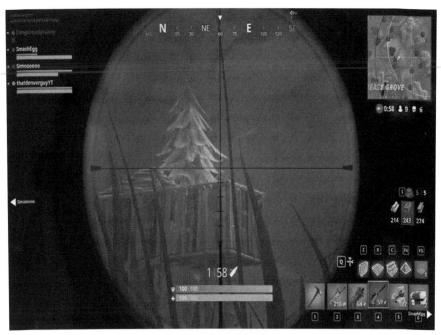

Either one of the three bolt action rifles will do over 100 damage, killing a player without shields outright, but have only one bullet in the magazine, meaning you need a solid cover between shots or have enough confidence that you'll take the enemy out with the first shot.

A headshot from a bolt action sniper rifle will instakill an enemy with full shields. Epic semi-auto sniper rifle deals 63 damage per shot (66 for legendary) and both hold 10 shots per magazine, meaning it will instakill the enemy only if you headshot them and they have 50 shields or less.

Use your sniper scope to rangefind and determine the bullet drop at a glance. Your sniper scope has four small and four large notches below the crosshairs, which you can use to estimate bullet drop at a distance. Length of one grid square on the map is 250m and if the height of a wall section neatly fits within the center of the crosshairs and the first big vertical notch of your scope, you're 250m away. If the player model fits between the crosshairs and the first notch, it's again 250m. If you're about 250m away from an enemy, place the first large vertical notch on top of his head to score a headshot.

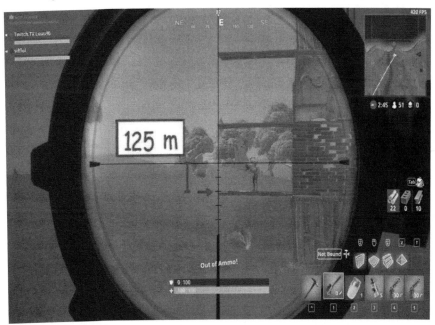

If you're about half that distance away (125m), check if the wall section/character model fits between the crosshairs and 2 big vertical notches of your scope. If so, align the first small notch with the player's head to score a headshot. Of course, you'll have trouble doing this kind of trigger trigonometry in the midst of a gunfight, but the main idea is to take out as much guesswork as possible from your sniper slaughter and finely tune your gut feeling for where to aim through practice.

Another major component of sniping is being able to hit enemies on the move by leading the crosshairs in front of them. The easiest targets are the ones standing still but an experienced opponent will move erratically and in a zig-zag pattern, especially if they know you're taking shots at them with a sniper rifle. This applies to you as well, so if you're sniping for a longer period of time, randomly crouch, jump or move a step to the left or right to minimize the chances of someone instakilling you with a sniper rifle.

Pre-aiming a sniper

A useful trick that can save your life is pre-aiming your sniper rifle. Bring up your scope and then strafe as you're going around corners – if the enemy happens to be there you can immediately shoot to kill. You can pre-aim when you can see your opponent but he can't see you, especially through gaps in wooden and brick walls. When you're crouched behind wooden or brick wall, line up your sights with the enemy position, stand up, shoot, quickly crouch down, move a few steps to the either side and repeat.

Pre-aiming is a very safe sniping strategy, that is, unless your enemy has explosives to blow up your cover. Metal walls don't have these gaps unless they're damaged, so hit them with your pickaxe but don't damage them too much. Firing a bullet while no-scoping makes it fly the same trajectory as it normally would, but doesn't really work unless you're willing to waste hours for that one Youtube highlight. Bolt action rifles are perfect for solo play and instakill headshots but semi-autos work better in squads and provide precious suppressive fire. Build platforms on unusual positions to quickly change your sniping angle and try shooting people through windows, they never see it coming.

How bloom can ruin your day

Bloom is a hotly debated mechanic that means a bullet shot from a gun can go anywhere within the circle covering the outer lines of the aiming reticle. In some cases and with certain weapons, bloom does not seem to be working properly, causing you to miss completely when aiming straight at the opponent in kiss range. Recoil and bloom are related concepts introduced to first-person shooters as a way to make gunfights more realistic and unpredictable but not quite the same: recoil will mostly move your gun upwards but bloom will send out your shots all around the reticle. When combined with panicky inexperienced players, the two often lead to the "spray and pray" behavior of weapons seen in many first-person shooter video games. Becoming competitive or rather just having an enjoyable experience playing *Fortnite* means understanding bloom and controlling for it whenever possible. To illustrate bloom, we'll take a look at a kiss-range gunfight.

In the screenshot above, the player we're following is using a hand cannon and aiming squarely at the opponent's left shoulder while both are strafing to the same side, trying to compensate for bloom. You can see that the reticle is very tight and the bullet should land somewhere on the opponent's chest no matter how you interpret bloom. However, as soon as he shoots the bullet misses completely, way outside of anything the reticle indicated.

You can actually see the miss, it's the tiny white speck beneath the opponent's gun, at a 45 degree angle down and left from the center of the crosshairs. As you can clearly see, bloom behaved erratically and caused a complete miss way outside the aiming reticle lines when it was meant to hit. *Fortnite* pros deal with these situations by not getting themselves in them to begin with, meaning they avoid hand cannon and strafe-shooting whenever possible. Some weapons simply aren't meant to be used, and hand cannon is definitely not something you want to be relying on in kiss-range combat whenever you have an alternative. In another example of failed hit detection caused by bloom, a player is aiming with a hunting rifle through an open doorway while his teammate is scouring a barn far out in the distance, as depicted by the red mark on the minimap.

An opponent runs into the open doorway and this seems like shooting fish in the barrel, but bloom still hasn't given its say. Aiming squarely at the opponent and with the reticle almost completely together, he takes the shot.

The bullet misses completely. Just like with the hand cannon screenshot above, the bullet goes to the down and left of the crosshairs, going somewhere above the opponent's right knee.

Observe the in-game clock and note how quickly all of this happened – within the span of a single second – which might lead to you just ignoring it when it happens in the heat of combat or, if you do notice it and try to talk about erratic bloom on *Fortnite* community forums, being dismissed as a salty fidgety noob. Bloom affects AR weapons in a similar fashion, it's just that the effect isn't as noticeable and their rate of fire is much faster, meaning that you're more likely to score at least a couple hits with a burst. As explained in the "Gamer etiquette" chapter, it's simply how the game works, so there's no reason to get upset about it.

Rapid twitch tracking

To deal with bloom when it comes to burst weapons, we should probably talk about general ways to hold your mouse and aim. Trying to keep your crosshairs on a moving target as you're shooting with a burst weapon is called "tracking." The most sensible and relaxed approach is to simply keep following your opponent and shooting at him when it seems like you've got a good shot. However, a smart opponent will try to swerve around you and jump, which combined with you always following his trajectory, recoil and bloom, means you'll simply pepper the spots he used to be, not the spots he's in right now. Worse yet is that standing still slightly increases your chances of hitting him but makes you a sitting duck, which is something a smart opponent will know how to exploit.

A better tracking technique is called "rapid twitch tracking" and is used by pros in *Fortnite* and other first-person shooters. It requires you to use constant tiny jerky movements with your crosshair as you're tracking the opponent the best you can. With this technique, bloom and recoil actually help you cover more of the opponent's path, providing a lot better results and higher hit ratio but it does require that you grip your mouse tightly. When it comes to holding your mouse, you should adapt to whatever your circumstances are, but note that the arms should be resting and the weight distributed evenly whenever possible to avoid unnecessary strain. This means to avoid leaning on your elbow but instead resting your mouse hand on the small round bone jutting out of your palm right above the wrist and opposite your thumb, called "pisiform."

Bloom is unlikely to ever be removed from *Fortnite*, even though the game is still in Early Access and all game mechanics and items are subject to radical change. This is an ironic consequence of rapid growth and success of a video game, since there is so much money at stake that game developers don't really want to mess with a game once it's taken off and risk removing well known mechanics, even if they're unintuitive and lead to degenerate gameplay. In a way it makes sense that bloom has to be in the game, as otherwise everyone would just camp from their fort and score headshots across the map.

With bloom, ARs can't function as snipers at long range and players are forced to close in to one another using building mechanics, movement, terrain and natural cover. Bloom is a balancing mechanic introduced to level off the playing field between pros and noobs, making the gameplay a bit more unpredictable, though it would be nice if the *Fortnite* devs acknowledged the problems and revealed the actual process going on behind the scenes so that players knew if their missed shot that should have landed is intended or not. Until then, understand how the weapon accuracy modifiers work and use them to your advantage.

Weapon accuracy modifiers

There are two actions that worsen your accuracy: sprinting and jumping/falling and three that improve it: crouching, standing still and aiming down sights (ADS). Each weapon has a slightly different formula for accuracy and benefits from different things so let's take a look at how they compare.

Suppressed and tactical SMG, pump shotgun, tactical shotgun, hand cannon, pistol, revolver and suppressed pistol are 7-30% more accurate with ADS than standing still, though with ordinary SMG there is no difference between ADS and standing still or even crouching. AR, burst AR, SCAR and minigun are 10% more accurate when standing still compared to ADS. Grenade launcher always has perfect accuracy no matter what you do and rocket launcher has a 20% boost to accuracy when standing still. Every higher quality weapon will have about 5% better accuracy than the common one while scoped weapons have zero spread when aiming down sights. Hunting rifle has a curious accuracy rating for ADS, namely it increases the chance of a successful shot to 95%, which explains the doorway screenshot we've examined previously. The devs seem to be aware that hunting rifle has some issues since *Fortnite* patch notes list it as a fixed bug, but whether it's been completely corrected remains to be seen. That's exactly the problem with bloom and lack of transparency – nobody really knows if a wayward shot is a bug, a glitch or a feature.

One interesting fact about weapon accuracy is that sprinting is in general worse than jumping/falling across all weapons. This explains why pro *Fortnite* players tend to jump at their opponent while shooting with a tactical shotgun – jumping actually provides about 5% more accurate shots than sprinting, closes you in better, gives you height advantage and makes headshots more likely. Every single thing a *Fortnite* pro does has a purpose, you just have to find out what it is.

Chapter 8 – Harvesting

You need as much cover as you can get, you build cover out of materials and you've got a pickaxe in a world filled with breakables that drop materials. Sounds logical what comes next, doesn't it? Chopping down trees to get wood seems like the most logical thing to do, but you can be wasting your time without even knowing it. There is no relation between how the object looks and how many resources it drops. For example, trees behind Retail Row give 20-25 wood, but go for the big pine trees and you'll be getting 50-60 wood per tree, netting you 1k wood in a minute or two of farming. You will typically have 10 times more wood than brick, so use wood for climbing over things and save stronger materials for late game.

Jump farming

When there's nobody around, get your pickaxe out, jump and hit things as you're going past them, switching to your weapon immediately after and before the pickaxe swing animation finishes so you don't lose running speed. If you don't do any other material collection, you can expect around 200 wood and 50 brick while doing this trick and still being able to optimize your looting route.

A marker will appear on the object you're harvesting - if you can hit it with your pickaxe you'll harvest twice as fast and gain double resources. If you harvest an object while standing next to it as closely as possible, the harvest marker won't move all that much and you can harvest everything without moving your camera. Never be stationary when harvesting, always throw glances behind your shoulder when harvesting or circle around the object you're harvesting. Breaking trees has a visible animation that can be seen from afar, so chop them down until they almost break and move on.

Harvest wooden pallets found indoors and on flatbed trucks for a lot of lumber without any risk. Break down wooden furniture inside houses, especially at the start of the game since you're protected. Cabbage plants and wooden fences drop some wood too, so grab whatever you can get. The amount of material gotten from certain sources is constantly being tweaked by the game developers, sometimes leading to nonsensical situations where a bathroom trashcan gives more wood than a small tree. In some locations

(Tilted Towers) you'll quickly run out of wood and find yourself having to smash buildings to get brick.

Cars and semis give the most metal, but some vehicles will start to blare a car alarm when you hit them, telling everyone exactly where you are and what you're doing. The pros harvest metal by picking it up from dead noobs who painstakingly harvested it. Other objects make a loud sound as you're harvesting them, masking what the opponents do. Stop once in a while and listen or all your resources will go to a sneaky opponent.

Chapter 9 – Combat

Most combat in *Fortnite* is done at medium to long range, meaning SMGs, ARs, shotguns and sniper rifles are what you want to get as soon as possible. But, you should aim to eventually become proficient with all weapons and use them with equal ease so don't give up if all you've got is a pistol or revolver. A headshot will typically do 200-250% damage compared to what the weapon normally does, so you always want to aim for the head and make yourself a cover that lets you hide your own noggin.

When you spot an opponent, look at the compass at the top and alert your squadmates by saying, "Rocket at 55" or "Sniper at 261." Within a team, you want to have different roles so you can focus on one task at all times. However, if you and your team get bolt action rifles, you can use them together and it's pretty much game over for everyone else. There is no matchmaker ranking (MMR) that would equalize squads based on skill when you're being paired up with other people in random squads; it's all completely random. Coordinate with your teammates, either through Discord or Teamspeak, and drop down pins on the map to agree where you're headed to next. In *Fortnite* squad modes those who communicate better have much greater chances to make it out alive.

Watch for signs of fighting or enemy presence. Leaving an obvious trail behind you invites your enemies to follow you, which includes stairs built, chests looted and objects harvested. People don't pay attention to this kind of thing to the point where you can safely draw a straight line through the doors opened and structures built right to the safe zone and know exactly where they are. If you have to drop something, tuck it in somewhere where it's difficult to see from a distance and close the doors behind you or set up a trap.

If you see an enemy in a fort but he hasn't spotted you, don't just blindly rush headfirst to your death. Wait until he starts building and then push him using the exact same material he is. His sounds of building will mask yours and you'll get a jump on him with his blueprint out in his hands. SMG is your disposable gun; you'll always find ammo for it and it's great at knocking down enemy structures.

All skins have the same hitbox but some skins (such as Dark Voyager) seem to have a larger helmet texture that gives people a bigger target. The same skin has an orange glow that was supposedly visible through smoke grenade cover and the pulsing orange bands can be distracting but it rocks with the rocket riding emote.

If your teammate dies straight away, leave the game and search again, but if it's late game then it's your duty to go Rambo and kill them all yourself. If you get a grenade launcher from a drop, you can roll over teams that don't have one. It's great at applying constant pressure and destroying the enemy fort at the same time. Don't glide directly for the gun you want to get; instead go a bit to the side to bait your opponents into thinking you'll move on, then quickly circle back, land, get the weapon and shoot the enemy just as he's landing right in front of you.

Never go into other player's building, they can set a tall tower with traps on top and a launchpad at the bottom that launches you into them. Just shoot at it from the outside, which is why having explosives is a must. They are great for just setting the opponent in panic mode where they tend to run out into the open and expose themselves. Even grenades will work well, since many people who build 1x1 bases or elaborate forts of other kinds leave an exposed roof at the very top, making it trivial to lob an explosive into it. The range and arc on grenades is huge, keep experimenting until you get the feel for them. When fighting an enemy with a high 1x1 base, shoot at the lowest level walls to knock down the entire thing and possibly kill the enemy with fall damage. Wood structure survives one shotgun blast while it's being built, unlike brick and metal, great for pushing the opponent.

Find a gun you feel comfortable with and just keep practicing with it. There's a lot to be learned about each weapon, so stick to one of them until you've found whatever works best for you, at least in the beginning. Tactical shotguns of higher quality dominate the game both at kiss and medium range, so you'll eventually want to learn how to handle one to instadown people but for a newbie any weapon is good enough to help him gain confidence and killer reflexes. The key idea is consistency. Playing in large teams is not recommended for newbies, who might get disoriented and overwhelmed by all the action and stress. Instead, go for Duo with a really good player to serve as your coach.

Enemies killed in Loot Lake drop their loot beneath the water texture, making it very difficult to know what they've dropped and whether it's worth getting. Crouch and look up slightly, which will bring your camera beneath the water texture and show you the loot. If you're isolated and your teammates are below 30 HP, you can have them jump off of a high position and then revive them to give them slight healing. Use the exact same weapon layout for each game to groove that muscle memory.

Retail Row has a tree that you can climb on and stay fairly hidden, sniping people as they pass near you. A ramp three blocks high means you won't take fall damage, but fourth step deals you 17 damage if you fall from there. Dropping from 5 blocks high deals 43 damage. If you get up too high, jump down and build a floor, ramp or even roof below you to land safely. Fall damage always ignores shields. Pay attention to weekly challenges and consider that many people will try completing them. You can set up so many ambushes and just keep piling on kills near key challenge points. Though this strategy may not win you matches, it's great as a way to gain confidence and practice your skills.

Resurrection

When you're downed, your HP bar will go red and start ticking down from 100 at a rate of 1 HP per second. When it reaches 0, you're dead. During this time you can only crawl around and can't build, shoot or use any items. Your teammates can resurrect you by standing still and holding the resurrect button for 10 seconds, during which time your HP drain is paused. If they let go of the button, the resurrect countdown resets and they have to do it all over again. Accidentally letting go during resurrect animation is something that happens to pro players too, so don't fret if that happens to you. When you are resurrected you start with 30 HP. Keep in mind that revival sound can be heard.

Healing

Bandages drop all the time, but they are the worst healing item due to how little they heal and how vulnerable they make you. Taking 3.5 seconds to apply, one bandage will heal you 15 HP up to 75. Share them with teammates whenever they need one and ideally have one of you carry all the bandages to save up on inventory slots. The most common healing combo you should go for is small shield potions and medkits: potions are gulped in two seconds flat and will help you survive chip damage whereas medkits will heal you back to full after an intense firefight.

Small shield potions (also called "minis") will give you 25 points of shields but can't raise it higher than 50. Slurp juice will regenerate 1 HP and 1 shields per second for 25 seconds up to 100 both but isn't all that good due to how slowly it acts. Chug jug takes a whole 15 seconds to consume, but grants full shields and full HP. Healing items arranged from best to worst are: chug jug, shield potion, small shield potion, med kit, slurp juice, bandages. Save the best for the final stages of the game and use the worst ones first. A regular shield potion gives 50 shields and can recharge them to 100.

Keep your HP and shields topped up at all times, though it might sometimes seem like you're wasting items. You might be tempted to save medkits and Shield potions for when you can get 100% value out of them, but don't you dare skimp on using resources that might put you ahead. It can be the right call to use a medkit to heal yourself for 1 HP from 99 to 100 when you and one other guy are the last ones remaining since that one HP might be the difference between you staying alive and dying on the spot. Think about it this way: whatever you use is one less item an enemy that kills you will get, and once the game is over the items remaining don't matter anyway.

Can you tie a match?

When it comes down to playing solo and having only one guy against you, it can literally come down to fractions of a second. If you both shoot at one another at the exact same time, whoever gets hit (and killed) first loses, with no other damage being applicable past that point. The *Fortnite* servers update player information 20 times a second, so it's not very likely that both players get killed at the exact same time, but if that does happen the one with the lower ping is considered the winner. People have actually tried tying a match by surviving to the very final Storm circle, building a floor section high up in the air, standing on it and destroying it so they fall at the exact same time, but a tie never occurred and the winner seemed to have always been the one with the lower ping, regardless of who was shown as touching the ground first.

Chapter 10 – Settings

Colorblind mode

Color blindness is a genetic disorder that makes the person unable to distinguish between certain color combinations and might be much more common than anyone ever suspected. In 2015, the entire web went into an uproar over a white/gold dress that some saw as black/blue, accidentally revealing just how many people seem to be having color blindness. Since it's not a critical condition, many colorblind people go through their lives just fine and without even realizing it, but this can manifest in *Fortnite* as difficulty seeing objects, items and character models. Luckily, *Fortnite* devs got you colored, I mean covered. The screenshot below shows six most common types of color blindness, each in its own circle.

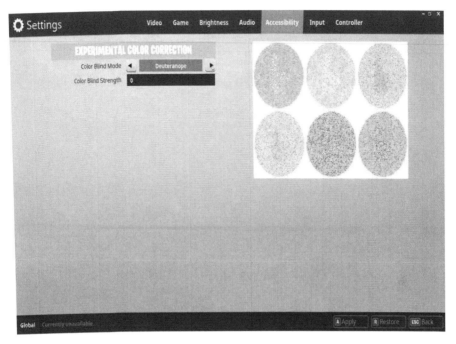

If you can see the silhouette in all six (spoilers: it's a llama), then you're fine, but you might still want to tinker with these settings if you're having trouble with things blending in the background.

Video settings

The goal of optimizing your video settings is to have as many frames-per-second (FPS) as possible. Use fullscreen rather than windowed or borderless windowed to maximize FPS and set the game's resolution to your monitor's native one. Set "Frame rate limit" to unlimited. The visual quality of graphics should really be secondary to performance but you want to be able to spot the opponent from as far away as possible, which largely depends on your hardware.

"View distance" taxes hardware the most and ideally you want it on epic, but if your machine can't handle that, lower it until you've found what gives you the best performance. On lower view distance settings you'll get a noticeable pop-in of smaller items, which can be distracting. "Shadows" should be set to off as they're purely cosmetic and act as a distraction most of the time. "Anti-aliasing" (AA) is a graphic trick that makes texture edges appear less jagged and shouldn't have any impact on game's performance, so choose whatever bothers you the least. The below screenshot shows Ninja's settings.

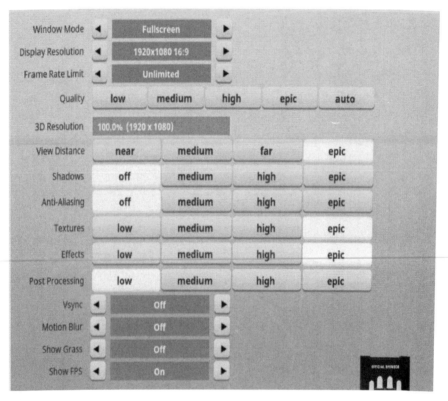

"Textures" determines how much detail is on objects within *Fortnite* game world. You should jump in a game and start from the lowest setting, observing how the world changes until you've lowered it to as low as you can tolerate. "Effects" are fancy animations, such as bubbles and trails, left behind by players and objects in the world. For example, on "epic" setting the water shimmers extra nicely but there is no combat situation that will help you in. So, down to the lowest setting effects go too.

"Post-processing" is another setting that helps graphical fidelity, adding more color to everything around you, which usually ends up making enemies blend into the background; lower it to minimize blurriness. This will make the picture darker, but you simply turn up the brightness to a medium value that works both during in-game day and night. The main idea is to find such a combination of video settings that strains you the least.

Sound

Use headphones for best sound control. You don't have to have a microphone if you're playing in a squad, but just do what you're told, drop map pins when everyone else does and you'll get along just fine.

Controller layout

As mentioned before, use Combat Pro as your button layout. It isn't the original controller button layout but makes you build much faster and sets bumpers for choosing which structure section to build. Toggle "reset building choice" to ON, otherwise the game will remember what you last built and use that rather than defaulting at the wall, which is the most useful in a cinch. Again, Ninja's settings.

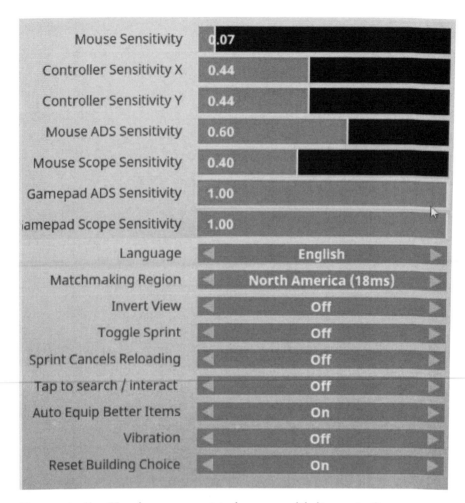

Mouse Sensitivity	0.07
Controller Sensitivity X	0.44
Controller Sensitivity Y	0.44
Mouse ADS Sensitivity	0.60
Mouse Scope Sensitivity	0.40
Gamepad ADS Sensitivity	1.00
Gamepad Scope Sensitivity	1.00
Language	◄ English ►
Matchmaking Region	◄ North America (18ms) ►
Invert View	◄ Off ►
Toggle Sprint	◄ Off ►
Sprint Cancels Reloading	◄ Off ►
Tap to search / interact	◄ Off ►
Auto Equip Better Items	◄ On ►
Vibration	◄ Off ►
Reset Building Choice	◄ On ►

For controller X axis, you want to have sensitivity up to 9 so you can turn around faster. If you're feeling uncomfortable with 9, lower it to 5-6 and slowly increase up. Because there's no quick turnaround button, the faster you can react when being shot at from behind the more likely it is you'll put up a wall and survive. Going to 10 sensitivity isn't recommended because you won't be able to register your shots properly. Eventually you want to end on 8 or 9 and slightly tweak based on how confident you are.

Streamer mode

Streamer mode hides the name of the person that kills you to discourage stream sniping; it doesn't stop the other person from knowing where you are, but it eliminates the bragging rights, which are pretty much the only incentive there is for stream sniping.

Mobile version

Right now, *Fortnite* is invite-only on mobile and only on iOS. If you do manage to get in and find yourself barely hitting anything despite aim assist, try putting the shoot button top right and the ADS button top left. This unfortunately only applies to huge devices, such as tablets and large iPhones, but should give you the experience closest to what PC players have. Since it's harder to aim up than down on mobile, high ground is essential for any kind of combat efficiency.

Chapter 11 – Most common causes of death for newbies

Impatience makes you reckless. You play video games to unwind, which involves smashing faces and slaying fools, but what do you do if there's no action for several minutes? You hear gunfights all around, your heart starts racing, you equip a pistol, jump out the nearest window and land right between three well-armed enemies: pew pew pew and you're dead. Going kamikaze style might seem like an honorable way to go, but *Fortnite* is about winning in any way possible, even if you do end up looking like a sleazy weasel. If you want to experience anything other than repeated frustration, you simply have to become patient and cautious. When you hear gunshots, you equip your pistol and sneak up to the window to scout the situation. You see three enemies below fighting to death, you wait until they've exchanged shots and only one remains. He crouches in the open to use Bandages – a big mistake. Now's your chance! You take careful aim: pew pew pew and he's dead. Now their loot is all yours. To put it this way – to win you merely have to survive, and that means having the instincts of a wounded mama wolf protecting her litter.

Picking a losing fight. If you watch pro *Fortnite* streamers, you'll notice they never pick a losing fight. At first glance this seems like the most sensible strategy ever, but if you were to know their thought process you'd be amazed just how nuanced their thinking is when it comes to sizing up the opponent and deciding when and where to engage the enemy or avoid them altogether. A pro player will constantly monitor his HP, weapons, ammo and material while trying to figure out the same thing for the opponent and estimate his chances of winning a firefight. If a pro player concludes he can't take out an enemy just yet, he'll fall back and wait for a window of opportunity to open so he can headshot him through it. Watching this kind of flexible mindset unfold is truly like watching an artist create his masterpiece and includes being able to recognize fights you're almost certainly going to lose and not engage in them. Once you're able to track a much stronger enemy than you through a peephole and not reveal your position, you've mastered this lesson.

Being even in a fight and barely losing. You were so close to killing that guy, he survived tons of shots and now he's dancing as you vomit your loot and get teleported out by that drone thingy. You narrowly lost – for the 20th time in a row. How can this happen? Are you the unluckiest *Fortnite* player ever? Are people hacking? In every game where there's RNG, there are streaks where it simply goes against you and there's nothing you can do about it. These streaks can actually last for dozens of games and the worst part is that human brain tends not to notice streaks of good RNG happening, so you can really start believing the game is rigged against you. In an even fight, there's an equal chance either of you will win, but if you're in the losing mindset you'll tend not to notice the situations where you've won and only remember those when you lost. If you now pay attention to how pros deal with such losing streaks, you'll realize they don't react at all and simply keep going. They know that once the losing streak is over it's time for some Youtube highlights, baby.

Suddenly changing your flight path and getting terrible gear. You had it all figured out right from the start, you were stoked to land in Pleasant Park for some juicy loots but once you saw other players swarming around your head like angry bees trying to find where they left their stingers, you felt a sense of dread overwhelm you. Panic mode got engaged, you took a sharp turn to a random direction, hit a tree, got stuck between the rock and the hard place and died an embarrassing death. There is an extended version of this scenario is which you landed safely but so far away from the chest spawn points that you couldn't get any solid weapons. The outcome is the same though – an embarrassing death that disgraces you and your clan. Sensei back home won't be proud of you. The main problem here is panicking. Once you experience panic, you lock up and lose control of your reflexes due to the "flight or flight" instinct. Again, pro players never panic for a very good reason – they know they can make a comeback as long as they stay as cool as cucumber, so even if they die they will never allow their emotions to take hold and dictate the game plan.

Getting pinned between two players. Not even Hercules can fight off two people, so what were you doing trying to take on two guys at once? It really bruises the pride when it just so happens that two enemies were fighting each other and accidentally kill you instead. This mistake is due to having poor game awareness and sense of direction, usually caused by ignoring sounds and visible signs of enemy presence, such as leftover loot strewn about. Pay attention to what you're hearing and always try to gauge the strength of your opponent, which is again something pros do all the time. If you find yourself surrounded, you have to react quickly and do whatever gives you the highest chances of survival. You should never allow yourself to be flanked or surrounded, even by accident. Of course, the easiest way to stop this from happening is if you play in a squad, where your teammates can actually help you pin down and encircle a hapless solitary enemy. If you're on your own, get on high ground and constantly scout your surroundings before the enemies have approached into kiss range. This gives you the most time to react and build whatever it takes to survive.

Died to the Storm because of bad luck. Ah, it's bad luck that got you this time, is it? In my day we walked uphill barefoot both ways inside the Storm and we used to say, "Thank you sir, may I have another?" There will be times when you'll die inside the Storm through no fault of your own but you should never attribute this to "bad luck." Whatever the outcome, it's your own doing; you made a mistake well before you actually died, so analyze your gameplan and realize where you've gone wrong. Then move on and keep playing to get better. For pro players there is no bad luck, there is only a poorly executed gameplan that relied on RNG and gambled the win away. As you realize how many choices you actually make with every passing second, you'll start taking control of the match, herding enemies to unfavorable positions where you can easily take them down. The more control you have, the better off you'll be until you're dominating the map and downing everyone with the shotgun. If at that point you read someone else's complaint about "bad luck," remember the learning experience you went through and explain this lesson to them in your own words.

Sniped out of nowhere. You got instakilled with a sniper between two buildings, through six windows and four eyes of the needle. It's understandable that it doesn't feel fair but just like with every other weapon in *Fortnite*, there's counterplay and you just happened to not be using it. In the case of snipers, you want to minimize the time you're out in the open and when having to cross the open field you want to zig-zag, randomly stop, duck or change direction. In some cases even doing a random emote that changes your stance can save your noggin from being ventilated. If you have enough shields, it's only the headshot that instakills you, so think of any ways you can keep your head behind cover at all times and you'll be just fine. You'll also notice pros do these rapid squats whenever they're drinking a potion even when they're behind cover just on the off chance someone might take a pot shot at them and have it glitch through the wall. The best strategy is to have multiple layers of cover from multiple angles and avoid peeking over ramps if you know there's someone sniping at you. In hectic combat situations you won't be able to get it perfect but you don't have to achieve perfection, just enough to survive.

Thinking you were behind cover. This one is actually justifiable and has something more to it than just player frustration. For whatever reason, the server collision detection that determines when players come in contact with bullets and structures can get wacky at times and allow you to get shot through a solid, freshly built wall. The reason for this is that software code, in this case hit detection, can sometimes glitch out and even if it works as intended 99.99% of the time it literally leaves a 1-in-10,000 type of thing that shouldn't upset you when it happens.

Player theory as to why this happens goes that if you place a structure section while a part of any character model (you or enemy) is clipping through the space where it's meant to appear, the section won't actually appear until the conflict is resolved and model moves away or through, even if the texture seems to be there. The support for this is that sometimes you'll place structure sections just as the enemy gets there and he'll be able to just walk through. In the case of getting shot through walls, it's probably a combination of unusual angles and distances that makes it occur. If you happen to be on the receiving end don't get tilted, just requeue straight away, as we all do.

Died to the Storm because of greed. Ah, it's greed that got you this time, is it? In my day we opened empty chests barehanded while walking uphill barefoot both ways inside the Storm and we used to say, "Thank you sir, may I have another?" The trick to not dying to the Storm is to constantly optimize your routes while in a match. There's always going to be more loot than you can possibly carry and use, so just go for having enough high-quality gear rather than all of it. Don't take needless risks, but do try to take calculated risks in which you can reasonably expect to get out ahead more times than not. A corollary to this is that you can sometimes do the smart thing and still die to the Storm, but as long as you made a solid decision that wasn't based on emotions, you did the right thing that just so happened to get you killed. You also want to trek across different sections enough times that you get a gut feeling how long it takes you and the Storm from here to there. It's like speedrunning where you have to cut corners and shave off seconds that will certainly save your life at some point in the game.

Chapter 12 – Gamer etiquette

Fortnite is a game for everyone: young and old, male and female, quick and slow. However, some younger players and those with poor impulse control tend to have negative emotional outbursts during and after a match whether they win or lose. Though that can lead to epic freak-out and rage videos on Youtube, this negativity tends to accumulate and can become so overwhelming that it infects the entire community (see *League of Legends*), repelling any newbies from wanting to join in. Sometimes presenting itself as toxic complaints about a particular weapon, item or mechanic (remember the section on bloom), this tidal wave of negativity can submerge everyone beneath it until you just give up and go do something else, which would be a shame.

To deal with this kind of problem, the more mature ones among us have to act like adults and not let the negativity affect them in any way. The best way to quench such drama coming from salty players is to communicate two phrases whenever you're given the chance: "GL HF" and "GG," the former meaning "good luck, have fun" and the latter "good game." Whenever you find yourself communicating with random people in *Fortnite,* make it a habit to wish them GL HF before and GG after every match and simply carry it over to any other video game you might end up playing. Don't accuse anyone of anything, don't argue, don't present excuses – just use "GL HF" and "GG" to spread some succinct cordiality and you'll come one step closer to becoming a professional gamer, since that's how they talk to one another.

Chapter 13 – Patch version history

Video games didn't use to get updates, let alone regular ones. In the 80s and 90s video games were painstakingly shipped on cassettes, floppy discs and CDs through the post office – any updates or improvements to the original were packaged as a separate game or expansion pack and sold separately. On one hand users couldn't really get extra value without opening their wallets but the games they did buy were much more polished and robust. On the other hand now we have speedy internet connections patching us on the opposite sides of the world and enabling constant updates at the cost of playing evergreen video games where no weapon, skill or gameplay mechanic is set in stone. There are no longer dedicated days or processes to patch a video game – every day is patch day and we'll see how a single patch in *Fortnite* gets rolled out over the course of a week or so, sometimes reverting what was just implemented, as if two developers were fighting over a keyboard.

Fortnite is a living, breathing video game, one that constantly changes and improves as its developers get cool new ideas, making the task of writing any kind of ultimate guide for it a sweet torment. This guide originally took about 3 weeks to write, by which time *Fortnite* developers had already released a new weapon and interactive in-game objects, tweaked damage and loot drop rates for almost all sources of loot and so on. This chapter represents an attempt to capture the evolution of *Fortnite* over time, both to help players stay up-to-date and see what the developers imagine the game being at some point.

The core gameplay mechanics and items are unlikely to ever change but we'll certainly see them tweaked and new stuff added so this chapter will focus on presenting new changes in chronological order. Before we get started one brief note on patch numbering: patches are numbered in a X.Y.Z format, where X is major, Y minor and Z (often omitted) minute version number. This number helps developers and users track the evolution of software and represents how well-developed the product is, with Z meaning "very little change", Y meaning "medium change" and X meaning "huge change".

Other than higher number being a newer patch version there is no logic behind the sequencing and a developer might release version 1.0 today and 2.1.5 tomorrow; the missing patches in between were tested internally but never released to the public. Huge developer teams behind browsers such as Chrome and Firefox have made version numbering all but meaningless since they push so many updates so quickly; Google Chrome is at 68.0.3440.84 and Mozilla Firefox at 61.0.1 as of August 1st, 2018. The first 12 chapters of this guide are current as of 27th March 2018, so let's see what was added afterwards.

Patch 3.4

Released March 28th 2018, this update added the Guided Missile to the game. It behaves like the one from *Half-Life*: the projectile shoots out a bit when fired and only then becomes guided. This idea was cool back in 1998 and it's still cool in 2018. The person firing the Guided Missile can't move, shoot or use items while the projectile is being controlled.

The Guided Missile shoots projectiles that outpace players; there's no running away from them and getting caught in the open is tantamount to death. The solution is to bob, weave and jump around since the projectile can't turn on the dime; the alternative is to hide inside or behind any complicated structure as the weapon had weird structural damage calculations. Whatever you do, just don't sit still.

Guided Missile uses Rocket ammo and comes in two rarities that initially did 105 (Epic) and 110 (Legendary) damage to players, instakilling an unshielded player. The projectile had enough fuel for 18 seconds of flight, giving out an audio warning during the last 3 seconds. If the fuel runs out, the projectile maintains its trajectory and behaves just like a regular rocket. It initially did 1,000 damage to structures and was meant to decimate them but had a fairly confusing rule on how it worked – the point of impact was taken as a centre of a sphere and damage to buildings was only to the first object within the centre's line of sight. That meant that if a chair and a wall were lined up with the centre, the chair would get destroyed but the wall would still stand even though both were caught in the blast radius.

This led to pretty awkward moments where the Guided Missile player would be sure they've destroyed a building but it would be barely scratched, pretty much necessitating multiple direct hits to knock down buildings. Thus the safest way to escape Guided Missiles is to run into a building where the attacking player has to tediously knock down one wall or object at a time (this will later get changed so explosives can kill through walls).

Teammates can ride the Guided Missile projectile but the timing is tricky and fall damage can still kill them. The Guided Missile has 100 HP and can be knocked out of the sky. The current drop rates for Guided Missile are, on average, 1.65% for both rarities except that Epic comes from floor loot and chests but Legendary can come from Supply Drops too.

This patch brought about a new interactive object to the game – Vending Machines. Originally thought to be an April Fools' joke, Vending Machine lets players exchange extra materials for goodies and works like this: when spawned, a Vending Machine randomly chooses a rarity (Common, Uncommon, Rare, Epic or Legendary) and offers 3 items of that rarity, one for each material type (wood, brick or metal). Costs starts from 100 for a Common and increase by hundred per rarity up to 500 for a Legendary. A Vending Machine cycles through 3 available items but can be made to go faster by hitting it with a pickaxe. Players may purchase as many items as they can afford. Location of a Vending Machine is random but always in the vicinity of a convenience store.

In this patch developers implemented First Shot Accuracy, probably in response to all the bloom furore. FSA means a weapon that's being aimed down sights while crouched will turn crosshairs into a solid dot and always have the first shot go 100% where it's aimed but FSA will persist if the player stands up, allowing for long-range crouch peek shots with many weapons that previously suffered greatly in the same situation.

The problem was that not all weapons got FSA and the ones added to the game afterwards again didn't have FSA, prompting all sorts of questions and discussions – is bloom intended or FSA? What's the logic for not adding it to all weapons? Why is this being changed?

FSA made pistols, especially Desert Eagle (called "hand cannon" in-game to avoid trademark issues), a brutal one-shot head remover, especially right after landing when players had no shields. Weapons that got FSA were penalized with a bigger damage falloff, meaning they weren't so good for medium- or long-range sniping; handguns also got a reduced headshot damage multiplier from 250% to 200%. As seen in the screenshots above and below, Desert Eagle was still good enough to ventilate players in a row from a safe position.

Players generally enjoyed FSA as it made low-tier loadouts valuable and able to compete even in late game where snipers dominated. The general feeling was that FSA made *Fortnite* the most balanced it's ever been, with skill factor ramped up to umpteen. That feeling of elation won't last long, as we're about to see.

The resource gain from objects was also tweaked so that there is less variance. For example, prior to this change an object that gave 100 wood on average could go up or down 30 but after the change went up or down 15; the average is still the same but the idea is that "feels bad man, only got 70 wood" situations shouldn't happen as often. As we mentioned previously the human mind doesn't understand probability correctly and often notices bad things when they happen in a row but ignores lucky streaks.

This patch also introduced something strange and ominous, only seen by the few who actually took some time to look at the sky – something akin to a meteor appeared and was slowly getting larger.

Players thought (or rather hoped) the meteor will hit Tilted Towers, thus ridding the game of this wretched place. Will it or won't it? Only time will tell. Meanwhile the alternate *Fortnite* gameplay mode called "Save the World" (StW) got the same comet in the sky and a storyline that hinted at its origins.

Patch 3.5

Released April 11th 2018, this patch added Port-a-Fort, an Epic rarity grenade that comes in singles and stacks up to 5. When thrown at a surface PaF creates a 3-tile-high 1x1 metal fort with a door at ground level, tires for jumping to the top and a funnel for cover. The structure outline builds instantly, faster than a player could ever do it manually, but the sections take a regular amount of time to fill up. PaFs can be stacked on top of one another. The screenshot below shows 4 stacked PaFs.

The intention behind PaF is that players with slower reaction times and those playing on console/mobile had trouble going toe to toe against experienced PC players in the later stages of the game – PaF gave newbies a chance to secure a position and take a more tactical approach. Of course, this doesn't solve the issue of PC players getting PaF too.

Guided Missile got the axe, with its turn rate decreased by 75% and movement speed decreased by 15%. This essentially meant players could easily outmanoeuvre the projectile and all but run circles around it. Developers finally realized double shot exploit was in the game, so they added a short time-to-equip animation for certain weapons (shotguns, handguns, snipers, crossbow and rocket launcher) to slow down the burst damage. Replay functionality was also added, allowing anyone to view any match they played in 5 different ways, including a free-floating drone's viewpoint that can explore the entire map.

A new weapon was added in this patch, Light Machine Gun. It's a Rare or Epic weapon with 100 rounds in the magazine and firing 8 bullets per second, each bullet doing 25 damage (26 for Epic). LMG is a cross between minigun and assault rifle, a weapon for bullies since it has the ability to provide suppressive fire while your teammate flanks the target.

LMG is meant to be used as a medium-range weapon that knocks down structures as they're being built and punishes turtling but isn't meant for sniping or even hitting moving targets due to poor accuracy. The best thing about LMG is it's got 100 bullets already loaded in the magazine and ready for use, outgunning entire teams especially if found immediately after landing. Has a 5 second reload time.

Patch 3.6

On April 24th 2018 players discovered that patch 3.6 increased FSA cooldown by 270% and made it more difficult to use, in particular that (un)crouching or switching weapons reset FSA cooldown. We can guesstimate this was because players exploited crouch peek shots with FSA. The community didn't like this change at all, noticing that hunting rifle is hurt a lot and basically behaved as if having bloom once again. Shooting with FSA now felt unintuitive and comments ranged from "this is so sloppy" to "what was the point?" SMGs were probably the worst at this point as they had FSA damage falloff but their single bullet damage is so low that there's no point in sniping with one, making them fairly useless.

There was a new grenade type added, the Clinger. It's an Uncommon grenade that sticks to a player or structure and explodes after 2.5 seconds, dealing 100 damage to all hostile players and 200 to neutral and hostile structures within 1 tile radius. The Clinger grenade will explode sooner if the supporting structure is destroyed.

Like all other grenades, Clinger is not meant to be used in exposed situations where the enemy knows your position; it's mostly in the game for humiliating newbies and making amazing highlights using the replay system.

Minigun was buffed in this patch, with 10% accuracy, recoil and damage boosts. This was probably done due to LMG hands down beating the minigun while not having any spin-up time.

We also got more clues trickled into the game, this time with some props in Tilted Towers showing a sketch of a meteor with a telescope nearby. Someone's been looking at the sky and trying to warn us. Uh, did I say "props"? That would imply *Fortnite* is actually a movie stage, wouldn't it?

Players made monumental efforts to save whatever they could (in this case Dusty Depot) but it just wasn't enough.

Patch 4.0

It was a comet all along and it crashed into the map! Released April 30, 2018, this patch marks the start of *Fortnite* season 4 and the addition of Hop Rocks, special consumables that allow the player to jump as if though under the launchpad effect at all times.

The map has been scarred by the meteor shards, with props getting chipped or outright nuked left, right and centre but others found something even weirder – giant dinosaur footprint in the ground.

It's like something came with the meteor or is it that we're on a movie stage? The debate raged on while developers kept tweaking the headshot mechanics.

Headshots are now given priority if the player aimed at the head but some other body part got in the way. The collision size of hands was also reduced to make the headshot detection go smoother. 4:3 aspect size support was added, making some streamers switch and claim it makes enemies easier to hit. This was disproven by players who compared *CS:Go*, in which the 4:3 aspect does work like that, to *Fortnite*.

The *CS:Go* example on the left shows the hitbox increased by roughly 47% while the *Fortnite* aspect ratio change on the right actually *decreased* the hitbox by roughly 32%. Crossbow was "vaulted" in this patch, meaning removed from the game until further notice. The idea is to have items and weapons cycled in and out the vault in order to keep the gameplay fresh and interesting.

It turned out the meteor was actually a spaceship, with the Visitor staggering out of it. Loading screens released at the time show a more complete story.

The most interesting theory about Visitor is that he's from the distant future and Hop Rocks are somehow related to his technology. The following week we got another loading screen, this time showing the Visitor building a rocket, possibly to go back whence he came.

Patch 4.2

May 15th 2018 meant the addition of a new weapon that's kind of already in the game except now it's better, Burst Assault Rifle. BAR is either Epic or Legendary and does 32 damage per bullet (33 for Legendary), firing at the same speed as other BARs in the game, 7 bullets in 4 seconds. BAR has a 30 bullet magazine and uses medium ammo.

A new consumable was also added – apples. They can't be carried in the inventory and picking them automatically consumes them. Each apple eaten restores 5 HP and they can be found in all loot containers, including floor loot, but also around certain trees.

This patch introduced a new item type called "backpacks". The first backpack is jetpack, always of Legendary rarity. When picked up jetpack visually replaces the cosmetic backpack, takes an inventory slot and allows the player to boost themselves up into the air. Jetpack has limited fuel, shown by the draining bar on the right side of the inventory icon. Fuel quantity persists through owner change, so you could potentially get one from an enemy with only a smidgen of fuel left.

Jetpack can overheat, which is shown as red vertical bars on the jetpack model itself (just like the HP bar in *Dead Space*). When jetpack isn't in use the red bars slowly fill up and quickly deplete when it's being flown. Not paying attention to this detail can cause you to learn about gravity the hard way – it's not the fall that kills but the sudden stop.

Players overwhelmingly disliked the jetpack, noting that there are very few instances where its use felt fair, for example when crossing Loot Lake under enemy fire. The main issue players had was that building to reach higher ground was made inferior and obsolete, but the jetpack player could also take insane risks with building sky bases and still survive them being knocked down. Someone with a jetpack during end game could simply fly up any amount of walls and shoot *from above* without having to build anything. True, it wasn't possible to shoot during ascent but the tactical advantage was simply disgusting.

Jetpack also caused issues for console players, who do have aim assist but it's notoriously bad on rapidly rising and dropping targets, meaning jetpack induced quite a few ragequits. Luckily the developers announced jetpack will be a LTI (limited time item), meaning it's going to be vaulted, which happened June 11th 2018.

SMG got a sizable buff, with damage increased by 16% and spread when firing full auto reduced by 25%; the damage falloff range was increased by 20% and damage penalty at long ranges reduced by about 6%. Damage Trap no longer instakilled unshielded players, with its damage being reduced from 125 to 75. Players felt both trap damage values were unwieldy and expressed a strong preference for them doing 100 flat. Remote Explosives now damaged everything within their blast radius rather than just the closest thing (remember the Guided Missile damage calculations), activated faster and could be thrown farther.

The meteor storyline continued, with trucks appearing to cart off the Hop Rocks. Eagle-eyed players noticed a familiar logo on them, one that resembled Vindertech company logo from StW found on skins and V-bucks, the in-game currency.

The wildest theory went that Vindertech was making robots out of the meteor metal, with *Fortnite* being a combat simulation where players practiced for the real invasion happening in StW, which would explain why there's a drone zapping players out when they "die" (it's a virtual reality type of thing). Those playing both Battle Royale and StW noticed there's a brand new enemy type in the latter made of metal that makes it revive after a little bit. Is that the meteor metal? Does that mean Vindertech are the bad guys?

Patch 4.3

May 25th 2018 saw the addition of a first rideable ground vehicle – shopping carts? Wait, what? Are we sure this isn't a typo? Not tanks or jeeps but *shopping carts*? Well they're in the game all right and players overwhelmingly *loved them*. Shopping carts have two movement modes, one in which it accelerates (the driver pushes with his foot) and the other where the driver runs behind it at a steady speed. The importance of the second mode is that it can be used to quickly go uphill. Two people can use the shopping cart at once, one driving and the other building, looting or shooting, with the passenger actually boosting the cart if rockets are shot backwards (developers will leave this in the game).

Shopping carts broke so many random things in *Fortnite*, for example speeding down a ramp with a shopping cart often meant ending up under the map. This was because a *Fortnite* server checks for collision a certain number of times per second (30 at that time); more checks means a smoother game, greater server load and more downtime so developers want to cut corners by finding the most balanced value but failed to account for shopping carts. Thanks to collision check players can't normally go through objects unless they achieve a certain speed; shopping carts were able to go so fast that they actually phased through the ground and into the void beneath the map.

Shopping carts are standalone objects, susceptible to gravity and inertia, making kids learn about Newton's laws in all sorts of fun ways. They also do *damage* if hitting the player at enough speed. In the screenshot above we see a stray shopping cart left on a hill slowly rolling to gain momentum and hitting a player to push him off the cliff. Players also used the minigun to quickly cross the Loot Lake by facing the front of the shopping cart and firing a continuous burst until the cart gained enough momentum.

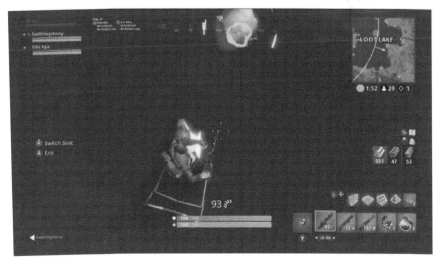

The fun was over June 17th when shopping carts were vaulted but returned back a few days later due to player demand. Another addition in this patch was Turbo Build, a way to burst build by holding down the build button, placing 18 structures in 1 second.

Mushrooms were added to the game. Similar to apples, mushrooms are consumables that are instantly used but they restore 5 shields upon use (up to 100). Can be found in wooded and swampy areas. Mushrooms take 1 second to pick up and 1 second to use.

New Rare trap was added, the Bouncer, dropping in stacks of 3 and placeable on floors and walls, ushering in a new age of flying out of the map at ludicrous speeds. Remember the collision check we just mentioned? The blue cone in the screenshot below is the entire *Fortnite* map.

Shotguns were slightly nerfed, with the official explanation being that they "are being used more often than we like". Traps had their 75 damage *doubled*, now doing 150, with players again complaining both values felt unwieldy. It's a pattern we'll see over and over again in *Fortnite*, with developers trying to tweak unused items or weapons but constantly missing the mark and not listening to player feedback.

Even trap damage set to 149 would make them interesting as it's fairly common to have 100 HP and 50 shields, meaning a 149 damage trap would allow the player to survive at 1 HP; surviving a 150 damage trap would often involve having 100 HP and 100 shields. This is a trap, as it were, game designers often fall into as they simply like clean, round numbers and would never think of putting trap damage at 102 because it feels off but maybe that's the best possible value.

Supply Llamas now dropped only 200 of each resource, down from 500, and no longer provided explosive ammo. Floor loot now gave 33% less materials in stacks and spawned them 33% less often. This was a huge nerf, meaning roughly 50% less mats in floor loot spawns. Minigun accuracy was again boosted by 10%.

Players also managed to crack open a meteor housed in Dusty Divot using (what else) a shopping cart hurtling down a ramp. The meteor shattered into a cloud of soot, revealing nothing inside. Is all of this just an elaborate ploy? Prior to that players used C4 and PaF to open the meteor, with each weapon getting a specific bug fix to prevent that.

Patch 4.4

Released 19th June 2018, this patch turned up the heat with a new weapon, Thermal Scope Assault Rifle, available as Epic and Legendary, with 15 bullets in the magazine and doing 35 damage per bullet (36 for Legendary). Despite the animation showing the bullet shot, TSAR is a hitscan weapon; the bullet doesn't have any travel time but aiming slightly in front of the target is advisable if it's moving to counter any lag.

The main advantage of TSAR over other scoped weapons in *Fortnite* is its scoped view that shows player, C4, supply drop and chest heat signatures, allowing you to see through player-built structures (not neutral solid ones) and spot the exact moment when they're about to do a peek shot. Damaged walls also show more of a player's silhouette.

The scope did not work as intended on low-end iOS devices at the time of patch release, showing a plain scoped view. The community consensus is that TSAR is better than scoped AR weapons in almost every regard.

To counter a player using TSAR, build redundant walls to hide your heat signature, such as a double wall in front of a double ramp. The campfire initially did not show up in TSAR as a heat signature but the second half of the patch fixed that. In this way it's possible to hide behind a campfire within your base.

The next addition was the Epic rarity Stink Bomb, an AoE denial grenade that deals 5 damage twice a second over 9 seconds (does a total of 90 damage, thus leaving a player at 10 HP). Found in stacks of 3, with the maximum inventory capacity of 5, the stink bomb is great for forcing campers out of hiding, especially if you rig a few traps at the exit. The bomb explodes on contact and the stink cloud goes through player structures but the damage does not stack with itself (don't throw more than one at the same target).

However, the cloud visibility reduction does stack, meaning it works just like the old smoke bomb when a couple are tossed next to one another. The cloud is roughly 1 tile in size; the damage ignores shields and directly chips away at HP. This bomb is a great addition to the game, especially for those who've been aching for a more tactical approach to *Fortnite* or just to see the good old smokes return.

This patch nerfed rocket launcher reload time and allowed players to set Bouncer traps on ramps but mostly focused on fixing the shopping carts and how the passenger physics worked to avoid ridiculous flying situations. Jetpack was also vaulted in this patch.

The villain base added to Snobby Shores after the meteor crash got what looked like a rocket launch countdown. Is Visitor leaving us?

Patch 4.5

Released 27th June 2018, this patch added Epic and Legendary Dual Pistol so everyone can pew-pew their way across the map like Lara Croft. Dual Pistol holds 18 medium bullets total (9 per pistol) and a single trigger press makes each pistol fire a bullet for 41 damage (43 for Legendary variety) *per bullet*. Each bullet travels separately so it's possible to headshot and bodyshot an enemy in the same shot.

Dual Pistol does not have FSA, does have bloom *and* recoil (note how wide the crosshair is in the screenshot above where Ninja is crouching and staying still); this is intentional to make the weapon worse at medium range. The community thought Dual Pistol is cool to use and really powerful, lauding developers' attempts to make weapons as strong as shotguns but decried that Dual Pistol is Epic and Legendary while shotguns are all over the place. Teammate map markers were added to the game so you can tell where everyone's headed at a glance.

The shotgun damage to structures was reduced 25-50% for pump, tactical and heavy shotguns to make them less useful against campers. Tactical SMG got the change we discussed earlier: its FSA was removed, base accuracy was buffed by 25%, sprinting accuracy was also buffed by 15%, damage was buffed by 2 and aiming down sights (ADS) accuracy was nerfed by 10%. This means SMG was tweaked so it's more of a run and gun kiss-range weapon fired at the hip meant for rushing players rather than a medium range sniper. However, silenced SMG got: 2 damage buff, ADS accuracy 20% buff and 10% base accuracy buff to help it parry all the other weapons.

Another weapon added was Uncommon and Rare Drum Gun (aka. Tommy gun). This SMG and rifle hybrid is a medium range suppressor and structure destroyer, doing 26 damage per bullet (27 for Rare), with a drum having 50 bullets. Drum Gun isn't all that accurate but the DPS (243 for Rare) more than makes up for it; only Epic Tactical SMG does more damage per second (260). The community welcomed Drum Gun with open arms, stating "this thing melts".

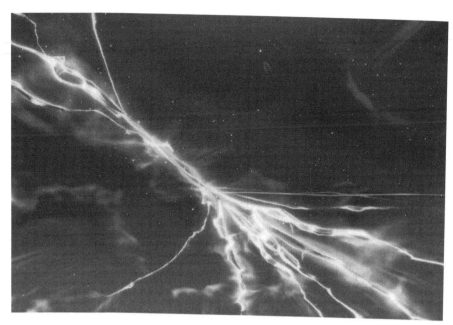

The sky appeared to be cracking wide open, leading some to believe they're under a protective dome while others thought the virtual reality they were all in was starting to fall apart. Of course, this issue was hotly debated and settled on the battlefield with bullets.

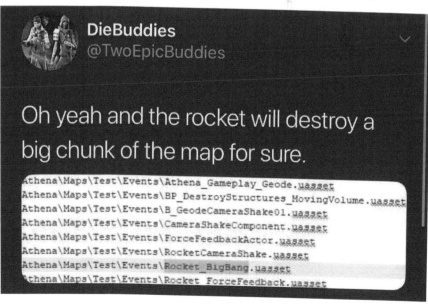

DieBuddies
@TwoEpicBuddies

Oh yeah and the rocket will destroy a big chunk of the map for sure.

Athena\Maps\Test\Events\Athena_Gameplay_Geode.uasset
Athena\Maps\Test\Events\BP_DestroyStructures_MovingVolume.uasset
Athena\Maps\Test\Events\B_GeodeCameraShake01.uasset
Athena\Maps\Test\Events\CameraShakeComponent.uasset
Athena\Maps\Test\Events\ForceFeedbackActor.uasset
Athena\Maps\Test\Events\RocketCameraShake.uasset
Athena\Maps\Test\Events\Rocket_BigBang.uasset
Athena\Maps\Test\Events\Rocket_ForceFeedback.uasset

Intrepid players dug through the game files and found something remarkable: there is a dedicated asset for a "Rocket_BigBang", implying it will destroy a huge part of the map once launched. Did developers know someone will look at this and put a red herring in?

The answer to that will come June 30th, when the rocket was launched way up into the sky. Now what? Those playing StW jumped in to help us out: first mission in StW revolves around the player launching a rocket that looks just like this one, except it's a *radar* used to uncover a new part of the map.

Patch 5.0

With this patch released 12th July 2018 *Fortnite* entered season 5, getting some curious Viking ships and ancient statues added to the map. There is now desert terrain (marked orange on the map) and two new locations: Paradise Palms and Lazy Links.

Players also got another vehicle, All Terrain Kart (ATK), to visit them all. It looks like a golf cart but drifting with it gives a small speed boost. Of course, passengers can shoot, harvest and loot everything within their reach. Let's go, War Boyz!

ATKs are extremely loud and fragile; half an AR clip will destroy an ATK and any hits on people inside will damage them. It can carry up to 4 players, including the driver. It's possible to do some huge jumps with an ATK, especially if all the passengers lean at the same time. The roof of an ATK acts as a bounce pad.

Rifts are a brand new addition that work like teleporters to the sky. They spawn randomly on the map and are best used for outrunning the storm. Player theory goes that Visitor's rocket launch is what caused rifts and all the weird ancient artefacts all over the map.

It's possible to drive through a Rift in an ATK and do some wild stunts; the ATK is extraordinarily resilient to fall damage and will likely survive the drop. It's unknown if that's a bug or intended.

The endgame was reworked – the centre of final storms in a match will now shrink *and* move to a random location to encourage fast thinking. Certain locations have also been removed from the map.

Shotguns now show how many pellets hit with each shot and the spread was made consistent rather than random. The double shot exploit was again addressed and shooting with a shotgun means any other shotgun carried by the player has a small forced cooldown where it can't be fired.

Another weapon was added, this time finally one that uses light ammo – Submachine Gun (SMG), spawning as common, uncommon and rare, doing 19-21 damage per bullet, with 30 rounds per magazine and firing 12 rounds per second, just like minigun.

Community described it as suppressed and tactical SMG combined. Tactical SMG has also been vaulted and semi-auto sniper rifle had its damage increased by roughly 20% (from 63/66 to 75/78).

Players noticed a bunker in Wailing Woods, joking it was the "vault" used to store weapons removed from the game. The hatch was invulnerable to any kind of damage but players managed to crack it open thanks to amazing shopping cart phase glitch. The inside contained nothing, it was just a square hole.

Patch 5.10

24th July 2018 saw the release of a compact SMG (trademark name P90) in a further attempt to depose shotguns as kings of kiss-range combat. Available as Epic and Legendary it does 23/24 damage per light ammo bullet, fires 11 of them a second and has a 50 round magazine. In theory a P90 can kill a 100 HP, 100 shields player behind a wall in under a second and just move on to the next guy and cut him down too without reloading.

Community thought and still thinks this weapon is outright bonkers. P90 cuts through buildings and players alike like hot katana through butter. It took developers an entire day before issuing a nerf for P90 and SMG: ADS accuracy bonus was reduced by 56%, drop rates were slightly nerfed, fire rate and damage got a 10% nerf. Slurp Juice was buffed to slowly regenerate HP (1 HP twice a second up to 75) and give shields if HP is already at 75 or higher.

Player-built structures got a nerf, with wood and stone losing 20% and 10% starting HP respectively. Metal walls were buffed however and got extra 25% maximum HP and a 20% build time buff. This was meant to incentivize players to build metal walls but the problem is simply how abundant wood and stone are compared to metal.

Storm timings were sped up, with almost all wait times between circles reduced 30-50%, putting pressure on players on the fringes to pick up the pace. Supply drops got their loot drop rates jumbled around, with emphasis on providing an assault rifle and no pistols. Finally, this patch returned Guided Missile from the vault but in a severely nerfed state: the missile now flies for 15 seconds, moves 10% slower, takes 10% longer to reload, does 25% less damage to players, mere 74 (77 if headshot), and a whopping 64% less damage to structures. The Guided Missile got the same treatment as all other explosives and was capable of damaging entities through walls if within blast radius.

Patch 5.20

Released August 7th 2018, we got a new weapon, this time a Double Shotgun. Spawning as Epic or Legendary, this blast from the past sends out 10 pellets for a total of up to 143 damage (150 for Legendary) *per shot*. It has a 2-second equip cooldown baked in, huge spread, very short range and lower crit damage bonus (125%).

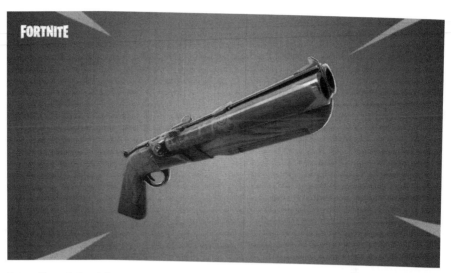

Vending Machines got tweaked as well, with the intention to have less Common ones and more other rarities. So, the Common Vending Machine spawn chance is reduced by 0.60% but Epic and Legendary got their spawn chances tripled and doubled respectively. All Vending Machines had their costs cut by 25% across the board.

Another interesting bug fix in this patch shows that the ramp peek shooting was actually a bug; quickly getting up from the crouching position no longer allows the player to shoot as if though he was standing before the animation finishes, which is what many players were abusing. One *Fortnite* developer actually made a detailed post on this issue, showing exactly how it was exploited before and how the bug was fixed.

To make the player models' feet line up nicely with sloped surfaces such as ramps, developers had to make some rough estimates with the game engine calculations. In the screenshot above the green sphere shows where the game places the rifle (green line is the bullet trajectory); the yellow sphere and line show the player's line of sight. In this case the player is capable of staying hidden behind a ramp while being able to see *and shoot* at everyone else. After the fix the player now has to actually expose herself (her head in particular) to retaliatory fire, as seen in the screenshot below.

This is an interesting turn of events that shows just how video game development works – a particular exploit can dominate the game to the point everyone does it but then it gets fixed, showing it wasn't meant to be. So why was it left in the game for so long? Developers set bigger things as their priorities: building the playerbase, adding cool stuff and writing a better story, making something as simple yet impactful as ramp peek exploit stay in the game for nearly a year before being fixed.

Conclusion

Having read this guide, you've got a glimpse into the vast world of *Fortnite* and the skills you need to come out on top in it. While it's still not fully fleshed out and we can certainly look forward to new weapons, items and cosmetics before it leaves Early Access, there are so many things to discover on your own, so many places to visit and so many new friends to make. Just go out there and have a blast.

Can you help me? If you enjoyed this book, I'd greatly appreciate if you would post a short review for it on Amazon. Thanks for your support!

Check out this book as well!

Printed in Great Britain
by Amazon

MOULTON'S
LIBRARY OF LITERARY CRITICISM
of English and American Authors

MOULTON'S LIBRARY

of English

THROUGH THE BEGINNING

IN FOUR VOLUMES

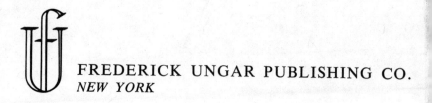

FREDERICK UNGAR PUBLISHING CO.
NEW YORK

OF LITERARY CRITICISM

and American Authors

OF THE TWENTIETH CENTURY

Abridged, revised, and with additions by

MARTIN TUCKER

Associate Professor of English
Long Island University

VOLUME III

The Romantic Period to the Victorian Age

Material that has been added to this revised edition is reprinted by permission
of the following:

Constable and Company Limited. For excerpt on George Meredith, from *Poetry
and Philosophy of George Meredith* by G. M. Trevelyan, published 1890.

Hutchinson & Co. Ltd. For excerpt on Ernest Dowson, in *Twenty Years in Paris*
by R. H. Sherard, published 1906.

Jonathan Cape Limited. For excerpt on Oscar Wilde and Ernest Dowson, in *The
Eighteen-nineties: A Review of Art and Ideas at the Close of the Nineteenth Century* by Holbrook Jackson, published 1927.

Macmillan & Co. Ltd. For excerpt on W. S. Gilbert, from *Coasting Bohemia* by
J. C. Carr, published 1914.

The Society of Authors, literary representative of the author's estate. For excerpt
on George Meredith, in *George Meredith* by Richard Le Gallienne, published 1890.

Every effort has been made to trace and to acknowledge properly all copyright
owners. If any acknowledgment has been inadvertently omitted, the necessary
correction will be made in the next printing.

CONTENTS

AUTHORS INCLUDED

BIBLIOGRAPHICAL NOTE

Below the introductory paragraph for each writer included in these volumes, the reader will find bibliographic entries of standard editions and biographical and/or critical studies published through 1964. The scheme of these entries is as follows:

The standard edition (or editions) of the writer's work is placed first; where one-volume texts and selected editions of excellence merit attention, these are listed next; on occasion convenient school texts are also noted; following the list of editions are standard biographical and critical studies. In cases where scholarly study has been particularly active, or literary issues remain in the realm of disputation and/or doubt, several biographical and critical works may be noted. Short titles are sometimes used, especially in editions of an author's work. In certain selected cases a study of a single work, as distinct from the collected edition of an author's work, will be found in the bibliographical listings.

Abbreviations used in the entries are: *repr.* for reprint; *rev.* for revision; *OSA* for Oxford Standard Authors one-volume editions; *ed.* for "edited by"; and *tr.* for "translated by."

Early standard editions listed in the original Moulton headnotes are usually not repeated in the bibliographical entries. Standard editions in the new listings, and their revisions and reprints, indicate availability, although they do not guarantee it.

THE NINETEENTH CENTURY:

Romanticism (continued)

WILLIAM BLAKE
1757-1827

Born, in London, 28 Nov. 1757. To drawing school, 1767. Began to write verse, 1768. Apprenticed to J. Basire, engraver to Soc. of Antiquaries, 1771-78. Student in Royal Academy, 1778. Engraved for magazines and books. Married Catharine Sophia Boucher, 18 Aug. 1782. Opened print-seller's shop in Broad Street, 1784. Exhibited at R. A. same year. Shop given up, 1787. At Felpham, 1800-04. Returned to London. Exhibited for last time at R. A. 1808. Died, 12 Aug. 1827. Buried at Bunhill Fields, Finsbury. WORKS, [all engraved and coloured by hand unless otherwise stated]: *Poetical Sketches* (printed), 1783; *Songs of Innocence* (with assistance of his wife), 1789; *The Book of Thel*, 1789; *The Marriage of Heaven and Hell*, 1790; *The French Revolution* (printed), 1791; *Prospectus*, 1793; *The Gates of Paradise*, 1793; *Visions of the Daughters of Albion*, 1793; *America*, 1793; *Europe*, 1794; *The Book of Urizen*, 1794; *Songs of Experience*, 1794; *The Song of Los*, 1795; *The Book of Ahania*, 1795; *Jerusalem*, 1804; *Milton*, 1804; *Descriptive Catalogue* (printed), 1809. COLLECTED WORKS: *Poems, edited* by R. H. Shepherd, 1868; by W. M. Rossetti (Aldine Series), 1874; Works, in facsimile of original editions, 1876. LIFE: By Gilchrist, 2nd ed. 1880.

R. Farquharson Sharp, 1897, *A Dictionary of
English Authors*, p. 27

SEE: *Writings*, ed. Geoffrey Keynes, 1925, 3 v.; *Complete Writings*, ed. Geoffrey Keynes, 1957; *Poetry and Prose*, ed. David V. Erdman, 1965; *The Prophetic Writings*, ed. D. J. Sloss and J. P. R. Wallis, 1926, 2 v.; *Notebooks*, ed. Geoffrey Keynes, 1935 [Facsimiles]; *Letters*, ed. Geoffrey Keynes, 1956; Alexander Gilchrist, *Life of William Blake*, 1863, 2 v., rev. 1942, 1945 (by Ruthven Todd); Mona Wilson, *The Life of Blake*, 1927, rev. 1949; S. Foster Damon, *William Blake: His Philosophy and Symbols*, 1924, repr. 1949; Max Plowman, *An Introduction to the Study of Blake*, 1927, repr. 1952; Mark Schorer, *William Blake: The Politics of Vision*, 1946; Northrop Frye, *Fearful Symmetry: A Study of William Blake*, 1947; Geoffrey Keynes, *Blake Studies*, 1949; H. M. Margoliouth, *William Blake*, 1951; David V. Erdman, *Blake: Prophet Against Empire*, 1954; Vivian de Sola Pinto, ed., *The Divine Vision: Studies in the Poetry and Art of William Blake*, 1957; Robert F. Gleckner, *The Piper and The Bard: A Study of William Blake*, 1959; E. D. Hirsch, Jr., *Innocence and Experience*, 1966; Darrell Figgis, *Paintings*, 1925; Laurence Binyon, *Engraved Designs*, 1926; *Engravings*, ed. Geoffrey Keynes, 1950; also see S. Foster Damon, *A Blake Dictionary: The Ideas and Symbols of William Blake*, 1965.

PERSONAL

Blake is a real name, I assure you, and a most extraordinary man, if he be still living. He is the Robert Blake, whose wild designs accompany a splendid folio edition of the *Night Thoughts,* which you may have seen. . . . He paints in water colours marvellous strange pictures, visions of his brain, which he asserts that he has seen. They have great merit. He has *seen* the old Welsh bards on Snowdon—he has seen the Beautifullest, the strongest, and the Ugliest Man, left alone from the Massacre of the Britons by the Romans, and has painted them from memory (I have seen his paintings), and asserts them to be as good as the figures of Raphael and Angelo, but not better, as they have precisely the same retro-visions and prophetic visions with themself (himself). The painters in oil (which he will have it that neither of them practised) he affirms to have been the ruin of art, and affirms that all the while he was engaged in his Water paintings, Titian was disturbing him, Titian the Ill Genius of Oil Painting. His Pictures—one in particular, "The Canterbury Pilgrims" (far above Stothard's)—have great merit, but hard, dry, yet with grace. He has written a Catalogue of them with a most spirited criticism on Chaucer, but mystical and full of Vision. . . . The man is flown, whither I know not—to Hades or a Mad House. But I must look on him as one of the most extraordinary persons of the age.

Charles Lamb, 1824, *Letter to Barton,* May 15;
Letters, ed. Ainger, vol. II, pp. 104, 105

Blake in an engraver by trade, a painter and poet also, whose works have been subjects of derision to men in general, but he has a few admirers, and some of eminence have eulogized his designs. He has lived in obscurity and poverty, to which the constant hallucinations in which he lives have doomed him. I do not mean to give you a detailed account of him; a few words will serve to inform you of what class he is. He is not so much a disciple of Jacob Boehme and Swedenborg as a fellow-visionary. He lives as they did, in a world of his own, enjoying constant intercourse with the world of spirits. He receives visits from Shakespeare, Milton, Dante, Voltaire, &c., and has given me repeatedly their very words in their conversations. His paintings are copies of what he sees in his visions. His books (and his MSS. are immense in quantity) are dictations from the spirits. A man so favoured, of course, has sources of wisdom and truth peculiar to himself. I will not pretend to give you an account of his religious and philosophical opinions; they are a strange compound of Christianity, Spinozism, and Platonism.

Henry Crabb Robinson, 1826, *Letter to Miss Wordsworth,* Feb.;
Reminiscences, ed. Sadler, vol. II, p. 38

She [Mrs. Blake] would get up in the night, when he was under his very fierce inspirations, which were as if they would tear him asunder, while he was yielding himself to the Muse, or whatever else it could be called, sketching and writing. And so terrible a task did this seem to be, that she had to sit motionless and silent, only to stay him mentally, without moving hand or foot: this for hours, and night after night.

John Thomas Smith, 1845, A Book for a Rainy Day, p. 14

I was much with him from 1810 to 1816, when I came abroad, and have remained in Italy ever since. I might have learned much from him. I was then a student of the Royal Academy, in the antique school, where I gained a medal, and thought more of form than anything else. I was by nature a lover of colour, and my *beau ideal* was the union of Phidias and Titian. Blake was the determined enemy of colourists, and his drawing was not very academical. His high qualities I did not prize at that time; besides, I thought him mad. I do not think so now. I never suspected him of imposture. His manner was too honest for that. He was very kind to me, though very positive in his opinion, with which I never agreed. His excellent old wife was a sincere believer in all his visions. She told me seriously one day, "I have very little of Mr. Blake's company; he is always in Paradise." She prepared his colours, and was as good as a servant. He had no other.

Seymour Kirkup, 1870, Letter to Lord Houghton, March 25;
The Life of Lord Houghton, ed. Reid, vol. II, p. 222

Now, this much is certain: that plain, commonplace, sober men, well acquainted with Blake in ordinary intercourse, saw in him one of themselves; that clever, shrewd, intelligent men thought him odd, but quite rational; and that men of high powers in art and literature, scholars, and sages of various schools, unanimously pronounced him sane. The evidence of his contemporaries is great in amount, and unvarying in substance. No one knew Blake, and thought him mad.

Lionel Johnson, 1893, The Academy, vol. 44, p. 163

ART

My friend Mr. D'Israeli possesses the largest collection of any individual of the very extraordinary drawings of Mr. Blake; and he loves his classical friends to disport with them, beneath the lighted Argand lamp of his drawing room, while soft music is heard upon the several corridors and recesses of his enchanted staircase. Meanwhile the visitor turns over the contents of the Blakëan portefeuille. Angels, Devils, Giants, Dwarfs, Saints, Sinners,

Senators, and Chimney Sweeps, cut equally conspicuous figures: and the *Concettos* at times border upon the burlesque, or the pathetic, or the mysterious. Inconceivably blest is the artist, in his visions of intellectual bliss. A sort of golden halo envelopes every object impressed upon the retina of his imagination; and (as I learn) he is at times shaking hands with Homer, or playing the pastoral pipe with Virgil. Meanwhile, shadowy beings of an unearthly form hang over his couch, and disclose to him scenes . . . such as no other Mortal hath yet conceived! Mr. Blake is himself no ordinary poet.

> Thomas Frognall Dibdin, 1824, *The Library Companion*,
> p. 734, note

Blake, no doubt, imported into the Bible a crowd of fantastic ideas that sprang from his own fertile, impetuous brain. He went to it for a revelation of facts, and seized chiefly upon those which other men were trying their best to be rid of. He was orientalized both by the Bible and by his passion for large, swelling conceptions of life, death and immortality. By degrees he peopled his mind with a strange crowd of figures, many with biblical outlines, many also, jostling these,—variations upon a few simple themes. The elemental facts of life, as has already been said, were those which were most luminous to him and for which he found visible shapes, which were repeated constantly in his designs.

> Horace E. Scudder, 1880, "William Blake, Painter and Poet,"
> *Scribner's Monthly*, vol. 20, p. 234

Blake, as an artist, is a more important figure than Blake the poet; and naturally so, for the smallest good poem involves a consecutiveness and complexity of thought which are required in paintings only of a character which Blake rarely attempted. Yet, even as a painter his reputation has until lately been much exaggerated. That exhibition of his collected drawings and paintings was a great blow to the fame which had grown up from a haphazard acquaintance by his admirers with a few sketches or an illustrated poem. Here and there there was a gleam of such pure and simple genius as is often revealed in the speech of a finely-natured child amid its ordinary chatter; here and there the expression of a tender or distempered dream which was not like anything else in the spectator's experience; now and then an outline that had a look of Michael Angelo, with sometimes hints which might have formed the themes of great works, and which justified the saying of Fuseli that "Blake is damned good to steal from"; but the effect of the whole collection was dejecting and unimpressive, and did little towards confirming its creator's opinion that Titian, Reynolds, and Gainsborough were bad artists, and Blake, Barry, and Fuseli good ones.

> Coventry Patmore, 1889-98, *Principle in Art*, p. 97

In art his aim was not merely to excite and satisfy the æsthetic sense; it was
to move and instruct—to elevate the soul above its mundane surroundings
—to create a desire for that life of the imagination in which alone "all things
exist." If that end were accomplished, all was accomplished. . . . His faculty
of invention was supreme. . . . It remains for ever true that as regards what
is commonly known as creative works, in that, namely, wherein the imagination reigns supreme, there have been few to equal and none to excel Blake
among our English artists.

> Alfred T. Story, 1893, *William Blake, His Life, Character
> and Genius*, pp. 155, 156

POETRY

Having spoken so far of Blake's influence as a painter, I should be glad
if I could point out that the simplicity and purity of his style as a lyrical poet
had also exercised some sway. But, indeed, he is so far removed from ordinary apprehensions in most of his poems, or more or less in all, and they
have been so little spread abroad, that it would be impossible to attribute
to them any decided place among the impulses which have directed the
extraordinary mass of poetry displaying power of one or another kind,
which has been brought before us from his day to our own. Perhaps some
infusion of his modest and genuine beauties might add a charm even to the
most gifted works of our present rather redundant time.

> Dante Gabriel Rossetti, 1863, *The Life of William Blake*, by
> Alexander Gilchrist, Supplementary Chapter, vol. I, p. 381

We are far from intending to disparage the real merits of these verses. Imi-
tative to the verge of plagiarism as they are, they are often so skilfully composed, and relieved by such graceful touches of fancy and sweet snatches
of melody, as to confer genuine pleasure in defiance of critical analysis.
Here Blake's artistic power makes itself felt, nor need we grudge him the
praise that belongs to it because his panegyrists perversely claim for him
honours to which he is not entitled. It was most creditable to his taste that
he rejected the inferior models of contemporary poetry in favour of the great
masters, but from the pother that Mr. Gilchrist and Mr. Swinburne make
about it, one would suppose that he was the only one of his generation who
manifested such sympathy. In fact, his was an age of poetic revival, and he
did but worship at shrines newly set up by others.

> Henry G. Hewlett, 1876, "Imperfect Genius: William Blake,"
> *Contemporary Review*, vol. 28, p. 765

It is to these essays of his youth and early manhood that we must look for the true sources of his fame. The *Poetical Sketches,* begun when the author was only twelve years of age, and finished when he was no more than twenty, must assuredly be reckoned among the most extraordinary examples of youthful production; and it is profoundly characteristic of the man and his particular cast of mind that many of these boyish poems are among the best that Blake at any time produced. For his was a nature that owed little to development or experience. The perfect innocence of his spirit, as it kept him safe from the taint of the world, also rendered him incapable of receiving that enlargement of sympathy and deepening of emotion which others differently constituted may gain from contact with actual life. His imagination was not of the kind that could deal with the complex problems of human passion; he retained to the end of his days the happy ignorance as well as the freshness of chilhood: and it is therefore perhaps less wonderful in his case than it would be in the case of a poet of richer and more varied humanity that he should be able to display at once and in early youth the full measure of his powers. But this acknowledgment of the inherent limitation of Blake's poetic gift leads us by a natural process to a clearer recognition of its great qualities. His detachment from the ordinary currents of practical thought left to his mind an unspoiled and delightful simplicity which has never been matched in English poetry.

J. Comyns Carr, 1880, The English Poets, ed. Ward,
vol. III, p. 598

We do not believe that the merely intelligent beholder, capable of admiring beauty and loving poetry, but without any settled creed in art or foregone conclusion, would ever of his own accord find in Blake the wonderful genius and grandeur with which it is now usual to credit him. Here and there he produces something by a sort of accidental inspiration, as in the beautiful creation, full of heavenly joy and beauty, of the "Morning stars singing together," by which the most insensible must be moved. But it is unfortunate that his exponents should strain their demands so far as to require us to applaud in an equal degree all those weird outlines flung about the windy skies, all the crouching horrors and staring wild apparitions which mope and gibber in so many of his extraordinary pages.

Margaret O. W. Oliphant, 1882, The Literary History of England,
XVIIIth-XIXth Century, vol. II, p. 240

If we wish to understand Blake as a poet, we must discard his Ossianic and prophetic aberrations, and read him as we would any other poet, not when he is at his worst, but when he is at his best, in his *Songs of Innocence,* and *Songs of Experience,* which was published five years later. Here we find a poet who differed from all his contemporaries, who had no predecessor, and has had no successor, but who was altogether unique, original and individual, primitive and elemental. The qualities which distinguish his verse at this time were simplicity and sincerity, sweetness and grace, an untutored, natural note which reminds one of the singing of a child who croones to himself in his happy moments, not knowing how happy he is, wise beyond his years, superior to time or fate. They seem never to have been written, but to have written themselves, they are so frank and joyous, so inevitable and final.

Richard Henry Stoddard, 1892, *Under the Evening Lamp*, p. 174

Indeed it must be owned that a singer of so faulty an ear, and a writer of so shaky a grammar as Blake, was hardly well equipped for a pioneer of literary reform. Even now a considerable amount of the little that Blake has left must be rejected by the impartial critic as neither poetry nor sense; but the high poetical quality, the exquisite charm and freshness of the residue, is not to be denied. The affinity of his highest work with that of Wordsworth's best is as striking as the resemblance of the two poets at their respective flattest is amusing. He anticipated the creator of Betty Foy, not in his noble simplicities alone, but in his irritating puerilities also. If he led the way for Wordsworth up the steep of Parnassus, he as certainly preceded him down the slope on the other side into the valley of Bathos. Blake's lack of humour seems to have been as complete as Wordsworth's, and in the elder poet there are lines of sudden descent into prose which startle us almost like a prophetic parody of the younger.

Henry Duff Traill, 1896, *Social England,* vol. V, p. 445

Blake's poetry is, from beginning to end, childish; it has the fresh simplicity, but also the vapid deficiences of its quality—the metre halts and is imperfect; the rhymes are forced and inaccurate, and often impress one with the sense that the exigencies of assonance are so far masters of the sense, that the word that ends a stanza is obviously not the word really wanted or intended by the author, but only approximately thrown out at it.

Arthur Christopher Benson, 1896, *Essays*, pp. 150, 151

This philosophy kept him more simply a poet than any poet of his time, for it made him content to express every beautiful feeling that came into his head without troubling about its utility or chaining it to any utility. . . . When one reads Blake, it is as though the spray of an inexhaustible fountain of beauty was blown into our faces, and not merely when one reads *The*

Songs of Innocence, or the lyrics he wished to call "The Ideas of Good and Evil"; but when one reads those "Prophetic Works" in which he spoke confusedly and obscurely because he spoke of things for whose speaking he could find no models in the world about him. He was a symbolist who had to invent his symbols; and his counties of England, with their correspondence to tribes of Israel, and his mountains and rivers, with their correspondence to parts of a man's body, are arbitrary as some of the symbolism in the *Axël* of the symbolist Villiers de l'Isle Adam is arbitrary, while they have an incongruity that *Axël* has not. He was a man crying out for a mythology, and trying to make one because he could not find one to his hand.

William Butler Yeats, 1897, "Academy Portraits," *The Academy,*
vol. 51, p. 634

GENERAL

His Design can ill be translated into words, and very inadequately by any engraver's copy. Of his Poems, tinged with the very same ineffable qualities, obstructed by the same technical flaws and impediments—a semi-utterance as it were, snatched from the depths of the vague and unspeakable—of these remarkable Poems, never once yet fairly placed before the reading public, specimens shall by-and-bye speak more intelligibly for themselves. Both form part in a Life and Character as new, romantic, pious—in the deepest natural sense—as they: romantic, though incident be slight; animated by the same unbroken simplicity, the same high unity of sentiment.

Alexander Gilchrist, 1863, *Life of William Blake,*
vol. 1, p. 4

During the last six years Blake has been a "fancy" with many people who had before hardly known his name; but the peculiar characteristics of his genius are such as to make him "caviare to the general." With two classes, however, he is likely to hold a high place permanently: with the mystics, as the most spiritual, intense, and imaginative of English mystics; and with artists, and true lovers of art, as painter and poet, with a genius of a curiously individual stamp, and as pure and lofty as it was original. Among modern artists, Blake forms a class by himself. With great inequalities, alike in conception and execution, his work is instinct with a spirit which distinguishes it from that of any of his predecessors or contemporaries. "William Blake, his mark," ineffaceably stamps every production of his pencil or his pen. In his highest reach of imagination he has never been surpassed; in the perfection of his technical execution at its best he is one of the great masters.

Charles Eliot Norton, 1869, "Blake's Songs and Poetical Sketches,"
North American Review, vol. 108, p. 641

Now that there is a movement in London to form a (William) Blake Society, on the lines of the Shelley and the Browning Societies, there will probably be something of the sort here. There is nobody on the face of the earth who could better serve as the centre of a Boston craze than William Blake. He was great enough to be utterly misunderstood; he wrote a good deal that is so absolutely incomprehensible to everybody that the wayfaring man, though a fool, cannot lack abundant excuse for all sorts of new and fantastic "interpretations" of it, while there is still enough that is beautiful and sublime, and at the same time intelligible, to hold the sensible, who are the saving salt of these societies. The fact that the Boston Art Museum has just accumulated the original Blake water-colors brought over here by Mr. Quaritch is an additional fact which may be counted upon as having some weight, and I live in hope that we may next winter have the amusement of a Blake Society, with all the exquisite fooling that this implies.

Arlo Bates, 1890, "Literary Topics in Boston,"
The Book Buyer, vol. 7, p. 199

WILLIAM HAZLITT
1778-1830

Born, at Maidstone, Kent, 10 April 1778. 1783, taken to the United States of America by his parents. 1786, returns to England. 1793, a scholar in the Unitarian College, Hackney. 1802, an art student in Paris. 1805, publishes *Essay on the Principles of Human Action*. 1806, publishes *Free Thoughts on Public Affairs*. 1808, marries Miss Sarah Stoddart. 1812, lectures upon philosophy, before the Russell Institute, London. 1814, contributes to the *Edinburgh Review*. Theatrical critic of the *Morning Chronicle*. 1817, *The Round Table* published, the joint work of Leigh Hunt and himself. Publishes *Characters of Shakespeare's Plays*. 1818, lectures upon the English poets, before the Surrey Institute, London. Publishes *A View of the English Stage*. 1819, lectures upon the English comic writers, before the Surrey Institute, London. 1820, lectures upon the dramatic literature of the age of Elizabeth, before the Surrey Institute, London. 1822, divorced from his wife. Writes for *The Liberal*. 1823, publishes *Liber Amoris*. 1824, marries Mrs. Bridgewater, a widow, and goes abroad with her. 1825, separated from his wife. Returns to England. Publishes *The Spirit of the Age*. 1828, publishes the *Life of Napoleon*, vols. 1 and 2. 1830, publishes the *Life of Napoleon*, vols. 3 and 4, and *Conversations of James Northcote*. Dies, September 18th.

Edward T. Mason, 1885, ed., *Personal Traits of British Authors*, p. 178

SEE: *Complete Works*, ed. P. P. Howe, 1930-34, 21 v.; *Selected Essays*, ed. Geoffrey Keynes, 1930; P. P. Howe, *The Life of Hazlitt*, 1922, rev. 1928, 1947; Lynn B. Bennion, *William Hazlitt's Shakespeare Criticism*, 1947; Herschel Baker, *William Hazlitt*, 1962.

PERSONAL

Heard Hazlitt's first lecture on the History of English Philosophy. He seems to have no conception of the difference between a lecture and a book. What he said was sensible and excellent, but he delivered himself in a low, monotonous voice, with his eyes fixed on his MS., not once daring to look at his audience; and he read so rapidly that no one could possibly give to the matter the attention it required. . . . The cause of his reading so rapidly was, that he was told to limit himself to an hour, and what he had prepared would have taken three hours, if it had been read slowly.

Henry Crabb Robinson, 1812, Diary, Jan. 14, 15;
Reminiscences, ed. Sadler, vol. I, p. 236

I found Hazlitt living in Milton's house, the very one where he dictated his *Paradise Lost,* and occupying the room where, tradition says, he kept the organ on which he loved to play. I should rather say Hazlitt sat in it, for, excepting his table, three chairs, and an old picture, this enormous room was empty and *un*occupied. It was white-washed, and all over the walls he had written in pencil short scraps of brilliant thoughts and phrases, half-lines of poetry, references, etc., in the nature of a commonplace-book. His conversation was much of the same kind, generally in short sentences, quick and pointed, dealing much in allusions, and relying a good deal on them for success; as, when he said, with apparent satisfaction, that Curran was the Homer of blackguards, and afterwards, when the political state of the world came up, said of the Emperor Alexander, that "he is the Sir Charles Grandison of Europe." On the whole, he was more amusing than interesting, and his nervous manner shows that this must be his character. He is now nearly forty, and when quite young lived several years in America, chiefly in Virginia, but a little while at our Dorchester.

George Ticknor, 1819, Journal; Life, Letters and Journals,
vol. I, p. 293

I really believe Hazlitt to be a disinterested and suffering man, who feels public calamities as other men do private ones; and this is perpetually redeeming him in my eyes. . . . I know that Hazlitt does *pocket* up wrongs in this way, to draw them out again some day or other. He says it is the only comfort which the friends of his own cause leave him.

Leigh Hunt, 1821, Correspondence, vol. I, p. 166

I stood well with him for fifteen years (the proudest of my life), and have ever spoken my full mind of him to some, to whom his panegyric must naturally be least tasteful. I never in thought swerved from him, I never betrayed him, I never slackened in my admiration of him; I was the same to him (neither better nor worse), though he could not see it, as in the days when he thought fit to trust me. At this instant, he may be preparing for me some compliment, above my deserts, as he has sprinkled many such among his admirable books, for which I rest his debtor; or, for anything I know, or can guess to the contrary, he may be about to read a lecture on my weaknesses. He is welcome to them (as he was to my humble hearth), if they can divert a spleen, or ventilate a fit of sullenness. I wish he would not quarrel with the world at the rate he does; but the reconciliation must be affected by himself, and I despair of living to see that day. But, protesting against much that he has written, and some things which he chooses to do; judging him by his conversation which I enjoyed so long, and relished so deeply; or by his books, in those places where no clouding passion intervenes—I should belie my own conscience, if I said less, than that I think W. H. to be, in his natural and healthy state, one of the wisest and finest spirits breathing. So far from being ashamed of that intimacy, which was betwixt us, it is my boast that I was able for so many years to have preserved it entire; and I think I shall go to my grave without finding or expecting to find, such another compaion.

Charles Lamb, 1823, The Tombs in the Abbey

Poor Hazlitt! He, too, is one of the victims to the Moloch Spirit of this Time. . . . In Hazlitt, as in Byron and Burns and so many others in their degree, there lay some tone of the "eternal melodies," which he could not fashion into terrestrial music, but which uttered itself only in harsh jarrings and inarticulate cries of pain. Poor Hazlitt. There is one star less in the heavens, though a twinkling, dimmed one; while the street-lamps and horn lanterns are all burning, with their whale-oil or coal gas, as before!

Thomas Carlyle, 1830, Letter; Life by Conway, p. 251

Mr. Hazlitt's life was particularly an intellectual one. . . . His personal and moral infirmities were the result of several combining circumstances; and his life displayed a continual conflict between a magnificent intellect and morbid, miserly physical influences. . . . On his behalf, if any new plea were capable of being urged, it would be this: that his irrepressible love of truth, and abhorrence of disguise in any shape or under any circumstances, have been the means of laying bare before us much that other men would have shrunk instinctively from divulging. We are bound to recollect that he has opened his whole heart to us; and allowances are to be made for that confessed addiction to taking the extreme view, and sailing over-closely to the wind.

W. Carew Hazlitt, 1867, Memoirs of William Hazlitt,
vol. I, Preface, pp. vii, xiii

Like so many another fierce combatant with the pen, he was a shy, timid, and morbidly, horribly sensitive creature. But shy, self-absorbed, diffident before others, he was at bottom proud, scornful, brimming over with every form of stirring and tumultuous passion. He himself spoke of himself as "the king of good haters"—which, indeed, he was not; for your real hater doth never unpack his heart with words; and our poor Hazlitt was constantly assailing some literary or political antipathy as a little blacker than Satan, and more destructive than sin. His strong personality can be read between every line that he wrote.

T. P. O'Connor, 1895, *Some Old Love Stories,* p. 150

Liber Amoris (1823)

Hazlitt at present gives me great pain by the folly with which he is conducting himself. He has fallen in love to a pitch of insanity, with a lodging-house hussy, who will be his death. He has been to Scotland and divorced his wife, although he has a fine little boy by her; and after doing this, to marry this girl, he comes back and finds she has been making a fool of him in order to get presents, and in reality has been admitting a lover more favored. Hazlitt's torture is beyond expression; you may imagine it. The girl really excited in him a pure, devoted, and intense love. His imagination clothed her with that virtue which her affected modesty induced him to believe in, and he is really downright in love with an ideal perfection, which has no existence but in his own head! He talks of nothing else day and night. He has written down all the conversations without color, literally as they happened; he has preserved all the love-letters, many of which are equal to anything of the sort, and really affecting; and I believe, in order to ease his soul of this burden, means, with certain arrangements to publish it as a tale of character. He will sink into idiotcy if he does not get rid of it. Poor Hazlitt! He who makes so free with the follies of his friends, is of all mortals the most open to ridicule. To hear him repeat in a solemn tone and with agitated mouth the things of love he said to her (to convince you that he made love in the true gallant way), to feel the beauty of the sentiment, and then look up and see his old, hard, weather-beaten, saturnine, metaphysical face—the very antidote of the sentiment—twitching all sorts of ways, is really enough to provoke a saint to laughter. He has a notion that women have never liked him. Since this affair he has dressed in the fashion, and keeps insinuating his improved appearance. *He springs up to show you his pantaloons!* What a being it is! His conversation is now a mixture of disappointed revenge, passionate remembrances, fiendish hopes, and melting lamentations.

Benjamin Robert Haydon, 1822, *Letter to Miss Mitford,* Sept. 8;
Life, Letters and Table Talk, ed. Stoddard, p. 210

Hazlitt paints her as a vision of rarest beauty, somewhat undeveloped and soulless, but into whom, like Pygmalion, his devotion would infuse life and soul. The truth seems to be, that his statue was a vulgar young woman, accustomed to flirt with the lodgers who came under her mother's roof, and that she could no more understand the feeling with which she was regarded by a man of genius than she could have returned it if it had been comprehensible to her.

Abby Sage Richardson, 1882, Old Love-Letters, p. 173

GENERAL

He seems pretty generally, indeed, in a state of happy intoxication—and has borrowed from his great original, not indeed the force and brilliancy of his fancy, but something of its playfulness, and a large share of his apparent joyousness and self-indulgence in its exercise. It is evidently a great pleasure to him to be fully possessed with the beauties of his author, and to follow the impulse of his unrestrained eagerness to impress them upon his readers.

Francis, Lord Jeffrey, 1817, "Hazlitt on Shakespeare,"
Edinburgh Review, vol. 28, p. 472

Hazlitt had [has] damned the bigoted and the blue-stockinged; how durst the man?! He is your only god damner, and if ever I am damned, I should ['nt] like him to damn me. *

John Keats, 1818, To Benjamin Robert Haydon,
March 21; Letters

We are not apt to imbibe half opinions, or to express them by halves; we shall, therefore, say at once, that when Mr. Hazlitt's taste and judgment are left to themselves, we think him among the best, if not the very best, living critic on our national literature. . . . As we have not scrupled to declare that we think Mr. Hazlitt is sometimes the very best living critic, we shall venture one step farther, and add, that we think he is sometimes the very worst. One would suppose he had a personal quarrel with all living writers, good, bad, or indifferent. In fact, he seems to know little about them, and to care less. With him, to be alive is not only a fault in itself, but it includes all other possible faults. He seems to consider life as a disease, and death as your only doctor. He reverses the proverb, and thinks a dead ass is better than a living lion. In his eyes, death, like charity, "covereth a multitude of sins."

---

*Hyder E. Rollins, in his edition of *The Letters of John Keats: 1814-1821* (1958), Vol. I. p. 252, Footnote 7, says of this last quoted sentence: " . . . a sentence that has been misquoted dozens of times. . . . Keats would hardly have wished to be damned by Hazlitt."

In short if you want his praise, you must die for it; and when such praise is deserved, and given really *con amore,* it is almost worth dying for.

John Wilson, 1818, "Hazlitt's Lectures on English Poetry," *Blackwood's Magazine,* vol. 3, p. 75

Though Mr. Hazlitt frequently shows great talent and taste, he is not qualified for the task he has undertaken. In the midst of what is good in him, he mistakes so grossly, that we are led to suspect that he has often picked up his opinions as well as his words from others, and that when he fails, it is when he relies upon himself. He is in the midst of men of genius in London, where it is no hard thing with a good memory and some smartness, and no conscience about thefts, to put together such a book as this. Of his conduct in life we know nothing; nor if we did should we speak of it, unless we might fairly with praise; neither do we altogether like giving an opinion of a man's secret principles and disposition, from his writings; yet we must say that Mr. Hazlitt appears too loose in the one, and too envious and spleeny, where there is room for it, in the other, to treat with a correct understanding and a right delicacy and truth of feeling and sentiment, upon a subject like poetry which concerns all that is moral and refined and intellectual in our natures. He is much too full of himself to have a sincere love and interest for what is abstractly good and great, and more intent upon displaying his own fine parts, than spreading before his readers the excellencies of others.

Richard Henry Dana, 1819, "Hazlitt's English Poets," *North American Review,* vol. 8, p. 320

Hazlitt was, in many respects, the most *natural* of critics. He was *born* to criticise, not in a small and captious way, but as a just, generous, although stern and rigorous judge. Nature had denied him great constructive, or dramatic, or synthetic power—the power of the highest kind of poet or philosopher. But he possessed that mixture in proper proportions of the acute and the imaginative, the profound and the brilliant, the cool and the enthusiastic, which goes to constitute the true critic. Hence his criticism is a fine compound—pleasing, on the one hand, the lover of analysis, who feels that its power can go no farther; and, on the other, the young and ardent votary of literature, who feels that Hazlitt has expressed in language what *he* only could "with the faltering tongue and the glistening eye."

George Gilfillan, 1855, *A Third Gallery of Portraits,* p. 176

Hazlitt's cynicism is the souring of a generous nature; and when we turn from the politician to the critic and the essayist, our admiration for his powers is less frequently jarred by annoyance at their wayward misuse. . . . Hazlitt's point of view was rather different, nor can we ascribe to him without qualification that exquisite appreciation of purely literary charm which is so rare and so often affected. Nobody, indeed, loved some authors more heartily or understood them better; his love is so hearty that he cannot preserve the true critical attitude. Instead of trying them on his palate, he swallows them greedily. His judgment of an author seems to depend upon two circumstances. He is determined in great measure by his private associations, and in part by his sympathy for the character of the writer. His interest in this last sense is, one may say, rather psychological than purely critical. . . . Hazlitt harps a good deal upon one string; but that string vibrates forcibly. His best passages are generally an accumulation of short, pithy sentences, shaped in strong feeling, and coloured by picturesque association; but repeating, rather than corroborating, each other. The last blow goes home, but each falls on the same place. He varies the phrase more than the thought; and sometimes he becomes obscure, because he is so absorbed in his own feelings that he forgets the very existence of strangers who require explanation. Read through Hazlitt, and this monotony becomes a little tiresome; but dip into him at intervals, and you will often be astonished that so vigorous a writer has not left some more enduring monument of his remarkable powers.

Leslie Stephen, 1875, *Hours in a Library, Second Series,*
vol. II, pp. 321, 322, 343

Hazlitt was beyond all question a great, a very great, critic—in not a few respects our very greatest. All his work, or almost all that has much merit, is small in individual bulk, though the total is very respectable. . . . Great as Hazlitt was as a miscellaneous and Montaignesque essayist, he was greater as a literary critic. Literature was, though he coquetted with art, his first and most constant love; it was the subject on which, as far as English literature is concerned (and he knew little and is still less worth consulting about any other), he had acquired the largest and soundest knowledge; and it is that for which he had the most original and essential genius. His intense prejudices and his occasional inadequacy make themselves felt here as they do everywhere, and even here it is necessary to give the caution that Hazlitt is never to be trusted when he shows the least evidence of dislike for which he gives no reason. But to any one who has made a little progress in criticism himself, to any one who has either read for himself or is capable of reading for himself, of being guided by what is helpful and of neglecting what is not, there is no greater critic than Hazlitt in any language. He will sometimes miss—he is never perhaps so certain as his friends Lamb and Hunt were to find—exquisite in individual points. Prejudice, accidental ignorance, or other causes may sometimes invalidate his account of authors or of subjects in general. But still the four great collections of his criticism, *The Characters of Shakespeare, The Elizabethan Dramatists, The English Poets,* and *The English Comic Writers,* with not a few scattered things in his other writings, make what is on the whole the best corpus of criticism by a single writer in English on English. He is the critics' critic as Spenser is the poets' poet; that is to say, he has, errors excepted and deficiencies allowed, the greatest proportion of the strictly critical excellencies—of the qualities which make a critic—that any English writer of his craft has ever possessed.

George Saintsbury, 1896, *A History of Nineteenth Century Literature*, pp. 185, 186

The four volumes [*Life of Napoleon*] certainly abound with magnificent passages, and when we look at the amount of technical detail and the fund of information brought together from scattered sources, we can hardly fail to admire the literary workmanship and intellectual penetration which are conspicuous throughout, and the power of the book is the more impressive when we recollect that it was produced under immense disadvantages and in declining health. He had never attempted anything on the same scale before; and he happened to undertake the task when he was, physically speaking, least qualified to carry it successfully out.

W. Carew Hazlitt, 1897, *Four Generations of a Literary Family,* vol. I, p. 192

HENRY MACKENZIE
1745-1831

Henry Mackenzie was born in Edinburgh, Scotland, July 28, 1745. He was educated at the University of Edinburgh, studied law, and became attorney for the crown. In 1804 he was appointed comptroller of taxes for Scotland. In 1771 he published anonymously a novel entitled *The Man of Feeling,* which at once became very popular. A young clergyman named Eccles, of Bath, laid claim to it, and to establish his claim transcribed with his own hand the entire book, making numerous corrections and interlineations. The question of authorship was settled by the formal declaration of the publishers. Mackenzie published *The Man of the World* in 1783; [1773] and afterward *Julia de Roubigné,* a tale in a series of letters. In 1779-80 he edited *The Mirror,* a semi-weekly modelled after Addison's *Spectator,* to which he contributed forty-two papers. Among these was the "Story of La Roche," which appeared in *The Mirror* for June 19, 22, and 26, 1779. In 1785-86 he edited a similar periodical called *The Lounger,* to which he contributed fifty-seven papers. Among these was an appreciative criticism on the poetry of Burns, which gave him the reputation of having first called attention to its merits. He wrote *The White Hypocrite,* a comedy, which was performed at Covent Garden, London; and two tragedies, *The Spanish*

Father, and *The Prince of Tunis.* The latter was brought out with great success in Edinburgh. Mackenzie's other works include biographies of Home and Dr. Blacklock, essays on dramatic poetry, and numerous Tory tracts. He married in 1776, and had a large family. He died in Edinburgh, January 14, 1831.

Rossiter Johnson, 1875, *Little Classics,* (Vol. XVI),
Authors, p. 168

SEE: *The Anecdotes and Egotisms of Henry Mackenzie,* ed. Harold William Thompson, 1927.

PERSONAL

A rare thing this literature, or love of fame or notoriety which accompanies it. Here is Mr. Henry Mackenzie on the very brink of human dissolution, as actively anxious about it as if the curtain must not soon be closed on that and everything else. He calls me his literary confessor; and I am sure I am glad to return the kindnesses which he showed me long since in George Square. No man is less known from his writings. You would suppose a retired, modest, somewhat affected man, with a white handkerchief, and a sign ready for every sentiment. No such thing: H. M. is alert as a contracting tailor's needle in every sort of business—a politician and a sportsman— shoots and fishes in a sort even to this day—and is the life of company with anecdotes and fun. Sometimes his daughter tells me he is in low spirits at home, but really I never see anything of it in society.

Sir Walter Scott, 1825, *Diary,* Dec. 6; *Life* by Lockhart, ch. lxv

The title of *The Man of Feeling* adhered to him ever after the publication of that novel; and it was a good example of the difference there sometimes is between a man and his work. Strangers used to fancy that he must be a pensive sentimental Harley; whereas he was far better,—a hard-headed practical man, as full of worldy wisdom as most of his fictitious characters are devoid of it; and this without in the least impairing the affectionate softness of his heart.

Henry, Lord Cockburn, 1830-54, *Memorials of His Time,* ch. v

The Man of Feeling (1771)

His *Man of Feeling* is the offspring of the *Sentimental Journal* and *Werther* schools: it is better regulated than the first, and less frantic than the second: the hero is possessed with a passion which he has too much modesty to utter, and dies, of true love and decline, when all wish him to live. The scene in the madhouse should be learned by heart.

Allan Cunningham, 1833, *Biographical and Critical History of*
the Last Fifty Years

The tender pleasure which *The Man of Feeling* excites is wholly without alloy. Its hero is the most beautiful personification of gentleness, patience, and meek sufferings which the heart can conceive.

> Thomas Noon Talfourd, 1842, *London New Monthly Magazine;*
> *Critical and Miscellaneous Writings,* p. 21

The novels of Henry Mackenzie have a charm of their own, which may be largely attributed to the fact that their author was a gentleman. Whoever has read, to any extent, the works of fiction of the eighteenth century, must have observed how perpetually he was kept in low company, how rarely he met with a character who had the instincts as well as the social position of a gentleman. A tone of refined sentiment and dignity pervades *The Man of Feeling,* which recalls *The Vicar of Wakefield,* and introduces the reader to better company and more elevated thoughts than the novels of the time usually afford. *The Man of Feeling* is hardly a narrative. Harley, the chief character, is a sensitive, retiring man, with feelings too fine for his surroundings. The author places him in various scenes, and traces the effect which each produces upon his character. The effect of the work is agreeable, though melancholy, and the early death of Harley contemplates the delineation of a man too gentle and too sensitive to battle with life.

> Bayard Tuckerman, 1882, *A History of English*
> *Prose Fiction,* p. 241

Written in a style alternating between the whims of Sterne and a winning plaintiveness, it enjoys the distinction of being the most sentimental of all English novels. One scene of it, in which the frail hero dies from the shock he receives when a Scotch maiden of pensive face and mild hazel eyes acknowledges that she can return his love for her, deserves to be remembered.

> Wilbur L. Cross, 1899, *The Development of the*
> *English Novel,* p. 83

SIR WALTER SCOTT
1771-1832

Born August 15, 1771. Scott, who began his study of the law in 1786, was certified for practice in 1792. Two years after his marriage in 1797, he was appointed Sheriff of Selkirkshire. Appointed Clerk of the Sessions in 1806. In 1812 he moved into Abbotsford. Created a baronet in 1820. In 1826 two tragedies struck him: the death of his wife and the failure of his publishers, Ballantyne. Scott, under no clear legal obligation, voluntarily worked to repay the debts of the publishing firm. His last years saw a considerable literary output under the strain of financial pressures.

In 1831 he travelled to Italy for a much-needed rest. He died September 21, 1832. WORKS: Published translation of Buerger's *Ballads,* 1796; translated Goethe's *Goetz von Berlichingen,* 1799; *The Eve of St. John: a Border Ballad,* 1800; *Minstrelsy of the Scottish Border,* 1802; edited *Sir Tristram,* a metrical romance by Thomas of Ercildoune, 1804; *The Lay of the Last Minstrel: a Poem,* 1805; edited *Memoirs,* 1806; *Marmion: a Tale of Flodden Field,* 1808; edited *The Works of John Dryden,* 18 vols., and *Life,* 1808; edited Strutt's *Queenhoo Hall: a Romance;* in 1809 he began his edition of State Papers and Somers' Collection of Tracts at which he worked until 1815; *The Lady of the Lake: a Poem,* 1810; in 1810 he edited *English Minstrelsy; The Vision of Don Roderick: a Poem,* 1811; *Rokeby: a Poem,* 1813; *The Bride of Triermain,* 1813; *Waverly,* 1814; edited *The Works of Swift,* 19 vols., and *Life,* 1814; *The Border Antiquities,* 1814-17; in 1815 he published *Guy Mannering; The Lord of the Isles; The Fields of Waterloo,* 1815; edited *Memoirs of the Somervilles,* 1815; *The Antiquary,* 1816; in 1817 he published the first of the series of *Tales of My Landlord,* which included *The Black Dwarf,* and *Old Mortality; Harold the Dauntless: a Poem,* 1817; *Rob Roy,* 1818; *Tales of my Landlord,* second series (includes *The Heart of Midlothian*), 1818; *Tales of My Landlord,* third series (*The Bride of Lammermoor; The Legend of Montrose*), 1819; *Ivanhoe,* 1820; *The Monastery,* 1820; *The Abbot,* 1820; *Kenilworth,* 1821; edited *Ballantyne's Novelists' Library,* 1821-24; *The Pirate,* 1822; *The Fortunes of Nigel,* 1822; *Peveril of the Peak,* 1822; *Halidon Hill: a Dramatic Sketch,* 1822; *Quentin Durward,* 1823; *Redgauntlet,* 1824; *St. Roman's Well,* 1824; *Tales of the Crusaders* (includes *The Betrothed* and *The Talisman*), 1825; *Woodstock: or the Cavalier,* 1826; *The Life of Napoleon Buonaparte,* 1827, 9 vols.; *Chronicles of the Canongate,* first series (includes *The Two Drovers; The Highland Widow; The Surgeon's Daughter*), 1827; *Chronicles of the Canongate,* second series (includes *The Fair Maid of Perth*), 1828; in 1828 a six-volume edition of his Miscellaneous Collected Works appeared; *Tales of a Grandfather,* two series, 1828-31; *Anne of Geierstein,* 1829; *The History of Scotland,* 1829-30; *Letters on Demonology and Witchcraft,* 1830; *Tales of My Landlord,* fourth series (includes *Count Robert of Paris* and *Castle Dangerous*), 1831. COLLECTED WORKS: *Novels and Tales,* 1819-33, 41 v.

SEE: *The Waverley Novels,* ed. Andrew Lang, 1892-94; *Complete Poetical Works,* ed. H. E. Scudder, 1900 (Cambridge ed.); *Poetical Works,* ed. J. Logie Robertson, 1904 (OSA); *Journal: 1825-1832,* ed. J. G. Tait and W. M. Parker, 1939-47, 3 v.; *Letters,* ed. H. J. C. Grierson and others, 1932-37, 12 v.; J. G. Lockhart, *Life of Sir Walter Scott,* 1837-38, 2 v., many reprints, one-volume abridgement by Andrew Lang, *Everyman* edition, 1906; H. J. C. Grierson, *Sir Walter Scott,* 1938 [supplement to Lockhart's *Life*]; John Buchan, *Sir Walter Scott,* 1932; David Cecil, *Sir Walter Scott,* 1933; W. L. Renwick, ed., *Sir Walter Scott Lectures,* 1950.

PERSONAL

On our mentioning Mr. Scott's name the woman of the house showed us all possible civility, but her slowness was really amusing. I should suppose it is a house little frequented, for there is no appearance of an inn. Mr. Scott, who she told me was a very clever gentleman, "goes there in the fishing season"; but indeed Mr. Scott is respected everywhere: I believe that by favour of his name one might be hospitably entertained throughout all the borders of Scotland.

Dorothy Wordsworth, 1803, *Journals,* Sept. 18, vol. II, p. 131

Tall, and rather robust than slender, but lame in the same manner as Mr. Hayley, and in a greater measure. Neither the contour of his face, nor yet his features, are elegant; his complexion healthy, and somewhat fair, without bloom. We find the singularity of brown hair and eyelashes, with flaxen eyebrows, and a countenance open, ingenuous, and benevolent. When seriously conversing or earnestly attentive, though his eyes are rather of a lightish gray, deep thought is on their lids. He contracts his brow, and the rays of genius gleam aslant from the orbs beneath them. An upper lip too long prevents his mouth from being decidedly handsome; but the sweetest emanations of temper and heart play about it when he talks cheerfully or smiles: and in company he is much oftener gay than contemplative. His conversation is an overflowing fountain of brilliant wit, apposite allusion, and playful archness; while, on serious themes, it is nervous and eloquent; the accent decidedly Scotch, yet by no means broad.

Anna Seward, 1807, *Letters*

My first impression was, that he was neither so large, nor so heavy in appearance as I had been led to expect by description, prints, bust, and picture. He is more lame than I expected, but not unwieldy; his countenance, even by the uncertain light in which I first saw it, pleased me much, benovelent, and full of genius without the slightest effort at expression; delightfully natural, as if he did not know he was Walter Scott or the Great Unknown of the North, as if he only thought of making others happy. . . . The impression left on my mind this night was, that Walter Scott is one of the best bred men I ever saw, with all the exquisite politeness which he knows so well how to describe, which is of no particular school or country, but which is of all countries, the politeness which arises from good and quick sense and feeling, which seems to know by instinct the characters of others, to see what will please, and put all his guests at their ease. As I sat beside him at supper, I could not believe he was a stranger, and forgot he was a great man.

Maria Edgeworth, 1823, *Letters,* vol. II, pp. 98, 99

An event has just been announced which has thrown our little world into complete astonishment. Constable the bookseller has become bankrupt for a very large sum,—I cannot exactly say how much, and Sir Walter Scott is involved in this misfortune. The grief I felt on this occasion was very different indeed from the qualified sympathy with which Rochefoucault supposes us to regard the misfortunes of our friends. It was keen, deep, and by no means transient; every time I hear any allusion to him I grieve anew. I do not care about Constable personally, yet I find room for a little corner for him, for he has had by two marriages ten children. Next to our Scottish Shakspeare I lament for the kind-hearted, talented, and liberal-minded James Ballantyne. . . . A person, who to so many high endowments adds a superior portion of sound common sense, could not be quite insensible to the coming storm; but after the blast has passed over he will still be able to say, "All is lost but honour."

> Anne Grant, 1826, *Letters,* Feb. 23;
> *Memoir and Correspondence,* ed. Grant, vol. III, pp. 72, 73

Sir Walter was the best formed man I ever saw, and, laying his weak limb out of the question, a perfect model of a man for gigantic strength. I remember of one day long ago, I think it was at some national dinner in Oman's Hotel, that at a certain time of the night, a number of the young heroes differed prodigiously in regard to their various degrees of muscular strength. A general measurement took place around the shoulders and chest, and I, as a particular judge in these matters, was fixed on as the measurer and umpire. Scott, who never threw cold water on any fun, submitted to be measured with the rest. He measured most round the chest, and to their great chagrin, I was next to him, and very little short. But when I came to examine the arms! Sir Walter's had double the muscular power of mine, and very nearly so of every man's who was there. I declare, that from the elbow to the shoulder, they felt as if he had the strength of an ox.

> James Hogg, 1834, *Familiar Anecdotes of Sir Walter Scott,* p. 237

The conversation of Scott was frank, hearty, picturesque and dramatic. During the time of my visit he inclined to the comic rather than the grave, in his anecdotes and stories, and such, I was told, was his general inclination. He relished a joke, or a trait of humor in social intercourse, and laughed with right good will. He talked not for effect, not display, but from the flow of his spirits, the stores of his memory, and the vigor of his imagination. He had a natural turn for narration, and his narratives and descriptions were without effort, yet wonderfully graphic. He placed the scene before you like a picture; he gave the dialogue with the appropriate dialect or peculiarities, and described the appearance and characters of his personages with that spirit and felicity evinced in his writings. Indeed, his conversation reminded me continually of his novels; and it seems to me, that during the whole time I was with him, he talked enough to fill volumes, and that they could not be filled more delightfully. He was as good a listener as talker, appreciating what others said, however humble might be their rank or pretensions, and was quick to testify his perception of any point in their discourse. He arrogated nothing to himself, but was perfectly unassuming and unpretending, entering with heart and soul into the business, or pleasure, or, I had almost said, folly, of the hour and the company. No one's concerns, no one's thoughts, no one's opinions, no one's tastes and pleasures seemed beneath him. He made himself so thoroughly the companion of those with whom he happened to be, that they forgot for a time his vast superiority, and only recollected and wondered, when all was over, that it was Scott with whom they had been on such familiar terms, and in whose society they had felt so perfectly at their ease. . . . I consider it one of the greatest advantages that I have derived from my literary career, that it has elevated me into genial communion with such a spirit.

Washington Irving, 1835, "Abbotsford," Crayon Miscellany

Many people are living who had a most intimate acquaintance with him. I know no more of him than I know of Dryden or Addison, and not a tenth part so much as I know of Swift, Cowper, or Johnson. Then again, I have not, from the little that I do know of him, formed so high an opinion of his character as most people seem to entertain, and as it would be expedient for the *Edinburgh Review* to express. He seems to me to have been most carefully and successfully on his guard against the sins which most easily beset literary men. On that side he multiplied his precautions, and set double watch. Hardly any writer of note has been so free from the petty jealousies, and morbid irritabilities, of our caste. But I do not think that he kept himself equally pure from the faults of a very different kind, from the faults of a man of the world. In politics, a bitter and unscrupulous partisan; profuse and ostentatious in expense; agitated by the hopes and fears of a gambler; perpetually sacrificing the perfection of his compositions, and the durability of his fame, to his eagerness for money; writing with the slovenly haste of Dryden, in order to satisfy wants which were not, like those of Dryden, caused by circumstances beyond his control, but which were produced by his extravagant waste or rapacious speculation; this is the way in which he appears to me. I am sorry for it, for I sincerely admire the greater part of his works; but I cannot think him a high-minded man, or a man of very strict principle.

Thomas Babington Macaulay, 1838, Letter to Napier, June 26;
Life and Letters of Macaulay, ed. Trevelyan

We were not long in reaching Abbotsford. The house, which is more compact, and of considerably less extent than I anticipated, stands in full view from the road, and at only a short distance from it, lower down towards the river. Its aspect disappointed me; but so does everything. It is but a villa, after all; no castle, nor even a large manor-house, and very unsatisfactory when you consider it in that light. Indeed, it impressed me, not as a real house, intended for the home of human beings,—a house to die in or to be born in,—but as a plaything,—something in the same category as Horace Walpole's Strawberry Hill. The present owner seems to have found it insufficient for the actual purposes of life; for he is adding a wing, which promises to be as extensive as the original structure. . . . On the whole, there is no simple and great impression left by Abbotsford; and I felt angry and dissatisfied with myself for not feeling something which I did not and could not feel. But it is just like going to a museum, if you look into particulars; and one learns from it, too, that Scott could not have been really a wise man, nor an earnest one, nor one that grasped the truth of life; he did but play, and the play grew very sad towards its close. In a certain way, however, I understand his romances the better for having seen his house; and his house the better for having read his romances. They throw light on one another.

Nathaniel Hawthorne, 1856, English Note-Books, vol. II, pp. 46, 52

POETRY

The muse of Scott lives only in reminiscences of the old songs of Scotland; his verse is, as it were, a mosaic composed of detached fragments of romantic legend and early chivalry adapted to Scottish customs, and knit together with wondrous skill and care: just as fragmentary portions of paintings on glass out of Gothic churches are sometimes found in country houses and hermitages at the present day, neatly cemented together for the sake of picturesque effect.

Frederick Schlegel, 1815-59, Lectures on the History
of Literature, p. 315

No writer of modern times has combined so much power of imagination with such shrewdness in the observation of human character, and so much of the painter's eye in his delineation of outward objects, more particularly as regards the dresses, armour, furniture, and other decorations of past ages, insomuch that he is apt to dwell on these to the prejudice of what is more important to the general effect of his story.

Henry Francis Cary, 1823, Notices of Miscellaneous English
Poets, Memoir, ed. Cary, vol. II, p. 300

Compared with true and great poets, our Scottish minstrel is but a "metre ballad-monger." We would rather have written one song of Burns, or a single passage in Lord Byron's *Heaven and Earth*, or one of Wordsworth's "fancies and good-nights," than all his epics. . . . He is a mere narrative and descriptive poet, garrulous of the old time. The definition of his poetry is a pleasing superficiality.

William Hazlitt, 1825, *The Spirit of the Age*

The poetic style of Scott is—(it becomes necessary to say so when it is proposed to "translate Homer into the melodies of Marmion")—. . . [when] tried by the highest standards, a bastard epic style; and that is why, out of his own powerful hands, it has had so little success. It is a less natural, and therefore a less good style, than the original ballad-style; while it shares with the ballad-style the inherent incapacity of rising into the grand style, of adequately rendering Homer.

Matthew Arnold, 1861, *Lectures on Homer*, p. 59

Scott has always been the poet of youthful and high-hearted readers: there seems to be no reason why he should not continue indefinitely to meet their requirements, and certainly they will be considerable losers if ever, in the lapse of time and shifting of poetic models, his compositions should pass out of ready currency. He is not, and never can be, the poet of literary readers: the student and the artist remember him as a cherished enchantment of their youth, and do not recur to him. Neither the inner recesses of thought nor the high places of art thrill to his appeal. But it is highly possible for the critical tendency and estimate to be too exclusively literary; the poetry of Scott is mainly amenable to a different sort of test, and to that it responds not only adequately but triumphantly.

William Michael Rossetti, 1878, *Lives of Famous Poets*, p. 233

Yet it seems to me impossible, on any just theory of poetry or of literature, to rank him low as a poet. He can afford to take his trial under more than one statute. To those who say that all depends on the subject, or that the handling and arrangement of the subject are, if not everything, yet something to be ranked far above mere detached beauties, he can produce not merely the first long narrative poems in English, which for more than a century had honestly enthralled and fixed popular taste, but some of the very few long narrative poems which deserve to do so. . . . In his own special divisions of the simpler lyric and of lyrical narrative he sometimes attains the exquisite, and rarely sinks below a quality which is fitted to give the poetical delight to a very large number of by no means contemptible

persons. It appears to me at least, that on no sound theory of poetical criticism can Scott be ranked as a poet below Byron, who was his imitator in
narrative and his inferior in lyric. But it may be admitted that this was not
the opinion of most contemporaries of the two, and that, much as the poetry
of Byron has sunk in critical estimation during the last half century, and slight
as are the signs of its recovery, those who do not think very highly of the
poetry of the pupil do not, as a rule, show much greater enthusiasm for that
of the master.

George Saintsbury, 1896, *A History of Nineteenth Century
Literature,* pp. 74, 75

His style was modelled at first chiefly on the Border ballads, and the word
picturesque may perhaps best define it. The landscape is often rather
touched-in by way of support to his figures than painted for its own sake or
as the mere background of earlier days; human interests and passions, or
those historical memories in which his soul delighted, in general, pervade it.
. . . Scott, after Chaucer, is the one of all our non-dramatic poets who puts
himself least forward; one of the few who thought little or nothing, personally, of themselves; the one who trusts most to letting his characters and
scenes speak for themselves. By inevitable natural law he is indeed, of
course, present in his work; but, like Homer, like Shakespeare, behind the
curtain; latent in his own creation.

Francis Turner Palgrave, 1896, *Landscape in Poetry,* pp. 183, 188

The Lay of the Last Minstrel (1805)

The author, enamoured of the lofty visions of chivalry, and partial to the
strains in which they were formerly embodied, seems to have employed all
the resources of his genius in endeavoring to recall them to the favour and
admiration of the public; and in adapting to the taste of modern readers a
species of poetry which was once the delight of the courtly, but has long
ceased to gladden any other eyes than those of the scholar and the antiquary.
This is a romance, therefore, composed by a minstrel of the present day; or
such a romance as we may suppose would have been written in modern
times, if that style of composition had continued to be cultivated, and par-
taken consequently of the improvements which every branch of literature
has received since the time of its desertion.

Francis, Lord Jeffrey, 1805-44, *Contributions to the
Edinburgh Review,* vol. II, p. 460

The truth is that the supernatural element, so far from being an excrescence,
overhangs, encompasses, and interpenetrates the human element in the

story. . . . We may, if we please, call this supernatural machinery grotesque, or childish, or ridiculous, but it is absurd to speak of it as an excrescence, or otherwise than thoroughly transfused with the human interest of the story. Only a born romancer, in full imaginative sympathy with such childish or childlike superstitions, could have effected so complete a transfusion.

> William Minto, 1886, ed., *The Lay of the Last Minstrel,*
> Preface, pp. 19, 21

Marmion (1808)

His modes of life, his personal feelings, are no where so detailed as in the epistles prefixed to the cantos of *Marmion*. These bring us close to his side, and leading us with him through the rural and romantic scenes he loved, talk with us by the way of all the rich associations of which he was master. His dogs are with him; he surveys these dumb friends with the eye of a sportsman and a philosopher, and omits nothing in the description of them which could interest either. An old castle frowns upon the road; he bids its story live before you with all the animation of a drama and the fidelity of ·a chronicle. Are topics of the day introduced? He states his opinions with firmness and composure, expresses his admiration with energy, and, where he dissents from those he addresses, does so with unaffected candor and cordial benignity. Good and great man!

> Margaret Fuller Ossoli, 1850?, *Art, Literature*
> *and the Drama,* p. 74

Skilfully as the character of Marmion has been constructed, the reader cannot help feeling that it has been put together; hence we never quite breathe in the story, as we do in the *Iliad* or the *Odyssey,* the ideal atmosphere which is produced by the perfection of metrical writing. Prose alone could secure the large and unfettered liberty that historical romance requires: when Scott employs his magic powers to clothe the spirit of the Past in the language of real life the verisimilitude of his creation is complete.

> William John Courthope, 1885, *The Liberal Movement*
> *in English Literature,* p. 130

The Lady of The Lake (1810)

He says Walter Scott is going to publish a new poem; I do not augur well of the title, *The Lady of the Lake*. I hope this lady will not disgrace him. . . . By great good fortune, and by the good nature of Lady Charlotte Rawdon, we had *The Lady of the Lake* to read just when the O'Beirnes were with us. A most delightful reading we had; my father, the Bishop, and Mr. Jephson reading it aloud alternately. It is a charming poem: a most interesting story, generous, finely-drawn characters, and in many parts the finest poetry. But for an old prepossession—an unconquerable prepossession—in favour of the old minstrel, I think I should prefer this to either the *Lay* or *Marmion*. Our pleasure in reading it was increased by the sympathy and enthusiasm of the guests.

Maria Edgeworth, 1810, Letters, vol. I, pp. 169, 173

Walter Scott is out and away the king of the romantics. *The Lady of the Lake* has no indisputable claim to be a poem beyond the inherent fitness and desirability of the tale. It is just such a story as a man would make up for himself, walking, in the best health and temper, through just such scenes as it is laid in. Hence it is that a charm dwells undefinable among these slovenly verses, as the unseen cuckoo fills the mountains with his note; hence, even after we have flung the book aside, the scenery and adventures remain present to the mind, a new and green possession, not unworthy of that beautiful name, *The Lady of the Lake,* or that direct, romantic opening,— one of the most spirited and poetical in literature,—"The stag at eve had drunk his fill."

Robert Louis Stevenson, 1881, Memories and Portraits

NOVELS

My dear Murray,—I have this moment finished the reading of 192 pages of our book—for ours it must be—and I cannot go to bed without telling you what is the strong and most favourable impression it has made upon me. If the remainder be at all equal, which it cannot fail to be from the genius displayed in what is now before me, we have been most fortunate indeed. The title is "The Tales of my Landlord; collected and reported by Jedediah Cleishbotham, Parish Clerk and Schoolmaster of Gandercleugh." There cannot be a doubt as to the splendid merit of the work. It would never have done to have higgled and protested about seeing more volumes. I have now neither doubts nor fears, and I anxiously hope you will have as little. I am so happy at the fortunate termination of all my pains and anxieties, that I cannot be in bad humour with you for not writing me two lines in answer to my two last letters.

William Blackwood, 1816, Letter to [Mr. John] Murray, Aug. 23;
William Blackwood and His Sons, vol. I, p. 68

The general name of these works, "the Scotch Novels," will always indicate an era in our literary history, for they add a new species to the catalogue of our native literary productions, and nothing of the same nature has been produced anywhere else. They are as valuable as history and descriptive travels for the qualities which render these valuable; while they derive a bewitching animation from the soul of poetry, and captivate the attention by the interest of romantic story. As pictures of national manners they are inestimable; as views of human nature, influenced by local circumstances, they are extremely curious; as enthusiastic appeals to the passions and the imagination, they supply a strong stimulus to these faculties; and by running the course of the story through the most touching incidents, and within sight of the grandest events, they carry the reader's sympathy perpetually with them.

John Scott, 1820, *London Magazine*, Jan.

Scott is certainly the most wonderful writer of the day. His novels are a new literature in themselves, and his poetry as good as any—if not better (only on an erroneous system)—and only ceased to be so popular, because the vulgar learned were tired of hearing "Aristides called the Just," and Scott the Best, and ostracised him. I like him, too, for his manliness of character, for the extreme pleasantness of his conversation, and his good nature towards myself, personally. May he prosper!—for he deserves it. I know no reading to which I fall with such alacrity as a work of W. Scott's.

Lord Byron, 1821, *A Journal in Italy*, Jan. 12

It is no wonder that the public repay with lengthened applause and gratitude the pleasure they receive. He writes as fast as they can read, and he does not write himself down. He is always in the public eye, and we do not tire of him. His worst is better than any other person's best. His *backgrounds* (and his later works are little else but back-grounds capitally made out)—are more attractive than the principal figures and most complicated actions of other writers. His works (taken together) are almost like a new edition of human nature. This is indeed to be an author!

William Hazlitt, 1825, *The Spirit of the Age*

We should only read what we admire, as I did in my youth, and as I now experience with Sir Walter Scott. I have just begun *Rob Roy,* and will read his best novels in succession. All is great—material, import, characters, execution; and then what infinite diligence in the preparatory studies! what truth of detail in the execution! We see, too, what English history is; and what a thing it is when such an inheritance falls to the lot of a clever poet.

Johann Wolfgang Goethe, 1831, *Conversations,*
ed. Eckermann, vol. II, p. 364

Scott's greatest glory, however, arises from the superior dignity to which he has raised the novel, not by its historic but its moral character, so that, instead of being obliged, as with Fielding's and Smollett's, to devour it, like Sancho Panza's cheesecakes, in a corner as it were, it is now made to furnish a pure and delectable repast for all the members of the assembled family. In all his multifarious fictions, we remember no line, which in a moral point of view he might wish to blot. Fortunate man, who, possessed of power sufficient to affect the moral destinies of his age, has possessed also the inclination to give that power a uniformly beneficent direction! Who beside him, amid the brilliant display of genius, or the wildest frolics of wit and fancy, has never been led to compromise for a moment the interest of virtue?

William Hickling Prescott, 1832, "English Literature of the Nineteenth Century," North American Review, vol. 35, p. 188

If literature had no task but that of harmlessly amusing indolent, languid men, here was the very perfection of literature; that a man, here more emphatically than ever elsewhere, might fling himself back, exclaiming, "Be mine to lie on this sofa, and read everlasting Novels of Walter Scott!" The composition, slight as it often is, usually hangs together in some measure, and *is* a composition. . . . The sick heart will find no healing here, the darkly struggling heart no guidance: the Heroic that is in all men no divine awakening voice. We say, therefore, that they do not found themselves on deep interests, but on comparatively trivial ones, not on the perennial, perhaps not even on the lasting. In fact, much of the interest of these novels results from what may be called contrasts of costume. The phraseology, fashion of arms, of dress and life, belonging to one age, is brought suddenly, with singular vividness, before the eyes of another. A great effect this; yet by the very nature of it, an altogether temporary one. Consider, brethren, shall not we too one day be antiques, and grow to have as quaint a costume as the rest?

Thomas Carlyle, 1838, "Memoirs of the Life of Scott," London and Westminster Review, vol. 28, pp. 334, 336

When I first arrived in Copenhagen, often walking about poor and forlorn, without sufficient money for a meal, I have spent the few pence I possessed to obtain from a library one of Walter Scott's novels, and, reading it, forgot hunger and cold, and felt myself rich and happy.

Hans Christian Andersen, 1846, Correspondence, p. 204

On the whole, and speaking roughly, these defects in the delineation which Scott has given us of human life are but two. He omits to give us a delineation of the soul: we have mind, manners, animation, but it is the stir of this world. We miss the consecrating power; and we miss it not only in its own peculiar sphere,—which, from the difficulty of introducing the deepest elements into a novel, would have been scarcely matter for a harsh criticism,—but in the place in which a novelist might most be expected to delineate it. There are perhaps such things as the love affairs of immortal beings, but no one would learn it from Scott. His heroes and heroines are well dressed for this world, but not for another; there is nothing even in their love which is suitable for immortality. As has been noticed, Scott also omits any delineation of the abstract side of unworldly intellect. This too might not have been so severe a reproach, considering its undramatic, unanimated nature, if it had stood alone; but taken in connection with the omission which we have just spoken of, it is most important. As the union of sense and romance makes the world of Scott so characteristically agreeable—a fascinating picture of this world in the light in which we like best to dwell on it; so the deficiency in the attenuated, striving intellect, as well as in the supernatural soul, gives to the "world" of Scott the cumbrousness and temporality—in short, the materialism which is characteristic of the world.

Walter Bagehot, 1858, *The Waverley Novels; Works,*
ed. Morgan, vol. II, p. 235

In the beginning of any art even the most gifted worker must be crude in his methods, and we ought to keep this fact always in mind when we turn, say, from the purblind worshippers of Scott to Scott himself, and recognize that he often wrote a style cumbrous and diffuse; that he was tediously analytical where the modern novelist is dramatic, and evolved his characters by means of long-winded explanation and commentary; that, except in the case of his lower-class personages, he made them talk as seldom man and never woman talked; that he was tiresomely descriptive; that on the simplest occasions he went about half a mile to express a thought that could be uttered in ten paces across lots; and that he trusted his readers' intuitions so little that he was apt to rub in his appeals to them. He was probably right; the generation which he wrote for was duller than this; slower-witted, æsthetically untrained, and in maturity not so apprehensive of an artistic intention as the children of to-day. All this is not saying Scott was not a great man; he was a great man, and a very great novelist as compared with the novelists who went before him. He can still amuse young people, but they ought to be instructed how false and how mistaken he often is, with his mediæval ideals, his blind Jacobitism, his intense devotion to aristocracy and royalty; his acquiescence in the division of men into noble and ignoble, patrician and plebeian, sovereign and subject, as if it were the law of God; for all which, indeed, he is not to blame as he would be if he were one of our contemporaries.

William Dean Howells, 1891, *Criticism and Fiction,* p. 21

Though Scott founded the historical novel, enunciated its most successful theory, and is, perhaps, still the greatest historical novelist, he is not the best exponent of his own theory. Attractive as is the theory of the romantic magnetization of history, overhanging it always is the shadow of the anger of the great god Verity. Scott was almost too ingrainedly honest for his theory. There are evidences of struggle when the Scotch lawyer becomes the romantic idealist in these historical novels. In truth, the novels never really desert fact; sometimes the story almost painfully and regretfully seems to cling to fact.

> Francis Hovey Stoddard, 1900, *The Evolution of*
> *the English Novel*, p. 104

The literary form under which Scott made the deepest impression upon the consciousness of his own generation and influenced most permanently the future literature of Europe, was prose fiction. As the creator of the historical novel and the ancestor of Kingsley, Ainsworth, Bulwer, and G. P. R. James; of Manzoni, Freytag, Hugo, Mérimée, Dumas, Alexis Tolstoi, and a host of others, at home and abroad, his example is potent yet. English fiction is directly or indirectly in his debt for *Romola, Hypatia, Henry Esmond,* and *The Cloister and the Hearth.* In several countries the historical novel had been trying for centuries to get itself born, but all its attempts had been abortive. *Waverley* is not only vastly superior to *Thaddeus of Warsaw* (1803) and *The Scottish Chiefs* (1809); it is something quite different in kind.

> Henry A. Beers, 1901, *A History of English Romanticism*
> *in the Nineteenth Century*, p. 30

Waverley (1814)

Walter Scott has no business to write novels, especially good ones. It is not fair. He has fame and profit enough as a poet, and should not be taking the bread out of the mouths of other people. I do not like him, and do not mean to like *Waverley* if I can help it, but fear I must.

> Jane Austen, 1814, *Letters,* vol. II, p. 317

Have you read Walter Scott's *Waverley?* I have ventured to say "Walter Scott's"; though I hear he denies it, just as a young girl denies the imputation of a lover: but, if there be any belief in internal evidence, it must be his. It is his by a thousand indications,—by all the faults and all the beauties; by the unspeakable and unrecollectable names; by the vile pedantry of French, Latin, Gaelic, and Italian; by the hanging the clever hero, and marrying the stupid one; by the praise (well deserved certainly,—for when has Scotland ever such a friend?—but thrust in by his head and shoulders) of the late Lord Melville; by the sweet lyric poetry; by the perfect costume; by the excellent keeping of the picture; by the liveliness and gayety of the dialogues; and last, not least, by the entire and admirable individuality of every character in the book, high as well as low,—the life and soul which animates them all with a distinct existence, and brings them before our eyes like the portraits of Fielding and Cervantes.

Mary Russell Mitford, 1814, Letter to Sir William Elford, Oct. 31

In my opinion it is the best novel that has been published these thirty years. The characters of Ebenezer Cruickshanks, mine host of the Garter, the Reverend Mr. Goukthrapple and Squire Bradwardine display a Cervantic vein of humour which has seldom been surpassed—whilst the descriptions of the gloomy caverns of the Highlands, and the delineations of the apathic Callum Beg and enterprising Vich Ian Vohr, show a richness of Scottean colouring which few have equalled.

Thomas Carlyle, 1814, Early Letters, ed. Norton, p. 10

When you have finished The Fair Maid of Perth, you must at once read Waverley, which is indeed from quite a different point of view, but which may, without hesitation, be set beside the best works that have ever been written in this world. We see that it is the same man who wrote The Fair Maid of Perth, but that he has yet to gain the favour of the public, and therefore collects his forces so that he may not give a touch that is short of excellence. The Fair Maid of Perth, on the other hand, is from a freer pen; the author is now sure of his public, and he proceeds more at liberty. After reading Waverley, you will understand why Walter Scott still designates himself the author of that work; for there he showed what he could do, and he has never since written anything to surpass, or even equal, that first published novel.

Johann Wolfgang Goethe, 1828, Conversations,
ed. Eckermann, vol. II, p. 83

Guy Mannering (1815)

Dandie Dinmont is, beyond all question, we think, the best rustic portrait that has ever yet been exhibited to the public—the most honourable to rustics, and the most creditable to the heart, as well as the genius of the artist—the truest to nature—the most interesting and the most complete in all its lineaments.—Meg Merrilees belongs more to the department of poetry. She is most akin to the witches of Macbeth, with some traits of the ancient

Sybil engrafted on the coarser stock of a Gipsy of the last century. Though not absolutely in nature, however, she must be allowed to be a very imposing and emphatic personage; and to be mingled, both with the business and the scenery of the piece, with the greatest possible skill and effect.—Pleydell is a harsh caricature; and Dirk Hatteric a vulgar bandit of the German school. The lovers, too, are rather more faultless and more insipid than usual,— and all the genteel persons, indeed, not a little fatiguing. Yet there are many passages of great merit, of a gentler and less obtrusive character.

> Francis, Lord Jeffrey, 1817-44, *"Tales of My Landlord,"*
> *Contributions to the Edinburgh Review,* vol. III, p. 446

There is a wide difference of opinion with regard to the relative rank of Scott's novels. Mr. Lowell once said that *The Bride of Lammermoor* was to him the most beautiful story in the language. Mr. Lang puts *Old Mortality* and *Quentin Durward* at the top of the list. But from any point of view, the popular instinct was not far astray in fastening upon *Ivanhoe,* as, on the whole, the most widely acceptable of these great stories. *Kenilworth* is not far behind, but *Guy Mannering* falls below the middle of the list for the very good reason that while the first two have clear movement and cumulative dramatic interest, the latter is very defective as a story. The hero is a secondary personage.

> Hamilton W. Mabie, "The Most Popular Novels in America,"
> *The Forum,* vol. 16, p. 512

The Antiquary (1816)

It unites to a considerable degree the merits of *Waverley* with the faults of the *Astrologer*; and we have no hesitation in placing it, with the crowd of modern novels, below the former, and, with very few modern novels, above the latter.

> William Gifford, 1816, *"The Antiquary,"*
> *Quarterly Review,* vol. 15, p. 125

As a novel of character, *The Antiquary* is the most remarkable of Scott's productions. Nowhere is he a more faithful observer of the turns which differing personalities take, nowhere does he give a more living picture of human beings, and this he does without aid from incident. Given the story of *Old Mortality,* there are many novelists who could have written not *Old Mortality* indeed, but a good novel. A bad one, with the story of *The Antiquary,* almost any novelist but Scott would have written. . . . To read the book is not certainly to have the imagination greatly quickened, but to read it—to read of Edie, of Oldbuck and his household—is to see the plain every-day world as we should not otherwise see it, till circumstances and trouble had enlarged and softened our vision.

Adolphus Alfred Jack, 1897, Essays on the Novel, pp. 92, 106

Old Mortality (1817)

Murray told me that Sir Walter Scott, on being taxed by him as the author of *Old Mortality,* not only denied having written it, but added, "In order to convince you that I am not the author, I will review the book for you in the *Quarterly"*—which he actually did, and Murray still has the MS. in his handwriting.

Richard Harris Barham, 1833, Life and Letters, vol. I, p. 214

Our evening's reading now is *Old Mortality.* When I read that romance on its appearance, about thirty years ago, I thought it, and as it has lived in my memory I have ever since considered it, the grandest and best of all that admirable novelist's works. My recurrence to it confirms the impression it then made on me.

W. C. Macready, 1855, Letter to Mrs. Pollock, March 26;
Reminiscences, ed. Pollock, p. 705

Ranking foremost among the *Waverley* novels for variety of character sketches, stirring incidents, and infinite humour, affords also an accurate picture of the disorders and abuses under which the Scottish people suffered during the reign of the last Stuarts. . . . Lord Evandale is probably the favourite with all young readers. There is an ardour and dashing gallantry about him which, combined with his unhappy fate, renders him peculiarly attractive, while Morton's restrained and serious nature wins on us more slowly, and it is not until the close of the story that we fully realise his historic qualities.

Gertrude Julian Young, 1893, Great Characters of Fiction,
ed. Townsend, pp. 59, 60

Rob Roy (1818)

This is not so good, perhaps, as some others of the family;—but it is better than any thing else; and has a charm and a spirit about it that draws us irresistibly away from our graver works of politics and science, to expatiate upon that which every body understands and agrees in; and after setting us diligently to read over again what we had scarce finished reading, leaves us no choice but to tell our readers what they all know already, and to persuade them of that of which they are most intimately convinced.

Francis, Lord Jeffrey, 1818-44, "Rob Roy," Contributions to
the Edinburgh Review, vol. III, p. 460

There is a peculiar fascination investing this story and its characters, and scenery that can be associated with them. Indeed, few of Scott's works have more readers, or so abound in picturesque incidents and persons, nearly all represented in romantic places, many of which can now be identified, and visited with pleasure; for this is the story of curious, old, half-haunted Osbaldistone Hall; of Glasgow Cathedral, and of the Highlands at Loch Ard; of the Scotch Robin Hood; of charming, miraculous Die Vernon; of inimitable Bailie Nichol Jarvie of the Saut Market; of that natural, calculating, conceited, semi-rascal, Andrew Fairservice; and of that wholly villainous Jesuit, Rashleigh.

James F. Hunnewell, 1871, *The Lands of Scott,* p. 164

The Heart of Midlothian (1818)

Our general admiration of the story of *The Heart of Mid-Lothian* does not, of course, extend to the management of all the details. The beginning, or rather the beginnings, for there are half a dozen of them, are singularly careless. The author, in his premature anxiety to get in medias res, introduces us at the point where the different interests converge; and then, instead of floating down the united streams of events, we are forced separately to ascend each of its tributary branches, like Humboldt examining the bifurcations of the Oroonoko, until we forget, in exploring their sources, the manner in which they bear on one another.

A. W. Senior, 1821, "Novels of the Author of *Waverley,*"
Quarterly Review, vol. 26, p. 116

During the Centenary festivities the Emperor of Brazil arrived in Edinburgh, and on the first morning of his stay he went at five o'clock in the morning, with *The Heart of Mid-Lothian* in his hand, to try and identify the localities about the region where the old Tolbooth formerly stood, described in the novel. A gentleman and lady at whose house he took luncheon assured me that the emperor had succeeded admirably in his identifications, which he declared to be due to the precision and vividness of Scott's descriptions.

M. D. Conway, 1872, "The Scott Centenary at Edinburgh,"
Harper's Magazine, vol. 44, p. 337

Last Evening I heard Jeanie Deans' Audience with Argyle, and then with the Queen. There I stop with the Book. Oh, how refreshing is the leisurely, easy, movement of the Story, with its true and well-harmonized Variety of Scene and Character! There is of course a Bore, Saddletree—as in Shakespeare, I presume to think—as in Cervantes—as in Life itself: somewhat too much of him in Scott, perhaps. But when the fuliginous and spasmodic Carlyle and Co. talk of Scott's delineating his Characters from without to within—why, he seems to have had a pretty good Staple of the inner Man of David, and Jeanie Deans, on beginning his Story.

> Edward Fitzgerald, 1877, *Letter to Fanny Kemble,*
> June 23; *Letters,* ed. Wright, p. 126

There we get his richest humour and his purest pathos, and especially that blending of the two, when the tears are close behind the smiles—as in *The Heart of Mid-Lothian* for instance—in which again he has been surpassed only by Shakespeare, and equalled, I think, only by Cervantes.

> Mowbray Morris, 1889, "Sir Walter Scott,"
> *Macmillan's Magazine,* vol. 60, p. 157

The Bride of Lammermoor (1819)

We see, even at the very beginning of the tale, the "little cloud, no bigger than a man's hand" which gradually overshadows the whole atmosphere, and at last bursts in ruin, in madness, and in despair over the devoted heads of Ravenswood and his betrothed. The catastrophe is tremendous, crushing, complete; and even the more comic scenes (the melancholy ingenuity of poor faithful Caleb) have a sad and hopeless gaiety, which forms a dismal and appropriate relief to the profoundly tragic tone of the action. One scene in this awful tale is truly terrific—the muttered cursing of the three hideous hags at the ill-omened marriage; nor is the interview between Ravenswood and the grave-digger, or the appearance of the unhappy hero to claim his promise from Lucy Ashton, inferior. They bear the impress of our elder dramatists; they might have been conceived by Ford, by Middleton, or by the sombre genius of Webster.

> Thomas B. Shaw, 1847, *Outlines of English Literature,* p. 328

Scott could neither have described nor even conceived the progress of jealousy in *Othello.* He could not have described nor even conceived that contrast between Curiace and either Horace, father or son, in which is so sublimely revealed the secret of the Roman ascendency. But, as an artist of Narrative and not of the Drama, Scott was perhaps the greater for his omissions. Let any reader bring to his recollection that passage in the grandest tragic romance our language possesses—*The Bride of Lammermoor*—in which, the night before the Master of Ravenswood vanishes from the tale, he shuts himself up in his fated tower, and all that is known of the emotions through which his soul travailed is the sound of his sleepless heavy tread upon the floor of his solitary room. What can be grander in narrative art

than the suppression of all dramatic attempt to analyse emotion and reduce
its expression to soliloquy?

Edward Bulwer-Lytton, Lord Lytton, 1863-68, "Caxtoniana,"
Miscellaneous Prose Works, vol. III, p. 473

"No man since Æschylus could have written *The Bride of Lammermoor*"—
such are the words of Mr. Gladstone, quoted in the *Life* of Lord Tennyson.
"The most pure and powerful of all the tragedies that Scott ever penned"—
such is the deliberate criticism of Lockhart. "Scott's first approach to failure
in prose"—such is the verdict of Professor Saintsbury on a book which,
whatever be its merits or demerits, is unique in the position which it holds
amongst the Waverley Novels. . . . He was supreme not by virtue of construction, but in the absence of it. And yet none the less it is true that in
this one novel he has fulfilled, as no other novelist has ever done, and as
he himself has never done elsewhere, dramatic conditions by which he was
not bound, and by which it would be absurd that romance should be fettered;
and that he has united in this single work the free play and variety of romance with the fundamental unity of the tragic drama. . . . That *The Bride
of Lammermoor* is his greatest novel few perhaps will maintain. But surely
the vast majority of critics will recognise in it, not "an approach to failure,"
but a combination of romance and dramatic tragedy which is absolutely
unique.

Sir Henry Craik, 1897, "*The Bride of Lammermoor,*"
Blackwood's Magazine, vol. 162, pp. 853, 857

To the merits in detail of *The Bride of Lammermoor* I never have hesitated
to do justice, though I think them more sparingly found than in the case of
most of the earlier novels. . . . I still maintain, for the reasons which "Maga"
permitted me to give three months ago, that the tragedy of *The Bride of
Lammermoor* is not "pure,"—is indeed distinctly faulty; and that, as I observed in the little book of which Sir Henry speaks so kindly, it is in its composition and general character as a novel, not indeed a failure, but Scott's
first approach to one.

George Saintsbury, 1897, "*The Bride of Lammermoor,*"
Blackwood's Magazine, vol. 162, p. 859

Ivanhoe (1820)

Never were the long-gathered stores of most extensive erudition applied to
the purposes of imaginative genius with so much easy, lavish, and luxurious
power; never was the illusion of fancy so complete.

John Wilson, 1819, "*Ivanhoe,*" *Blackwood's Magazine*,
vol. 6, p. 263

Ivanhoe was received throughout England with a more clamorous delight than any of the Scotch novels had been. The volumes were now for the first time of the post 8vo. form, with a finer paper than hitherto, the press-work much more elegant, and the price accordingly raised from eight shillings a volume to ten; yet the copies sold in this original shape were twelve thousand. . . . The publication of *Ivanhoe* marks the most brilliant epoch in Scott's history as the literary favorite of his contemporaries. With the novel which he next put forth the immediate sale of them began gradually to decline.

> John Gibson Lockhart, 1836, *Memoirs of the Life of Sir Walter Scott*, ch. xlvi

Perhaps the most favourite novel in the English language.

> Anthony Trollope, 1879, *Thackeray* (*English Men of Letters*), p. 142

We believe it is not generally known that the honor of having been the prototype and inspiration of the character of Rebecca the Jewess, in *Ivanhoe*, belongs to an American lady, whose beauty and noble qualities were described to Scott by a friend. The friend was Washington Irving, and the lady Rebecca Gratz, of an honorable Jewish family of Philadelphia.

> Gratz Van Rensselaer, 1882, "The Original of Rebecca in *Ivanhoe*," *The Century*, vol. 24, p. 679

Tested by . . . the magic by which it evokes the past, the skill with which legend and history are used to create a poetic atmosphere . . . the masterly delineation of nationalities and professions, and representatives of every order and rank; above all its fundamental rightness, . . . tested by these qualities, *Ivanhoe* deserves its fame as one of the great romances of the world.

> Bliss Perry, 1897, ed. *Ivanhoe* (*Longman's English Classics*), Introduction

Ivanhoe, which appeared at the end of 1819, marked a new departure. Scott was now drawing upon his reading instead of his personal experience, and the book has not the old merit of serious portraiture of real life. But its splendid audacity, its vivid presentation of mediæval life, and the dramatic vigour of the narrative, may atone for palpable anachronisms and melodramatic impossibilities. The story at once achieved the popularity which it has always enjoyed, and was more successful in England than any of the so-called "Scottish novels." It was Scott's culminating success in a bookselling sense, and marked the highest point both of his literary and his social prosperity.

Leslie Stephen, 1897, *Dictionary of National Biography,*
vol. LI, p. 92

It did not seem desirable to point out in special notes the many inaccuracies and errors, grammatical and rhetorical, that may be found in *Ivanhoe.* If the student is sensitive to such things he will easily discover them; and if he does not detect them he is probably destined to be a soldier, a sailor, or some such bold and active person to whom the technicalities of expression will not matter. . . . In *Ivanhoe* we breathe the sane and wholesome air of a heroic simple life—the life of objective deeds and sheer accomplishment. To the brave company that peoples our world of dreams it adds many fig-ures, noble, beautiful, gay—knights and ladies, merry-men and trouba-dours, pilgrim and crusader, friar and jester. It touches the past with a glow of poetry, lighting up situations, institutions, and men, making real and rich for us those things that in the technical records seem meagre and colorless. Its style gives us the refreshment of writing which, though it may not be delicately correct, is also not consciously fine nor painfully precise, but which moves buoyantly forward without strain and without weariness.

Porter Lander MacClintock, 1900, ed. *Ivanhoe,*
Introduction, pp. xxi, xxiii

Kenilworth (1821)

Though *Kenilworth* must rank high among his works, we think it inferior, as a whole, to his other tragedies, *The Bride of Lammermoor,* the historical part of *Waverley,* and the *Abbot,* both in materials and in execution. Amy Robsart and Elizabeth occupy nearly the same space upon the canvas as Catherine Seyton and Mary. But almost all the points of interest, which are divided between Amy and Elizabeth, historical recollections, beauty, talents, attractive virtues and unhappy errors, exalted rank and deep mis-fortune, are accumulated in Mary; and we want altogether that union of the lofty and the elegant, of enthusiasm and playfulness, which enchanted us in Catherine. . . . It is a fault perhaps of the conclusion, that it is too uniformly tragical. . . . The immediate circumstances of Amy's death, as she rushes to meet, what she supposes to be, her husband's signal, almost pass the limit that divides pity from horror.

A. W. Senior, 1821, "Novels by the Author of *Waverley,*"
Quarterly Review, vol. 26, pp. 143, 147

The Life of Napoleon Buonaparte (1827)

You are the first person from whom I have heard a word in favour of Scott's *Napoleon,* and I am really glad to hear some good of it, as I was afraid it was too probable that he had been bookmaking. The defect which you mention is attributable to the defect of moral force in Scott's character; invariable candour and moderation in judging men is generally accompanied by such a defect. Scott seems to be always disposed to approve of rectitude of conduct and to acquiesce in the general rules of morality, but without any instinctive or unconquerable aversion from vice—witness his friendship for Byron.

Sir Henry Taylor, 1827, *to Edward Villiers,* Oct. 15;
Correspondence, ed. Dowden, p. 19

I am reading Walter Scott's *Napoleon,* which I do with greatest pleasure. I am as much surprised at it as at any of his works. So current, so sensible, animated, well arranged; so agreeable to take up, so difficult to put down, and, for him, so candid! there are, of course, many mistakes, but that has nothing to do with the general complexion of the work.

Sydney Smith, 1828, *To Lord Holland,* July;
Letters, ed. Mrs. Austin

It is true that the author may be reproached with great inaccuracy, and equally great partiality, but even these two defects give to his work particular value in my eyes. The success of the book, in England, was great beyond all expectation; and hence we see that Walter Scott, in this very hatred for Napoleon and the French, has been the true interpreter and representative of the English popular opinion and national feeling. His book will not be by any means a document for the history of France, but it will be one for the history of England. At all events, it is a voice which could not be wanting in this important historical process.

Johann Wolfgang Goethe, 1830, *Conversations,*
ed. Eckermann, vol. II, p. 213

The paper and print of the first and second edition, in nine volumes, brought the creditors £18,000—an amount of gain, in relation to amount of labour, unexampled in the history of literature, and which will probably have no parallel for ages to come.

Robert Chambers, 1835-71, *Life of Sir Walter Scott,* p. 81

The Fair Maid of Perth (1828)

To me, one of the most remarkable figures he ever drew was that of Conachar. Nothing could be more difficult than to provoke at once pity, contempt, and sympathy for a coward. Yet he has successfully achieved this feat; and as far as I can recollect, it is the sole instance in English literature where such an attempt was ever made. More than this, he has drawn two cowards in this remarkable novel,—each quite different from the other and contrasted with eminent skill—the comic, swaggering, good-natured, fussy little coward, Oliver Proudfute, who provokes a perpetual smile; and the sullen, irritable, proud, and revengeful coward, Conachar, whom we cannot but pity, while we despise him. *The Fair Maid of Perth* was always a favorite of mine. It has perhaps more variety of interest, incident, and characters than any he ever wrote, and it never flags.

William Wetmore Story, 1890, Conversations in a Studio,
vol. I, p. 273

GENERAL

Criticism on his works is now superfluous. They have taken their enduring station in the literature of the world. If the applause of foreign nations be equivalent, as it is said, to the voice of posterity, no author who ever wrote has obtained that honor in so large a measure. His novels, his poems, have been translated into every civilized language; his heroes and heroines have become household words all over the world. The painter, the sculptor, the engraver, the musician, have sought inspiration from his pages. The names of his works, or the personages introduced into them, are impressed on the man-of-war or the quadrille, the race-horse or the steamboat. The number of persons who became famous by following in their different lines, the ideas of Sir Walter, is immense, and comprehends all classes of intellect or enterprise. The tribes of imitators, whether of his verse or prose, whom he has called into existence, are countless. Many of them are persons of great abilities and unquestioned genius. Which of them will be named in competition with the master? Not one.

William Maginn, 1832, "The Death of Sir Walter Scott,"
Fraser's Magazine, vol. 6, p. 380

The illustrious painter of Scotland seems to me to have created a false class; he has, in my opinion, confounded history and romance: the novelist has set about writing historical romances, and the historian romantic histories. . . . I refuse, therefore, to sit in judgment on any English author whose merit does not appear to me to reach that degree of superiority which it has in the eyes of his countrymen.

François René, Vicomte de Chateaubriand, 1837, *Sketches of English Literature,* vol. II, pp. 306, 307

Scott was, in truth, master of the picturesque. He understood, better than any historian since the time of Livy, how to dispose his lights and shades so as to produce the most striking result. This property of romance he had a right to borrow. This talent is particularly observable in the animated parts of his story—in his battles, for example. No man ever painted those terrible scenes with greater effect. He had a natural relish for gunpowder; and his mettle roused, like that of the war-horse, at the sound of the trumpet. His acquaintance with military science enabled him to employ a technical phraseology, just technical enough to give a knowing air to his descriptions, without embarrassing the reader by a pedantic display of unintelligible jargon. This is a talent rare in a civilian. Nothing can be finer than many of his battle-pieces in his *Life of Bonaparte,* unless, indeed, we except one or two in his *History of Scotland*: as the fight of Bannockburn, for example, in which Burns's "Scots, wha hae" seems to breathe in every line.

William Hickling Prescott, 1839, "Chateaubriand's English Literature," *Biographical and Critical Miscellanies,* p. 284

The defects of his prose are the more serious ones of slipshod and tawdry sentences, of clumsy and lumbering paragraphs. Where he is solemn or dignified, he rarely troubles himself with the virtues of restraint or selection; he never attempts the subtle harmony of words, or balances his style to suit with nicety the sentiments he wishes to convey. A certain amount of grandiloquence has often a quaint flavour of humour, but it is seldom so with Scott. His phrases are often rotund and ornate, but this seems to come from a careless conventionality of habit, and not from deliberate art. He pours out his words without discrimination, and frequently with an absence of all taste for style, which is perhaps akin to the insensibility of perception which his biographer admits—his obtuseness to what was disagreeable in smell or colour, his lack of musical ear, his bluntness to some of the more common tastes. He himself recognised the lack with his usual magnanimity, and neither resented its suggestion nor defended its faults. . . . The wonder is not that Scott's style had defects, but that it was not much worse. He never studied it. His mind was filled with the picturesque in scenery and in conception, and he had neither room nor leisure for more. And if the instrument was sometimes defective, no one used it with a more consummate ease. His style is best where we notice it least; and often the thrilling force

and fire of genius, burning underneath, sublimes it into a certain unconscious grandeur. Nay, even this very common-placeness of Scott's style is
not without its value. An artistic style must be redolent both of the writer
and of his age; and the impersonality of Scott's style rather adds to, than
detracts from, the perennial interest of his romance.

Henry Craik, 1896, *English Prose,* vol. V, pp. 9, 10

GEORGE CRABBE
1754-1832

Born, at Aldeborough, 24 Dec. 1754. Educated at private schools at
Bungay and Stowmarket. After leaving school, worked in warehouse at
Slaughden; apprenticed as errand-boy to a doctor at Wickham Brook, near
Bury St. Edmunds, 1768; to a surgeon at Woodbridge, 1771. Contrib. to
Wheble's Mag., 1772. Returned to Aldeborough, 1775, to work in warehouse. Studied medicine. After a visit to London, became assistant to
surgeon in Aldeborough, and afterwards set up in practice there. To
London to make living by literature, April 1780. Ultimate success, mainly
through assistance of Burke. Ordained Deacon, 21 Dec. 1781, as curate
to Rector of Aldeborough. Ordained Priest, Aug. 1782. To Belvoir, as
chaplain to Duke of Rutland, 1782. Given degree of LL.B. by Archbishop
of Canterbury, and presented (by Thurlow) with livings of Frome, St.
Quentin and Evershot, Dorsetshire. Married Sarah Elmy, Dec. 1783. Ac-
cepted curacy of Stathern, 1785. Contrib. to *Annual Register,* 1784.
Voluminous writer, but published little. Exchanged Dorsetshire livings for
Rectorship of Muston and Allington, and settled at Muston 25 Feb. 1789.
Removed to Parham as curate of Sweffling and Great Glemham, 1792.
Took Great Glenham Hall, 1796. Returned to Muston, Oct. 1805. Wife
died, 31 Oct. 1813. Rector of Trowbridge Wiltshire, and Croxton, near
Belvoir, June 1814. Visited London, 1817 and 1822. Visited Scott in
Edinburgh, autumn 1822. Died, at Trowbridge, 3 Feb. 1832. Buried there.
WORKS: *Inebriety* (anon.), 1775; *The Candidate,* 1780; *The Library*
(anon.), 1781; *The Village,* 1783; *The Newspaper,* 1785; *A Discourse
. . . after the funeral of the Duke of Rutland,* 1788; *Poems,* 1807; *The
Parish Register,* 1807; *The Borough,* 1810; *Tales,* 1812; *The Variation of
public opinion and feelings considered,* 1817; *Tales of the Hall,* 1819.
POSTHUMOUS: *Posthumous Sermons,* ed. by J. D. Hastings, 1850. COL-
LECTED WORKS: with letters, and *Life* by his son George, 1834.

R. Farquharson Sharp, 1897, *A Dictionary of
English Authors,* p. 68

SEE: *Poems,* ed. A. W. Ward, 1905-7, 3 v.; *Poetical Works,* ed. A. J. and
R. M. Carlyle, 1908(OSA); *New Poems,* ed. Arthur Pollard, 1960;
George Crabbe, *The Life of Crabbe by His Son,* ed. E. M. Forster, 1932,
ed. Edmund Blunden, 1947; Lilian Haddakin, *The Poetry of Crabbe,* 1955.

PERSONAL

The people with whom I live perceive my situation, and find me to be indigent and without friends. About ten days since, I was compelled to give a note for seven pounds, to avoid an arrest for about double that sum which I owe. I wrote to every friend I had, but my friends are poor likewise. . . . Having used every honest means in vain, I yesterday confessed my inability, and obtained, with much entreaty, and as the greatest favour, a week's forbearance, when I am positively told, that I must pay the money, or prepare for a prison. You will guess the purpose of so long an introduction. I appeal to you, Sir, as a good, and, let me add, a great man. I have no other pretensions to your favour than that I am an unhappy one. . . . Can you, Sir, in any degree, aid me with propriety?—Will you ask any demonstrations of my veracity? I have imposed upon myself, but I have been guilty of no other imposition. Let me, if possible, interest your compassion. I know those of rank and fortune are teased with frequent petitions, and are compelled to refuse the requests even of those whom they know to be in distress: it is, therefore, with a distant hope I venture to solicit such favour; but you will forgive me, Sir, if you do not think proper to relieve.

George Crabbe, 1781, *Letter to Edmund Burke;*
Life of Crabbe by His Son, vol. I, p. 92

Crabbe is absolutely delightful—simple as a child, but shrewd, and often good-naturedly reminding you of the best parts of his poetry. He took his wine cheerfully—far from excess; but his heart really seemed to expand; and he was full of anecdote and social feeling.

Thomas Campbell, 1817, *To His Sister,* July 15;
Life and Letters, ed. Beattie, vol. II, ch. iv

Perhaps no man of origin so very humble ever retained so few traces of it as he did, in the latter years, at least, of his long and chequered life. There was no shade of subserviency in his courtesy, or of coarseness in his hilarity; his simplicity was urbane;—the whole demeanour exactly what any one would have pronounced natural and suitable in an English clergyman of the highest class, accustomed, from youth to age, to refined society and intellectual pursuits—gentle, grave, and venerable—and only rendered more interesting by obvious unfamiliarity with some of the conventional nothings of modern town-bred usage.

John Gibson Lockhart, 1834, *"Life of Crabbe by His Son,"*
Quarterly Review, vol. 50, p. 471

He was stern only in verse. His was the gentle, kindly nature of one who loving God loved man, and all the creatures God has made. His early struggles, less for fame than the bare means of existence, may surely furnish a lesson, and, in their result, an encouragement, to those who labor for either through difficulties it might seem impossible to overcome.

Samuel Carter Hall, 1883, *Retrospect of a Long Life*, p. 315

His preaching attracted large congregations. He was a clergyman of the old-fashioned school, a good friend to the poor, for whose benefit he still practiced medicine, and a preacher of good homespun morality. But he was indifferent to theological speculations, suspicious of excessive zeal, contemptuous towards "enthusiasts," and heartily opposed to Wesleyans, evangelicals, and other troublesome innovators.

Leslie Stephen, 1887, *Dictionary of National Biography*,
vol. XII, p. 429

GENERAL

I have sent you back Mr. Crabbe's poem, which I read with great delight. It is original, vigorous, and elegant. The alterations which I have made I do not require him to adopt, for my lines are, perhaps, not often better [than] his own; but he may take mine and his own together, and perhaps between them produce something better than either. He is not to think his copy wantonly defaced; a wet sponge will wash all the red lines away, and leave the pages clean. His Dedication will be least liked: it were better to contract it into a short sprightly address. I do not doubt of Mr. Crabbe's success.

Samuel Johnson, 1783, *To Sir Joshua Reynolds*, March 4;
Letters, ed. Hill, vol. II, p. 287

> Truth will sometimes lend her noblest fires,
> And decorate the verse herself inspires:
> This fact in Virtue's name let Crabbe attest;
> Though Nature's sternest painter, yet the best.
>
> Lord Byron, 1809, *English Bards and Scotch Reviewers*

It is very pleasing to perceive, that, in his best passages, Mr. Crabbe is, practically at least, a convert to the good old principle of paying some regard to fancy and taste in poetry. In these passages he works expressly for the imagination; not perhaps awakening its loftiest exertions, yet studiously courting its assistance, and conciliating its good will. He now accommodates himself to the more delicate sympathies of our nature, and flatters our prejudices by attaching to his pictures agreeable and interesting associations. Thus it is that, for his best success, he is indebted to something more than ungarnished reality. He is the Paladin, who on the day of decisive combat, laid aside his mortal arms, and took only the magic lance.

> William Gifford, 1810, "Crabbe's *Borough*,"
> *Quarterly Review,* vol. 4, p. 295

Original, terse, vigorous, and popular. He is the Hogarth of modern bards: or rather, I should say, if he display Hogarth's power of *conception,* his pictures are finished with the point and brilliancy of Teniers. Every body reads, because every body understands, his poems: but the subjects are too frequently painful, by being too true to nature.

> Thomas Frognall Dibdin, 1824, *The Library Companion,*
> p. 742, note

Crabbe with all his defects stands immeasurably above Wordsworth as the Poet of the Poor.

> John Wilson, 1825, *Blackwood's Magazine,* Sep.

He not only deals in incessant matters of fact, but in matters of fact of the most familiar, the least animating, and the most unpleasant kind; but he relies for the effect of novelty on the microscopic minuteness with which he dissects the most trivial objects—and for the interest he excites, on the unshrinking determination with which he handles the most painful. His poetry has an official and professional air. He is called in to cases of difficult births, of fractured limbs, or breaches of the peace; and makes out a parochial list of accidents and offenses. He takes the most trite, the most gross and obvious and revolting part of nature, for the subject of his elaborate descriptions; but it is Nature still, and Nature is a great and mighty Goddess! . . . Mr. Crabbe is one of the most popular and admired of our living authors. That he is so, can be accounted for on no other principle than the strong ties that bind us to the world about us, and our involuntary yearnings after whatever in any manner powerfully and directly reminds us of it.

> William Hazlitt, 1825, *The Spirit of the Age,* p. 239

Crabbe is a cold and remorseless dissector, who pauses with the streaming knife in his hands, to explain how strongly the blood is tainted, what a gangrene is in the liver, how completely the sources of health are corrupted, and that the subject is a bad one. . . . Deliver us from Crabbe in the hour of depression! Pictures of moral, and mental, and bodily degradation, are frequent through all his works; he is one of Job's chief comforters to the people.

Allan Cunningham, 1833, *Biographical and Critical History*
of Literature of the Last Fifty Years

I think Crabbe and Southey are something alike; but Crabbe's poems are founded on observation and real life—Southey's on fancy and books. In facility they are equal, though Crabbe's English is of course not upon a level with Southey's, which is next door to faultless. But in Crabbe there is an absolute defect of the high imagination; he gives me little or no pleasure: yet, no doubt, he has much power of a certain kind, and it is good to cultivate, even at some pains, a catholic taste in literature. I read all sorts of books with some pleasure, except modern sermons and treatises on political economy.

Samuel Taylor Coleridge, 1834, *Table-Talk,*
ed. Ashe, March 5, p. 276

I take no pleasure in Crabbe's unpoetical representations of human life. And though no one can dispute that he had a powerful pen, and could truthfully portray what he saw, yet he had an eye only for the sad realities of life. As Mrs. Barbauld said to me many years ago, "I shall never be tired of Goldsmith's *Deserted Village,*—I shall never look again into Crabbe's *Village.*" Indeed, this impression is so strong, that I have never read his later works, and know little about them.

Henry Crabb Robinson, 1835, *Diary,* Dec. 29;
Reminiscences, ed. Sadler, vol. II, p. 219

I have given a larger space to Crabbe in this republication than to any of his contemporary poets; not merely because I think more highly of him than of most of them, but also because I fancy that he has had less justice done him. The nature of his subjects was not such as to attract either imitators or admirers, from among the ambitious or fanciful lovers of poetry; or, consequently, to set him at the head of a School, or let him surround himself with the zealots of a Sect: And it must also be admitted, that his claims to distinction depend fully as much on his great powers of observation, his skill in touching the deeper sympathies of our nature, and his power of inculcating, by their means, the most impressive lessons of humanity, as on any fine play of fancy, or grace and beauty in his delineations. I have great faith, however, in the intrinsic worth and ultimate success of those more substantial attributes; and have, accordingly, the strongest impression that the citations I have here given from Crabbe will strike more, and sink deeper into the minds of readers to whom they are new (or by whom they may have been partially forgotten), than any I have been able to present from other writers.

Francis, Lord Jeffrey, 1844, "Crabbe's Poems,"
Contributions to the Edinburgh Review, vol. III, p. 3, note

I am awfully sleepy and stupid, or should try to say something about the only book I have read for a long while back—Crabbe, whose poems were known to me long ago, but not at all familiarly till now. I fancy one might read him much oftener and much later than Wordsworth—than almost any one.

Dante Gabriel Rossetti, 1855, *Letters to William Allingham,*
ed. Hill, p. 102

It is difficult to find a single passage, not too long for quotation, which will convey any tolerable notion of the power and beauty of Crabbe's poetry, where so much of the effect lies in the conduct of the narrative—in the minute and prolonged but wonderfully skillful as well as truthful pursuit and exposition of the course and vicissitude of passions and circumstances.

George L. Craik, 1861, *A Compendious History of English
Literature and of the English Language,* vol. II, p. 513

The Village was intended as an antithesis to Goldsmith's idyllic sentimentalism. Crabbe's realism, preceding even Cowper and anticipating Wordsworth, was the first important indication of one characteristic movement in the contemporary school of poetry. His clumsy style and want of sympathy with the new world isolated him as a writer, as he was a recluse in his life. But the force and fidelity of his descriptions of the scenery of his native place and of the characteristics of the rural population give abiding interest to his work. His pathos is genuine and deep, and to some judgments his later works atone for the diminution in tragic interest by their gentleness and simple humour. Scott and Wordsworth had some of his poetry by heart. Scott, like Fox, had Crabbe read to him in his last illness (Lockhart, ch. lxxxiii). Wordsworth said that the poems would last as long as anything written in verse since their first appearance (note to *Village,* bk. i. in *Collected Works*). Miss Austen said that she could fancy being Mrs. Crabbe. Jeffrey reviewed him admiringly, and in later years E. FitzGerald, the translator of *Omar Khayyám,* wrote (1882) an admiring preface to a selection in which he says that Lord Tennyson appreciates them equally with himself. Cardinal Newman speaks of the "extreme delight" with which he read *Tales of the Hall,* on their appearance.

Leslie Stephen, 1887, *Dictionary of National Biography,*
vol. XII, p. 430

It is superfluous to say that a writer who has been so lauded by the greatest poet, the most ardent orator, the most honored novelist, and the most refined letter-writer of England in a century must himself have possessed extraordinary qualities. Yet it remains true that Crabbe is not read, is not even likely to be much read for many years to come; and the reason of this is perfectly simple: his excellencies lie in a direction apart from the trend of modern thought and sentiment, while his faults are such as most strongly repel modern taste. . . . To me personally there is no tedium, but only endless delight, in these mated rhymes which seem to pervade and harmonize the whole rhythm. And withal they help to create the artisic illusion, that wonderful atmosphere, I may call it, which envelops Crabbe's world. No one, not even the most skeptical of Crabbe's genius, can deny that he has succeeded in giving to his work a tone or atmosphere peculiarly and consistently his own.

Paul Elmer More, 1901, "A Plea for Crabbe,"
Atlantic Monthly, vol. 88, p. 851

PHILIP FRENEAU
1752-1832

Journalist, poet, and essayist, Freneau produced patriotic verse and essays during the American Revolution which proved effective and popular. He entered Princeton University when he was sixteen years old; in college he became a close friend of James Madison and a follower of Whig principles. While in college Freneau wrote part of a novel, "Father Bombo's Pilgrimage to Mecca in Arabia," in collaboration with Hugh Henry Brackenridge, and a Commencement poem, *The Rising Glory of America.* He lived in the West Indies and Bermuda for two years, and in 1778 returned to the United States where he served as a propagandist for the Revolution, mainly through his writings in *The United States Magazine.* Freneau was captured by the British while on a blockade runner; this experience culminated in his bitter *The British Prison-Ship,* and a flood of anti-British satires and ballads. After the war Freneau worked as a seaman, free-lance writer, and magazine editor while continuing to produce his poetry. Among his works are *The Poems of Philip Freneau,* 1786, and *The Miscellaneous Works of Mr. Philip Freneau Containing His Essays and Additional Poems,* 1788.

SEE: *Poems,* ed. Fred L. Pattee, 1902-7, 3 v.; *Last Poems,* ed. Lewis Leary, 1946; Lewis Leary, *That Rascal Freneau: A Study in Literary Failure,* 1941.

PERSONAL

On the eighteenth of December, 1832, an old man, sprightly and vigorous under the weight of nearly eighty-one years, started, just as the evening was coming on, to walk from the village of Monmouth, in New Jersey, to his home in the open country, a distance of about two miles. At that home, a paternal estate of a thousand acres, this man had passed, at intervals, many years of his long life—filled as it had been with manifold employments on land and sea. He was still a fine specimen of active and manly old age; in person somewhat below the ordinary height, but muscular and compact; his face pensive in expression and with a careworn look; his dark gray eyes sunken deep in their sockets, but sending out gleams and flashes of fire when aroused in talk; his hair once abundant and beautiful, now thinned and bleached by time; stooping a little as he walked; to those who knew him, accustomed to give delight by a conversation abounding in anecdotes of the great age of the American Revolution. On the evening just referred to, he had started alone on his walk toward his home, but the night passed away without his arrival there; and the next morning his lifeless body was found in a swampy meadow, into which, as it seemed, he must have wandered,—missing his way in the darkness, and in his exhaustion and bewilderment surrendering at last to death. That dead old man was Philip Freneau, incomparably the bitterest and the most unrelenting, and, in some respects the most powerful, of the satirical poets belonging to the insurgent side of the Revolution.

> Moses Coit Tyler, 1897, *The Literary History of the*
> *American Revolution*, 1763-1783, vol. I, p. 171

Extremely hospitable, Freneau always warmly welcomed his friends at Mount Pleasant, where he devoted his declining years to reading and answering his numerous correspondents, and in occasionally penning an article for the press. He always retained his original frankness in expressing himself, but it was softened down considerably as he advanced in years. In fact it was his pen, as some author has said, more than his heart that was so acrimonious in his early years; no personal malice ever rested in his mind, and he was ever ready to pardon those who had injured him. Even his adversaries, some of whom he had treated pretty roughly with his pen in early days, in later times claimed him as a friend. In his friendships he was ardent and sincere, and they were usually life-long.

> Mary S. Austin, 1901, *Philip Freneau the Poet of*
> *the Revolution*, p. 202

GENERAL

Philip Freneau was the most distinguished poet of our revolutionary time. He was a voluminous writer, and many of his compositions are intrinsically worthless, or, relating to persons and events now forgotten, are no longer interesting; but enough remain to show that he had more genius and more enthusiasm than any other bard whose powers were called into action during the great struggle for liberty.

Rufus W. Griswold, 1842-46, *The Poets and Poetry of America*, p. 1

He wrote many songs and ballads in a patriotic and historical vein, which attracted and somewhat reflected, the feelings of his contemporaries, and were not destitute of merit. Their success was owing, in part, to the immediate interest of the subjects, and in part to musical versification and pathetic sentiment. One of his Indian ballads has survived the general neglect to which more artistic skill and deeper significance in poetry have banished the mass of his verses; to the curious in the metrical writings, however, they yet afford a characteristic illustration of the taste and spirit of the times.

Henry T. Tuckerman, 1852, *A Sketch of American Literature*

The poems of Philip Freneau represent his times, the war of wit and verse no less than of sword and stratagem of the Revolution; and he superadds to this material a humorous, homely simplicity peculiarly his own, in which he paints the life of village rustics, with their local manners fresh about them, of days when tavern delights were to be freely spoken of, before temperance societies and Maine laws were thought of; when men went to prison at the summons of inexorable creditors, and when Connecticut deacons rushed out of meeting to arrest and waylay the passing Sunday traveller. When these homors of the day were exhausted, and the impulses of patriotism were gratified in song, when he had paid his respects to Rivington and Hugh Gaine, he solaced himself with higher themes, in the version of an ode of Horace, a visionary meditation on the antiquities of America, or a sentimental effusion on the loves of Sappho. These show the fine tact and delicate handling of Freneau, who deserves much more consideration in this respect from critics than he has ever received.

Evert A. and George L. Duyckinck, 1855-65-75, *Cyclopædia of American Literature*, ed. Simons, vol. I

The headlong mass of his verse far exceeded his powers to keep it up to the highest standard of that age, far less to escape the anathemas of our own when every graduate can make fair jingle on moon or glacier, on love or war. Nine-tenths of his patriotic hymns, of his odes valedictory, worshipful, or comminative, are such as are consigned to the corners of weekly newspapers. Some half dozen pieces, however, remain to prove that Philip Freneau was a poet.

John Nichol, 1880-85, *American Literature*, p. 94

Freneau was a genius in his way, and had brilliant instincts. Some of his poetry sprung from the intense flame of oppression, and as a poet he blew it to a white heat. He was possessed of an impetuous flow of song for freedom, and his wit was pungent and stinging. That he used this with effect can be readily seen by any person who reads his supposed interview with King George and Fox. Then take his exquisite dirge of the heroes of Eutaw Springs, his odes like *Benedict Arnold's Departure;* some parts of them unrivalled. His works show that he imitated in some degree both Gray and Shelley.

James D. Murray, 1883, *Lecture Before the
Long Island Historical Society*

Philip Freneau is talked about, but is not read. His name is known, in a vague way, as that of "the Poet of the Revolution;" and those unfamiliar with his voluminous verse are ready to believe that he was a patriot, a wit, and a successful lyrist. . . . Freneau's masterpiece, which seems to me the best poem written in America before 1800, is *The House of Night, a Vision,* in one hundred and thirty-six four-line stanzas, which appeared in his 1786 collection. Its occasional faults of expression and versification are manifest, but in thought and execution, notwithstanding the influence of Gray, it is surprisingly original and strong, distinctly anticipating some of the methods of Coleridge, Poe, and the English pre-Raphaelite poets, none of whom, probably, ever read a line of it. To those who enjoy a literary "find," and like to read and praise a bit of bizarre genius unknown to the multitude, I confidently commend *The House of Night*.

Charles F. Richardson, 1888, *American Literature,*
1607-1885, vol. II, pp. 13, 15

Freneau's patriotic verses and political lampoons are now unreadable; but he deserves to rank as the first real American poet, by virtue of his "Wild Honeysuckle," "Indian Burying-Ground," "Indian Student," and a few other little pieces, which exhibit a grace and delicacy inherited, perhaps, with his French blood. Indeed, to speak strictly, all of the "poets" hitherto mentioned were nothing but rhymers; but in Freneau we meet with something of beauty and artistic feeling; something which still keeps his verses fresh.

Henry A. Beers, 1895, Initial Studies in American Letters, p. 62

SAMUEL   TAYLOR   COLERIDGE
1772-1834

1772—Born at Ottery St. Mary, Oct. 21. 1782—Admitted to Christ's Hospital, 1791—Enters Cambridge University. 1793—Enlists in the Light Dragoons. 1794—Returns to Cambridge; meets Southey at Oxford; Pantisocracy hatched; leaves Cambridge and goes to London. 1795—Goes to Bristol; marries Miss Fricker, and settles at Clevedon. 1796—First volume of poems; *The Watchman.* 1797—Removes to Nether Stowey; first meeting with Wordsworth; *Lyrical Ballads* begun. 1798—*Lyrical Ballads* published; visits Germany with the Wordsworths. 1799—Returns to England; *Morning Post* and *Wallenstein.* 1800—Removes to Greta Hall, Keswick. 1801—Broken health; the "Kendal Black Drop." 1802—Dejection and family discord. 1803—Visits Scotland with the Wordsworths. 1804—Sails for Malta; made secretary to Sir Alexander Ball. 1905—Visits Sicily and Rome. 1806-10—At Coleorton with Wordsworth; lectures on the poets at the Royal Institution, London; at Grasmere; projects the *Friend.* 1811-12—In London; lectures on Shakespeare and Milton. 1813-16—*Remorse* at Drury Lane; lectures at Bristol; goes to Calne; settles at Highgate with the Gillmans; publishes *Christabel.* 1817—*Biographia Literaria* and *Sibylline Leaves.* 1818—Lectures in London; meets Thomas Allsop and Keats. 1818—Failure of publishers. 1820-22—Hackwork. 1825—*Aids to Reflection;* Pension. 1825-34—Last years at Highgate.

Andrew J. George, 1897, ed. Coleridge's
The Ancient Mariner, p. 27

WORKS: *Fall of Robespierre* (act I by Coleridge; acts II., III. by Southey), 1794; *Moral and Political Lecture delivered at Bristol,* 1795; *Conciones ad Populum,* 1795; *The Plot Discovered,* 1795; *The Watchman,* 1796; *Ode on the Departing Year,* 1796; *Poems on various subjects,* 1796; *Fears in Solitude,* 1798; *France,* 1798; *Frost at Midnight,* 1798; *Ancient Mariner* contributed to *Lyrical Ballads,* 1798; Poems contributed to *Annual Anthology,* 1800; *The Friend,* 1809-10; contributions to Southey's *Omniana,* 1812; *Remorse,* 1813; *Christabel, Kubla Khan and Pains of Sleep,* 1816; *The Statesman's Manual,* 1816; *Blessed are ye that sow beside all waters: a lay Sermon,* 1817; *Biographia Literaria,* 1817; *Sibylline Leaves,* 1817; *Zapolya,* 1817; *Aids to Reflection in the formation of a Manly Character,* 1825; *Poetical Works, including Dramas,* 1829; *On the Constitution of Church and State,* 1830. POSTHUMOUS: *Table-Talk,* 1835; *Literary Remains,* 1836-38; *Letters,* ed. by T. Allsop, 1836; *Confessions of an Enquiring Spirit,* 1840; *Treatises on Method* (from *Encyclopædia Metropolitana*), 1845; *Hints towards a formation of a more comprehensive Theory of Life,* 1848; *Notes and Lectures upon Shakespeare,* 1849; *Essays on his Own Times, forming a second series of "The Friend,"* 1850;

The Relation of Philosophy to Theology, 1851; Lay Sermons, 1852; Notes upon English Divines, 1853; Notes theological, political and miscellaneous, 1853; Anima Poetæ; from the unpublished notebooks of S. T. Coleridge, ed. by E. H. Coleridge, 1895; Letters; edited by E. H. Coleridge, 1895. He translated: Schiller's Wallenstein, 1800. COLLECTED WORKS: in 7 vols., ed. by W. G. T. Stedd, 1884; Poems, ed. by W. Bell Scott, 1894. LIFE: by H. D. Traill, 1884.

R. Farquharson Sharp, 1897, A Dictionary of
English Authors, p. 60

SEE: Complete Poetical Works, ed. E. H. Coleridge, 1912, 2 v.; Poetical Works, ed. J. D. Campbell, 1909; Christabel, ed. E. H. Coleridge, 1907; Biographia Literaria, ed. John Shawcross, 1908, 2 v.; Shakespearean Criticism, ed. T. M. Raysor, 1930, 2 v.; Philosophical Lectures, 1818-1819, ed. Kathleen Coburn, 1949; Collected Letters, ed. Earl Leslie Griggs, 1956-59, 4 v.; Select Poetry and Prose, ed. Stephen Potter, 1933, rev. 1950, repr. 1962; E. K. Chambers, S. T. Coleridge, 1938, repr. 1950; Laurence Hanson, The Life of S. T. Coleridge: The Early Years, 1938; John Livingston Lowes, The Road to Xanadu, 1927, rev. 1930; Arthur H. Nethercot, The Road to Tryermaine, 1939; N. P. Stallknecht in Strange Seas of Thought, 1945; Humphry House, Coleridge, 1953 (Clark Lectures).

PERSONAL

My Father was very fond of me, and I was my Mother's darling: in consequence whereof I was very miserable. For Molly, who had nursed my brother Francis, and was immoderately fond of him, hated me because my Mother took more notice of me than of Frank; and Frank hated me because my Mother gave me now and then a bit of cake when he had none. . . . So I became fretful and timorous, and a tell-tale; and the school-boys drove me from play, and were always tormenting me. And hence I took no pleasure in boyish sports, but read incessantly. . . . And I used to lie by the wall, and mope; and my spirits used to come upon me suddenly, and in a flood;—and then I was accustomed to run up and down the church-yard, and act over again all I had been reading on the docks, the nettles and the rank grass. At six years of age I remember to have read Belisarius, Robinson Crusoe, and Philip Quarles; and then I found the Arabian Nights' Entertainments, one tale of which . . . made so deep an impression on me . . . that I was haunted by spectres, whenever I was in the dark: . . . So I became a dreamer, and acquired an indispositon to all bodily activity; and I was fretful and inordinately passionate; and as I could not play at anything, and was slothful, I was despised and hated by the boys; and because I could read and spell, and had, I may truly say, a memory and understanding forced into almost unnatural ripeness, I was flattered and wondered at by all the old women.

Samuel Taylor Coleridge, 1797, Letter to Mr. Poole, Oct. 9;
Biographia Literaria, Biographical Supplement, ed. H. N. Coleridge

Every sight and every sound reminded me of him—dear, dear fellow, of his many talks to us, by day and by night, of all dear things. I was melancholy, and could not talk, but at last I eased my heart by weeping—nervous blubbering says William. It is not so. O! how many, many reasons have I to be anxious for him.

Dorothy Wordsworth, 1801, *Journals,* Nov. 10,
ed. Knight, vol. I, p. 64

O capacious Soul!
Placed on this earth to love and understand,
And from thy presence shed the light of love,
Shall I be mute, ere thou be spoken of?
Thy kindred influence to my heart of hearts
Did also find its way.

William Wordsworth, 1805, *The Prelude,* bk. xiv

His countenance is the most variable that I have ever seen; sometimes it is kindled with the brightest expression, and sometimes all its light goes out, and is utterly extinguished. Nothing can convey stronger indications of power than his eye, eyebrow, and forehead. Nothing can be more imbecile than all the rest of the face; look at them separately, you would hardly think it possible that they could belong to one head; look at them together, you wonder how they came so, and are puzzled what to expect from a character whose outward and visible signs are so contradictory.

Robert Southey, 1808, *Letter to Matilda Betham,* June 3;
Fraser's Magazine, vol. 98, p. 80

Coleridge has a grand head, but very ill balanced, and the features of the face are coarse—although, to be sure, nothing can surpass the depth of meaning in his eyes, and the unutterable dreamy luxury in his lips.

John Gibson Lockhart, 1819, *Peter's Letters to
His Kinsfolk,* Letter liv

His complexion was at that time [1798] clear, and even bright—
   "As are the children of yon azure sheen."
His forehead was broad and high, light as if built of ivory, with large projecting eyebrows, and his eyes rolling beneath them, like a sea with darkened lustre. "A certain tender bloom his face o'erspread," a purple tinge as we see it in the pale thoughtful complexions of the Spanish portrait-painters, Murillo and Velasquez. His mouth was gross, voluptuous, open, eloquent; his chin good-humoured and round; but his nose, the rudder of the face, the index of the will, was small, feeble, nothing—like what he has

done. . . . His hair (now, alas! gray) was then black and glossy as the raven's, and fell in smooth masses over his forehead.

William Hazlitt, 1821-22, "My First Acquaintance
with Poetry," *Table Talk*

In height he might seem to be about five feet eight (he was, in reality, about an inch and a-half taller, but his figure was of an order which drowns the height); his person was broad and full, and tended even to corpulence; his complexion was fair, though not what painters technically style fair, because it was associated with black hair; his eyes were large, and soft in their expression; and it was from the peculiar appearance of haze or dreaminess which mixed with their light that I recognised my object. . . . I examined him steadfastly for a minute or more; and it struck me that he saw neither myself nor any other object in the street. He was in a deep reverie; for I had dismounted, made two or three trifling arrangements at an inn-door, and advanced close to him, before he had apparently become conscious of my presence. The sound of my voice, announcing my own name, first awoke him: he started, and for a moment seemed at a loss to understand my purpose or his own situation; for he repeated rapidly a number of words which had no relation to either of us. There was no *mauvaise honte* in his manner, but simple perplexity, and an apparent difficulty in recovering his position amongst daylight realities. This little scene over, he received me with a kindness of manner so marked that it might be called gracious. . . . In the evening, when the heat of the day had declined, I walked out with him; and rarely, perhaps never, have I seen a person so much interrupted in one hour's space as Coleridge, on this occasion, by the courteous attentions of young and old.

Thomas De Quincey, 1834-54, *Autobiography from 1803
to 1808, Collected Writings,* ed. Masson, vol. II, pp. 150, 151

His benignity of manner placed his auditors entirely at their ease; and inclined them to listen delighted to the sweet, low tones in which he began to discourse on some high theme. Whether he had won for his greedy listener only some raw lad, or charmed a circle of beauty, rank, and wit, who hung breathless on his words, he talked with equal eloquence; for his subject, not his audience, inspired him. At first his tones were conversational; he seemed to dally with the shadows of the subject and with fantastic images which bordered it; but gradually the thought grew deeper, and the voice deepened with the thought; the stream gathering strength, seemed to bear along with it all things which opposed its progress, and blended them with its current; and stretching away among regions tinted with ethereal colors, was lost at airy distance in the horizon of fancy. His hearers were unable to grasp his theories, which were indeed too vast to be exhibited in the longest conversation; but they perceived noble images, generous suggestions, affecting pictures of virtue, which enriched their minds and nurtured their best affections. . . . He usually met opposition by conceding the point to the object, and then went on with his high argument as if it had never been raised; thus satisfying his antagonist, himself, and all who heard him; none of whom desired to hear his discourse frittered into points, or displaced by the near encounter even of the most brilliant wits.

> Thomas Noon Talfourd, 1837, *The Life and Letters of*
> *Charles Lamb*, p. 223

Whatever might have been his habits in boyhood, in manhood he was scrupulously clean in his person, and especially took great care of his hands. . . . In his dress also he was cleanly as the liberal use of snuff would permit, though the clothes-brush was often in requisition to remove the wasted snuff. "Snuff," he would facetiously say, "was the final cause of the nose, though troublesome and expensive in its use."

> James Gillman, 1838, *The Life of Samuel Taylor Coleridge,*
> p. 19, note

Coleridge was as little fitted for action as Lamb, but on a different account. His person was of a good height, but as sluggish and solid as the other's was light and fragile. He had, perhaps, suffered it to look old before its time, for want of exercise. His hair was white at fifty; and as he generally dressed in black, and had a very tranquil demeanor, his appearance was gentlemanly, and for several years before his death was reverend. Nevertheless, there was something invincibly young in the look of his face. It was round and fresh-colored, with agreeable features, and an open, indolent, good-natured mouth. This boy-like expression was very becoming in one who dreamed and speculated as he did when he was really a boy, and who passed his life apart from the rest of the world, with a book, and his flowers. His forehead was prodigious—a great piece of placid marble; and his fine eyes, in which all the activity of his mind seemed to concentrate, moved under it with a sprightly ease, as if it was pastime to them to carry all that thought.

> Leigh Hunt, 1850-60, *Autobiography*

Every body has heard the often told story of Coleridge's enlisting in a cavalry regiment under a feigned name, and being detected as a Cambridge scholar in consequence of his writing some Greek lines, or rather, I believe, some Greek words, over the bed of a sick comrade, whom, not knowing how else to dispose of him, he had been appointed to nurse. It has not been stated that the arrangement for his discharge took place at my father's house at Reading. Such, however, was the case.

Mary Russell Mitford, 1851, *Recollections of a Literary Life*, p. 394

Coleridge sat on the brow of Highgate Hill, in those years, looking down on London and its smoke-tumult, like a sage escaped from the inanity of life's battle; attracting towards him the thoughts of innumerable brave souls still engaged there. . . . The good man, he was now getting old, sixty perhaps; and gave you an idea of a life that had been full of sufferings; a life heavy-laden, half-vanquished, still swimming painfully in seas of manifold physical and other bewilderment. Brow and head were round and of massive weight, but the face was flabby and irresolute. The deep eyes, of a light hazel, were as full of sorrow as of inspiration; confused pain looked mildly from them, as in a kind of mild astonishment. The whole figure and air, good and amiable otherwise, might be called flabby and irresolute; expressive of weakness under possibility of strength. He hung loosely on his limbs, with knees bent, and stooping attitude; in walking, he rather shuffled than decisively stept; and a lady once remarked, he never could fix which side of the garden walk would suit him best, but continually shifted, in corkscrew fashion, and kept trying both. A heavy-laden, high-aspiring, and surely much-suffering man. His voice, naturally soft and good, had contracted itself into a plaintive snuffle and singsong; he spoke as if preaching,—you would have said, preaching earnestly and almost hopelessly the weightest things. I still recollect his "object" and "subject," terms of continual recurrence in the Kantean province; and how he sang and snuffled them into "om-m-mject" and "sum-m-mject," with a kind of solemn shake or quaver, as he rolled along. No talk, in his century or in any other, could be more surprising.

Thomas Carlyle, 1851, *The Life of John Sterling*

Coleridge was a marvellous talker. One morning he talked three hours without intermission about poetry, and so admirably that I wished every word he uttered had been written down. But sometimes his harangues were quite unintelligible, not only to myself but to others. Wordsworth and I called upon him one forenoon when he was lodging in Pall Mall. He talked uninterruptedly for about two hours, during which Wordsworth listened to him with profound attention, every now and then nodding his head as if in assent. On quitting the lodging I said to Wordsworth, "Well, for my own part I could not make head or tail of Coleridge's oration; pray, did you understand it?" "Not one syllable of it," was Wordsworth's reply.

Samuel Rogers, 1855, *Recollections of Table Talk,* ed. Dyce

I recollect him only as an eloquent but intolerable talker; impatient of the speech and opinions of others; very inconsecutive, and putting forth with a plethora of words misty dogmas in theology and metaphysics, partly of German origin, which he never seemed to me to clear up to his own understanding or to that of others. What has come out posthumously of his philosophy has not removed this imputation upon it.

Sir Henry Holland, 1871, Recollections of Past Life, p. 205

If Coleridge was at any period guilty of offence against the moral law it must have been in those early days when, as he says, he knew "just so much of folly" as "made maturer years more wise." In later years his walk became, more than ever, that of a man who had never so much as a temptation to such offence. It is a curious fact, which any careful reader of his letters may verify, that when he became a slave to opium, his spiritual consciousness became more active, and his watchfulness of the encroachments of the baser impulses of his nature more keen. If his excesses in this regard were what Southey described them, guilty animal indulgences, it is a strange problem in psychology why the whole spiritual nature of the man should undergo a manifest exaltation. Every one who was brought into contact with Coleridge in the darkest days of his subjection to opium, observed this extraordinary moral transfiguration.

Hall Caine, 1887, Life of Samuel Taylor Coleridge
(Great Writers), p. 136

Coleridge's domestic life was not fortunate or wisely managed, but at Clevedon, for some time after his early marriage, he was as happy as a lover. Every one who knows his early verse remembers the frequent references to his beloved Sara, which are provoking in their lack of real characterisation. With the most exquisite feeling for womanhood in its general features, he seems to have been incapable of drawing strongly the features of any individual woman. His nearest approach to the creation of a heroine is perhaps in his Illyrian queen, Zapolya. Even Christabel is a figure somewhat too faintly drawn, a figure expressing indeed the beauty, innocence, and gentleness of maidenhood, but without any of the traits of a distinctive personality. All his other imaginings of women are exquisite abstractions, framed of purely feminine elements, but representing Woman rather than being themselves veritable women.

Edward Dowden, 1895, New Studies in Literature, p. 321

Coleridge's life glided slowly away, calm outwardly, but animated by inner and never resting intellectual and emotional forces. The close of his life was attended with many physical sufferings. He was troubled greatly by nightmare. . . . What Coleridge appeared to me to lack was force of character and individuality. His life was centred in his imagination. His world was not our every-day working world, but one created out of his own inner consciousness. Coleridge was a Richter without his vivid humanity and humour. He was about 5 feet 9½ inches in height, but looked shorter. When a youth, his hair was black and glossy; but it was white at fifty. His complexion was fair; his countenance thoughtful and benevolent. In advanced years he was a great snuff-taker; but always scrupulously clean.

Joseph Forster, 1897, *Great Teachers*

POETRY

Shall gentle Coleridge pass unnoticed here.
To turgid ode and tumid stanza dear?
Though themes of innocence amuse him best,
Yet still obscurity's a welcome guest.
If Inspiration should her aid refuse
To him who takes a pixy for a muse,
Yet none in lofty numbers can surpass
The bard who soars to elegize an ass.
How well the subject suits his noble mind,
He brays, the laureat of the long-ear'd kind.
—Lord Byron, 1809, *English Bards and Scotch Reviewers*

He was a mighty poet—and
   A subtle-soul'd psychologist;
All things he seem'd to understand,
Of old or new—of sea or land—
   But his own mind—which was a mist.
This was a man who might have turn'd
   Hell into Heaven—and so in gladness
A Heaven unto himself have earn'd;
But he in shadows undiscern'd
   Trusted,—and damn'd himself to madness.
Percy Bysshe Shelley, 1819, *Peter Bell the Third*

He is superior, I think, to almost all our poets, except Spenser, in the deliciousness of his numbers. This charm results more from melody than measure, from a continuity of sweet sounds than from an apt division or skilful variation of them. There is no appearance of preparation, effort or artifice; they rise or fall with his feelings, like the unbidden breathings of an Æolian harp, from the deep intonations of passion to the light skirmishes of fancy. On the generality of readers it is to be feared this is all so much thrown away. Rapidity of reading hinders attraction to it. To enjoy the instrument one had need be in some such happy Castle of Indolence as Thomson has placed it in.

Henry Francis Cary, 1823, Notices of Miscellaneous
English Poets, Memoir, ed. Cary, vol. II, p. 299

His poetry is another matter. It is so beautiful, and was so quietly content with its beauty, making no call on the critics, and receiving hardly any notice, that people are but now beginning to awake to a full sense of its merits. Of pure poetry, strictly so called, that is to say, consisting of nothing but its essential self, without conventional and perishing helps, he was the greatest master of his time. If you could see it in a phial, like a distillation of roses (taking it, I mean, at its best), it would be found without a speck. . . . Oh! it is too late now; and habit and self-love blinded me at the time, and I did not know (much as I admired him) how great a poet lived in that grove at Highgate; or I would have cultivated its walks more, as I might have done, and endeavoured to return him, with my gratitude, a small portion of the delight his verses have given me.

Leigh Hunt, 1844, Imagination and Fancy, pp. 250, 255

Few minds are capable of fathoming his by their own sympathies, and he has left us no adequate manifestation of himself as a poet by which to judge him. For his dramas, I consider them complete failures, and more like visions than dramas. For a metaphysical mind like his to attempt that walk, was scarcely more judicious than it would be for a blind man to essay painting the bay of Naples. Many of his smaller pieces are perfect in their way, indeed no writer could excel him in depicting a single mood of mind, as Dejection, for instance. . . . Give Coleridge a canvass, and he will paint a single mood as if his colors were made of the mind's own atoms. Here he is very unlike Southey. There is nothing of the spectator about Coleridge; he is all life; not impassioned, not vehement, but searching, intellectual life, which seems "listening through the frame" to its own pulses.

Margaret Fuller Ossoli, 1850, Art, Literature and
the Drama, pp. 97, 98

As a poet his place is indisputable. It is high among the highest of all time. An age that should forget or neglect him might neglect or forget any poet that ever lived. At least, any poet whom it did remember such an age would remember as something other than a poet; it would prize and praise in him, not the absolute and distinctive quality, but something empirical or accidental. That may be said of this one which can hardly be said of any but the greatest among men; that come what may to the world in course of time, it will never see his place filled. Other and stronger men, with fuller control and concentration of genius, may do more service, may bear more fruit; but such as his was they will not have in them to give. The highest lyric work is either passionate or imaginative; of passion Coleridge's has nothing; but for height and perfection of imaginative quality he is the greatest of lyric poets. This was his special power, and this is his special praise.

Algernon Charles Swinburne, 1875, Essays and Studies, p. 274

There is no one of Coleridge's sonnets which can be pronounced distinctly satisfactory. The one I have given seems to me on the whole the best. The famous one on Schiller's *Robbers* has been much overrated—though Coleridge himself had a high opinion of it. Wordsworth showed his critical faculty when, on receipt of Dyce's *Sonnet-Anthology,* he referred to the insertion of *The Robbers* as a mistake, on the ground of "rant." . . . There are probably few readers of mature taste who would not consider Wordsworth's epithet "rant" as literally applicable. One learns with a sense of uncomfortable wonder that Coleridge himself—this supreme master of metrical music—considered the last six lines "strong and fiery!" What a difference between this Schiller sonnet and the beautiful poem in fourteen lines entitled "Work without Hope." If these lines had only been adequately set in sonnet-mould, the result would have been a place for this poetic gem among the finest sonnets in the language.

William Sharp, 1886, Sonnets of this Century, p. 238, note

The poetic genius of Coleridge, the highest of his many gifts, found brilliant and fascinating expression. His poems—those in which his fame lives—are as unique as they are memorable; and though their small number, their confined range, and the brief period during which his faculty was exercised with full freedom and power, seem to indicate a narrow vein, yet the remainder of his work in prose and verse leaves an impression of extraordinary and abundant intellectual force. In proportion as his imaginative creations stand apart, the spirit out of which they came must have possessed some singularity: and if the reader is not content with simple æsthetic appreciation of what the gods provide, but has some touch of curiosity leading him to look into the source of such remarkable achievement and its human history, he is at once interested in the personality of the "subtle-souled psychologist," as Shelley with his accurate critical insight first named him.

George E. Woodberry, 1897, Library of the World's Best
Literature, ed. Warner, vol. VII, p. 3844

No other poet, perhaps, except Spenser, has been an initial influence, a generative influence, on so many poets. Having with that mild Elizabethan much affinity, it is natural that he also should be "a poets' poet" in the rarer sense—the sense of fecundating other poets. As with Spenser, it is not that other poets have made him their model, have reproduced essentials of his style (accidents no great poet will consciously perpetuate). The progeny are sufficiently unlike the parent. It is that he has incited the very sprouting in them of the laurel-bough, has been to them a fostering sun of song. Such a primary influence he was to Rossetti—Rossetti, whose model was far more Keats than Coleridge. Such he was to Coventry Patmore, in whose work one might trace many masters rather than Coleridge. . . . For the last thirty years criticism has unburdened its suppressed feelings about Coleridge, which it considerately spared him while he was alive; and his position is clear, unquestioned; his reputation beyond the power of wax or wane. Alone of modern poets, his fame sits above the power of fluctuation. Wordsworth has fluctuated; Tennyson stands not exactly as he did; there is reaction in some quarters against the worship of Shelley; though all are agreed Keats is a great poet, not all are agreed as to his place. But around Coleridge the clamour of partisans is silent: none attacks, none has need to defend. . . . Over that wreck, most piteous and terrible in all our literary history, shines, and will shine for ever, the five-pointed star, of his glorious youth; those poor five resplendent poems, for which he paid the devil's price of a desolated life and unthinkably blasted powers. Other poets may have done greater things; none a thing more perfect and uncompanioned. Other poets belong to this class or that; he to the class of Samuel Taylor Coleridge.

Francis Thompson, 1897, *Academy Portraits,*
The Academy, vol. 51, pp. 179, 180

The Ancient Mariner (1798)

His *Ancient Mariner* is the most remarkable performance, and the only one that I could point out to any one as giving an adequate idea of his great natural powers. It is high German, however, and in it he seems to "conceive of poetry but as a drunken dream, reckless, careless, and heedless, of past, present, and to come."

William Hazlitt, 1818, *Lectures on the English Poets,* Lecture viii

A wild, mystical, phantasmagoric narrative, most picturesquely related in the old English ballad measure, and in language to which is skillfully given an air of antiquity in admirable harmony with the spectral character of the events. The whole poem is a splendid dream, filling the ear with the strange

and floating melodies of sleep, and the eye with a shifting, vaporous succession of fantastic images, gloomy or radiant.

Thomas B. Shaw, 1847, English Literature, p. 426

The Ancient Mariner is a poem of which (in the experience of most of
us) the first impression dates back to those earliest years when the Bible and
Pilgrim's Progress made up the whole body of serious reading; but if we
could encounter it first of all late in life, after the stream of more modern
literature had filtered into our minds, it would probably seem to us like
meeting for the first time in person some great writer of whom we have
known much through his books. For just as in the one case, many qualities
of mind and heart which have endeared the writer to us, find to our heightened sense a kind of visible embodiment in the face, voice, gait and gesture
of the man in whose work we recognised them; so in the other, many exquisite and original imaginative fantasies which we must have seen wandering
through uncertain channels, would find their true place and fitting mission
in the beautiful and complete conception from which they were borrowed.

Hall Caine, 1883, Cobwebs of Criticism, p. 59

It is enough for us here that he has written some of the most poetical poetry
in the language, and one poem, *The Ancient Mariner,* not only unparalleled, but unapproached in its kind, and that kind of the rarest. It is
marvellous in its mastery over that delightfully fortuitous inconsequence
that is the adamantine logic of dreamland. Coleridge has taken the old
ballad measure and given to it by an indefinable charm wholly his own
all the sweetness, all the melody and compass of a symphony. And how
picturesque it is in the proper sense of the word. I know nothing like it.
There is not a description in it. It is all picture.

James Russell Lowell, 1885-90, Address on Unveiling the Bust
of Coleridge in Westminster Abbey, 7 May; Prose Works,
Riverside ed., vol. VI, p. 73

If in outward form the poem cannot be called religious, in its spirit it is
steeped in religious thought and conviction. Into it has passed, perhaps unconsciously to the poet himself, the profoundest human experiences which
are indicative of the energy of the religious consciousness.

W. Boyd Carpenter, 1901, The Religious Spirit in the Poets, p. 150

Christabel (1805-16)

Christabel—I won't have any one sneer at *Christabel*: it is a fine wild
poem.

Lord Byron, 1816, Letter to Mr. Murray, Sept. 30

It is common to hear everything which Mr. Coleridge has written condemned with bitterness and boldness. His poems are called extravagant; and his prose works, poems too, and of the noblest breed, are pronounced to be mystical, obscure, metaphysical, theoretical, unintelligible, and so forth; just as the same phrases have over and over been applied, with as much sagacity, to Plato, St. Paul, Cudworth, and Kant. But *Christabel* is the only one of his writings which is ever treated with unmingled contempt. . . . Throughout the poem there runs and lives one especial excellence, the beauty of single lines and expressions, perfect flowers in themselves, yet interfering as little with the breadth and unity of the general effect, as the primroses and hawthorns of the valley with its sweeping perspective of light and shadow. No one, I imagine, can fail to recognise in it the original germ of the *Lay of the Last Minstrel*: but how superior is it to that spirited and brilliant tale, in the utter absence both of defect and superfluity in the diction,—in the thrilling interest and beauty of every, the slightest circumstance,—in the relation of each atom to the whole,—and in the deep reflection, which is the very atmosphere and vital air of the whole composition!

John Sterling, 1828-58, "On Coleridge's Cristabel,"
Essays and Tales, ed. Hare, vol. I, pp. 101, 110

The thing attempted in *Christabel* is the most difficult of execution in the whole field of romance—witchery by daylight; and the success is complete. Geraldine, so far as she goes, is perfect. She is *sui generis*. The reader feels the same terror and perplexity that Christabel in vain struggles to express, and the same spell that fascinates her eyes. Who and what is Geraldine— whence come, whither going, and what designing? What did the poet mean to make of her? What could he have made of her? Could he have gone on much farther without having had recourse to some of the ordinary shifts of witch tales? Was she really the daughter of Roland de Vaux, and would the friends have met again and embraced? . . . We are not amongst those who wish to have Christabel finished. It cannot be finished. The poet has spun all he could without snapping. The theme is too fine and subtle to bear much extension. It is better as it is, imperfect as a story, but complete as an exquisite production of the imagination, differing in form and colour from the "Ancient Mariner," yet differing in effect from it only so as the same powerful faculty is directed to the feudal or the mundane phases of the preternatural.

John Gibson Lockhart, 1834, "The Poetical Works of
S. T. Coleridge," <i>Quarterly Review</i>, vol. 52, pp. 29, 30</div>

Out of a hundred readers of *Christabel,* fifty will be able to make nothing of its rhythm, while forty-nine of the remaining fifty will, with some ado, fancy they comprehend it after the fourth or fifth perusal. The one out of the whole hundred who shall both comprehend and admire it at first sight must be an unaccountably clever person; and I am by far too modest to assume, for a moment, that that very clever person is myself.

Edgar Allan Poe, 1848, *The Rationale of Verse, Works of Poe,*
ed. Stedman and Woodberry, vol. VI, p. 76

For my part, I cannot compare *Kubla Khan* with *Christabel.* The magical beauty of the latter has been so long canonized in the world's estimate, that to praise it now would be unseemly. It brought into English poetry an atmosphere of wonder and mystery, of weird beauty and pity combined, which was quite new at the time it appeared, and has never since been approached. The movement of its subtle cadences has a union of grace with power, which only the finest lines of Shakespeare can parallel. As we read *Christabel* and a few other of Coleridge's pieces, we recall his own words:

> "In a half-sleep we dream,
> And dreaming hear thee still, O singing lark!
> That singest like an angel in the clouds."

John Campbell Shairp, 1881, "Poetic Style in Modern
English Poetry," *Aspects of Poetry*

Kubla Khan (1816)

Were we compelled to the choice, I for one would rather preserve *Kubla Khan* and *Christabel* than any other of Coleridge's poems. It is more conceivable that another man should be born capable of writing the *Ancient Mariner* than one capable of writing these. The former is perhaps the most wonderful of all poems. In reading it we seem rapt into that paradise revealed to Swedenborg, where music and colour and perfume were one, where you could hear the hues and see the harmonies of heaven. For absolute melody and splendour it were hardly rash to call it the first poem in the language.

Algernon Charles Swinburne, 1875, *Essays and Studies,* p. 264

Were there left of Coleridge nothing but *Kubla Khan,* from this gem one might almost reconstruct, in full brightness, its great author's poetic work, just as the expert zoölogist reconstructs the extinct megatherium from a single fossil bone. Of this masterpiece, the chief beauty is not the noted music of the versification, but the range and quality of the imaginings embodied in this music. Were there in these no unearthly breathings, no mysterious grandeur, the verse could not have been made to pulsate so rhythmically. The essence of the melody is in the fineness of the conception, in the poetic imaginations.

George H. Calvert, 1880, *Coleridge, Shelley, Goethe,* p. 12

To us *Kubla Khan* is a splendid curiosity, a lyrical landscape fairy tale, which we know not what to make of. Ninety years ago this specimen of emotional inspiration evinced a bold and powerful reaction. Shelley borrowed many a curiosity from it; for example, in *Marianne's Dream* we have the Fata Morgana towers—the half-joyful, half-demoniacal sound in the lady's ears—the bursting streams of light, and the feverishly-tossing floods—all without any practical object. And again, in the *Skylark,* the "high-born maiden" in a palace, and the harmonious madness of the singer. This is why Byron, Shelley, and Keats indulge so commonly in visions, distinctly so entitled—for example, *Darkness, Vision of the Sea, On a Dream*—seeking in all seriousness to forecast the future, and even placing the truth of the dream before that of the waking eye. The poetic atmosphere became purified, but, in the zeal for reform, too much rarefied.

> Alois Brandl, 1887, *Samuel Taylor Coleridge and the English Romantic School,* tr. Lady Eastlake, p. 186

GENERAL

Beyond all other political speculators, our author mingles important moral philosophical principles with his reasonings. . . . We cannot conclude without expressing an earnest wish, that this original thinker and eloquent writer may be persuaded to put the literary public speedily in possession, by successive volumes of essays, of an ample portion of those refined speculations, the argument and the strongest illustrations of which he is well known to have in an almost complete state in his mind—and many of which will never be in any other mind, otherwise than as communicated from him. The chief alteration desirable, for his reader's sake, to be made in his mode of writing, is a resolute restriction on that mighty profusion and excursiveness of thought, in which he is tempted to suspend the pursuit and retard the attainment of the one distinct object which should be clearly kept in view; and, added to this, a more patient and prolonged effort to reduce the abstruser part of his ideas, as much as their subtle quality will possibly admit, to a substantial and definable form.

> John Foster, 1811, "Coleridge," *Critical Essays,* ed. Ryland, vol. II, pp. 20, 23

> Coleridge, too, has lately taken wing,
> But like a hawk encumber'd with his hood,—
> Explaining metaphysics to the nation—
> I wish he would explain his Explanation.

> Lord Byron, 1819, *Don Juan,* Dedication

> You will see Coleridge—he who sits obscure
> In the exceeding lustre and the pure
> Intense irradiation of a mind,
> Which, with its own internal lightning blind,
> Flags wearily through darkness and despair—
> A cloud-encircled meteor of the air,
> A hooded eagle among blinking owls.

Percy Bysshe Shelley, 1820, Letter to Maria Gisborne

If Mr. Coleridge had not been the most impressive talker of his age, he would probably have been the finest writer; but he lays down his pen to make sure of an auditor, and mortgages the admiration of posterity for the stare of an idler. If he had not been a poet, he would have been a powerful logician; if he had not dipped his wing in the Unitarian controversy, he might have soared to the very summit of fancy. But in writing verse, he is trying to subject the Muse to *transcendental* theories: in his abstract reasoning, he misses his way by strewing it with flowers. All that he has done of moment, he had done twenty years ago: since then, he may be said to have lived on the sound of his own voice. . . . He walks abroad in the majesty of an universal understanding, eyeing the "rich strond," or golden sky above him, and "goes sounding on his way," in eloquent accents, uncompelled and free!

William Hazlitt, 1825, The Spirit of the Age, pp. 38, 39

Taken absolutely and in itself, the *Remorse* is more fitted for the study than the stage; its character is romantic and pastoral in a high degree, and there is a profusion of poetry in the minor parts, the effect of which could never be preserved in the common routine of representation. What this play wants is dramatic movement; there is energetic dialogue and a crisis of great interest, but the action does not sufficiently grow on the stage itself.

John Gibson Lockhart, 1834, "The Poetical Works of
S. T. Coleridge," Quarterly Review, vol. 52, p. 23

The Opium-eater calls Coleridge "the largest and most spacious intellect, the subtlest and most comprehensive that has yet existed among men." Impiety to Shakspeare! treason to Milton! I give up the rest, even Bacon. Certainly, since their day, we have seen nothing at all comparable to him. Byron and Scott were but as gunflints to a granite mountain! Wordsworth has one angle of resemblance.

Walter Savage Landor, 1835, Letter to Lady Blessington,
March 16; Literary Life and Correspondence, ed. Madden,
vol. II, p. 123

I think with all his faults Old Sam was more of a great man than any one that has lived within the four seas in my memory. It is refreshing to see such a union of the highest philosophy and poetry, with so full a knowledge, in so many points at least, of particular facts.

Thomas Arnold, 1836, *Letter to W. W. Hull,* Nov. 16;
Life and Correspondence, ed. Stanley, vol. II, p. 61

The name of Coleridge is one of the few English names of our own time which are likely to be oftener pronounced, and to become symbolical of more important things, in proportion as the inward workings of the age manifest themselves more and more in outward facts. Bentham excepted, no Englishman of recent date has left his impress so deeply in the opinions and mental tendencies of those among us who attempt to enlighten their practice by philosophical meditation. . . . The influence of Coleridge, like that of Bentham, extends far beyond those who share in the peculiarities of his religious or philosophical creed. He has been the great awakener in this country of the spirit of philosophy, within the bounds of traditional opinions. . . . It is hardly possible to speak of Coleridge, and his position among his contemporaries, without reverting to Bentham: they are connected by two of the closest bonds of association—resemblance and contrast. It would be difficult to find two persons of philosophic eminence more exactly the contrary of one another. Compare their modes of treatment of any subject, and you might fancy them inhabitants of different worlds. They seem to have scarcely a principle or a premise in common. Each of them sees scarcely anything but what the other does not see. Bentham would have regarded Coleridge with a peculiar measure of the good-humoured contempt with which he was accustomed to regard all modes of philosophizing different from his own. Coleridge would probably have made Bentham one of the exceptions to the enlarged and liberal appreciation which (to the credit of *his* mode of philosophizing) he extended to most thinkers of any eminence, from whom he differed.

John Stuart Mill, 1840, "Coleridge," *London and Westminster Review,* vol. 33, pp. 257, 258, 259

A new era of critical opinion upon Shakspere, as propounded by Englishmen, may be dated from the delivery of the lectures of Samuel Taylor Coleridge, at the Surrey Institution, in 1814. What that great man did for Shakspere during the remainder of his valuable life can scarcely be appreciated by the public. For his opinions were not given to the world in formal treatises and ponderous volumes. They were fragmentary; they were scattered, as it were, at random; many of them were the oral lessons of that wisdom and knowledge which he poured out to a few admiring disciples. But they have had their effect. For ourselves, personally, we owe a debt of gratitude to that illustrious man that can never be repaid. If in any degree we have been enabled to present Shakspere to the popular mind under new aspects, looking at him from a central point, which should permit us, however imperfectly, to comprehend something of his wondrous *system,* we owe the desire so to understand him ourselves to the germs of thought which are scattered through the works of that philosopher; to whom the homage of future times will abundantly compensate for the partial neglect of his contemporaries. We desire to conclude this outline of the opinions of others upon the works of Shakspere, in connection with the imperfect expression of our own sense of those opinions, with the name of COLERIDGE.

Charles Knight, 1845, *Studies of Shakspere,* p. 560

Coleridge was the first who made criticism interpretative both of the spirit and the form of works of genius, the first who founded his principles in the nature of things. . . . He had a clear notion of the difference lying at the base of all poetic criticism, between *mechanical regularity* and *organic form.*

Edwin P. Whipple, 1846, *Essays and Reviews,* vol. II, pp. 183, 184

Coleridge, a catholic mind, with a hunger for ideas; with eyes looking before and after to the highest bards and sages, and who wrote and spoke the only high criticism in his time, is one of those who save England from the reproach of no longer possessing the capacity to appreciate what rarest wit the island has yielded. Yet the misfortune of his life, his vast attempts but most inadequate performings, failing to accomplish any one masterpiece,— seems to mark the closing of an era. Even in him, the traditional Englishman was too strong for the philosopher, and he fell into *accommodations;* and as Burke had striven to idealize the English State, so Coleridge "narrowed his mind" in the attempt to reconcile the Gothic rule and dogma of the Anglican Church, with eternal ideas. But for Coleridge, and a lurking taciturn minority uttering itself in occasional criticism, oftener in private discourse, one would say that in Germany and in America is the best mind in England rightly respected.

Ralph Waldo Emerson, 1856-84, "Literature," *English Traits;*
Works, Riverside ed., vol. V, p. 236

Coleridge had less delicacy and penetration than Joubert, but more richness and power; his production, though far inferior to what his nature at first seemed to promise, was abundant and varied. Yet in all his production how much is there to dissatisfy us! How many reserves must be made in praising either his poetry, or his criticism, or his philosophy! How little either of his poetry, or of his criticism, or of his philosophy, can we expect permanently to stand! But that which will stand of Coleridge is this; the stimulus of his continual effort,—not a moral effort, for he had no morals,—but of his continual instinctive effort, crowned often with rich success, to get at and to lay bare the real truth of his matter in hand, whether that matter were literary, or philosophical, or political, or religious; and this in a country where at that moment such an effort was almost unknown. . . . Coleridge's great action lay in his supplying in England, for many years and under critical circumstances, by the spectacle of this effort of his, a stimulus to all minds, in the generation which grew up round him, capable of profiting by it. His action will still be felt as long as the need for it continues. When, with the cessation of the need, the action too has ceased, Coleridge's memory, in spite of the disesteem,—nay, repugance,—which his character may and must inspire, will yet forever remain invested with that interest and gratitude which invests the memory of founders.

Matthew Arnold, 1865, "Joubert," Essays in Criticism

The literary life of Coleridge was a disinterested struggle against the relative spirit. With a strong native bent towards the tracking of all questions, critical or practical, to first principles, he is ever restlessly scheming to "apprehend the absolute," to affirm it effectively, to get it acknowledged. It was an effort, surely, an effort of sickly thought, that saddened his mind, and limited the operation of his unique poetic gift. . . . Perhaps the chief offence in Coleridge is an excess of seriousness, a seriousness arising not from any moral principle, but from a misconception of the perfect manner.

Walter Pater, 1865-80, Appreciations, pp. 67, 68

The influence of Coleridge has been scattered and fragmentary. In church, in state, in literature, his spirit has descended to many whose theories and purposes are otherwise widely different. John Henry Newman and Frederick D. Maurice alike owe their inspiration to him; John Stuart Mill can call him one of the two great moving forces of the century; Thomas Carlyle and Matthew Arnold carried on in their different fashions his European and cosmopolitan culture of England. His literary criticism is of the same scattered and frutiful sort. In his suggestions lies the germ of a higher development, the spirit that must inform the great and enduring work of the future. Fragmentary as his writings are, there is yet opened through them an ideal criticism that has never been reached, and for which we can only hope if the clear intellectuality of the eighteenth century shall come to blend with the spirituality that complemented and destroyed it.

Laura Johnson Wylie, 1894, Evolution of English Criticism, p. 204

One is a little apt to forget that his metaphysical bent was no less innate than his poetical,—even at Christ's hospital, his spiritual potation was a half-and-half in which the waters of a more or less authentic Castaly, and the "philosophic draughts" from such fountains as Jamblichus and Plotinus, were equally mingled. Whether or not a born "maker," he was certainly a born theorist; and we believe not only that under all his most important artistic achievements there was a basis of intellectual theory, but that the theory, so far from being an alien and disturbing presence, did duty as the unifying principle which co-ordinated the whole.

William Watson, 1893, *Excursions in Criticism,* p. 98

The contributions which Coleridge made to modern thought, rich, ample, and suggestive as they are, have all the characteristics of his varied and eventful life. In Poetry, Criticism, and Philosophy he drove the shaft deep and gave us samples of the wealth of ore lying in their confines. Although he worked these mines only at irregular intervals and passed rapidly from one to the other, yet, by stimulating and quickening activity in his associates and followers, he caused the entire territory to be explored as it never was before in English history. If it cannot be said of him that he left us a rounded and complete system, yet it can be said—and it is a far nobler tribute—that he made it possible for us to grasp those principles which underlie all systems. His contribution to the literature of power is certainly unsurpassed by that of any writer of modern times.

Andrew J. George, 1895, ed. *Coleridge's Principles of Criticism,* p. vii

Like Nelson's letter to Lady Hamilton, Coleridge's "Letters," to everybody almost, are not always agreeable reading. One lesson of Mr. Carlyle's, a lesson which he preached by precept rather than example, we have partly learned. "Consume your own smoke," said the sage. Coleridge, in his private correspondence, blew abroad the vapor of smoke which rose from, and often dimmed the fire of his unexampled genius. On that sacred flame it is no metaphor to say that he poured too many drugs, heaped "poppy buds and laudanum." Hence ascended the smoke which he did not restrain or consume, but allowed to take its free way through heaven and earth. It may be said that there is an affectation, now, of reticence, and an affectation of manliness. Affectations if they be, these at least are imitations of virtues which Coleridge did not possess. He had a kind of mania for confessing himself, and crying *mea culpa.* Like the bad man in Aristotle, he is "full of repentance," or of remorse. He is an erring creature, and knows it, and his confessions occasionally suggest, in a sense, the Scotch proverbial policy of "taking the first word of flyting." One would rather see him more hardened, less "sensible." To moralise about Coleridge is temptingly easy and absolutely useless.

Andrew Lang, 1895, "The Letters of Coleridge,"
Contemporary Review, vol. 67, p. 876

In disburthening himself of the ideas and imaginations which pressed upon his consciousness, in committing them to writing and carefully preserving them through all his wanderings, Coleridge had no mind that they should perish utterly. The invisible pageantry of thought and passion which forever floated into his spiritual ken, the perpetual hope, that half belief that the veil of the senses would be rent in twain, and that he and not another would be the first to lay bare the mysteries of being, and to solve the problem of the ages—of these was the breath of his soul. It was his fate to wrestle from night to morn with the Angel of the Vision, and of that unequal combat he has left, by way of warning or encouragement, a broken but an inspired and inspiring record.

Ernest Hartley Coleridge, 1895, *Anima Poetæ from the
Unpublished Note-Books of Samuel Taylor Coleridge*,
Preface, p. ix

Coleridge's Shakespeare criticism is from first to last a continual quest of the evidences of organic structure, thus conceived. It illustrates both the value of the method and its perils. He made the first serious effort to grasp the totality of Shakespeare's work, and to trace out the inner history of his mind through the chronological chaos in which the dramas were still involved. The method gives subtlety, sometimes over-subtlety, to his appreciation of character. Every obvious trait becomes the mask of an alien quality which it conceals. He insists upon the inadequacy of the traditional classifications. He refuses to see sheer folly or villainy; dwells on the intellectual greatness of Iago, of Richard; repudiates the "cowardice" of Falstaff, and finds in Polonius a wise man past his prime. He elicits the hidden pathos of humour, and is somewhat too prone to find profound judgement in a pun.

C. H. Herford, 1897, *The Age of Wordsworth*, p. 87

CHARLES LAMB
1775-1834

1775—Born February 10, Crown Office Row, Temple. 1782—Enters Christ's Hospital School. 1789—Leaves school and enters service of South

Sea House. 1792—Enters service East India Company. 1795—Resides at No. 7 Little Queen St., Holborn. 1796—Publishes four Sonnets in volume of *Poems by S. T. Coleridge.* 1797—Removes to No. 45 Chappel St., Pentonville.—Contributes to *Poems by S. T. Coleridge, Charles Lamb, and Charles Lloyd.* 1800—Writes Epilogue to Godwin's *Antonio.* 1801—Removes to No. 16 Mitre-Court Buildings, Temple. 1802—Publishes *John Woodvil.* 1806—Produces *Mr. H*—a Farce, at Drury Lane. 1807—Publishes *Tales from Shakespear*—*Mrs. Leicester's School.*—Writes Prologue for *Faulkener,* by Godwin. 1808—Publishes *Specimens of Dramatic Poets* —*The Adventures of Ulysses.* 1809—Publishes *Poetry for Children.*— Removes to No. 4 Inner Temple Lane.—Lives at No. 34 Southampton Buildings. 1811—Publishes *Prince Dorus.* 1813—Writes Prologue for Coleridge's *Remorse.* 1817—Removes to No. 20 Russell St., Covent Garden. 1818—Publishes *Collected Works,* 2 vols. 1820—Contributes to the *London Magazine.* 1823—Removes to Colebrooke (Colnbrooke) Row, Islington.—Publishes *Essays of Elia,* First Series. 1825—Retires from East India House.—Contributes numerous articles to Hone's *Every Day Book.* 1826—Removes to Enfield. 1827—Contributes Introduction to *The Garrick Plays,* in Hone's *Table Book.* 1829—Lodges in Enfield. 1830— Publishes *Album Verses.*—Contributes "De Foe's Works of Genius" to Wilson's *Memoirs of Daniel De Foe.* 1831—Publishes *Satan in Search of a Wife.* 1832—Removes to Bay Cottage, Edmonton. 1833—Publishes *Last Essays of Elia.*—Contributes Epilogue to *The Wife,* by J. Sheridan Knowles. 1834—Charles Lamb dies, December 27, at Edmonton.

Ernest D. North, 1890-94, *In the Footprints of Charles Lamb,* by Benjamin Ellis Martin, Bibliography, p. 149

SEE: *Works of Charles and Mary Lamb,* ed. E. V. Lucas, 1903-5, 7 v., rev. 1912, 6 v.; *Works in Prose and Verse,* ed. Thomas Hutchinson, 1924 (two volumes in one); *The Portable Charles Lamb,* ed. John Mason Brown, 1948; *Letters of Charles and Mary Lamb,* ed. E. V. Lucas, 1935, 3 v.; E. V. Lucas, *Life of Charles Lamb,* 1905, 2 v., rev. 1921; Edmund Blunden, *Lamb and His Contemporaries,* 1933 (Clarke lectures); also see Walter Pater, in *Appreciations,* 1889.

PERSONAL

I am glad that you think of him as I think; he has an affectionate heart, a mind *sui generis;* his taste acts so as to appear like the unmechanic simplicity of an instinct—in brief, he is worth an hundred men of *mere* talents. Conversation with the later tribe is like the use of leaden bells—one warms by exercise, Lamb every now and then *irradiates,* and the beam, though single and fine as a hair, is yet rich with colours, and I both see and feel.

Samuel Taylor Coleridge, 1800, *Letter to William Godwin,* May 21; *William Godwin his Friends and Contemporaries,* ed. Paul, vol. II, p. 3

I forget whether I had written my last before my Sunday evening at Haydon's—no, I did not, or I should have told you, Tom, of a young man you met at Paris, at Scott's, of the [name of] Ritchie. I think he is going to Fezan, in Africa; then to proceed if possible like Mungo Park. He was very polite to me, and inquired very particularly after you. Then there was Wordsworth, Lamb, Monkhouse, Landseer, Kingston, and your humble servant. Lamb got tipsy and blew up Kingston—proceeding so far as to take the candle across the room, hold it to his face, and show us what a soft fellow he was.

John Keats, 1818, *Letter to his Brothers,* Jan. 5;
Poetry and Prose, ed. Forman, vol. V, p. 78

There was L— himself, the most delightful, the most provoking, the most witty and sensible of men. He always made the best pun, and the best remark in the course of the evening. His serious conversation, like his serious writing, is his best. No one ever stammered out such fine, piquant, deep, eloquent things in half a dozen half-sentences as he does. His jests scald like tears: and he probes a question with a play upon words. . . . There was no fuss of cant about him: nor were his sweets or his sours ever diluted with one particle of affectation.

William Hazlitt, 1821-22, *On the Conversation of Authors,*
Table Talk

Charles Lamb, born in the Inner Temple, 10th February, 1775; educated in Christ's Hospital; afterwards a clerk in the Accountants' Office, East India House; pensioned off from that service, 1825, after thirty-three years' service; is now a gentleman at large; can remember few specialities in his life worth noting, except that he once caught a swallow flying (*teste sua manu*). Below the middle stature; cast of face slightly Jewish, with no Judaic tinge in his complexional religion; stammers abominably, and is therefore more apt to discharge his occasional conversation in a quaint aphorism, or a poor quibble, than in set and edifying speeches; has consequently been libelled as a person always aiming at wit; which, as he told a dull fellow who charged him with it, is at least as good as aiming at dullness. A small eater, but not drinker; confesses a partiality for the production of the juniper berry; was a fierce smoker of tobacco, but may be resembled to a volcano burnt out, emitting only now and then an occasional puff. Has been guilty of obtruding upon the public a tale in prose, called "Rosamond Gray," a dramatic sketch named "John Woodvil," a "Fairewell Ode to Tobacco," with sundry other poems and light prose matter, collected in two slight crown octavos, and pompously christened his works, though, in fact, they were his recreations; and his true works may be found on the shelves of Leadenhall Street, filling some hundred folios. He is also the true Elia, whose essays are extant in a little volume. He died 18— much lamented.

Charles Lamb, 1827, *Autobiography,* April 18

Heigh ho! Charles Lamb I sincerely believe to be in some considerable degree insane. A more pitiful, rickety, gasping, staggering, stammering Tomfool I do not know. He is witty by denying truisms and abjuring good manners. His speech wriggles hither and thither with an incessant painful fluctuation, not an opinion in it, or a fact, or a phrase that you can thank him for—more like a convulsion fit than a natural systole and diastole. Besides, he is now a confirmed, shameless drunkard; *asks* vehemently for gin and water in strangers' houses, tipples till he is utterly mad, and is only not thrown out of doors because he is too much despised for taking such trouble with him. Poor Lamb! Poor England, when such a despicable abortion is named genius!

> Thomas Carlyle, 1831, *Journal, Life* by Froude, vol. II, p. 170

Once, and once only have I seen thy face,
Elia! once only has thy tripping tongue
Run o'er my heart, yet never has been left
Impression on it stronger and more sweet,
Cordial old man! what youth was in thy years,
What wisdom in thy levity, what soul
In every utterance of thy purest breast!
Of all that ever wore man's form, 'tis thee
I first would spring to at the gate of Heaven.

I say *tripping* tongue for Charles Lamb stammered and spoke hurriedly. He did not think it worth while to put on a fine new coat to come down to see me in, as poor Coleridge did, but met me as if I had been a friend of twenty years' standing; indeed, he told me I had been so, and showed me some things I had written much longer ago and had utterly forgotten. The world will never see again two such delightful volumes as *The Essays of Elia;* no man living is capable of writing the worst twenty pages of them. The Continent has Zadig and Gil Blas, we have Elia and Sir Roger de Coverley.

> Walter Savage Landor, 1834, *Letter to the Countess of Blessington, Literary Life and Correspondence,* ed. Madden, vol. II, p. 381

Genius triumphed over seeming wrong,
And poured out truth in works by thoughtful love
Inspired—works potent over smiles and tears.
And as round mountain-tops thy lightning plays,
Thus innocently sported, breaking forth
As from a cloud of some grave sympathy,
Humour and wild instinctive wit, and all
The vivid flashes of his spoken words. . . .

At the centre of his being, lodged
A soul by resignation sanctified:
And if too often, self-reproached, he felt
That innocence belongs not to our kind,
A power that never ceased to abide in him,
Charity, 'mid the multitude of sins
That she can cover, left not his exposed
To an unforgiving judgment from just Heaven,
Oh, he was good, if e'er a good Man lived.

William Wordsworth, 1835, *Written After the Death of*
Charles Lamb

Mr. Lamb's personal appearance was remarkable. It quite realized the expectations of those who think that an author and a wit should have a distinct air, a separate costume, a particular cloth, something positive and singular about him. Such unqestionably had Mr. Lamb. Once he rejoiced in snuff-color, but latterly his costume was inveterately black—with gaiters which seemed longing for something more substantial to close in. His legs were remarkably slight,—so indeed was his whole body, which was of short stature, but surmounted by a head of amazing fineness. . . . His face was deeply marked and full of noble lines—traces of sensibility, imagination, suffering, and much thought. His wit was in his eye, luminous, quick, and restless. The smile that played about his mouth was ever cordial and good-humored; and the most cordial and delightful of his smiles were those with which he accompanied his affectionate talk with his sister, or his jokes against her.

John Forster, 1835, "Charles Lamb," *New Monthly Magazine*,
vol. 43, p. 205

In these miscellaneous gatherings, Lamb said little, except when an opening arose for a pun. And how effectual that sort of small shot was from *him*, I need not say to anybody who remembers his infirmity of stammering, and his dexterous management of it for purposes of light and shade. He was often able to train the roll of stammers into settling upon the words immediately preceding the effective one; by which means the key-note of the jest or sarcasm, benefiting by the sudden liberation of his embargoed voice, was delivered with the force of a pistol shot. That stammer was worth an annuity to him as an ally of his wit. Firing under cover of that advantage, he did triple execution; for, in the first place, the distressing sympathy of the hearers with *his* distress of utterance won for him unavoidably the silence of deep attention; and then, whilst he had us all hoaxed into this attitude of mute suspense by an appearance of distress that he perhaps did not really feel, down came a plunging shot into the very thick of us, with ten times the effect it would else have had.

Thomas De Quincey, 1850, "Charles Lamb," Biographical Essays

Lamb was not a saint. He drank sometimes to excess. He also smoked tobacco. But if ever a good, great man walked the earth—good and great in the profoundest and noblest sense—full of that simple human charity, and utter renunciation of self, which is the fulfilling of the highest law and the holiest instinct—it was that man with a face of "quivering sweetness," nervous, tremulous; . . . so slight of frame that he looked only fit for the most placid fortune,—but who conquered poverty and hereditary madness, and won an imperishable name in English literature, and a sacred place in every generous heart, all in silence, and with a smile.

George William Curtis, 1859, "Notes of Charles Lamb to
Thomas Allsop," Harper's Magazine, vol. 20, p. 97

No one who has passed an hour in the company of Charles Lamb's "dear boy" can ever lose the impression made upon him by that simple, sincere, shy, and delicate soul. His small figure, his head, not remarkable for much besides its expression of intelligent and warm goodwill, and its singular likeness to that of Sir Walter Scott; his conversation, which had little decision or "point" in the ordinary sense, and often dwelt on truths which a novelty-loving society banishes from its repertory as truisms, never disturbed the effect, in any assemblage, of his real distinction. His silence seemed wiser, his simplicity subtler, his shyness more courageous than the wit, philosophy, and assurance of others.

Coventry Patmore, 1877, in Bryan Waller Procter,
Autobiographical Fragment, ed. Coventry Patmore, p. 5

POETRY

There is much quaint feeling in his verses: he has used the style of the good old days of Elizabeth in giving form and utterance to his own emotions; and, though often unelevated and prosaic, every line is informed with thought or with some vagrant impulse of fancy. . . . He gives portraits of men whose manners have undergone a city change; records sentiments which are the true offspring of the mart and the custom-house, and attunes his measure to the harmony of other matter than musical breezes and melodious brooks.

Allan Cunningham, 1833, Biographical and Critical History
of the Literature of the Last Fifty Years

Charles Lamb was a true poet, but not a great one. His genius was peculiar and wayward, and his mind seemed so impregnated with the dramatists preceding or contemporary with Shakspeare—Marlowe, Webster, Ford, Shirley, Marston, Massinger, and their compeers—that he could not help imitating their trains of thought. Yet he struck out a few exquisite things,—sparks from true genius, which can never be extinguished; as *The Old Familiar Faces; To Hester; The Virgin of the Rocks;* and the descriptive forest-scene in *John Woodvil,* which, it is said, Godwin, having found somewhere extracted, was so enchanted with, that he hunted—of course vainly—through almost all the earlier poets in search of it:

"To see the sun to bed, and to arise," &c.

D. M. Moir, 1850-51, *Poetical Literature of the Past Half-Century,* p. 89

Lamb's poems, as a rule, are insipid, are *artificially natural;* he belongs to that school of which Ambrose Phillips is generally—though without sufficent ground, perhaps—regarded as the founder. Namby-pambyism is surely not so modern.

William Carew Hazlitt, 1874, *Mary and Charles Lamb,* p. 172

It is of course true that his popularity rests more with his essays than with his poems, which form only the smaller portion of his writings, but the same qualities which make his prose such delightful reading are found crystallised and perfected in his verse. His distinctive characteristic is quaint originality, coloured, but not formed by his keen appreciation of, and familiar acquaintance with, the works of our old poets and dramatists. He never has any tendency to fall into the manner of "the lake poets," though he was the intimate friend of Wordsworth, Coleridge, and Southey. He was not insensible to the beauties of nature, or to the charm of fine scenery; but he was more at home amidst the world of books and the haunts of men. . . . As an original humourist he has never been surpassed, and this quality, no less than the depth of sensibility and pathetic power, in his poems attests that the mild jocularity of Wordsworth, who called him "Lamb, the frolic and the gentle," was not misplaced.

Thomas Archer, 1895, *The Poets and Poetry of the Century, Robert Southey to Percy Bysshe Shelley,* ed. Miles, pp. 131, 136

Rosamund Gray (1798)

Rosamund, with the pale blue eyes and the "yellow Hertfordshire hair," is but a fresh copy of his Anna and his Alice. That Rosamund Gray had an actual counterpart in real life seems certain, and the little group of cottages, in one of which she dwelt with her old grandmother, is still shown in the village of Widford, about half a mile from the site of the old mansion of Blakesware. And it is the tradition of the village, and believed by those who have the best means of judging, that *Rosamund Gray* (her real name was equally remote from this, and from Alice W—n) was Charles Lamb's first and only love. Her fair hair and eyes, her goodness, and (we may assume) her poverty, were drawn from life. The rest of the story in which she bears a part is of course pure fiction. The real Anna of the sonnets made a prosperous marriage, and lived to a good old age.

Alfred Ainger, 1882, *Charles Lamb* (*English Men of Letters*), p. 39

It is crude and formless, the raw elements of a story clumsily thrust into a common frame. The idyllic picture of Rosamund and her grandmother (embalming probably a memory of his Anna Simmons) has a charm; but the horrible fate of the young girl is a jarring dissonance, sudden and arbitrary as the invading shock of madness in which that early love had issued.

C. H. Herford, 1897, *The Age of Wordsworth,* p. 61

Letters

Lamb's letters are not indeed model letters like Cowper's. Though natural to Lamb, they cannot be called easy. "Divine chit-chat" is not the epithet to describe them. His notes are all high. He is sublime, heartrending, excruciatingly funny, outrageously ridiculous, sometimes possibly an inch or two overdrawn. He carries the charm of incongruity and total unexpectedness to the highest pitch imaginable.

Augustine Birrell, 1892, *Res Judicatæ,* p. 240

As for Lamb, those who love him at all love him so well that it matters little which of his letters they read, or how often they have read them before. Only it is best to select those written in the meridian of his life. The earlier ones are too painful, the later ones too sad. Let us take him at his happiest, and be happy with him for an hour; for, unless we go cheerfully to bed, the portals of morn open for us with sullen murmur, and fretful dreams, more disquieting than even the troubled thoughts of day, flit batlike round our melancholy pillows.

Agnes Repplier, 1894, *In the Dozy Hours,* p. 8

His correspondence must remain an integral part of the age, which it immediately concerns, as much as that of Walpole; and in this capacity and aspect, if in no other, he has laid himself, so to speak, across an epoch. Any one who bestows even a cursory study on these inimitable productions must perceive and allow that the serious style largely preponderates, and that of broad fun there is little more than an occasional vein. His wit is more usually delicate and playful—sometimes bordering on pathos. Here and there, among the letters, there are spasms of boisterous and rollicking gaiety parallel with the horse-play in the Inner Temple Lane times; but it makes little indeed in so voluminous a body of matter.

William Carew Hazlitt, 1897, *The Lambs, their Lives,*
their Friends and their Correspondence, p. 13

GENERAL

Elia in his happiest moods delights me: he is a fine soul; but when he is dull, his dulness sets human stupidity at defiance. He is like a well-bred, ill-trained pointer. He has a fine nose, but he won't or he can't range. He keeps always close to your foot, and then he points larks and titmice. You see him snuffing and smoking and brandishing his tail with the most impassioned enthusiasm, and then drawn round into a semicircle, he stands beautifully—dead-set. You expect a burst of partridges or a towering cock-pheasant, when lo, and behold! away flits a lark, or you discover a mouse's nest, or there is absolutely nothing at all. Perhaps a shrew has been there the day before. Yet if Elia were mine, I would not part with him, for all his faults.

John Wilson, 1822, *Noctes Ambrosianæ,* April

Read *Elia,* if the book has not fallen in your way. It is by my old friend Charles Lamb. There are some things in it which will offend, and some which will pain you, as they do me; but you will find in it a rich vein of pure gold.

Robert Southey, 1823, *Letters*

His style runs pure and clear, though it may often take an underground course, or be conveyed through old-fashioned conduit-pipes. . . . There is a fine tone of *chiaro-scuro,* a moral perspective in his writings. He delights to dwell on that which is fresh to the eye of memory; he yearns after and covets what soothes the frailty of human nature. That touches him most nearly which is withdrawn to a certain distance, which verges on the borders of oblivion:—that piques and provokes his fancy most, which is hid from a superficial glance. That which, though gone by, is still remembered, is in his view more genuine, and has given more "vital signs that it will live," than a thing of yesterday, that may be forgotten tomorrow. Death has in this sense the spirit of life in it; and the shadowy has to our author something substantial in it.

William Hazlitt, 1825, *The Spirit of the Age,* pp. 262, 263

We never rise from one of his essays without a feeling of contentment. He leads our thoughts to the actual, available springs of enjoyment. He reconciles us to ourselves; causing home-pleasures, and the charms of the way-side, and the mere comforts of existence, to emerge from the shadow into which our indifference has cast them, into the light of fond recognition. The flat dull surface of common life, he causes to rise into beautiful *basso-relievo*. In truth, there are few better teachers of gratitude than Lamb.

Henry T. Tuckerman, 1849, Characteristics of Literature, p. 167

Charles Lamb was no teacher of his time, and had no commanding or immediate influence on his contemporaries. He lifted up no banner, sum-moned no contending hosts to the conflict, did no battle on the side of faction or party, and was possessed of no vast intellectual powers. But this he *was*—one of the most affectionate, most lovable, most piquantly imper-fect of dear, good fellows that ever won their way into the human heart, and one of the most hearty, most English, most curiously felicitous humor-ists—emphatically one of the *best* that ever lived. He has left us in his works a perennial source of refining pleasure, full of freshness and moral health, and kindly communicative warmth, over which countless readers will bend with smiling face or moistened eye; and the sad will feel a solace, the weary gather heart's-ease, the cold and narrow of nature may warm them and expand in the generous glow to be found in the writings of Charles Lamb.

Gerald Massey, 1867, "Charles Lamb," Fraser's Magazine,
vol. 75, p. 672

In the making of prose he realises the principle of art for its own sake, as completely as Keats in the making of verse. And, working ever close to the concrete, to the details, great or small, of actual things, books, persons, and with no part of them blurred to his vision by the intervention of mere abstract theories, he has reached an enduring moral effect also, in a sort of boundless sympathy. Unoccupied, as he might seem, with great matters, he is in immediate contact with what is real, especially in its caressing littleness, that littleness in which there is much of the whole woeful heart of things, and meets it more than half-way with a perfect understanding of it. What sudden, unexpected touches of pathos in him!—bearing witness how the sorrow of humanity, the *Welt-schmerz,* the constant aching of its wounds, is ever present with him; but what a gift also for the enjoyment of life in its subtleties, of enjoyment actually refined by the need of some thoughtful economies and making the most of things!

Walter Pater, 1878, Appreciations

It is in vain to attempt to convey an idea of the impression left by Lamb's style. It evades analysis. One might as well seek to account for the perfume of lavender, or the flavour of quince. It is in truth an essence, prepared from flowers and herbs gathered in fields where the ordinary reader does not often range. And the nature of the writer—the alembic in which these various simples were distilled——was as rare for sweetness and purity as the best of those enshrined in the old folios—his "midnight darlings." If he had by nature the delicate grace of Marvell, and the quaint fancy of Quarles, he also shared the chivalry of Sidney, and could lay on himself "the lowliest duties," in the spirit of his best-beloved of all, John Milton. It is the man, Charles Lamb, that constitutes the enduring charm of his written words. He is, as I have said, an egotist—but an egotist without a touch of vanity or self-assertion—an egotist without a grain of envy or ill-nature.

Alfred Ainger, 1882, *Charles Lamb*
(*English Men of Letters*), p. 120

In some respects, though in some only, Charles Lamb's humour anticipates the type of humour which we now call, in the main, American. When, for instance, he gravely narrated the origin of the Chinese invention of roast pig, in the burning down of a house,—when he told a friend that he had moved just forty-two inches nearer his beloved London,—and again, when he wrote to Manning in China that the new Persian Ambassador was called "Shaw Ali Mirza," but that the common people called him "Shaw Non-sense," we might think we were listening to Artemus Ward's or Mark Twain's minute and serious nonsense. But for the most part, Charles Lamb's humour is more frolicsome, more whimsical, and less subdued in its extrava-gance; more like the gambolling of a mind which did not care to conceal its enjoyment of paradox, and less like the inward invisible laughter in which the Yankees most delight.

Richard Holt Hutton, 1882-94, *Criticisms on Contemporary Thought and Thinkers*, vol. I, p. 105

Lamb's use of the short sentence was incomparably freer, and as Mr. Pater might have said, "blither" than that of any of his predecessors. In sentence-length, indeed, he exhibits all the variability of insanity. . . . In spite of now and then a long but harmless parenthesis, Lamb knew the value of the paragraph structure—knew it better than Coleridge did, or DeQuincey. Hardly one of his shorter sections but is an artistic whole. The order is loose. The mass is often perfect—the topic striking the eye instantly, and the paragraph ending with words that deserves emphasis. . . . The fact is that Lamb's style, on any subject Lamb would have been willing to touch, would be easier to follow than Coleridge's, no matter how far afield the whimsical Elia might wander. For there are no long intervals between Lamb's propositions, no involved restrictions of those propositions, no necessity of supplying anything except a few obvious verbs and the sense of a few freakish vocables.

Edwin Herbert Lewis, 1894, *The History of the English Paragraph*, pp. 132, 133

Elia is a name of the imagination; but it was borne by an old acquaintance, an Italian who was a fellow-clerk at the South-Sea House when Lamb was a boy there, thirty years before he sat down to write these Essays; and, as a piece of pleasantry, he borrowed his friend's true face to mask his own. He went, he tells us, to see the Elia of flesh and blood, and laugh over the liberty he had taken, but found the Italian dead; and the incident—the playfulness of the odd plagiarism ending unexpectedly in a solemn moment, a pathetic close—is so in character with the moods of these pages, that even their maker could not have invented better what life gave into his hands. The name had devolved upon him now, he said; he had, as it were, unknowingly adopted a shade, and it was to go about with him thenceforth, and watch at his grave after he too should depart. For two years he used the ruse of this ghost of a name, but the uncanniness of it was his own secret; to the reader of the *London Magazine,* in which he published, Elia was— what it is to us—a name of the eternal humorist in life's various crowd.

George Edward Woodberry, 1900, *Makers of Literature*, p. 109

JAMES HOGG
1770-1835

Born, at Ettrick, Selkirkshire, 1770; baptised, 9 Dec. 1770. Employed as shepherd in various quarters till 1800. Managed his father's farm at Ettrick, 1801-03. Made unsuccessful attempts at sheep-farming on his own account. Having by this time published some poems, settled in Edinburgh, 1810, to take up literary career. Ed. *The Spy,* Sept. 1810 to 1811. Presented by Duke of Buccleuch with the farm of Altrive Lake, Yarrow, 1816. Settled there. Helped to start *Blackwood's Mag.,* 1817; became frequent contributor. Married Margaret Phillips, 1820. Visit to London, 1832. Entertained at a public dinner there; also at Peebles in 1833. Died, 21 Nov. 1835. Buried in Ettrick churchyard. WORKS: *Scottish Pastorals,* 1801; *The Shepherd's Guide,* 1807; *The Mountain Bard,* 1807; *The Forest Minstrel* (mainly by Hogg), 1810; *The Queen's Wake,* 1813; *The Hunting of Badlewe* (under pseud. of "J. H. Craig"), 1814; *The Pilgrims of the Sun,* 1815; *Madoc of the Moor,* 1816; *The Poetic Mirror* (anon.), 1816; *Dramatic Tales* (anon.), 1817; *Long Pack* (anon.), 1817; *The Brownie of*

Bodsbeck (2 vols.), 1818; *Jacobite Relics of Scotland* (2 vols.), 1819-20; *Winter Evening Tales,* 1820; *The Royal Jubilee* (anon.), 1822; *The Three Perils of Man* (3 vols.), 1822; *The Three Perils of Woman* (3 vols.), 1823; *The Private Memoirs and Confessions of a Justified Sinner* (anon.), 1824; *Queen Hynde,* 1825; *The Shepherd's Calendar,* 1829; *Songs* (anon.), 1831; *Altrive Tales,* 1832; *A Queer Book* (anon.), 1832; *A Series of Lay Sermons,* 1834; *The Domestic Manners and Private Life of Sir Walter Scott,* 1834; *Tales of the Wars of Montrose,* 1835. COLLECTED WORKS: in 2 vols., ed. by Blackie, with LIFE by Rev. T. Thomson, 1865-66.

R. Farquharson Sharp, 1897, A Dictionary of
English Authors, p. 134

SEE: *Selected Poems,* ed. J .W. Oliver, 1940; Edith C. Batho, *The Ettrick Shepherd,* 1927; Louis Simpson, *James Hogg: A Critical Study,* 1962.

PERSONAL

I have had the most amusing letter from Hogg, the Ettrick minstrel and shepherd. He wants me to recommend him to Murray; and, speaking of his present bookseller, whose "bills" are never "lifted," he adds, *totidem verbist,* "God d—n him and them both." I laughed, and so would you too, at the way in which this execration is introduced. The said Hogg is a strange being, but of great, though uncouth, powers. I think very highly of him, as a poet; but he, and half of these Scotch and Lake troubadours, are spoilt by living in little circles and petty societies.

Lord Byron, 1814, Letter to Moore, Aug. 3

I had no method of learning to write save by following the Italian alphabet; and though I always stripped myself of coat and vest when I began to pen a song, yet my wrist took a cramp, so that I could rarely make above four or five lines at a sitting. Whether my manner of writing it out was new, I knew not, but it was not without singularity. Having very little spare time from my flock, which was unruly enough, I folded and stitched a few sheets of paper, which I carried in my pocket. I had no ink-horn, but in place of if I borrowed a small phial, which I fixed in a hole in the breast of my waistcoat; and having a cork fastened by a piece of twine, it answered my purpose fully as well. Thus equipped, whenever a leisure minute or two offered, and I had nothing else to do, I sat down and wrote out my thoughts as I found them. This is still my invariable practice in writing prose. I cannot make out one sentence by study without the pen in my hand to catch the ideas as they rise, and I never write two copies of the same thing. My manner of composing poetry is very different, and, I believe, much more singular. Let the piece be of what length it will, I compose and correct it wholly in my mind, or on a slate, ere ever I put pen to paper; and then I write it down as fast as the A, B, C. When once it is written, it remains in that state; it being with the utmost difficulty that I can be brought to alter one syllable.

James Hogg, 1832? *Autobiography*

Hogg is a little red-skinned stiff sack of a body, with quite the common air of an Ettrick shepherd, except that he has highish though sloping brow (among his yellow grizzled hair), and two clear little beads of blue or grey eyes that sparkle, if not with thought, yet with animation. Behaves himself quite easily and well; speaks Scotch, and mostly narrative absurdity (or even obscenity) therewith. Appears in the mingled character of zany and rare show. All bent on bantering him, especially Lockhart; Hogg walking through it as if unconscious, or almost flattered. His vanity seems to be immense, but also his good-nature. I felt interest for the poor "herd body," wondered to see him blown hither from his sheepfolds, and how, quite friendless as he was, he went along cheerful, mirthful, and musical. I do not well understand the man; his significance is perhaps considerable. His poetic talent is authentic, yet his intellect seems of the weakest; his morality also limits itself to the precept "be not angry." Is the charm of this poor man chiefly to be found therein, that he *is* a real product of nature, and able to speak naturally, which not one in a thousand is? An "unconscious talent," though of the smallest, emphatically *naïve*. Once or twice in singing (for he sung of his own) there was an emphasis in poor Hogg's look—expression of feeling, almost of enthusiasm.

Thomas Carlyle, 1832, *Journal*, Jan. 21;
Life by Froude, vol. II, p. 189

I likewise formed an acquaintance with James Hogg, the Ettrick Shepherd, and was amused with his blunt simplicity of character and good-nature. It did not seem as if he had the slightest veneration for any one more than another whom he addressed, no matter what was their rank or position; and I could quite believe that he sometimes took the liberty, as is alleged of him, of familiarly addressing Sir Walter Scott as "Watty," and Lady Scott as "Charlotte." The Shepherd, however, was a genuinely good creature, and an agreeable acquaintance.

William Chambers, 1882, *Story of a Long and Busy Life*, p. 46

GENERAL

Who is there that has not heard of the Ettrick Shepherd—of him whose inspiration descended as lightly as the breeze that blows along the mountainside—who saw, amongst the lonely and sequestered glens of the south, from eyelids touched with fairy ointment, such visions as are vouchsafed to the minstrel alone—the dream of sweet Kilmeny, too spiritual for the taint of earth? I shall not attempt any comparison—for I am not here to criticise— between his genius and that of other men, on whom God in His bounty has bestowed the great and the marvellous gift. The songs and the poetry of the Shepherd are now the nation's own, as indeed they long have been; and amidst the minstrelsy of the choir who have made the name of Scotland and her peasantry familiar throughout the wide reach of the habitable world, the clear wild notes of the forest will forever be heard to ring.

William Edmondstoune Aytoun, 1844, The Burns Festival,
Memoir, ed. Martin, p. 102

All the verses of Hogg exhibit that kind of imaginative awe which lives on the fruit and food yielded by Superstition. His images from Nature are all surrounded with the beings of another day: what an array of fairies, witches, bogies, ghosts, we have! He seems to transport his mind back to the time when every object in Nature was the home, and beneath the guardianship of some spiritual being; when there was a spirit in every dingle, and the muttering of some potent power in every gale; when Superstition was priviliged to erect her gibbets, and kindle her fires in every village and town. . . . His eye had beheld, his soul had sported, in all the strange amplitude of nature's vast boundless theatre. Whatever else he felt, the soul of the forest was strong within him; he wrote beneath the glare of its lightnings, and the gleam of its sunsets and sunrisings. The roar of its woods and waters was forever sounding on his ear; the snatches of old songs, the carol and the lilt of old wild lyrics, these were the pages of the book whence he gathered his ideas.

Edwin Paxton Hood, 1859-70, The Peerage of
Poverty, pp. 338, 339

No Scottish poet has dealt with the power and the realm of Fairy more vividly and impressively than the Bard of Ettrick. He caught up several of the floating traditions which actually localised the fairy doings, and this, as he haunted the hills and moors where they were said to have taken place, brought the old legend home to his every day life and feeling. He was thus led to an accurate observation and description of the reputed scenes of the story, and of the haunts of the Fairies. These had received only bare mention in the tradition itself, and little more than this even when they had been put into verse in the older time. But all these spots he knew well; many of them were the daily round of the shepherd and his collie. The legend he had learned thus acquired something of the reality which he felt. Hence Hogg's poems of Fairy are remarkable for the fulness, the richness, and the accuracy of the description of the country—of hill, glen, and moor.

John Veitch, 1878, *The History and Poetry of the Scottish Border*, p. 358

The combination of rough humour with sweetness of purity and sentiment is by no means rare; but Hogg is one of the most eminent examples of it; all the more striking that both qualities were in him strongly accentuated by his demonstrative temperament. His humour often degenerates into deliberate loutishness, affected oddity; and his tenderness of fancy sometimes approaches "childishness," or, as the Scotch call it, "bairnliness." But with all his extravagances, there is a marked individuality in the Shepherd's songs and poems; he was a singer by genuine impulse, and there was an open-air freshness in his note.

William Minto, 1880, *The English Poets*, ed. Ward, vol. IV, p. 227

WILLIAM COBBETT
1762-1835

Born at Farnham, Surrey, England, March 9, 1762; died near Farnham, June 18, 1835. A noted English political writer. He was the son of a peasant, obtained a meager education, enlisted in the army about 1783, obtained his discharge about 1791, and in 1792 emigrated to America. From 1797 to 1799 he published at Philadelphia *Porcupine's Gazette*, a Federalist daily newspaper. He returned to England in 1800. In January, 1802, he began at London the publication of *Cobbett's Weekly Political Register*, which, with trifling interruptions, was continued until his death; and in 1803 began to publish the *Parliamentary Debates*, which in 1812 passed into the hands of T. C. Hansard. He at first supported the government, but about 1804 joined the opposition, with the result that he was several times fined for libel, and in 1810 sentenced to imprisonment for two years. He was elected to Parliament as member for Oldham in 1832, and again in 1834. Author of *Porcupine's Works* (1801-02), *A Grammar of the English Language* (1818), a grammar and a dictionary of the French language, *Cottage Economy* (1821), *The Emigrant's Guide* (1828), *Advice to Young Men, and, incidentally, to Young Women* (1830), etc.

Benjamin E. Smith, ed. 1894-97, *The Century Cyclopedia of Names*, p. 262

SEE: *Selections*, ed. A. M. D. Hughes, 1923; *The Opinions of Cobbett*, ed. G. D. H. and Margaret Cole, 1944; G. D. H. Cole, *Life of Cobbett*, 1924, rev. 1927.

PERSONAL

I had this day as a visitor one of the most distinguished literary and political characters which ever adorned this or any other country, namely Mr. William Cobbett. . . . Mr. Cobbett is now in his sixty-seventh year. He is above six feet high, stout made, of a plump, ruddy countenance, and has a most winning and engaging smile. His hair is as white as the driven snow. His whole appearance is of the most engaging and gentlemanly kind. He is a singularly abstemious and temperate man; never eating anything after dinner, with the exception of a little bread to his tea. He avoids spirits, wine, ale, porter. His dislike to all these things is so great that he will not sit down in a room where they are used. His common drink is a little skim milk. He goes to bed at eight or nine o'clock, and rises by four or five in the morning.

Robert Blakey, 1832, *Memoirs*, pp. 68, 70

Mr. Cobbett, in personal stature, was tall and athletic. I should think he could not have been less than six feet, while his breadth was proportionally great. He was, indeed, one of the stoutest men in the house. I have said there was a tendency to corpulency about him. His hair was of a milk-white colour, and his complexion ruddy. His features were not strongly marked. What struck you most about his face was his small, sparkling, laughing eyes. When disposed to be humorous himself, you had only to look at his eyes and you were sure to sympathise in his merriment. When not speaking, the expression of his eyes and his countenance was very different. He was one of the most striking refutations of the principles of Lavater I ever witnessed. Never were the books of any man more completely at variance with his character. There was something so dull and heavy about his whole appearance, that any one who did not know him, would at once have set him down for some country clodpole—to use a favourite expression of his own—who not only never read a book, or had a single idea in his head, but who was a mere mass of mortality, without a particle of sensibility of any kind in his composition. He usually sat with one leg over the other, his head slightly drooping, as if sleeping, on his breast, and his hat down almost to his eyes.

James Grant, 1835, *Random Recollections of the House of Commons from the Year 1830 to the Close of 1835*, p. 198

He made but a poor figure in the House; had not a scintillation of eloquence, and his manner was brusque almost to coarseness. The rudeness that is so often mistaken for independence never at any time "told" there, where the greatest and the humblest are certain to find their true level; and if there be any who recall him to memory, with a faint idea that they may accord to it respect, it will not be as seated on the Opposition bench of the House of Commons. Though he spoke often, he never made what might have been called "a speech." He seemed always on guard lest he might commit himself; indeed, in the House he never seemed at home, and was by no means the virtuous contemner of his superiors he was expected to have been; few who listened to him would have thought they heard the author of much envenomed bitterness— the quality that so continually character- ized his written words.

Samuel Carter Hall, 1883, *Retrospect of a Long Life,* p. 137

GENERAL

Have you seen Cobbett's last number? It is the most plausible and the best written of anything I have seen from his pen, and apparently written in a less fiendish spirit than the average of his weekly effusions. The self- complacency with which he assumes to himself exclusively, truths which he can call his own only as a horse-stealer can appropriate a stolen horse, by adding mutilation and deformities to robbery, is as artful as it is amusing.

Samuel Taylor Coleridge, 1819, *Table Talk,* ed. Ashe,
Dec. 13, p. 308

This [*Cottage Economy*] is an excellent little book—written not only with admirable clearness and good sense, but in a very earnest and entertaining manner—and abounding with kind and good feelings, as well as with most valuable information: And as we have never scrupled openly to express our disapprobation of Mr. Cobbett's conduct and writings, when we thought him in the wrong, we shall scarcely be suspected of partiality in the grati- tude we now profess to him, and the endeavour we make to assist his exer- tions for the benefit of by far the most numerous and important part of society—the labouring classes.

Francis, Lord Jeffrey, 1823 ,"Cobbett's Cottage Economy,"
Edinburgh Review, vol. 38, p. 105

Had he full scholastic instruction, and the benefit of extensive reading, his abilities, cultivated and improved, might have placed his name with many of the highest in literature. As it was, his boldness wanted knowledge and judgment to control it; he was ignorant of much that the most ordinary writers ought to understand; he had no proper conception of the estimate in which the giants of literature are to be held. He pronounced it easy to imitate Shakspeare because the public had been partially deluded for a while by Ireland's "Vortigern;" and easy to copy Milton, because any one could make angels and devils fight like men. Having sense to see the vanity of pretending to be what he was not, he affected to decry what he did not possess; and yet, though he proclaimed his contempt for the learned languages as useless, he would fain have had his public think that he was not altogether ignorant of them, as was shown by his writing always *per centum,* and introducing now and then a Latin expression. . . . In the style in which he set forth his declarations, however extravagant, there was sure to be something attractive; whatever he supported or assailed, his readers would never fail to find something to interest or amuse them.

John Selby Watson, 1870, Biographies of John Wilkes and
William Cobbett, pp. 397, 399

As a writer of pure English, Cobbett stands out almost unrivalled, and hundreds of passages might be quoted from his writings which are masterpieces of diction. He did not draw his illustrations from the fantasies of a perplexed brain, but from that nature which is always ready to reveal her secrets to those who love her. You will find his descriptions of scenery as true as those of Sir Walter Scott, and flowers and trees and coppices and wolds and woodlands and the birds and beasts that belong to them, are all put in their proper places. His word-paintings savour sometimes of almost an excessive realism.

Charles Milnes Gaskell, 1886, "William Cobbett,"
The Nineteenth Century, vol. 19, p. 255

Nobody now would say of him as William Hazlitt said, under the more direct influence of his personal energy and power, that "he might be said to have the cleverness of Swift, the naturalness of Defoe, and the picturesque satirical description of Mandeville." He was perhaps as strong a man as Bernard Mandeville; but he had the cleverness of Swift without the genius, and Defoe's naturalness without the imagination that enabled Defoe to shape the real into an ideal, and in *Robinson Crusoe* to produce a work having some part of the nature of a poem, though Defoe, like Cobbett, was essentially a man of prose. Cobbett belaboured to good purpose the big drum of politics, and blew a trumpet all his own. But the plain speech of Cobbett was as honest and as resolute as the plain speech of Luther; and Luther in the conflict did not measure his words.

Henry Morley, 1887, ed., Advice to Young Men
by William Cobbett, Introduction, p. 6

The total is huge; for Cobbett's industry and facility of work were both appalling, and while his good work is constantly disfigured by rubbish, there is hardly a single parcel of his rubbish in which there is not good work. . . . As happens with all writers of his kind he is not easily to be characterised. Like certain wines he has the *goût du terroir;* and that gust is rarely or never definable in words. It is however I think critically safe to say that the intensity and peculiarity of Cobbett's literary savour are in the ratio of his limitation. He was content to ignore so vast a number of things, he so bravely pushed his ignorance into contempt of them and almost into denial of their real existence, that the other things are real for him and in his writings to a degree almost unexampled. I am not the first by many to suggest that we are too diffuse in our modern imagination, that we are cumbered about too many things. No one could bring this accusation against Cobbett; for immense as his variety is in particulars, these particulars group themselves under comparatively few general heads. I do not think I have been unjust in suggesting that this ideal was little more than the bellyful, that Messer Gaster was not only his first but his one and sufficient master of arts.

George Saintsbury, 1891, "William Cobbett,"
Macmillan's Magazine, vol. 65, pp. 95, 108

A brutal personality, excellently muscular, snatching at words as the handiest weapons wherewith to inflict itself, and the whole body of its thoughts and preferences, on suffering humanity, is likely enough to deride the daintiness of conscious art. Such a writer is William Cobbett, who has often been praised for the manly simplicity of his style, which he raised into a kind of creed. His power is undeniable; his diction, though he knew it not, both choice and chaste; yet page after page of his writing suggests only the reflection that here is a prodigal waste of good English. He bludgeons all he touches, and spends the same monotonous emphasis on his dislike of tea and on his hatred of the Government. His is the simplicity of a crude and violent mind, concerned only with giving forcible expression to its unquestioned prejudices. Irrelevance, the besetting sin of the ill-educated, he glories in, so that his very weakness puts on the semblance of strength, and helps to wield the hammer.

Walter Raleigh, 1897, *Style,* p. 106

WILLIAM GODWIN
1756-1836

Born, at Wisbeach, Cambs., 3 March, 1756. Family removed to Debenham, Suffolk, 1758; to Guestwick, Norfolk, 1760. At school at Guestwick, 1760-64; at Hindolveston, 1764-67; with tutor, 1767-71. Master at Hindolveston School, 1771-73. To Hoxton Academy, London, 1773. Minister at

Ware, Herts, 1778. In London, 1779. Minister at Stowmarket, Suffolk, 1780-82; returned to London, 1782. Minister at Beaconsfield in 1783; gave up ministry that year and took to literature. Intimacy with Mary Wollstonecraft begun, 1796; married her, 29 March 1797. Daughter Mary (afterwards Mrs. Shelley) born 30 Aug. 1797; wife died, 10 Sept. 1797. Married Mrs. Mary Jane Clairmont, Dec. 1801. Friendship with Coleridge, Lamb, Wordsworth. *Tragedy of Antonio* produced at Drury Lane, 13 Dec. 1800; *Faulkener* produced, Dec. 1807. Financial troubles. Wife started publishing business. Friendship with Shelley begun, 1811. Bankrupt, 1822. Yeoman Usher of Exchequer, 1833-36. Died, in London, 7 April 1836. Buried in Old St. Pancras Churchyard. WORKS: *Life of Chatham* (anon.), 1783; *Sketches of History*, 1784; *Enquiry concerning Political Justice*, 1793; *Things as they are; or, the Adventures of Caleb Williams*, 1794; *Cursory Strictures on the Charge of Chief-Justice Eyre*, 1794; *The Enquirer*, 1797; *Memoirs of the Author of a Vindication of the Rights of Women*, 1798 (2nd edn. same year); *St. Leon*, 1799; *Antonio*, 1800; *Thoughts occasioned by . . . Dr. Parr's Spital Sermon*, 1801; *Life of Geoffrey Chaucer*, 1803; *Fleetwood*, 1805 (French trans. same year); *Fables* (under pseud. "Edward Baldwin"), 1805; *The Looking-Glass* (under pseud. "Theophilus Marcliffe," attrib. to Godwin), 1805; *Faulkener*, 1807; *Essay on Sepulchres*, 1809; *Dramas for Children* (anon.), 1809; *History of Rome* (by "E. Baldwin"), 1809; *New and improved Grammar of the English Language* (anon.), 1812; *Lives of Edward and John Philips*, 1815; *Mandeville*, 1817; *Of Population*, 1820; *Life of Lady Jane Grey* (by "E. Baldwin"), 1824; *History of the Commonwealth of England* (4 vols.), 1824-28; *The History of England for the use of Schools* (by "E. Baldwin"), 1827; *History of Greece* (by "E. Baldwin"), 1828; *Cloudesley* (anon.), 1830; *Thoughts on Man*, 1831; *Deloraine*, 1833; *Lives of the Necromancers*, 1834. POSTHUMOUS: *Essays*, 1873. He *translated*: Lord Lovat's *Memoirs* 1797; and *edited*: Mary Godwin's *Posthumous Works*, 1798; his son (W. Godwin's) *Transfusion*, 1835. LIFE: by C. Kegan Paul, 1876.

R. Farquharson Sharp, 1897, *A Dictionary of English Authors*, p. 113

SEE: *Enquiry Concerning Political Justice*, ed. F. E. L. Priestley, 1946, 3 v. (Facsimiles); George Woodcock, *William Godwin*, 1946; David Fleischer, *William Godwin: A Study in Liberalism*, 1951; James A. Preu, *The Dean [Swift] and the Anarchist*, 1959.

PERSONAL

I was disgusted at heart with the grossness and vulgar insanocecity of this dim-headed prig of a philosophocide, when, after supper, his ill stars impelled him to renew the contest. I begged him not to goad me, for that I feared my feeling would not long remain in my power. He (to my wonder and indignation) persisted (I had not deciphered the cause), and then, as he well said, I did "thunder and lighten at him" with a vengeance for more than an hour and a half. Every effort of self-defence only made him more ridiculous. If I had been Truth in person, I could not have spoken more accurately; but it was Truth in a war chariot, drawn by the three Furies, and the reins had slipped out of the goddess's hands!

Samuel Taylor Coleridge, 1804, *To Robert Southey,* Feb. 20;
Letters, ed. E. H. Coleridge, vol. II, p. 465

The name of Godwin has been accustomed to excite in me feelings of reverence and admiration. I have been accustomed to consider him as a luminary too dazzling for the darkness which surrounds him, and from the earliest period of my knowledge of his principles, I have ardently desired to share in the footing of intimacy that intellect which I have delighted to contemplate in its emanations. Considering, then, these feelings, you will not be surprised at the inconceivable emotion with which I learned your existence and your dwelling. I had enrolled your name on the list of the honourable dead. I had felt regret that the glory of your being had passed from this earth of ours. It is not so. You still live, and I firmly believe are still planning the welfare of human kind. . . . When I come to London I shall seek for you. I am convinced I could represent myself to you in such terms as not to be thought wholly unworthy of your friendship. At least, if any desire for universal happiness has any claim upon your preference, that desire I can exhibit.

Percy Bysshe Shelley, 1811, *Letter to Godwin,* Jan. 3;
William Godwin by C. K. Paul, vol. II, p. 202

Godwin is as far removed from everything feverish and exciting as if his head had never been filled with anything but geometry. He is now about sixty-five, stout, well-built, and unbroken by age, with a cool, dogged manner, exactly opposite to everything I had imagined of the author of *St. Leon* and *Caleb Williams.* He lives on Snowhill, just about where Evelina's vulgar relations lived. His family is supported partly by the labors of his own pen and partly by those of his wife's, but chiefly by the profits of a shop for children's books, which she keeps and manages to considerable advantage. She is a spirited, active woman, who controls the house, I suspect, pretty well; and when I looked at Godwin, and saw with what cool obstinacy he adhered to everything he had once assumed, and what a cold selfishness lay at the bottom of his character, I felt a satisfaction in the thought that he had a wife who must sometimes give a start to his blood and a stir to his nervous system.

George Ticknor, 1819, *Journal; Life, Letters and Journals,*
vol. I, p. 294

The Spirit of the Age was never more fully shown than in its treatment of this writer—its love of paradox and change, its dastard submission to prejudice and to the fashion of the day. Five-and-twenty years ago he was in the very zenith of a sultry and unwholesome popularity; he blazed as a sun in the firmament of reputation; no one was more talked of, more looked up to, more sought after, and wherever liberty, truth, justice was the theme, his name was not far off:—now he has sunk below the horizon, and enjoys the supreme delight of a doubtful immortality. Mr. Godwin, during his lifetime, has secured to himself the triumphs and the mortifications of an extreme notoriety and of a sort of posthumous fame.

William Hazlitt, 1825, The Spirit of the Age, pp. 19, 33

He rose between seven and eight, and read some classic author before breakfast. From nine till twelve or one he occupied himself with his pen. He found that he could not exceed this measure of labour with any advantage to his own health, or the work in hand. While writing *Political Justice,* there was one paragraph which he wrote eight times over before he could satisfy himself with the strength and perspicuity of his expressions. On this occasion a sense of confusion of the brain came over him, and he applied to his friend Mr. Carlisle, afterwards Sir Anthony Carlisle, the celebrated surgeon, who warned him that he had exerted his intellectual faculties to their limit. In compliance with his direction, Mr. Godwin reduced his hours of composition within what many will consider narrow bounds. The rest of the morning was spent in reading and seeing his friends. When at home he dined at four, but during his bachelor life he frequently dined out. His dinner at home at this time was simple enough. He had no regular servant; an old woman came in the morning to clean and arrange his rooms, and if necessary she prepared a mutton chop, which was put in a Dutch oven.

Mary Wollstonecraft Shelley, 1851? Fragmentary Notes,
in William Goodwin, by C. K. Paul, vol. I, p. 79

Godwin, though overrated in his generation, and almost ludicrously idealized by Shelley, was a man whose talents verged on genius. But he was by no means consistent. His conduct in money-matters shows that he could not live the life of a self-sufficing philosopher; while the irritation he expressed when Shelley omitted to address him as Esquire, stood in comic contradiction with his published doctrines.

John Addington Symonds, 1879, Shelley
(English Men of Letters), p. 93

Caleb Williams (1794)

One word respecting the MS. itself, and I have done. The incidents are ill chosen; the characters unnatural, distorted; the phraseology intended to mark the humorous ones inappropriate; the style uncouth; everything upon stilts; the whole uninteresting; written as a man would make a chair or a table that had never handled a tool. I got through it, but it was as I get over a piece of ploughed-up ground, with labour and toil. By the way, judging from the work in question, one might suppose some minds not to be unlike a piece of ground. Having produced a rich crop, it must lie fallow for a season, that it may gain sufficient vigour for a new crop. You were speaking for a motto for this work—the best motto in my opinion, would be a *Hic jacet;* for depend upon it, the world will suppose you to be exhausted; or rather what a few only think at present, will become a general opinion, that the Hercules you have fathered is not of your begetting.

James Marshal, 1793, *Letter to Godwin,* May 31;
William Godwin by Paul, vol. I, p. 90

In the writings of Godwin, some of the strongest of our feelings are most forcibly awakened, and there are few novels which display more powerful painting, or excite higher interest, than his *Caleb Williams.* The character of Falkland, the chief actor, which is formed on visionary principles of honour, is perhaps not strictly an invention, as it closely resembles that of Shamont, in Beaumont and Fletcher's *Nice Valour.* But the accumulated wretchedness with which he is overwhelmed, the inscrutable mystery by which he is surrounded, and the frightful persecutions to which he subjects the suspected possessor of his dreadful secret, are peculiar to the author, and are represented with a force which has not been surpassed in the finest passages and scenes of poetic or dramatic fiction.

John Dunlop, 1814-42, *The History of Fiction,* vol. II, p. 405

The novel had very great success, and was dramatized by Colman under the name of *The Iron Chest.* In spite of the amazing impossibilities of the story and its unrelieved gloom; in spite of the want of almost any character to admire—since Mr. Clare, by whom Godwin probably intended to repre-sent his friend Fawcet, dies early in the tale; though there is no real heroine and scarcely mention of love, the story has survived and has probably been read by very many persons who, but for it, have never heard of Godwin. It is a very powerful book, and the character of Falkland the murderer is unique in literature.

C. Kegan Paul, 1876, *William Godwin: his Friends
and Contemporaries,* vol. I, p. 117

In *Caleb Williams* we have before us a revolutionary work of art, the imag-inative work of a theorist, a tale which enforces a doctrine. It gains and loses by the concentration of spirit with which Godwin in it studies and works out a moral problem. To read it is to enter and explore a cavern; it is narrow; it is dark; we lose the light and air, and the clear spaces of the firmament; but the explorer's passion seizes upon us, and we grope along the narrowing walls with an intensity of curious desire. As the work of a political thinker, the book is an indictment of society. . . . *Caleb Williams* is the one novel of the days of Revolution, embodying the new doctrine of the time, which can be said to survive.

> Edward Dowden, 1897, *The French Revolution*
> *and English Literature,* pp. 66, 76

GENERAL

Godwin was a man of great powers, insufficiently balanced; and, as the European world was, in his youth, a mighty conflict of great powers insufficiently balanced, he was just the man to make an impression of vast force on the society of his day. Soon after his *Political Justice* was published, working-men were seen to club their earnings to buy it, and to meet under a tree or in an ale-house to read it. It wrought so violently that Godwin saw there must be unsoundness in it; and he modified it considerably before he reissued it. His mind was acute, and, through the generosity of his heart, profound; but it was one-sided.

> Harriet Martineau, 1849, *A History of the Thirty Years' Peace,*
> *A. D.* 1815-1846, vol. IV, p. 79

Godwin is essentially a prose-writer, and his style, though it has been over-praised, is of considerable merit. Although his exaggerated anarchism and determination to regard everything as an open question are absurd enough in principle and lead to the most unimaginable absurdities in detail, yet they give his thought always the appearance, and sometimes the reality of freer play than had been enjoyed by any English writer since Hobbes. . . . It was Godwin, more than any one else, who introduced the mischievous but popular practice of bolstering out history by describing at great length the places and scenes which his heroes might have seen, the transactions in which, being contemporary, they might have taken an interest, and the persons with whom they either were, or conceivably might have been, acquainted. In this, as in other things, he belonged to the class of "germinal" writers. And his influence on the early, although impermanent, creeds and tempers of the most brilliant young men of his day was quite extraordinary.

> George Saintsbury, 1898, *A Short History of*
> *English Literature,* pp. 634, 635

FRANCES BURNEY
(MADAME D'ARBLAY)
1752-1840

Frances Burney (Madame D'Arblay), 1752-1840. Born, at King's Lynn, 13 June 1752. Family removed to London, 1760. Mother died, 1761. Father married again, 1766. No regular education. Began early to write stories, plays, poems, etc. First novel published anonymously, Jan. 1778. Intimacy with Mrs. Thrale, Dr. Johnson, Sheridan, Burke, etc. Appointed Second Keeper of Robes to Queen, 17 July 1786. Bad health; retired, 7 July 1791, with pension of £100 a year. Travelled in England. Made acquaintance of Gen. D'Arblay at Mickleham, where her sister lived. Married to him, 31 July 1793. Settled at Bookham, near Norbury. Tragedy, *Edwy and Elvina,* performed at Drury Lane, 21 March 1795; withdrawn after first night. Built a cottage at West Humble, near Mickleham; removed there, 1797. Comedy, *Love and Fashion,* accepted for Covent Garden, but withdrawn before performance, 1800. Husband went to seek employment in France, 1801. In Paris with him, 1802-05; at Passy, 1805-14. Visit to England with son, Aug. 1812. In Paris, 1814-15. In Belgium, March to July, 1815. Returned to England, Oct. 1815. At Bath, Feb. 1816 to June 1817; at Ilfracombe, June to Oct., 1817; at Bath, Oct. 1817 to Sept. 1818. Husband died, 3 May 1818. To London, Oct. 1818. Son died, 19 Jan. 1837. Severe illness, 1839. Died, in London, 6 Jan. 1840. WORKS: *Evelina* (anon.), 1778; *Cecilia* (anon.), 1782; *Brief Reflections relative to the French Emigrant Clergy* (anon.), 1793; *Camilla,* 1796; *The Wanderer,* 1814; *Memoirs of Dr. Burney,* 1832. POSTHUMOUS: *Diary and Letters* (7 vols.), 1842-46.

R. Farquharson Sharp, 1897, *A Dictionary of
English Authors,* p. 41

SEE: *Diary and Letters,* ed. Charlotte Barrett and Austin Dobson, 1904-5, 6 v.; *Fanny Burney's Diary: A Selection from the Diary and Letters,* ed. John Wain, 1962; Joyce Hemlow, *The History of Fanny Burney,* 1958.

PERSONAL

Mrs. Byron, who really loves me, was disgusted at Miss Burney's carriage to me, who have been such a friend and benefactress to her: not an article of dress, not a ticket for public places, not a thing in the world that she could not command from me: yet always insolent, always pining for home, always preferring the mode of life in St. Martin's Street to all I could do for her. She is a saucy-spirited little puss, to be sure, but I love her dearly for all that; and I fancy she has a real regard for me, if she did not think it beneath the dignity of a wit, or of what she values more,—the dignity of Dr. Burney's daughter,—to indulge it. Such dignity! the Lady Louisa of Leicester Square! In good time!

Hester Lynch Thrale (Mrs. Piozzi), 1780, *Thraliana,* July 1;
Autobiography, Letters and Literary Remains,
ed. Hayward, p. 485

There are few—I believe I may say fairly there are none at all—that will not find themselves better informed concerning human nature, and their stock of observation enriched, by reading your *Cecilia*. . . . I might trespass upon your delicacy if I should fill my letter to you with what I fill my conversation to others; I should be troublesome to you alone if I should tell you all I feel and think on the natural vein of humour, the tender pathetic, the comprehensive and noble moral and the sagacious observation, that appear quite throughout this extraordinary performance. . . . In an age distinguished by producing extraordinary women, I hardly dare to tell where my opinion would place you amongst them.

Edmund Burke, 1782, *Letter to Miss Burney,* July 29

Was introduced by Rogers to Mad. D'Arblay, the celebrated authoress of *Evelina* and *Cecilia*—an elderly lady, with no remains of personal beauty, but with a simple and gentle manner, a pleasing expression of countenance, and apparently quick feelings. She told me she had wished to see two persons—myself, of course, being one, the other George Canning. This was really a compliment to be pleased with—a nice little handsome pat of butter, made up by a "neat-handed Phillis" of a dairy-maid, instead of the grease, fit only for cart-wheels, which one is dosed with by the pound. Mad. D'Arblay told us that the common story of Dr. Burney, her father, having brought home her own first work, and recommended it to her perusal, was erroneous. Her father was in the secret of *Evelina* being printed. But the following circumstance may have given rise to the story:— Dr. Burney was at Streatham soon after the publication, where he found Mrs. Thrale recovering from her confinement, low at the moment, and out of spirits. While they were talking together, Johnson, who sat beside in a kind of reverie, suddenly broke out, "You should read this new work, madam—you should read *Evelina,* every one says it is excellent, and they are right." The delighted father obtained a commission from Mrs. Thrale to purchase his daughter's work and retired the happiest of men. Madame D'Arblay said she was wild with joy at this decisive evidence of her literary success, and that she could only give vent to her rapture by dancing and skipping round a mulberry-tree in the garden. She was very young at this time.

Sir Walter Scott, 1826, *Journal,* Nov. 18;
Life by Lockhart, ch. lxxii

The Queen was persuaded to appoint Miss Burney, Mrs. Delany and Mr. Smelt having deceived themselves into believing her capable of adapting herself to her place, and of performing her new duties satisfactorily; their earnest desire to insure Miss Burney a certain salary instead of the precarious income arising from her works, having blinded their better judgment. Miss Burney was elated to such a degree by the appointment that she gradually lost all consciousness of her actual or relative position. She lived in an ideal world of which she was, in her own imagination, the centre. She believed herself possessed of a spell which fascinated all those she approached. She became convinced that all the equerries were in love with her, although she was continually the object of their ridicule, as they discovered her weaknesses and played upon her credulity for their own amusement. Many entertaining anecdotes might be collected of the ludicrous effect produced by Miss Burney's far-fetched expressions when she desired to be especially eloquent, and *particularly courtly.*

> Lady Llanover, 1862, ed., *The Autobiography and
> Correspondence of Mary Granville, Mrs. Delaney,*
> Second Series, vol. III, p. 361

I attended her during the last twenty years of her long life. . . . She lived in almost total seclusion from all but a few members of her own family; changed her lodgings more frequently than her dresses and occupied herself laboriously in composing those later works which retain so little of the charm of her earlier writings. Mr. Rogers was the only literary man who seemed to know of her existence.

> Sir Henry Holland, 1871, *Recollections of Past Life,* pp. 204, 205

Evelina (1778)

This year was ushered in by a grand and most important event! At the latter end of January, the literary world was favored with the first publication of the ingenious, learned, and most profound Fanny Burney! . . . This admirable authoress has named her most elaborate performance, *Evelina; or, a Young Lady's Entrance into the world.* Perhaps this may seem a rather bold attempt and title for a female whose knowledge of the world is very confined, and whose inclinations, as well as situation, incline her to a private and domestic life. All I can urge is, that I have only presumed to trace the accidents and adventures to which a "young woman" is liable; I have not pretended to shew the world what it actually *is,* but what it *appears* to a girl of seventeen: and so far as that, surely, any girl who is past seventeen may safely do?

> Fanny Burney, 1778, *Early Diary,* ed. Ellis, vol. II, p. 213

Evelina seems a work that should result from long experience, a deep and intimate knowledge with the world: yet it has been written without either. Miss Burney is a real wonder. What she is, she is intuitively. Dr. Burney told me she had the fewest advantages of any of his daughters, from some peculiar circumstances. And such has been her timidity, that he himself had not any suspicion of her powers. . . . Modesty with her is neither pretense nor decorum; it is an ingredient of her nature; for she who could part with such a work for twenty pounds, could know so little of its worth or of her own, as to leave no possible doubt of her humility.

Samuel Johnson, 1778, On Miss Burney's Evelina

The publication of *Evelina,* in 1778, made a sensation which the merits of the work fully justified. . . . *Evelina* fully deserved the praise and interest which it then obtained and still excites. . . . This novel presents to the reader a variety of social scenes which gives it a value possessed by no other work of fiction of the eighteenth century. No novelist of the theatres, of Vauxhall and Ranelagh, of Bath in the season, of the ridottos and assemblies of the London fashionable world. The shops, the amusements and the manners of the middle classes are made familiar to Evelina by her association with the Brangtons, and add greatly to the breadth of this valuable picture of metropolitan life. With a feminine attention to detail, and a quick perception of salient characteristics, Miss Burney described the world about her so faithfully and picturesquely as to deserve the thanks of every student of social history. . . . In the painting of manners Miss Burney was eminently successful. But she was hardly less so in a point in which excellence could not have been expected in so youthful a writer. The plot of *Evelina* is constructed with a skill worthy of a veteran. Fielding alone, of the eighteenth century novelists, can be said to surpass Miss Burney in this respect. . . . In regard to her sketches of character, it may be objected that Miss Burney lacked breadth of treatment, that she dwelt on one distinctive characteristic at the expense of the others. But still, Lord Orville, though somewhat too much of a model, and Mrs. Selwyn, though somewhat too habitually a wit, are vivid and life-like characters. The Brangtons and Sir Clement Willougby are nature itself, and the girlish nature of Evelina is betrayed in her letters with great felicity.

Bayard Tuckerman, 1882, A History of English
Prose Fiction, pp. 251, 252, 253

It was the masterly nautral freshness of the character-drawing, the clear, unencumbered vivacity of the incidents, the frankness of the humour,—in a word, the originality, the absence of literary artificiality,—that signalized *Evelina* as a work of genius, and set everybody talking about the new writer. Miss Burney was not the first woman novelist, but she was the first with a distinct vein of her own who wrote with her eyes on the subject, and not on any established model of approved style.

William Minto, 1894, The Literature of the Georgia Era,
ed. Knight, p. 120

The novel, as we know, was reported, before its author's name was known, to be the work of a girl of seventeen, and perhaps some part of its extraordinary vogue may have been due to this flattering mistake. But the main element in its success must surely, I should think, be sought in the fact that it was the first "novel of manners," in the later sense of the word, that had ever been offered to the public. It was a picture of life in London, life at Bath, life at the Bristol Hot Wells, in the later eighteenth century —principally, indeed, of modish life, but with just so much of a side glance at the gaieties and affectations of the middle class as would give it additional piquancy to the taste of the superiors whom they strove to imitate. . . . No tenderness towards this subject of a hundred-years-old nine-days' wonder ought to induce a candid critic of to-day to conceal his conviction that *Evelina* is a very crude performance.

Henry Duff Traill, 1898, The New Fiction, pp. 147, 149

Cecilia (1782)

Though the world saw and heard little of Madame D'Arblay during the last forty years of her life, and though that little did not add to her fame, there were thousands, we believe, who felt a singular emotion when they learned that she was no longer among us. The news of her death carried the minds of men back at one leap, clear over two generations, to the time when her first literary triumphs were won. All those whom we had been accustomed to revere as intellectual patriarchs, seemed children when compared with her; for Burke had sat up all night to read her writings, and Johnson had pronounced her superior to Fielding when Rogers was still a school-boy, and Southey still in petticoats. Yet more strange did it seem that we should just have lost one whose name had been widely celebrated before anybody had heard of some illustrious men who, twenty, thirty, or forty years ago, were, after a long and splendid career, borne with honour to the grave. Yet so it was. Frances Burney was at the height of fame and popularity before Cowper had published his first volume, before Porson had gone up to college, before Pitt had taken his seat in the House of Commons, before the voice of Erskine had been once heard in Westminster Hall. Since the appearance of her first work, sixty-two years had passed; and this interval had been crowded, not only with political, but also with intellectual revolutions.

Thomas Babington Macaulay, 1843, "Madame D'Arblay,"
Edinburgh Review; Critical and Miscellaneous Essays

She wrote *Cecilia* because the world told her it was amused by her, and that she could make her fortune by going on amusing it. But even in this second book there were indications that the natural spring was pretty nearly exhausted, while a deterioration of style betrayed the fact that her mastery of the means of literary expression was not sufficient to keep her works up to the mark when the vivacity of the first spontaneous impulse should be spent.

Mary Elizabeth Christie, 1882, "Miss Burney's Novels,"
Contemporary Review, vol. 42, p. 897

GENERAL

She is a quick, lively, and accurate observer of persons and things; but she always looks at them with a consciousness of her sex, and in that point of view in which it is the particular business and interest of women to observe them. There is little in her works of passion or character, or even manners, in the most extended sense of the word, as implying the sum-total of our habits and pursuits; her *forte* is in describing the absurdities and affectations of external behaviour, or the manners of people in company. . . . In one of her novels, for example, a lady appears regularly every ten pages, to get a lesson in music for nothing. She never appears for any other purpose; this is all you know of her; and in this the whole wit and humour of the character consists. Meadows is the same, who has always the cue of being tired, without any other idea. It has been said of Shakspeare, that you may always assign his speeches to the proper characters; and you may infallibly do the same thing with Madame D'Arblay's, for they always say the same thing. The Braughtons are the best. Mr. Smith is an exquisite city portrait. *Evelina* is also her best novel, because it is the shortest; that is, it has all the liveliness in the sketches of character, and smartness of comic dialogue and repartee, without the tediousness of the story, and endless affectation of sentiment which disfigures the others. . . . There is little other power in Madame D'Arblay's novels than that of immediate observation; her characters, whether of refinement or vulgarity, are equally superficial and confined.

William Hazlitt, 1818, *Lecture on the English Novelists*

Miss Burney did for the English novel what Jeremy Collier did for the English drama; and she did it in a better way. She first showed that a tale might be written in which both the fashionable and the vulgar life of London might be exhibited with great force, and with broad comic humour, and which yet should not contain a single line inconsistent with rigid morality, or even with virgin delicacy. She took away the reproach which lay on a most useful and delightful species of composition. She vindicated the right of her sex to an equal share in a fair and noble province of letters. Several accomplished women have followed in her track. At present, the novels which we owe to English ladies form no small part of the literary glory of our country. No class of works is more honourably distinguished by fine observation, by grace, by delicate wit, by pure moral feeling. Several among the successors of Madame D'Arblay have equalled her; two, we think, have surpassed her. But the fact that she has been surpassed gives her an additional claim to our respect and gratitude; for in truth we owe to her, not only *Evelina, Cecilia,* and *Camilla,* but also *Mansfield Park* and the *Absentee.*

Thomas Babington Macaulay, 1843, "Madame D'Arblay,"
Edinburgh Review; Critical and Miscellaneous Essays

Fanny Burney is one of the best examples of what has been called the originality of ignorance. She was positively illiterate. . . . Quick observation, quick fancy, were her chief gifts. A little more study of the writings of others, a few more ideas, would have stifled her genius. Had she had a spark of imagination with her limited intellect, she would probably have been unable to write at all; but the absence of any transcendental quality made her fearless and successful in paths where more distinguished abilities dared not tread.

John Davidson, 1895, *Sentences and Paragraphs,* p. 42

The most difficult figure to fit in to any progressive scheme of English fiction is Frances Burney, who was actually alive with Samuel Richardson and with Mr. George Meredith. She wrote seldom, and published at long intervals; her best novels, founded on a judicious study of Marivaux and Rosseau, implanted on a strictly British soil, were produced a little earlier than the moment we have now reached. Yet *The Wanderer* was published simultaneously with *Waverley.* She is a social satirist of a very sprightly order, whose early *Evelina* and *Cecilia* were written with an ease which she afterwards unluckily abandoned for an aping of the pomposity of her favourite lexicographer. Miss Burney was a delightful novelist in her youth, but she took no part in the progressive development of English literature.

Edmund Gosse, 1897, *A Short History of
Modern English Literature,* p. 294

ROBERT   SOUTHEY
1774-1843

1774—Born, August 12th, in Bristol. 1788—A scholar at Westminster. 1792—Expelled from Westminster School, for printing an article upon flogging. 1793—Enters Oxford University. 1794—Studies medicine for a short time. Publishes a volume of poems, the joint work of himself and Robert Lovell. Leaves Oxford. Plans a Pantisocracy, with Coleridge and others. 1795—Marries Miss Edith Fricker, privately. Goes to Lisbon with his uncle. Publishes *Joan of Arc.* 1796—Returns to England, and lives with his wife in Bristol. 1797—Resides in London, in order to study law. 1800—Goes to Lisbon with his wife. 1801—Returns to England. Publishes *Thalaba.* Becomes private secretary to the Irish Lord Chancellor of the Exchequer. 1802—Resigns his position as Secretary. Lives at Bristol with his wife. 1803—Takes his wife to Greta Hall, at Keswick. 1805—Publishes *Madoc.* 1807—Receives a pension of two hundred pounds per annum. 1809—Contributes to the first numbers of *The Quarterly Review.* 1810—Publishes the *Curse of Kehama,* and the first volume of *The History of Brazil.* 1813—Becomes Poet Laureate. Publishes *The Life of Nelson.* 1814—Publishes *Roderick.* 1817—*Wat Tyler,* a revolutionary sketch, written in Southey's youth, is published, without his consent. 1820—Publishes *The Life of Wesley.* 1824—Publishes *The Book of the Church.* 1826—Elected to Parliament, but declines to serve. 1829—Publishes *Colloquies.* 1834—Publishes *The Doctor.* 1835—Publishes *The Life of Cowper.* Declines a baronetcy, offered to him by Sir Robert Peel. Receives an addition of 300*l.* per annum to his pension. 1837—His wife dies. 1839—Marries Miss Catherine Bowles. 1843—Dies, March 21st.

Edward T. Mason, 1885, *Personal Traits of British Authors, Byron-Landor,* p. 214

SEE: *Poetical Works,* ed. H. T. Tuckerman, 1884, 5 v.; *Poems,* ed. Edward Dowden, 1895, repr. 1930; *Select Prose,* ed. Jacob Zeitlin, 1916; *Letters: A Selection,* ed. Maurice H. Fitzgerald, 1912; *New Letters,* ed. Kenneth Curry, 1965 (Vols. I, II); Cuthbert J. Southey, *Life and Correspondence,* 1849-50, 6 v.; Jack Simmons, *Southey,* 1945.

PERSONAL

Literature is now Southey's trade; he is a manufacturer, and his workshop is his study,—a very beautiful one certainly, but its beauty and the delightful environs, as well as his own celebrity, subject him to interruptions. His time is his wealth, and I shall therefore scrupulously abstain from stealing any portion of it.

Henry Crabb Robinson, 1816, *Diary,* Sept. 9; *Diary, Reminiscences and Correspondence,* ed. Sadler, vol. I, p. 340

> Bob Southey! You're a poet—Poet-Laureate,
>   And representative of all the race,
> Although 'tis true that you turn'd out a Tory at
>   Last—yours has lately been a common case,—
> And now, my Epic Renegade! what are ye at?
>   With all the Lakers, in and out of place?

Lord Byron, 1819, *Don Juan,* Dedication

He is certainly an extraordinary man, one of those whose character I find it difficult to comprehend, because I hardly know how such elements can be brought together, such rapidity of mind with such patient labour and weari-some exactness, so mild a disposition with so much nervous excitability, and a poetical talent so elevated with such an immense mass of minute, dull learning.

George Ticknor, 1819, *Journal; Life, Letters and Journals,* vol. I, p. 286

His figure is rather tall and slim, but apparently muscular, and has altogether an air of gentility about it. He has nothing whatever about him of the stiffness or awkwardness of a great student; but, on the contrary, were he a mere ordinary person, I should describe him as a genteel-looking man, possessing much natural elegance, or even grace. But his head and countenance bespeak the poet. His hair is black, and bushy, and strong, and gives him a bold, free, and even dignified look; his face is sharp; his nose high; and his eyes, without having that piercing look which is often felt to be disagreeable, because too searching, in the eyes of men of genius, are, without any exception, the most acute and intelligent I ever beheld. Yet I believe he is near-sighted; and this seems to have given him a habit of elevating his face when he speaks, as if he were looking up, which brings all his features fully before you, and seemed to me to impart to his whole demeanour a singular charm of sincerity and independence. His voice seemed to me at first to be shrill and weak, and perhaps it is so, but there is in it a kind of musical wildness, which I could not help considering to be characteristic of the author of *Thalaba;* and when he chanced to recite a few lines of poetry it became quite empassioned.

John Gibson Lockhart (Philip Kempferhausen), 1819, "Letters from the Lakes," *Blackwood's Magazine,* vol. 4, p. 401

Mr. Southey's conversation has a little resemblance to a common-place book; his habitual deportment to a piece of clock-work. He is not remarkable either as a reasoner or an observer: but he is quick, unaffected, replete with anecdotes, various and retentive in his reading, and exceedingly happy in his play upon words as most scholars are who give their minds this sportive turn. We have chiefly seen Mr. Southey in company where few people appear to advantage, we mean in that of Mr. Coleridge. He has not certainly the same range of speculation, nor the same flow of sounding words, but he makes up by the detail of knowledge, and by a scrupulous correctness of statement for what he wants in originality of thought, or impetuous declamation.

William Hazlitt, 1825, *The Spirit of the Age*

Southey certainly is as elegant a writer as any in the kingdom. But those who would love Southey as well as admire him, must see him, as I did, in the bosom, not only of one lovely family, but of three, all attached to him as a father, and all elegantly maintained and educated, it is generally said, by his indefatigable pen. The whole of Southey's conversation and economy, both at home and afield, left an impression of veneration on my mind, which no future contingency shall ever either extinguish or injure. Both his figure and countenance are imposing, and deep thought is strongly marked in his dark eye; but there is a defect in his eyelids, for these he has no power of raising, so that when he looks up he turns up his face, being unable to raise his eyes; and when he looks towards the top of one of his romantic mountains, one would think he was looking at the zenith. This peculiarity is what will most strike every stranger in the appearance of the accomplished laureate. He does not at all see well at a distance, which made me several times disposed to get into a passion with him, because he did not admire the scenes which I was pointing out.

James Hogg, 1832, *Autobiography*

Some people assert that genius is inconsistent with domestic happiness, and yet Southey was happy at home and made his home happy, he not only loved his wife and children *though* he was a poet, but he loved them better *because* he was a poet. He seems to have been without taint of worldliness. London with its pomps and vanities, learned coteries with their dry pedantry, rather scared than attracted him. He found his prime glory in his genius, and his chief felicity in home affections. I like Southey.

Charlotte Brontë, 1850, *Letter to W. S. Williams,* April 12;
Charlotte Brontë and her Circle, ed. Shorter, p. 399

In associating with Southey, not only was it necessary to salvation to refrain from touching his books, but various rites, ceremonies, and usages must be rigidly observed. At certain appointed hours only was he open to conversation; at the seasons which had been predestined from all eternity for holding intercourse with his friends. Every hour of the day had its commission— every half-hour was assigned to its own peculiar, undeviating function. The indefatigable student gave a detailed account of his most painstaking life, every moment of which was fully employed and strictly pre-arranged, to a certain literary Quaker lady. "I rise at five throughout the year; from six till eight I read Spanish; then French for one hour; Portuguese next, for half an hour,—my watch lying on the table; I give two hours to poetry: I write prose for two hours; I translate so long; I make extracts so long," and so of the rest until the poor fellow had fairly fagged himself into his bed again. "And, pray when dost thou think, friend?" she asked, dryly, to the great discomfiture of the future Laureate.

Thomas Jefferson Hogg, 1858, *The Life of
Percy Bysshe Shelley,* vol. II, p. 27

An English worthy, doing his duty for fifty noble years of labour, day by day storing up learning, day by day working for scant wages, most charitable out of his small means, bravely faithful to the calling which he had chosen, refusing to turn from his path for popular praise or princes' favour; I mean *Robert Southey*. We have left his old political landmarks miles and miles behind; we protest against his dogmatism; nay, we begin to forget it and his politics; but I hope his life will not be forgotten, for it is sublime in its simplicity, its energy, its honour, its affection! In the combat between Time and Thalaba, I suspect the former destroyer has conquered; Kehama's curse frightens very few readers now; but Southey's private letters are worth piles of epics, and are sure to last among us as long as kind hearts like to sympathize with goodness and purity and love and upright life.

William Makepeace Thackeray, 1861, "George the Fourth,"
The Four Georges

The change in Southey's political and religious opinions which made the republican of 1793 a tory, the author of *Wat Tyler* a poet laureate, and the independent thinker whom Coleridge had just managed to convert from deism to unitarianism a champion of the established church, inevitably exposed Southey to attack from the advocates of the opinions he had forsaken. There can be no question of Southey's perfect sincerity. The evalution of his views did not differ materially from that traceable in the cases of Wordsworth and Coleridge. But the immediate advantage to the convert was more visible and tangible, and Southey provoked retaliation by the uncharitable tone he habitually adopted in controversy with those whose sentiments had formerly been his own. Every question presented itself to him on the ethical side. But constitutionally he was a bigot; an opinion for him must be either moral or immoral; those which he did not himself share inevitably fell into the latter class, and their propagators appeared to him enemies of society. At the same time his reactionary tendencies were not unqualified. He could occasionally express liberal sentiments.

Richard Garnett, 1898, *Dictionary of National Biography,*
vol. LIII, p. 287

Poems

O Southey! Southey! cease thy varied song!
A bard may chant too often and too long:
As thou art strong in verse, in mercy, spare!
A fourth, alas! were more than we could bear,
But if, in spite of all the world can say,
Thou still wilt verseward plod thy weary way;

If still in Berkeley ballads most uncivil,
Thou wilt devote old women to the devil,
The babe unborn thy dread intent may rue;
"God help thee" Southey, and thy readers too.

Lord Byron, 1809, English Bards and Scotch Reviewers

His Laureate odes are utterly and intolerably bad, and, if he had never written anything else, must have ranked him below Colley Cibber in genius, and above him in conceit and presumption.

Francis, Lord Jeffrey, 1816, "The Lay of the Laureate,"
Edinburgh Review, vol. 26, p. 449

The poetry of Mr. Southey occupies not fewer than 14 volumes in crown octavo; and it embraces subjects of almost every description. *Thalaba* has long been, and will long continue to be, very generally known and admired. It was abundantly popular at the period of its publication. The *Curse of Kehama* is perhaps the greatest effort of the author's genius; but his *Roderic,* or the *Last of the Goths,* is that which seems to have received his most careful elaboration and finishing. It is a grand poem. *Madoc,* though full of wild imagery, and with verse of occasionally uncouth structure, is not destitute of some of the most brilliant touches of the poet.

Thomas Frognall Dibdin, 1824, The Library Companion,
p. 737, note

His poems, taken in the mass, stand far higher than his prose works. The Laureate Odes, indeed, among which the *Vision of Judgment* must be classed, are, for the most part, worse than Pye's and as bad as Cibber's; nor do we think him generally happy in short pieces. But his longer poems, though full of faults, are nevertheless very extraordinary productions. We doubt greatly whether they will be read fifty years hence; but that, if they are read, they will be admired, we have no doubt whatever.

Thomas Babington Macaulay, 1830, "Southey's Colloquies on
Society," Edinburgh Review; Critical and Miscellaneous Essays

Southey's *Madoc, Don Roderick,* and the *Curse of Kehama* are splendid metrical histories, but they do not contain the traits which speak at once to all mankind: they are addressed to the learned and studious, and these are a mere fragment of the human race. Admired, accordingly, by the well-informed, they are already comparatively unknown to the great body of readers; and the author's poetical fame rests chiefly on *Thalaba,* in which his brilliant imagination revelled without control, save that of high moral feeling, in the waterless deserts and palm-shaded fountains and patriarchal life of the Happy Arabia.

> Sir Archibald Alison, 1853-59, *History of Europe, 1815-1852,* vol. I, ch. v

I am not sure whether it might not be put as a test of the existence or otherwise of a pure love of the art in any man that he should like or dislike these achievements of Southey; and if Ariosto is able to retain his readers, it appears hardly creditable to the public taste of our time that Southey should entirely lose his. It is at least certain that for many subtle and pleasing varieties of rhythm, for splendor of invention, for passion and incident sustained often at the highest level, and for all that raises and satisfies wonder and fancy, there will be found in *Thalaba, Kehama,* and *Roderick* passages of unrivalled excellence ("perfect," even Byron thought); and these may here excuse, if they do not wholly justify, the hopes that once centered in them, and to which exalted expression is given in the correspondence of the friends.

> John Forster, 1869, *Walter Savage Landor,* p. 129

Joan of Arc (1796)

With *Joan of Arc* I have been delighted, amazed; I had not presumed to expect anything of such excellence from Southey. Why the poem is alone sufficient to redeem the character of the age we live in from the imputation of degenerating in Poetry.

> Charles Lamb, 1796, *Letter to Coleridge, Final Memorials,* ed. Talfourd

He gave the publick a long quarto volume of epick verses, *Joan of Arc,* written, he says in the preface, in *six weeks.* Had he meant to write well, he should have kept it at least six years.—I mention this, for I have been much pleased with many of the young gentleman's little copies of verses. I wish also that he would review *some of his principles.*

> Thomas James Mathias, 1798, *The Pursuits of Literature,* Eighth ed., p. 352

Mr. Southey's *Joan of Arc,* though incorrect, and written with inexcusable rapidity, reflects great credit on his genius and abilities; the sentiments are noble and generous, and burn with an enthusiastic ardour for liberty; the characters, especially that of his Heroine, are well supported, and his visionary scenes are rich with bold and energetic imagery. His fable, however, I can not but consider peculiarly unfortunate, as directly militating against national pride and opinion. . . . The versification of this poem is in many parts very beautiful, and would have been altogether so, had the author condescended to bestow more time on its elaboration.

Nathan Drake, 1798-1820, Literary Hours, vol. II, p. 107

Thalaba the Destroyer (1801)

The first thing that strikes the reader of *Thalaba* is the singular structure of of the versification, which is a jumble of all the measures that are known in English poetry (and a few more), without rhyme, and without any sort of regularity in their arrangement. Blank odes have been known in this country about as long as English sapphics and dactylics; and both have been considered, we believe, as a species of monsters, or exotics, that were not very likely to propagate, or thrive, in so unpropitious a climate. Mr. Southey, however, has made a vigorous effort for their naturalization, and generously endangered his own reputation in their behalf. The melancholy fate of his English sapphics, we believe, is but too generally known; and we can scarcely predict a more favourable issue to the present experiment.

Francis, Lord Jeffrey, 1802, "Southey's Thalaba,"
Edinburgh Review, vol. I, p. 72

Thalaba was the first fruits of one of Southey's earliest ambitions, for he tells us himself that even in his schooldays he had formed the design of writing a great poem on each of the more important mythologies. *Thalaba* is based upon the Mahometan and is written in an irregular form of blank verse. . . . Southey describes it as "the Arabesque ornament of an Arabian tale," and as such it is perhaps the fitting garb of an Oriental fiction—a lawless measure for a lawless song. The poem recounts the adventures and triumphs of an Arabian hero at war with the powers of evil, but though often characterized by beauty of expression and grandeur of scene, lacks the human interest which attaches only to the record of the thoughts, feelings, and actions of men and women moving within the limits of natural law, and the sphere of human sympathy.

Alfred H. Miles, 1892, The Poets and the Poetry of the Century,
Southey to Shelley, p. 4

Roderick (1814)

This is the best, we think, and the most powerful of all Mr. Southey's poems. It abounds with lofty sentiments, and magnificent imagery; and contains more rich and comprehensive descriptions—more beautiful pictures of pure affection—and more impressive representations of mental agony and exaltation than we have often met with in the compass of a single volume. . . . The author is a poet undoubtedly; but not of the highest order. There is rather more of rhetoric than of inspiration about him—and we have oftener to admire his taste and industry in borrowing and adoring, than the boldness or felicity of his inventions. He has indisputably a great gift of amplifying and exalting; but uses it, we must say, rather unmercifully. He is never plain, concise, or unaffectedly simple, and is so much bent upon making the most of every thing, that he is perpetually overdoing. . . . This want of relief and variety is sufficiently painful of itself in a work of such length; but its worst effect, is that it gives an air of falsetto and pretension to the whole strain of the composition, and makes us suspect the author of imposture and affectation, even when he has good enough cause for his agonies and raptures.

> Francis, Lord Jeffrey, 1815-44, "Southey's *Roderick*,"
> *Contributions to the Edinburgh Review*, vol. III, p. 133

In *Kehama* he has exhibited virtue struggling against the most dreadful inflictions with heavenly fortitude, and made manifest to us the angel-guards who love to wait on innocence and goodness. But in *Roderic* the design has even a higher scope, is more difficult of execution; and, so far as I know, unique. The temptations which beset a single soul have been a frequent subject, and one sure of sympathy if treated with any power. Breathlessly we watch the conflict, with heartfelt anguish mourn defeat, or with heart-expanding triumph hail a conquest. But, where there *has* been defeat, to lead us back with the fallen one through the thorny and desolate paths of repentance to purification, to win not only our pity, but our sympathy, for one crushed and degraded by his own sin; and finally, through his faithful though secret efforts to redeem the past, secure to him, justly blighted and world-forsaken as he is, not only our sorrowing love, but our respect;—*this* Southey alone has done, perhaps alone could do.

> Margaret Fuller Ossoli, 1850? *Art, Literature and
> the Drama*, p. 96

Wat Tyler (1817)

The poem *Wat Tyler,* appeared to him to be the most seditious book that was ever written; its author did not stop short of exhorting to general anarchy; he vilified kings, priests, and nobles, and was for universal suffrage and perfect equality. The Spencean plan could not be compared with it; that miserable and ridiculous performance did not attempt to employ any arguments; but the author of *Wat Tyler* constantly appealed to the passions, and in a style which the author, at that time, he supposed, conceived to be eloquence. Why, then, had not those who thought it necessary to suspend the Habeas Corpus Act taken notice of this poem? Why had not they discovered the author of that seditious publication, and visited him with the penalties of the law? The work was not published secretly, it was not handed about in the darkness of night, but openly and publicly sold in the face of day. It was at this time to be purchased at almost every bookseller's shop in London: it was now exposed for sale in a bookseller's shop in Pall-Mall, who styled himself bookseller to one or two of the royal families. He borrowed the copy from which he had just read the extract from an honourable friend of his, who bought it in the usual way; and, therefore, he supposed there could be no difficulty in finding out the party that wrote it.

William Smith, 1817, *Speech in the House of Commons,*
March 14; *Hansard's Parliamentary Debates,* vol. 35, p. 1091

As to *Wat Tyler.* Now, sir, though you are not acquainted with the full history of this notable production, yet you could not have been ignorant that the author whom you attacked at such unfair advantage was the aggrieved, and not the offending, person. You knew that this poem had been written very many years ago, in his early youth. You knew that a copy of it had been surreptitiously obtained and made public by some skulking scoundrel, who had found booksellers not more honorable than himself to undertake the publication. You knew that it was published without the writer's knowledge, for the avowed purpose of insulting him, and with the hope of injuring him, if possible. You knew that the transaction bore upon its face every character of baseness and malignity. You knew that it must have been effected either by robbery or by breach of trust. These things, Mr. William Smith, you knew! and, knowing them as you did, I verily believe, that if it were possible to revoke what is irrevocable, you would at this moment be far more desirous of blotting from remembrance the disgraceful speech, which stands upon record in your name, than I should be of canceling the boyish composition which gave occasion to it. *Wat Tyler* is full of errors, but they are the errors of youth and ignorance; they bear no indication of an ungenerous spirit or of a malevolent heart.

Robert Southey, 1817, *A Letter to William Smith, M. P.*

Many years after this was written, and, as Southey fondly hoped, forgotten, he being at the time a pensioned supporter of the Government, he was startled by reading an advertisement of *Wat Tyler,* by Robert Southey, "a Dramatic Poem, with a preface suitable to recent circumstances, London, W. Hone," and shortly afterwards he received a copy of the drama, addressed to *Robert Southey, Poet Laureate, and Renegade.* By the advice of his friends, Southey applied for an injunction to restrain the publication; Lord Eldon refused to grant this protection, on the plea that "a person cannot recover damages upon a work which in its nature is calculated to do injury to the public." This decision was not only extremely annoying to Southey, but greatly increased the notoriety of the reprint of the drama, of which no less than 60,000 copies were sold in a very short time, and it is even now much more frequently met with than any of his other poems. Southey's political opponents did not let the matter rest here, for both Lord Brougham and Mr. William Smith, member for Norwich, drew attention in the House to Southey's inconsistent writings, contrasting *Wat Tyler* with his later Conservative articles in *The Quarterly Review,* and inquiring why the Government had taken no steps to prosecute the author of that treasonable play. These proceedings reflected little credit on either party.

> Walter Hamilton, 1879, "Robert Southey," *The Poets Laureate of England, being a History of the Office of Poet Laureate,* p. 224

A Vision of Judgment (1821)

It hath been wisely said, that "One fool makes many," and it hath been poetically observed
    "That fools rush in where angels fear to tread."
If Mr. Southey had not rushed in where he had no business, and where he never was before, and never will be again, the following poem would not have been written. It is not impossible that it may be as good as his own, seeing that it cannot, by any species of stupidity, natural or acquired, be *worse.* The gross flattery, the dull impudence, the renegado intolerance, and impious cant, of the poem by the author of *Wat Tyler,* are something so stupendous as to form the sublime of himself—containing the quintessence of his own attributes.

> Lord Byron, 1824, *The Vision of Judgment,* Preface

Byron's satire has given that poem an immortality which it would never otherwise have gained. But Southey's poem is more profane than even Byron's. Southey really ventured on anticipating the judgment of heaven; Byron only intended to sneer at Southey's gross presumption.

> Spencer Walpole, 1878, *A History of England from the Conclusion of the Great War in 1815,* vol. I, p. 355

In this most impious work, he fearlessly condemns or rewards political personages at the day of judgment, according as their opinions coincide or not with his own, in a manner so little short of blasphemy, as to disgust his best friends and create greater activity amongst his foes.

> Walter Hamilton, 1879, *The Poets Laureate of England,* p. 227

It is always to be regretted that in his anxiety to do his whole duty, to fulfill all the obligations of his office, Southey should have written *A Vision of Judgment.* The error was also partly due to a wish to strike out a new path in a somewhat dreary field, to write something different from the tiresome odes of his predecessors, to be original at the expense of good taste.

Frances Louise Howland (Kenyon West), 1895,
The Laureates of England, p. 154

Life of Nelson (1813)

His prose is perfect. Of his poetry there are various opinions. There is, perhaps, too much of it for the present generation; posterity will probably select. He has *passages* equal to any thing. At present he has *a party,* but no *public,*—except for his prose writings. The *Life of Nelson* is beautiful.

Lord Byron, 1813, *Journal,* Nov. 22; *Moore's Life of Lord Byron*

But though in general we prefer Mr. Southey's poetry to his prose, we must make one exception. The *Life of Nelson* is, beyond all doubt, the most perfect and the most delightful of his works. The fact is, as his poems most abundantly prove, that he is by no means so skilful in designing as filling up. It was therefore an advantage to him to be furnished with an outline of characters and events, and to have no other task to perform than that of touching the cold sketch into life. No writer, perhaps, ever lived, whose talents so precisely qualified him to write the history of the great naval warrior.

Thomas Babington Macaulay, 1830, "Southey's Colloquies on Society," *Edinburgh Review; Critical and Miscellaneous Essays*

The *Life of Nelson* is a model of unaffected, direct narrative, allowing the facts to speak for themselves through the clearest possible medium of expression; and yet this most popular of Southey's books, far from being the offspring of any strong personal sympathy or perception, was so entirely a literary job, that he says it was thrust upon him, and that he moved among the sea-terms like a cat among crockery.

Henry T. Tuckerman, 1857, *Essays, Biographical and Critical,* p. 73

That Southey should live mainly by a book which was merely a publisher's commission, and not by the works which he and his contemporaries deemed immortal, is one of the ironies of literature.

Clement K. Shorter, 1897, "Victorian Literature," *Sixty Years of Books and Bookmen,* p. 6

GENERAL

Reflect but on the variety and extent of his acquirements! He stands second to no man, either as a historian or as a bibliographer; and when I regard

him as a popular essayist (for the articles of his composition in the reviews
are, for the greater part, essays on subjects of deep or curious interest
rather than criticisms on particular works)—I look in vain for any writer,
who has conveyed so much information, from so many and recondite
sources, with so many just and original reflections, in a style so lively and
poignant, yet so uniformly classical and perspicuous; no one, in short, who
has combined so much wisdom with so much wit, so much truth and knowledge with so much life and fancy. His prose is always intelligible, and always
entertaining. In poetry he has attempted almost every species of composition
known before, and he has added new ones; and if we except the highest
lyric—(in which how few, how very few, even of the greatest minds have
been fortunate)—he has attempted every species successfully. . . . It is
Southey's almost unexampled felicity, to possess the best gifts of talent and
genius free from all their characteristic defects. . . . As son, brother,
husband, father, master, friend, he moves with firm yet light steps, alike
unostentatious and alike exemplary. As a writer, he has uniformly made
his talents subservient to the best interests of humanity, of public virtue,
and domestic piety; his cause has ever been the cause of pure religion and
of liberty, of national independence and of national illumination.   ·

Samuel Taylor Coleridge, 1817, Biographia Literaria, ch. iii

But the most various, scholastic, and accomplished of such of our literary
contemporaries as have written works as well as articles, and prose as well
as poetry—is, incontestably, Mr. Southey. The Life of Nelson is acknowledged to be the best biography of the day. The Life of Wesley and The
Book of the Church, however adulterated by certain prepossessions and
prejudices, are, as mere compositions, characterized by an equal simplicity
and richness of style,—an equal dignity and an equal ease. No writer blends
more happily the academical graces of the style of the last century with
the popular vigor of that which distinguishes the present. . . . The great
charm of that simple power which is so peculiarly Southeian. . . . Southey's
rich taste and antique stateliness of mind.

Edward Bulwer-Lytton, Lord Lytton, 1833, England and the English

There is not, perhaps, any single work of Southey's the loss of which would
be felt by us as a capital misfortune. But the more we consider his total
work, its mass, its variety, its high excellence, the more we come to regard
it as a memorable, an extraordinary achievement.

Edward Dowden, 1880, Southey (English Men of Letters), p. 1

Although the concise humour and simplicity of his lines on The Battle of
Blenheim ensure it a place among the best known short poems in the

language, there are not half a dozen of his lyrical pieces, some of his racy ballads excepted, that have any claim to poetic distinction. The *English Eclogues,* however, have an important place in literature as prototypes of Tennyson's more finished performances, but are hardly poetry. As a writer of prose Southey is entitled to very high praise, although, as De Quincey justly points out, the universally commended elegance and perspicuity of his style do not make him a fine writer. But within his own limits he is a model of lucid, masculine English—"sinewy and flexible, easy and melodious."

Richard Garnett, 1898, Dictionary of National Biography,
vol. LIII, p. 289

NOAH WEBSTER
1758-1843

> Born at Hartford, Conn., Oct. 16, 1758: died at New Haven, Conn., May 28, 1843. An American lexicographer and author. He entered Yale in 1774; served in the Revolutionary War in 1777; graduated at Yale in 1778; and was admitted to the bar in 1781. He taught in various places, and in 1788 settled in New York as a journalist. In 1798 he removed to New Haven, and in 1812 to Amherst, Massachusetts, where he took part in the founding of the college and was the first president of its board of trustees. He returned to New Haven in 1822. He published *A Grammatical Institute of the English Language* (1783-85; comprising spelling-book, grammar, and reader), *Dissertations on the English Language* (1789), *A Compendious Dictionary of the English Language* (1806), and *A Grammar of the English Language* (1807). He is best known from his large *American Dictionary of the English Language* (1828: 2d ed. 1841). Among his other works are *Rights of Neutrals* (1802), *Collection of Papers on Political, Literary, and Moral Subjects* (1843), and a brief history of the United States (1823).
>
> Benjamin E. Smith, ed., 1894-97, The Century
Cyclopedia of Names, p. 1053

PERSONAL

I have never been a hard student, unless a few years may be excepted; but I have been a steady, persevering student. I have rarely used lamp or candle light, except once, when reading law, and then I paid for my imprudence, for I injured my eyes. My practice has usually been to rise about half an hour before the sun, and make use of all the light of that luminary. But I have never or rarely been in a hurry. When I first undertook the business of supporting General Washington's administration, I laboured too hard in writing or translating from the French papers for my paper, or in composing pamphlets. In two instances I was so exhausted that I expected to die, for I could not perceive any pulsation in the radial artery; but I recovered. While engaged in composing my *Dictionary*, I was often so much excited by discoveries I made, that my pulse, whose ordinary action is scarcely 60 beats to the minute, was accelerated to 80 or 85. My exercise has not been violent nor regular. While I was in Amherst I cultivated a little land, and used to work at making hay, and formerly I worked in my garden, which I cannot now do. Until within a few years, I used to make my fires in the morning, but I never or rarely walked before breakfast. My exercise is now limited to walking about the city to purchase supplies for my family. . . . I began to use spectacles when fifty years of age, or a little more, and that was the time when I began to study and prepare materials for my *Dictionary*. I had had the subject in contemplation some years before, and had made memorandums on the margin of Johnson's *Dictionary,* but I did not set myself to the work till I wore spectacles. When I finished my copy I was sitting at my table in Cambridge, England, January, 1825. When I arrived at the last word, I was seized with a tremor that made it difficult to proceed. I, however, summoned up strength to finish the work, and then walking about the room I soon recovered.

Noah Webster, 1836, Letter to Dr. Thomas Miner, Nov. 21

To men of the present generation, Dr. Webster is known chiefly as a learned philologist; and the natural inference would be, that he spent his whole life among his books, and chiefly in devotion to a single class of studies. The fact, however, was far otherwise. Though he was always a close student,— reading, thinking, and writing at every period of his life,—he never withdrew himself from the active employments of society. After his first removal to New Haven, he was for a number of years one of the aldermen of the city, and judge of one of the state courts. He also frequently represented that town in the legislature of the state. During his residence at Amherst, he was called, in repeated instances, to discharge similar duties, and spent a part of several winters at Boston as a member of the General Court.

Chauncey A. Goodrich, 1847, Memoir of Noah Webster

Spelling Book

Noah Webster, who wrote the earliest American spelling-book, was the first author whose writing I ever read; and what a work it was to my young imagination! In its externals, as well as its internals, it is before me now precisely as it was nearly half a century ago. The narrow yellow-white leathern back, with not quite all the hairs tanned out of it in some copies; the palish-blue cover; the thick, whitish paper, whose smell I inhale as freshly at this moment as when it first pervaded my young nostrils—all are "present with me." And its contents! How palpable are their first impressions upon the mind!—from the pregnant moral inculcations in one syllable, onward to the reading-lessons in wider and taller words, which, in certain parts, sometimes bothered "us boys" not a little: yet not much, either, after encountering the spelling-lessons that preceded them, which enabled me generally to conquer the most formidable of them; especially after I had "gone up to the head" in spelling them in the longest class in the old log school-house. The moral and patriotic inculcations of those one-syllable lessons are familiar to tens of thousands of readers at this moment, who perhaps have not looked into the good old book for the last thirty years; and yet of which more than *one million* of copies have been sold every twelve months.

Lewis Gaylord Clark, 1870, "Noah Webster,"
Lippincott's Magazine, vol. 5, p. 448

The final success of the little book has been quite beyond definite computation, but a few figures will show something of the course it has run. In 1814, 1815, the sales averaged 286,000 copies a year; in 1828 the sales were estimated to be 350,000 copies. In 1847 the statement was made that about twenty-four million copies of the book had been published up to that time, and that the sale was then averaging a million of copies a year. It was also then said, that during the twenty years in which he was employed in compiling his *American Dictionary,* the entire support of his family was derived from the profits of this work, at a premium for copyright of five mills a copy. The sales for eight years following the Civil War, namely 1866-1873, aggregated 8,196,028.

Horace E. Scudder, 1881, *Noah Webster*
(*American Men of Letters*), p. 70

American Dictionary (1828-41)

For the learned I am fully convinced that Mr. Webster's *Dictionary* will have great value, although it may contain objectionable points and peculiarities, which a mind of another cast would not have admitted. The preface will be the most difficult part for him to execute. In all his publications he has manifested a singular want of judgment in estimating the comparative value of his own attainments, and in setting forth what he deems the most important discoveries which he has made. His friends in New Haven are aware of this foible, and they are resolved to counteract it in the present instance as far as the nature of the case will admit.

Jared Sparks, 1826, *Journal of a Southern Tour,* June 29;
Life and Writings, ed. Adams, vol. I, pp. 500, 501, 502

About thirty-five years ago, I began to think of attempting the compilation of a Dictionary. I was induced to this undertaking, not more by the suggestion of friends, than by my own experience of the want of such a work while reading modern books of science. In this pursuit I found almost insuperable difficulties, from the want of a dictionary for explaining many new words which recent discoveries in the physical sciences had introduced into use. To remedy this defect in part, I published my *Compendious Dictionary* in 1806, and soon after made preparations for undertaking a larger work. . . . I had not pursued this course more than three or four years before I discovered that I had to unlearn a great deal that I had spent years in learning, and that it was necessary for me to go back to the first rudiments of a branch of erudition which I had before cultivated, as I had supposed, with success. I spent ten years in this comparison of radical words, and in forming a "Synopsis of the principal Words in twenty Languages, arranged in Classes under their primary Elements or Letters." The result has been to open what are to me new views of language, and to unfold what appear to be the genuine principles on which these languages are constructed. After completing this "Synopsis," I proceeded to correct what I had written of the *Dictionary,* and to complete the remaining part of the work. But before I had finished it, I determined on a voyage to Europe, with the view of obtaining some books and some assistance which I wanted, of learning the real state of the pronunciation of our language in England, as well as the general state of philology in that country, and of attempting to bring about some agreement or coincidence of opinions in regard to unsettled points in pronunciation and grammatical construction. In some of these objects, I failed; in others, my designs were answered. . . . . To that great and benevolent Being, who, during the preparation of this work, has sustained a feeble constitution amidst obstacles and toils, disappointments, infirmities and depression,—who has borne me and my manuscripts in safety across the Atlantic, and given me strength and resolution to bring the work to a close,—I would present the tribute of my most grateful acknowledgments. And if the talent which he intrusted to my care has not been put to most profitable use in his service, I hope that it has not been "kept laid up in a napkin," and that any misapplication of it may be graciously forgiven.

Noah Webster, 1828, *American Dictionary of the*
English Language, Preface, pp. xv, xvi

I imagine that Webster's dictionary will never be current. The plan of citing *names,* instead of *passages,* is unsatisfactory and unfair.

James W. Alexander, 1829, *Letter,* July 15;
Forty Years' Familiar Letters, vol. I, p. 132

He was regarded with suspicion, and frequently openly opposed: for his well known views as a reformer of the language laid him particularly open to attack; since speech being common property, every one was bound more or less to question his proceedings. Though the dictionary bearing Webster's name is now in very general use, it has secured this result by the number of its words, and particularly the extent of its scientific terms and the accuracy of their definitions, in spite of the peculiar Websterisms of orthography. His mistake, as the compiler of a dictionary, at the outset was, in seeking to amend the language, while his duty was simply to record the use of words by the best authors. In the attempt to impose new conditions, and with his American innovations, he placed himself beyond the recognition of the highest authorities of the language in the universities of England and the colleges of America.

> Evert A. and George L. Duyckinck, 1855-65-75,
> *Cyclopædia of American Literature,* ed. Simons

He worked alone, and his solitariness was not wholly due to his idiosyncrasies. It was in part the penalty paid by a student of the time. The resolution and self-reliance of an American were his, and so was the individuality. That such enterprises are not now conducted single-handed is owing not to a lack of courage but to the greater complexity of life, the more constant sense of interdependence, the existence of greater solidarity in intellectual pursuits. Webster was unable to believe that a company of scholars could ever be formed who should carry forward a revision of the Bible, and therefore, he made the attempt himself. Individual criticism has been abundant ever since, but no one, however learned or popular, has even been able to impress his work upon the community. The most carefully organized body of scholars submits the results of ten years' conference to the votes of the world. The history of Webster's Dictionary is parallel with the growth of national life out of individualism.

> Horace E. Scudder, 1881, *Noah Webster*
> (*American Men of Letters*), p. 293

THOMAS CAMPBELL
1777-1844

Born, in Glasgow, 27 July, 1777. Educated at Glasgow Grammar School, 1784-91; at Glasgow University, Oct. 1791 to Spring, 1796. As private tutor at Downie, 1796-97. Returned to Glasgow. Removed to Edinburgh to study Law. A few weeks later undertook literary work for Messrs. Mundell and Co., publishers. Also gave private tuition. First poems published,

April 1799. To Germany, 1800; studied and wrote poems. Returned to London, April 1801. Married Matilda Sinclair, 10 Oct. 1803. Devoted himself to literary work, and lived in London for rest of life. Crown pension of £200 granted him, 1805. Lectured on poetry at Royal Institution, 1810. Visit to Paris, 1814. Royal Institution lectures repeated at Liverpool and Birmingham, 1819. In Germany and Austria, May to Nov. 1820. Edited *New Monthly Magazine*, Nov. 1820 to 1830. Scheme of London University conceived, 1824. Visit to Berlin University, Sept. 1825. Lord Rector of Glasgow University, 1826-29. Wife died, 1828. Edited *Metropolitan Magazine*, 1831-32. Founded Polish Association, 1832. Visit to Paris and Algiers, 1834. Returned to London, 1835. Settled in Victoria Square, Pimlico, with niece (Mary Campbell) as companion. Edited *The Scenic Annual* for 1838. To Boulogne for health, June 1843. Died there, 15 June 1844. Buried in Westminster Abbey. WORKS: *The Pleasures of Hope*, 1799; *Annals of Great Britain* (anon.), 1807; *Gertrude of Wyoming*, 1809; *Essay on English Poetry*, 1819; *Specimens of the British Poets* (7 vols.), 1819; *Miscellaneous Poems*, 1824; *Theodric*, 1824 [?] (2nd edn., 1824); *Rectorial Address*, 1827; *Poland*, 1831 [?] (2nd edn., 1831); *Life of Mrs. Siddons* (2 vols.), 1834; *Letters from the South* (2 vols.), 1837; *Life of Petrarch* (2 vols.), 1841; *The Pilgrim of Glencoe*, 1842; *History of Our Own Times* (anon.), 1843. POSTHUMOUS: *Life and Letters*, ed. by W. Beattie, 1849. He *edited*: Byron's Works (with Moore, Scott, etc.), 1835; Shakespeare's Plays, 1838; *Frederick the Great; his Court and Times*, 1842-43. COLLECTED POEMS: in 2 vols., 1810, 1815; in 2 vols., 1828; in 2 vols., 1833, 1837, 1839, 1851 (ed. by W. A. Hill, illustrated by Turner), etc.

R. Farquharson Sharp, 1897, A Dictionary of
English Authors, p. 47

SEE: *Complete Works*, ed. J. Logie Robertson, 1907; William Beattie, *Life and Letters*, 1849-50, 3 v.; J. Cuthbert Hadden, *Thomas Campbell*, 1899.

PERSONAL

When I first saw this eminent person, he gave me the idea of a French Virgil. Not that he was like a Frenchman, much less the French translator of Virgil. I found him as handsome, as the Abbé Delille is said to have been ugly. But he seemed to me to embody a Frenchman's ideal notion of the Latin poet; something a little more cut and dry than I had looked for; compact and elegant, critical and acute, with a consciousness of authorship upon him; a taste over-anxious not to commit itself and refining and diminishing nature as in a drawing-room mirror. This fancy was strengthened in the course of conversation, by his expatiating on the greatness of Racine. . . . His skull was sharply cut and fine; with plenty, according to the phrenologists, both of the reflective and amative organs: and his poetry will bear them out. . . . His face and person were rather on a small scale; his features regular; his eye lively and penetrating; and when he spoke, dimples played about his mouth; which, nevertheless had something restrained and close in it.

Leigh Hunt, 1850, Autobiography, ch. x

Campbell's appearance was more in unison with his writings than is generally the case with authors. He was about thirty-seven years of age; of the middle size, lightly and genteelly made; evidently of a delicate, sensitive organization, with a fine intellectual countenance and a beaming poetic eye. He had now been about twelve years married. Mrs. Campbell still retained much of the personal beauty for which he praises her in his letters written in the early days of matrimony; and her mental qualities seemed equally to justify his eulogies: a rare circumstance, as none are more prone to dupe themselves in affairs of the heart than men of lively imaginations. She was, in fact, a more suitable wife for a poet than poet's wives are apt to be; and for once a son of song had married a reality and not a poetical fiction.

Washington Irving, 1850, Life and Letters of Thomas Campbell,
ed. Beattie, Introduction, vol. I, p. xii

He had never sufficient control over himself, never sufficient command of his intellectual condition and movements, to be sure he might not be tempted, at a moment's warning, to abandon the wide and populous solitude of his little study at Sydenham, or the sweet society of his own Gertrude of Wyoming. . . . for the boisterous good-fellowship . . .of Tom Hill's after-dinner table, with its anomalous ollapodrida of "larking" stockbrokers, laughing punsters, roaring [?] farce-writers, and riotous practical jokers. . . . To sum up this speculation in a word, . . . Tom Campbell was a very good fellow, and a very pleasant one withal; but he prevented Thomas Campbell from being a great poet, though not from doing great things in poetry.

P. G. Patmore, 1854, My Friends and Acquaintance,
vol. I, pp. 146, 148

I remember being told by a personage who was both a very popular writer and a very brilliant converser, that the poet Campbell reminded him of Goldsmith—his conversation was so inferior to his fame. I could not deny it; for I had often met Campbell in general society, and his talk had disappointed me. Three days afterwards, Campbell asked me to come up and sup with him tête-àtête. I did so. I went at ten o'clock. I stayed till dawn; and all my recollections of the most sparkling talk I have ever heard in drawing-rooms, affords nothing to equal the riotous affluence of wit, of humour, of

fancy, of genius, that the great lyrist poured forth in his wondrous monologue. Monologue it was; he had it all to himself.

Edward Bulwer-Lytton, Lord Lytton, 1863-68, Caxtoniana,
Miscellaneous Prose Works, vol. III, p. 114

Campbell's career was deeply weighted in other ways. His only son, whose
childhood had been beautiful beyond expression to the tender father, who
felt, as young parents often do, his own child a revelation from heaven, was
a life-long grief and disappointment to him, and spent most of his life in a
lunatic asylum. His wife died early; and he was left to make up to himself,
as far as he could, by a hundred gentle flirtations, chiefly with ladies under
the age of ten, for the absence of a woman's society, and the bright faces of
children. Some of his innocent adventures in this way are at once amusing
and pathetic.

Margaret O. W. Oliphant, 1882, Literary History of England,
XVIII-XIX Century, vol. II, p. 166

Gertrude of Wyoming (1809)

We rejoice to see once more a polished and pathetic poem in the old style of
English pathos and poetry. This is of the pitch of *The Castle of Indolence,*
and the finer parts of Spenser; with more feeling, in many places, than the
first, and more condensation and diligent finishing than the latter. If the true
tone of nature be not everywhere maintained, it gives place, at least, to art
only, and not to affectation—and, least of all, to affectation of singularity
or rudeness. . . . There are but two noble sorts of poetry—the pathetic, and
the sublime; and we think he has given very extraordinary proofs of his
talents for both.

Francis, Lord Jeffrey, 1809, "Campbell's Gertrude of Wyoming,"
Edinburgh Review, vol. 14, pp. 1, 19

The greatest effort of Campbell's genius, however, was his *Gertrude of Wyoming,* nor is it ever likely to be excelled in its own peculiar style of excellence. It is superior to *The Pleasures of Hope* in the only one thing in which
that poem could be surpassed—purity of diction; while in pathos, and in
imaginative power, it is no whit inferior.

D. M. Moir, 1851-52, Sketches of the Poetical Literature
of the Past Half-Century

The construction of the entire poem is loose and incoherent. Even the love
scenes, which, as Hazlitt says, breathe a balmy voluptuousness of sentiment,
are generally broken off in the middle. Then he was unwise in adopting the
Spenserian stanza. It was quite alien to his style; even Thomson, living long

before the romantic revival, managed it more sympathetically than Campbell. The necessities of the rhyme led Campbell to invert his sentences unduly, to tag his lines for the mere sake of the rhyme, and to use affected archaisms with a quite extraordinary clumsiness. Anything more unlike the sweet, easy, graceful compactness of Spenser could scarcely be imagined. Nor are the characters of the poem altogether successful; indeed, with the single exception of the Indian, they are mere shadows. Gertrude herself makes a pretty portrait; but as Hazlitt has remarked, she cannot for a moment compare with Wordsworth's Ruth, the true infant of the woods and child-nature.

> J. Cuthbert Hadden, 1899, *Thomas Campbell*
> (*Famous Scots Series*), p. 96

GENERAL

The exquisite harmony of his versification is elaborated, perhaps, from the *Castle of Indolence* of Thomson, and the serious pieces of Goldsmith;—and it seems to be his misfortune, not to be able to reconcile himself to any thing which he cannot reduce within the limits of this elaborate harmony. This extreme fastidiousness, and the limitation of his efforts to themes of unbroken tenderness or sublimity, distinguish him from the careless, prolific, and miscellaneous authors of our primitive poetry;—while the enchanting softness of his pathetic passages, and the power and originality of his more sublime conceptions, place him at a still greater distance from the wits, as they truly called themselves, of Charles II. and Queen Anne.

> Francis, Lord Jeffrey, 1811-44, *Contributions to the*
> *Edinburgh Review,* vol. II, p. 295

Campbell's poetry has little need of critical illustration. His chief merit is rhetorical. There is not vagueness of mysticism in his verse. The scenes and feelings he delineates are common to human beings in general, and the impressive style with which these are unfolded, owes its charm to vigor of language and forcible clearness of epithet. Many of his lines ring with a harmonious energy, and seem the offspring of the noblest enthusiasm. This is especially true of his martial lyrics, which in their way are unsurpassed.

> Rufus W. Griswold, 1844, *The Poets and Poetry of England*
> *in the Nineteenth Century,* p. 114

It is by his shorter pieces that Campbell will retain his hold upon posterity. It is difficult to imagine a time in which human hearts will not thrill with patriotic ardour at the recital of "Hohenlinden," "Ye Mariners of England," and the "Battle of the Baltic" or throb with sympathy at the recital of "The Soldier's Dream," and the story of "Lord Ullin's Daughter." There are a lofty tone and rhythmic movement in these ballads which one would think could never fail to please. "The Last Man" is one of the grander of these shorter pieces, and well-nigh rises to the level of its sublime theme. "O'Connor's Child" is a more sustained effort, full of passion, pathos, and poetic fervour. Campbell was at his best when his heart was stirred by patriotic emotion or sympathy for the suffering and the oppressed. Had he written no more than this small group of poems, with "O'Connor's Child" for his longest effort, he would have written himself deep in human hearts, and therefore high in human estimation.

Alfred H. Miles, 1892, The Poets and the Poetry of the Century,
Southey to Shelley, p. 154

The three splendid war-songs . . . the equals, if not the superiors, of anything of the kind in English, and therefore in any language—set him in a position from which he is never likely to be ousted. In a handful of others —*Lochiel,* the exquisite lines on "A Deserted Garden in Argyleshire," with, for some flashes at least the rather over-famed *Exile of Erin, Lord Ullin's Daughter,* and a few more—he also displays very high, though rather unequal and by no means unalloyed, poetical faculty; and *The Last Man,* which, by the way, is the latest of his good things, is not the least. But his best work will go into a very small compass; a single octavo sheet would very nearly hold it, and it was almost all written before he was thirty. . . . It is to be noted that even in Campbell's greatest things there are distinct blemishes, and that these blemishes are greatest in that which in his best parts reach the highest level—*The Battle of the Baltic.* Many third and some tenth rate poets would never have left in their work such things as "The might of England flushed *To anticipate the scene,"* which is half fustian and half nonsense; no very great poet could possibly have been guilty of it. Yet for all this Campbell holds, as has been said, the place of best singer of war in a race and language which are those of the best singers and not the worst fighters in the history of the world—in the race of Nelson and the language of Shakespeare. Not easily shall a man win higher praise than this.

George Saintsbury, 1896, A History of Nineteenth
Century Literature, pp. 93, 94

THOMAS HOOD
1799-1845

Born, in London, 23 May 1799. At school in London. In mercantile house, 1813-15. Health failed. At Dundee, 1815-18; contrib. to local Press from

1814. Articled to firm engravers in London, 1818; but owing to ill-health devoted himself to literature. On staff of *London Mag.,* 1821-23. Married Jane Reynolds, 5 May 1824. Edited *The Gem,* 1829; edited *The Comic Annual,* 1830-42. Financial losses, 1834. Lived at Coblentz, 1835-37; at Ostend, 1837-40. Returned to England, April 1840. Joined staff of *New Monthly Mag.,* 1840; editor, Aug. 1841 to Jan. 1844. "The Song of the Shirt," published in *Punch,* Christmas 1843. Started *Hood's Mag.,* Jan. 1844. Crown Pension of £100 granted to his wife, Nov. 1844. Died, at Hampstead, 3 May 1845. Buried in Kensal Green Cemetery. WORKS: *Odes and Addresses to Great People* (anon.), 1825; *Whims and Oddities* (2 ser.), 1826-27; *National Tales* (2 vols.), 1827; *The Plea of the Midsummer Fairies,* 1827; *The Epping Hunt,* 1829; *The Dream of Eugene Aram,* 1831; *Tylney Hall* (3 vols.), 1834; *Hood's Own,* 1839; *Up the Rhine,* 1840 (2nd edition same year); *Whimsicalities* (2 vols.), 1844. POSTHUMOUS: *Fairy Land,* (with his daughter, Mrs. Broderip), 1861 (1860); *Hood's Own,* 2nd series, ed. by his son, 1861. COLLECTED WORKS: *Poems* (2 vols.), 1846; *Works,* ed. by his son and daughter (10 vols.), 1869-73. LIFE: *Memorials,* by Mrs. Broderip, 1860.

R. Farquharson Sharp, 1897, *A Dictionary of English Authors,* p. 135

SEE: *Complete Poetical Works,* ed. Walter Jerrold, 1906; *Letters,* ed. Leslie A. Marchand, 1945; Walter Jerrold, *Hood: His Life and Times,* 1907.

PERSONAL

I think Hood, perhaps the most taking lion I have seen, perhaps because he does not try to take, and his wit comes out really because it cannot stop in, there is so much behind.

Henry F. Chorley, 1834, *Autobiography, Memoirs and Letters,* p. 99

He possessed the most refined taste and appreciation for all the little luxuries and comforts that make up so much of the enjoyments of life; and the cares and annoyances that would be scarcely perceptible to a stronger and rougher organisation, fell with a double weight on the mind overtasked by such constant and harassing occupation. He literally fulfilled his own words, and was one of the "master minds at journey-work—moral magistrates greatly underpaid—immortals without a living—menders of the human heart, breaking their own—mighty intellects, without their mite." The income his works now produce to his children, might *then* have prolonged his life for many years; although, when we looked on the calm happy face after death, free at last from the painful expression that had almost become habitual to it, we dared not regret the rest so long prayed for, and hardly won.

Frances Freeling (Hood) Broderip, 1860, *Memorials of Thomas Hood,* vol. I, p. 2

When they were getting up a subscription in London for his monument, some of the most distinguished names in England were prominent on the list; but, to my thinking, those small sums that came up from the working-people of Manchester and Bristol and Preston, far outweighed the piles of guineas poured out by the great ones. Some of those little packages, that were sent in from the working-districts, were marked, "From a few poor needle-women," "From seven dressmakers," "From twelve poor men in the coal-mines." The rich gave of their abundance to honor the wit; the Englishman of genius, the great author; but the poor women of Britain remembered who it was that sang *The Song of the Shirt,* and *The Bridge of Sighs,* and, down there in their dark dens of sorrow and poverty, they resolved to send up their mite, though coined out of heart's blood, for the good man's monument. They had heard all about their dying friend, who had been pleading their cause through so many years. They knew that he had been sending out from his sick-chamber lessons of charity and forbearance, reminding Wealth of Want, Feasting of Fasting, and Society of Solitude and Despair.

James T. Fields, 1885, "Thomas Hood," Some Princes, Authors and Statesmen of Our Time, ed. Parton, p. 154·

GENERAL

Mr. Hood possesses an original wealth of humour, invention and an odd sort of wit that should rather be called whimsicality, or a faculty of the "high fantastic." Among comic writers he is one of those who also possess genuine pathos; it is often deep, and of much tenderness, occasional of expression, and full of melancholy memories. The predominating characteristics of his genius are humorous fancies grafted upon melancholy impressions.

Richard H. Horne, 1844, A New Spirit of the Age

We look upon this writer as a quaint masquer—as wearing above a manly and profound nature, a fantastic and deliberate disguise of folly. He reminds us of Brutus, cloaking under pretended idiocy, a stern and serious design, which burns his breast, but which he chooses in this way only to disclose. Or, he is like Hamlet—able to form a magnificent purpose, but, from constitutional weakness, not able to incarnate it in effective action. A deep message has come to him from the heights of his nature, but, like the ancient prophet, he is forced to cry out, "I cannot speak—I am a child!" Certainly there was, at the foundation of Hood's soul, a seriousness, which all his puns and mummeries could but indifferently conceal. Jacquez, in the forest of Arden, mused not with a profounder pathos, or in quainter language, upon the sad pageant of humanity, than does he; and yet, like him, his "lungs" are ever ready to "crow like a chanticleer" at the sight of its grotesquer absurdities. Verily, the goddess of melancholy owes a deep grudge to the mirthful magician, who carried off such a promising victory.

George Gilfillan, 1847, "Thomas Hood," *Tait's Edinburgh Magazine*, vol. 14, p. 69

Hood's pathos culminates in *The Song of the Shirt, The Lay of the Laborer,* and *The Bridge of Sighs.* These are marvellous lyrics. In spirit and in form they are singular and remarkable. We cannot think of any poems which more show the mystic enchantment of genius. How else was a ragged sempstress in a squalid garret made immortal, nay, made universal, made to stand for an entire sisterhood of wretchedness? Here is direst poverty, blear-eyed sorrow, dim and dismal suffering,—nothing of the romantic. A stern picture it is, which even the softer touches render sterner; still there is nought in it that revolts or shocks; it is deeply poetic, calls into passionate action the feelings of reverence and pity, and has all the dignity of tragedy. Even more wonderful is the transformation that a rustic mind undergoes in *The Lay of the Laborer,* in which a peasant out of work personifies, with eloquent impressiveness, the claims and calamities of toiling manhood. But an element of the sublime is added in *The Bridge of Sighs.* In that we have the truly tragic; for we have in it the union of guilt, grief, despair, and death. An angel from heaven, we think, could not sing a more gentle dirge, or one more pure; yet the ordinary associations suggested by the corpse of the poor, ruined, self-murdered girl are such as to the prudish and fastidious would not allow her to be mentioned, much less bring her into song.

Henry Giles, 1860, "Thomas Hood," *Atlantic Monthly*, vol. 6, p. 522

Like other men, Hood had his "fixed ideas" in life—permanent thoughts and convictions, in behalf of which he could become pugnacious or even savage, or under the excitement of which every show of humour would fall off from him, and he would appear as a man purely sorrowful and serious. The sentiment of Anti-Pharisaism may be regarded as traditional in all men of popular literary genius; and back from our own days to those of Burns and still farther, British Literature has abounded with expressions of it, each more or less powerful in its time, but not superseding the necessity of another, and still another, in the times following. Almost last in the long list of these poets of Anti-Pharisaism comes the name of Hood. His writings are full of this sentiment, and especially of protests against over-rigid Sabbatarianism. On no subject did he so systematically and resolutely exert his powers of sarcasm and wit; and perhaps the English language does not contain any single poem from which the opponents of extreme Sabbatarianism and of what is called religious formality in general can borrow more pungent quotations, or which is really in its way a more eloquent assertion of personal intellectual freedom, than the *Ode to Rae Wilson, Esquire.*

David Masson, 1860, "Thomas Hood,"
Macmillan's Magazine, vol. 2, p. 323

A genius of a high class cutting capers and making jokes, an author of the humour and deeper calibre of the highest Elizabethan poets, and with the gentle satire of Touchstone, an essayist in his way as subtile as Charles Lamb, a tale-maker with the *drolatique* power and capability of Rabelais, and a poet with much of the sweetness and more than the pathos of Keats; —these together would make up Thomas Hood.

James Hain Friswell, 1869, *Essays on English Writers,* p. 348

Hood was not one of those men of commanding intellect who arise but once or twice at most in a nation's history. He did not signalize himself by being the first to climb the slippery steps of Pisgah, and catch sublime glimpses of the promised land with which to gladden the heart of the world. He is no cold unapproachable idol of the intellect—to be worshipped from afar with awe and trembling. Rather is he enshrined amid the Lares and Penates of our hearts—our household favorites—our Charley Lambs and Sir Philip Sidneys; a kind, genial, honest-hearted man of genius, whom one feels it is good to know and pleasant to remember, whose laugh has a hearty ring wherewith to blow away the cobwebs of sorrow and care, and the shake of whose hand does one's heart good. There have been three or four greater writers in our nation's history, and a few more as great, but there has been no one whose noble efforts on behalf of the poor, the outcast, and the sinning, will serve to embalm his memory and his works in a kindlier affection and regard than Thomas Hood, "the darling of the English heart."

J. Fraser, 1871, "Thomas Hood," *The Westminster Review,*
vol. 95, p. 354

Whether, under favourable circumstances, he would have produced more work of a high character is a question that it is scarcely profitable to discuss; but it is manifest that during his life-time the somewhat coarse-palated public welcomed most keenly not so much his best as his second-best. The "Tom Hood" they cared for was not the delicate and fanciful author of the *Plea of the Midsummer Fairies,* but the Hood of *Miss Kilmansegg and her Precious Leg,*—the master of broad-grin and equivoque, the delightful parodist, the impressible and irresistible joker and Merry-Andrew. It is not to be denied that much of his work in this way is excellent of its kind, admirable for its genuine drollery and whim, having often at its core, more-over, that subtle sense of the *lacrimæ rerum,* which lends a piquancy of sadness and almost a quality of permanence to much of our modern jesting. But the rest!—the larger part! Nothing except the record of his over-strained, over-burdened life can enable us to understand how the author of the *Ode to Rae Wilson,* the *Lament for Chivalry,* and the lines *On a distant Prospect of Clapham Academy* could ever have produced such mechanical and melancholy mirth as much of that which has been preserved appears to be. Yet his worst work is seldom without some point; it is better than the best of many others; and, with all its drawbacks, it is at least always pure. It should be remembered too that the fashions of fun pass away like other fashions.

Austin Dobson, 1880, The English Poets, ed. Ward, vol. IV, p. 531

Hood, it is true, was too great a man to be dismissed as merely a writer of the transition; yet, just because of his greatness, his history shows better than that of any other man how earnestness was discouraged and triviality fostered. Seldom have so great poetic gifts been so squandered—with no dishonour to Hood—on mere puns. The poet, as an early critic pointed out, was a man of essentially serious mind; but he had to earn bread for himself and his children, and as jesting paid, while serious poetry did not, he was compelled to jest. . . . Perhaps the most original fruit of Hood's genius is *Miss Kilmansegg,* which conceals under a grotesque exterior deep feeling and effective satire. It has been sometimes ranked as Hood's greatest work; and if comparison be made with his longer pieces only, or if we look principally to the uniqueness of the poem, the judgment will hardly be disputed; but probably the popular instinct which has seized upon *The Song of the Shirt* and *The Bridge of Sighs,* and the criticism which exalts *The Haunted House,* are in this instance sounder.

Hugh Walker, 1897, The Age of Tennyson, pp. 54, 55

EMILY BRONTE
1818-1848

Emily Brontë was born at Hartshead-cum-Clifton, near Leeds, in 1818, and lived at the parsonage at Haworth from 1820 to her death. The monotony of this existence was broken only by a brief attempt to be a governess and by a short stay at Brussels in 1842, all exile from home being excessively painful and hurtful to her. She died of consumption at Haworth on the 19th of December, 1848. She published, in conjunction with her sisters, *Poems by Currer, Ellis, and Acton Bell,* in 1846, and, alone, the novel of *Wuthering Heights* in 1847.

Thomas Humphry Ward, 1880, ed., *The English Poets,*
vol. IV, p. 581

SEE: *Heather Edition of the Works of the Brontë Sisters,* ed. Phyllis *Bentley,* 1949, 6 v.; *Complete Poems,* ed. Philip Henderson, 1951; *Gondal Poems,* ed. H. Brown and J. Mott, 1938; F. E. Ratchford, *The Brontës' Web of Childhood,* 1941; also see *The Brontës: Their Lives Recorded by Their Contemporaries,* ed. E. M. Delafield, 1935.

PERSONAL

> No coward soul is mine,
> No trembler in the world's storm-troubled sphere:
> I see Heaven's glories shine,
> And faith shines equal, arming me from fear,

Emily Brontë, 1848, *Last Lines*

> . . . she
> (How shall I sing her?) whose soul
> Knew no fellow for might,
> Passion, vehemence, grief,
> Daring, since Byron died,
> That world-famed son of fire—she, who sank
> Baffled, unknown, self-consumed;
> Whose too bold dying song
> Stirr'd, like a clarion-blast, my soul.

Matthew Arnold, 1855-85, *Haworth Churchyard,* April

The feeling which in Charlotte partook of something of the nature of an affection, was, with Emily, more of a passion. Some one speaking of her to me, in a careless kind of strength of expression, said, "she never showed regard to any human creature; all her love was reserved for animals." The helplessness of an animal was its passport to Charlotte's heart; the fierce, wild, intractability of its nature was what often recommended it to Emily. Speaking of her dead sister, the former told me that from her many traits in Shirley's character were taken; her way of sitting on the rug reading, with her arm round her rough bull-dog's neck; her calling to a strange dog, running past, with hanging head and lolling tongue, to give it a merciful draught of water, its maddened snap at her, her nobly stern presence of mind, going right into the kitchen, and taking up one of Tabby's red-hot Italian irons to sear the bitten place, and telling on one, till the danger was well-nigh over, for fear of the terrors that might beset their weaker minds. All this, looked upon as a well-invented fiction in *Shirley,* was written by Charlotte with streaming eyes; it was the literal true account of what Emily had done.

Elizabeth Cleghorn Gaskell, 1857, *Life of Charlotte Brontë,* ch. xii

Not even the unstinted praise of three great and very dissimilar poets has given to Emily Brontë her due rank in popular esteem. Her work is not universally acceptable, even to imaginative readers; her personality is almost repulsive to many who have schooled themselves to endure the vehemence of genius but not its ominous self-restraint. Most people were afraid of Emily Brontë's "whitening face and set mouth" when she was alive, and even now that she is dead her memory seems to inspire more terror than affection. Against an instinctive repugnance it is in vain to reason, and in discussing her poetical quality we must assume that her power has at least been felt and not disliked by the reader, since "you must love her, ere to you she should seem worthy to be loved." Those who have come under the spell of her genius will expect no apology for her intellectual rebellion, her stoic harshness of purpose, her more than manlike strength. She was a native blossom of those dreary and fascinating moorlands of which Charlotte has given, in a few brilliant phrases, so perfect a description, and like the acrid heaths and gentians that flourish in the peat, to transplant her was to kill her. Her actions, like her writings, were strange, but consistent in their strangeness. Even the dreadful incident of her death, which occurred as she stood upright in the little parlour at Haworth, refusing to go to bed, but just leaning one hand upon the table, seems to me to be no unfit ending for a life so impatient of constraint from others, so implacable in its slavery to its own principles.

Edmund Gosse, 1880, *The English Poets,* ed. Ward, vol. IV, p. 581

In 1833 Emily was nearly fifteen, a tall, long-armed girl, full grown, elastic of tread; with a slight figure that looked queenly in her best dresses, but loose and boyish when she slouched over the moors whistling to her dogs, and taking long strides over the rough earth. A tall, thin, loose-jointed girl—not ugly, but with irregular features and a pallid, thick complexion. Her dark-brown hair was naturally beautiful, and in later days looked well loosely fastened with a tall comb at the back of her head; but in 1833 she wore it in an unbecoming tight curl and frizz. She had very beautiful eyes of haze color. . . . Two lives went on side by side in her heart, neither ever mingling with or interrupting the other. Practical housewife with capable hands, dreamer of strange horrors: each self was independent of the companion to which it was linked by day and night. People in those days knew her but as she seemed—"t' Vicar's Emily"—a shy awkward girl, never teaching in Sunday-school like her sisters, never talking with the villagers

like merry Branwell, but very good and hearty in helping the sick and
distressed: not pretty in the village estimation—a "slinky lass," no prim,
trim little body like pretty Anne, nor with Charlotte Brontë's taste in dress;
just a clever lass with a spirit of her own. So the village judged her. At
home they loved her with her strong feelings, untidy frocks, indomitable
will and ready contempt for the commonplace; she was appreciated as a
dear and necessary member of the household. Of Emily's deeper self, her
violent genius, neither friend nor neighbor dreamed in those days.

A. Mary F. Robinson, 1883, *Emily Brontë*
(Famous Women), pp. 65, 69

Wuthering Heights (1847)

I trust you have not, as we have, wasted your time on "that little family in
Hell," living and dying at *Wuthering Heights*. It is a most signal waste of
talent. There is a certain resemblance to *Jane Eyre,* like a family look; the
energy of thought and style, the northern mind as well as air that breathes
through it, the intimate and masterly acquaintance with a location and
coterie, and exclusion from the world, the remarkable directness of style,
are all qualities peculiar, and marvelously like *Jane Eyre,* so that I think
the author must be her brother, the masculine of her masculine mind.

Catharine M. Sedgwick, 1848, *To Mrs. K. S. Minot,* May 27;
Life and Letters, ed. Dewey, p. 307

Wuthering Heights was hewn in a wild workshop, with simple tools, out of
homely materials. The statuary found a granite block on a solitary moor;
gazing thereon he saw how from the crag might be elicited a head, savage,
swart, sinister: a form moulded with at least one element of grandeur—
power. He wrought with a rude chisel, and from no model but the vision of
his meditations. With time and labour the crag took human shape; and
there it stands, colossal, dark, and frowning, half statue, half rock; in the
former sense, terrible and goblin-like; in the latter, almost beautiful, for its
colouring is of mellow gray, and moorland moss clothes it; and heath, with
its blooming bells and balmy fragrance, grows faithfully close to the giant's
foot.

Charlotte Brontë, 1851, *Wuthering Heights,* Preface

Emily Brontë—for it is now time that we should say something of the two
other persons in this remarkable trio—was, in certain respects, the most
extraordinary of the three sisters. She has this distinction at any rate, that
she has written a book which stands as completely alone in the language as
does the *Paradise Lost* or the *Pilgrim's Progress.* . . . Its power is absolutely

Titanic: from the first page to the last it reads like the intellectual throes of a giant. It is fearful, it is true, and perhaps one of the most unpleasant books ever written: but we stand in amaze at the almost incredible fact that it was written by a slim country girl who would have passed in a crowd as an insignificant person, and who had had little or no experience of the ways of the world. . . . We challenge the world to produce another work in which the whole atmosphere seems so surcharged with suppressed electricity, and bound in with the blackness of tempest and desolation.

George Barnett Smith, 1875, "The Brontës,"
Poets and Novelists, pp. 236, 239, 240

Twice or thrice especially the details of deliberate or passionate brutality in Heathcliff's treatment of his victims make the reader feel for a moment as though he were reading a police report or even a novel by some French "naturalists" of the latest and brutallest order. But the pervading atmosphere of the book is so high and healthy that the effect even of those "vivid and fearful scenes" which impaired the rest of Charlotte Brontë is almost at once neutralized—we may hardly say softened, but sweetened, dispersed, and transfigured—by the general impression of noble purity and passionate straightforwardness, which removes it at once and forever from any such ugly possibility of association or comparison. The whole work is not more incomparable in the effect of its atmosphere or landscape than in the peculiar note of its wild and bitter pathos; but most of all is it unique in the special and distinctive character of its passion. The love which devours life itself, which devastates the present and desolates the future with unquenchable and raging fire, has nothing less pure in it than flame or sunlight. And this passionate and ardent chastity is utterably and unmistakably spontaneous and unconscious. Not till the story is ended, not till the effect of it has been thoroughly absorbed and digested, does the reader even perceive the simple and natural absence of any grosser element, any hint or suggstion of a baser alloy in the ingredients of its human emotion than in the splendour of lightning or the roll of a gathered wave.

Algernon Charles Swinburne, 1883-86, Miscellanies, p. 269

As to the capability of Branwell to write Wuthering Heights, not much need be said here. Those who read this book will see that, despite his weaknesses and his follies, Branwell was, indeed, unfortunate in having to bear the penalty, in ceaseless open discussion, of "une fanfaronnade des vices qu'il n'avait pas," and that, moreover, his memory has been darkened, and his acts misconstrued, by sundry writers, who have endeavoured to find in his character the source of the darkest passages in the works of his sisters. Far from being hopelessly a miserable fellow," an "unprincipled dreamer," an "unnerved and garrulous prodigal," as we have been told he was, he had, in fact, within him, an abundance of worthy ambition, a modest confidence in his own ability, which he was never known to vaunt, and a just pride in the celebrity of his family, which, it may be trusted, will remove from him, at any rate, the imputation of a lack of moral power to do anything good or forcible at all. Those who have heard fall from the lips of Branwell Brontë —and they are few now—all those weird stories, strange imaginings, and vivid and brilliant disquisitions on the life of the people of the West Riding, will recognize that there was at least no opposition, but rather an affinity, between the tendency of his thoughts and those of the author of "Wuthering Heights."

Francis A. Leyland, 1886, *The Brontë Family with Special Reference to Patrick Branwell Brontë,* vol. II, p. 191

The heroines of Emily Brontë have not the artistic completeness of Charlotte Brontë's. They are blocked out with hysterical force, and in their character there is something elemental, as if, like the man who beat and browbeat them, they too were close to the savagery of nature. The sort of super-naturalism, which appears here and there in their story, wants the refine-of the telepathy and presentiment which play a part in Jane Eyre, but it is still more effectual in the ruder clutch which it lays upon the fancy. In her dealing with the wild passion of Heathcliff for the first Catharine, Emily Brontë does not keep even such slight terms with convention as Charlotte does in the love of Rochester and Jane Eyre; but this fierce longing, stated as it were in its own language, is still farther from anything that corrupts or tempts; it is as wholesome and decent as a thunder-storm, in the conscious-ness of the witness. The perversities of the mutual attraction of the lovers are rendered without apparent sense on the part of the author that they can seem out of nature, so deeply does she feel them to be in nature, and there is no hint from her that they need any sort of proof.

William Dean Howells, 1900, "Heroines of Nineteenth Century Fiction," *Harper's Bazar,* vol. 33, p. 2224

POEMS

Some of Emily's poems in this book are full of such original and intense— though hardly attractive—writing as gives her quite a unique and lofty posi-tion among our poets. The note of these poems comes very near despair, but such is the strength of Emily's character that it is rather a desperate courage. Self-dependent in every act and thought of her life, she will recog-nise nothing in the universe but the beauty of the external world and the strength of her own intellectual being. She expresses no hope in the future or

in a God other than a vague pantheistic hope; she throws abroad small sympathy for her fellow-beings. The history of the world does not entice her to be its prophetess; she breathes into her poetry only her individual self, but expresses that self so nobly that we find in some of her verses the elements of such a character as in different circumstances might have turned her into a Maid of Orleans, or a Madam Roland. The soul of Emily Brontë was ever
> "Struggling fierce toward Heaven's free wilderness."

with strong wings, and with the loneliness of wings.

Eric S. Robertson, 1883, English Poetesses, p. 324

Her poetry, in general less powerful, is more pleasing than her fiction; harsh and forbidding as her view of life seems at first, it gains upon us as we realise her proud superiority to external circumstances, and the passionate affection for those she really loves, which redeems her unamiability towards the rest. . . . Almost all the poetry which Emily Brontë published during her lifetime was of this character, though not always attaining the same careless beauty, graceful in its apparent negligence. Not until nigh to death did she compose a strain of quite another sort, which, if it were just to judge her solely by one supreme inspiration, would place her above every other female lyrist since Sappho. The grandeur and eloquence of her last verses have in our judgement never been rivalled by any English poetess: the question whether she could have maintained herself at such an elevation, were it capable of an answer, would help to elucidate the deeper problem how far poetical inspiration is the result of favourable conditions, and how far it is a visitation from above. It must remain for ever unanswered.

Richard Garnett, 1892, The Poets and the Poetry of the Century,
Joanna Baillie to Mathilde Blind, ed. Miles, pp. 284, 285

EDGAR ALLAN POE
1809-1849

January 19, 1809—Born at Boston, Massachusetts. December 8, 1811—His mother died at Richmond, Virginia. 1811—[Edgar Poe adopted by Mr. John Allan]. 1816—Brought to Europe, and placed at school in Stoke Newington. 1821—Returns to the United States. 1822—Placed at school in Richmond, Virginia. February 1, 1826—Enters University of Virginia. [Signs matriculation book, 14th February 1826]. December 15, 1826—Leaves University of Virginia. 1827—*Tamerlane and other Poems* printed at Boston. June? 1827—Departs for Europe. March, 1829—Returns to Richmond, Virginia. 1829—Publishes *Al Aaraaf, Tamerlane, and Minor Poems,* at Baltimore. July 1, 1830—Admitted as cadet to West Point Military Academy. March 6, 1831—Dismissed the Military Academy. March,

1831—Publishes *Poems,* New York. Autumn, 1833—Gains prize from *Saturday Visitor* (Baltimore). December, 1835—Editor of the *Southern Literary Messenger* (Richmond, Virginia). May 16, 1836—Married to his cousin, Virginia Clemm, at Richmond. [Virginia C. born August 13th, 1822]. January, 1837—Resigns editorship of *Southern Literary Messenger.* 1837-8—Resides in New York. July, 1838—*Arthur Gordon Pym* published, New York and London. Autumn, 1838—Removes to Philadelphia. July, 1839—Editor of the *Gentleman's Magazine,* Philadelphia. 1840—*Tales of the Grotesque and Arabesque* published, Philadelphia. 1840—*The Conchologist's First Book* published, Philadelphia. June, 1840 —Resigns editorship of *Gentleman's Magazine.* January, 1841—Editor of *Graham's Magazine,* Philadelphia. April, 1842, Resigns editorship of *Graham's Magazine.* Spring, 1843—Gains $100 prize for "The Gold Bug." Autumn, 1844—Sub-editor of the *Evening Mirror,* New York. January 29, 1845—"The Raven" published in *Evening Mirror.* February 28, 1845— Lectures in New York Historical Society's room. March 8, 1845—Joint- editor of the *Broadway Journal.* July, 1845—*Tales* published, New York and London. July, 1845—Sole-editor of the *Broadway Journal.* November 1, 1845—Proprietor of *Broadway Journal.* November, 1845—*The Raven and Other Poems* published, New York and London. Winter, 1845—Lec- tures at Boston Lyceum. December, 1845—*Broadway Journal* disposed of. February, 1846—*The Literati* begun in Godey's *Lady's Book.* June 23, 1846—*Evening Mirror* publishes libel. June 28, 1846—"Reply" to libel in Philadelphia *Saturday Gazette.* Summer, 1846—Removes to Fordham. January 30, 1847—His wife dies. February 17, 1847—Gains libel suit against *Evening Mirror.* February 3, 1848—Lectures in New York His- torical Society's room. Summer, 1848—"Eureka" published, New York. Summer, 1848—Richmond, Virginia, revisited. Summer, 1848—Lectures at Lowell, Mass., and Providence, R. I. October, 1848—Betrothed to Mrs. Whitman. December, 1848—Engagement with Mrs. Whitman broken off. June 30, 1849—Departs for the South. Autumn, 1849—In Richmond and neighbourhood. October 7, 1849—Dies at Baltimore, Maryland. Novem- ber 17, 1875—Monument Inaugurated, Baltimore.

> John H. Ingram, 1880, *Edgar Allan Poe, His Life,*
> *Letters and Opinions,* vol. I, p. xi

SEE: *Works,* ed. George E. Woodberry and Edmund C. Stedman, 1894-5, 10 v.; *Complete Works,* ed. James A. Harrison, 1902, 17 v.; Killis Camp- bell, *The Poems of Edgar Allan Poe,* 1917; *Letters,* ed. J. W. Ostrom, 1948, 2 v.; Arthur H. Quinn, *Edgar Allan Poe: A Critical Biography,* 1941; Edward Davidson, *Poe: A Critical Study,* 1957.

PERSONAL

Dear Sir—Poe did right in referring to me. He is very clever with his pen— classical and scholarlike. He wants experience and direction, but I have no doubt he can be made very useful to you. And, poor fellow! he is *very* poor. I told him to write something for every number of your magazine, and that you might find it to your advantage to give him some permanent employ.

He has a volume of very bizarre tales in the hands of—, in Philadelphia, who for a year past has been promising to publish them. This young fellow is highly imaginative, and a little given to the *terrific*. He is at work on a tragedy, but I have turned him to drudging upon whatever may make money, and I have no doubt you and he will find your account in each other.

John Pendleton Kennedy, 1835, Letter to J. W. White, April 13;
Poe Memorial, ed. Rice, p. 13

He really does not possess one tithe of greatness which he seems to regard as an uncomfortable burden. He mistakes coarse abuse for polished invective, and vulgar insinuation for sly satire. He is not alone thoroughly unprincipled, base, and depraved, but silly, vain, and ignorant,—not alone an assassin in morals, but a quack in literature. His frequent quotations from languages of which he is entirely ignorant, and his consequent blunders, expose him to ridicule; while his cool plagiarisms, from known or forgotten writers, excite the public amazement. He is a complete evidence of his own assertion, that "no spectacle can be more pitiable than that of a man without the commonest school education, busying himself in attempts to instruct mankind on topics of polite literature."

Thomas Dunn English, 1846, New York Evening Mirror

Edgar Allen Poe is dead. He died in Baltimore on Sunday, October 7th. This announcement will startle many, but few will be grieved by it. . . . His conversation was at times almost supra-mortal in its eloquence. His voice was modulated with astonishing skill, and his large and variably expressive eyes looked repose or shot fiery tumult into theirs who listened, while his own face glowed, or was changeless in pallor, as his imagination quickened his blood or drew it back frozen to his heart. His imagery was from the worlds which no mortals can see but with the vision of genius.—Suddenly starting from a proposition, exactly and sharply defined, in terms of utmost simplicity and clearness, he rejected the forms of customary logic, and by a crystalline process of accretion, built up his acular demonstrations in forms of gloomiest and ghastliest grandeur, or in those of the most airy and delicious beauty—so minutely and distinctly, yet so rapidly, that the attention which was yielded to him was chained till it stood among his wonderful creations—till he himself dissolved the spell, and brought his hearers back to common and base existence, by vulgar fancies or exhibitions of the ignoblest passion. He was at all times a dreamer—dwelling in ideal realms —in heaven or hell—peopled with the creatures and the accidents of his brain. He walked the streets, in madness or melancholy, with lips moving in indistinct curses, or with eyes upturned in passionate prayer (never for himself, for he felt, or professed to feel, that he was already damned, but) for their happiness who at the moment were objects of his idolatry;—or, with his glances introverted to a heart gnawed with anguish, and with a face shrouded in gloom, he would brave the wildest storms; and all night, with drenched garments and arms beating the winds and rains, would speak as if to spirits that at such times only could be evoked by him from the Aidenn, close by whose portals his disturbed soul sought to forget the ills to which his constitution subjected him—close by the Aidenn where were those he loved—the Aidenn which he might never see, but in fitful glimpses, as its gates opened to receive the less fiery and more happy natures whose destiny to sin did not involve the doom of death.

Rufus Wilmot (Ludwig) Griswold, 1849, "The Death of
Edgar A. Poe," New York Tribune

I can sincerely say, that although I have frequently *heard* of aberrations on his part from the "straight and narrow path," I have never *seen* him otherwise than gentle, generous, well-bred, and fastidiously refined. To a sensitive and delicately-nurtured woman, there was a peculiar and irresistible charm in the chivalric, graceful, and almost tender reverence with which he invariably approached all women who won his respect. It was this which first commanded and always retained my regard for him. . . . It was in his own simple yet poetical home, that to me the character of Edgar Poe appeared in it most beautiful light. Playful, affectionate, witty, alternately docile and wayward as a petted child—for his young, gentle, and idolized wife, and for all who came, he had, even in the midst of his most harassing literary duties, a kind word, a pleasant smile, a graceful and courteous attention. At his desk, beneath the romantic picture of his loved and lost Lenore, he would sit, hour after hour, patient, assiduous, and uncomplaining, tracing, in an exquisitely clear chirography, and with almost superhuman swiftness, the lightning thoughts—the "rare and radiant" fancies as they flashed through his wonderful and ever-wakeful brain.

Frances Sargent Osgood, 1850, "Reminiscences of Poe by
Griswold," International Magazine, vol. I

Literature with him was religion; and he, its high-priest, with a whip of scorpions scourged the money-changers from the temple. In all else he had the docility and kind-heartedness of a child. No man was more quickly touched by a kindness—none more prompt to atone for an injury. For three or four years I knew him intimately, and for eighteen months saw him almost daily; much of the time writing or conversing at the same desk; knowing all his hopes, his fears and little annoyances of life, as well as his high-hearted struggle with adverse fate—yet he was always the same polished gentleman—the quiet, unobtrusive, thoughtful scholar—the devoted husband—frugal in his personal expenses—punctual and unwearied in his industry—*and the soul of honor* in all his transactions.

George R. Graham, 1850, *To N. P. Willis,* Feb. 2;
Graham's Magazine

In character he was certainly one of the strangest anomalies in the history of mankind. . . . He was no more a gentleman than he was a saint. His heart was as rotten as his conduct was infamous. He knew not what the terms honor and honorable meant. He had absolutely no virtue or good quality, unless you call remorse a virtue, and despair a grace. Some have called him mad; but we confess we see no evidence of this in his history. He showed himself, in many instances, a cool, calculating, deliberate blackguard. His intellect was of the clearest, sharpest, and most decisive kind. A large heart has often beat in the bosom of a debauchee; but Poe had not one spark of genuine tenderness, unless it were for his wife, whose heart, nevertheless, and constitution, he broke—hurrying her to a premature grave, that he might write *Annabel Lee* and *The Raven!* . . . He died, as he had lived, a raving, cursing, self-condemned, conscious cross between the fiend and the genius, believing nothing, hoping nothing, loving nothing, fearing nothing— himself his own god and his own devil—a solitary wretch, who had cut off every bridge that connected him with the earth around and the heavens above. This, however, let us say in his favor—he has died "alone in his iniquity;" he has never, save by his example (so far as we know his work), sought to shake faith or sap morality. His writings may be morbid, but they are pure. . . . He has gone far away from the misty mid-region of Weir; his dreams of cosmogonies have been tested by the searching light of eternity's truth; his errors have received the reward that was meet; and we cannot but say, ere we close, peace even to the well-nigh putrid dust of Edgar A. Poe.

George Gilfillan, 1855, *A Third Gallery of Portraits,* pp. 327, 330, 338

The next number of the *Saturday Visitor* [1833] contained the "MS. Found in a Bottle," and announced the author. My office, in those days, was in the building still occupied by the Mechanics' Bank, and I was seated at my desk on the Monday following the publication of the tale, when a gentleman entered and introduced himself as the writer, saying that he came to thank me, as one of the committee, for the award in his favor. Of this interview, the only one I ever had with Mr. Poe, my recollection is very distinct indeed, and it requires but a small effort of imagination to place him before me now, as plainly almost as I see any one of my audience. He was, if anything, be- low the middle size, and yet could not be described as a small man. His figure was remarkably good, and he carried himself erect and well, as one who had been trained to it. He was dressed in black, and his frock-coat was buttoned to the throat, where it met the black stock, then almost universally worn. Not a particle of white was visible. Coat, hat, boots and gloves had very evidently seen their best days, but so far as mending and brushing go, everything had been done, apparently, to make them presentable. On most men his clothes would have looked shabby and seedy, but there was something about this man that prevented one from criticising his garments, and the details I have mentioned were only recalled afterwards. The impression made, however, was that the award in Mr. Poe's favor was not inopportune. *Gentleman* was written all over him. His manner was easy and quiet, and although he came to return thanks for what he regarded as deserving them, there was nothing obsequious in what he said or did. His features I am unable to describe in detail. His forehead was high and remarkable, for the great development at the temple. This was the characteristic of his head, which you noticed at once, and which I have never forgotten. The expression of his face was grave, almost sad, except when he was engaged in conversation, when it became animated and changeable. His voice, I remember, was very pleasing in its tone and well modulated, almost rhythmical, and his words were well chosen and unhesitating.

John H. B. Latrobe, 1875, "Reminiscences of Poe,"
Poe Memorial, ed. Rice, p. 60

There is no necessity for us to touch heavily upon this terrible *trait* in the character of Edgar Poe—this sad, sickening infirmity of his "lonesome latter years;" his error, if such it may be styled—the impulse which blindly impelled him to his destruction—injured no one but himself; but certainly no one before or since has suffered so severely in character as a consequence of such a fault. Other children of genius have erred far worse than Poe ever did, inasmuch as their derelictions have injured others; but with them the world has dealt leniently, accepting *their* genius as a compensation. But for poor Edgar Poe, who wronged no one but himself, the world, misled greatly, it is true, as to his real character, has hitherto, had no mercy. The true story of his life has now been told; henceforth let his errors be forgotten, and to his name be assigned that place which is due to it in the glory-roll of fame.

John H. Ingram, 1876, "A Biographical Sketch,"
Poe Memorial, ed. Rice, p. 35

Poe's eyes, indeed, were his most striking feature, and it was to these that his face owed its peculiar attraction. I have never seen other eyes at all resembling them. They were large, with long, jetblack lashes,—the iris dark steel-gray, possessing a crystalline clearness and transparency, through which the jet-black pupil was seen to expand and contract with every shade of thought and emotion, I observed that the lids never contracted, as is so usual in most persons, especially when talking; but his gaze was ever full, open, and unshrinking. His usual expression was dreamy and sad. He had a way of sometimes turning a slightly askance look upon some person who was not observing him, and with a quiet, steady gaze, appear to be mentally taking the caliber of the unsuspecting subject.

Mrs. Susan A. T. Weiss, 1878, "Last Day of Edgar A. Poe,"
Scribner's Magazine, vol. 15, p. 711

All that makes Poe's career least defensible—his vices, quarrels, desperate straits, attempted suicides, ardent and sometimes simultaneous love-affairs —all these afford great resources for the biographer, who has reason to be grateful for a subject who did not dwell in decencies for ever. It is almost amusing to see how each new memoir of Poe professes to be the first to tell the real story of his life; and how each, while denouncing the obvious malice of Griswold, ends by re-establishing almost all the damaging facts which Griswold left only half-proved. If Poe fared ill at the hands of his enemy, he has fared worse, on the whole, at those of his friends.

Thomas Wentworth Higginson, 1880, "Recent Works on
Edgar Poe," *The Nation,* vol. 31, p. 360

In a dream I once had, I saw a vessel on the sea, at midnight, in a storm. It was no great full-rigged ship, nor majestic steamer, steering firmly through the gale, but seemed one of those superb little schooner yachts I had often seen lying anchored, rocking so jauntily, in the waters around New York, or up Long Island Sound; now flying uncontrolled with torn sails and broken spars through the wild sleet and winds and waves of the night. On deck was a slender, slight, beautiful figure, a dim man, apparently enjoying all the terror, the murk, and the dislocation of which he was the centre and the victim. That figure of my lurid dream might stand for Edgar Poe, his spirit, his fortunes, and his poems—themselves all lurid dreams.

Walt Whitman, 1882, "Edgar Poe's Significance,"
The Critic, vol. 2, p. 147

I now felt it necessary that I should determine the nature of his disease and make out a correct diagnosis, so as to treat him properly. I did not then know but he might have been drinking, and so to determine the matter, I said, "Mr. Poe, you are extremely weak, pulse very low; I will give you a glass of toddy." He opened wide his eyes, and fixed them so steadily upon me, and with such anguish in them that I had to look from him to the wall beyond the bed. He then said, "Sir, if I thought its potency would transport me to the Elysian bowers of the undiscovered spirit world, I would not take it." "I will then administer an opiate, to give you sleep and rest," I said. Then he rejoined, "Twin sister, spectre to the doomed and crazed mortals of earth and perdition." I was entirely shorn of my strength. Here was a patient supposed to have been drunk, very drunk, and yet refuses to take liquor. The ordinary response is, "Yes, Doctor, give me a little to strengthen my nerves." I found there was no tremor of his person, no unsteadiness of his nerves, no fidgeting with his hands, and not the slightest odor of liquor upon his breath or person. I saw that my first impression had been a mistaken one. He was in a sinking condition, yet perfectly conscious. I had his body sponged with warm water, to which spirits were added, sinapisms applied to his stomach and feet, cold applications to his head, and then administered a stimulating cordial. . . . The appearance of the dead poet had not materially changed; his face was calm and placid; a smile seemed to play around his mouth, and all who gazed upon him remarked how natural he looked; so much so, indeed, that it seemed as though he only slept.

> Dr. John J. Moran, 1885, *A Defense of Edgar Allan Poe,*
> *Life, Character and Dying Declarations of the Poet, An Official*
> *Account of his Death by his Attending Physician*, pp. 65, 82

It was a positive privilege to hear Poe talk. I have known times when at a dinner party, warmed with wine, and in a genial, glowing mood, he would pour out torrents of learning, and say hundreds of Rochefoucauld-like things apropos of literature and art, which, had they found their way into print, would have delighted cultivated society. It is a pity there was not in his audience a Boswell to take them down. Some of his utterances reminded one of the worldly wise sayings of Tacitus and Seneca. . . . In personal appearance Poe was a slight, small-boned, delicate looking man, with a well developed head, which, at a glance, seemed out of proportion to his slender body. His features were regular, his complexion pale; his nose was Grecian and well molded, his eyes large and luminous, and when excited, peculiarly vivid and penetrating. He dressed with neatness, and there was a suggestion of hauteur in his manner towards strangers. He was impatient of restraint or contradiction, and when his Southern blood was up, as the saying goes, he could be cuttingly rude and bitterly sarcastic.

> Howard Paul, 1892, "Recollections of Edgar Allan Poe,"
> *Munsey's Magazine*, vol. 7, pp. 555, 557

He spent much of his time with Mrs. Shelton, and finally asked her to marry him, and was, it must be believed from the correspondence, accepted. She was older than he, a plain woman, and wealthy. Poe got the wedding ring, and after his death she wore mourning for him. At the last moment, he still wavered when he thought of "Annie," who was evidently the nearest to him of all, except Mrs. Clemm,—but that was impossible. He was in doubt whether to have Mrs. Clemm come on to Richmond, or to go himself and bring her. He decided on the latter course, and on Sunday, as is conjectured, September 30, or else on the following day, he left his friends in Richmond, and went on the boat sober and cheerful. After reaching Baltimore, it is said that he took the train to Philadelphia, but was brought back, being in the wrong car, from Havre de Grace in a state of stupor. It is also said that he dined with some old military friends, became intoxicated, and was captured by politicians, who kept him stupefied, and made him vote at several booths on Wednesday, election day. All that is known is that, being then partially intoxicated, he called upon his friend, Dr. Brooks, on an afternoon, and, not finding him, went away; and that on Wednesday, October 3, about noon, he was recognised at a rum shop used as a voting-place,— Ryan's Fourth Ward Polls,—and on his saying that he was acquainted with Dr. Snodgrass, word was sent to that gentleman, who had him taken to the Washington Hospital. He was admitted at five o'clock, and word was sent to his relatives, who attended to his needs. He remained, except for a brief interval, in delirium; and on Sunday, Oct. 7, 1849, at about five o'clock in the morning, he died. The funeral was taken charge of by his relatives, and took place the next day. Five persons, including the officiating minister, followed his body to the grave.

George E. Woodberry, 1894, The Works of Edgar Allan Poe,
ed. Stedman and Woodberry, Memoir, vol. I, p. 86

POETRY

His poems are constructed with wonderful ingenuity, and finished with consummate art. They display a somber and weird imagination, and a taste almost faultless in the apprehension of that sort of beauty which was most agreeable to his temper. But they evince little genuine feeling, and less of that spontaneous ecstasy which gives its freedom, smoothness and naturalness to immortal verse. . . . He was not remarkably original in invention. Indeed some of his plagiarisms are scarcely paralleled for their audacity in all literary history.

Rufus Wilmot Griswold, 1850, "Edgar Allan Poe,"
The International Magazine, vol. 1, p. 340

So many faculties were brought into play in the expression of Poe's poetical compositions, that readers in whom the critical intellect prevails over the imaginative, often acknowledge the refined art, the tact, the subtlety, the faultless method, while the potent *magnetism* of his genius utterly escapes them. There are persons whom nature has made non-conductors to this sort of electricity. . . . It is not to be questioned that Poe was a consummate master of language; that he had sounded all the secrets of rhythm; that he understood and availed himself of all its resources,—the balance and poise of syllables, the alternations of emphasis and cadence, of vowel-sounds and consonants, and all the metrical sweetness of "phrase and metaphrase." Yet this consummate art was in him united with a rare simplicity. He was the most genuine of enthusiasts, as we think we shall presently show. His genius would follow no leadings but those of his own imperial intellect. With all his vast mental resources, he could never write an occasional poem, or adapt himself to the taste of a popular audience. His graver narratives and fantasies are often related with an earnest simplicity, solemnity, and apparent fidelity, attributable not so much to a deliberate artistic purpose, as to that power of vivid and intense conception that made his dreams realities, and his life a dream.

Sarah Helen Whitman, 1860-65, Edgar Poe and
his Critics, pp. 34, 35

Once as yet, and once only, has there sounded out of it all [America] one pure note of original song—worth singing, and echoed from the singing of no other man; a note of song neither wide nor deep, but utterly true, rich, clear, and native to the singer; the short exquisite music, subtle and simple and sombre and sweet, of Edgar Poe. All the rest that is not of mocking-birds is of corncrakes, varied but at best for an instant by some scant-winded twitter of linnet or of wren.

Algernon Charles Swinburne, 1872, Under the Microscope

Of Edgar Poe's poems,—except The Raven, which will always owe a certain popularity to the skill with which rhyme and metre reflect the dreary hopelessness and shudderiness, if I may coin a word, of the mood depicted —it is impossible to speak very highly. His imagination was not high enough for the sphere of poetry, and when he entered it he grew mystical and not a little bombastic.

Richard Holt Hutton, 1874, Criticisms on Contemporary
Thought and Thinkers, vol. I, p. 68

It is not difficult to understand that there were many sides on which Poe was likely to be long distasteful to Boston, Cambridge, and Concord. The intellectual weight of the man, though unduly minimised in New England, was inconsiderable by the side of that of Emerson. But in poetry, as one has to be always insisting, the battle is not to the strong; and apart from all faults, weaknesses, and shortcomings of Poe, we feel more and more clearly, or we ought to feel, the perennial charm of his verses. The posy of his still fresh and fragrant poems is larger than that of any other deceased American writer, although Emerson may have one or two single blossoms to show which are more brilliant than any of his. If the range of the Baltimore poet had been wider, if Poe had not harped so persistently on his one theme of remorseful passion for the irrecoverable dead, if he had employed his extraordinary, his unparalleled gifts of melodious invention, with equal skill, in illustrating a variety of human themes, he must have been with the greatest poets.

Edmund Gosse, 1888-89, "Has America Produced a Poet?"
Questions at Issue, pp. 89, 90

Poe's keen sensitiveness to criticism either of himself or of his writings is a noteworthy trait. The melody of his best poems is haunting, but tended ever to degenerate into mere mechanical jingle. His tone is spiritous, never spiritual. Alone among our poets, Poe links us to European literature by his musical despair—so similar to that of Leopardi, Pushkin, Heine, Lenau, Petöfi, and DeMusset (all descendants of Byron).

Greenough White, 1890, *Sketch of the Philosophy of
American Literature,* p. 59

Poe, like Swinburne, was a verbal poet merely; empty of thought, empty of sympathy, empty of love for any real thing: a graceful and nimble skater up and down over the deeps and shallows of life,—deep or shallow, it was all the same to him. Not one real thing did he make more dear to us by his matchless rhyme; not one throb of the universal heart, not one flash of the universal mind, did he seize and put in endearing form for his fellow men. . . . I am not complaining that Poe was not didactic: didacticism is death to poetry. I am complaining that he was not human and manly, and that he did not touch life in any helpful and liberating way. His poems do not lay hold of real things. I do not find the world a more enjoyable or beautiful place because he lived in it. I find myself turning to his poems, not for mental or spiritual food, as I do to Wordsworth or Emerson or Whitman, or for chivalrous human sentiments as in Tennyson, but to catch a glimpse of the weird, the fantastic, and, as it were, of the night-side or dream-side of things. . . . I would not undervalue Poe. He was a unique genius. But I would account for his failure to deeply impress his own countrymen, outside the professional literary guild. His fund of love and sympathy was small. He was not broadly related to his fellows, as were Longfellow and Whittier and Whitman. His literary equipment was remarkable; his human equipment was not remarkable: hence his failure to reach the general fame of the New England poets.

John Burroughs, 1893, "Mr. Gosse's Puzzle over Poe,"
The Dial, vol. 15, pp. 214, 215

And yet in the eyes of foreigners he is the most gifted of all authors of America; he is the one to whom the critics of Europe would most readily accord the full title of genius. At the end of this nineteenth century Poe is the sole man of letters born in the United States whose writings are read eagerly in Great Britain and in France, in Germany, in Italy, and in Spain, where Franklin is now but a name, and where the fame of James Fenimore Cooper, once as widely spread, is now slowly fading away. . . . That his scheme of poetry was highly artificial, that the themes of his poems were vague and insubstantial, and that his stanzas do not stimulate thought— these things may be admitted without disadvantage. What the reader does find in Poe's poetry is the succession of departed but imperishable beauty, and the lingering grace and fascination of haunting melancholy. His verses throb with an inexpressible magic and glow with intangible fantasy. His poems have no other purpose; they convey no moral; they echo no call to duty; they celebrate beauty only—beauty immaterial and evanescent; they are their own excuse for being.

Brander Matthews, 1896, *An Introduction to the Study
of American Literature*, pp. 156, 166

The Bells

If I were called upon to express my opinion of Poe as a poetic artist, I should say that *The Bells* was the most perfect example of his "power of words," if not, indeed, the most perfect example of that kind of power in all poetic literature. I should also say that *Alexander's Feast,* which our ancestors thought so incomparable, was not to be named in the same day with it.

Richard Henry Stoddard, 1875-84, *The Life of Edgar Allan Poe,
Poe's Works,* vol. I, p. 172

Poe's doctrine of "rhythm and rhyme" finds its amplest verification in *The Bells*. Reason and not "ecstatic intuition," led him to conclude that English versification is exceedingly simple, that "one tenth of it, possibly, may be called ethereal; nine-tenths, however, appertain to the mathematics; and the whole is included within the limits of the commonest common-sense." It must be believed that Poe appropriated, with the finest artistic discernment, the vitalizing power of rhythm and rime, and nowhere with more skill than in *The Bells*. It is the climax of his art on its technical side.

John Phelps Fruit, 1899, *The Mind and Art of Poe's Poetry*, p. 136

Ulalume

Muffled in an unusual number of thicknesses of elaborate rigmarole in rhyme, this is the pith of a ballad, which borrows interest from its position as the last exponent of the perpetual despair that enshrouded Poe's manhood, and the last visit of his tortured soul to the tomb of his lost beautiful, typified by the dead Ulalume. The *geist* of the ballad—that which transfuses it with meaning, and redeems it from the criticism so often passed upon it, that it is mere words—lies solely in the fact of its interpenetration with a kind psychological significance. Thus sang he, then died.

Francis Gerry Fairfield, 1875, "A Mad Man of Letters,"
Scribner's Monthly, vol. 10, p. 698

All things considered, the most singular poem that he ever produced, if not, indeed, the most singular poem that anybody ever produced, in commemoration of a dead woman, which I take to have been Poe's object, or one of his objects, when he sat down to write it. The mood of mind in which it was conceived was no doubt an imaginative one, but it was not, I think, on the hither side of the boundary between sense and madness. I can perceive no touch of grief in it, no intellectual sincerity, but a diseased determination to create the strange, the remote, and the terrible, and to exhaust ingenuity in order to do so. No healthy mind was ever impressed by *Ulalume,* and no musical sense was ever gratified with its measure, which is little beyond a jingle, and with its repetitions, which add to its length without increasing its general effect, and which show more conclusively than any thing in the language, the absurdity of the refrain when it is allowed to run riot, as it does here.

Richard Henry Stoddard, 1875-84, *Life of Edgar Allan Poe,*
Poe's Works, vol. I, p. 149

The ballad of *Ulalume* was written in 1847. The poet, still distraught by the death of his idolized child-wife, shattered in health, and impoverished in fortune, was nearing the borderland of insanity. Though not yet out of his thirties, he lived among the ghosts and shadows of a wasted life, in a world peopled with the horrors of a Dantean Inferno.

> "There sighs, complaints, and ululations loud
> Resounded through the air without a star."

It was under such circumstances that the poet composed his *Ulalume,* pronounced by a competent critic, "the extreme limit of Poe's original genius." The poem will not stand criticism. Many of its lines and rhymes are indefensible. Yet, in spite of its faults, it is an exquisite lyric. It comes like a wail of suffering, wrenched from a tortured, baffled soul, whose very anguish finds expression only in a melodious rhythm. The vagueness of its fantasies is forgotten in the effect of its irresistible music. In spite of the bitter arraignment by Mr. R. H. Stoddard, all classes of minds, healthy and otherwise, have been impressed by the little poem, and if, as that critic asserts, "no musical sense was ever gratified with its measure," it is difficult to explain away its subtle charm.

James L. Onderdonk, 1899-1901, *History of*
American Verse, p. 247

The Raven

We regard it as the most effective single example of fugitive poetry ever published in this country.

Nathaniel Parker Willis, 1845, *The Evening Mirror,* Jan. 29

Your friend, Mr. Poe, is a speaker of strong words "in both kinds." But I hope you will assure him from me that I am grateful for his reviews, and in no complaining humor at all. As to *The Raven* tell me what you shall say about it. There is certainly a power—but it does not appear to me the natural expression of a sane intellect in whatever mood; and I think that this should be specified in the title of the poem. There is a fantasticalness about the "sir or madam," and things of the sort which is ludicrous, unless there is a specified insanity to justify the straws. Probably he—the author— intended to be read in the poem, and he ought to have intended it. The rhythm acts excellently upon the imagination, and the "never more" has a solemn chime with it.

Elizabeth Barrett Browning, 1845, *Letter to R. H. Horne,* May 12

It is my design to render it manifest that no one point in its composition is referrable either to accident or intuition—that the work proceeded, step by step, to its completion with the precision and rigid consequence of a mathematical problem. . . . The reader begins now to regard the Raven as emblematical—but it is not until the very last line of the very last stanza that the intention of making him emblematical of *Mournful and Never-ending Remembrance* is permitted distinctly to be seen.

Edgar Allan Poe, 1846, *The Philosophy of Composition,*
Works, ed. Stedman and Woodberry, vol. VI, pp. 33, 46

The Raven room is little altered since the time Poe occupied it. It has a modern mantlepiece, painted black and most elaborately carved. Poe's name may be found in fine letters cut upon one side of it. His writing-table stood by one of the front windows, and, while seated before it, he could look down upon the rolling waters of the Hudson and over at the Palisades beyond. It was a fitting dwelling for a poet, and though not far from the city's busy hum, the atmosphere of solitude and remoteness was as actual, as if the spot had been in the heart of the Rocky Mountains. The explanations of the composition of *The Raven* given by Poe, even to his most intimate friends, were very conflicting, except that all these agree in stating that the analysis given in *The Philosophy of Composition* was pure fiction, —one of the poet's mischievous caprices to catch the critics, which proved successful beyond his expectation. Mrs. Weiss states that, not only Poe assured her that his published account of the alleged method of the composition of *The Raven* was not genuine, but that he also said that he had never intended it should be seriously received as such.

William Fearing Gill, 1877, The Life of Edgar Allan Poe, p. 149

His reputation rests upon three or four short poems, chiefly remarkable for their melody, and half a dozen tales, distinguished by their weirdness of colouring, their analytic power, and their subtle skill of construction. The best known of his poems is also the most elaborate—*The Raven,* and of this it may fairly be said that, in spite of its want of adequate motive, it is unique in conception as in execution, and it occupies a place of its own in our English literature.

W. H. Davenport Adams, 1880, Wrecked Lives, vol. II, p. 310

The Philosophy of Composition, his analysis of *The Raven,* is a technical dissection of its method and structure. Neither his avowal of cold-blooded artifice, nor his subsequent avowal to friends that an exposure of this artifice was only another of his intellectual hoaxes, need be wholly credited. If he had designed the complete work in advance, he scarcely would have made so harsh a prelude of rattle-pan rhymes to the delicious melody of the second stanza,—not even upon his theory of the fantastic. Of course an artist, having perfected a work, sees, like the first Artist, that it is good, and sees why it is good. A subsequent analysis, coupled with a disavowal of any sacred fire, readily enough may be made. My belief is that the first conception and rough draft of this poem came as inspiration always comes; that its author then saw how it might be perfected, giving it the final touches described in his chapter on Composition, and that the latter, therefore, is neither wholly false nor wholly true.

Edmund Clarence Stedman, 1884, The Raven, Illustrated by
Gustave Doré, Comment on the Poem, p. 13

In the *Evening Mirror,* January 29, 1845, *The Raven* was published, with a highly commendatory card from Willis; and a few days later *The American Whig Review* for February, from the advance sheets of which this poem had been copied, was the centre of literary interest and the prey of editorial scissors throughout the length and breadth of the country. In the magazine the author was masked under the pseudonym "Quarles," but in this journal he had been named as E. A. Poe. The popular response was instantaneous and decisive. No great poem ever established itself so immediately, so widely, and so imperishably in men's minds. *The Raven* became, in some sort, a national bird, and the author the most notorious American of the hour.

George E. Woodberry, 1885, *Edgar Allan Poe*
(*American Men of Letters*), p. 221

My brother Dante Gabriel and myself must have been among the earliest readers of Poe's Raven when that classical bird reached the English shore, and how many and many times did we not re-peruse it, and (more especially my brother) recite it!

William Michael Rossetti, 1899, *Letter to the Poe Memorial,*
ed. Kent, p. 64

Tales

You are mistaken in supposing that you are not "favorably known to me." On the contrary, all that I have read from your pen has inspired me with a high idea of your power; and I think you are destined to stand among the first romance-writers of the country, if such be your aim.

Henry Wadsworth Longfellow, 1841, *To Edgar Allan Poe,*
May 19; *Life of Longfellow* by Samuel Longfellow, vol. I, p. 377

In his tales, Mr. Poe has chosen to exhibit his power chiefly in that dim region which stretches from the very utmost limits of the probable into the weird confines of superstition and unreality. He combines in a very remarkable manner two faculties which are seldom found united: a power of influencing the mind of the reader by the impalpable shadows of mystery, and a minuteness of detail which does not leave a pin or a button unnoticed.

James Russell Lowell, 1845, "Edgar Allan Poe,"
Graham's Magazine, Feb.

It is through his tales that Mr. Poe is best known, and in them is displayed the real bent of his genius. Their chief characteristic is a grim horror,— sometimes tangible, but usually shadowy and dim. He revelled in faintly sketching scenes of gastly gloom, in imagining the most impossible plots, and in making them seem real by minute detail. His wild and weird conceptions have great power; but they affect the fears only, rarely the *heart;* while sometimes his morbid creations are repulsive and shocking; yet, in the path which he has chosen, he is unrivalled.

Charles D. Cleveland, 1859, A Compendium of
American Literature, p. 638

Although it may be doubted whether the fiery and tumultuous rush of a volcano, which might be taken to typify Poe, is as powerful or impressive in the end as the calm and inevitable progression of a glacier, to which, for the purposes of this comparison only, we may liken Hawthorne, yet the weight and influence of Poe's work are indisputable. One might hazard the assertion that in all Latin countries he is the best known of American authors. Certainly no American writer has been so widely accepted in France. Nothing better of its kind has ever been done than the "Pit and the Pendulum," or than the "Fall of the House of Usher" (which has been compared aptly with Browning's "Childe Roland to the Dark Tower Came" for its power of suggesting intellectual desolation). Nothing better of its kind has ever been done than the "Gold Bug," or than the "Purloined Letter," or than the "Murders in the Rue Morgue." The "Murders in the Rue Morgue" is indeed a story of the most marvellous skill: It was the first of its kind, and to this day it remains a model, not only unsurpassed, but unapproachable. It was the first of detective stories; and it has had thousands of imitations and no rival. The originality, the ingenuity, the verisimilitude of this tale and of its fellows are beyond all praise. Poe had a faculty which one may call imaginative ratiocination to a degree beyond all other writers of fiction.

Brander Matthews, 1885-1901, The Philosophy of
the Short-story, p. 44

Closely akin to this dryness of treatment is a certain insincerity of tone or flourish of manner, that often interferes with our enjoyment of Poe. We become suddenly aware of the gleaming eye and complacent smile of the concealed manipulator in the writing-automaton. The author is too plainly lying in wait for us; or he is too ostentatiously exhibiting his cleverness and resource, his command of the tricks of the game. One of the worst things that can be said of Poe from this point of view is that he contains the promise and potency of Mr. Robert Hichens, and of other cheap English decadents. Poe himself is never quite a mere acrobat; but he suggests the possible coming of the acrobat, the clever tumbler with ingenious grimace and the palm itching for coppers.

Lewis E. Gates, 1900, Studies and Appreciations, p. 125

Criticisms

The harshness of his criticisms I have never attributed to anything but the irritation of a sensitive nature, chafed by some indefinite sense of wrong.

> Henry Wadsworth Longfellow, 1849, *Southern
> Literary Messenger*, November

Had he been really in earnest, with what a solid brilliancy his writings might have shone forth to the world. With the moral proportioned to the intellectual faculty he would have been in the first rank of critics. In that large part of the critic's perceptions, he has been unsurpassed by any writer in America; but lacking sincerity, his forced and contradictory critical opinions are of little value as authorities, though much may be gathered from them by any one willing to study the peculiar mood in which they were written.

> Evert A. and George L. Duyckinck, 1855-65-75, *Cyclopædia
> of American Literature,* ed. Simons, vol. II, p. 404

As a critic, Poe spent himself upon questions of detail, and, in all cases, belittled his subject. He did not exercise the most engaging faculties of his mind. He is brilliant, caustic, stinging, personal without geniality, expressing an irritated mind. Reading his criticisms, we think his literary being might be said to resemble a bush that blossoms into a few perfect flowers, but always has its thorns in thickest profusion. Poe was what may be called a *technical critic*. He delighted to involve his reader in the mechanism of poetry, and convict his victim of ignorance, while he used his knowledge as a means to be exquisitely insolent. He was like an art critic stuffed with the jargon of studies, talking an unknown language; careless about the elements of the subject which, properly, are the chief and only concern of the public. That Poe was acute, that he was exact, that he was original, no one can question; but he was not stimulating, and comprehensive, and generous, like the more sympathetic critics, as, for example, Diderot or Carlyle.

> Eugene Benson, 1868, "Poe and Hawthorne,"
> *The Galaxy,* vol. 6, p. 747

There was but little literary criticism in the United States at the time Hawthorne's earlier works were published; but among the reviewers Edgar Poe perhaps held the scales the highest. He, at any rate, rattled them loudest, and pretended, more than any one else, to conduct the weighing-process on scientific principles. Very remarkable was this process of Edgar Poe's, and very extraordinary were his principles; but he had the advantage of being a man of genius, and his intelligence was frequently great. His collection of critical sketches of the American writers flourishing in what M. Taine would call his *milieu* and *moment,* is very curious and interesting reading, and it has one quality which ought to keep it from ever being completely forgotten. It is probably the most complete and exquisite specimen of *provincialism* ever prepared for the edification of men. Poe's judgments are pretentious, spiteful, vulgar; but they contain a great deal of sense and discrimination as well, and here and there, sometimes at frequent intervals, we find a phrase of happy insight imbedded in a patch of the most fatuous pedantry.

Henry James Jr., 1880, *Nathaniel Hawthorne*
(*English Men of Letters*), p. 62

In fact, his reputation as a critic would now suffer rather for the mercy he showed than for the vengeance he took. With what hesitancy he suggests that Mrs. Sigourney might profitably forget Mrs. Hemans; with what consideration he hints a fault in Mrs. Ellet, or just notices a blemish in Miss Gould; with what respect he treats Mellen and Gallagher! And if he asserts that Drake had an analogical rather than a creative mind, and insinuates that Halleck's laurel was touched with an artificial green,—these were the names that a lesser man would have let pass unchallenged. The whole mass of this criticism—but a small portion of which deals with imaginative work —is particularly characterized by a minuteness of treatment which springs from a keen, artistic sensibility, and by that constant regard to the originality of the writer which is so frequently an element in the jealousy of genius. One wearies in reading it now; but one gains thereby the better impression of Poe's patience and of the alertness and compass of his mental curiosity.

George E. Woodberry, 1885, *Edgar Allan Poe*
(*American Men of Letters*), p. 90

I read with no less zest than his poems the bitter, and cruel, and narrow-minded criticisms which mainly filled one of the volumes. As usual, I accepted them implicitly, and it was not till long afterward that I understood how worthless they were.

William Dean Howells, 1895, *My Literary Passions,* p. 119

His discriminations with respect to writers of importance have for the most part been confirmed. Sometimes they were affected by gratitude, as in the cases of Kennedy and Willis, the peculiar status of the latter affording Poe a chance to express his conviction that the mere man of letters could not then hold his own in America, but needed the aid of some factitious social position. But he might as well have said this of Bulwer and Disraeli in England. He was not far out in his estimates of Cooper and Bryant; he saw that Hawthorne, Longfellow, and Lowell were to be among the foremost builders of our imaginative literature, and his rally to the defence of young Bayard Taylor was quick and fine. He ranked Lowell high among our poets, on the score of his imagination, but found his ear for rhythm imperfect. Whittier seemed to him distinctly unimaginative, and as a Southerner and artist he was opposed to the poet-reformer's themes; but he recognized his *vivida vis,* his expressional fervor. Poe was among the first to do homage, in an outburst of genuine delight, to the rising genius of Tennyson.

> Edmund Clarence Stedman, 1895, *Works of Edgar Allan Poe,*
> ed. Stedman and Woodberry, vol. VI, p. xxii

GENERAL

There is poetry in the man, though, now and then, seen between the great gaps of bathos. . . . *Politian* will make you laugh—as *The Raven* made *me* laugh, though with something in it which accounts for the hold it took upon such as Mr. N. P. Willis and his peers—it was sent to me from *four* different quarters besides the author himself, before its publication in this form, and when it had only a newspaper life. Some of the other lyrics have power of a less questionable sort. For the author, I do not know him at all—never heard from him nor wrote to him—and in my opinion, there is more faculty shown in the account of that horrible mesmeric experience (mad or not mad) than in his poems. Now do read it from the beginning to the end. That *going out* of the hectic, struck me very much . . . and the writhing *away* of the upper lip. Most horrible! Then I believe so much of mesmerism, as to give room for the full acting of the story on me . . . without absolutely giving full credence to it, understand.

> Elizabeth Barrett Browning, 1846, *To Robert Browning,* Jan. 26;
> *The Letters of Robert Browning and Elizabeth Barrett Browning,*
> vol. I, p. 429

There comes Poe, with his "Raven," like "Barnaby Rudge,"
Three-fifths of him genius and two-fifths sheer fudge,
Who talks like a book of iambs and pentameters,
In a way to make people of common sense damn metres,
Who has written some things quite the best of their kind,
But the heart somehow seems all squeezed out by the mind.

> James Russell Lowell, 1848, *A Fable for Critics*

Just look at the dreadful, the unquenchable, the infernal *life* of Poe's *Lyrics and Tales*. No one can read these without shuddering, without pity, and sorrow, and condemnation of the author, without a half-muttered murmur of inquiry at his Maker—"Why this awful anomaly in thy works?" And yet no one can avoid reading them, and reading them again, and hanging over their lurid and lightning-blasted pages, and thinking that this wondrous being wanted only two things to have made him the master of American minds—virtue and happiness.

George Gilfillan, 1855, *A Third Gallery of Portraits,* p. 130

Poe is a kind of Hawthorne and *delirium tremens*. What is exquisitely fanciful and airy in the genuine artist is replaced in his rival by an attempt to overpower us by dabblings in the charnel-house and prurient appeals to our fears of the horribly revolting. After reading some of Poe's stories one feels a kind of shock to one's modesty. We require some kind of spiritual ablution to cleanse our minds of his disgusting images.

Leslie Stephen, 1874, *Hours in a Library,* First Series

My firm conviction that widely as the fame of Poe has already spread, and deeply as it is already rooted, in Europe, it is even now growing wider and striking deeper as time advances; the surest presage that time, the eternal enemy of small and shallow reputations, will prove in this case also the constant and trusty friend and keeper of a true poet's full-grown fame.

Algernon Charles Swinburne, 1875, *Letter to the
Poe Memorial,* Nov. 9, ed. Rice

A literary *Erinaceus*. . . . Professing himself the special apostle of the beautiful in art, he nevertheless forces upon us continually the most loathsome hideousness and the most debasing and unbeautiful horror. This passionate, unhelmed, errant search for beauty was in fact not so much a normal and intelligent desire, as an attempt to escape from interior discord; and it was the discord which found expression, accordingly, instead of the sense of beauty,—except (as has been said) in fragments. Whatever the cause his brain had a rift of ruin in it, from the start, and though his delicate touch often stole a new grace from classic antiquity, it was the frangibility, the quick decay, the fall of all lovely and noble things, that excited and engaged him. . . . Always beauty and grace are with him most poetic in their overthrow, and it is the shadow of ruined grandeur that he receives, instead of the still living light so fair upon them, or the green growth clinging around them.

George Parsons Lathrop, 1876, *A Study of
Hawthorne,* pp. 206, 309

Edgar Allen Poe was fastidious—even morbidly fastidious—in his love of beautiful form; but he had no root of humanity in him, and little passion for actual external nature. He was not an interpreter. He had no mission, save to create dreams. A greater dreamer in prose than in verse, he has yet added to American literature a few poems of the most striking originality; but of deep spirituality he has none. His loftiest flights of imagination in verse, like his boldest efforts in prose fiction, rise into no more empyreal realm than the fantastic. His sense of beauty in language was usually fine. Like Gautier, he loved to work "in" onyx and enamel.

Eric S. Robertson, 1886, *Life of Henry Wadsworth Longfellow*
(*Great Writers*), p. 173

Oblivious of what I may have said, but fully conscious of what I mean to say, Poe was a curious compound of the charlatan and the courtly gentleman; a mixture of Count Cagliostro, of Paracelsus, who was wisely named Bombastes, and of Cornelius Agrippa,—the three beings intermoulded from the dust of Apollonius of Tyana and Elymas the Sorcerer. His first master in verse was Byron, in prose Charles Brockden Brown, and later Hawthorne. Most men are egoists; he was egotistical. His early poems are exquisite, his later ones are simply melodious madness. The parent of *Annabel Lee* was Mother Goose, who in this instance did *not* drop a golden egg. Always a plagiarist, he was always original. Like Molière, whom he derided, he took his own wherever he found it. Without dramatic instinct, he persuaded himself (but no one else) that he was a dramatist. The proof of this assertion is his drama of *Politian,* which was never ended, and which should never have been begun.

Richard Henry Stoddard, 1889, "Edgar Allan Poe,"
Lippincott's Magazine, vol. 43, p. 109

Turning aside from his own special field of literature, Baudelaire talked and wrote to make the name of Edgar Poe famous; and he was successful, for, as a Frenchman has himself certified, "It was through the labour and genius of Baudelaire that Edgar Poe's tales have become so well known in France, and are now regarded as classical models." Further, it should be noticed that Edgar Poe is the only American writer who has become popular in that land where the literature of the nineteenth century has reached a perfection which after-ages will certainly record and admire. But we ask ourselves, Is this result due to the exquisite style Baudelaire employed in his translation? and would his magic pen have endowed any foreign author, however unworthy, with fame? Did the strange influence lie in the rich fancy of the American author or in the richer setting given to it by the Frenchman?

Baudelaire must evidently have known English well; but did he, whilst reading it, simultaneously clothe the English words in his own French dress, or did English style and New World fancy win his admiration? These questions are difficult to answer. Baudelaire's explanation does not altogether clear up the difficulty. "Believe me or not, as you like," he says, "but I discovered in Edgar Poe's works, poems and stories which had been lying dormant in my own brain, vague, confused, ill-assorted, whilst he had known how to combine, to transcribe, and to bring them to perfection." Here was, according to the French poet, the secret of his success. He had discovered his affinity; he had but to collect his own floating ideas, finding no difficulty in the setting, for all was clear to him. The two authors were of one mind, and the result was this gift of classic work to France, created with alien thought.

> Esmè Stuart, 1893, "Charles Baudelaire and Edgar Poe,"
> *The Nineteenth Century,* vol. 34, p. 66

It is the first and perhaps the most obvious distinction of Edgar Allan Poe that his creative work baffles all attempts to relate it historically to antecedent conditions; that it detached itself almost completely from the time and place in which it made its appearance, and sprang suddenly and mysteriously from a soil which had never borne its like before. There was nothing in the America of the third decade of the century which seemed to predict *The City in the Sea, Israfel,* and the lines, "To Helen." . . . Poe stood alone among his contemporaries by reason of the fact that, while his imagination was fertilized by the movement of his time, his work was not, in theme or sympathy, representative of the forces behind it. The group of gifted men, with whom he had for most part only casual connections, reflected the age behind them or the time in which they lived; Poe shared with them the creative impulse without sharing the specific interests and devotions of the period. He was primarily and distinctively the artist of his time; the man who cared for his art, not for what he could say through it, but for what it had to say through him. . . . Poe alone, among men of his eminence, could not have been foreseen. This fact suggests his limitations, but it also brings into clear view the unique individuality of his genius and the originality of his work. His contemporaries are explicable; Poe is inexplicable. He remains the most sharply-defined personality in our literary history. His verse and his imaginative prose stand out in bold relief against a background which neither suggests nor interprets them. One may go further, and affirm that both his verse and his prose have a place by themselves in the literature of the world.

> Hamilton W. Mabie, 1899, "Poe's Place in American Literature,"
> *Poe Memorial,* ed. Kent, pp. 44, 46, 47

MARIA EDGEWORTH
1767-1849

Born, at Black Burton, Oxfordshire, Jan. 1, 1767. In Ireland with father, 1773-75. To School in Derby, 1775; in London, 1780. Home to Edgeworthstown 1782. Began to write stories. To Clifton with parents, Dec. 1791; returned to Edgeworthstown, winter of 1793. Visit to France with father, Oct. 1802 to March 1803. Visit to London, spring of 1803; to Bowood, autumn of 1818; to London, 1819; to Paris and Switzerland, 1820 to March 1821. Returned to Edgeworthstown and lived there for rest of life. Occasional visits to London. Visit to Scotland, spring of 1823. Friendship with Sir Walter Scott; he visited her at Edgeworthstown, 1825. Active philanthropy during famine of 1846. Died, at Edgeworthstown, 22 May 1849. WORKS: *Letters to Literary Ladies,* 1795; *Parent's Assistant* (anon.), pt. i., 1796; in 6 vols. 1800; *Practical Education,* 1798; *Castle Rackrent* (anon.), 1800; *Early Lessons,* 1801; *Belinda,* 1801; *Moral Tales,* 1801; *Irish Bulls,* 1802; *Popular Tales,* 1804; *Modern Griselda,* 1804; *Leonora,* 1806; *Tales from Fashionable Life,* 1809; 2nd series, 1812; *Patronage,* 1814; *Continuation of Early Lessons,* 1815; *Harington,* 1817; *Ormond,* 1817; *Comic Dramas,* 1817; vol. ii. of R. L. Edgeworth's *Memoirs,* 1820; *Frank,* 1822; *Harry and Lucy, concluded,* 1825; *Garry Owen,* 1832; *Helen,* 1834. COLLECTED WORKS: in 14 vols., 1825; in 18 vols., 1832-33; in 12 vols., 1893. LIFE: by H. Zimmern, 1883 ("Eminent Women" series); *Life and Letters,* ed. by Augustus J. C. Hare, 1894.

R. Farquharson Sharp, 1897, *A Dictionary of
English Authors,* p. 90

SEE: *Tales,* ed. Austin Dobson, 1903; *Castle Rackrent,* ed. George Watson, 1965; *Chosen Letters,* ed. F. V. Barry, 1931; Elizabeth Inglis-Jones, *The Great Maria: A Portrait of Maria Edgeworth,* 1959.

PERSONAL

I had persuaded myself that the author of the work on Education, and of other productions, useful as well as ornamental, would betray herself by a remarkable exterior. I was mistaken. A small figure, eyes nearly always lowered, a profoundly modest and reserved air, with expression in the features when not speaking: such was the result of my first survey. But when she spoke, which was too rarely for my taste, nothing could have been better thought, and nothing better said, though always timidly expressed.

Marc-Auguste Pictet, 1802, *Voyage de trois mois en
Angleterre,* tr. Oliver

Mr., Mrs., and Miss Edgeworth are just come from Ireland, and are the general objects of curiosity and attention. I passed some hours with them yesterday afternoon, under pretence of visiting the new Mint, which was a great object to them, as they are all proficients in mechanics. Miss Edgeworth is a most agreeable person, very natural, clever, and well informed, without the least pretensions of authorship. She had never been in a large society before, and she was followed and courted by all the persons of distinction in London, with an avidity almost without example. The court paid to her gave her an opportunity of showing her excellent understanding and character. She took every advantage of her situation, either for enjoyment or observation; but she remained perfectly unspoiled by the homage of the great.

Sir James Mackintosh, 1813, Journal, May 11;
Memoirs of Mackintosh, ed. his Son, vol. II, p. 267

She was a nice little unassuming "Jeanie Deans'-looking bodie" as we Scotch say—and if not handsome certainly not ill-looking. One could never have guessed that she could write *her name;* whereas her father talked, *not* as if he could write nothing else, but as if nothing else was worth writing.

Lord Byron, 1821, Journal, Jan. 19

To have repeatedly met and listened to Miss Edgeworth, seated familiarly with her by the fireside, may seem to her admirers in America a sufficient payment for the hazards of crossing the Atlantic. Her conversation, like her writings, is varied, vivacious, and delightful. Her forgetfulness of self and happiness in making others happy are marked traits in her character. Her person is small and delicately proportioned, and her movements full of animation. The ill-health of the lovely sister, much younger than herself, at whose house in London she was passing the winter, called forth such deep anxiety, untiring attention, and fervent gratitude for every favourable symptom, as seemed to blend features of maternal tenderness with sisterly affection.

Lydia Huntley Sigourney, 1842, Pleasant Memories
of Pleasant Lands

Maria Edgeworth's life did not pass without the romance of love. She received an offer of marriage from a Swedish gentleman, while she was staying in Paris with her family in 1803. She returned his affections, but refused to marry him, sacrificing herself and him to what she believed to be her duty to her father and family. Her third and last step-mother wrote that for years "the unexpected mention of his name, or even that of Sweden, in a book or newspaper, always moved her so much that the words and lines in the page became a mass of confusion before her eyes, and her voice lost all power." Her suitor, M. Edelcrantz, never married. At the altar of filial piety she sacrificed much.

Millicent Garrett Fawcett, 1889, Some Eminent
Women of Our Times, p. 160

Castle Rackrent (1800)

The inimitable *Castle Rackrent* I consider one of the very best productions of genius in the language, in its own way. I only lament that others are not as well qualified as I am to judge of the faithful drawing and vivid colouring of that admirable work. To do this, one must have lived in Ireland, or the West Highlands, which contain much rack-rent; but one must not have lived always there, as, in that case, the force of these odd characters would be lost in their familiarity.

> Anne Grant, 1809, *To Mrs. Fletcher,* July 6;
> *Memoir and Correspondence,* ed. Grant, vol. I, p. 214

Miss Edgeworth's *Castle Rackrent* and *Fashionable Tales* are incomparable in depicting truly several traits of the rather modern Irish character: they are perhaps on one point somewhat overcharged; but, for the most part, may be said to exceed Lady Morgan's Irish novels. The fiction is less perceptible in them: they have a greater air of reality—of what I have myself often and often observed and noted in full progress and actual execution throughout my native country. The landlord, the agent, and the attorney, of *Castle Rackrent* (in fact, every person it describes) are neither fictitious nor even uncommon characters: and the changes of landed property in the country where I was born (where perhaps they have prevailed to the full as widely as in any other united Empire) owed, in nine cases out of ten, their origin, progress, and catastrophe, to incidents in no wise differing from those so accurately painted in Miss Edgeworth's narrative.

> Sir Jonah Barington, 1830, *Personal Sketches
> of his Own Times,* p. 375

One of the most powerful and impressive of her books is devoted to the miserable story of improvidence, recklessness, and folly, by which so many families have been ruined, and which is linked with so much that is attractive in the way of generosity and hospitality and open-handedness, that the hardest critic is mollified unawares, and the sympathetic populace, which is no adept in moral criticism, admires with enthusiasm while he lasts, and pities, when he has fallen, the culprit who is emphatically nobody's enemy but his own.

> Margaret O. W. Oliphant, 1882, *Literary History of England,
> XVIII-XIX Century,* vol. III, p. 174

GENERAL

As a writer of tales and novels, she has a very marked peculiarity. It is that of venturing to dispense common sense to her readers, and to bring them within the precincts of real life and natural feeling. She presents them with no incredible adventures, or inconceivable sentiments, no hyperbolical representations of uncommon character, or monstrous exhibitions of exaggerated passion. Without excluding love from her pages, she knows how to assign to it, its just limits. She neither degrades the sentiment from its true dignity, nor lifts it to a burlesque elevation. It takes its proper place among the other passions. Her heroes and heroines, if such they may be called, are never miraculously good, nor detestably wicked. They are such men and women as we see and converse with every day of our lives; with the same proportionate mixture in them of what is right and what is wrong, of what is great and what is little.

William Gifford, 1809, "Tales of Fashionable Life,"
Quarterly Review, vol. 2, p. 146

Thinking as we do, that her writings are, beyond all comparison, the most useful of any that have come before us since the commencement of our critical career, it would be a point of conscience with us to give them all the notoriety that they can derive from our recommendations, even if their executions were in some measure liable to objection. In our opinion, however, they are as entertaining as instructive; and the genius, and wit, and imagination, they display, are at least as remarkable as the justness of the sentiments they so powerfully inculcate.

Francis, Lord Jeffrey, 1809-44, "Miss Edgeworth,"
Contributions to the Edinburgh Review, vol. III, p. 408

Where, then, is Miss Edgeworth's merit, her extraordinary merit, both as a moralist and a woman of genius? It consists in her having selected a class of virtues far more difficult to treat as the subject of fiction than others, and which had, therefore, been left by former writers to her. This is the merit both of originality and utility; but it never must be stated otherwise, unless we could doubt that superiority of the benevolent virtues over every other part of morals, which is not a subject of discussion, but an indisputable truth.

Sir James Mackintosh, 1810, *Letter to Mrs. Mackintosh*

Most of her characters are formed from the most genuine and ordinary materials of human nature,—with very little admixture of anything derived from heaven, or the garden of Eden, or the magnificent part of the regions of poetry. There is rarely anything to awaken for one moment the enthusiasm of an aspiring spirit, delighted to contemplate, and ardent to resemble, a model of ideal excellence. . . . She is very expert at contriving situations for bringing out all the qualities of her personages, for contrasting those personages with one another, for creating excellent amusement by their mutual reaction, and for rewarding or punishing their merits or faults. She appears intimately acquainted with the prevailing notions, prejudices, and habits of the different ranks and classes of society. She can imitate very satirically the peculiar diction and slang of each; and has contrived (but indeed it needed very little contrivance) to make the fashionable dialect of the upper ranks sound exceedingly silly. As far as she has had opportunities for observation, she has caught a very discriminative idea of national characters: that of the Irish is delineated with incomparable accuracy and spirit. It may be added, that our author, possessing a great deal of general knowledge, finds many lucky opportunities for producing it, in short arguments and happy allusions.

John Foster, 1810, *The Morality of Works of Fiction;*
Critical Essays, ed. Ryland, vol. I, p. 427

She is the author of works not to be forgotten; of works, which can never lose their standard value as "English classics," and deserve that honourable name infinitely more than half the dull and licentious trash bound up in our libraries under that title. . . . Her novels always found an eager reception at a time when the poetry of Scott, of Campbell, and of Crabbe, was issuing in its freshness from the press, when the Edinburgh and Quarterly Reviews, then splendid novelties, were to be duly read and studied, when Madame de Staël was at her zenith, and, in a word, when the competition of the noblest wits was only less keen, than at the present day.

Edward Everett, 1823, "Miss Edgeworth,"
North American Review, vol. 17, pp. 388, 389

She paints character as it presented itself to her view, sometimes well and sometimes ill, but her men and women have not a life in themselves. Her short tales are excellent, and superior to her novels, for the reason that the things required in a short tale are incident and moral point, not character. In the invention or adaption of incident she is very clever; she also has a large share of the faculty, most conspicuous in Defoe, of giving fiction the air of reality by minute elaboration of detail. She writes decidedly well, and often says witty or sparkling things, of which but few are to be found in Jane Austen.

Goldwin Smith, 1883, "Miss Edgeworth," *The Nation,* vol. 36, p. 322

Her novels have been described as a sort of essence of common sense, and even more happily it has been said that it was her genius to be wise. We must content to take that which she can offer; and since she offers so much, why should we not be content? Miss Edgeworth wrote of ordinary human life, and not of tremendous catastrophes or highly romantic incidents. Hers was not heated fancy. She had no comprehension of those fiery passions, those sensibilities that burn like tinder at contact with the feeblest spark; she does not believe in chance, that favorite of so many novelists; neither does she deal in ruined castles, underground galleries nor spectres, as was the fashion in her day.

Helen Zimmern, 1883, Maria Edgeworth (Famous Women), p. 180

Her style is easy, pliant, and vigorous; timid, perhaps, in its avoidance of all eccentricities, and somewhat overburdened by imitation of accredited literary models, but always correct, and free from tawdriness and exaggeration. Like the other attributes of her work, it shows earnestness and thoroughness of care and attention: and we are not surprised, when we watch the result, to read in one of her father's prefaces, that every page of her printed writing represents "twice as many pages as were written;" and yet not the least convincing proof of this care is that she has been able to avoid any obtrusive evidence of toil: and that if she spent much *labor limæ* she has given no sign of it in cumbrousness or pedantry of style.

Henry Craik, 1895, English Prose, vol. IV, p. 621

THOMAS LOVELL BEDDOES
1803-1849

Born, at Clifton, 20 July 1803. Educated at Bath Grammar School; and at Charterhouse, June 1817-20; Contrib. sonnet to *Morning Post,* 1819. Wrote *The Bride's Tragedy,* 1819. To Pembroke Coll., Oxford, 1 May 1820; B. A., 25 May 1825; M. A., 16 April 1828. Assisted in publication of Shelley's Posthumous Poems, 1824. To Italy in summer of 1824. Göttingen Univ., studying medicine, July 1825-29. To Würzburg, 1829; degree of M. D. there, 1832. At Zurich, June 1835 to March 1840. To Berlin, 1841. In England, 1842; at various towns in Germany and Switzerland, 1844-46; in England, 1846-47; settled in Frankfort, June 1847. Died, in Basle Hospital, 26 Jan. 1849. Buried in Hospital cemetery. WORKS: *The Improvisatore,* 1821; *The Bride's Tragedy,* 1822. POSTHUMOUS: *Death's Jest-Book, or the Fool's Tragedy,* 1850; *Poems, Posthumous and Collected,* ed. by T. F. Kelsall (2 vols.), 1851; *Poetical Works,* ed. by E. Gosse (2 vols.), 1890; *Letters,* ed. by E. Gosse, 1894.

R. Farquharson Sharp, 1897, A Dictionary of
English Authors, p. 21

SEE: *Works,* ed. H. W. Donner, 1935, rev. 1950 (*Muses Library* edition); R. H. Snow, *Thomas Lovell Beddoes: Eccentric and Poet,* 1928; H. W. Donner, *Beddoes: The Making of a Poet,* 1935.

PERSONAL

I first knew Thomas Lovell Beddoes at the Charter-house in 1817 or 1818. We were in the same house (Mr. Watkinson's No. 15 in the square). Beddoes was near the top of the school; I was his fag, and in constant attendance upon him. The expression of his face was shrewd and sarcastic, with an assumption of sternness, as he affected the character of a tyrant and bully, though really not much of either; but a persevering and ingenious tormentor, as I knew to my cost. With a great natural turn for humour, and a propensity to mischief; impatient of control, and indisposed to constituted authority over him, he suggested and carried out many acts of insubordination, in the contrivance of which he shewed as much wit, as spirit in their execution; and even when detected in positive rebellion, his invincible assurance and deliberate defiance of the masters, together with the grim composure of his countenance, was so irresistibly comic, that I have seen them unable to speak for laughing when he was brought up for punishment.

> Charles Dacres Bevan, 1851, *Letter to Revell Phillips, The Poems
> Posthumous and Collected of Thomas Lovell Beddoes,*
> ch. i, p. cxxviii

Beddoes in person and otherwise was not unlike Keats. Both were short in stature, and independent in manner, and very brief and decided in conversation. Beddoes was too fond of objecting and carping, when the merits of any modern books came into discussion. Not that he was at all vain or envious himself, but he was at all times unwilling to yield homage to any poets, except Shelley and Keats and Wordsworth. Of these Shelley was undoubtedly his favorite. Like that great poet, Beddoes had much love for philosophical questions, although the poetical element was predominant in him.

> Bryan Waller Procter (Barry Cornwall), 1874?
> *Recollections of Men of Letters*

His mother was a sister of Maria Edgeworth, and his father a distinguished physician and an intimate friend of Sir Humphry Davy. In the father's character we may trace the principal traits of the son: a strong scientific bent, a fondness for poetic dreams, an invincible independence, were predominant in both. The character of Lovell Beddoes' poetry was the natural outgrowth of his poetry studies. His schoolfellows at the Charterhouse speak of him at the age of fourteen as already thoroughly versed in the best English literature and a close student of the dramatists, from the Elizabethan to those of his own day. He was always ready to invent and carry out acts of insubordination, which he informed with so much wit and spirit that the very authorities were often subdued by their own irresistible laughter. It was one phase of his dramatic genius, that seemed to be constantly impelling him to get up some striking situation wherein he might pose as a youthful Ajax defying the lightnings. At Oxford his restless independence was continually prompting him to affront his tutors. He was always in opposition to the spirit of the occasion, whatever it might be.

Kate Hilliard, 1873, "A Strayed Singer,"
Lippincott's Magazine, vol. 12, p. 551

GENERAL

How stately or enduring a monument he may, by the earnest cultivators of English poetic literature, be deemed to have himself erected in his works, this is not perhaps the fitting place in which to venture a prediction. In his life time, he may certainly be said to have strangely missed his fame: the most golden bough of "the everlasting singing-tree,"—the laudarier a laudatis,—as posthumous events have shown, lay already within his reach, would he but have stretched his hands to gather it. But even the full and open requital of these his actual, though hidden, claims of distinction, would still have left, for those who best knew that creative mind in all its undeveloped power, the larger portion of their Hope unsatisfied.

Thomas Forbes Kelsall, 1851, *The Poems Posthumous and Collected of Thomas Lovell Beddoes,* Memoir, vol. I, p. cxvi

Beddoes is a poet for poets, and few other readers will enjoy him. He is "of imagination all compact." His works scarcely contain a single passage of purely subjective feeling. He is, perhaps, the most concrete poet of his day, the most disposed to express sentiment by imagery and material symbolism. In this he resembles Keats, and may be termed a Gothic Keats, the Teutonic counterpart of his more celebrated contemporary's Hellenism. The spirit of Gothic architecture seems to live in his verse, its grandeur and grotesqueness, its mystery and its gloom. His relation to the Elizabethan dramatists, moreover, is nearly the same as that of Keats to the Elizabethan pastoral poets; but the resemblance is one of innate temperament; he borrowed nothing, either from his Elizabethan precursors or the chief objects of his admiration among his contemporaries, Keats and Shelley. The want of constructive power which mars his dramas is even more prejudicial to his lyrics; but some few songs, where the right key note has been struck from the first, rank among the most perfect in our language.

Thomas Spencer Baynes, 1877, *Encyclopædia Britannica,*
Ninth ed., vol. III, p. 415

The quality of youth is still more distinctly discernible in some of Thomas Beddoes' dazzling little songs, stolen straight from the heart of the sixteenth century, and lustrous with that golden light which set so long ago. It is not in spirit only, nor in sentiment, that this resemblance exists; the words, the imagery, the swaying music, the teeming fancies of the younger poet, mark him as one strayed from another age, and wandering companionless under alien skies.

Agnes Repplier, 1891, "English Love-Songs," *Points of View,* p. 60

Beddoes is always large, impressive; the greatness of his aim gives him a certain claim on respectful consideration. That his talent achieved itself, or ever could have achieved itself, he himself would have been the last to affirm. But he is a monumental failure, more interesting than many facile triumphs. . . . Beddoes' genius was essentially lyrical: he had imagination, the gift of style, the mastery of rhythm, a strange choiceness and curiosity of phrase. But of really dramatic power he had nothing. He could neither conceive a coherent plot, nor develop a credible situation. He had no grasp on human nature, he had no conception of what character might be in men and women, he had no faculty of expressing emotion convincingly. Constantly you find the most beautiful poetry where it is absolutely inappropriate, but never do you find one of those brief and memorable phrases—words from the heart—for which one would give much beautiful poetry. . . . A beautiful lyrist, a writer of charming, morbid, and magnificent poetry in dramatic form, Beddoes will survive to students not to readers, of English poetry, somewhere in the neighborhood of Ebenezer Jones and Charles Wells.

Arthur Symons, 1891, "The Poetical Works of Thomas Lovell Beddoes," *The Academy,* vol. 40, p. 129

Except Donne, there is perhaps no English poet more difficult to write about, so as to preserve the due pitch of enthusiasm on the one hand and criticism on the other, than Thomas Lovell Beddoes. . . . Beddoes has sometimes been treated as a mainly bookish poet deriving from the Elizabethans and Shelley. I cannot agree with this. His very earliest work, written when he could not know much either of Shelley or Keats, shows as they do technique perhaps caught from Leigh Hunt. But this is quite dropped later; and his Elizabethanism is not imitation but inspiration. In this inspiration he does not follow but shares with, his greater contemporaries. His is a younger and tragic counterpart to Charles Lamb in the intensity with which he has imbibed the Elizabethan spirit, rather from the nightshade of Webster and Tourneur than from the vine of Shakespeare. As wholes, his works are naught, or naught but nightmares; though *Death's Jest-Book,* despite its infinite disadvantages from constant rewriting and uncertainty of final form, has a strong grasp. But they contain passages, especially lyrics, of the most exquisite fancy and music, such as since the seventeenth century none but Blake and Coleridge had given.

George Saintsbury, 1896, *A History of Nineteenth Century Literature*, p. 114

JAMES CLARENCE MANGAN
1803-1849

James Clarence Mangan was born in Dublin in 1803. His father was a grocer, and became bankrupt. At the age of fifteen James entered a scrivener's office, and seven years later he became a solicitor's clerk, in which occupation he spent three years. Concerning this period he wrote: "I was obliged to work seven years of the ten from five in the morning, winter and summer, to eleven at night; and during the remaining three years nothing but a special providence could have saved me from suicide." The misery of his situation drove him to drink, and he was also an opium-eater. At about the age of twenty-five, just after a grievous disappointment in love, he became connected with the library of Trinity College, Dublin, where he acquired a knowledge of many languages, including several Oriental tongues, and from nearly all of them he made poetical translations, some of which are said to surpass the originals. These translations, together with numerous short original poems, were published in an illustrated weekly in Dublin, and afterward in the penny journals and the famous *Nation,* and finally Mangan became a regular contributor to the *Dublin University Magazine.* His heart was with the revolutionary movement of 1842-48, and he wrote several ringing ballads to help it on. Broken down by his intemperate habits, he died in a hospital in Dublin, June 20, 1849.

Rossiter Johnson, 1875, *Little Classics, Authors*, p. 169

SEE: *Poems,* ed. D. J. O'Donoghue, 1903; *Selected Poems,* ed. Louise I. Guiney, 1897; *Prose Writings,* ed. D. J. O'Donoghue, 1904; D. J. O'Donoghue, *Life and Writings of James Clarence Mangan,* 1897; J. D. Sheridan, *James Clarence Mangan,* 1937.

PERSONAL

Mangan was not only an Irishman,—not only an Irish papist,—not only an Irish papist rebel;—but throughout his whole literary life of twenty years, he never deigned to attorn to English criticism, never published a line in any English periodical, or through any English bookseller, never seemed to be aware that there was a British public to please. He was a rebel politically, and a rebel intellectually and spiritually,—a rebel with his whole heart and soul against the whole British spirit of the age. The consequence was sure, and not unexpected. Hardly anybody in England knew the name of such a person. . . . The first time the present biographer saw Clarence Mangan, it was in this wise—Being in the college library, and having occasion for a book in that gloomy apartment of the institution called the "Fagel Library," which is the innermost recess of the stately building, an acquaintance pointed out to me a man perched on the top of a ladder, with the whispered information that the figure was Clarence Mangan. It was an unearthly and ghostly figure, in a brown garment; the same garment (to all appearance) which lasted till the day of his death. The blanched hair was totally unkept; the corpse-like features still as marble; a large book was in his arms, and all his soul was in the book. I had never heard of Clarence Mangan before, and knew not for what he was celebrated; whether as a magician, a poet, or a murderer; yet [I] took a volume and spread it on a table, not to read, but with pretence of reading to gaze on the spectral creature upon the ladder. Here Mangan laboured mechanically, and dreamed, roosting on a ladder, for certain months, perhaps years; carrying the proceeds in money to his mother's poor home, storing in his memory the proceeds which were not in money but in another kind of ore, which might feed the imagination indeed, but was not available for board and lodging. All this time he was the bond-slave of opium.

John Mitchel, 1859, ed., *Poems by James Clarence Mangan,*
Memoir, pp. 8, 13

Life was to Mangan one long interval. "No one wish of his heart," says Mitchel, "was ever fulfilled; no aspiration satisfied." . . . If he could have faced the denials of destiny with an austere renunciation, if he could have opposed a monastic fortitude to the buffets of the world, his might have been a serener if not a happier story. But a passionate longing after the ideal drove him to those deadly essences which fed for a time the hot flame of his genius at the price of his health, his reason, and his life. Genius and misery have been bed-fellows and board-brothers often enough, but they have seldom indeed been yoked together under conditions as tragic as those which make Mangan's story a record of despair.

Justin Huntly McCarthy, *Hours with Great Irishmen*

GENERAL

He is inimitable—the very prince of translators. He is among the few writers of any time or country who have succeeded in transfusing into their own language not merely the literal meaning, graces of style, and musical movement of foreign poems, but also their true spirit and suggestiveness. Often his translation far surpasses the original. He was a most accomplished linguist, and translated from the Irish, French, German, Spanish, Italian, Danish, as well as Turkish and other Asiatic tongues.

John Kane Murray, 1877-84, *Lessons in English Literature,* p. 367

In many respects, both in life and genius, Mangan bears a resemblance to Edgar A. Poe, and, if he did not achieve a single marked success like *The Raven,* his poetical faculty was of the same sombre sort, and his command of original and musical rhythm almost equally great. . . . His original poems are quite few in number, but display the same command of original and powerful rhythm and impressive diction as his translations, while their spirit of hopelessness is beyond any artificial pathos. There is hardly anything more profoundly affecting in English literature than such a poem as *The Nameless One,* read with a knowledge of the life of which it was a confession; and it is the more impressive that it has no bitterness nor maudlin arraignment of fortune, such as is apparent in much of the poetry of genius wrecked by its own errors. His political odes were those of a dreamer of noble things for his country, rather than of practical knowledge or faith, notwithstanding their exalted and noble sentiment, and in all things except his personal misery he was not of the actual life of the world.

Alfred M. Williams, 1881, *The Poets and Poetry of Ireland,* pp. 325, 328

In 1845, under the title of *Anthologia Germania,* he published two volumes of translations from the German, and in them much of his best work is to be found. His renderings from the Irish, on the other hand, which were issued in two posthumous publications, are very disappointing and inferior; generally they are poor in execution and spiritless in tone, while in the mystic and weird ministrelsy of the Teuton, Mangan found a longing for something beyond this life akin to his own vague aspirations. . . . Great as his merits undoubtedly are, Mangan has been so overpraised by his countrymen, who have endeavoured to give a political colouring to his writings, that English critics have been prejudiced against him, and have deemed him a mere provincial poetaster. As an original poet, it is difficult to assign him as high a rank as his countrymen claim, but as a translator his merits are great; no one has transmitted the *spirit* of German ballad lore better than Mangan has, often, indeed, giving it a charm greater than the original possesses.

John H. Ingram, 1894, *The Poets and the Poetry of the Century, John Keats to Lord Lytton,* ed. Miles, pp. 453, 457, 458

Mangan's position in Irish poetry is a matter of difference of opinion among Irishmen. Even many of those who admire his work extremely are not altogether disposed to place him above Moore. Yet in lyrical power and range, vigour of expression, variety of treatment, originality of form, mastery of technique, keenness of perception, and in other qualities, Mangan seems to be quite unapproached by any Irish poet. Some of these qualities are possessed in a greater degree by other Irish poets, but in none are they combined in such perfection as in Mangan. Some attributes there are which Mangan lacks, or possesses only in a slender degree, and his perverseness in certain directions has been to no small extent detrimental to his reputation; but, with all deductions, it is perfectly certain that no other Irish poet is his peer in sheer imaginative power or fertility of invention. Those who admire his writings at all must admire them warmly; indifference is impossible in such a case.

D. J. O'Donoghue, 1897, The Life and Writings of
James Clarence Mangan, pp. 199, 232

Mangan's great work has never been overpraised: not so his less great. He was an Irishman writing English verse during the first half of the century: his wide and genuine if straggling culture, his range of literary interest, his technical mastery of verse, filled his audience with a feeling of novelty. It was a portent, a presage, of an outburst of Irish poetry in English verse such as had not before been heard: and it is not unnatural that Mangan's poetry was received, is often still received, with too lavish an applause, too indiscriminate a welcome. . . . Mangan's flight is highest, his music is noblest, when ancient Ireland speaks to him of her glories, her sorrows, her hopes. He is the poet of much else that is imperishable; but above all he is the poet of a poem foremost among the world's poems of inspired patriotism. It were enough for Mangan's fame that he is the poet of the *Dark Rosaleen*.

Lionel Johnson, 1900, A Treasury of Irish Poetry,
eds. Brooke and Rolleston, pp. 243, 248, 249

WILLIAM WORDSWORTH
1770-1850

Born, at Cockermouth, Cumberland, 7 April 1770. Early education at Hawkshead Grammar School, 1778-87. Matric. St. John's Coll., Camb., Oct. 1787; B. A., 1791. Travelled on Continent, July to Oct., 1790. Visited Paris, Nov. 1791. Settled with his sister near Crewkerne, Dorsetshire, autumn of 1795. First visit from Coleridge, June 1797. Removed to Alfoxden, Nether Stowey, Somersetshire, July 1797. Friendship with

Charles Lamb and Hazlitt begun. In Bristol, 1798. In Germany, Sept. 1798 to July 1799. Settled at Grasmere, Dec. 1799. Visit to France, July to Aug. 1802. Married Mary Hutchinson, 4 Oct. 1802. Friendship with Scott and Southey begun, 1803. Removed to Coleorton, Leicestershire, 1806. Returned to Grasmere, 1808. Contrib. to *The Friend*, 1810. Removed to Rydal Mount, spring of 1813. Distributor of stamps for Westmorland, March 1813 to 1842. Visits to Continent, 1820, 1823, 1828, 1837. Hon. D. C. L., Durham, 1838. Hon. D. C. L., Oxford, 12 June 1839. Crown Pension, 1842. Poet Laureate, 1843. Died, at Rydal Mount, 23 April 1850. Buried in Grasmere Churchyard. WORKS: *An Evening Walk*, 1793; *Descriptive Sketches in Verse*, 1793; *Lyrical Ballads, with a Few Other Poems* (2 vols.), 1798-1800; *Poems* (2 vols.) 1807; *On the Relations of Great Britain, Spain, and Portugal to each other*, 1809; *The Excursion*, 1814; *The White Doe of Rylstone*, 1815; *Poems* (3 vols.), 1815-20; *Thanksgiving Ode*, 1816; *Letter to a Friend of Robert Burns*, 1816; *Peter Bell*, 1819; *The Waggoner*, 1819; *The River Duddon*, 1820; *The Little Maid and the Gentleman; or, We Are Seven* (anon.), [1820?]; *Memorials of a Tour on the Continent*, 1822; *Ecclesiastical Sketches*, 1822; *Description of the Scenery of the Lakes in the North of England*, 1822; *Yarrow Revisited*, 1835; *Sonnets*, 1838; *Poems*, 1842; *Poems on the Loss and Rebuilding of St. Mary's Church*, by W. Wordsworth, J. Montgomery, and others, 1842; *Ode on the Installation of Prince Albert at Cambridge*, [1847]; *The Prelude*, 1850. COLLECTED WORKS: *Poetical Works*, ed. by E. Dowden (7 vols.), 1892-93; *Prose Works*, ed. by W. Knight (2 vols.), 1896. LIFE: by C. Wordsworth, 1851; by E. P. Hood, 1856; by J. M. Sutherland, 2nd edn., 1892.

R. Farquharson Sharp, 1897, *A Dictionary of English Authors*, p. 304

SEE: *Poetical Works*, ed. Ernest de Selincourt and Helen Darbishire, 1940-49, rev. 1952, 5 v.; *Poetical Works*, ed. Thomas Hutchinson, 1911 (OSA), rev. 1936 (by Ernest de Selincourt); *Prefaces and Essays*, ed. *George Sampson*, 1920; *The Prelude*, ed. Ernest de Selincourt, 1926, rev. 1959 (by Helen Darbishire); *Letters of William and Dorothy Wordsworth*, ed. Ernest de Selincourt, 1935-39, 6 v.; G. M. Harper, *William Wordsworth: His Life, Works and Influence*, 1916, 2 v., rev. 1929, one vol.; Emile Legouis, *William Wordsworth and Annette Vallon*, 1922; Mary Moorman, *William Wordsworth: The Later Years, 1803-1850*, 1965; C. H. Herford, *Wordsworth*, 1930; Herbert Read, *Wordsworth*, 1930, rev. 1949; R. D. Havens, *The Mind of a Poet: A Study of Wordsworth's Thought with Particular Reference to 'The Prelude'*, 1941; J. C. Smith, *A Study of Wordsworth*, 1944; J. V. Logan, *Wordsworthian Criticism*, 1947; Helen Darbishire, *The Poet Wordsworth*, 1950 (Clark Lectures); Markham L. Peacock, *The Critical Opinions of William Wordsworth*, 1950; Lascelles Abercrombie, *The Art of Wordsworth*, 1952; John Jones, *The Egotistical Sublime: A History of Wordsworth's Imagination*, 1954; also see Judson Stanley Lyon, *The Excursion: A Study*, 1950; Abbie Findlay Potts, *Wordworth's 'Prelude': A Study of Its Literary Form*, 1954; *Journals of Dorothy Wordsworth*, ed. Ernest de Selincourt, 1941, 2 v., rev. 1958 (by Helen Darbishire); *Letters of Mary Wordsworth*, ed. Mary E. Burton, 1958.

PERSONAL

On Monday, 4th October 1802, my brother William was married to Mary Hutchinson. I slept a good deal of the night, and rose fresh and well in the morning. At a little after eight o'clock, I saw them go down the avenue towards the church. William had parted from me upstairs. When they were absent, my dear little Sara prepared the breakfast. I kept myself as quiet as I could, but when I saw the two men running up the walk, coming to tell us it was over, I could stand it no longer, and threw myself on the bed, where I lay in stillness, neither hearing nor seeing anything till Sara came upstairs to me, and said, "They are coming." This forced me from the bed where I lay, and I moved, I knew not how, straight forward, faster than my strength could carry me, till I met my beloved William, and fell upon his bosom. He and John Hutchinson led me to the house, and there I stayed to welcome my dear Mary. As soon as we had breakfasted, we departed. It rained when we set off.

Dorothy Wordsworth, 1802, Journals, vol. I, p. 148

A visit from Wordsworth. . . . His conversation was long and interesting. He spoke of his own poems with the just feeling of confidence which a sense of his own excellence gives him. He is now convinced that he never can derive emolument from them; but, being independent, he willingly gives up all idea of doing so. He is persuaded that if men are to become better and wiser, the poems will sooner or later make their way.

Henry Crabb Robinson, 1812, Diary, May 8;
Diary, Reminiscences and Correspondence, vol. I, p. 245

Wordsworth's residence and mine are fifteen miles asunder—a sufficient distance to preclude any frequent interchange of visits. I have known him nearly twenty years, and for about half that time intimately. The strength and the character of his mind you see in The Excursion; and his life does not belie his writings, for in every relation of life, and every point of view, he is a truly exemplary and admirable man. In conversation he is powerful beyond any of his contemporaries; and as a poet—I speak not from the partiality of friendship, nor because we have been so absurdly held up as both writing upon one concerted system of poetry, but with the most deliberate exercise of impartial judgment whereof I am capable, when I declare my full conviction that posterity will rank him with Milton.

Robert Southey, 1814, Letter to Bernard Barton, Dec. 19;
Life and Correspondence, ed. C. C. Southey

There seemed to me, in his first appearance, something grave almost to austerity, and the deep tones of his voice added strength to that impression of him. There was not visible about him the same easy and disengaged air that so immediately charmed me in Southey—his mind seemed to require an effort to awaken itself thoroughly from some brooding train of thought, and his manner, as I felt at least, at first reluctantly relaxed into blandness and urbanity. . . . The features of Wordsworth's face are strong and high, almost harsh and severe—and his eyes have, when he is silent, a dim, thoughtful, I had nearly said melancholy expression—so that when a smile takes possession of his countenance, it is indeed the most powerful smile I ever saw. . . . Never saw I a countenance in which Contemplation so reigns. His brow is very lofty—and his dark brown hair seems worn away, as it were, by thought, so thinly is it spread over his temples. The colour of his face is almost sallow; but it is not the sallowness of confinement or ill-health, it speaks rather of the rude and boisterous greeting of the mountain-weather.

John Gibson Lockhart, 1819, "Letters from the Lakes,"
Blackwood's Magazine, vol. 4, pp. 739, 740

More than all The Excursion and the Platonic Ode is developed in his dome-like forehead. And his manner and conversation are full of the pleasant playful sincerity and kindness which are so observable in his works. The utter absence of pretension in all he says and looks is very striking. He does not say many things to be remembered; and most of his observations are chiefly noticeable for their delicate taste, strong good sense, and stout healthy diction, rather than for imagery or condensed principles of philosophy. You see in him the repose or the sport, but neither the harlequinade, nor the conflict of genius. I believe he has long turned the corner of life; and yet there is not about him the slightest tendency to be wearied or disgusted with human nature, or to be indifferent toward the common little objects, occurrences, and people round him. All his daily fireside companionable sympathies are as sensitive and good-humoured as ever.

John Sterling, 1828, Letters

I must say I never saw any manifestation of small jealousy between Coleridge and Wordsworth; which . . . I thought uncommonly to the credit of both. I am sure they entertained a thorough respect for each other's intellectual endowments. . . . Wordsworth was a single-minded man: with less imagination than Coleridge, but with a more harmonious judgment, and better balanced principles. Coleridge, conscious of his transcendent powers, rioted in a licence of tongue which no man could tame. Wordsworth, though he could discourse most eloquent music, was never unwilling to sit still in Coleridge's presence, yet could be as happy in prattling with a child as in communing with a sage. If Wordsworth condescended to converse with me, he spoke to me as if I were his equal in mind, and made me pleased and proud in consequence. If Coleridge held me by the button, for lack of fitter audience, he had a talent for making me feel *his* wisdom and my own stupidity; so that I was miserable and humiliated by the sense of it.

Charles Mayne Young, 1828, Journal, July 6;
Memoir by Julian Charles Young

He was, upon the whole, not a well made man. His legs were pointedly condemned by all female connoisseurs in legs; not that they were bad in any way which *would* force itself upon your notice—there was no absolute deformity about them; and undoubtedly they had been serviceable legs beyond the average standard of human requisition; for I calculate, upon good data, that with these identical legs Wordsworth must have traversed a distance of 175,000 to 180,000 English miles—a mode of exertion which, to him, stood in the stead of alcohol and all other stimulants whatsoever be the animal spirits; to which, indeed, he was indebted for a life of unclouded happiness, and we for much of what is most excellent in his writings. But, useful as they have proved themselves, the Wordsworthian legs were certainly not ornamental; and it was really a pity, as I agreed with a lady in thinking, that he has not another pair for evening dress parties. . . . I do not conceive that Wordsworth *could* have been an amiable boy; he was austere and unsocial, I have reason to think, in his habits; not generous; and not self-denying. I am pretty certain that no consideration would ever have induced Wordsworth to burden himself with a lady's reticule, parasol, shawl, or anything exacting trouble and attention. Mighty must be the danger which would induce him to lead her horse by the bridle. Nor would he, without some demur, stop to offer his hand over a stile. Freedom—unlimited, careless, insolent freedom—unoccupied possession of his own arms—absolute control over his own legs and motions—these have always been so essential to his comfort, that, in any case where they were likely to become questionable, he would have declined to make one of the party.

Thomas DeQuincey, 1839-54, The Lake Poets:
William Wordsworth, Works, ed. Masson, vol. II, pp. 242, 262

Just for a handful of silver he left us,
Just for a riband to stick in his coat—
Found the one gift of which fortune bereft us,
Lost all the others she lets us devote;
They, with gold to give, doled him out silver,
So much was theirs who so little allowed:
How all our copper had gone for his service!
Rags—were they purple, his heart had been proud!

We that had loved him so, followed him, honoured him,
Lived in his mild and magnificent eye,
Learned his great language, caught his clear accents,
Made him our pattern to live and to die!
Shakespeare was of us, Milton was for us,
Burns, Shelley, were with us—they watch from their graves!
He alone breaks from the van and the freemen,
—He alone sinks to the rear and the slaves!

Robert Browning, 1842, The Lost Leader

He led me out into his garden, and showed me the gravel walk in which thousands of his lines were composed. . . . He had just returned from a visit to Staffa, and within three days had made three sonnets on Fingal's Cave, and was composing a fourth, when he was called in to see me. He said, "If you are interested in my verses, perhaps you will like to hear these lines." I gladly assented, and he recollected himself for a few moments, and then stood forth and repeated, one after the other, the three entire sonnets with great animation. . . . This recitation was so unlooked-for and surprising—he, the old Wordsworth, standing apart, and reciting to me in a garden-walk, like a schoolboy declaiming,—that I at first was near to laugh; but recollecting myself, that I had come thus far to see a poet, and he was chanting poems to me, I saw that he was right and I was wrong, and gladly gave myself up to hear.

Ralph Waldo Emerson, 1856, English Traits, ch. i

For the rest, he talked well in his way; with veracity, easy brevity, and force; as a wise tradesman would of his tools and work-shop,—and as no unwise one could. His voice was good, frank and sonorous, though practically clear, distinct and forcible, rather than melodious; the tone of him business-like, sedately confident, no discourtesy, yet no anxiety about being courteous; a fine wholesome rusticity, fresh as his mountain breezes, sat well on the stalwart veteran, and on all he said and did. You would have said he was a usually taciturn man; glad to unlock himself, to audience sympathetic and intelligent, when such offered itself. His face bore marks of much, not always peaceful, meditation; the look of it not bland nor benevolent, so much as close, impregnable and hard: a man *multa tacere loquive paratus,* in a world where he had experienced no lack of contradictions as he strode along! The eyes were not very brilliant, but they had quite a clearness; there was enough of brow, and well-shaped; rather too much of cheek ("horse-face," I have heard satirists say), face of squarish shape and decidedly longish, as I think the head itself was (*its* "length" going *horizontal*): he was large-boned, lean but still firm-knit, tall, and strong-looking when he stood; a right good old steel-gray figure, with a fine rustic simplicity and dignity about him, and a veracious *strength* looking through him which might have suited one of those old steel-gray *Markgrafs* (Graf-Grau, "Steel-gray") whom Henry the Fowler set up toward the "marches," and to do battle with the intrusive Heathen, in a stalwart and judicious manner.

Thomas Carlyle, 1867, "Wordsworth," *Reminiscences,*
ed. Norton, vol. II, p. 301

Wordsworth and Dickens did not *take* to each other. Indeed, there was a mutual contempt between them, although they met only once. This was about the year 1843. Some days after, the gentleman whose guest Wordsworth was, in the suburbs of London, asked the Poet, how he liked the great Novelist? Wordsworth had a great contempt for young men, and, after pursing up his lips in a fashion peculiar to him, and swinging one leg over the other, the bare flesh of his ankles appearing over his socks, slowly answered: "Why, I am not much given to turn critic on people I meet; but, as you ask me, I will candidly avow that I thought him a very talkative, vulgar young person,—but I dare say he may be very clever. Mind, I don't want to say a word against him, for I have never read a line he has written." Some time after this, the same querist guardedly asked Dickens how he had liked the Poet Laureate?—"Like him? Not at all. He is a dreadful Old Ass."

R. Shelton Mackenzie, 1870, *Life of Charles Dickens,* p. 243

Old "Daddy Wordsworth," as he was sometimes called, I am afraid, from my Christening, he is now, I suppose, passing under the Eclipse consequent on the Glory which followed his obscure Rise. I remember fifty years ago at our Cambridge, when the Battle was fighting for him by the Few against the Many of us who only laughed at "Louisa in the Shade" &c. His brother was then Master of Trinity College; like all Wordsworths (unless the drowned Sailor) pompous and priggish. He used to drawl out the Chapel responses so that we called him the "Meeserable Sinner" and his brother the "Meeserable Poet."

Edward Fitzgerald, 1876, *Letters,* vol. I, p. 381

Can a man be reckoned a favourite of fortune when he has lost his mother during his eighth year, and his father at sixteen; when he has been arbitrarily deprived of his inheritance, has had to endure a humiliating existence under the roof of stern and narrow-minded grandparents, and for years has been coldly treated by his relations on account of his indolence, his obstinacy, and his refusal to embark upon any of the safe careers suggested to him; when he is kept apart from the sister whom he loves beyond everything else, apparently from fear that she may become contaminated by his disobedience and his subversive opinions; when he entrusts all his dreams of happiness to the French Revolution, only to see them borne under in the tempest, and loses not only his respect and love for his native country, but all hope of progress as well; when, meanwhile, his existence is so straitened, so penurious even, and so utterly without promise for the morrow, that he is compelled to postpone indefinitely his union with his sister's friend, that maiden, chosen long ago, and now beloved, whom he knows not whether he can ever make his wife?

> Emile Legouis, 1896, *The Early Life of William Wordsworth,*
> *1770-1798*, tr. Matthews, p. 386

Some readers of Wordsworth are misled in their judgment of the poet by the vulgar error that he was before all else tranquil, mild, gentle, an amiable pastoral spirit. He sang of the daisy and the celandine, the linnet and the lamb; and therefore he must have been always a serene, tender, benign contemplator of things that make for peace. There can be no greater mistake; at the heart of his peace was passion; his benignity was like the greensward upon a rocky hillside. As a boy, Wordsworth was violent and moody; in his early manhood he was stern, bold, worn by exhausting ardours.

> Edward Dowden, 1897, *The French Revolution and*
> *English Literature,* p. 197

Descriptive Sketches in Verse (1793)

During the last year of my residence at Cambridge, 1794, I became acquainted with Mr. Wordsworth's first publication, entitled *Descriptive Sketches*: and seldom, if ever, was the emergence of an original poetic genius above the literary horizon more evidently announced. In the form, style, and manner of the whole poem, and in the structure of the particular lines and periods, there is a harshness and acerbity connected and combined with words and images all a-glow, which might recall those products of the vegetable world, where gorgeous blossoms rise out of a hard thorny rind and shell, within which the rich fruit is elaborating. The language is not only peculiar and strong, but at times knotty and contorted, as by its own impatient strength; while the novelty and struggling crowd of images, acting in conjunction with the difficulties of the style, demands always a greater closeness of attention than poetry,—at all events, than descriptive poetry—has a right to claim.

> Samuel Taylor Coleridge, 1817, *Biographia Literaria,* ch. iv

Wordsworth's first poetical ventures, which were published three years before Scott's translations from Bürger, were *An Evening Walk*—an attempt to paint a series of landscape views in his own country, and *Descriptive Sketches*, an attempt to paint the scenery of the Alps, among which he had lately made a pedestrian tour with a college friend. The most that can be said of these productions is that they are fairly well written, and that there are touches of natural description in them which could only have been the result of actual observation.

> Richard Henry Stoddard, 1883, *English Verse,*
> *Lyrics of the Nineteenth Century,* Introduction, p. xx

The Borderers (1795-96)

I must be allowed to observe that however unjust and however absurd it would be to cite this play of *The Borderers,* completed by Wordsworth at the age of twenty-six and published by Wordsworth at the age of seventy-two, as an adequate and important specimen of his work, it is a hundred times more unjust and it is a thousand times more absurd to cite the poem of *Queen Mab* as an adequate and important selection of Shelley's. And none but a very rash and very ignorant partisan will venture to deny that if this burlesque experiment in unnatural horror had been attempted by any poet of less orthodox and correct reputation in ethics and theology than Wordsworth's, the general verdict of critical morality would almost certainly have described it and dismissed it as the dream of a probably incurable and possibly a criminal lunatic. I am very far from thinking that this would have been a justifiable or a reasonable verdict: but I have no manner of doubt that it would have been a popular one.

> Algernon Charles Swinburne, 1886, "Wordsworth and Byron,"
> *Miscellanies,* p. 119

Taking the piece upon its own claim to merit as a study in the genesis of sin and in the inequalities of justice, it is not altogether a success. Its characterisation is unclear, and its treatment is unconvincing. With the most amenable disposition to the didactic purpose of the play, the reader is left perplexed. Wordsworth was grappling with a great idea, but the form which he chose was neither suitable to it nor consistent with itself.

> Laurie Magnus, 1897, *A Primer of Wordsworth*
> *with a Critical Essay,* p. 49

Lyrical Ballads (1798-1800)

The principal object, then, which I proposed to myself in these Poems was to chuse incidents and situations from common life, and to relate or describe them, throughout, as far as was possible, in a selection of language really used by men, and, at the same time, to throw over them a certain colouring of imagination, whereby ordinary things should be presented to the mind in an unusual way; and, further, and above all, to make these incidents and situations interesting by tracing in them, truly though not ostentatiously, the primary laws of our nature: chiefly, as far as regards the manner in which we associate ideas in a state of excitement. Low and rustic life was generally chosen, because, in that condition, the essential passions of the heart find a better soil in which they can attain their maturity, are less under restraint, and speak a plainer and more emphatic language; because in that condition of life our elementary feelings co-exist in a state of greater simplicity, and, consequently, may be more accurately contemplated, and more forcibly communicated; because the manners of rural life germinate from these elementary feelings; and from the necessary character of rural occupations, are more easily comprehended, and are more durable; and, lastly, because in that condition the passions of men are incorporated with the beautiful and permanent forms of nature.

William Wordsworth, 1800, *Lyrical Ballads,*
Second Edition, Preface

A careful and repeated examination of these confirms me in the belief, that the omission of less than a hundred lines would have precluded nine-tenths of the criticism on this work. I hazard this declaration, however, on the supposition, that the reader has taken it up, as he would have done any other collection of poems purporting to derive their subjects or interests from the incidents of domestic or ordinary life, intermingled with higher strains of meditation which the poet utters in his own person and character; with the proviso, that these poems were perused without knowledge of, or reference to, the author's peculiar opinions, and that the reader had not had his attention previously directed to those peculiarities. . . . In the critical remarks, therefore, prefixed and annexed to the Lyrical Ballads, I believe, we may safely rest, as the true origin of the unexampled opposition which Mr. Wordsworth's writings have been since doomed to encounter.

Samuel Taylor Coleridge, 1817, *Biographia Literaria,* ch. iv

His Muse . . . is a levelling one. . . . Fools have laughed at, wise men scarcely understand them. He takes a subject or a story merely as pegs or loops to hang thought and feeling on; the incidents are trifling, in porportion to his contempt for imposing appearances; the reflections are profound, according to the gravity and the aspiring pretensions of his mind.

William Hazlitt, 1825, *The Spirit of the Age,* p. 124

This volume contained several poems which have been justly blamed for triviality—as "The Thorn," "Goody Blake," "The Idiot Boy"; several in which, as in "Simon Lee," triviality is mingled with much real pathos; and some, as "Expostulation and Reply" and "The Tables Turned," which are of the very essence of Wordsworth's nature. It is hardly too much to say that, if these two last-named poems—to the careless eye so slight and trifling—were all that had remained from Wordsworth's hand, they would have "spoken to the comprehending" of a new individuality, as distinct and unmistakable in its way as that which Sappho has left engraven on the world forever in words even fewer than these. And the volume ended with a poem which Wordsworth composed in 1798, in one day, during a tour with his sister to Tintern and Chepstow. The "Lines written above Tintern Abbey" have become, as it were, the *locus classicus,* or consecrated formulary of the Wordsworthian faith. They say in brief what it is the work of the poet's biographer to say in detail.

F. W. H. Myers, 1881, *Wordsworth*
(*English Men of Letters*), p. 33

The tribute which the Poet paid [in *Tintern Abbey*] to his sister is the highest which one soul can pay to another: he was never weary of singing her praise, nor was she ever tired of trying to make herself worthy of his praise. Endowed with faculties capable of gaining distinction in the same sphere of work, she nevertheless chose to let him sing of what she felt and saw. To those familiar with the close of her life these words seem prophetic; for she lingered a few years after her brother's death, and her chief solace seemed to be the remembrance of days passed in his companionship. More has been written of this poem than of any other of his unless it be the "Platonic Ode."

Andrew J. George, 1889, ed., *Selections from
Wordsworth*, p. 342, note

There was, indeed, one poem in the volume, the "Lines written above Tintern Abbey," in which a fresh theme was handled with a power that nobody could be insensible to. If all had been like this, the acknowledgment of Wordsworth's greatness would not have been checked and held back by astonishment at the grotesque strangeness of the lyrical ballads, to which the title of the volume challenged special attention. . . . This poem is characteristic of the loftiest side of Wordsworth's genius. In it he struck for the first time the sublime note that has drawn men after him as the prophet of a new delight, a full-voiced speaker of things that all feel dimly and vaguely, but which no poet before him had expressed with such force.

William Minto, 1894, *The Literature of the
Georgian Era,* ed. Knight, pp. 176, 180

Peter Bell (1798; pub. 1819)

> Wordsworth informs us he was nineteen years
>   Considering and re-touching Peter Bell;
> Watering his laurels with the killing tears
>   Of slow, dull care, so that their roots to hell
> Might pierce, and their wide branches blot the spheres
>   Of heaven with dewey leaves and flowers; this well
> May be, for heaven and earth conspire to foil
> The ever-busy gardener's blundering toil.
>
> Percy Bysshe Shelley, 1820, *The Witch of Atlas*, Proem

None of Wordsworth's productions are better known by name than *Peter Bell,* and yet few, probably, are less familiar, even to convinced Wordsworthians. The poet's biographers and critics have commonly shirked the responsibility of discussing this poem, and when the Primrose stanza has been quoted, and the Parlour stanza smiled at, there is usually no more said about *Peter Bell.* A puzzling obscurity hangs around its history. We have no positive knowledge why its publication was so long delayed; nor, having been delayed, why it was at length determined upon. Yet a knowledge of this poem is not merely an important, but, to a thoughtful critic, an essential element in the comprehension of Wordsworth's poetry. No one who examines that body of literature with sympathetic attention should be content to overlook the piece in which Wordsworth's theories are pushed to their furthest extremity.

> Edmund Gosse, 1891, *Gossip in a Library,* p. 253

It is by his matter that Wordsworth must primarily be judged, and, fortunately, when it was not complicated by technicalities in the telling, his style was always equal to it. The material of Peter Bell's story does not fall below the level of the best of Wordsworth's work. Its theme is true. As knowledge widens, it is recognised more and more that man is not divorced from the rest of nature.

> Laurie Magnus, 1897, *A Primer of Wordsworth*
> *with a Critical Essay,* pp. 77, 78

Intimations of Immortality (1803-6)

It is for every one who takes thought of the deep things of his nature, the mysteries of his being, memories of early innocence and yearnings for eternity, that Wordsworth struck his lofty lyric the most sublime ode in this and, perhaps, any language, on the birth—the life—the undying destiny of the soul of man.

> Henry Reed, 1850-55, *Lectures on English Literature,*
> *from Chaucer to Tennyson,* p. 33

His "Ode on Immortality" is the high-water mark which the intellect has reached in this age. New means were employed, and new realms added to the empire of the muse, by his courage.

Ralph Waldo Emerson, 1856-84, English Traits

What is valuable in Wordsworth's poetry is very valuable indeed; and I think a true lover of what is highest and best in poetic expression, would rather have written his Ode on the Intimations of Immortality than any other existing piece of the same length.

James Hain Friswell, 1869, Essays on English Writers, p. 332

That famous, ambitious, and occasionally magnificent poem—which by the way is no more an ode than it is an epic—reveals the partiality and inequality of Wordsworth's inspiration as unmistakably as its purity and its power. Five stanzas or sections—from the opening of the fifth to the close of the ninth—would be utterly above all praise, if the note they are pitched in were sustained throughout: but after its unspeakably beautiful opening the seventh stanza falls suddenly far down beneath the level of those five first lines, so superb in the majesty of their sweetness, the magnificence of their tenderness, that to have written but the two last of them would have added glory to any poet's crown of fame. The details which follow on the close of this opening cadence do but impair its charm with a sense of incongruous realism and triviality, to which the suddenly halting and disjointed metre bears only too direct and significant a correspondence. No poet, surely, ever "changed his hand" with such inharmonious awkwardness, or "checked his pride" with such unreasonable humility, as Wordsworth.

Algernon Charles Swinburne, 1886, "Wordsworth and Byron,"
Miscellanies, p. 135

In the famous Ode on Intimations of Immortality, the poet doubtless does point to a set of philosophic ideas, more or less complete; but the thought from which he sets out, that our birth is but a sleep and a forgetting, and that we are less and less able to perceive the visionary gleam, less and less alive to the glory and the dream of external nature, as infancy recedes farther from us, is, with all respects for the declaration of Mr. Ruskin to the contrary, contrary to notorious fact, experience, and truth.

John Morley, 1888, ed., The Complete Poetical Works of
William Wordsworth, Introduction, p. lxv

The Excursion (1814)

This will never do! It bears no doubt the stamp of the author's heart and fancy: But unfortunately not half so visibly as that of his peculiar system.

His former poems were intended to recommend that system, and to bespeak favour for it by their individual merit;—but this, we suspect, must be recommended by the system—and can only expect to succeed where it has been previously established. It is longer, weaker, and tamer, than any of Mr. Wordsworth's other productions; with less boldness of originality, and less even of that extreme simplicity and lowliness of tone which wavered so prettily, in the *Lyrical Ballads,* between silliness and pathos. We have imitations of Cowper, and even of Milton here; engrafted on the natural drawl of the Lakers—and all diluted into harmony by that profuse and irrepressible wordiness which deluges all the blank verse of this school of poetry, and lubricates and weakens the whole structure of their style.

Francis, Lord Jeffrey, 1814-44, "Wordsworth's Excursion,"
Contributions to the Edinburgh Review, vol. III, p. 233

The causes which have prevented the poetry of Mr. Wordsworth from attaining its full share of popularity are to be found in the boldness and originality of his genius. The times are past when a poet could securely follow the direction of his own mind into whatever tracts it might lead. . . . If from living among simple mountaineers, from a daily intercourse with them, not upon the footing of a patron, but in the character of an equal, he has detected, or imagines that he has detected, through the cloudy medium of their unlettered discourse, thoughts and apprehensions not vulgar; traits of patience and constancy, love unwearied, and heroic endurance, not unfit (as he may judge) to be made the subject of verse, he will be deemed a man of perverted genius by the philanthropist who, conceiving of the peasantry of his country only as objects of a pecuniary sympathy, starts at finding them elevated to a level of humanity with himself, having their own loves, enmities, cravings, aspirations, &c., as much beyond his faculty to believe, as his beneficence to supply. . . . Those who hate *Paradise Lost* will not love this poem. The steps of the great master are discernible in it; not in direct imitation or injurious parody, but in the following of the spirit, in free homage and generous subjection.

Charles Lamb, 1814, "Wordsworth's Excursion,"
Quarterly Review, vol. 12, pp. 110, 111

This week I finished Wordsworth's poem. It has afforded me less intense pleasure on the whole, perhaps, than I had expected, but it will be a source of frequent gratification. The wisdom and high moral character of the work are beyond anything of the same kind with which I am acquainted, and the spirit of the poetry flags much less frequently than might be expected. There are passages which run heavily, tales which are prolix, and reasonings which are spun out, but in general the narratives are exquisitely tender. That of the courtier parson, who retains in solitude the feelings of high society, whose vigour of mind is unconquerabie, and who, even after the death of his wife, appears able for a short time to bear up against desolation and wretchedness, by the powers of his native temperament, is most delightful.

Henry Crabb Robinson, 1814, Diary, Nov. 23; Diary,
Reminiscences and Correspondence, ed. Sadler, vol. I, p. 296

And Wordsworth, in a rather long "Excursion"
(I think the quarto holds five hundred pages),
Has given a sample from the vasty version
Of his new system to perplex the sages;
'Tis poetry—at least by his assertion,
And may appear so when the dog-star rages—
And he who understands it would be able
To add a story to the Tower of Babel.

Lord Byron, 1819, Don Juan, Dedication

It affects a system without having an intelligible clue to one; and, instead of unfolding a principle in various and striking lights, repeats the same conclusions till they become flat and insipid. . . . *The Excursion,* we believe, fell still-born from the press. There was something abortive, and clumsy, and ill-judged in the attempt. It was long and laboured. The personages, for the most part, were low, the fare rustic: the plan raised expectations which were not fulfilled, and the effect was like being ushered into a stately hall and invited to sit down to a splendid banquet in the company of clowns, and with nothing but successive courses of apple-dumpling served up. It was not even *toujours perdrix!*

William Hazlitt, 1825, The Spirit of the Age, p. 129

Judged by ordinary standards *The Excursion* appears an epic without action, and with two heroes, the Pastor and the Wanderer, whose characters are identical. Its form is cumbrous in the extreme, and large tracts of it have little claim to the name of poetry. Wordsworth compares *The Excursion* to a temple of which his smaller poems form subsidiary shrines; but the reader will more often liken the small poems to gems, and *The Excursion* to the rock from which they were extracted. The long poem contains, indeed, magnificent passages, but as a whole it is a diffused description of scenery which the poet has elsewhere caught in brighter glimpses; a diffused statement of hopes and beliefs which have crystallized more exquisitely elsewhere round the moments of inspiring emotion. *The Excursion,* in short, has the drawbacks of a didactic poem as compared with lyrical poems; but, judged as a didactic poem, it has the advantage of containing teaching of true and permanent value.

> F. W. H. Myers, 1881, *Wordsworth* (*English Men of Letters*)

Wordsworth's *Excursion* was published in 1814, in a two guinea quarto volume, but it took six years to exhaust an edition of five hundred copies.

> Henry B. Wheatley, 1898, *Prices of Books*, p. 97

The Prelude (1850)

> Friend of the wise! and teacher of the good!
> Into my heart have I received that lay
> More than historic, that prophetic lay
> Wherein (high theme by thee first sung aright)
> Of the foundations and the building up
> Of a Human Spirit thou hast dar'd to tell
> What may be told, to the understanding mind
> Revealable; and what within the mind
> By vital breathings secret as the soul
> Of vernal growth, oft quickens in the heart
> Thoughts all too deep for words!—

> Samuel Taylor Coleridge, 1807, *To William Wordsworth,*
> *Composed on the night after his recitation of a Poem*
> *on the growth of an individual mind*

We have finished Wordsworth's *Prelude*. It has many lofty passages. It soars and sinks, and is by turns sublime and commonplace. It is Wordsworth as he was at the age of thirty-five or forty.

> Henry Wadsworth Longfellow, 1850, *Journal,* July 21;
> *Life* by S. Longfellow, vol. II, p. 175

I brought home, and read, *The Prelude*. It is a poorer *Excursion*; the same sort of faults and beauties; but the faults greater, and the beauties fainter, both in themselves, and because faults are always made more offensive, and beauties less pleasing, by repetition. The story is the old story. There are the old raptures about mountains and cataracts; the old flimsy philosophy about the effect of scenery on the mind; the old crazy mystical metaphysics; the endless wilderness of dull, flat, prosaic twaddle; and here and there fine descriptions and energetic declamations interspersed. The story of the French Revolution, and of its influence on the character of a young enthusiast, is told again at greater length, and with less force and pathos, than in the *Excursion*. The poem is to the last degree Jacobinical, indeed Socialist. I understand perfectly why Wordsworth did not choose to publish it in his lifetime.

Thomas Babington Macaulay, 1850, *Journal*, July 28;
Life and Letters, ed. Trevelyan, vol. II, ch. xii

At the time when *The Prelude* was fresh from the press, he [Macaulay] was maintaining against the opinion of a large and mixed society that the poem was unreadable. At last, overborne by the united indignation of so many of Wordsworth's admirers, he agreed that the question should be referred to the test of personal experience: and on inquiry it was discovered that the only individual present who had got through *The Prelude* was Macaulay himself.

George Otto Trevelyan, 1876, *Life and Letters*
of Lord Macaulay, vol. I, ch. ii

In Wordworth's case, the posthumous decline may have been owing in part to disappointment occasioned by *The Prelude,* which was given to the public a few months after the author's death. For myself, I must confess that I was greatly taken back on first reading that work; it disappointed me sadly: but Coleridge's grand poem in its praise had raised very high expectations in me; which were so far from being met, and indeed so badly dashed, that I did not venture upon a second reading for several years. But I still remembered Coleridge's poem, still had faith in his judgment, and so committed the rather unusual folly of suspecting that the fault, after all, might be in myself. So, at length, I gave it a second perusal, and was then even more disappointed than I had been at first, but disappointed just the other way; and so repented my hasty dislike, that I soon after tried it a third time: this led to a fourth trial, and this to a fifth. Thus its interest kept mounting higher and higher on every fresh perusal; and now for some eighteen years I have not been able to let a year pass without reading it at least twice. And it still keeps its hold on me, still keeps pulling me back to it.

Henry N. Hudson, 1884, *Studies in Wordsworth*, p. 96

The Prelude, in which Wordsworth gives an account of his own spiritual development, is one of the numerous echoes of the *Confessions* of Rousseau; but it is an echo in which the morbid and unhealthy self-analysis of the *Confessions* has all but disappeared, and in which the interest of the reader is claimed on grounds which are all but independent of the mere individual. Wordsworth seeks to exhibit to us, not so much of his own personal career, as the way in which, amid the difficulties of the time, a human soul might find peace and inward freedom.

Edward Caird, 1892, "Wordsworth," Essays on Literature
and Philosophy, vol. I, p. 186

No autobiography, however, is so free from the taint of vanity as *The Prelude*. There are no theatrical attitudes, no arrangements of drapery for the sake of effect. The poet takes no pains to give statuesque beauty to his gestures, or dramatic sequence to his actions. Wordsworth had too much pride—if the word may be used to denote justifiable self-confidence—to be vain. He felt, he knew, that he was a great poet, and did not disguise the fact. He was unconscious of any obligation to wrap himself in the detestable cloak of false modesty.

Emile Legouis, 1896, The Early Life of William Wordsworth,
1770-1798, A Study of "The Prelude," tr. Matthews, p. 13

SONNETS

To Wordsworth has been vouchsafed the last grace of the self-denying artist: you think neither of him nor his style, but you cannot help thinking of—you *must* recall—the exact phrase, the *very* sentiment he wished. Milton's purity is more eager. In the most exciting parts of Wordsworth—and these sonnets are not very exciting—you always feel, you never forget, that what you have before you is the excitement of a recluse. There is nothing of the stir of life; nothing of the brawl of the world.

Walter Bagehot, 1864, "Wordsworth, Tennyson and Browning,"
Works, ed. Morgan, vol. I, p. 218

Wordsworth, the greatest of modern poets, is perhaps the greatest of English sonnet writers. Not only has he composed a larger number of sonnets than any other of our poets; he has also written more that are of first-rate excellence. There is no intensity of passion in Wordsworth's sonnets; and herein he differs from Shakespeare, and from Mrs. Browning, for whose sonnets the reader may feel an enthusiastic admiration that Wordsworth's thoughtful and calm verse rarely excites; neither has he attained the "dignified simplicity" which marks the sonnets of Milton; but for purity of language, for variety and strength of thought, for the *curiosa felicitas* of poetical diction, for the exquisite skill with which he associates the emotions of the mind and the aspects of nature, we know of no sonnet writer who can take precedence of Wordsworth. In his larger poems his language is sometimes slovenly, and occasionally, as Sir Walter Scott said, he chooses to crawl on all-fours; but this is rarely the case in the sonnets, and though he wrote upwards of four hundred, there are few, save those on the "Punishment of Death" and some of those called *Ecclesiastical* (for neither argument nor dogma find a fiitting place in verse) that we could willingly part with. Wordsworth's belief that the language of the common people may be used as the language of poetry was totally inoperative when he composed a sonnet. He wrote at such times in the best diction he could command, and the language like the thought is that of a great master.

John Dennis, 1873-80, English Sonnets: A Selection, note

Wordsworth's predilection for the sonnet, and the success wherewith he has cultivated a kind which might seem somewhat artificial for a poet of nature and of the fields, are things to be observed, and important to take account of in the final estimate. He has really excelled in it, and many of his sonnets approach perfection. Although English literature is singularly rich in poetical jewels of this kind, Wordsworth, to my taste, has in this respect rivals, but no superiors. The piece on the sonnet itself, that composed on Westminster Bridge, that addressed to Milton, and half a hundred others (he wrote four hundred), show that combination of ingenious turn and victorious final touch which is the triumph of the kind.

Edmond Scherer, 1880-91, "Wordsworth and Modern Poetry
in England," Essays on English Literature, tr. Saintsbury, p. 196

He had a right to think highly of his sonnets; for when they are good they surpass those of his contemporaries; but, unfortunately, the number of his good sonnets is small. He has written hundreds (say five hundred in round figures), of which it would be difficult to name twenty that substantiate his poetic greatness. He wrote upon all occasions, and many of his occasions, it must be confessed, are of the slightest. To stub his toe was to set his poetic feet in motion, and to evolve a train of philosophical musings upon toes in particular and things in general. His prime defect *(me judice)* is his stupendous egotism, which dwarfed that of Milton, great as it was, and which led him to worship himself, morning, noon, and night. Sacred in his own eye, he could not be otherwise in the eyes of others. That he was, or could be tedious, never entered into his calculation. I honor his memory this side of idolatry, as Ben Jonson wrote of Shakspere, but when I read his sonnets I am constrained to say, with the wicked Jeffrey, "This will never do."

Richard Henry Stoddard, 1881, "The Sonnet in English Poetry,"
Scribner's Monthly, vol. 22, p. 918

In the sonnets, on the other hand, we find much of Wordsworth's finest work, alike in substance and in form. "The sonnet's scanty plot of ground" suited him so well because it forced him to be at once concise and dignified, and yet allowed him to say straight out the particular message or emotion which was possessing him. . . . Taking them at their best you will find that nowhere in his work has he put so much of his finest self into so narrow a compass. Nowhere are there so many splendid single lines, lines of such weight, such imaginative ardour. And these lines have nothing to lose by their context, as almost all the fine lines which we find in the blank verse poems have to lose.

Arthur Symons, 1902, "Wordsworth,"
Fortnightly Review, vol. 77, p. 42

GENERAL

Southey's *Madoc* is in the press, I understand, and will make its appearance the beginning of winter. Wordsworth's Poems, for he has two great ones, that is, long ones, will not be published so soon. One of these is to be called *The Recluse,* and the other is to be a history of himself and his thoughts; this philosophy of egotism and shadowy refinements really spoils a great genius for poetry. We shall have a few exquisite gleams of natural feeling, sunk in a dull ugly ground of trash and affectation. I cannot forgive your expression, "Wordsworth & Co"; he merits criticism, but surely not contempt; to class him with his imitators is the greatest of all contempt. I thought our perusal of the *Lyrical Ballads* in the Temple would have prevented this; we found much to admire, but you will not admire. Sharp, however, is in the other extreme, I admit; but I insist it is the better of the two: he has been living at the Lakes, with these crazed poets; Wordsworth read him some thousand lines, and he repeated to me a few of these one day, which I could not worship as he wished me.

Francis Horner, 1804, *Letter to Francis Jeffrey,* Aug. 13;
Memoirs and Correspondence, vol. I, p. 272

Trouble not yourself about their present reception; of what moment is that compared with what I trust is their destiny? To console the afflicted; to add sunshine to daylight, by making the happy happier; to teach the young, and the gracious of every age, to see, to think, and feel, and therefore to become more actively and securely virtuous—this is their office, which I trust they will faithfully perform, long after we (that is, all that is mortal of us) are mouldered in our graves.

William Wordsworth, 1807, *Letter to Lady Beaumont,* May 21;
Knight's *Life of Wordsworth,* vol. II, p. 88

I have just got, by a most lucky chance, Wordsworth's new Poems. I owe them some most delightful hours of abstraction from the petty vexations of the little world where I live, and the horrible dangers of the great world, to which my feelings are attached. I applied to him his own verses:—

> Blessings be with them, and eternal praise,
> Who gave us nobler loves and nobler cares—the Poets.

The Sonnets on Switzerland and on Milton are sublime. Some of the others are in a style of severe simplicity, sometimes bordering on the harshness and dryness of some of Milton's Sonnets. Perhaps it might please him to know, that his poetry has given these feelings to one at so vast a distance: it is not worth adding, to one who formerly had foolish prejudices against him.

Sir James Mackintosh, 1808, *Journal,* July 6;
Memoirs of Mackintosh, ed. his Son, vol. I, p. 409

First; an austere purity of language, both grammatically and logically; in short, a perfect appropriateness of the words to the meaning. . . . The second characteristic excellence of Mr. Wordsworth's work is: a correspondent weight and sanity of the Thoughts and Sentiments,—won, not from books; but—from the poet's own meditative observation. They are *fresh* and have the dew upon them. . . . Even throughout his smaller poems there is scarcely one, which is not rendered valuable by some just and original reflection. . . . Third; . . . the sinewy strength and originality of single lines and paragraphs; the frequent *curiosa felicitas* of his diction. . . . Fourth; the perfect truth of nature in his images and descriptions, as taken immediately from nature, and proving a long and genial intimacy with the very spirit which gives the physiognomic expression to all the works of nature. . . . Fifth; a meditative pathos, a union of deep and subtle thought with sensibility; a sympathy with man as man,—the sympathy of a contemplator, rather than a fellow-sufferer or co-mate (*spectator, haud particeps*), but of a contemplator, from whose views no difference of rank conceals the sameness of nature; no injuries of wind or weather, or toil, or even of ignorance, wholly disguise the human face divine. . . . Here the man and Poet find themselves in each other . . . Last, and pre-eminently, I challenge for this poet the gift of Imagination in the highest and strictest sense of the word. In the play of *fancy,* Wordsworth, to my feelings, is not always graceful, and sometimes recondite. The *likeness* is occasionally too strange, or demands too peculiar a point of view, or is such as appears the creature of predetermined research, rather than spontaneous presentation. Indeed, his fancy seldom displays itself, as mere and unmodified fancy. But in imaginative power he stands nearest of all modern writers to Shakspeare and Milton; and yet in a kind perfectly unborrowed and his own. To employ his own words, which are at once an instance and an illustration, he does indeed to all thoughts and to all objects—

> Add the gleam,
> The light that never was, on sea or land,
> The consecration, and the poet's dream.

Samuel Taylor Coleridge, 1817, *Biographia Literaria*, ch. xxii

Mr. Wordsworth is the most original poet now living. He is the reverse of Walter Scott in all his defects and excellences. He has nearly all that the other wants, and wants all that the other possesses. His poetry is not external, but internal; it does not depend upon tradition, or story, or old song; he furnishes it from his own mind and is his own subject. He is the poet of mere sentiment. . . . He has produced a deeper impression, and on a smaller circle, than any other of his contemporaries. His powers have been mistaken by the age, nor does he exactly understand them himself. He cannot form a whole. He has not the constructive faculty. He can give only the fine tones of thought, drawn from his mind by accident or nature, like the sounds drawn from the Æolian harp by the wandering gale. He is totally deficient in all the machinery of poetry.

William Hazlitt, 1818, *Lectures on the English Poets,*
Lecture viii

> He had as much imagination
>   As a pint-pot;—he never could
> Fancy another situation,
> From which to dart his contemplation,
>   Than that wherein he stood.

Percy Bysshe Shelley, 1819, *Peter Bell the Third*

The descriptive poetry of the present day has been called by its cultivators a return to nature. Nothing is more impertinent than this pretension. Poetry cannot travel out of the regions of its birth, the uncultivated lands of semi-civilised men. Mr. Wordsworth, the great leader of the returners to nature, cannot describe a scene under his own eyes without putting into it the shadow of a Danish boy or the living ghost of Lucy Gray, or some similar phantastical parturition of the moods of his own mind.

Thomas Love Peacock, 1820, "The Four Ages of Poetry,"
Calidore and Miscellanea, p. 64

I do not know a man more to be venerated for uprightness of heart and loftiness of genius. Why he will sometimes choose to crawl upon all fours, when God has given him so noble a countenance to lift to heaven, I am as little able to account for, as for his quarrelling (as you tell me) with the wrinkles which time and meditation have stamped his brow withal.

Sir Walter Scott, 1820, *Letter to Allan Cunningham,* Nov.;
Life of Scott by Lockhart, ch 1

The highest quality of art is to conceal itself: these peasants of Schiller's are what every one imagines he could imitate successfully; yet in the hands of any but a true and strong-minded poet they dwindle into repulsive coarseness or mawkish insipidity. Among our own writers, who have tried such subjects, we remember none that has succeeded equally with Schiller. One potent but ill-fated genius has, in far different circumstances and with far other means, shown that he could have equalled him: *The Cotter's Saturday Night* of Burns is, in its own humble way, as quietly beautiful, as *simplix munditiis,* as the scenes of *Tell.* No other has even approached them; though some gifted persons have attempted it. Mr. Wordsworth is no ordinary man; nor are his pedlars, and leech-gatherers, and dalesmen, without their attractions and their moral; but they sink into whining drivellers beside *Rösselmann the Priest, Ulric the Smith, Hans of the Wall,* and the other sturdy confederates of Rütli.

Thomas Carlyle, 1825-45, *Life of Friedrich Schiller,* pt. iii, p. 205

Next to Byron, there is no poet whose writings have had so much influence on the taste of the age as Wordsworth. Byron drove on through the upper air till the thunder of his wheels died on the ear. Wordsworth drove to Parnassus by the lower road, got sometimes lost in bushes and lowland fogs, and was much molested by mosquito critics.

Henry Wadsworth Longfellow, 1829, *Note Book,*
Life by S. Longfellow, vol. I, p. 172

I have only a single remark to make on the poetry of Wordsworth, and I do it because I never saw the remark made before. It relates to the richness of his works for quotations. For these they are a mine that is altogether inexhaustible. There is nothing in nature that you may not get a quotation out of Wordsworth to suit, and a quotation too that breathes the very soul of poetry. There are only three books in the world that are worth the opening in search of mottos and quotations, and all of them are alike rich. These are, the Old Testament, Shakspeare, and the poetical works of Wordsworth, and strange to say, *The Excursion* abounds most in them.

James Hogg, 1832, *Autobiography*

I shall never forget with what feeling my friend Bryant, some years ago, described to me the effect produced upon him by his meeting for the first time with Wordsworth's Ballads. He lived, when quite young, where but a few works of poetry were to be had; at a period, too, when Pope was still the great idol in the Temple of Art. He said that, upon opening Wordsworth, a thousand springs seemed to gush up at once in his heart, and the face of Nature, of a sudden, to change into a strange freshness and life. He had felt the sympathetic touch from an according mind; and you see how instantly his powers and affections shot over the Earth and through his kind.

Richard Henry Dana, 1833, *The Idle Man,* Preface

Genius is not a creator, in the sense of fancying or feigning what does not exist. Its distinction is, to discern more of truth than common minds. It sees under disguises and humble forms everlasting beauty. This it is the prerogative of Wordsworth to discern and reveal in the walks of life, in the common human heart. He has revealed the loveliness of the primitive feelings, of the universal affections, of the human soul. The grand truth which pervades his poetry is that the beautiful is not confined—the rare, the new, the distant,—to scenery and modes of life open only to the few; but that it is poured forth profusely on the common earth and sky, that it gleams from the loneliest flower, that it lights up the humblest sphere, that the sweetest affections lodge in lowly hearts, that there is sacredness, dignity, and loveliness in lives which few eyes rest on,—that, even in the absence of all intellectual culture, the domestic relations can quietly nourish that disinterestedness which is the element of all greatness, and without which intellectual power is a splendid deformity. Wordsworth is the poet of humanity; he teaches reverence for our universal nature; he breaks down the fictitious barriers between human hearts.

William Ellery Channing, 1841, *The Present Age,* Addresses

Subsequently to Shakspere, these notices, as of all phenomena whatsoever that demanded a familiarity with nature in the spirit of love, became rarer and rarer. At length, as the eighteenth century was winding up its accounts, forth stepped William Wordsworth; of whom, as a reader of all pages in nature, it may be said that, if we except Dampier, the admirable buccaneer, the gentle *filibustier,* and some few professional naturalists, he first and he last looked at natural objects with the eye that neither will be dazzled from without nor cheated by preconceptions from within. Most men look at nature in the hurry of a confusion that distinguishes nothing; *their* error is from without. Pope, again, and many who live in towns, make such blunders as that of supposing the moon to tip with silver the hills *behind* which she is rising, not by erroneous use of their eyes (for they use them not at all), but by inveterate preconceptions. Scarcely has there been a poet with what could be called a learned eye, or an eye *extensively* learned, before Wordsworth. Much affectation there has been of that sort since *his* rise, and at all times much counterfeit enthusiasm; but the sum of the matter is this,—that Wordsworth had his passion for nature fixed in his blood; it was a necessity, like that of the mulberry-leaf to the silkworm; and through his commerce with nature did he live and breathe. Hence it was—viz. from the *truth* of his love—that his knowledge grew; whilst most others, being merely hypocrites in their love, have turned out merely sciolists in their knowledge. This chapter, therefore, of *sky*-scenery may be said to have been revivified amongst the resources of poetry by Wordsworth— rekindled, if not absolutely kindled.

Thomas De Quincey, 1845-57, *On Wordsworth's Poetry,*
Works, ed. Masson, vol. XI, p. 318

My admiration of Wordsworth is composed of two different elements, namely, my admiration of what is peculiar to his genius, and my admiration of what he has in common with other first-class poets; I must therefore adjust the balance between these two admirations; and therefore I cannot agree with those who admire even the inferior poems of his earlier and most characteristic manner more than the best poems written in his later style. . . . Without what is absolutely peculiar to his genius, and to it alone, Wordsworth would not have been a very great, that is, an original poet; but if this, his special merit, had been his only merit, he would have lacked several of those perfections which, in their aggregate alone, make up a first-class poet, as well as an original poet.

Sara Coleridge, 1845, *Letter to Aubrey DeVere;*
Recollections, pp. 203, 204

Wordsworth, I am told, does not care for music! And it is very likely, for music (to judge from his verses) does not seem to care for him. I was astonished the other day, on looking in his works for the first time after a long interval, to find how deficient he was in all that may be called the musical side of a poet's nature,—the genial, the animal-spirited or bird-like,—the happily accordant. Indeed he does not appear to me, now, more than half the man I once took him for, when I was among those who came to the "rescue" for him, and exaggerated his works in the heat of "reaction." . . . Wordsworth is indeed "cold and diffuse," notwithstanding "all the fine things" which, you justly add, he contains. He seems to like nothing heartily, except the talking about it; and is in danger of being taken by posterity (who will certainly never read two-thirds of him) for a kind of puritan retainer of the Establishment, melancholy in his recommendations of mirth, and perplexed between prudence and pragmaticalness, subserviency and ascendency, retrospection and innovation. I should infallibly (or far as lay in my power) have deposed the god I helped to set up, and put Coleridge in his stead (I mean in the last edition of *The Feast of the Poets*), but I did not like to hurt his feelings in his old age.

Leigh Hunt, 1848, *Correspondence,* vol. II, pp. 92, 93

A breath of the mountains, fresh born in the regions majestic,
That look with their eye-daring summits deep into the sky.
The voice of great Nature; sublime with her lofty conceptions,
Yet earnest and simple as any sweet child of the green lowly vale.

George Meredith, 1851, *Works,* vol. XXXI, p. 140

Never, perhaps, in the whole range of literary history, from Homer downwards, did any individual, throughout the course of a long life, dedicate himself to poetry with a devotion so pure, so perfect, and so uninterrupted, as he did. It was not his amusement, his recreation, his mere pleasure—it was the main, the serious, the solemn business of his being. . . . It was his morning, noon, and evening thought, the object of his out-of-doors rambles; the subject of his in-door reflections; and, as an art, he studied it as severely as ever Canova did sculpture, or Michael Angelo painting.

D. M. Moir, 1851-52, *Sketches of the Poetical Literature of the Past Half-Century,* p. 66

Wordsworth is more like Scott, and understands how to be happy, but yet cannot altogether rid himself of the sense that he is a philosopher, and ought always to be saying something wise. He has also a vague notion that Nature would not be able to get on well without Wordsworth; and finds a considerable part of his pleasure in looking at himself as well as at her.

John Ruskin, 1856, *Modern Painters,* vol. III, pt. iv

He's good, you know, but unbearable.

Dante Gabriel Rossetti, 1859, *Letters to William Allingham,* p. 218

Byron's merits are on the surface. This is not the case with Wordsworth. You must love Wordsworth ere he will seem worthy of your love.

Alfred, Lord Tennyson, 1869, *Life* by his son, vol. II, p. 69

His fame has slowly climbed from stage to stage until now his influence is perceived in all the English poetry of the day. If this were the place to criticise his poetry, I should say, of his more stately poems in blank verse, that they often lack compression,—that the thought suffers by too great expansion. Wordsworth was unnecessarily afraid of being epigrammatic. He abhorred what is called a point as much as Dennis is said to have abhorred a pun. Yet I must own that even his most diffuse amplifications have in them a certain grandeur that fills the mind.

William Cullen Bryant, 1870, *A New Library of Poetry and Song,* Introduction, vol. I, p. 42

Does it not sometimes come over one (just the least in the world) that one would give anything for a bit of nature pure and simple, without quite so strong a flavor of W. W.? W. W. is, of course, sublime and all that—but! For my part, I will make a clean breast of it, and confess that I can't look at a mountain without fancying the late laureate's gigantic Roman nose thrust between me and it, and thinking of Dean Swift's profane version of *Romanos rerum dominos* into *Roman nose! a rare 'ur! dom your nose!*

James Russell Lowell, 1871, "A Good Word for Winter," *My Study Windows,* p. 37

A new Cowper, with less talent and more ideas than the other, was essentially an interior man, that is, engrossed by the concerns of the soul. . . . He saw a grandeur, a beauty, lessons in the trivial events which weave the woof of our most common-place days. He needed not for the sake of emotion, either splendid sights or unusual actions. The dazzling glare of the lamps, the pomp of the theatre, would have shocked him; his eyes are too delicate, accustomed to sweet and uniform tints. He was a poet of the twilight. Moral existence in common-place existence, such was his object— the object of his preference. His paintings are cameos with a grey ground, which have a meaning; designedly he suppresses all which ought to please the senses, in order to speak solely to the heart. . . . Half of his pieces are childish, almost foolish; dull events described in a dull style, one nullity after another, and that on principle.

H. A. Taine, 1871, *History of English Literature,* tr. Van Laun, vol. II, bk. iv, ch. i, pp. 260, 261, 262

What made Wordsworth's poems a medicine for my state of mind, was that they expressed, not mere outward beauty, but states of feeling, under the excitement of beauty. They seemed to be the very culture of the feelings which I was in quest of. In them I seemed to draw from a source of inward joy, of sympathetic and imaginative pleasure, which could be shared in all by human beings, which had no connexion with struggle or imperfection, but would be made richer by every improvement in the physical or social condition of mankind. From them I seemed to learn what would be the perennial sources of happiness, when all the greater evils of life shall have been removed. And I felt myself at once better and happier as I came under their influence.

John Stuart Mill, 1873, *Autobiography,* p. 148

Wordsworth has dug out of nature the stones and moss and crumbling matters which common men tread upon, and contemplated them through his intellectual microscope, until they have yielded up all their beauty and meaning, and shown on what their motion and vitality depend. And all this knowledge he has kneaded and intermingled with such human matter as is allied to the earthy material of his themes. The peasant, the beggar, the wagoner, the idiot and his mother, become the actors in his dramas, and we are moved by them and the common objects around them, instead of by those fierce internal throes and terrible disasters which make up the stature and grandeur of antique tragedy.

Bryan Waller Procter (Barry Cornwall), 1874,
Recollections of Men of Letters, p. 140

Those who wish to understand his influence, and experience his peculiar savour, must bear with patience the presence of an alien element in Wordsworth's work, which never coalesced with what is really delightful in it, nor underwent his special power. Who that values his writings most has not felt the intrusion there, from time to time, of something tedious and prosaic? . . . And this duality there—the fitfulness with which the higher qualities manifest themselves in it, gives the effect in his poetry of a power not altogether his own, or under his control, which comes and goes when it will, lifting or lowering a matter, poor in itself; so that that old fancy which made the poet's art an enthusiasm, a form of divine possession, seems almost literally true of him. . . . He meets us with the promise that he has much, and something very peculiar, to give us, if we will follow a certain difficult way, and seems to have the secret of a special and privileged state of mind. And those who have undergone his influence, and followed this difficult way, are like people who have passed through some initiation, a *disciplina arcani,* by submitting to which they become able constantly to distinguish in art, speech, feeling, manners, that which is organic, animated, expressive, from that which is only conventional, derivative, inexpressive.

Walter Pater, 1874, *Appreciations,* pp. 38, 39, 40

I gladly take for granted—what is generally acknowledged—that Wordsworth in his best moods reaches a greater height than any other modern Englishman. The word "inspiration" is less forced when applied to his loftiest poetry than when used of any of his contemporaries. With defects too obvious to be mentioned, he can yet pierce furthest behind the veil; and embody most efficiently the thoughts and emotions which come to us in our most solemn and reflective moods. Other poetry becomes trifling when we are making our inevitable passages through the Valley of the Shadow of Death. Wordsworth's alone retains its power. We love him the more as we grow older and become more deeply impressed with the sadness and seriousness of life; we are apt to grow weary of his rivals when we have finally quitted the regions of youthful enchantment. And I take the explanation to be that he is not merely a melodious writer, or a powerful utterer of deep emotion, but a true philosopher. His poetry wears well because it has solid substance. He is a prophet and a moralist as well as a mere singer. His ethical system, in particular, is as distinctive and capable of systematic exposition as that of Butler. By endeavouring to state it in plain prose, we shall see how the poetical power implies a sensitiveness to ideas which, when extracted from the symbolical embodiment, fall spontaneously into a scientific system of thought.

Leslie Stephen, 1874-79, "Wordsworth's Ethics,"
Hours in a Library, Second Series, p. 276

I firmly believe that the poetical performance of Wordsworth is, after that of Shakspeare and Milton, of which all the world now recognises the worth, undoubtedly the most considerable in our language from the Elizabethan age to the present time. . . . If it is a just claim, if Wordsworth's place among the poets who have appeared in the last two or three centuries is after Shakspeare, Molière, Milton, Goethe, indeed, but before all the rest, then in time Wordsworth will have his due. We shall recognise him in his place, as we recognise Shakspeare and Milton; and not only we ourselves shall recognise him, but he will be recognised by Europe also. . . . His best work is in his shorter pieces, and many indeed are there of these which are of first-rate excellence. But in his seven volumes the pieces of high merit are mingled with a mass of pieces very inferior to them; so inferior to them that it seems wonderful how the same poet should have produced both.

Matthew Arnold, 1879, ed., *Poems of Wordsworth,*
Preface, pp. x, xi

Wordsworth was, and felt himself to be, a discoverer, and like other great discoverers, his victory was in seeing by faith things which were not yet seen, but which were obvious, or soon became so, when once shown. He opened a new world of thought and enjoyment to Englishmen; his work formed an epoch in the intellectual and moral history of the race. But for that very reason he had, as Coleridge said, like all great artists, to create the taste by which he was to be relished, to teach the art by which he was to be seen and judged. And people were so little prepared for the thorough and systematic way in which he searched out what is deepest or highest or subtlest in human feeling under the homliest realities, that not being able to understand him they laughed at him. Nor was he altogether without fault in the misconceptions which occasioned so much ridicule and scorn.

Richard William Church, 1879, Wordsworth,
Dante and Other Essays, p. 202

Of sluggish or unmusical rhythm there are abundant specimens, especially in his earlier works. In reading Wordsworth, I often feel about his rhythm as if I were wading against a stream instead of floating along with it. This would never be so were the feeling of form in the poet's soul as sensitive as his thought. We could dispense with much profundity of thought, were we only borne along by a musical motion which wedded itself spontaneously to the idea. A perfect poem demands a fine accord between the body and the soul of thought. We are often moved by the *soul* of Wordsworth's thought; not often, I think, by the soul in intimate conjunction of form with his thought.

Christopher P. Cranch, 1880, "Wordsworth,"
Atlantic Monthly, vol. 45, p. 248

Devotion to Wordsworth, if it has a tendency to exalt, has also a tendency to infatuate the judicial sense and spirit of his disciples; to make them, even as compared with other devotees, unusually prone to indulgence in such large assertions and assumptions on their master's behalf as seem at least to imply claims which it may be presumed that their apparent advocates would not seriously advance or deliberately maintain. It would in some instances be as unreasonable to suppose that they would do so as to imagine that Mr. Arnold really considers the dissonant doggerel of Wordsworth's halting lines to a skylark equal or superior to Shelley's incomparable transfusion from notes into words of the spirit of a skylark's song. Such an instance is afforded us by the most illustrious—with a single exception—of all Wordsworth's panegyrists. . . . If Wordsworth's claims as a poet can only be justified on grounds which would prove him a deeper student of nature, a saner critic of life, a wiser man and a greater poet than Shakespeare, the inference is no less obvious than inevitable: Wordsworth's claims as a poet must in that case go by the board altogether, and at once, and for ever. . . . Meditation and sympathy, not action and passion, were the two main strings of his serene and stormless lyre. On these no hand ever held more gentle yet more sovereign rule than Wordsworth's. His command of all qualities and powers that are proper to the natural scope and adequate to the just application of his genius was as perfect as the command of those greater than he—of the greatest among all great poets—over the worlds of passion and of action.

Algernon Charles Swinburne, 1886, "Wordsworth and Byron,"
Miscellanies, pp. 113, 115, 117

Take him for all in all, in his spiritual history as well as his poetic achievement, Wordsworth is probably a better exponent than Shelley of the democratic ideal in all its length and breadth. In spite of *The Warning,* his conservatism was pure matter of surface opinion. He grew despondent over the political tendencies of the day; but his very despondency, however misguided, had its deep source in the love of the common people. The radiance of his democratic faith did indeed as he grew older fade into the light of common day; yet those first affections, those shadowy recollections of a divine glory once shed on human life, remained to the end the master-light of all his seeing, a power to cherish and to uphold. His poetry made incursions into stupid regions as he grew older, and we miss the old concentrated intensity of phrase. But through mistaken dissertation on politics, as through his glorified contemplation of human life, pulses the same unwavering interest and faith in men and women as they are.

Vida D. Scudder, 1895, *The Life of the Spirit
in the Modern English Poets,* p. 58

Wordsworth's example redeemed his theories, and Coleridge had no theories to redeem. The latter's influence was therefore the earlier in its operation, while that of the former has been perhaps the greater in the long run. Yet, by a somewhat ironical fate, it has turned out that Coleridge, who concerned himself rather with the matter than the mechanism of poetry, has taken rank as one of the greatest English masters of poetic form, while Wordsworth, who believed himself to be the inventor of a new, or at any rate the restorer of the true, language of poetry, owes his place in our literature to a force and depth of poetic feeling which even his many defects of form have proved unable to outweigh. The matchless music of the one singer has enriched the note, as the inspired vision of the other has enlarged the outlook, of all English poetry since their day.

Henry Duff Traill, 1896, *Social England,* vol. V, p. 582

FRANCIS, LORD JEFFREY
1773-1850

Born, in Edinburgh, 23 Oct. 1773. At Edinburgh High School, Oct. 1781 to 1787, at Glasgow Univ., 1787-89. Studied Law in Edinburgh, 1789-91. Matric. Queen's Coll., Oxford, 17 Oct. 1791. Left Oxford, 5 July, 1792. Studied Law in Edinburgh, 1792-93. Called to Scotch Bar, 16 Dec. 1794. Visit to London, 1798. Married Catherine Wilson, 1 Nov. 1801; settled in Edinburgh. Contrib. to *Monthly Rev.*, 1802. Started *Edinburgh Review*, with Sydney Smith and others; first number appeared, 10 Oct. 1802; he edited it till June 1829; contrib. to it, Oct. 1802 to Jan. 1848. Joined Volunteer regiment, 1803. One of founders of "Friday Club," 1803. Visit to London, 1804. Wife died, 8 Aug. 1805. Visit to London, 1806. Duel with Moore (followed by reconciliation), Chalk Farm, 11 Aug. 1806. Legal practice in Scotland increasing. Fell in love with Charlotte Wilkes, 1810; followed her to America, 1813; married her in New York, Nov. 1813. Tour with her in America. Returned to England, Feb. 1814. Settled at Craigcrook, near Edinburgh, 1815. Visit to Continent same year. Joined Bannatyne Club, 1826. Dean of Faculty of Advocates, Edinburgh, 2 July 1829; Lord Advocate, 1830. M. P. for Forfarshire Burghs, 1830; unseated owing to irregularity in election. M. P. for Malton, April and June 1831. Ill-health, in London, 1831. M. P. for Edinburgh, Dec. 1832 to 1834. Judge of Court of Sessions, as Lord Jeffrey, June 1834. Ill-health, 1841. Died, in Edinburgh, 26 Jan. 1850. Buried in Dean Cemetery. WORKS: *A Summary View of the right and claims of the Roman Catholics of Ireland* (anon.), 1808; *A Short Vindication of the late Major A. Campbell* (anon.), 1810; *Contributions to the Edinburgh Review* (4 vols.), 1844. He *edited*: J. Playfair's *Works*, 1822; Byron's *Poems*, 1845. LIFE: (with selected correspondence) by Lord Cockburn, 1852.

R. Farquharson Sharp, 1897, *A Dictionary of English Authors,* p. 149

SEE: *Literary Criticism,* ed. D. Nichol Smith, 1910; J. A. Greig, *Francis Jeffrey of the Edinburgh Review,* 1948.

PERSONAL

His manner is not at first pleasing; what is worse, it is of that cast, which almost irresistibly impresses upon strangers the idea of levity and superficial talents. Yet there is not any man, whose real character is so much the reverse; he has indeed a very sportive and playful fancy, but it is accompanied with very extensive and varied information, with a readiness of apprehension almost intuitive, with judicious and calm discernment, with a profound and penetrating understanding. Indeed, both in point of candour and of vigour in the reasoning powers, I have never personally known a finer intellect than Jeffrey's, unless I were to except Allen's.

Francis Horner, 1802, *Memoirs and Correspondence,* vol. I, p. 212

There is no subject on which he is not *au fait*: no company in which he is not ready to scatter his pearls for sport. . . . His only difficulty seems to be, not to speak, but to be silent. . . . He is never absurd, nor has he any favourite points which he is always bringing forward. It cannot be denied that there is something bordering on petulance of manner, but it is of that least offensive kind which may be accounted for from merit and from success, and implies no exclusive pretensions nor the least particle of ill-will to others. On the contrary Mr. Jeffrey is profuse of his encomiums and admiration of others, but still with a certain reservation of a right to differ or to blame. He cannot rest on one side of a question: he is obliged, by a mercurial habit and disposition, to vary his point of view. If he is ever tedious it is from an execess of liveliness: he oppresses from a sense of airy lightness. He is always setting out on a fresh scent: there are always *relays* of topics. New causes are called; he holds a brief in his hand for every possible question. This is a fault. Mr. Jeffrey is not obtrusive, is not impatient of opposition, is not unwilling to be interrupted; but what is said by another, seems to make no impression on him; he is bound to dispute, to answer it, as if he was in Court, or as if he were in a paltry Debating Society, where young beginners were trying their hands. . . . He cannot help cross-examining a witness, or stating the adverse view of the question. He listens not to judge, but to reply. In consequence of this, you can as little tell the impression your observations make on him as what weight to assign to his.

> William Hazlitt, 1825, *The Spirit of the Age,* pp. 188, 189

Poor dear Jeffrey! I bought a *Times* at the station yesterday morning, and was so stunned by the announcement, that I felt it in that wounded part of me, almost directly; and the bad symptoms (modified) returned within a few hours. I had a letter from him in extraordinary good spirits within this week or two—he was better, he said, than he had been for a long time —and I sent him proof-sheets of the number only last Wednesday. I say nothing of his wonderful abilities and great career, but he was a most affectionate and devoted friend to me; and though no man could wish to live and die more happily, so old in years and yet so young in faculties and sympathies, I am very, very deeply grieved for his loss.

> Charles Dickens, 1850, *Letter to John Forster,* Jan. 29;
> *Life of Dickens,* ed. Forster, vol. II, p. 483

No artist could paint Jeffrey. His expression was so variable, that in different moods he seemed a different man. At the Bar, in Parliament, on the Bench, or in the romantic scenery of his own Craig-Crook, there was a different man—and yet there were not half-a-dozen Jeffreys, but one! To hear him talk, in that sharp shrill voice, whose lowest whisper floated through the air, and was heard by all, was indeed a pleasure and delight. Above all, he had the gentlest courtesy towards women, irrespective of their age. And, to crown all, he was fond, really and truly, of children. (I never knew a bad man who was. I am, and the inference is inevitable!) It was at home, that Jeffrey was ever seen to full advantage.

R. Shelton Mackenzie, 1854, ed., *Noctes Ambrosianæ*
vol. III, p. 429, note

There was something of Voltaire in him; something even in bodily features: those bright-beaming swift and piercing hazel-eyes, with their accompaniment of rapid keen expressions in the other lineaments of face, resembled one's notion of Voltaire; and in the voice too, there was a fine, half-plangent, kind of a metallic ringing tone, which used to remind me of what I fancied Voltaire's voice might have been: *"voix sombre et majesteuse,"* Duvernet calls it.

Thomas Carlyle, 1867, "Lord Jeffrey," *Reminiscences,* ed. Norton

He never took up his pen till the candles were lit, . . . he did most of his work in those fatal hours of inspiration from ten at night till two or three o'clock in the morning. . . . His manuscript was inexpressibly vile; for he wrote with great haste, . . . generally used a wretched pen, . . . and altered, erased, and interlined without the slightest thought either of the printer or his correspondent. . . . The explanation is, of course, the usual one with men of Jeffrey's temperament and genius. He had a horror and hatred of the work of the desk. . . . His favourite hours of reading were in the morning and in bed, unless he had to deal with a subject of peculiar difficulty, and in that case he read it up . . . at night; for he had a notion that hints and suggestions, facts and thoughts, illustrations and authorities, picked up promiscuously over-night, assorted themselves in sleep round their proper centres, and thus reappeared in the morning in logical order.

Charles Pebody, 1870, "The Edinburgh Reviewers,"
Gentleman's Magazine, n. s., vol. 5, p. 42

Editor's Note: Some confirmation of the preceding passage may be attained by the following comment.

My dear Jeffrey—We are much obliged by your letter, but should be still more so were it legible. I have tried to read it from left to right, and Mrs. Sydney from right to left, and we neither of us can decipher a single word of it.

Sydney Smith, 1822, *Letter to Francis Jeffrey; Memoir of Rev. Sydney Smith* by Lady Holland, chap. viii

GENERAL

> Health to immortal Jeffrey! once, in name,
> England could boast a judge almost the same;
> In soul as like, so merciful, yet just,
> Some think that Satan has resign'd his trust,
> And given the spirit to the world again
> To sentence letters, as he sentenced men.
>
> Lord Byron, 1809, *English Bards and Scotch Reviewers*

Our very ideas of what is poetry, differ so widely, that we rarely talk upon these subjects. There is something in his mode of reasoning that leads me greatly to doubt whether, notwithstanding the vivacity of his imagination, he really has any *feeling* of poetical genius, or whether he has worn it all off by perpetually sharpening his wit on the grindstone of criticism.

> Sir Walter Scott, 1812, *Letter to Joanna Baillie*, Jan. 17;
> Lockhart's *Life of Scott*, ch. xxiv

When I compare him with Sydney and myself, I feel, with humility perfectly sincere, that his range is immeasurably wider than ours. And this is only as a writer. But he is not only a writer; he has been a great advocate, and he is a great judge. Take him all in all, I think him more nearly an universal genius than any man of our time.

> Thomas Babington Macaulay, 1843, *Letter to Macvey Napier*,
> Dec. 13; *Correspondence*, ed. his son

A prominent defect of Jeffrey's literary criticism arose from his lack of earnestness,—that earnestness which comes, not merely from the assent of the understanding to a proposition, but from the deep convictions of a man's whole nature. He is consequently ingenious and plausible, rather than profound,—a man of expedients, rather than of ideas and principles. In too many of his articles, he appears like an advocate, careless of the truth, or skeptical as to its existence or possibility of being reached, and only desirous to make out as good a case for his own assumed position as will puzzle or unsettle the understandings of his hearers. His logical capacity is shown in acute special pleading, in sophistical glosses, more than in fair argument.

> Edwin P. Whipple, 1845, *North American Review;*
> *Essays and Reviews*, vol. II, p. 128

Jeffrey, who took the lead in this great revolution in literature, was a very remarkable man, but more so from the light, airy turn of his mind, and the felicity of illustration which he possessed, than from either originality of thought or nervous force of expression. His information was far from extensive: he shared in the deficiency of his country at that period in classical knowledge; he was ignorant of Italian and German; and his acquaintance with French literature was chiefly confined to the gossiping memoirs of the day, and, with that of his own country, to the writings of the Scotch metaphysicians or the old English dramatists. But these subjects he knew thoroughly; within these limits he was thoroughly master. He was fitted by nature to be a great critic. A passionate admirer of poetry, alive to all the beauties and influences of nature, with a feeling mind and a sensitive heart, he possessed at the same time the calm judgment which enabled him to form an impartial opinion on the works submitted to his examination, and the correct taste which, in general, discovered genius and detected imperfections in them.

Sir Archibald Alison, 1853-59, *History of Europe, 1815-52*, ch. v

In his criticisms of Wordsworth we see vividly at once his own character and his failure to appreciate a character very different from his own. He was an affectionate man, intensely attached to his friends, and uncontrollably fond of their society; and the passages that he admires in Wordsworth are chiefly passages of tenderness. He loved natural scenery, too, in a way, and does justice to Wordsworth's more striking word-pictures; but he was too much attracted to "the busy haunts of men" to follow the raptures of a genuine nature-worshipper, and he found Wordsworth's minute descriptions intolerably tedious. But what he chiefly failed to understand, and what chiefly offended him, were the meditations natural to a recluse, and the glorification of children and of country personages to a degree altogether out of keeping with their conventional place in the social scale. He was constantly accusing Wordsworth of clothing the commonest commonplaces with unintelligible verbiage, and of debasing tenderness with vulgarity. A similar narrowness, the same tendency to lay down the law without a suspicion that other people were differently constituted from himself, appears in his essay on "Beauty." Himself defective in the feeling for colour, he denies that colour possesses any intrinsic beauty, and is utterly sceptical regarding the statements of artists and connoisseurs, suspecting them of pedantry and jargon. His style is forcible and copious, without any pretence to finished or elegant structure. His diction is perhaps too overflowing; his powers of amplification and illustration sometimes ran away with him; "his memory," says Lockhart, "appeared to range the dictionary from A to Z, and he had not the self-denial to spare his readers the redundance which delighted himself." His collected works give but a feeble idea of the cleverness of his ridicule; he refused to republish the most striking specimens of his satirical skill.

William Minto, 1872-80, *Manual of English
Prose Literature*, p. 530

The peculiar value of Jeffrey is not, as that of Coleridge, of Hazlitt, or of Lamb, in his very subtle, very profound, or very original views of his subjects. He is neither a critical Columbus nor a critical Socrates: he neither opens up undiscovered countries, nor provokes and stimulates to the discovery of them. His strength lies in the combination of a fairly wide range of sympathy with an extraordinary shrewdness and good sense in applying that sympathy. Tested for range alone, or for subtlety alone, he will frequently be found wanting; but he almost invariably catches up those who have thus outstripped him when the subject of the trial is shifted to soundness of estimate, intelligent connection of view, and absence of eccentricity. And it must be again and again repeated that Jeffrey is by no means justly chargeable with the Dryasdust failings so often attributed to academic criticism. They said that on the actual Bench he worried counsel a little too much, but that his decisions were on the whole invariably sound. Not quite so much perhaps can be said for his other exercise of the judicial function. But however much he may sometimes seem to carp and complain, however much we may sometimes wish for a little more equity and a little less law, it is astonishing how weighty Jeffrey's critical judgments are after three quarters of a century which has seen so many seeming heavy things grow light. There may be much that he does not see: there may be some things which he is physically unable to see; but what he does see, he sees with a clearness, and co-ordinates in its bearings on other things seen with a precision which are hardly to be matched among the fluctuating and diverse race of critics.

George Saintsbury, 1887, "Francis Jeffrey,"
Macmillan's Magazine, vol. 56, p. 267

Jeffrey was before all things a literary critic, and, within the limits of his discernment, one of the acutest and liveliest of his time. His point of view was that of refined but positive common-sense, qualified by a rooted distrust of innovation. To the simple and obvious poetry of Rogers, Campbell, Crabbe, he brought a keen if somewhat excessive appreciation; mawkish sentiment and pseudo-mediævalism he exposed with signal effect. We cannot now wholly disapprove of the stricture upon *Marmion* which angered Scott, nor share his effusive penitence for those upon Byron's *Hours of Idleness*. But he was, unfortunately, as proof against the true Romantics as against the false, and comprehended the mysticism of imaginative poetry in the same anathema with the crude supernaturalism of the school of horrors. The manifesto against the "Lake school" with which he opened the review is one of the most striking examples in literature of the fatuous efforts of a clever man to interpret a larger world than his own. The naked simplicity of Wordsworth, the tumultuous energy of Coleridge, the irregular metres of Southey were equally offensive to him, and he classed them together, as if innovators formed one brotherhood.

C. H. Herford, 1897, *The Age of Wordsworth*, p. 52

SARAH MARGARET FULLER
MARCHIONESS OSSOLI

1810-1850

Educator and philosopher, born in Cambridge, Mass., 23 May, 1810, lost at sea 15th July, 1850. She received a broad education and early felt a deep interest in social questions. She learned French, German and the classics, and her associates in Cambridge were persons of culture, experience and advanced ideas. In 1833 the family removed to Groton, Mass., where she gave lessons to private classes in languages and other studies. Her father, Timothy Fuller, died of cholera, 26th September, 1835, and his death threw the family upon Margaret for support, and her plans for a trip to Europe were abandoned. In 1836 she went to Boston, where she taught Latin and French in A. Bronson Alcott's school, and taught private classes of girls in French, German and Italian. In 1837 she became a teacher in a private school in Providence, R. I., which was organized on Mr. Alcott's plan. She translated many works from the German and other languages. In 1839 she removed to Jamaica Plain, Mass., and took a house on her own responsibility, to make a home for the family. The next year they returned to Cambridge. In 1839 she instituted in Boston her conversational class, which was continued for several years. She did much writing on subjects connected with her educational work. In 1840 she became the editor of *The Dial*, which she managed for two years. Her contributions to that journal were numerous. Several volumes of translations from the German were brought out by her. In 1843 she went on a western tour with James Freeman Clarke and his artist-sister, and her first original work, *Summer on the Lakes,* was the result of that trip. In 1844 she removed to New York City, where for two years she furnished literary criticisms for the *Tribune*. In 1846 she published her volume, *Papers on Literature and Art*. After twenty months of life in New York she went to Europe. She met in Italy, in 1847, Giovani Angelo, Marquis Ossoli, a man younger than she and of less intellectual culture, but a simple and noble man, who had given up his rank and station in the cause of the Roman Republic. They were married in 1847. Their son, Angelo Philip Eugene Ossoli, was born in Rieti, 5th September, 1848. After the fall of the republic it was necessary for them to leave Rome, and Madame Ossoli, desiring to print in America her history of the Italian struggle, suggested their return to the

United States. They sailed on the barque "Elizabeth" from Leghorn, 17th May, 1850. The trip was a disastrous one. Capt. Hasty died of the small-pox and was buried off Gibraltar. Mme. Ossoli's infant son was attacked by the disease on 11th June, but recovered. On 15th July the "Elizabeth" made the New Jersey coast at noon, and during a fog the vessel ran upon Fire Island and was wrecked. Madame Ossoli refused to be separated from her husband, and all three were drowned. The body of their child was found on the beach and was buried in the sand by the sailors, to be after-wards removed to Mount Auburn Cemetery, near Boston. The bodies of Marquis and Madame Ossoli were never found.

Charles Wells Moulton, 1893, A Woman of the Century,
eds. Willard and Livermore, p. 551

SEE: The Writings, ed. Mason Wade, 1941; Mason Wade, Margaret Fuller: Whetstone of Genius, 1940; Arthur W. Brown, Margaret Fuller, 1964.

PERSONAL

Yesternight there came a bevy of Americans from Emerson, one Margaret Fuller, the chief figure of them, strange, lilting, lean old maid, not nearly such a bore as I expected.

Thomas Carlyle, 1846, Letter, Oct. 8; Thomas Carlyle: A History
of his Life in London, ed. Froude, vol. I, p. 342

I still remember the first half hour of Margaret's conversation. She was then twenty-six years old. She had a face and frame that would indicate fullness and tenacity of life. She was rather under the middle height; her complexion was fair, with strong, fair hair. She was then, as always, carefully and be-comingly dressed, and of lady-like self-possession. For the rest, her ap-pearance had nothing prepossessing. Her extreme plainness—a trick of incessantly opening and shutting her eyelids—the nasal tone of her voice—all repelled; and I said to myself, we shall never get far. It is to be said that Margaret made a disagreeable first impression on most persons, in-cluding those who became afterwards her best friends, to such an extreme that they did not wish to be in the same room with her. This was partly the effect of her manners, which expressed an overweening sense of power, and slight esteem of others, and partly the prejudice of her fame. She had a dangerous reputation for satire, in addition to her great scholarship. The men thought she carried too many guns, and the women did not like one who despised them. I believe I fancied her too much interested in personal history; and her talk was a comedy in which dramatic justice was done to everybody's foibles. I remember that she made me laugh more than I liked. . . . She had an incredible variety of ancedotes, and the readiest wit to give an absurd turn to whatever passed; and the eyes, which were so plain at first, soon swam with fun and drolleries, and the very tides of joy and superabundant life. This rumor was much spread abroad, that she was sneering, scoffing, critical, disdainful of humble people, and of all but the intellectual. . . . It was a superficial judgment. Her satire was only the pastime and necessity of her salient, the play of superabundant animal spirits. . . . Her mind presently disclosed many moods and powers, in successive platforms or terraces, each above each, that quite effaced this first impression, in the opulence of the following pictures.

> Ralph Waldo Emerson, 1851, *Memoirs of Margaret Fuller Ossoli,* vol. I, pp. 202, 203

Her temperament was predominantly what the physiologists would call nervous-sanguine; and the gray eyes, rich brown hair, and light complexion, with the muscular and well-developed frame, bespoke delicacy balanced by vigor. Here was a sensitive, yet powerful being, fit at once for rapture or sustained effort, intensely active, prompt for adventure, firm for trial. She certainly had not beauty; yet the high arched dome of the head, the changeful expressiveness of every feature, and her whole air of mingled dignity and impulse, gave her a commanding charm. Especially characteristic were two physical traits. The first was a contraction of the eyelids almost to a point—a trick caught from near-sightedness—and then a sudden dilatation, till the iris seemed to emit flashes; an effect, no doubt, dependent on her highly-magnetized condition. The second was a singular pliancy of the vertebræ and muscles of the neck, enabling her by a mere movement to denote varying emotion; in moments of tenderness, or pensive feeling, its curves were swan-like in grace, but when she was scornful or indignant, it contracted, and made swift turns like that of a bird of prey. Finally, in the animation yet *abandon* of Margaret's attitude and look, were rarely blended the fiery force of northern, and the soft langour of southern races.

> William Henry Channing, 1851, *Memoirs of Margaret Fuller Ossoli,* vol. II, p. 35

Though we were members of the same household, we scarcely met save at breakfast; and my time and thoughts were absorbed in duties and cares, which left me little leisure or inclination for the amenities of social intercourse. Fortune seemed to delight in placing us two in relations of friendly antagonism, or rather, to develop all possible contrasts in our ideas and social habits. She was naturally inclined to luxury and a good appearance before the world. My pride, if I had any, delighted in bare walls and rugged fare. She was addicted to strong tea and coffee, both which I rejected and contemned, even the most homœopathic dilutions; while, my general health being sound, and hers sadly impaired, I could not fail to find in her dietetic habits the causes of her almost habitual illness; and once, while we were still barely acquainted, when she came to the breakfast-table with a very severe headache, I was tempted to attribute it to her strong potations of the Chinese leaf the night before. She told me quite frankly that she "declined being lectured on the food or beverage [I see] she saw fit to take," which was but reasonable in one who had arrived at her maturity of intellect and fixedness of habits. So the subject was henceforth tactly avoided between us; but, though words were suppressed, looks and involuntary gestures could not so well be; and an utter divergency of views on this and kindred themes created a perceptible distance between us.

Horace Greeley, 1851, *Memoirs of Margaret Fuller Ossoli,*
vol. II, p. 153

From first to last she was a woman of noble aims, and, with all her egotism, unselfish in action. The longer I live, the more presumptuous and futile it seems to me to attempt judgment of character, and Miss Fuller's was exceptional. Her self-esteem was so inordinate as to be almost insane, but it appears (and it is, I think, so stated) to have been a constitutional and inherited defect, and certainly without moral taint. Her truth was exemplary, and all her conduct after she had left off theorizing and began the action of life in the accustomed channels was admirable, her Italian life beautiful. The close had the solemnity of a fulfilled prophecy, and, with all its apparent horrors, was it not merciful? Had she come safely to our shores, she must have encountered harassing struggles for the mere means of existence, anxiety, and all the petty cares that perplex and obstruct a noble nature, and, worse than all, disappointment!

Catharine M. Sedgwick, 1852, *Letter to Mrs. Channing;*
Life and Letters, p. 340

She was a person anxious to try all things, and fill up her experience in all directions; she had a strong and coarse nature, which she had done her utmost to refine, with infinite pains; but of course it could only be superficially changed. The solution of the riddle lies in this direction, nor does one's conscience revolt at the idea of thus solving it, for (at least, this is my own experience) Margaret has not left in the hearts and minds of those who knew her any deep witness of her integrity and purity. She was a great humbug—of course, with much talent and much moral reality, or else she could never have been so great a humbug. But she had stuck herself full of borrowed qualities, which she chose to provide herself with, but which had no root in her. . . . There never was such a tragedy as her whole story, the sadder and sterner, because so much of the ridiculous was mixed up with it, and because she could bear anything better than to be ridiculous. It was such an awful joke, that she should have resolved—in all sincerity, no doubt—to make herself the greatest, wisest, best woman of the age. And to that end she set to work on her strong, heavy, unpliable, and, in many respects, defective and evil nature, and adorned it with a mosaic of admirable qualities, such as she chose to possess; putting in here a splendid talent and there a moral excellence, and polishing each separate piece, and the whole together, till it seemed to shine afar and dazzle all who saw it. She took credit to herself for having been her own Redeemer, if not her own Creator; and, indeed, she is far more a work of art than any of Mozier's statues. But she was not working on an inanimate substance, like marble or clay; there was something within her that she could not possibly come at, to re-create or refine it; and, by and by, this rude old potency bestirred itself, and undid all her labor in the twinkling of an eye. On the whole, I do not know but I like her the better for it; because she proved herself a very woman after all.

> Nathaniel Hawthorne, 1857-59, *Extract from Roman Journal;*
> *Nathaniel Hawthorne and his Wife,* by Julian Hawthorne,
> vol. I, pp. 260, 261

It was a strange history and a strange destiny, that of this brilliant, restless, and unhappy woman—this ardent New Englander, this impassioned Yankee, who occupied so large a place in the thoughts, the lives, the affections, of an intelligent and appreciative society, and yet left behind her nothing but the memory of a memory. Her function, her reputation, were singular, and not altogether reassuring: she was a talker; she was *the* talker; she was the genius of talk.

> Henry James, Jr., 1880, *Nathaniel Hawthorne*
> *(English Men of Letters)*, p. 76

Her life seems to me, on the whole, a triumphant rather than a sad one, in spite of the prolonged struggle with illness, with poverty, with the shortcomings of others and with her own. In later years she had the fulfillment of her dreams; she had what Elizabeth Barrett, writing at the time of her marriage to Robert Browning, named as the three great desiderata of existence, "life and love and Italy." She shared great deeds, she was the counselor of great men, she had a husband who was a lover, and she had a child. They loved each other in their lives, and in death they were not divided. Was not that enough?

> Thomas Wentworth Higginson, 1884, *Margaret Fuller Ossoli*
> *(American Men of Letters)*, p. 314

Woman in the Nineteenth Century

Was perhaps framed on too large a scale for one who had so little constructive power. It was noble in tone, enlightened in its statement, and full of suggestion; yet after all it was crude and disconnected in its execution.

Thomas Wentworth Higginson, 1868, *Eminent Women of the Age*, p. 193

In 1840, Margaret Fuller published an essay in *The Dial,* entitled "The Great Lawsuit, or Man *vs.* Woman: Woman *vs.* Man." In this essay she demanded perfect equality for woman, in education, industry, and politics. It attracted great attention and was afterwards expanded into a work entitled *Woman in the Nineteenth Century.* This, with her parlor conversations, on art, science, religion, politics, philosophy, and social life, gave a new impulse to woman's education as a thinker.

Anthony and Gage Stanton, eds., 1881-87, *History of Woman Suffrage*, vol. I, p. 40

Before Margaret Fuller's day the agitation regarding woman's career and work in the world was practically unknown here; and all the ideas which have now become incorporated into the platform of the woman's party found in her their first and perhaps their best exponent. Very little that is new has since been urged upon this question. Her powerful mind seemed to have grasped the whole subject, and to have given it the best expression of which it was capable. She embodied her ideas after a time in her book, *Woman in the Nineteenth Century,* and although the literature of the subject is now voluminous, that book is still read and referred to.

Hattie Tyng Griswold, 1886, *Home Life of Great Authors,* p. 305

GENERAL

It is for dear New England that I want this review [*The Dial*], for myself, if I had wished to write a few pages now and then, there were ways and means enough of disposing of them. But in truth I have not much to say; for since I have had leisure to look at myself, I find that, so far from being an original genius, I have not yet learned to think to any depth, and that the utmost I have done in life has been to form my character to a certain consistency, cultivate my tastes, and learn to tell the truth with a little better grace than I did at first. For this the world will not care much, so I shall hazard a few critical remarks only, or an unpretending chalk sketch now and then, till I have learned to do something.

Margaret Fuller Ossoli, 1840, *Memoirs of Margaret Fuller Ossoli*, vol. II, p. 26

In spite of these things, however, and of her frequent unjustifiable Carlyle-isms (such as that of writing sentences which are no sentences, since, to be parsed, reference must be had to sentences preceding), the style of Miss Fuller is one of the very best with which I am acquainted. In general effect, I know no style which surpasses it. It is singularly piquant, vivid, terse, bold, luminous; leaving details out of sight, it is everything that a style need be.

Edgar Allan Poe, 1846, *The Literati; Works*
ed. Stedman and Woodberry, vol. VIII, p. 81

Margaret is an excellent soul: in real regard with both of us here. Since she went, I have been reading some of her Papers in a new Book we have got; greatly superior to all I knew before; in fact the undeniable utterances (now first undeniable to me) of a true heroic mind;—altogether unique, so far as I know, among the Writing Women of this generation; rare enough, too, God knows, among the Writing Men. She is very narrow, sometimes; but she is truly high.

Thomas Carlyle, 1847, *Letter to Emerson*, March 2;
Correspondence of Carlyle and Emerson, ed. Norton,
vol. II, p. 155

Those who knew her in early youth, who witnessed her extraordinary intel-lectual developments, who experienced her wonderful power in conversa-tion, and who cast the horoscope of the woman from the brilliant promise of the girl, predicted for her a distinguished literary career. They saw in her a future D'Arblay or De Staël. . . . For ourselves, we incline to the belief that in no circumstances, by no favor of fortune, would Margaret have produced a work which should have worthily expressed her genius. With all her mental wealth and race faculty, we doubt whether she pos-sessed the organic power, the concentration and singleness of purpose, necessary for such an undertaking. Her mind was critical, not construc-tive; impulsive, not laborious. Her strength lay rather in oracular judg-ments, in felicitous statements and improvisations, than in patient elabora-tion. True, she has written much and well. Her critical essays, and especially her papers on Goethe, in *The Dial*, are unsurpassed in their kind. But all that she has written is fragmentary; nothing epic, nothing that possesses formal excellence, no one complete work.

Frederick Henry Hedge, 1856, "Madame Ossoli's At Home
and Abroad," *North American Review*, vol. 83, p. 261

In her published works there are passages of great power and beauty. Her descriptions of scenery—that of Niagara, for instance—are given with a few bold strokes, that suggest much more than at first meets the eye. She paints, in fact, our inward emotion in presence of the scene, and so gives us the ideal of nature. Her critical articles often show insight, and the power of clear statement; but either she was warped by personal dislikes or she took pleasure in demolishing popular idols. In her view there were but half a dozen people with brains in America. In her way of writing, the editorial we had a royal sound, that would have been offensive if it had not been so often absurd. . . . It was some time before it was discovered that philosophic diction did not always clothe philosophic thought. Perhaps Margaret Fuller had passed through her *destructive* stage, and was ready to build. Perhaps if she had lived, she would have justified the opinions of her admirers by the creation of some artistic work. If this were so, the calamity of the shipwreck is the more to be lamented. As in the case of great orators, actors, and singers, who, after charming a generation, die and leave only a tradition of their powers, this extraordinary woman will be a mere name in our literary history. Something of her influence survives. The advocates for the elevation of woman hold her in high regard as a pioneer in their cause. In this, as in everything else in which she took part, she put her own intense personality forward, and did much to win for her sex the right of discussion and the privilege of being heard.

Francis H. Underwood, 1872, *A Hand-Book of*
English History, American Authors

In many respects Margaret Fuller stands, like Poe, solitary in our literature. Her strong, masculine personality which placed her alone among American women, and her keen, peculiar intellect which made her a powerful influence on the intellectual men of her generation, defy classification. If judged alone by her actual literary product, she would deserve but a passing notice, yet she is ranked with the great builders of American literature. Concerning few American writers, save Poe and Whitman, can one find such extremes of opinion. Some of her contemporaries characterized her as superficially learned, disagreeable, warped by intense personal likes and dislikes, domineering, oracular, inordinately fond of monologue; while others, like Emerson, Carlyle, Channing, and Higginson, declared her a rare genius, a profound thinker and scholar. . . . She is almost the only American author who, like a great singer or actor, keeps a place in our memories chiefly through the testimony of contemporaries. . . . The place which Margaret Fuller will ultimately occupy in the history of American letters can only be conjectured. "Her genius was not quick to clothe itself in the written word," and it seems but fair to judge that any literary fame that rests largely upon tradition must ultimately be lost. . . . She held frequent "Conversations," during which her admirers listened with bated breath as to a goddess. She drew about her with scarcely an effort a circle of the purest and most spiritual men and women of New England and she ruled it with singular power. And after her death the noblest and best minds of both hemispheres united to do honor to her memory.

Fred Lewis Pattee, 1896, *A History of American Literature with a View to the Fundamental Principles Underlying its Development*, pp. 231, 234

JAMES FENIMORE COOPER
1789-1851

Born at Burlington, N. J., Sept. 15, 1789. Father, of Quaker descent and a congressman; mother, of Swedish descent. Family settled in Cooperstown, N. Y., 1790, where Mr. Cooper owned much land. Attended the village school; then became the private pupil of an Albany rector; entered Yale, 1802; dismissed for participation in a frolic, 1805. Served before the mast in a merchant vessel, 1806-07; served as midshipman in the navy, part of the time on Lakes Ontario and Champlain, 1807-11. Married Miss DeLancey, 1811; five daughters and two sons were born to him. Resided at Mamaroneck, 1811-1814; Cooperstown, 1814-1817; Scarsdale, 1817-1822; New York, 1822-1826. Lived in Europe, chiefly in France and Italy, 1826-1833; consul at Lyons, 1826-1829. Returned to America, 1833; lived by turns at New York and at Cooperstown. Died at Cooperstown, Sept. 14, 1851; wife died four months later. An Episcopalian. WORKS: *Precaution*, 1820. *The Spy*, 1821. *The Pioneers*, 1823. *The Pilot*, 1824 (imprint, 1823). *Lionel Lincoln*, 1825. *The Last of the Mohicans*, 1826. *The Prairie*, 1827. *The Red Rover*, 1828. *The Wept of Wish-ton-Wish* (= *The Borderers*), 1829. *The Water-Witch*, 1830. *The Bravo*, 1831. *The Heidenmauer*, 1832. *The Headsman*, 1833. *The Monikins*, 1835. *Homeward Bound*, 1838. *Home as Found* (= *Eve Effingham*), 1838. *The History of the Navy of the United States of America*, 1839; abridged edition, 1841. *The Pathfinder*, 1840. *Mercedes of Castile*, 1840. *The Deerslayer*, 1841. *The Two Admirals*, 1842. *The Wing-and-Wing* (= *The Jack o'Lantern*), 1842. *Wyandotte*, 1843. *Ned Myers* [the life of one of Cooper's shipmates], 1843. *Afloat and Ashore*, 1844. *Miles Wallingford* (= *Lucy Hardinge*) [sequel to *Afloat and Ashore*], 1844. *Satanstoe*, 1845. *The Chainbearer*, 1846. *Lives of Distinguished American Naval Officers*, 1846. *The Redskins* (= *Ravensnest*), 1846. *The Islets of the Gulf*, 1846-1848 in *Graham's Magazine;* 1848 in book form, as *Jack Tier* (= *Captain Spike*). *The Crater* (= *Mark's Reef*), 1847. *The Oak Openings* (= *The Bee Hunter*), 1848. *The Sea Lions*, 1849. *The Ways of the Hour*, 1850. The titles of the English editions, when they differed from the American, are given in parentheses. Cooper also wrote several tales for *Graham's Magazine*, ten volumes of travels, and a good deal of controversial matter.

Walter C. Bronson, 1900, *A Short History of American Literature*, p. 126, note

SEE: *Works*, New York, 1895-1900, 33 v.; *Representative Selections*, ed. Robert E. Spiller, 1936; *Gleanings in Europe*, ed. Robert E. Spiller,

1928-30, 2 v.; *The American Democrat,* ed. H. L. Mencken, 1931; *Correspondence,* ed. James F. Cooper, 1922, 2 v.; *Letter and Journals,* ed. James Franklin Beard, 1960 (Vols. I, II), 1965 (Vols. III, IV); Robert E. Spiller, *Fenimore Cooper: Critic of His Times,* 1931; James Grossman, *James Fenimore Cooper,* 1949; also see Robert E. Spiller and P. C. Blackburn, *Descriptive Bibliography of the Writings of James Fenimore Cooper,* 1934.

PERSONAL

Visited Princess Galitzin, and also Cooper, the American novelist. This man, who has shown so much genius, has a good deal of the manners, or want of manners, peculiar to his countrymen.

Sir Walter Scott, 1826. *Journal,* Nov. 3;
Life by Lockhart, ch. lxxii

I met this evening (for the first time) with Cooper, the American writer. He is the author of *The Pioneers, The Spy,* etc. He has a dogged, discontented look, and seems ready to affront or to be affronted. His eye is rather deep-set, dull, and with little motion. One might imagine that he had lost his life in gazing at seas and woods and rivers, and that he would gaze—gaze on for ever. His conversation is rough, abrupt, and unamusing; yet I am told that he can recount an adventure well, and I can easily believe it. There was something peculiar in his physiognomy, but I could not make out what it was. . . . He resembles very much a caricature that I remember to have seen indicative of "Damme, who cares?"

Bryan Waller Procter (Barry Cornwall), 1828, May 17;
Autobiographical Fragments, pp. 74, 76

Mr. Cooper's manuscript is very bad—*unformed,* with little of distinctive character about it, and varying greatly in different epistles. In most of those before us a steel pen has been employed, the lines are crooked, and the whole chirography has a constrained and school-boyish air.

Edgar Allan Poe, 1841, *A Chapter on Autobiography,*
Works, ed. Stedman and Woodberry, vol. IX, p. 212

We are among those who regard Mr. Cooper as a wronged and persecuted man. We conceive that his countrymen have done him gross injustice—that they have not only shown themselves ungenerous but ungrateful, and that, in lending a greedy ear to the numerous malicious aspersions which have assailed his person and his reputation, they have only given confirmation and strength to the proverbial reproach, of irreverence and ingratitude, to which countries, distinguished by popular governments, have usually been thought obnoxious. We do not mean to regard him as wholly faultless—on the contrary, we look upon Mr. Cooper as a very imprudent person; one whose determined will, impetuous temperament, and great self-esteem, continually hurry forward into acts and expressions of error and impatience.

William Gilmore Simms, 1845, *Views and Reviews in American Literature, History and Fiction,* p. 210

Of his failings I have said little; such as he had were obvious to all the world; they lay on the surface of his character; those who knew him least made the most account of them. With a character so made up of positive qualities—a character so independent and uncompromising, and with a sensitiveness far more acute than he was willing to acknowledge, it is not surprising that occasions frequently arose to bring him, sometimes into friendly collision, and sometimes into graver disagreements and misunderstandings with his fellow-men. For his infirmities, his friends found an ample counterpoise in the generous sincerity of his nature. He never thought of disguising his opinions, and he abhorred all disguise in others; he did not even deign to use that show of regard towards those of whom he did not think well, which the world tolerates, and almost demands. A manly expression of opinion, however different from his own, commanded his respect. . . . His character was like the bark of the cinnamon, a rough and astringent rind without, and intense sweetness within. Those who penetrated below the surface found a genial temper, warm affections, and a heart with ample place for his friends, their pursuits, their good name, their welfare. They found him a philanthropist, though not precisely after the fashion of the day; a religious man, most devout where devotion is most apt to be a feeling rather than a custom, in the household circle; hospitable, and to the extent of his means liberal-handed in acts of charity.

William Cullen Bryant, 1852, *Orations and Addresses,* p. 85

Mr. Cooper was in person solid, robust, athletic; in voice, manly; in manner, earnest, emphatic, almost dictatorial,—with something of self-assertion, bordering on egotism. The first effect was unpleasant, indeed repulsive, but there shone through all this a heartiness, frankness, which excited confidence, respect, and at last affection.

Samuel Griswold Goodrich, 1856, *Recollections of a Lifetime,*
Letter xxxvi

A man of unquestioned talent,—almost genius,—he was aristocratic in feeling and arrogant in bearing, altogether combining in his manners what a Yankee once characterized as "winning ways to make people hate him."

Retiring to his parental acres near Cooperstown, N. Y., he was soon involved in a difficulty with the neighboring villagers, who had long been accustomed, in their boating excursions on the Lake (Otsego), to land and make themselves at home for an hour or two on a long, narrow promontory or "point," that ran down from his grounds into the lake, and whom he had now dissuaded from so doing by legal force. The Whig newspaper of the village took up the case for the villagers, urging that their exclusion from "The Point," though legal, was churlish, and impelled by the spirit of the dog in the manger; whereupon Cooper sued the editor for libel, recovered a verdict, and collected it by taking the money—through a sheriff's officer—from the editor's trunk.

Horace Greeley, 1868, *Recollections of a Busy Life,* p. 261

I had known Mr. Cooper during the later years of his life, and used to see him occasionally when he visited New York. He was an amazingly fluent talker as well as speaker and writer; and he affected an intense bitterness against the institutions of his native country in his conversation as well as in his writings. I can see him now, in my mind's eye, standing with his back to the fire-place in my office, with his legs apart and his coat-tails under his arms, pouring out diatribes which did not seem half in earnest.

Maunsell B. Field, 1873, *Memories of Many Men
and of Some Women,* p. 178

The Spy (1821)

Quite new scenes and characters, humour and pathos, a picture of America in Washington's time; a surgeon worthy of Smollett or Moore, and quite different from any of their various surgeons; and an Irishwoman, Betty Flanagan, incomparable.

Maria Edgeworth, 1821, *To Mrs. Rexton,* July 8;
Letters, vol. II, p. 29

The Spy was an event. It was the boldest and best attempt at the historical romance which had ever been made in America. It is somewhat the practice, at this day, to disparage that story. This is in very bad taste. The book is a good one,—full of faults, perhaps, and blunders; but full also of decided merits, and marked by a boldness of conception, and a courage in progress, which clearly showed the confidence of genius in its own resources. The conception of the Spy, as a character, was a very noble one.

William Gilmore Simms, 1845, *Views and Reviews in
American Literature, History and Fiction,* p. 211

That "Spy" made the groundwork of Cooper's fame in this country, in England, and on the Continent. There were men who modelled their lives on lines traceable in the career of Harvey Birch, and were proud to do it. His devotion, his trueness to the cause he loved and served—his modesty, his strength of purpose, his self-effacement made up the preaching of a good moral sermon; none the less effective because his story was founded upon actual occurrences detailed to Mr. Cooper by his host, upon the occasion of some visit to the Jay homestead in Westchester.

Donald G. Mitchell, 1897, *American Lands and Letters,*
The Mayflower to Rip-Van-Winkle, p. 234

The success of *The Spy* was not altogether due to the novelty of its subject. With many of Cooper's characteristic faults, it has also his characteristic merits. It is full of scenes that show the vigor and dash of his narrative power; and its central character, the humble peddler Harvey Birch, cool, brave, incorruptible, quick in resource in times of peril, is a noble example of that homely heroism in the portrayal of which Cooper excelled.

Henry S. Pancoast, 1898, *An Introduction to*
American Literature, p. 133

General

Has the almost singular merit of writing American novels which everybody reads, and which we are of course bound to review now and then. For these last five or six years he has supplied the reading public annually with a repast of five or six hundred pages of such matter; so that we have a right to consider him as publicly professing this department of elegant literature. It is too late to say, that he does not excel in it; or at least, that he has not some considerable merit; for, however far he may fall short of our ideal standards, or wherever we may rank him among living writers, the public voice has long since confirmed to him the apellation of the American novelist, a title which was but sparingly and timidly suggested for the author of *The Spy.* No one has yet appeared among us who has been wholly able to cope with him in his proper walk; and we see no good reason why he should not be allowed, for the present at least, to maintain the distinction.

W. H. Gardiner, 1826, "Cooper's Novels,"
North American Review, vol. 23, p. 150

Mr. Cooper is admitted by very general consent to have distanced every other competitor in the route struck out by the author of Waverley. We would not be understood by this language, to imply any thing like a servile imitation, in the detracting spirit of some English journals; for Cooper is no more an imitator of Scott, than Milton is of Shakspeare, because they both wrote in blank verse, or than Scott himself is of this latter, whom he resembles in the *fond,* though not the form of his writings. If this be imitation, it is more glorious than most originality. . . . Cooper's great defect is his incapacity to seize the tone of good society; we say incapacity, for his repeated failures, we think, put it beyond a doubt. Nothing can be more lamentable than the compound of affectation, primness, and pedantry, a sort of backwoods gentility, which makes up with him the greater part of its dialogue and its manners. Defects like these would seem to be the natural result of an imperfect education, as well as a want of familiarity with well-bred society. But this last can scarcely be imputed to Mr. Cooper, and his experience of late years must have abundantly enlarged the sphere of his social observation, for all practical purposes. Has he shown a corresponding improvement?

William Hickling Prescott, 1832, "English Literature of the Nineteenth Century," *North American Review,* vol. 35, p. 190

Mr. Cooper's works, for the last three or four years, seem to have been written under no higher inspiration than that of spleen. They abound in uncalled-for political disquisitions, filled up with expressions of the bitterest scorn and hatred. They are deformed by perpetual out-breaks of a spirit, which might be expected to show itself in the pages of a ruthless partisan, careless of truth in aiming at the reputation of an opponent whom he wishes to ruin; but from which the writings of the poet and the man of letters, sitting apart, "in the still air of delightful studies," ought to be wholly exempt. He has added nothing to the range of characters in fiction, which amuse and occupy our hours of leisure, and to which the mind returns, as to old familiar scenes, or the faces of friends; he has told no new tale of human passions, for our instruction or warning; but he has given us, both in his books of travels, and his last novel, a few brilliant descriptions of natural scenery, both by land and sea.

Francis Bowen, 1838, "Cooper's *Homeward Bound,*" *North American Review,* vol. 47, p. 488

The first enthusiasm about Cooper having subsided, we remember more his faults than his merits. His ready resentment and way of showing it in cases which it is the wont of gentlemen to pass by in silence, or meet with a good humoured smile, have caused unpleasant associations with his name, and his fellow citizens, in danger of being tormented by suits for libel, if they spoke freely of him, have ceased to speak of him at all. But neither these causes, nor the baldness of his plots, shallowness of thought, and poverty in the presentation of character, should make us forget the grandeur and originality of his sea-sketches, nor the redemption from oblivion of our forest-scenery, and the noble romance of the hunter-pioneer's life. Already, but for him, this fine page of life's romance would be almost forgotten. He has done much to redeem these irrevocable beauties from the corrosive acid of a semi-civilized invasion.

Margaret Fuller Ossoli, 1850, "Modern British Poets," *Art, Literature and the Drama*, p. 305

One of the most widely known of Cooper's novels is *The Last of the Mohicans,* which forms the third volume of the [Leatherstocking] series, and which, with all the elements of a vulgar popularity, combines excellences of a far higher order. It has, nevertheless, its great and obtrusive faults. It takes needless liberties with history; and though it would be folly to demand that an historical novelist should always conform to received authorities, yet it is certainly desirable that he should not unnecessarily set them at defiance; since the incidents of the novel are apt to remain longer in the memory than those of the less palatable history. But whatever may be the extent of the novelist's license, it is, at all events, essential that his story should have some semblance of probability, and not run counter to nature and common sense. In *The Last of the Mohicans,* the machinery of the plot falls little short of absurdity. Why a veteran officer, pent up in a little fort, and hourly expecting to be beleaguered by a vastly superior force, consisting in great part of bloodthirsty savages, should at that particular time desire or permit a visit from his two daughters, is a question not easy to answer. Nor is the difficulty lessened when it is remembered, that the young ladies are to make the journey through a wilderness full of Indian scalping parties. It is equally difficult to see why the lover of Alice should choose, merely for the sake of a romantic ride, to conduct her and her sister by a circuitous and most perilous by-path through the forests, when they might more easily have gone by a good road under the safe escort of a column of troops who marched for the fort that very morning. The story founded on these gross inventions is sustained by various minor improbabilities, which cannot escape the reader unless his attention is absorbed by the narrative. . . .

In respect to the delineation of character, *The Last of the Mohicans* is surpassed by several other works of the author. Its distinguishing merit lies in its descriptions of scenery and action. . . .

It is easy to find fault with *The Last of the Mohicans;* but it is far from easy to rival or even approach its excellences. The book has the genuine game flavor; it exhales the odors of the pine woods and the freshness of the mountain wind. Its dark and rugged scenery rises as distinctly on the eye as the images of the painter's canvas, or rather as the reflection of nature herself. But it is not as the mere rendering of material forms, that these wood paintings are most highly to be esteemed. They are instinct with life, with the very spirit of the wilderness; they breathe the sombre poetry of solitude and danger. In these achievements of his art, Cooper, we think, has no equal, unless it may be the author of that striking romance, Wacousta or the Prophecy, whose fine powers of imagination are, however, even less under the guidance of a just taste than those of the American novelist.

Francis Parkman, Jan., 1852, *North American Review,* pp. 153-156

He is colonel of the literary regiment; Irving, lieutenant-colonel; Bryant, the major; while Longfellow, Whittier, Holmes, Dana, and myself may be considered captains. . . . Two or three of Cooper's characters I consider the first in American fiction. Which are they? Why, Leatherstocking, Long Tom Coffin, and Uncas. Why this noble creation has been so neglected by painters and sculptors I am at a loss to understand. Certainly there is no nobler Indian character depicted in our literature. Thackeray calls the first of these immortal creations—and he was certainly a competent judge —one of "the great prize-men" of fiction, better perhaps than any of Scott's men, and ranks dear old "Natty Bumppo" with Uncle Toby, Sir Roger de Coverley, and Falstaff—heroic figures all.

Fitz-Greene Halleck, 1867?, *Bryant and His Friends,*
by Wilson, p. 238

When he began writing he stood almost alone where now an innumerable crowd are contesting every inch of vantage-ground; and although his style has its defects, his novels are powerful and interesting in themselves, besides presenting valuable pictures of the infancy of our country, the life of the pioneer, the characteristics of the Indians, and the struggle for national liberty both on land and sea. All public libraries are obliged to provide themselves with numerous copies of his works, and no private library is considered complete without a costly edition. As an evidence of his popularity abroad, it may be mentioned that in Holland alone there are three different translations of his novels into three different dialects of the country.

Constance Fenimore Woolson, 1871, "The Haunted Lake,"
Harper's Magazine, vol. 44, p. 26

Characteristics there are of Cooper's writings which would and do repel many. Defects exist both in manner and matter. Part of the unfavorable judgment he has received is due to the prevalence of minor faults, disagreeable rather than positively bad. These, in many cases, sprang from the quantity of what he did and the rapidity with which he did it. . . . In the matter of language this rapidity and carelessness often degenerated into downright slovenliness. . . . He too often passed the bounds that divide liberty from license. It scarcely needs to be asserted that in most of these cases the violation of idiom arose from haste or carelessness. But there were some blunders which can only be imputed to pure unadulterated ignorance. He occasionally used words in senses, unknown to past or present use. He sometimes employed grammatical forms that belong to no period in the history of the English language. . . . All this is, in itself, of slight importance when set off against positive merits. . . . There are imperfections far more serious than these mistakes in language. He rarely attained to beauty of style. The rapidity with which he wrote forbids the idea that he ever strove earnestly for it. Even the essential but minor grace of clearness is sometimes denied him. . . . These are imperfections that have led to the undue depreciation of Cooper among highly cultivated men. Taken by themselves they might seem enough to ruin his reputation beyond redemption. It is a proof of his real greatness that he triumphs over defects which would utterly destroy the fame of a writer of inferior power. . . . The more uniform excellence of Cooper, however, lies in the pictures he gives of the life of nature.

Thomas R. Lounsbury, 1882, James Fenimore Cooper
(American Men of Letters), pp. 271, 272, 273, 274, 275, 281, 283

Though he could draw very well a sailor's sweetheart, like Mary Pratt, or a soldier's daughter, like Mabel Dunham, yet of *fine* women he had only a chivalrous notion, and painted them from a respectful distance. They were delicate creatures, to be handled like porcelain. Dressed out and beautified, they were to be protected and worshipped. They walk through the halls of his heroes, and take seats at the upper end to distribute the prizes after the tournament.

James Herbert Morse, 1883, "The Native Element in
American Fiction," The Century, vol. 26, p. 290

With all his foibles, Cooper was inspired by an intense patriotism, and he had a bold, vigorous, aggressive nature. He freed his talents at a stroke, and giving them full play attained at once a world-wide reputation, which no man of colonial mind could ever have dreamed of reaching. Yet his countrymen, long before his days of strife and unpopularity, seem to have taken singularly little patriotic pride in his achievements, and the well bred and well educated shuddered to hear him called the "American Scott"; not because they thought the epithet inappropriate and misapplied, but because it was a piece of irreverent audacity toward a great light of English literature.

Cooper was the first, after the close of the war of 1812, to cast off the colonial spirit and take up his position as a representative of genuine American literature.

Henry Cabot Lodge, 1884, *Studies in History,* p. 353

No Hamlets or Werthers or Renés or Childe Harolds were allowed to tenant his woods or appear on his quarter-decks. Will, and the trained sagacity and experience directing will, were the invigorating elements of character which he selected for romantic treatment. Whether the scene be laid in the primitive forest or on the ocean, his men are always struggling with each other or with the forces of nature. This primal quality of robust manhood all men understand, and it shines triumphantly through the interposing fogs of French, German, Italian, and Russian translations. A physician of the mind could hardly prescribe a more efficient tonic for weak and sentimental natures than a daily diet made up of the most bracing passages in the novels of Cooper. Another characteristic of Cooper, which makes him universally acceptable, is his closeness to nature. He agrees with Wordsworth in this, that in all his descriptions of natural objects he indicates that he and nature are familiar acquaintances, and, as Dana says, have "talked together."

Edwin Percy Whipple, 1886, *American Literature and Other Papers,* ed. Whittier, p. 46

One of the very greatest characters in fiction, the old woodsman, Natty Bumppo. . . . The five tales vary in value, no doubt, but taken altogether they reveal a marvelous gift of narration, and an extraordinary fullness of invention. . . . Time may be trusted safely to make a final selection from any author's works, however voluminous they may be, or however unequal. Cooper died almost exactly in the middle of the nineteenth century; and already it is *The Spy,* and the *Leatherstocking Tales* and four or five of the *Sea Tales* which survive, because they deserve to survive, because they were at once new and true when they were written, because they remain to-day the best of their kind. Cooper's men of the sea, and his men of the forest and the plain, are alive now though other fashions in fiction have come and gone. Other novelists have a more finished art nowadays, but no one of them all succeeds more completely in doing what he tried to do than did Cooper at his best. And he did a great service to American literature by showing how fit for fiction were the scenes, the characters, and the history of his native land.

Brander Matthews, 1896, *An Introduction to the Study of American Literature,* pp. 62, 63, 67

It seems to me that it was far from right for the Professor of English Literature in Yale, the Professor of English Literature in Columbia, and Wilkie Collins to deliver opinions on Cooper's literature without having read some of it. It would have been much more decorous to keep silent and let persons talk who have read Cooper. Cooper's art has some defects. In one place in *Deerslayer,* and in the restricted space of two-thirds of a page, Cooper has scored 114 offences against literary art out of a possible 115. It breaks the record. There are nineteen rules governing literary art in the domain of romantic fiction—some say twenty-two. In *Deerslayer* Cooper violated eighteen of them. . . . Cooper's gift in the way of invention was not a rich endowment; but such as it was he liked to work it, he was pleased with the effects, and indeed he did some quite sweet things with it. In his little box of stage properties he kept six or eight cunning devices, tricks, artifices for his savages and woodsmen to deceive and circumvent each other with, and he was never so happy as when he was working these innocent things and seeing them go. A favorite one was to make a moccasined person tread in the tracks of the moccasined enemy, and thus hide his own trail. Cooper wore out barrels and barrels of moccasins in working that trick. Another stage-property that he pulled out of his box pretty frequently was his broken twig. He prized his broken twig above all the rest of his effects, and worked it the hardest. It is a restful chapter in any book of his when somebody doesn't step on a dry twig and alarm all the reds and whites for two hundred yards around. Every time a Cooper person is in peril, and absolute silence is worth four dollars a minute, he is sure to step on a dry twig. There may be a hundred handier things to step on, but that wouldn't satisfy Cooper. Cooper requires him to turn out and find a dry twig; and if he can't do it, go and borrow one. In fact, the Leather Stocking Series ought to have been the Broken Twig Series.

> Samuel Langhorne Clemens (Mark Twain), 1897,
> "Fenimore Cooper's Literary Offences," *How to Tell a
> Story and Other Essays,* pp. 93, 97

His long introductions he shared with the other novelists of the day, or at least with Scott, for both Miss Austen and Miss Edgeworth are more modern in this respect and strike more promptly into the tale. His loose-jointed plots are also shared with Scott, but he knows as surely as Scott how to hold the reader's attention when once grasped. Like Scott's, too, is his fearlessness in giving details, instead of the vague generalizations which were then in fashion, and to which his academical critics would have confined him. . . . Balzac, who risked the details of buttons and tobacco pipes as fearlessly as Cooper, said of *The Pathfinder,* "Never did the art of writing tread closer upon the art of the pencil. This is the school of study for literary landscape painters." He says elsewhere: "If Cooper had succeeded in the painting of character to the same extent that he did in the painting of the phenomena of nature, he would have uttered the last word of our art." Upon such praise as this the reputation of James Fenimore Cooper may well rest.

Thomas Wentworth Higginson, 1898, American Prose,
ed. Carpenter, p. 151

The gist of the matter is that Cooper was not a verbal artist, and that his endowment of what we are pleased to call literary conscience was scant. With no special training as a writer, when, at thirty or thereabouts, it accidentally came into his head to try his hand at a novel, he struck boldly out, not particularly considering whither. Some of his early books, written for his own pleasure, brought him popularity which surprised no one more than himself. The art of writing engaged his attention far less than the panorama and the story. Robust and impetuous, he disdained details of style and academic standards. To apply to him academic standards is as if one should inquire whether Hard-Heart's horsemanship conforms to the rules of the riding-school; for nobody cares. It is to miss the point that, heaven knows how or why, he struck—Heaven be praised!—a new trail which, admitting all the shortcomings in style that any one may choose to allege, the world is not yet weary of following. The indisputable, the essential fact is that, entering unheralded and possessing the land, he founded a realm, and became by divine right king of American fiction.

W. B. Shubrick Clymer, 1900, James Fenimore Cooper
(Beacon Biographies), p. 59

He did not begin writing with any sense of a heaven-bestowed commission to reform American fiction, but felt his way like any ordinary mortal, following up his successes and, in general, forsaking his failures; so that his Leather Stocking Tales when read in the order of their hero's experiences seem to show a falling off in artistic achievement, whereas, if they are read in the actual order of their appearance one sees the advance made from *The Pioneers* to *The Pathfinder* and *The Deerslayer*. In building his earlier tales around a conventional romance of youthful lovers, Cooper had the excellent example of Scott to follow, as well as that of the countless minor novelists of the day.

From the use of this sentimental machinery arises that fruitful source of controversy, the question of Cooper's heroines. Professor Lounsbury has made merry over them. Mr. Brownell has achieved the more difficult, but not impossible, feat of admiring them, assuring the curious reader that the quiet scholastic atmosphere of New Haven is responsible for

Professor Lounsbury's craving for "more ginger" in fiction. One gathers that Mr. Brownell himself finds a certain repose in contemplating the elegant vacuity of a Cecilia Howard or a Louisa Grant. One's own ideal is, of course, a matter of taste, but there is no real ground for supposing that these gentle beings were necessarily Cooper's ideal. They belong to one of the most elderly and respectable traditions of fiction—that of the fine lady or "elegant female"—and they could be inserted in any romance as simply as could a comma or an interrogation point. The romance of two young persons aristocratic, either by birth or by reason of wealth or position, has always, with few exceptions, turned the wheels of the tale of romantic adventure,—and in tales of this sort the heroine usually belongs to one of three simple types, the hoyden, the cat, or the imbecile. Cooper was far too polite to introduce the hoyden, too chivalrous to believe in the cat—there remained only the imbecile, who had the further advantage of being much the easiest to manage. . . .

Cooper's Indian, if less a source of controversy than Cooper's heroine, has been even more hardly judged. The assertion that Cooper "idealized" the Indian has acquired the greyhaired respectability of established tradition. . . . Cooper can hardly be said to have idealized his Indians any more than Charles Brockden Brown idealized them. Both saw their picturesque possibilities. Brown emphasizes the picturesqueness of their faults, —Cooper that of their virtues. But the virtues which he attributed to them are those with which they are generally credited by people who knew the Indian before he came into contact with the blessings of civilization as disseminated by the trader. Snelling, who wrote his *Tales of the Northwest* to correct the popular idea of Indian character and manners, did not adduce anything to disprove Cooper's general estimate of Indian character. The real idealization of the Indian was carried on by Cooper's contemporaries and imitators—some of them excellent Massachusetts ladies— whose Indians are white men painted red, and endowed with all the virtues and a figurative turn of speech. Cooper shows his sincerity when he allows Chingachgook, the only one of his Indian heroes whose career is followed at length, to fulfill the sordid tragedy of his race by degrading his old age with drink.

Lillie Deming Loshe, 1907, *The Early American Novel,* pp. 86-89

JOHN JAMES AUDUBON
1780-1851

Born near New Orleans, May 4, 1780: died at New York, Jan. 27, 1851. A noted American ornithologist, of French descent, chiefly celebrated for his drawings of birds. He was educated in France, where he was a pupil of the painter David, and on his return to the United States made various unsuccessful attempts to establish himself in business in New York, Louisville, and New Orleans. His time was chiefly devoted to his favorite study, in the pursuit of which he made long excursions on foot through the United States. His chief work, *Birds of America,* was published, 1827-30, by subscription, the price of each copy being $1,000. In 1831-39 he published *Ornithological Biography* (5 volumes). His *Quadrupeds of America* (chiefly by John Bachman and Audubon's sons) appeared 1846-54.

> Benjamin E. Smith, ed., 1894-97, *The Century Cyclopedia of Names,* p. 94

SEE: *Audubon's America: The Narratives and Experiences of John James Audubon,* ed. Donald C. Peattie, 1940; Francis H. Herrick, *Audubon the Naturalist,* 1917, 2 v.; Constance Rourke, *Audubon,* 1936.

PERSONAL

I cannot help thinking Mr. Audubon a dishonest man. Why did he make you believe that he was a man of property? How is it his circumstances have altered so suddenly? In truth I do not believe you fit to deal with the world, or at least the American world.

> John Keats, 1819, *Letter to George Keats,* Sept. 17; *The Poetical Works and other Writings of John Keats,* ed. Forman, vol. IV, p. 5

He is the greatest artist in his own work that ever lived, and cannot fail to reap the reward of his genius and perseverance and adventurous zeal in his own beautiful branch of natural history, both in fame and fortune. The man himself—whom I have had the pleasure of frequently meeting—is just what you would expect from his works,—full of fine enthusiasm and intelligence—most interesting in looks and manners—a perfect gentleman—and esteemed by all who know him for the simplicity and frankness of his nature.

> John Wilson, 1827, *Noctes Ambrosianæ,* Jan.

His love of nature was not philosophic, like that of Wordsworth, nor scientific, like that of Humboldt, nor adventurous, like that of Boone; but special and artistic—circumstances, rather than native idiosyncrasy, made him a naturalist; and his knowledge was by no means so extensive in this regard as that of others less known to fame. But few men have indulged so genuine a love of nature for her own sake, and found such enjoyment in delineating one of the most poetical and least explored departments of her boundless kingdom. To the last his special ability, as an artistic naturalist, was unapproached; and, while one of his sons drew the outline, and another painted the landscape, or the foreground, it was his faithful hand that, with a steel-pen, made the hairy coat of the deer, or, with a fine pencil, added the exquisite plumage to the sea-fowl's breast. . . . His high-arched brow, dark-gray eye, and vivacious temperament, marked him as fitted by nature to excel in action as well as thought—a destiny which his pursuits singularly realized. There was something bird-like in the very physiognomy of Audubon, in the shape and keenness of his eye, the aquiline form of the nose, and a certain piercing and vivid expression when animated. He was thoroughly himself only amid the freedom and exuberance of nature; the breath of the woods exhilarated and inspired him; he was more at ease under a canopy of boughs than beneath gilded cornices, and felt a necessity to be within sight either of the horizon or the sea. Indeed, so prevailing was this appetite for nature, if we may so call it, that from the moment the idea of his last-projected expedition was abandoned,—in accordance with the urgent remonstrances of his family, mindful of his advanced age,—he began to droop, and the force and concentration of his intellect visibly declined.

Henry T. Tuckerman, 1857, Essays, Biographical
and Critical, pp. 305, 309

The interval of about three years which passed between the time of Audubon's return from the West and the period when his mind began to fail, was a short and sweet twilight to his adventurous career. His habits were simple. Rising almost with the sun, he proceeded to the woods to view his feathered favorites till the hour at which the family usually breakfasted, except when he had drawing to do, when he sat closely to his work. After breakfast he drew till noon and then took a long walk. At nine in the evening he generally retired. He was now an old man, and the fire which had burned so steadily in his heart was going out gradually. Yet there are but few things in his life more interesting and beautiful than the tranquil happiness he enjoyed in the bosom of his family, with his two sons and their children under the same roof, in the short interval between his return from his last earthly expedition, and the time when his sight and mind began to grow dim, until mental gloaming settled on him, before the night of death came.

Mrs. John J. Audubon, 1869, The Life of
John James Audubon, pp. 435, 436

GENERAL

That work, while it reflects such great credit on our country, and contributes so largely to the advancement of one of the most delightful departments of science, is likely, from the extreme expense attendant upon it, to repay but poorly the indefatigable labor of a lifetime. The high price necessarily put on the copies of Mr. Audubon's magnificent work places it beyond the means of the generality of private individuals. It is entitled therefore to the especial countenance of our libraries and various other public institutions. It appears to me, that the different departments in Washington ought each to have a copy deposited in their libraries or archives.

Washington Irving, 1836, *Letter to Martin Van Buren,* Oct. 19;
Life of John James Audubon, ed. his widow, p. 395

The great naturalist of America, John James Audubon, left behind him, in his *Birds of America* and *Ornithological Biography,* a magnificent monument of his labors, which through life were devoted to the illustration of the natural history of his native country. His grand work on the Biography of Birds is quite unequaled for the close observation of the habits of birds and animals which it displays, its glowing pictures of American scenery, and the enthusiastic love of nature which breathes throughout its pages. The sunshine and the open air, the dense shade of the forest, and the boundless undulations of the prairies, the roar of the sea beating against the rock-ribbed shore, the solitary wilderness of the Upper Arkansas, the savannas of the South, the beautiful Ohio, the vast Mississippi, and the green steeps of the Alleghanies,—all were as familiar to Audubon as his own home. The love of birds, of flowers, of animals,—the desire to study their habits in their native retreats,—haunted him like a passion from his earliest years, and he devoted almost his entire life to the pursuit. . . . While you read Audubon's books, you feel that you are in the society of no ordinary naturalist. Everything he notes down is the result of his own observation. Nature, not books, has been his teacher. You feel the fresh air blowing in your face, scent the odor of the prairie-flowers and the autumn-woods, and hear the roar of the surf along the sea-shore.

Samuel Smiles, 1860, *Brief Biographies,* pp. 98, 100

The journals of this trip are of surpassing interest. To the historian and student of Americana they furnish glimpses of early frontier life, and notes, interspersed with prophetic visions, of commerce and conditions along the Missouri River; to the ethnologist they give truthful pictures of the appearance, dress, and character of the Indians; to the naturalist they offer entertaining accounts of the discovery and habits of new or little known species, of the abundance and manner of hunting wolves, buffaloes, and other big game, and observations concerning the former ranges of animals no longer found in the region.

C. H. Merriam, 1898, "Audubon," *The Nation,* vol. 66, p. 152

MARY WOLLSTONECRAFT SHELLEY
1797-1851

[Daughter of William Godwin]. Born, in London, 30 Aug. 1797. Met Shelley, 1814. Eloped to Continent with him, 28 July 1814; returned, Sept. 1814. Married to Shelley, after his wife's suicide, 30 Dec. 1816. Lived at Marlow, 1817-18. To Italy, on account of Shelley's health, March 1818; he was drowned there, 8 July 1822. She returned to London, 1823; devoted herself to literature. Travelled on Continent, 1840, 1842-43. Died, in London, 21 Feb. 1851. Buried in Bournemouth Churchyard. WORKS: *History of a Six Weeks' Tour through a Part of France, etc.* (with her husband; anon.), 1817; *Frankenstein* (anon.), 1818; *Valperga* (anon.), 1823; *The Last Man* (anon.), 1826; *The Fortunes of Perkin Warbeck* (anon.), 1830; *Lodore* (anon.), 1835; *Falkner* (anon.), 1837; *Lives of the Most Eminent, Literary, and Scientific Men of France* (anon.; 2 vols.), 1838-39; *Rambles in Germany and Italy* (2 vols.), 1844. POSTHUMOUS: *The Choice,* ed. by H. B. Forman (priv. ptd.), 1876. She edited: Shelley's *Posthumous Poems* [1824]; *Poetical Works,* 1839; *Essays, etc.,* 1840. COLLECTED WORKS: *Tales and Stories,* ed. by R. Garnett, 1891. LIFE: *Life and Letters,* by F. A. Marshall, 1889.

> R. Farquharson Sharp, 1897, *A Dictionary of*
> *English Authors,* p. 254

SEE: *Tales and Stories, now First Collected,* ed. Richard Garnett, 1891; *Letters,* ed. Frederick L. Jones, 1944, 2 v.; *Mary Shelley's Journal,* ed. F. L. Jones, 1947; Elizabeth Nitchie, *Mary Shelley,* 1953.

PERSONAL

And what art thou? I know, but dare not speak:
Time may interpret to his silent years.
Yet in the paleness of thy thoughtful cheek,
And in the light thine ample forehead wears,
And in thy sweetest smiles, and in thy tears,
And in thy gentle speech, a prophecy
Is whispered, to subdue my fondest fears:
And, through thine eyes, even in thy soul I see
A lamp of festal fire burning internally.
They say that thou wert lovely from thy birth,
Of glorious parents thou aspiring child.
I wonder not—for One then left this earth
Whose life was like a setting planet mild,
Which clothed thee in the radiance undefiled
Of its departing glory; still her fame
Shines on thee, through the tempests dark and wild

Which shake these latter days; and thou canst claim
The shelter, from thy sire, of an immortal name.

Percy Bysshe Shelley, 1817, *The Revolt of Islam,* Dedication

Mrs. Shelley was, I have been told, the intimate friend of my son in the lifetime of his first wife, and to the time of her death, and in no small degree, as I suspect, estranged my son's mind from his family, and all his first duties in life; with that impression on my mind, I cannot agree with your Lordship that, though my son was unfortunate, Mrs. Shelley is innocent; on the contrary, I think that her conduct was the very reverse of what it ought to have been, and I must, therefore, decline all interference in matters in which Mrs. Shelley is interested.

Sir Timothy Shelley, 1823, *Letter to Lord Byron,* Feb. 6;
The Life and Letters of Mary Wollstonecraft Shelley,
ed. Marshall, vol. II, p. 66

At the time I am speaking of Mrs. Shelley was twenty-four. Such a rare pedigree of genius was enough to interest me in her, irrespective of her own merits as an authoress. The most striking feature in her face was her calm, grey eyes; she was rather under the English standard of woman's height, very fair and light-haired, witty, social and animated in the society of friends, though mournful in solitude; like Shelley, though in a minor degree, she had the power of expressing her thoughts in varied and appropriate words, derived from familiarity with the works of our vigorous old writers. Neither of them used obsolete or foreign words. This command of our language struck me the more as contrasted with the scanty vocabulary used by ladies in society, in which a score of poor hackneyed phrases suffice to express all that is felt or considered proper to reveal.

Edward John Trelawny, 1858-78, *Records of*
Shelley, Byron and the Author, p. 15

Frankenstein (1818)

When we have thus admitted that *Frankenstein* has passages which appall the mind and make the flesh creep, we have given it all the praise (if praise it can be called) which we dare to bestow. Our taste and our judgment alike revolt at this kind of writing, and the greater the ability with which it may be executed the worse it is.

Sir Walter Scott, 1818, *"Frankenstein,"*
Quarterly Review, vol. 13, p. 385

How changed is the taste of verse, prose, and painting, since *le bon vieux temps,* dear madam! Nothing attracts us but what terrifies, and is within—

if within—a hair's breadth of positive disgust. Some of the strange things they write remind me of Squire Richard's visit to the Tower Menagerie, when he says: "Odd, they are *pure* grim devils,"—particularly a wild and hideous tale called *Frankenstein.*

> Hester Lynch (Thrale) Piozzi, 1818, *Letter to Mme. D'Arblay;*
> *Diary and Letters of Mme. D'Arblay,* ed. Woolsey

Your talents are truly extraordinary. *Frankenstein* is universally known, and though it can never be a book for vulgar reading, is everywhere respected. It is the most wonderful work to have been written at twenty years of age that I ever heard of. You are now five and twenty, and, most fortunately, you have pursued a course of reading, and cultivated your mind in a manner the most admirably adapted to make you a great and successful author. If you cannot be independent, who should be?

> William Godwin, 1823, *Letter to Mrs. Shelley,* Feb. 18;
> *The Life and Letters of Mary Wollstonecraft Shelley,*
> ed. Marshall, vol. II, p. 68

That a young creature of this age should have produced anything at once so horrible and so original as the hideous romance of *Frankenstein,* is one of the most extraordinary accidents in literature; and that she should never, having made such a beginning, have done anything more, is almost equally wonderful. . . . Mary Shelley's individual appearances afterwards are only those of a romantically-desolate widow, pouring out her grief and fondness in sentimental gushes, which look somewhat overstrained and ridiculous in print, whatever they may have done in fact; but to hear her read, with her girlish lips, this most extraordinary and terrible of imaginations, must have been a sensation unparalleled. It is one of the books adopted into the universal memory, which everybody alludes to, and thousands who can never have read it understand the main incidents of—which is a wonderful instance of actual fame. That this should be merely stated as a fact in the history, and no one pause to wonder at it, is another odd instance of the insensibility of contemporaries.

> Margaret O. W. Oliphant, 1882, *Literary History of England,*
> *XVIII-XIX Century,* vol. III, p. 58

GENERAL

Mrs. Shelley has published, besides a *Frankenstein,* a romance entitled *Valperga,* which is less known than the former, but is of high merit. She exhibits in her hero, a brave and successful warrior, arriving at the height of his ambition, endowed with uncommon beauty and strength, and with many good qualities, yet causes him to excite emotions of reprobation and pity, because he is cruel and a tyrant, and because in the truth of things he is unhappy. This is doing a good work, taking the false glory from the eyes and showing things as they are. There are two female characters of wonderful power and beauty. The heroine is a lovely and noble creation. The work taken as a whole, if below *Frankenstein* in genius, is yet worthy of its author and of her high rank in the aristocracy of genius, as the daughter of Godwin and Mary Wollstonecraft, and the widow of Shelley.

Richard Hengist Horne, 1844, A New Spirit of the Age, p. 321

In spite of much descriptive and analytic talent she shared the inaptitude for history which marked the Godwinian and Radcliffian schools alike. *The Last Man* . . . has a pathetic significance as shadowing her own tragic loneliness,—the "Loneliness of Crusoe"—as she herself long afterwards declared it to have been.

C. H. Herford, 1897, The Age of Wordsworth, p. 98

THOMAS MOORE
1779-1852

Born, in Dublin, 28 May 1779. At school in Dublin. Contrib. verses to *Anthologia Hibernica*, 1793. To Trin. Coll., Dublin, 1794; B. A., 1798 [or 1799?]. Student at Middle Temple, 1799. Admiralty Registrar at Bermuda, Aug. 1803. Left deputy in office and removed to New York, 1804; travelled in U. S. A. Returned to London, Nov. 1804. Contrib. to *Edinburgh Rev.* from 1806. Married Bessie Dyke, 25 March 1811. Settled near Ashbourne. Friendship with Byron begun, 1811. Visit to Paris, 1817. His deputy at Bermuda proved defaulter for £6,000, 1818. In Paris and Italy, 1819-22. Returned to England, April 1822; debt to Admiralty reduced to £1,000, and paid by Lord Lansdowne's help. Settled in Wiltshire again, Nov. 1822. Literary Fund Pension, 1835; Civil List Pension, 1850. Died, 25 Feb. 1852. Buried at Bromham. WORKS: *The Poetical Works of the Late Thomas Little* (pseud.), 1801; *Epistles, Odes, and Other Poems*, 1806; *Irish Melodies* (10 nos.), 1807-34; *Corruption and Intolerance* (anon.), 1808; *The Sceptic* (anon.), 1809; *Letter to the Roman Catholics of Dublin*, 1810 (2nd edn. same year); *M. P.*, 1811; *Intercepted Letters; or, the Twopenny Post-Bag* (under pseud. "Thomas Brown the Younger"), 1813 (11th edn. same year); *National Airs*, 1815; *Lines on the Death of ——* (*i.e.*, Sheridan), (anon.), 1816; *The World at Westminster* (anon.), 1816; *Sacred Songs*, 1816; *Lalla Rookh*, 1817 (6th edn. same year); *The Fudge Family in Paris* (by "Thomas Brown the Younger"), 1818 (8th edn. same year); *Tom Crib's Memorial* (anon.), 1819 (4th edn. same year); *Rhymes on the Road* (by "Thomas Brown the Younger"), 1823; *The Loves of the Angels*, 1823 (5th edn. same year); *Fables for the Holy Alliance* (by

"Thomas Brown the Younger"), 1823; *Evenings in Greece* [1825?]; *The Fudges in England* (by "Thomas Brown the Younger"), 1825; *Memoirs of Captain Rock* (anon.), 1824; *Memoirs of the Life of Sheridan*, 1825 (3rd edn. same year); *The Epicurean*, 1827 (with addition of "Alciphron," 1839); *Rhymes of the Times* (anon.), 1827; *Odes upon Cash, Corn, Catholics and other matters* (anon.), 1828; *Legendary Ballads* [1830?]; *The Life and Death of Lord Edward Fitzgerald* (2 vols.), 1831; *The Summer Fête* [1831]; *Travels of an Irish Gentleman in Search of a Religion* (anon.), 1833; *History of Ireland* (in Lardner's *Cabinet Cyclopædia*, 4 vols.), 1835-46; *Poetical Works*, 1840; *Songs, Ballads and Sacred Songs*, 1809. POSTHUMOUS: *Memoirs, Journals and Correspondence*, ed. by Lord John Russell (8 vols.), 1853-56. He translated: *Odes of Anacreon*, 1800; and edited Byron's *Letters and Journals*, 1830; Sheridan's Works, 1833; Byron's Works, 1835.

R. Farquharson Sharp, 1897, A Dictionary of
English Authors, p. 201

SEE: *Poetical Works*, ed. A. D. Godley, 1910; *Tom Moore's Diary: A Selection*, ed J. B. Priestley, 1925; Howard Mumford Jones, *The Harp That Once —: The Life of Moore*, 1937.

PERSONAL

Moore has a peculiarity of talent, or rather talents,—poetry, music, voice, all his own; and an expression in each which never was, nor will be, possessed by another. . . . There is nothing Moore may not do, if he will but seriously set about it. In society, he is gentlemanly, gentle, and altogether more pleasing than any individual with whom I am acquainted.

Lord Byron, 1813, Journals, Nov. 22

I saw Moore (for the first time I may say) this season. We had indeed met in public twenty years ago. There is a manly frankness, with perfect ease and good breeding about him which is delightful. Not the least touch of the poet or pedant. A little—very little man. Less, I think, than Lewis, and something like him in person; God knows not in conversation, for Matt, though a clever fellow, was a bore of the first description. Moreover, he always looked like a schoolboy. Now Moore has none of this insignificance. His countenance is plain, but the expression so animated, especially in speaking or singing, that it is far more interesting than the finest features could have rendered it.

Sir Walter Scott, 1825, Journal, Nov. 22;
Life by Lockhart, ch. lxv

His forehead is bony and full of character, with "bumps" of wit, large and radiant enough to transport a phrenologist. His eyes are as dark and fine, as you would wish to see under a set of vine-leaves; his mouth generous and good-humored, with dimples; his nose sensual, prominent and at the same time the reverse of acquiline. There is a very peculiar character in it, as if it were looking forward, and scenting a feast or an orchard. The face, upon the whole, is Irish, not unruffled with care and passion, but festivity is the prominent expression.

Leigh Hunt, 1828, *Lord Byron and some of his*
Contemporaries, vol. I, p. 282

With a keen sense of enjoyment, he loved music and poetry, the world and the playhouse, the large circle of society, and the narrow precincts of his home. His heart was thrilled by deep feelings of devotion, and his mind expatiated over the wide field of philosophy. In all that he did, and wrote, and spoke, there was a freedom and a frankness which alarmed and delighted:—frightened old men of the world, and charmed young men and young women who were something better than the world. . . . Mrs. Moore brought him no fortune; indeed it was intended that she should earn her living by the stage, and Moore, afraid that so unworldly a match might displease his parents, at first concealed from them the fact of his marriage. But the excellence of his wife's moral character; her energy and courage; her abhorrence of all meanness; her disinterested abstinence from amusement; her persevering economy; made her a better, and even a richer partner to Moore, than an heiress of ten thousand a year would have been with less devotion to her duty, and less steadiness of conduct.

Lord John Russell, 1853, ed., *Memoirs, Journal and*
Correspondence of Thomas Moore, Preface, vol. VI, pp. v, xviii

Moore's democracy did not prevent his being remarkably fond of the society of aristocrats. In his journal, he duly chronicles with what untiring perseverance he went to the mansions of noble lords and lovely or fashionable ladies; and how constantly he was inventing excuses for going to London, that he might mingle in their society,—they, to do justice to both, being as happy to receive him as he was to visit them. The compliment, in his case, was as much *bestowed* as *received,* if he only would have thought so. It was mean for Byron to say of Moore, as reported by Leigh Hunt on his return from Italy, "Tommy dearly loves a lord"; but it was meaner still, besides being spiteful, for Hunt to repeat it. Nevertheless, it was true. Moore was, I will not say happiest,—for he was a domestic man in his way, —but very happy, in the society of the peerage.

R. Shelton Mackenzie, 1871, *Sir Walter Scott:*
The Story of His Life, p. 374

His *Journals* curiously indicate what I repeatedly witnessed in my own house and elsewhere, his morbid sensitiveness when singing his Irish Ballads, to the effect they produced on those around him. In the most touching passages his eye was wandering around the room scrutinising jealously the influence of his song.

Sir Henry Holland, 1871, *Recollections of Past Life*, p. 208

Thomas Moore (or Tom Moore, as he was usually called) was small in stature and almost girlish in appearance when he came to the United States in 1804. He had been a "show child"—attractive and noteworthy almost from babyhood. He was a clever rhymer at the age of fourteen years, and at twenty he had earned fame as a poet, and was "patronized" and flattered by the Prince of Wales, afterward King George the Fourth. His face was small and intellectual in expression, sweet and gentle. His eyes were dark and brilliant; his mouth was delicately cut and full-lipped; his nose was slightly upturned, giving an expression of fun to his face; his complexion was fair and somewhat ruddy; his hair was a rich dark brown, and curled all over his head; his forehead was broad and strongly marked; and his voice, not powerful, was exquisitely sweet, especially when he was singing. Such is a description of Moore's personal appearance at the time of his visit here, which was given me by Mrs. M—r, an elderly lady at Fredericksburg, Virginia, almost thirty years ago.

Benson J. Lossing, 1877, "Tom Moore in America,"
Harper's Magazine, vol. 55, p. 537

Odes of Anacreon (1800)

If we open a collection of his poems now, and read his *Odes of Anacreon,* to which the Prince of Wales and other notabilities of rank subscribed, we desist after a time with something of the disgust we should feel at a profuse display of pretty, sham jewelry. The ample, brimming bowls and goblets of wine, the wreaths and garlands of roses, the rich perfumes, the sparkling eyes, and the golden tresses, and the snowy necks, are well enough in moderation, but some eighty odes of such materials pall for lack of variety. Any variety that there is lies within the narrowest limits; now it is a bowl and now it is a goblet, now we drink and now we quaff, now it is a bud and now it is a full-blown rose, now a garland and now a cluster, now ringlets and now tresses; but it is always wine and flower, with little variation of phrase. We are soon surfeited with such sentiment, and disposed to laugh at its artificiality. Moore's prettiness, always expressed in soft and melodious verse, were probably a pleasant surprise to a generation weary of didactic poems; but if we have a liking for such things now, we can find more genuine articles of the same kind, compounded with much higher art, in the poetry of the seventeenth century, the volumes of Queen Henrietta's poets, Lovelace, and Carew, and Suckling, and above all, Herrick.

> William Minto, 1894, *The Literature of the
> Georgian Era*, ed. Knight

Irish Melodies (1807-1834)

There is a liquid ease, a dance of words, and a lyrical grace and brevity in them all; but there is, likewise, an epigrammatic point and smartness, a courtly and a knowing air, so to speak, alien to the simplicity of the music and to the nature of song. . . . In one word, there is not a little affectation in them, put-on graces, and artificial raptures. These faults are nearly balanced by beauties.

> Allan Cunningham, 1833, *Biographical and Critical History
> of the Literature of the Last Fifty Years*

It provided him with a solid basis for his reputation of making him the national lyrist of Ireland, a character which, notwithstanding the numerous charges which may justly be brought against his *Irish Melodies,* on the ground both of false poetry and false patriotism, he must retain until some one arises to deprive him of it. Better isolated pieces have no doubt been written by some of his successors, but he, and he alone, has produced an imposing body of national song; nor have his fancy, melody, and pathos, on the whole, been yet equalled by any competitor.

> Richard Garnett, 1894, *Dictionary of National Biography,*
> vol. XXXVIII, p. 381

No such distinguished success was ever before, or has ever since, been achieved in the not very distinguished art of "writing up to" music. The *Irish Melodies,* it is true, show many marks of their conventional origin; they are in a certain sense artificial products, altogether wanting in the freshness and *naïveté,* the epic force and simplicity of the genuine folk-song; but they were the work of a man in whom the melancholy charm of his country and of his country's music inspired a feeling so genuine and, indeed, so intense as continually to lift, if it could not consistently maintain, his expression above the level of the commonplace. It is the lack of this emotional sincerity which leaves his more ambitious efforts comparatively cold and lifeless, and has consigned *Lalla Rookh* to an oblivion which the *Irish Melodies* and a few other lyrics of Moore's have escaped.

> Henry Duff Traill, 1896, *Social England,* vol. V, p. 587

Lalla Rookh (1817)

I have read two pages of *Lalla Rookh,* or whatever it is called. Merciful Heaven! I dare read no more, that I may be able to answer at once to any questions, "I have but just looked at the work." O Robinson! if I could, or if I dared, act and feel as Moore and his set do, what havoc could I not make amongst their crockery-ware! Why, there are not three lines together without some adulteration of common English, and the ever-recurring blunder of using the possessive case, *"compassion's* tears," &c., for the preposition "of,"—a blunder of which I have found no instances earlier than Dryden's slovenly verses written for the trade.

Samuel Taylor Coleridge, 1817, *Letter to H. C. Robinson,* June;
Robinson's Diary, Reminiscences and Correspondence,
ed. Sadler, vol. I, p. 363

There is something very extraordinary, we think, in the work before us— and something which indicates in the author, not only a great exuberance of talent, but a very singular constitution of genius. While it is more splendid in imagery—(and for the most part in very good taste)—more rich in sparkling thoughts and original conceptions, and more full indeed of exquisite pictures, both of all sorts of beauties and virtues, and all sorts of sufferings and crimes, than any other poem that has yet come before us; we rather think we speak the sense of most readers when we add, that the effect of the whole is to mingle a certain feeling of disappointment with that of admiration! to excite admiration rather than any warmer sentiment of delight—to dazzle, more than to enchant—and, in the end, more frequently to startle the fancy, and fatigue the attention, by the constant succession of glittering images and high-strained emotions, than to maintain a rising interest, or win a growing sympathy, by a less profuse or more systematic display of attractions. The style is, on the whole, rather diffuse, and too unvaried in its character. But its greatest fault, in our eyes, is the uniformity of its brilliancy—the want of plainness, simplicity and repose.

Francis, Lord Jeffrey, 1817-44, "Moore's *Lalla Rookh,*"
Contributions to the Edinburgh Review, vol. III, p. 200

Mr. Moore ought not to have written *Lalla Rookh,* even for three thousand guineas. His fame is worth more than that. He should have minded the advice of Fadladeen. It is not, however, a failure, so much as an evasion and a consequent disappointment of public expectation. He should have left it to others to break conventions with nations, and faith with the world. He should, at any rate, have kept his with the public. *Lalla Rookh* is not what people wanted to see whether Mr. Moore could do—namely, whether he could write a long epic poem. It is four tales. The interest, however, is often high wrought and tragic, but the execution still turns to the effeminate and voluptuous side.

William Hazlitt, 1818, *Lectures on the English Poets,*
Lecture viii

It is still possible to read *Lalla Rookh* with pleasure, and even with a sort of indulgent enthusiasm. Rococo prettiness could hardly reach a higher point of accomplishment, and the sham-oriental is perhaps not more hope-lessly antiquated than our own sham-mediæval will be sixty years hence. The brilliance of Moore's voluptuous scenes has faded; he gilded them too much with the gold of Mrs. Tighe's *Psyche,* a preparation that was expressly made to tarnish. But underneath the smooth and faded surface lie much tenderness and pathos in the story of the Peri, much genuine patriotism in the fate of the Fire Worshippers, much tropical sweetness in the adventures of the "Light of the Haram." These narratives possess more worth, for instance, than all but the very best of Byron's tales, and would be read with more pleasure than those were they not overburdened by a sensuous richness of style. This quality, which Moore considered his chief claim to immortality, was in point of fact a great snare to him.

Edmund Gosse, 1880, *The English Poets,* ed. Ward, vol. IV, p. 310

Life of Lord Byron (1830)

We have read this book with the greatest pleasure. Considered merely as a composition, it deserves to be classed among the best specimens of English prose which our age has produced. It contains, indeed, no single passage equal to two or three which we could select from the *Life of Sheridan*; but, as a whole, it is immeasurably superior to that work. The style is agreeable, clear, and manly; and when it rises into eloquence, rises without effort or ostentation. Nor is the matter inferior to the manner. It would be difficult to name a book which exhibits more kindness, fairness, and modesty. It has evidently been written, not for the purpose of show-ing, what, however, it often shows, how well its author can write; but for the purpose of vindicating, as far as truth will permit, the memory of a celebrated man.

Thomas Babington Macaulay, 1830, "Moore's *Life of
Lord Byron*," *Edinburgh Review; Critical and
Miscellaneous Essays*

The poet could not forecast that Moore would get the money and not pub-lish the book; that his bibliopolist's compilation—all puff and laudation to sell his stock—would be substituted—a lifeless life, giving no notion of the author, nothing told as Byron told it, and, excepting the letters it contains, unreadable and unread. Byron could not escape the poet's fate—his true life suppressed, and a bookish, elaborate eulogy of his poetry to sell his works substituted.

Edward John Trelawny, 1858-78, *Records of Shelley,*
Byron and the Author, p. 38

Moore's vice is cautious, soft, seductive, slippery, and covered at times with a thin, tremulous veil of religious sentimentalism. In regard to Byron, he was an unscrupulous, committed partisan: he was as much bewitched by him as ever man has been by woman; and therefore to him, at last, the task of editing Byron's Memoirs was given. This Byron, whom they all knew to be obscene beyond what even their most drunken tolerance could at first endure; this man, whose foul license *spoke out* what most men conceal from mere respect to the decent instincts of humanity; whose "honor was lost,"—was submitted to this careful manipulator, to be turned out a perfected idol for a world longing for one, as the Israelites longed for the calf in Horeb.

Harriet Beecher Stowe, 1870, *Lady Byron Vindicated,* p. 99

It was exactly the biography which that age required: by no means complete or entirely authentic, nor claiming to be so, but presenting Byron in the light in which contemporaries desired to regard him, and in every respect a model of tact and propriety. The fearless criticism and the deep insight which are certainly missing were not at that time required, and until they are supplied elsewhere the work will rank as a classic, even though its interest be less due to the efforts of Moore's own pen than to the charm of the letters which he was the first to give to the world.

Richard Garnett, 1894, *Dictionary of National Biography,*
vol. XXXVIII, p. 383

History of Ireland (1830-46)

Moore wasted much time on uncongenial tasks, such as his *History of Ireland.* He bestowed great pains upon it, but the result proved that he had spent his strength in vain. His great and lasting achievement is to have set forth and lamented in exquisite verse the sorrows and wrongs of his native land. Moore's admirers can forgive his shortcomings as the historian of Erin when they regard him as its bard.

W. Fraser Rae, 1885, "The Bard of Erin,"
Temple Bar, vol. 75, p. 45

The last years of his life were spent in writing a *History of Ireland,* now quite unknown. He persisted in this work, and this gives us a higher idea of his character. With all his apparent affectation he was a genuine patriot, an industrious worker, and a most exemplary son and husband, and there is no doubt that it was these qualities that helped to make him the darling of the London drawing-rooms.

William Minto, 1894, *The Literature of the Georgian Era,*
ed. Knight, p. 234

GENERAL

He . . . may boast, if the boast can please him, of being the most licentious of modern versifiers, and the most poetical of those who, in our times, have devoted their talents to the propagation of immorality. We regard his book, indeed, as a public nuisance, and would willingly trample it down by one short movement of contempt and indignation, had we not reason to apprehend that it was abetted by patrons who are entitled to a more respectful remonstrance and by admirers who may require a more extended exposition of their dangers. . . . It seems to be his aim to impose corruption upon his readers by concealing it under the mask of refinement; to reconcile them imperceptibly to the most vile and vulgar sensuality by blending its language with that of exalted feeling and tender emotion; and to steal impurity into their hearts, by gently perverting the most simple and generous of their affections. In the execution of this unworthy task he labours with a perseverance at once ludicrous and detestable. . . . A publication which we would wish to see consigned to universal reprobation.

Francis, Lord Jeffrey, 1806, "Moore's Poems,"
Edinburgh Review, vol. 8, pp. 456, 457, 465

Mr. Moore's Muse is another Ariel, as light, as tricksy, as indefatigable, and as humane a spirit. His fancy is forever on the wing, flutters in the gale, glitters in the sun. Every thing lives, moves, and sparkles in his poetry, while over all love waves his purple light. . . . The fault of Mr. Moore is an exuberance of involuntary power. His facility of production lessens the effect of, and hangs as a dead weight upon, what he produces. His levity at last oppresses. The infinite delight he takes in such an infinite number of things, creates indifference in minds less susceptible of pleasure than his own. He exhausts attention by being inexhaustible. His variety cloys; his rapidity dazzles and distracts the sight. The graceful ease with which he lends himself to every subject, the genial spirit with which he indulges in every sentiment, prevents him from giving their full force to the masses of things, from connecting them into a whole. He wants intensity, strength, and grandeur. His mind does not brood over the great and permanent; it glances over the surfaces, the first impressions of things, instead of grappling with the deep-rooted prejudices of the mind, its inveterate habits, and that "perilous stuff that weighs upon the heart." His pen, as it is rapid and fanciful, wants momentum and passion. It requires the same principle to make us thoroughly like poetry, that makes us like ourselves so well, the feeling of continued identity.

William Hazlitt, 1818, *Lectures on the English Poets,*
Lecture viii

Moore had in his time many imitators, but all his gayety, his brilliant fancy, his somewhat feminine graces, and the elaborate music of his numbers, have not saved him from the fate of being imitated no more.

William Cullen Bryant, 1870, *A New Library of Poetry and Song,* Introduction, vol. I, p. 43

Nearly every line he wrote is pregnant with platitude and literary affectations; nearly every song he sang is either playfully, or forlornly, or affectedly, genteel; and though he had a musical ear, he was deficient in every lofty grace, every word-compelling power, of the divine poetic gift. Above all, he lacked simplicity—that one unmistakable gift of all great national poets, from Homer downwards. And the cardinal defect of the verse was the true clue to the thoroughly artificial character of the man. . . . I have granted the merit of Moore's verses and the amusing nature of his personality; but I must protest in the name of justice against his acceptance as the national poet of Ireland. If Irishmen accept him and honour him as such, so much the worse for Irishmen, since his falsehood of poetic touch must respond to something false and unpoetic in their own natures.

Robert Buchanan, 1886, "The Irish 'National' Poet,"
A Look Round Literature, pp. 205, 206

It was a society which loved bric-à-brac, and Moore gave it bric-à-brac poetry of the best kind. Never was it better done; and the verse had a melodious movement, as of high-bred and ignorant ladies dancing on enamelled meadows, which pleased the ear and almost seemed to please the eye. He was quite, then, in harmony with the society for which he wrote, and it would be rather surly of us if we judged him altogether from our standard of poetry and abused him for complying with the taste of his time. No one dreams of comparing him with the greater men, or of giving his poetry too important a place in the history of English song. But the man whose work Byron frankly admired; whom Scott did not dispraise; who received letters of thanks and appreciation from readers in America, Europe, and Asia; who fulfilled Matthew Arnold's somewhat foolish criterion of a poet's greatness by being known and accepted on the Continent; whom the Italians, French, Germans, Russians, Swedes, and Dutch translated; whose *Lalla Rookh* was partly put into Persian, and became the companion of Persians, on their travels and in the streets of Ispahan; to whom publishers like Longmans gave 3,000*l.* for a poem before they had even seen it, "as a tribute to reputation already acquired"—can scarcely be treated with the indifferent contempt which some have lavished upon him. He pleased, and he pleased a very great number. Time has altered that contemporary verdict, and rightly—but when it is almost universal, not merely the verdict of a clique, it counts.

Stopford A. Brooke, 1900, *A Treasury of Irish Poetry,*
ed. Brooke and Rolleston, p. 36

JOHN GIBSON LOCKHART
1794-1854

Born, at Cambusnethan, Lanarkshire, 14 July 1794. At school in Glasgow. At Glasgow Univ., 1805-09. Matric. Balliol Coll., Oxford, as Exhibitioner, 16 Oct. 1809; B. C. L., 1817. Studied Law in Edinburgh, 1813-16; Advocate, 1816. Travelled in Germany, 1816-17; visited Goethe at Weimar. Contrib. to *Blackwood's Magazine,* from Oct. 1817. Friendship with Sir Walter Scott begun, May 1818. Married Sophia Scott, 29 April 1820. Lived at Chiefswood, near Abbotsford. Active literary life. Removed to London, 1825. Edited *Quarterly Review,* 1825-53. Called to Bar at Lincoln's Inn, 22 Nov. 1831. D. C. L., Oxford, 13 June 1834. Auditor of the Duchy of Lancaster, 1843. Withdrew from society in later years. In Italy, winter 1853-54. Died, at Abbotsford, 25 Nov. 1854. Buried in Dryburgh Abbey. WORKS: *Peter's Letters to his Kinsfolk* (under pseud. "Peter Morris"), 1819; *Valerius* (anon.), 1821; *Some passages in the life of Mr. Adam Blair* (anon.), 1822; *Reginald Dalton* (anon.), 1823; *The History of Matthew Wald* (anon.), 1824; *Life of Robert Burns,* 1828; *History of Napoleon Buonaparte* (anon.), 1829; *History of the late War,* 1832; *Memoirs of the Life of Sir Walter Scott* (7 vols.), 1836-38; *Songs of the Edinburgh Squadron* (anon.), 1839; *The Ballantyne Humbug Handled,* 1839; *Theodore Hook* (anon.), 1852; He edited Motteux's translation of *Don Quixote,* 1822; Sir W. Scott's *Poetical Works* (under initials J. G. L.), 1833-34; Byron's Works (with Sir W. Scott), 1835; and translated *Ancient Spanish Ballads,* 1823. LIFE: *Life and Letters,* ed. by A. Lang, 1897.

R. Farquharson Sharp, 1897, *A Dictionary of
English Authors,* p. 171

SEE: abridgement of *Memoirs of Life of Sir Walter Scott* (1837-38, 7 v.), by Andrew Lang, 1906; *Literary Criticism,* ed. M. C. Hildyard, 1931;

Andrew Lang, *The Life and Letters of John Gibson Lockhart,* 1897, 2 v.; Gilbert Macbeth, *John Gibson Lockhart: A Critical Study,* 1935; Marion C. Lochhead, *John Gibson Lockhart,* 1954.

PERSONAL

To Moore, Lockhart offers a strong and singular contrast. Tall, and slightly, but elegantly formed, his head possesses the noble contour, the precision and harmony of outline, which distinguish classic sculpture. It possesses, too, a striking effect of color, in a complexion pale yet pure, and hair as black as the raven's wing. Though his countenance is youthful (he seems scarce more than thirty), yet I should designate reflection as the prominent, combined expression of that broad, white forehead; those arched and pencilled brows; those retired, yet full, dark eyes; the accurately chiselled nose; and compressed, though curved lips. His face is too thin, perhaps, for mere beauty; but this defect heightens its intellectual character.

Edmund D. Griffin, 1829, Pencillings

When it is considered what literary celebrity Lockhart has gained so early in life, and how warm and disinterested a friend he has been to me, it argues but little for my sagacity that I scarcely recollect anything of our first encounters. He was a mischievous Oxford puppy, for whom I was terrified, dancing after the young ladies, and drawing caricatures of every one who came in contact with him. But then I found him constantly in company with all the better rank of people with whom I associated, and consequently it was impossible for me not to meet with him. I dreaded his eye terribly; and it was not without reason, for he was very fond of playing tricks on me, but always in such a way that it was impossible to lose temper with him. I never parted company with him that my judgment was not entirely jumbled with regard to characters, books and literary articles of every description. Even his household economy seemed clouded in mystery; and if I got any explanation, it was sure not to be the right thing.

James Hogg, 1832, Autobiography, p. 469

A precise, brief, active person of considerable faculty, which, however, had shaped itself *gigmanically* only. Fond of quizzing, yet not *very* maliciously. Has a broad black brow, indicating force and penetration, but the lower half of face diminishing into the character at best of distinctness, almost of triviality. Rather liked the man, and shall like to meet him again.

Thomas Carlyle, 1832, Journal, Jan. 21; Early Life of
Thomas Carlyle, ed. Froude, vol. II, p. 188

He has been spoken of as cold, heartless, incapable of friendship. We have written in vain, and his own letters are vainly displayed, if it be not now recognised that the intensity of his affections rivalled, and partly caused, the intensity of his reserve. Garrulous lax affections and emotions are recognised and praised: ready tears, voluble sorrows, win sympathy,— and may have forsaken the heart they tenanted almost in the hour of their expression. Lockhart felt too strongly for words, and his griefs were "too great for tears," as the Greek says. His silence was not so much the result of a stoical philosophy, as of that constitutional and ineradicable play of nature which, when he was a child, left his cheeks dry while others wept, and ended in a malady of voiceless grief. He was born to be so, and to be misconstrued. . . . Unfortunate in so much, Lockhart was most happy in a wife and daughter who inherited the sweetness of spirit of their father and their grandfather. To their influence, in part, we may trace the admirable qualities which, in his later years, contrasted with the acerbity of his early manhood. To adapt the noble phrase of the Greek historian, "Being a man, he bore manfully such things as mortals must endure."

Andrew Lang, 1896, ed., The Life and Letters of
John Gibson Lockhart, vol. II, pp. 408, 412

Life of Sir Walter Scott (1836-38)

Fortunate as Sir Walter Scott was in his life, it is not the least of his good fortunes that he left the task of recording it to one so competent as Mr. Lockhart, who to a familiarity with the person and habits of his illustrious subject unites such entire sympathy with his pursuits, and such fine tact and discrimination in arranging the materials for publication.

William Hickling Prescott, 1838, Biographical and
Critical Miscellanies

Executed with so much skill, and in so admirable a manner, that, next to Boswell's *Life of Johnson,* it will probably always be considered as the most interesting work of biography in the English language.

Sir Archibald Alison, 1853-59, History of Europe, 1815-52, ch. v

The defect of Lockhart's book is that he devotes too much space to a discussion of the connection between Scott and the Ballantynes. The tone and temper of this discussion are equally out of keeping with the biography and its author's intention of exhibiting Scott in a favorable light. The executors of James Ballantyne replied, in a voluminous pamphlet, the object of which was to show that Ballantyne was more sinned against than sinning. Lockhart retorted, in a bitter publication called *The Ballantyne Humbug Handled*. It was contemptuous and personal. Then followed a rejoinder, going closely into detail, in which they showed how constantly Scott used to draw on Ballantyne for money, and how improvident he was. To this there was no reply, but the discussion, which was provoked by Lockhart's aspersions, did not tend to exalt Scott in public estimation.

> R. Shelton Mackenzie, 1854, ed. *Noctes Ambrosianæ,*
> *Memoir of John Gibson Lockhart,* vol. III, p. xiv

As a man of letters, Lockhart is a fascinating, if not a prominent, figure in the history of the earlier half of our century; but to the majority he will never be more than the biographer of Scott.

> T. Hutchinson, 1896, *The Academy,* vol. 50, p. 344

GENERAL

Has been universally accepted [*Life of Burns*] as a graceful treatment of the subject; kind, without being partial, towards Burns, and informed with a fine spirit of criticism. It adds, however, little to the details previously known, and certainly any effort made by the author to attain correctness in the statement and arrangement of facts, was far from what would appear to have been necessary in the case.

> Robert Chambers, 1850, *The Life and Works of*
> *Robert Burns,* Preface, vol. I, p. vi

Its present accomplished editor [of the *Quarterly Review*] Lockhart, who at a short interval succeeded Gifford in its direction, brought to his arduous task qualities which eminently fitted him for its duties. He is not political in his disposition, at least so far as engaging in the great strife of public questions is concerned: he is one of the light, not the heavy armed, infantry, and prefers exchanging thrusts with a court rapier to wielding the massy club of Hercules. But in the lighter branches of literature he has deservedly attained the very highest eminence. As a novelist, a critic, and a biographer, he has taken a lasting place in English literature.

> Sir Archibald Alison, 1853-59, *History of Europe, 1815-52,* ch. v

No student of biography can afford to overlook Lockhart. Apart from his skill in choosing significant circumstances, he is peculiarly distinguished by his faithful adherence to reality: his biographies are remarkably free from the distortions of romance and hero-worship. He objected on several grounds to the writing of the lives of persons recently deceased; but he held that if "contemporaneous biography," as he called it, is to be permitted the biographers should be peculiarly careful not to make in favour of the hero suppressions that might do injustice to other persons concerned. It was probably in pursuance of this principle that he made revelations concerning Scott which extreme admirers of the poet would rather he had left unsaid. Lockhart's is not a studied, finished style, but he had a great mastery of language, and is exceedingly fresh and varied in his diction. His characteristic qualities are keen incisive force, and sarcastic exuberant wit.

William Minto, 1872-80, *Manual of English Prose Literature*, p. 544

Only a word on his novels,—*Valerius, a Roman Story,* coldly and sternly classical as a romance of Apuleius or Barclay; *Adam Blair,* with its burning passion and guilt, which startled the kirk like a bombshell; *Reginald Dalton,* light, easy and superficial, in which the author sought to depict, with a difference,—as *Tom Brown* has done for us in later days,—undergraduate life at Oxford, as it was during the earlier period of his own academical career; and lastly, not the least remarkable, *Matthew Wald* forcibly portraying a character, which, though redeemed by some better impulses, gradually sinks downward, by reason of its innate selfishness, to degradation and madness. These storys are, one and all, powerfully written; they exhibit force of narrative, passages of surpassing beauty and pathos, and elegance of style; but they have failed to gain for their writer an exalted or permanent place among the great masters of fiction.

William Bates, 1874-98, *The Maclise Portrait-Gallery of Illustrious Literary Characters*, p. 9

THE NINETEENTH CENTURY:

Victorianism
American Literature

CHARLOTTE BRONTE

("Currer Bell")

1816-1855

Born, at Thornton, 21 April 1816. Early life spent at Haworth. At school at Cowan's Bridge, Sept. 1824 to autumn of 1825. At Miss Wooler's school at Roehead, Jan. 1831 to 1832. Returned there as a teacher, 29 July 1835 to spring of 1838. Situation as governess in 1839. At home, 1840. Governess, March to Dec. 1841. To school at Brussels with her sister Emily, Feb. 1842. Returned to Haworth, Nov. 1842. Returned to Brussels school as teacher, Jan. 1843. Returned to Haworth, 2 Jan. 1844. Published poems with her sisters, 1846. *Jane Eyre* published 1847. Visits to London: with Emily, June 1848; Nov. 1849 (when she was made acquainted with Thackeray); 1850; 1851; 1853. Married to The Rev. Arthur Nicholls, 29 June 1854. Visited Ireland with her husband, and returned with him to Haworth. Died there, 31 March 1855. WORKS: Contrib. to *Poems: by Currer, Ellis and Acton Bell**, 1846; *Jane Eyre,* 1847; *Shirley,* 1849; *Villette,* 1853; all under pseudonym of Currer Bell. POSTHUMOUS: *The Professor: by Currer Bell,* 1857; *Emma* (a fragment), pub. in *Cornhill Magazine,* April 1860. She edited (under pseud. of "Currer Bell") a new edition of *Wuthering Heights,* and *Agnes Grey,* with selections and prefaces, 1850. COLLECTED WORKS: with those of her sisters Anne and Emily (7 vols.), 1872-73. LIFE: by Mrs. Gaskell, 4th edn., 1858; by Clement K. Shorter, 1896.

R. Farquharson Sharp, 1897, A Dictionary of
English Authors, p. 32

SEE: *The Shakespeare Head Brontë,* ed. Thomas J. Wise and J. A. Symington, 1932-38, 8 v.; *Heather Edition of the Works of the Brontë Sisters,* ed. Phyllis Bentley, 1949, 6 v.; *Complete Poems,* ed. Clement Shorter and C. W. Hatfield, 1923; E. M. Delafield, ed., *The Brontës: Their Lives Recorded by Their Contemporaries,* 1935; Margaret Lane, *The Brontë Story: A Reconsideration of Mrs. Gaskell's Life,* 1953; F. E. Ratchford, *The Brontës' Web of Childhood,* 1941.

PERSONAL

I sent a dose of cooling admonition to the poor girl whose flighty letter reached me at Buckland. It was well taken, and she thanked me for it. It seems she is the eldest daughter of a clergyman, has been expensively educated, and is laudably employed as a governess in some private family.

---

* Pseudonyms of Charlotte, Emily, and Anne Brontë.

About the same time that she wrote to me, her brother wrote to Wordsworth, who was disgusted with the letter, for it contained gross flattery to him, and plenty of abuse of other poets, including me. I think well of the sister from her second letter, and probably she will think kindly of me as long as she lives.

> Robert Southey, 1837, *To Caroline Bowles; The Correspondence of Robert Southey with Caroline Bowles,* p. 348

I think the poems of Currer much better than those of Acton and Ellis, and believe his novel is vastly better than those which they have more recently put forth. I know nothing of the writers, but the common rumour is that they are brothers of the weaving order in some Lancashire town. At first it was generally said that Currer was a lady, and Mayfair circumstantialized by making her the *chère amie* of Mr. Thackeray. But your skill in "dress" settles the question of sex. I think, however, some women have assisted in the school scenes of *Jane Eyre,* which have a striking air of truthfulness to me—an ignoramus, I allow, on such points.

> John Gibson Lockhart, 1848, *Letter to Miss Rigby.* Nov. 13;
> *Correspondence of Lady Eastlake,* ed. Smith, vol. I, p. 222

Averse to personal publicity, we veiled our names under those of Currer, Acton and Ellis Bell,—the ambiguous choice being dictated by a sort of conscientious scruple at assuming Christian names positively masculine, while we did not like to declare ourselves women, because—without at that time suspecting that our mode of writing and thinking was not what is called "feminine"—we had a vague impression that authoresses are likely to be looked on with prejudice; we had noticed how critics sometimes use for their chastisement the weapon of personality, and for their reward a flattery which is not true praise.

> Charlotte Brontë, 1850, *Biographical Notice by Currer Bell*

Lewes was describing Currer Bell to me yesterday as a little, plain, provincial, sickly looking old maid. Yet what passion, what fire in her! Quite as much as in George Sand, only the clothing is less voluptuous.

> George Eliot, 1853, *Letter to Sarah Hennell,* March 28;
> *George Eliot's Life as related in her Letters and Journals,*
> ed. Cross, vol. I, p. 221

Between the appearance of *Shirley* and that of *Villette,* she came to me;— in December, 1850. Our intercourse then confirmed my deep impression of her integrity, her noble conscientiousness about her vocation, and her consequent self-reliance in the moral conduct of her life. I saw at the same time tokens of a morbid condition of mind, in one or two directions;—much less than might have been expected, or than would have been seen in almost any one else under circumstances so unfavourable to health of body and mind as those in which she lived; and one fault which I pointed out to her in *Villette* was so clearly traceable to these unwholesome influences that I would fain have been spared a task of criticism which could hardly have been of much use while the circumstances remained unchanged. . . . She might be weak for once; but her permanent temper was one of humility, candour, integrity and conscientiousness. She was not only unspoiled by her sudden and prodigious fame, but obviously unspoilable.

Harriet Martineau, 1855-77, *Autobiography*,
ed. Chapman, vol. II, p. 24

I remember the trembling little frame, the little hand, the great honest eyes. An impetuous honesty seemed to me to characterize the woman. Twice I recollect she took me to task for what she held to be errors in doctrine. Once about Fielding we had a disputation. She spoke her mind out. She jumped too rapidly to conclusions. . . . She formed conclusions that might be wrong, and built up whole theories of character upon them. New to the London world, she entered it with an independent, indomitable spirit of her own; and judged of contemporaries, and especially spied out arrogance or affectation, with extraordinary keenness of vision. She was angry with her favourites if their conduct or conversation fell below her ideal. Often she seemed to me to be judging the London folk prematurely: but perhaps the city is rather angry at being judged. I fancied an austere little Joan of Arc marching in upon us, and rebuking our easy lives, our easy morals. She gave me the impression of being a very pure, and lofty, and high-minded person. A great and holy reverence of right and truth seemed to be with her always. Such, in our brief interview, she appeared to me.

William Makepeace Thackeray, 1860, "The Last Sketch,"
Cornhill Magazine, vol. 1, p. 486

In the sombre web of her existence there shone one thread of silver, all the brighter and more blessed for the contrast—it was the warm, steady, unfailing friendship of her school-fellow "E." [Ellen Nussey.] "Ma bien aimée, ma précieuse E., mon amie chère et chérie," she calls her in one of her earlier letters. "If we had but a cottage and a competency of our own, I do think we might live and love on till death, without being dependent on any third person for happiness." "What am I compared to you?" she exclaims; "I feel my own utter worthlessness when I make the comparison. I am a very coarse, commonplace wretch." But the affection that overflowed in such loving extravagance was no passing sentiment. As life deepened and grew more and more intense—and fuller of pain—for each, the closer became their attachment, the more constantly Charlotte turned for sympathy and support to her faithful companion. . . . In her, indeed, she found all the greater rest and refreshment because of the difference in their natures. Her individuality colors the Caroline Helstone of *Shirley*.

Richard Watson Gilder, 1871, "The Old Cabinet,"
Scribner's Monthly, vol. 2, p. 100

The garden is less spacious than it was in Charlotte's time, new classrooms having been added, which cut off something from its length. But the whole place was strangely familiar and pleasant to our eyes. Shut in by surrounding houses, more than one window overlooks its narrow space. Down its length upon one side extends the shaded walk, the "allée défendue," which Charlotte paced alone so many weary hours, when Emily had returned to England. Parallel to this is the row of giant pear-trees—huge, misshapen, gnarled—that bore no fruit to us but associations vivid as memories. From behind these in the summer twilight the ghost of *Villette* was wont to steal, and buried at the foot of "Methuselah," the oldest, we knew poor Lucy's love-letters were hidden to-day. A seat here and there, a few scattered shrubs, evergreen, laurel, and yew, scant blossoms, paths damp, green-crusted—that was all. Not a cheerful place at its brightest; not a sunny spot associated in one's mind with summer and girlish voices.

Adeline Trafton, 1871, "A Visit to Charlotte Brontë's
School at Brussels," *Scribner's Monthly*, vol. 3, p. 188

The loving admirers of Charlotte Brontë can never feel much enthusiasm for Mr. Nicholls. Mrs. Gaskell states that he was not attracted by her literary fame, but was rather repelled by it; he appears to have used her up remorselessly, in their short married life, in the routine drudgery of parish work. She did not complain, on the contrary, she seemed more than contented to sacrifice everything for him and his work; but she remarks in one of her letters, "I have less time for thinking." Apparently she had none for writing. Surely the husband of a Charlotte Brontë, just as much as the wife of a Wordsworth or a Tennyson, ought to be attracted by literary fame. To be the life partner of one to whom the most precious of Nature's gifts is confided, and to be unappreciative of it and even repelled by it, shows a littleness of nature and essential meanness of soul. A true wife or husband of one of these gifted beings should rather regard herself or himself as responsible to the world for making the conditions of the daily life of their distinguished partners favourable to the development of their genius.

But pearls have before now been cast before swine, and one cannot but regret that Charlotte Brontë was married to a man who did not value her place in literature as he ought.

Millicent Garrett Fawcett, 1889, *Some Eminent Women of our Times*, p. 109

Story-telling, as we shall see, was a hereditary gift in the Brontë family, and Patrick inherited it from his father. Charlotte's friend, Miss Ellen Nussey, has often told me of the marvellous fascination with which the girls would hang on their father's lips as he depicted scene after scene of some tragic story in glowing words and with harrowing details. The breakfast would remain untouched till the story had passed the crisis, and sometimes the narration became so real and vivid and intense, that the listeners begged the vicar to proceed no farther. Sleepless nights succeeded story-telling evenings at the vicarage.

William Wright, 1893, *The Brontës in Ireland*, p. 15

Taken as a whole, the life of Charlotte Brontë was among the saddest in literature. At a miserable school, where she herself was unhappy, she saw her two elder sisters stricken down and carried home to die. In her home was the narrowest poverty. She had, in the years when that was most essential, no mother's care; and perhaps there was a somewhat too rigid disciplinarian in the aunt who took the mother's place. Her second school brought her, indeed, two kind friends; but her shyness made that school-life in itself a prolonged tragedy. Of the two experiences as a private governess I shall have more to say. They were periods of torture to her sensitive nature. The ambition of the three girls to start a school on their own account failed ignominiously. The suppressed vitality of childhood and early womanhood made Charlotte unable to enter with sympathy and toleration into the life of a foreign city, and Brussels was for her a further disaster. Then within two years, just as literary fame was bringing its consolation for the trials of the past, she saw her two beloved sisters taken from her. And, finally, when at last a good man won her love, there were left to her only nine months of happy married life. "I am not going to die. We have been so happy." These words to her husband on her death-bed are not the least piteously sad in her tragic story.

Clement K. Shorter, 1896, *Charlotte Brontë and Her Circle*, p. 21

I must confess that my first impression of Charlotte Brontë's personal appearance was that it was interesting rather than attractive. She was very small, and had a quaint old-fashioned look. Her head seemed too large for her body. She had fine eyes, but her face was marred by the shape of the mouth and by the complexion. There was but little feminine charm about her; and of this fact she herself was uneasily and perpetually conscious. It may seem strange that the possession of genius did not lift her above the weakness of an excessive anxiety about her personal appearance. But I believe that she would have given all her genius and her fame to have been beautiful. Perhaps few women ever existed more anxious to be pretty than she, or more angrily conscious of the circumstance that she was *not* pretty.

Sir George Murray Smith, 1901, "In the Early Forties,"
The Critic, vol. 38, p. 53

The Professor

Charlotte Brontë wrote *The Professor* long before "George Eliot" took up her pen; and she must at least receive credit for having been in the field as a reformer of fiction before her fellow-labourer was heard of. She was true to the conditions she had laid down for herself in writing *The Professor.* Nothing more sober and matter-of-fact than that story is to be found in English literature. And yet, though the landscape one is invited to view is but a vast plain, without even a hillock to give variety to the prospect, it has beauties of its own which commend it to our admiration. . . . Though a sad, monotonous book, has life and hope, and a fair faith in the ultimate blessedness of all sorrowful ones, shining through all its pages; and it closes in a scene of rest and peace.

T. Wemyss Reid, 1877, *Charlotte Brontë, A Monograph,* pp. 221, 222

Jane Eyre (1847)

I now send you per rail a MS. entitled, *Jane Eyre,* a novel in three volumes, by Currer Bell. I find I cannot prepay the carriage of the parcel, as money for that purpose is not received at the small station-house where it is left. If, when you acknowlege the recepit of the MS. you would have the goodness to mention the amount charged on delivery, I will immediately transmit it in postage stamps. It is better in future to address Mr. Currer Bell, under cover to "Miss Brontë, Haworth, Bradford, Yorkshire," as there is a risk of letters otherwise directed not reaching me at present. To save trouble, I enclose an envelope.

Charlotte Brontë, 1847, *Letter to Messrs. Smith and Elder,* Aug. 24

I have finished the adventures of Miss Jane Eyre, and think her far the cleverest that has written since Austen and Edgeworth were in their prime. Worth fifty Trollopes and Martineaus rolled into one counterpane, with fifty Dickenses and Bulwers to keep them company—but rather a brazen Miss.

John Gibson Lockhart, 1847, *Letter to Mrs. Hope,* Dec. 29;
Life of J. G. Lockhart, ed. Lang, vol. I, p. 310

Altogether the autobiography of Jane Eyre is pre-eminently an anti-Christian composition. There is throughout it a murmuring against the comforts of the rich and against the privations of the poor, which, as far as each individual is concerned, is a murmuring against God's appointment —there is a proud and perpetual assertion of the rights of man, for which we find no authority either in God's word or in God's providence—there is that pervading tone of ungodly discontent which is at once the most prominent and the most subtle evil which the law and the pulpit, which all civilized society in fact has at the present day to contend with. We do not hesitate to say that the tone of mind and thought which has overthrown authority and violated every code human and divine abroad, and fostered Chartism and rebellion at home, is the same which has also written *Jane Eyre.* . . . If we ascribe the book to a woman at all, we have no alternative but to ascribe it to one who has, for some sufficient reason, long forfeited the society of her own sex.

Elizabeth Rigby (Lady Eastlake), 1848, *"Vanity Fair* and
Jane Eyre," Quarterly Review, vol. 84, pp. 173, 176

I have read *Jane Eyre,* and shall be glad to know what you admire in it. All self-sacrifice is good, but one would like it to be in a somewhat nobler cause than that of a diabolical law which chains a man soul and body to a putrefying carcass. However, the book *is* interesting; only I wish the characters would talk a little less like the heroes and heroines of police reports.

George Eliot, 1848, *Letter to Charles Bray,* June;
George Eliot's Life as related in her Letters and Journals,
ed. Cross, vol. I, p. 138

We take Currer Bell to be one of the most remarkable of *female* writers; and believe it is now scarcely a secret that Currer Bell is the pseudonyme of a woman. An eminent contemporary, indeed, has employed the sharp vivacity of a female pen to prove "upon irresistible evidence" that *Jane Eyre must be* the work of a man! But all that " irresistible evidence" is set aside by the simple fact that Currer Bell *is* a woman. We never, for our own parts, had a moment's doubt on the subject. That Jane herself was drawn by a woman's delicate hand, and that Rochester equally betrayed the sex of the artist, was to our minds so obvious, as absolutely to shut our ears to all the evidence which could be adducted by the erudition even of a *marchande des modes*; and that simply because we know that there were women profoundly ignorant of the mysteries of the toilette, and the terminology of fashion (independent of the obvious solution, that such ignorance might be counterfeited, to mislead), and felt that there was no man who *could so* have delineated a woman—or *would so* have delineated a man. The fair and ingenious critic was misled by her own acuteness in the perception of details; and misled also in some other way, and more uncharitably, in concluding that the *author* of *Jane Eyre* was a heathen educated among heathens—the *fact* being, that the *authoress* is the daughter of a clergyman! This question of authorship, which was somewhat hotly debated a little while ago, helped to keep up the excitement about *Jane Eyre*; but, independently of that title to notoriety, it is certain that, for many years, there had been no work of such power, piquancy, and originality. Its very faults were faults on the side of vigour; and its beauties were all original. The grand secret of its success, however,—as of all genuine and lasting success,—was its *reality*. From out of the depths of a sorrowing experience, here was a voice speaking to the experience of thousands. The aspects of external nature, too, were painted with equal fidelity,—the long cheerless winter days, chilled with rolling mists occasionally gathering into the strength of rains,—the bright spring mornings,—the clear solemn nights, —were all painted to your *soul* as well as to your eye, by a pencil dipped into a soul's experience for its colours. Faults enough the book has undoubtedly; faults of conception, faults of taste, faults of ignorance, but in spite of all, it remains a book of singular fascination. A more masculine book, in the sense of vigour, was never written. Indeed that vigour often amounts to coarseness,—and is certainly the very antipode to "lady like."

George Henry Lewes, 1850, "Currer Bell's *Shirley*,"
Edinburgh Review, vol. 91, p. 158

Those who remember that winter of nine-and-twenty years ago know how something like a *Jane Eyre* fever raged among us. The story which had suddenly discovered a glory in uncomeliness, a grandeur in overmastering passion, moulded the fashion of the hour, and "Rochester airs" and "Jane Eyre graces" became the rage. The book, and its fame and influence, travelled beyond the seas with a speed which in those days was marvellous. In sedate New England homes the history of the English governess was read with an avidity which was not surpassed in London itself, and within a few months of the publication of the novel it was famous throughout two continents. No such triumph has been achieved in our time by any other English author; nor can it be said, upon the whole, that many triumphs have been better merited. It happened that this anonymous story, bearing the unmistakable marks of an unpracticed hand, was put before the world at the very moment when another great masterpiece of fiction was just beginning to gain the ear of the English public. But at the moment of publication *Jane Eyre* swept past *Vanity Fair* with a marvellous and impetuous speed which left Thackeray's work in the distant back-ground; and its unknown author in a few weeks gained a wider reputation than that which one of the master minds of the century had been engaged for long years in building up. The reaction from this exaggerated fame, of course set in, and it was sharp and severe.

T. Wemyss Reid, 1877, *Charlotte Brontë, A Monograph,* p. 8

The gift of which I would speak is that of a power to make us feel in every nerve, at every step forward which our imagination is compelled to take under the guidance of another's, that thus and not otherwise, but in all things altogether even as we are told and shown, it was and it must have been with the human figures set before us in their action and their suffering; that thus and not otherwise they absolutely must and would have felt and thought and spoken under the proposed conditions. It is something for a writer to have achieved if he has made it worth our fancy's while to consider by the light of imaginative reason whether the creatures of his own fancy would in actual fact and life have done as he has made them or not; it is something, and by comparison it is much. But no definite terms of comparison will suffice to express how much more than this it is to have done what the youngest of capable readers must feel on their first opening *Jane Eyre* that the writer of its very first pages has shown herself competent to do. In almost all other great works of its kind, in almost all the sovereign masterpieces even of Fielding, of Thackeray, of the royal and imperial master, Sir Walter Scott himself—to whose glorious memory I need offer no apology for the attribution of epithets which I cannot but regret to remember that even in their vulgar sense he would not have regarded as other than terms of honour—even in the best and greatest works of these our best and greatest we do not find this one great good quality so innate, so immanent as in hers.

Algernon Charles Swinburne, 1877, *A Note on Charlotte Brontë,* p. 13

I hope I shall not be called a Puritan or a Philistine if I say that the morality of Charlotte Brontë's work always strikes me as being radically unhealthy. The ethical quality of the productions of any novelist whose experience of life was so narrow and so painful as hers must be either morbidness or weakness; and it is hard to see how *Jane Eyre* can be considered anything but morbid in spite of its singular power. The objection to its whole conception is that the abnormal is treated as if it were the normal, and the reader is led to make wide ethical generalizations from a series of really exceptional instances. . . . In *Jane Eyre* the furnace of emotion is heated seven times more than it is wont to be heated in the healthy life of every day; the atmosphere is that of a Turkish bath, but there is no welcome douche to brace up the relaxed tissues of feeling.

James Ashcroft Noble, 1886, *Morality in
English Fiction*, pp. 48, 49

Miss Brontë's novels are day-dreams and memories rather than stories. In *Jane Eyre* she is dealing with the eternal day-dream of the disinherited; the unfortunate guest at life's banquet. It is a vision that has many shapes: some see it in the form of a buried treasure to make them suddenly wealthy —this was the day-dream of Poe; or of a mine to be discovered, a company to be formed—thus it haunted Balzac. The lodging house servant straight out of foundlings dreams, and behold she is a young countess, changed at nurse and kept out of her own. The poor author dreams of a "hit," and (in this novel) Miss Brontë dwelt in fantasy on the love and the adventures that might come to a clever governess, who was not beautiful. . . . *Jane Eyre* is her best story, and far the most secure of life, because it has plenty of good, old-fashioned, foolish, immortal romance.

Andrew Lang, 1889, "Charlotte Brontë," *Good Words,* vol. 30, p. 239

I do not think that she was exactly what can be called a great genius, or that she would ever have given us anything much better than she did give; and I do not think that with critical reading *Jane Eyre* improves, or even holds its ground very well. It has strength, or at any rate force; it has sufficient originality of manner; it has some direct observation of life within the due limits of art; and it has the piquancy of an unfashionable unconventionality at a very conventional time. These are good things, but they are not necessarily great; and it is to me a very suspicious point that quite the best parts of Charlotte Brontë's work are admittedly something like transcripts of her personal experience.

George Saintsbury, 1895, *Corrected Impressions*, p. 159

A study of Charlotte Brontë's novels suggests the judgment that while in all of them there is much that is of high value and interest, there is only one part of one of them that leaves the distinct impression of unmistakable greatness, namely, the relation between Rochester and Jane Eyre. This may seem a small achievement on which to base security of fame, but it is not to be measured by the number of pages in which it is contained. It struck a new note in the history of fiction—a note which has added many grand

and subtle harmonies to itself in the works of succeeding writers, and the sweetness and power of which will never die away.

> James Oliphant, 1899, *Victorian Novelists*, p. 77

Shirley (1849)

I have read *Shirley* lately; it is not equal to *Jane Eyre* in spontaneousness and earnestness. I found it heavy, I confess, though in the mechanical part of the writing—the compositional *savoir faire*—there is an advance.

> Elizabeth Barrett Browning, 1850, *To Mrs. Jameson*, April 2;
> *The Letters of Elizabeth Barrett Browning*, ed. Kenyon,
> vol. I, p. 442

Shirley has, and deserves to have, many friends, and contains passages of great daring and beauty; but, as a whole, it must be pronounced (by me) inferior alike to its predecessor, and its successor. It lacks the splendid unity of *Jane Eyre,* the uniqueness of *Villette*. It is a series of portraits and exteriors—all good, some superb; but to pursue the metaphor, one walks through a book as through a picture gallery, always ready to go on, but never averse to turn back, since continuity of impression is of necessity impossible.

> Augustine Birrell, 1887, *Life of Charlotte Brontë*
> (*Great Writers*), p. 122

Her second book, *Shirley* (1848), was less powerful than her first, and much more artificial. It showed perhaps something of the strain the writer put on her mettle, and fully bent on exceeding, if possible, the previous natural and spontaneous effort. But it was also revolutionary to the highest degree, casting aside the discreet veil of the heroine which almost all previous novelists had respected, and representing the maiden on the tip-toe of expectation, no longer modestly awaiting the coming of Prince Charming, but craning her neck out of every window in almost fierce anticipation, and upbraiding heaven and earth, which kept her buried in those solitudes, out of his way.

> Margaret O. W. Oliphant, 1892, *The Victorian Age*
> *of English Literature*, p. 307

Villette (1853)

I am only just returned to a sense of the real world about me, for I have been reading *Villette,* a still more wonderful book than *Jane Eyre*. There is something almost preternatural in its power.

> George Eliot, 1853, *Letter to Mrs. Bray,* Feb. 15; *George Eliot's*
> *Life as related in her Letters and Journals,* ed. Cross, vol. I, p. 220

Something has already been said of the true character of that marvellous book, in which her own deepest experiences and ripest wisdom are given to the world. Of the manner in which it was written her readers know nothing. Yet this, the best beloved child of her genius, was brought forth with a travail so bitter that more than once she was tempted to lay aside her pen and hush her voice forever. Every sentence was wrung from her as though it had been a drop of blood, and the book was built up by bit and bit, amid paroxysms of positive anguish, occasioned in part by her own physical weakness and suffering, but still more by the torture through which her mind passed as she depicted scene after scene from the darkest chapter in her own life, for the benefit of those for whom she wrote. It is from her letters at this time also we get the best indications of what she was passing through. Few, perhaps, reading these letters would suppose that their writer was at that very time engaged in the production of a great master-piece, destined to hold its own among the ripest and finest fruits of English genius.

T. Wemyss Reid, 1877, *Charlotte Brontë, A Monograph*, p. 127

Villette is full of scenes which one can trace to incidents which occurred during Miss Brontë's visits to us. The scene at the theatre at Brussels in that book, and the description of the actress, were suggested by Rachel, whom we took her to see more than once. The scene of the fire comes from a slight incident to the scenery at Devonshire House, where Charles Dickens, Mr. Foster, and other men of letters gave a performance. . . . In *Villette* my mother was the original of "Mrs. Bretton"; several of her expressions are given *verbatim*. I myself, as I discovered, stood for "Dr. John." Charlotte Brontë admitted this herself to Mrs. Gaskell, to whom she wrote: "I was kept waiting longer than usual for Mr. Smith's opinion of the book, and I was rather uneasy, for I was afraid he had found me out, and was offended."

Sir George Murray Smith, 1901, "In the Early Forties,"
The Critic, vol. 38, p. 59

GENERAL

It seems to us, that the authoress of *Jane Eyre* combines all the natural and incidental attributes of the novelist of her day. In the ecclesiastical ten-dencies of her education and habits—in the youthful ambiguity of her politics—in a certain old-world air, which hangs about her pictures, we see her passports into circles which otherwise she would never reach. Into them she is carrying, unperceived, the elements of infallible disruption and revolution. In the specialties of her religious belief, her own self-grown and glorious heterodoxies—in the keen satiric faculty she has shown—in the exuberant and multiform vigour of her idiosyncrasy—in her unmistakable hatred of oppression, and determination to be free—in the onward tendencies of a genius so indisputably original, and in the reaction of a time on which, if she lives, she cannot fail to act strongly, we acknowledge the best pledge that the passport, already torn, will be one day scattered to the winds.

Sydney Dobell, 1850, "Currer Bell," *Life and Letters of Sydney Dobell*, ed. Jolly, vol. I, p. 183

Say that two foreigners have passed through Staffordshire, leaving us their reports of what they have seen. The first, going by day, will tell us of the hideous blackness of the country, but yet more, no doubt, of that awful, patient struggle of man with fire and darkness, of the grim courage of those unknown lives; and he would see what they toil for, women with little children in their arms; and he would notice the blue sky beyond the smoke, doubly precious for such horrible environment. But the second traveller has journeyed through the night; neither squalor nor ugliness, neither sky nor children, has he seen, only a vast stretch of blackness shot through with flaming fires, or here and there burned to a dull red by heated furnaces; and before these, strange toilers, half naked, scarcely human, and red in the leaping flicker and gleam of the fire. The meaning of their work he could not see, but a fearful and impressive phantasmagoria of flame and blackness and fiery energies at work in the encompassing night. So differently did the black country of this world appear to Charlotte, clear-seeing and compassionate, and to Emily Brontë, a traveller through the shadows.

A. Mary F. Robinson, 1883, *Emily Brontë (Famous Women)*, p. 5

Charlotte Brontë had, in the highest degree, that which Ruskin had called the "pathetic fallacy," the eye which beholds Nature coloured by the light of the inner soul. In this quality she really reaches the level of fine poetry. Her intense sympathy with her native moors and glens is akin to that of Wordsworth. She almost never attempts to describe any scenery with which she is not deeply familiar. But how wonderfully she catches the tone of her own moorland, skies, storm-winds, secluded hall or cottage. . . . Charlotte Brontë is great in clouds, like a prose Shelley. . . . Charlotte Brontë painted not the world, hardly a corner of the world, but the very soul of one proud and loving girl. That is enough; we need ask no more. It was done with consummate power. We feel that we know her life, from ill-used childhood to her proud matronhood; we know her home, her school, her professional duties, her loves and hates, her agonies and her joys, with that intense familiarity and certainty of vision with which our own personal memories are graven on our brain.

> Frederic Harrison, 1895, *Studies in Early Victorian Literature*, pp. 154, 155, 162

Charlotte Brontë was likewise deficient in humour. This might be safely inferred from her works, where there are hardly any humourous characters or situations; and the inference would be confirmed by her life. Her letters, often excellent for their common sense and their high standards of duty, and sometimes for their dignity, are almost destitute of playfulness. Neither does she seem to have readily recognized humour in others. She admired Thackeray above almost all men of her time, but she was completely puzzled by him when they met. She lectured him on his faults and quaintly adds that his excuses made them worse. The humourist was playing with too serious a mind. Had Miss Brontë been as Irish in nature as she was by blood she would not have made this mistake.

> Hugh Walker, 1897, *The Age of Tennyson*, p. 105

In one direction Miss Brontë's experience was adequate, namely, in her contact with nature. From her books one comes to know how largely in her life the clouds, the ragged hills, the wide spaces of the Yorkshire moors under sunset or moonlight, made up for the inadequacy of human society and interests. It is true, she has the Gothic trick of setting off her incidents by a sympathetic background; but in a deeper fashion than this she makes nature enter into the warp and woof of her stories through the part which it plays in the most essential elements in them, the inner life of her heroines.

> William Vaughn Moody and Robert Morss Lovett, 1902, *A History of English Literature*, p. 375

SAMUEL ROGERS
1763-1855

Born at Stoke Newington, 30 July 1763. Educated at schools at Stoke Newington and Hackney. Entered his father's bank about 1775. Contrib. to *Gentleman's Mag.*, 1781. Visit to Scotland 1789; to Paris 1802. Gained prominent position as poet; also as collector and patron of fine arts. Visits to Italy, 1815 and 1822. Offered Laureateship, but declined it, 1850. Died, in London, 18 Dec. 1855. Buried in Hornsey Churchyard. Unmarried. WORKS: *An Ode to Superstition* (anon.), 1786; *The Pleasures of Memory* (anon.), 1792; *Epistle to a Friend* (anon.), 1798; *Verses written in West-minster Abbey after the funeral of the Rt. Hon. C. J. Fox* (anon.), [1806]; *The Voyage of Columbus* (anon.), 1810 (priv. ptd., 1808); *Poems*, 1812; *Miscellaneous Poems* (with E. C. Knight and others; anon.), 1812; *Jac-queline* (anon.), 1814; *Human Life*, 1819; *Italy*, pt. i. (anon.), 1822; pt. ii., 1828; revised edn. of the whole, 1830; *Poems* (2 vols.), 1834. POSTHUMOUS: *Poetical Works*, 1856; *Table Talk*, ed. by A. Dyce, 1856; *Recollections*, ed. by W. Sharpe, 1859 (2nd edn. same year). LIFE: *Early Life*, by P. W. Clayden, 1887; *Rogers and his Contemporaries*, by P. W. Clayden, 1889.

R. Farquharson Sharp, 1897, A Dictionary of
English Authors, p. 240

SEE: *Poetical Works*, ed. Edward Bell, 1875; Richard Ellis Roberts, *Samuel Rogers and His Circle*, 1910; J. R. Hale, *The Italian Journal of Samuel Rogers*, 1957.

PERSONAL

He is a good poet, has a refined taste in all the arts, has a select library of the best editions of the best authors in all languages, has very fine pictures, very fine drawings, and the finest collection of Etruscan vases I ever saw; and moreover, he gives the best dinners to the best company of men of talents and genius I know; the best served, and with the best wines, liqueurs, etc. . . . His books of prints of the greatest engravers from the greatest masters in history, architecture, and antiquities, are of the first class. His house in St. James's Place, looking into the Green Park, is deliciously sit-uated, and furnished with great taste.

Charles Burney, 1804, Diary, May 1

Rogers is silent,—and, it is said, severe. When he does talk, he talks well; and, on all subjects of taste, his delicacy of expression is pure as his poetry. If you enter his house—his drawing-room—his library—you of yourself say, this is not the dwelling of a common mind. There is not a gem, a coin, a book, thrown aside on his chimney-piece, his sofa, his table, that does not bespeak an almost fastidious elegance in the possessor. But this very delicacy must be the misery of his existence. Oh the jarrings his disposition must have encountered through life!

Lord Byron, 1813, Journal, Nov. 22

I think you very fortunate in having Rogers at Rome. Show me a more kind and friendly man; secondly, one, from good manners, knowledge, fun, taste, and observation, more agreeable; thirdly, a man of more strict politi-cal integrity, and of better charcter in private life. If I were to choose any

Englishman in foreign parts whom I should wish to blunder upon, it should be Rogers.

> Sydney Smith, 1815, *To Lady Holland,* Feb. 1;
> *Letters,* ed. Austin

There is something preternatural in the cold, clear, marbly paleness that pervades, and, as it were, penetrates his features to a depth that seems to preclude all change, even that of death itself. Yet there is nothing in the least degree painful or repulsive in the sight, nothing that is suggestive of death.

> Peter George Patmore, 1854, *My Friends and Acquaintance,* vol. I, p. 160

The death of the poet Rogers seems almost like the extinction of an institution. The world by his departure has one object the less of interest and reverence. The elegant hospitality which he dispensed for nearly three quarters of a century, and in which Americans had a large share, is brought to an end, and a vacuity is created which no Englishman can supply. . . . Rogers's breakfasts were the pleasantest social meetings that can be conceived of. There you met persons of every variety of intellectual and social distinction, eminent men and attractive women, wits, orators, dramatists, travelers, artists, persons remarkable for their powers of conversation, all of whom found themselves on the easiest terms with their venerable host, whose noon of life was reached in the last century. Even bores, in his society, which discouraged all tediousness, and in the respect which his presence inspired, seemed to lose their usual character, and to fall involuntarily into the lively and graceful flow of conversation of which he gave the example. . . . Mr. Rogers was of low stature, neither slightly nor sturdily proportioned; his face was rather full and broad than otherwise, and his complexion colorless. . . . In conversation, Mr. Rogers was one of the most agreeable and interesting of men; he was remarkable for a certain graceful laconism, a neatness and power of selection in telling a story or expressing a thought, with its accessories, which were the envy of the best talkers of his time. His articulation was distinct, just deliberate enough to be listened to with pleasure, and during the last ten to twelve years of his life slightly —and but very slightly—marked with the tremulousness of old age. His ordinary manner was kind and paternal; he delighted to relate anecdotes illustrative of the power of the affections, which he did with great feeling. On occasion, however, he could say caustic things; and a few examples of this kind, which were so epigrammatic as to be entertaining in their repetition, have given rise to the mistake that they were frequent in his conversation.

William Cullen Bryant, 1855, "Samuel Rogers,"
New York Evening Post, Editorial Article

Whatever place may be assigned to Samuel Rogers among poets, he deserves to hold the highest place among men of taste; not merely of taste for this or that, but of general good taste in all things. He was the only man I have ever known (not an artist) who felt the beauties of art like an artist. He was too quiet to exercise the influence he should have maintained among the patrons of art; but, as far as his own patronage extended, it was most useful. He employed, and always spoke his mind in favor of Flaxman, Stothard, and Turner, when they were little appreciated by their countrymen. The proof of his superior judgment to that of any contemporary collector of art or *vertu* is to be found in the fact that there was nothing in his house that was not valuable.

Charles Robert Leslie, 1860, *Autobiographical Recollections,*
ed. Taylor, p. 155

My first look at the poet then in his seventy-eighth year, was an agreeable surprise, and a protest in my mind against the malignant injustice which had been done him. As a young man he might have been uncomely if not as ugly as his revilers had painted him, but as an old man there was an intellectual charm in his countenance and a fascination in his manner which more than atoned for any deficiency of personal beauty.

Charles Mackay, 1877, *Forty Years' Recollections of
Life, Literature and Public Affairs, from 1830 to 1870*

You could not fancy, when you looked upon him, that you saw a good man. It was a repulsive countenance; to say it was ugly would be to pay it a compliment, and I verily believe it was indicative of a naturally shrivelled heart and contracted soul. . . . With enormous power to do good, how did Rogers use it? If he lent—and it was seldom he did—to a distressed brother of the pen, he required the return of a loan with interest—when it could be had; if he gave, it was grudgingly and with a shrug. He was prudence personified; some one said of him: "I am sure that as a baby he never fell down unless he was pushed, but walked from chair to chair in the drawing-room, steadily and quietly, till he reached a place where the sunbeams fell on the carpet.

Samuel Carter Hall, 1883, *Retrospect of a Long Life,* pp. 370, 371

GENERAL

I can visit the justly-admired author of *The Pleasures of Memory,* and find myself with a friend, who together with the brightest genius possesses elegance of manners and excellence of heart. He tells me he remembers the day of our first meeting at Mr. Dilly's; I also remember it, and though his modest, unassuming nature held back and shrunk from all appearances of ostentation and display of talents, yet even then I take credit for discovering a promise of good things to come, and suspected him of holding secret commerce with the Muse, before the proof appeared in shape of one of the most beautiful and harmonious poems in our language. I do not say that he has not ornamented the age he lives in, though he were to stop where he is, but I do hope he will not so totally deliver himself over to the arts as to neglect the Muses; and I now publicly call upon Samuel Rogers to answer to his name, and stand forth in the title page of some future work that shall be in substance greater, in dignity of subject more sublime, and in purity of versification not less charming than his poem above mentioned.

Richard Cumberland, 1807, *Memoirs Written by Himself,*
vol. II, p. 229

I confess that I cannot understand the popularity of his poetry. It is pleasant and flowing enough, less monotonous than most of the imitations of Pope and Goldsmith, and calls up many agreeable images and recollections. But that such men as Lord Granville, Lord Holland, Hobhouse, Lord Byron, and others of high rank in intellect, should place Rogers, as they do, above Southey, Moore, and even Scott himself, is what I cannot conceive. But this comes of being in the highest society in London. What Lady Jane Granville called the Patronage of Fashion can do as much for a middling poet as for a plain girl like Miss Arabella Falconer.

Thomas Babington Macaulay, 1831, *To Hannah M. Macaulay,*
June 3; *Life and Letters,* ed. Trevelyan, ch. iv

Rogers was a poet of *culture.* His workmanship is artistic in a high degree, his diction as clear and polished as art can make it, and his versification everywhere elegant, refined, and graceful. He paints us finely-finished pictures, suffused with soft and mellow light, and exhibits them in carefully carven frames—pictures that awaken gentle sympathy and stimulate quiet thought—pictures that please without moving us. He is often tender in sentiment and wise in reflection; but lacks force and originality, and is altogether destitute of passion. He never annoys us with the faults of taste and style which disfigure the writings of some greater poets; but, on the other hand, he never thrills our emotions nor fires our imaginations as they do. He manipulates the heroic couplet with skill and grace.

Alfred H. Miles, 1891, *The Poets and the Poetry
of the Century, Crabbe to Coleridge*, p. 127

THOMAS BABINGTON MACAULAY
BARON MACAULAY
1800-1859

Born, at Rothley Temple, Leicestershire, 25 Oct. 1800. Early education at a dayschool at Clapham; at school at Little Shelford, near Cambridge, and afterwards at Aspenden Hall, Herts., 1812-18. Matric. Trin. Coll., Camb., Oct. 1818; English Prize Poem, 1819 and 1821; Craven Scholarship, 1821; B. A. 1822; Fellow of Trin. Coll., Oct. 1824 to 1831; M. A. 1825. Student of Lincoln's Inn; called to Bar, 1826. Contrib. to periodicals from 1823. Commissioner in Bankruptcy, Jan. 1828. M. P. for Calne, Feb. 1830. Commissioner of Board of Control, June 1832. Sec. to Board, Dec. 1832. M. P. for Leeds, Dec. 1832. In India, as Mem. of Supreme Council, 1834-38. M. P. for Edinburgh, 1839; re-elected, 1841 and 1846. Sec. for War, 1839-41. Paymaster-General, 1846-48. Defeated at Edinburgh 1847; withdrew from political life. Lord Rector, Glasgow Univ., Nov. 1849. F. R. S. Nov. 1849. Prof. of Ancient Hist., Royal Acad., 1850. Fellow of University of London, 1850-59. Trustee of British Museum, 1847. Re-elected M. P. for Edinburgh, July 1852. Mem. of Institute of France, 1853. Knight of Prussian Order of Merit, 1853. Hon. D. C. L., Oxford, June 1854. Pres. of Philosophical Inst., Edinburgh, 1854. Member of Academies of Utrecht, Munich, and Turin. Created Baron Macaulay, 10 Sept. 1857. High Steward of Borough of Cambridge, 1857. Died, in London, 28 Dec. 1859. Buried in Westminster Abbey. WORKS: *Pompeii* 1819; *Evening,* 1821; *Critical and Miscellaneous Essays* (Philadelphia, 5 vols.), 1841-44; *Lays of Ancient Rome,* 1842; *Critical and Historical Essays* (from *Edinburgh Rev.*), 1843; *History of England,* vols. I, II, 1849, vols. III, IV, 1855; vol. V (*posthumous*), ed. by Lady Trevelyan, 1861; *Inaugural Address* [at Glasgow], 1849; *Speeches* (2 vols.), 1853 (edn. "corrected by himself," 1854). POSTHUMOUS: *Biographies contributed to the Encyclopædia Britannica,* 1860; *Miscellaneous Writings,* ed. by T. F. Ellis, 1860; vol. V of *History of England* (*see* above), 1861. COLLECTED WORKS: ed. by Lady Trevelyan (8 vols.), 1866. LIFE: By Sir G. O. Trevelyan, 1876.

R. Farquharson Sharp, 1897, *A Dictionary of
English Authors,* p. 178

SEE: *Complete Writings,* 1899-1900, 20 v. (Boston, Houghton, Mifflin edition); *Prose and Poetry,* ed. G. M. Young, 1952; *The Reader's Macaulay,* ed. W. H. French and G. D. Sanders, 1936; *Speeches, with His Minute on Indian Education,* ed. G. M. Young, 1953; G. O. Trevelyan, *Life and Letters of Lord Macaulay*, 1876, 2 v., repr. 1932 with preface by G. M. Trevelyan; Arthur Bryant, *Macaulay*, 1933.

PERSONAL

I poke one line into Tom's vile scrawl to say that he goes on in the usual Pindaric style; much desultory reading, much sitting from bower to bower; Spenser, I think, is the favourite poet to-day. As his time is short, and health, I think, the chief object just now, I have not insisted on much system. He read in the sun yesterday and got a little headache. Since "Childe Hugh," a long poem on Hunt's election, really a good parody, has been shown us, I have discovered in the writing-box an Epithalamium of many folio pages on Mr. Sprague's marriage. I do compel him to read two or three scenes of Metastasio every day, and he seems to like it. His talents are very extraordinary and various, and his acquirements wonderful at his age. His temper is good, and his vivacity a great recommendation to me, but this excess of animal spirits makes some certain studies seem a little dry and dull. I will tell you honestly as a true friend, what indeed you know already and mentioned to me, that his superiority of talents makes competitors necessary for him, for that he is a little inclined to under-value those who are not considerable or distinguished in some way or other. I have talked with him gently on the subject, telling him how valuable and worthy people may be who are neither brilliant in talent nor high in situation.

Hannah More, 1810, *Letter*, May; *Life and Letters of Zachary Macaulay*, ed. Knutsford, p. 288

I had a most interesting companion in young Macaulay, one of the most promising of the rising generation I have seen for a long time. . . . He has a good face,—not the delicate features of a man of genius and sensibility, but the strong lines and well-knit limbs of a man sturdy in body and mind. Very eloquent and cheerful. Overflowing with words and not poor in thought. Liberal in opinion, but no radical. He seems a correct as well as a full man. He showed a minute knowledge of subjects not introduced by himself.

Henry Crabb Robinson, 1826, *Diary*, Nov. 29; *Diary, Reminiscences and Correspondence*, ed. Sadler

An emphatic, hottish, really forcible person, but unhappily without divine idea.

Thomas Carlyle, 1832, *Journal*, Jan. 13; *Thomas Carlyle, A History of the First Forty Years of his Life*, ed. Froude, vol. II, p. 187

His memory is prodigious, surpassing any thing I have ever known, and he pours out its stores with an instructive but dinning prodigality. He passes from the minutest dates of English history or biography to a discussion of the comparative merits of different ancient orators, and gives you whole strophes from the dramatists at will. He can repeat every word of every article he has written, without prompting; but he has neither grace of body, face, nor voice; he is without intonation or variety; and he pours on like Horace's river, while we, poor rustics, foolishly think he will cease; and if you speak, he does not respond to what you say, but, while your last words are yet on your lips, takes up again his wondrous tale. He will not confess ignorance of any thing, though I verily believe that no man would ever have less occasion to make the confession. I have heard him called the most remarkable person of his age; and again the most overrated one. You will see that he has not left upon me an entirely agreeable impression; still I confess his great and magnificent attainments and powers. I wish he had more address in using them, and more deference for others.

Charles Sumner, 1839, *To George Hillard*, Feb. 16;
Memoir and Letters of Sumner, ed. Pierce, vol. II, p. 65

He is absolutely renowned in society as the greatest bore that ever yet appeared. I have seen people come in from Holland House, breathless and knocked up, and able to say nothing but "Oh dear, oh mercy." What's the matter? being asked. "Oh, Macaulay." Then every one said, "That accounts for it—you're lucky to be alive," etc.

Henry, Lord Brougham, 1842, *To Napier*, Aug. 14; *Selections from the Correspondence of Macvey Napier*, ed. Napier, p. 403

In Parliament, he was no more than a most brilliant speaker; and in his speeches there was the same fundamental weakness which pervades his writings,—unsoundness in the presentment of his case. Some one element was sure to be left out, which falsified his statement, and vitiated his conclusions; and there never was perhaps a speaker or writer of eminence, so prone to presentments of cases, who so rarely offered one which was complete and true. My own impression is, and always was, that the cause of the defect is constitutional in Macaulay. The evidence seems to indicate that he wants heart. He appears to be wholly unaware of this deficiency; and the superficial fervour which suns over his disclosures probably deceives himself, as it deceives a good many other people; and he may really believe that he has a heart. To those who do not hold this key to the interpretation of his career, it must be a very mysterious thing that a man of such imposing and real ability, with every circumstance and influence in his favour, should never have achieved any complete success. As a politician, his failure has been signal, notwithstanding his irresistible power as a speaker, and his possession of every possible facility. As a practical legislator, his failure was unsurpassed, when he brought home his Code from India.

Harriet Martineau, 1855-77, Autobiography, ed. Chapman,
vol. I, p. 262

One paper I have read regarding Lord Macaulay says "he had no heart." Why, a man's books may not always speak the truth, but they speak his mind in spite of himself; and it seems to me this man's heart is beating through every page he penned. He is always in a storm of revolt and indignation against wrong, craft, tyranny. How he cheers heroic resistance; how he backs and applauds freedom struggling for its own; how he hates scoundrels ever so victorious and successful; how he recognizes genius, though selfish villains possess it! The critic who says Macaulay had no heart, might say that Johnson had none; and two men more generous, and more loving, and more hating, and more partial, and more noble, do not live in our history. Those who knew Lord Macaulay knew how admirably tender and generous, and affectionate he was. It was not his business to bring his family before the theatre footlights, and call for bouquets from the gallery as he wept over them.

William Makepeace Thackeray, 1860, "Nil Nisi Bonum,"
Roundabout Papers

One late grave has been opened in the Historical Aisle of the South Transept, to receive the remains of the poet and historian who, perhaps, of all who have trod the floor of the Abbey or lie buried within its precincts, most deeply knew and felt its manifold interests, and most unceasingly commemorated them. Lord Macaulay rests at the foot of the statue of Addison, whose character and genius none had painted as he; carrying with him to his grave the story of the reign of Queen Anne, which none but he could have told.

Arthur Penrhyn Stanley, 1868, Historical Memorials of
Westminster Abbey, p. 319

There are some men who gain such mastery over their libraries for practical purposes, that it would be a crime to curtail their collections. Such preeminently was Lord Macaulay, of whom one might say what Dryden did of Ben Jonson, "He invaded authors like a monarch." Surrounded by his many thousand volumes, he could summon any one to his hands in a moment; and, by a felicity of memory which might well be called instinct, could put his finger almost instantly on the passage sought for. How he used this and his other faculties his works sufficiently tell. No writer had ever his intellectual materials more thoroughly in hand. When his memory failed as to facts it told him at once where to look for them.

Sir Henry Holland, 1871, *Recollections of a Past Life,* p. 395

His clothes, though ill put on, were good, and his wardrobe was always enormously overstocked. Later in life he indulged himself in an apparently inexhaustible succession of handsome embroidered waistcoats, which he used to regard with much complacency. He was unhandy to a degree quite unexampled in the experience of all who knew him. When in the open air he wore perfectly new dark kid gloves, into the fingers of which he never succeeded in inserting his own more than half way.

George Otto Trevelyan, 1876, *Life and Letters of Lord Macaulay*

He was a boy in spirit all his life long, and yet, when he was a boy, it was one of a queer kind. What would the boys themselves say to a boy who never knew how to skate, or swim, or shoot, or row, or drive, and didn't care enough about his ignorance to try to mend it? a boy who never liked dogs? What would the boys of an older growth say to a boy who was so clumsy that when a barber said he might pay him whatever he usually gave the person who shaved him, he replied, "In that case, I should give you a great gash on each cheek"? a boy who, when he reached the kid-glove age, always wore out-doors perfect new dark gloves, into which he never got his fingers more than half way; who has left on record only one instance in which he knew one tune from another, and who seems never to have been in love in all his life? And yet he was the exact opposite of a little prig. He was the life and soul of his father's big family of boys and girls—Selina, Jane, John, Henry, Fanny, Hannah, Margaret, and Charles. In this circle he was king. . . . Nothing could be more beautiful than Macaulay's love for his sisters Hannah and Margaret, which they repaid with a devotion all the more profound because the brother they loved was a brother to be very proud of. They were the nearest to him of all the children in sympathies, but not in age, being respectively ten and twelve years younger than he. . . . It was one of the good things about Tom Macaulay that he was just as fond of his sisters' society when he was a great and busy man as he was before, and that when his little nephews and nieces began to grow up about him, they never knew that he was any body in particular, except dear Uncle Tom, who was always giving them great treats and taking them to see the shows.

D. D. Lloyd, 1879, "The 'Tom' Side of Macaulay,"
Harper's Magazine, vol. 58, pp. 605, 606, 607

I used . . . to look in during the course of the day, upon whatever circle might be gathered in the drawing or morning rooms, for a few minutes at a time, and remember, on this occasion of my meeting Macaulay at Bowood, my amazement at finding him always in the same position on the hearth-rug, always talking, always answering everybody's questions about everything; and I used to listen to him till I was breathless with what I thought ought to have been *his* exhaustion. As one approached the room, the loud, even, declamatory sound of his voice made itself heard like the uninterrupted flow of a fountain. He stood there from morning till evening, like a knight in the lists, challenging and accepting the challenge of all comers. There never was such a speech-"power," and as the volume of his voice was full and sonorous, he had immense advantages in sound as well as sense over his adversaries. Sydney Smith's humorous and good-natured rage at his prolific talk was very funny. Rogers's of course, was not good-humored.

Frances Ann Kemble, 1882, Records of Later Life, p. 281

I have much pleasure in giving you any information in my power respecting Lord Macaulay. He died in his library at Holly Lodge. For some time before he had been in ill-health from weak heart. His servant, who had left him feeling rather better, found on his return his master fainting in his chair. I was quickly sent for, got him removed to his couch, where he expired in a few moments. None of his family were with him. His sister, Mrs. Trevelyan, arrived soon after his death, accompanied by her son, then a very young man, but now, I believe, the Irish Secretary. At the time of his seizure Lord Macaulay was reading a number of the *Cornhill Magazine,* then a new publication; and, as far as my memory serves me, he was reading Thackeray's *Adventures of Philip.* Holly Lodge is still standing and is, I believe, unaltered. You will find it on the top of Campden Hill, next the Duke of Argyll's.

Dr. Thomas Joyce, 1883, Letter to Laurence Hutton,
Literary Landmarks of London, p. 203

ESSAYS

Edinburgh Review came last night. A smart, vigorous paper by Macaulay on Horace Walpole. Ambitious, too antithetic; the heart of the matter not struck. What will that man become? He has more force and emphasis in him than any other of my British contemporaries (coevals). Wants the root of belief, however. May fail to accomplish much. Let us hope better things.

Thomas Carlyle, 1833; Journal, Nov. 1; Thomas Carlyle,
A History of the First Forty Years of his Life,
ed. Froude, vol. II, p. 301

The *Bacon* is, as you say, very striking, and no doubt is the work of an extremely clever man. It is so very long that I think you might have cut it in two, there being an obvious division. But (not to trouble you with the superfluous enumeration of its good qualities), it has two grievous defects, —a redundancy, an over-crowding of every one thing that is touched upon, that almost turns one's head; for it is out of one digression into another, and each thought in each is illustrated by twenty different cases and anecdotes, all of which follow from the first without any effort. This is a sad defect in Macaulay, and it really seems to get worse instead of better. I need not say that it is the defect of a very clever person—it is indeed exuberance. But it is a defect also that *old age* is liable to.

> Henry, Lord Brougham, 1837, *To Napier*, July 28; *Selections from the Correspondence of Macvey Napier*, ed. Napier, p. 196

Macaulay's style, like other original things, has already produced a school of imitators. Its influence may distinctly be traced, both to the periodical and daily literature of the day. Its great characteristic is the shortness of the sentences, which often equal that of Tacitus himself, and the rapidity with which new and distinct ideas of facts succeed each other in his richly-stored pages. He is the Pope of English prose: he often gives two sentiments or facts in a single line. No preceding writer in prose, in any modern language with which we are acquainted, has carried this art of abbreviation, or rather cramming of ideas to such a length; and to its felicitous use much of the celebrity which he has acquired is to be ascribed. There is no doubt that it is a most powerful engine for the stirring of the mind, and when not repeated too often, or carried too far, has a surprising effect. Its introduction forms an era in our historical compositon.

> Sir Archibald Alison, 1859, "Macaulay's History of England," *Blackwood's Magazine*, vol. 65, p. 387

His *Essays* are as good as a library; they make an incomparable manual and vademecum for a busy, uneducated man who has curiosity and enlightenment enough to wish to know a little about the great lives and great thoughts, the shining words and many-coloured complexities of action, that have marked the journey of man through the ages. Macaulay had an intimate acquaintance both with the imaginative literature and the history of Greece and Rome, with the literature and the history of modern Italy, of France, and of England. Whatever his special subject, he contrives to pour into it with singular dexterity a stream of rich, graphic, and telling ilustrations from all these widely diversified sources.

> John Morley, 1876, "Macaulay," *Fortnightly Review*, vol. 25, p. 499

With the "Essay on Milton" began Macaulay's career, and, brilliant as the career was, it had few points more brilliant than its beginning. . . . A style to dazzle, to gain admirers everywhere, to attract imitators in multitude! A style brilliant, metallic, exterior; making strong points, alternating invective with eulogy, wrapping in a robe of rhetoric the thing it represents; not, with the soft play of life, following and rendering the thing's very form and pressure. For, indeed, in rendering things in this fashion, Macaulay's gift did not lie.

Matthew Arnold, 1879, "A French Critic on Milton,"
Mixed Essays, pp. 237, 238

Macaulay's essays are lively and entertaining, but their literary merit has been overestimated. They are really the chips and <i>débris</i> of his history, and though there are brilliant passages among them, they are for the most part carelessly written. The best that can be said of some of them is that they are more interesting than the books which Macaulay pretended to review. In others, serious subjects are treated in a wanton and superficial manner. They are rather dangerous reading for young people, or indeed for any who cannot discriminate readily between the true and false in literature. He has a bad habit of cumulative repetition and deals too frequently in sharp antitheses. His style of argument in reply to what he calls Sadler's Refutation is in the most domineering parliamentary vein. We feel less compunction in exposing the errors in Macaulay's writing, for he was always most unmerciful in his criticism of others.

Frank Preston Stearns, 1897, Modern English Prose Writers, p. 52

As an essayist Macaulay occupies an almost unique position in English literature. He created the historical essay, a form of literature exactly suited to the time in which he lived, a brief, clear, and illuminating introduction to some great era or some dominating personality. It is perfectly true that the more one knows about the era or the personality, the less one cares for Macaulay's introduction; but it is none the less valuable to the beginner for its stimulating quality, its power to awaken the interest in the past and the far away. Macaulay has been well called an almost unsurpassed leader to reading, and his essays have been to hundreds and thousands the door through which they entered into the great world of past politics, history, and literature. Macaulay is seldom a good critic, never an impartial judge; he is always, as in the "Essay on Milton," an advocate pleading his cause. But—and this is the great merit of his work—his causes are almost always right. He is biased indeed, but in favor of liberty, toleration, decency, and good faith.

Thomas Marc Parrott, 1900, ed. Essays on Milton and Addison
by Thomas Babington Macaulay, Introduction, p. xix

POEMS

It is a great merit of these poems that they are free from ambition and exaggeration. Nothing seems overdone; no tawdry piece of finery disfigures the simplicity of the plan that has been chosen. They seemed to have been framed with great artistical skill, with much self-denial and abstinence from anything incongruous, and with a very successful imitation of the effects intended to be represented. Yet here and there images of beauty and expressions of feeling are thrown out that are wholly independent of Rome or the Romans, and that appeal to the widest sensibilities of the human heart. In point of homeliness of thought and language there is often a boldness which none but a man conscious of great powers of writing would have ventured to show.

John Wilson, 1842, *"Lays of Ancient Rome,"*
Blackwood's Magazine, vol. 52, p. 823

These poems, therefore, are not the worse for being un-Roman in their form; and in their substance they are Roman to a degree which deserves great admiration. . . . We have not been able to detect, in the four poems, one idea or feeling which was not, or might not have been, Roman; while the externals of Roman life, and the feelings characteristic of Rome and of that particular age, are reproduced with great felicity, and without being made unduly predominant over the universal features of human nature and human life. Independently, therefore, of their value as poems, these compositions are a real service rendered to historical literature; and the author has made this service greater by his prefaces, which will do more than the work of a hundred dissertations in rendering that true conception of early Roman history, the irrefragable establishment of which has made Niebuhr illustrious, familiar to the minds of general readers.

John Stuart Mill, 1843, "Macaulay's *Lays of Ancient Rome,"*
Westminster Review, vol. 39, p. 106

Mr. Macaulay's *Lays of Ancient Rome* differed initially from Mr. Lockhart's Spanish translations in this, that the latter worked from the native materials, which he refined and improved; the former simply from the general scope and spirit of ancient legends. Taking it for granted, according to the very probable theory of Niebuhr, that the semi-fabulous traditions of all infant nations must have existed primarily in a metrical form, he re-transferred some of the portions of early Roman history back into the shape which might be supposed to have been their original one ere historicized by Livy, and this with great consummate imaginative and artistic ability. He is entirely of the Homer, the Chaucer, and Scott school, his poetry being thoroughly that of action; and sentiment is seldom more than interjectionally introduced—the utmost fidelity being thus shown to the essential characteristics of that species of composition which he has so triumphantly illustrated.

D. M. Moir, 1851-52, *Sketches of the Poetical Literature*
of the Past Half-Century, p. 300

Lord Macaulay's *Lays of Ancient Rome* was a literary surprise, but its poetry is the rhythmical outflow of a vigorous and affluent writer, given to splendor of diction and imagery in his flowing prose. He spoke once in verse, and unexpectedly. His themes were legendary, and suited to the author's heroic cast, nor was Latinism ever more poetical than under his thoroughly sympathetic handling. I am aware that the *Lays* are criticised as being stilted and false to the antique, but to me they have a charm, and to almost every healthy young mind are an immediate delight. Where in modern ballad-verse will you find more ringing stanzas, or more impetuous movement and action? Occasionally we have a noble epithet or image. Within his range—little as one who met him might have surmised it— Macaulay was a poet, and of the kind which Scott would have been first to honor. "Horatius" and "Virginius" among the Roman lays, and that resonant battle-cry of "Ivry" have become, it would seem, a lasting portion of English verse.

Edmund Clarence Stedman, 1875-87, *Victorian Poets,* p. 250

Macaulay was, perhaps, at his best in his four *Lays of Ancient Rome.* Whatever else he wrote required some qualities of mind other than those which have made all that he wrote popular. The *Lays of Ancient Rome* called into play just those powers which he had in perfection, and required no more. . . . Macaulay caught the swing of Scott's romance measure, made it a little more rhetorical, without loss—some might say rather with increase of energy,—and brought into play his own power of realizing in his mind all that he told.

Henry Morley, 1887, ed. *Lays of Ancient Rome,* Preface

The Lays are dated 1842; they have passed through edition after edition; and if Matthew Arnold disliked and contemned them, the general [reader] is wise enough to know them by heart. But a book that is "a catechism to fight" (in Johnson's phrase) would have sinned against itself had it taken no account of them, and I have given "Horatius" in its integrity. . . . As for "The Armada," I have preferred it to "The Battle of Naseby," first, because it is neither vicious nor ugly, and the other is both; and, second, because it is so brilliant an outcome of that capacity for dealing with proper names which Macaulay, whether poet or not, possesses in common with none but certain among the greater poets.

> William Ernest Henley, 1891, ed. *Lyra Heroica,* p. 353, note

I believe the critics of the grand style call them "pinchbeck," which I fancy is meant to be scornful—I can only say that they are still ringing in my ears with a note as fresh as they had fifty years back. I have said them over on their own ground; I have proved the truth of every epithet; and now, with the Sicilian deeds of Pyrrhus as my day's work, it is the notes of the "Prophecy" of Capys" which come first home to me at the thought of the "Red King" and his bold Epirotes.

> Edward A. Freeman, 1892, "A Review of My Opinions,"
> *The Forum,* vol. 13, p. 153

It is a gross and vulgar critical error to deem Macaulay's poetical effects vulgar or gross. They are *popular;* they hit exactly that scheme of poetry which the general ear can appreciate and the general brain understand. They are coin for general circulation; but they are not base coin. Hundreds and thousands of immature and 'prentice tastes have been educated to the enjoyment of better things by them; thousands and tens of thousands of tastes, respectable at least, have found in them the kind of poetry which they can like, and beyond which they are not fitted to go. And it would be a very great pity if there were ever wanting critical appreciations, which, while relishing things more exquisite and understanding things more esoteric, can still taste and savour the simple genuine fare of poetry which Macaulay offers.

> George Saintsbury, 1896, *A History of*
> *Nineteenth Century Literature,* p. 227

The History of England (1849-1855)

The mother that bore you had she been yet alive, would scarcely have felt prouder or happier than I do at this outburst of your graver fame. I have long had a sort of parental interest in your glory, and it is now mingled with a feeling of deference to your intellectual superiority which can only consist, I take it, with the character of a female parent.

> Francis, Lord Jeffrey, 1848, *Letter to Macaulay,*
> *Life and Letters of Lord Macaulay,* ed. Trevelyan, ch. xi

The first two volumes of Macaulay's *History* have had a most brilliant success, but I cannot help thinking that the work has meretricious attractions which may pall upon the public taste. There can be no doubt that, to produce a startling effect, the author does exaggerate very much, if he may be defended from positive misrepresenting. I rejoice that such good principles as those which he inculcates should be found in such a popular work.

John Lord Campbell, 1849, Journal, Jan. 11;
Life, ed. Mrs. Hardcastle, vol. II, p. 248

Macaulay's success has been enormous; indeed, such as to convince one his book cannot be worth much—that is, in a high sense, for in a low one his two volumes have got him £10,000. A young officer said to me, "That is what I call history. We took five copies at our depot."

Richard Monckton Milnes (Lord Houghton), 1849,
To Mrs. MacCarthy, May 19; Life, Letters, and
Friendships,</i> ed. Reid, vol. I, p. 432</div>

He has written some very brilliant essays—very transparent in artifice, and I suspect not over honest in scope and management, but he has written *no history;* and he has, I believe, committed himself ingeniously in two or three points, which, fitly exposed, would confound him a good deal, and check his breeze from El Dorado. Chiefly, his bitter hatred of the Church of England all through is evident; it is, I think, the only very strong feeling in the book; and his depreciation of the station and character of the clergy of Charles II. and James II. to-day is but a symptom. . . . I doubt if Macaulay's book will go down as a standard edition to our *historical* library, though it must always keep a high place among the specimens of English rhetoric.

John Gibson Lockhart, 1849, To Mr. Croker, July 12;
The Croker Papers, ed. Jennings, vol. III, pp. 192, 193

The sect of Quakers has been in high dudgeon with Macaulay, for what they consider an unjust attack upon Penn in his History. They demanded an interview, which he at once granted, and they remonstrated with him upon what they considered his aspersions on their fame, particularly as referring to the transaction of the money which was extorted from the girls who went out to meet Monmouth for the use of the maids of honour, and which was carried on by Penn. The Quakers denied the facts, but Macaulay produced all the official documents on which he had founded his statement, and they were entirely *floored*. Macaulay offered to print the documents from which he had gathered his facts, but they were in no hurry to accept this proposal, and said they would confer further before they gave their answer. Macaulay was much amused by this incident, and contrived to please the Quakers by his courtesy.

Henry Greville, 1849, Leaves from His Diary, Feb. 7,
ed. Enfield, p. 320

Mr Macaulay's historical narrative is poisoned with a rancour more violent than even the passions of the time; and the literary qualities of the work, though in some respects very remarkable, are far from redeeming its substantial defects. There is hardly a page—we speak literally, hardly a page— that does not contain something objectionable either in substance or in colour: and the whole of the brilliant and at first captivating narrative is perceived on examination to be impregnated to a really marvelous degree with bad taste, bad feeling, and, we are under the painful necessity of adding—bad faith. These are grave charges: but we make them in sincerity, and we think that we shall be able to prove them; and if, here or hereafter, we should seem to our readers to use harsher terms than good taste might approve, we beg in excuse to plead that it is impossible to fix one's attention on, and to transcribe large portions of a work, without being in some degree infected with its spirit; and Mr. Macaulay's pages, what ever may be their other characteristics, are as copious a repertorium of vituperative eloquence as, we believe, our language can produce, and especially against everything in which he chooses (whether right or wrong) to recognise the shiboleth of Toryism. . . . Mr. Macaulay's Historical Novel. . . . We accuse him of a habitual and really injurious perversion of his authorities. This unfortunate indulgence, in whatever juvenile levity it may have originated, and through whatever steps it may have grown into an unconscious habit, seems to us to pervade the whole work—from Alpha to Omega—from Procopius to Mackintosh—and it is on that very account the more difficult to bring to the distinct conception of our readers. Individual instances can be, and shall be, produced; but how can we extract and exhibit the minute particles that colour every thread of the texture?—how extract the impalpable atoms that have fermented the whole brewing? We must do as Dr. Faraday does at the Institution when he exhibits in miniature the larger processes of Nature.

John Wilson Croker, 1849, "Mr. Macaulay's History of England,"
Quarterly Review, vol. 84, pp. 550, 553, 561

But as he announced a History, the public received as a *bona fide* History the work on which he purposes to build his fame. If it had been announced as a historical romance, it might have been read with almost unmixed delight, though exception might have been taken to his presentment of several characters and facts. He has been abundantly punished, for instance, for his slanderous exhibition of William Penn. But he has fatally manifested his loose and unscrupulous method of narrating, and, in his first edition, gave no clue whatever to his authorities, and no information in regard to dates which he could possibly suppress. Public opinion compelled, in future editions, some appearance of furnishing references to authorities, such as every conscientious historian finds it indispensable to his peace of mind to afford, but it is done by Macaulay in the most ineffectual and baffling way possible,—by clubbing together the mere names of his authorities at the bottom of the page, so that reference is all but impracticable. Where it is made, by painstaking readers, the inaccuracies and misrepresentations of the historian are found to multiply as the work of verification proceeds. In fact, the only way to accept his History is to take it as a brilliant fancy-piece,—wanting not only the truth but the repose of history,—but stimulating, and even, to a degree, suggestive.

Harriet Martineau, 1855-77, *Autobiography,*
ed. Chapman, vol. I, p. 263

His history is like a cavalry charge. Down go horse and man before his rapid and reckless onset. His "rush" is irresistible save by the coolest judgment and the most cultivated intellects. Ranks are broken, guns are spiked, and away sweeps the bold dragoon to arrive at a fresh square.

Thomas Edward Kebbel, 1864, *Essays upon History and Politics*

He has brought to this work a new method of great beauty, extreme power. . . . When he is relating the actions of a man or a party, he sees in an instant all the events of his history, and all the maxims of his conduct; he has all the details present; he remembers them every moment, in great numbers. He has forgotten nothing; he runs through them as easily, as completely, as surely, as on the day when he enumerated or wrote them. No one has so well taught or known history. . . . He is not a poet like Michelet; he is not a philosopher like Guizot; but he possesses so well all the oratorical powers, he accumulates and arranges so many facts, he holds them so closely in his hand, he manages them with so much ease and vigour, that he succeeds in recomposing the whole and harmonious woof of history, not losing or separating one thread. The poet reanimates the dead; the philosopher formulates creative laws; the orator knows, expounds, and pleads causes. The poet resuscitates souls, the philosopher composes a system, the orator redisposes chains of arguments; but all three march towards the same end by different routes, and the orator, like his rivals, and by other means than his rivals, reproduces in his work the unity and complexity of life.

H. A. Taine, 1871, *History of English Literature,* tr. Van Laun,
vol. II, bk. v, ch. iii, pp. 423, 425, 426

The day of their publication, 17th Dec., 1855, will be long remembered in the annals of Paternoster Row. It was presumed that 25,000 copies would be quite sufficient to meet the first public demand; but this enormous pile of books, weighing fifty-six tons, was exhausted the first day, and eleven thousand applicants were still unsatisfied. In New York one house sold 73,000 volumes (three different styles and prices) in ten days, and 25,000 more were immediately issued in Philadelphia—10,000 were stereo-typed, printed, and in the hands of publishers within fifty working hours. The aggregate sale in England and America, within four weeks of publica-tion, is said to have exceeded 150,000 copies. Macaulay is also stated to have received £16,000 from Mr. Longman for the copyright of the third and fourth volumes.

Henry Curwen, 1873, *A History of Booksellers,* p. 106

There is here a wide field of choice. Shall we go back to the art of which Macaulay was so great a master? We could do worse. It must be a great art that can make men lay aside the novel and take up the history, to find there, in every fact, the movement and drama of life. What Macaulay does well he does incomparably. Who else can mass the details as he does, and yet not mar or obscure, but only heighten, the effect of the picture as a whole? Who else can bring so amazing a profusion of knowledge within the strait limits of a simple plan, nowhere encumbered, everywhere free and obvious in its movement? How sure the strokes, and how bold and vivid the result! Yet when we have laid the book aside, when the charm and the excitement of the telling narrative have worn off, when we have lost step with the swinging gait at which the style goes, when the details have faded from our recollection, and we sit removed and thoughtful, with only the greater outlines of the story sharp upon our minds, a deep misgiving and dissatisfaction take possession of us. We are no longer young, and we are chagrined that we should have been so pleased and taken with the glitter and color and mere life of the picture. . . . Macaulay the artist, with an exquisite gift for telling a story, filling his pages with little vignettes it is impossible to forget, fixing these with an inimitable art upon the surface of a narrative that did not need the ornament they gave it, so strong and large and adequate was it; and Macaulay, the Whig, subtly turning narrative into argument, and making history the vindication of a party. The mighty nar-rative is a great engine of proof. It is not told for its own sake. It is evidence summed up in order to justifiy a judgment. We detect the tone of the ad-vocate, and though if we are just we must deem him honest, we cannot deem him safe. The great story-teller is discredited; and, willingly or un-willingly, we reject the guide who takes it upon himself to determine for us what we shall see.

Woodrow Wilson, 1896, *Mere Literature and
Other Essays,* pp. 167, 168

His brilliant success was largely due to the artistic use of infinite detail in narrative and in the portrayal of character. But, as he soon found when he began to write, this method required vast space. He cannot fairly be charged with diffuseness in the *History,* except, perhaps, in some cases where he develops a general statement with redundant illustration. On the other hand, he often condenses into a few words or sentences the results of wide reading and laborious research. A careful study of almost any chapter will show that, relatively to the mass of particulars which he communicates, his style is, on the whole, compact. But even a greater conciseness of language could not have materially reduced the amount of room which his plan, by its very nature, demanded.

> Sir Richard Claverhouse Jebb, 1900, *Macaulay,*
> *a Lecture Delivered at Cambridge on Aug. 10,* p. 9

The general accusation against Macaulay really resolves itself into this, that he overstated his case and was too much of his own opinion. I do not think it is altogether wise to deny that there is some truth in this charge. The proper answer is that the vehemence of Macaulay's Whiggery and the unqualified manner in which he condemns Marlborough and Penn are incidental defects of a very noble quality, the quality of moral indignation. Macaulay was no arm-chair politician judging of temptations which he had never felt, and of circumstances in which he had never been placed. He sat in the House of Commons, in the Cabinet, in the Council of the Governor-General of India. He knew public life as well as any man of letters ever knew it.But the knowledge did not make him a cynic or a pessimist. He had an almost passionate belief in the progress of society and in the greatness of England.

> Herbert Paul, 1901, "Macaulay and his Critics,"
> *Men and Letters,* pp. 289, 295

GENERAL

Take at hazard any three pages of the *Essays* or *History,* and, glimmering below the stream of the narrative you, as it were, you, an average reader, see one, two, three, a half-score of allusions to other historic facts, characters, literature, poetry, with which you are acquainted. . . . Your neighbor, who has *his* reading, and his little stock of literature stowed away in his mind, shall detect more points, allusions, happy touches, indicating not only the prodigious memory and vast learning of this master, but the wonderful industry, the honest, humble previous toil of this great scholar. He reads twenty books to write a sentence; he travels a hundred miles to make a line of description.

> William Makepeace Thackeray, 1860, *"Nil Nisi Bonum,"*
> *Roundabout Papers*

Macaulay, divested of all the exorbitancies of his spirit and his style, would have been a Samson shorn of the locks of his strength. . . . He never wrote an obscure sentence in his life, and this may seem a small merit, until we remember of how few writers we could say the same. . . . Macaulay is like the military king who never suffered himself to be seen, even by the attendants in his bedchamber, until he had time to put on his uniform and jackboots. His severity of eye is very wholesome; it makes his writing firm, and firmness is certainly one of the first qualities that good writing must have. But there is such a thing as soft and considerate precision, as well as hard and scolding precision. Those most interesting English critics of the generation slightly anterior to Macaulay,—Hazlett, Lamb, De Quincey, Leigh Hunt,—were fully his equals in precision, and yet they knew how to be clear, acute, and definite without that edginess and inelasticity which is so conspicuous in Macaulay's criticisms, alike in their matter and their form.

John Morley, 1876, "Macaulay," *Fortnightly Review,*
vol. 25, pp. 496, 505, 507

The truth which explains if it does not harmonize the conflicting opinions about Macaulay is that his distinctive merits and defects are merely the obverse and reverse aspects of one and the same quality. The association between seeing clearly and seeing narrowly is a well-nigh universal law of the human mind; and the undeniable narrowness of Macaulay's view was due neither to willful blindness nor yet to defect of vision, but to the preter-human vividness with which he saw whatever he happened at the moment to be looking at. Any object, or event, or quality which he sets himself to contemplate is illuminated as with an electric light, and, amid the dazzling brilliance which it rays around, all sense of shade and gradation is lost. This is the explanation of that luminous clearness of his color which has been so much and so justly admired: it is also the explanation of that lack of proportion and relation and that total absence of perspective which have been equally complained of in his compositions.

Clarence H. Jones, 1880, *Lord Macaulay,
His Life and Writings,* p. 246

It can hardly be said that Macaulay belonged to the very highest order of minds. I do not think that he did. In no department except the historical did he show preeminent capacity, and even his *History* is open to the charge of being only a splendid and ornate panorama. . . . Macaulay unquestionably *had* genius of a kind: the genius which moulds the results of immense industry into a coherent and consistent whole. This is a fine and a most rare gift; and we are not wrong when we assert that its owner must always be, even when not of the highest order, a man of genius. . . . He

is one of the greatest masters of the English tongue. The march of his
ordered prose is measured and stately. Still it is ponderous, compared at
least with the unaffected freedom and flexible life of Shakespeare's, or
Fielding's, or Charles Lamb's. But the art with which this defect is concealed is, like every other detail of Lord Macaulay's art, perfect in its way.
The style is ponderous, but there is no monotony. Short sentences, which,
like the fire of sharpshooters through cannon, break the volume of sound,
are introduced at stated intervals into each paragraph. A Junius-like epigram follows the imposing burst of eloquence with which Burke or Brougham might have clenched a great harangue. There is no slovenliness in these
finished pages.

John Skelton, 1883, *Essays in History and Biography,* pp. 279, 280

One of the most remarkable qualities in his style is the copiousness of expression, and the remarkable power of putting the same statement in a
large number of different ways. This enormous command of expression corresponded with the extraordinary power of his memory. At the age of eight
he could repeat the whole of Scott's poem of *Marmion.* He was fond, at
this early age, of big words and learned English; and once, when he was
asked by a lady if his toothache was better, he replied, "Madam, the agony
is abated!" He knew the whole of Homer and of Milton by heart; and it
was said with perfect truth that, if Milton's poetical works could have been
lost, Macaulay would have restored every line with complete exactness.
Sydney Smith said of him: "There are no limits to his knowledge, on small
subjects as on great; he is like a book in breeches." His style has been
called "abrupt, pointed, and oratorical." He is fond of the arts of surprise
—of antithesis—and of epigram.

J. M. D. Meiklejohn, 1887, *The English Language:
Its Grammar, History and Literature,* p. 351

No writer is placed at such a disadvantage as Macaulay, when his worst
passages are taken up and criticised minutely. With no writer is criticism
so apt to be unjust, simply because it is impossible to represent in detail
a genius which was great by the extent of its empire, rather than by any
mystery of its inner shrines. To remember particular bits of Macaulay's
prose is not always as satisfactory as to remember his heroic ballads. But
in the variegated mass of his writings, and in the impression of life and
zest in all that he wrote, the particular faults and fallacies may easily and
rightly pass out of notice.

W. P. Ker, 1896, *English Prose,* ed. Craik, vol. V, pp. 410, 417

THOMAS DE QUINCEY
1785-1859

Born, in Manchester, 15 Aug. 1785. Educated privately at Salford; at Bath Grammar School, 1797[?]-99; at school at Winkfield, Wilts, 1799-1800. To Manchester Grammar School, winter of 1800. Ran away from latter, July 1802. Lived a roving life in Wales, July to Nov., 1802. To London, Nov. 1802; after great distress there reconciled with family. Matric. Worcester Coll., Oxford, 17 Dec. 1803; left, without degree, 1807. Friendship with Coleridge begun, 1807. Visit to Oxford, and in London 1808. Student of Middle Temple, 1808 [?]. With Wordsworth at Grasmere, Dec. 1808 to Feb. 1809. Settled in cottage at Townend, Westmoreland, Nov. 1809. In Edinburgh with Professor Wilson, winters of 1814-15 and 1815-16. Habitual taking of opium began, 1813. Married Margaret Simpson, winter of 1816. Contrib. to *Blackwood* and *Quarterly Review*. Edited *Westmoreland Gazette,* 1819-1820. To London, 1821. Through Lamb's introduction, became contributor to *London Magazine,* in which the *Confessions of an Opium-Eater* appeared, Oct. to Nov., 1821. Contrib. to *London Magazine,* 1821-24; to Knight's *Quarterly Magazine,* 1824. In Westmoreland, 1825. Contrib. to *Blackwood,* 1826-49. Settled in Edinburgh, 1828; wife and children joined him there, 1830. Contrib. to *Edinburgh Literary Gazette,* 1828-30; to *Tait's Magazine,* 1834-51. Relapse into opium habit after wife's death in 1837; improvement in 1844. In Glasgow, March 1841 to June 1847. To Edinburgh, 1847. Died there, 8 Dec. 1859. Buried in West Churchyard, Edinburgh. WORKS: *Confessions of an English Opium-Eater* (anon.), 1822; *Klosterheim* (anon.), 1832; *The Logic of Political Economy,* 1844; *Selections, grave and gay, from his writings,* edited by himself (4 vols.), 1853-60. COLLECTED WORKS: in 20 vols., 1853-55. LIFE: by H. A. Page, 1877; by Prof. Masson, 1881.

> R. Farquharson Sharp, 1897, *A Dictionary of English Authors,* p. 77

SEE: *Collected Writings,* ed. David Masson, 1889-90, 14 v.; *Selected Writings,* ed. Philip Van Doren Stern, 1937; *De Quincey at Work: New Letters,* ed. W. H. Bonner, 1936; Horace A. Eaton, *De Quincey,* 1936; Edward Sackville-West, *A Flame in Sunlight: The Life and Work of Thomas De Quincey,* 1936.

PERSONAL

His person is small, his complexion fair, and his air and manner are those of a sickly and enfeebled man. From this circumstance his sensibility, which I have no doubt is genuine, is in danger of being mistaken for effeminateness. At least coarser and more robustly healthful persons may fall into this mistake.

> Henry Crabb Robinson, 1812, *Diary,* June 17;
> *Diary, Reminiscences and Correspondence,* ed. Sadler

On Wednesday the 28th, and Thursday, 29th of October, 1821, I passed the evening at Taylor and Hessey's in company with the author of *Confessions of an English Opium-Eater,* published in Nos. 21 and 22 of the *London Magazine.* I had formed to myself the idea of a tall, thin, pale, gentlemanly-looking, courtier-like man; but I met a short, sallow-looking person, of a very peculiar cast of countenance, and apparently much an invalid. His demeanour was very gentle, modest, and unassuming; and his conversation fully came up to the idea I had formed of what would be that of the writer of those articles. . . . The Opium-Eater appears to have read a great deal, and to have thought much more. I was astonished at the depth and *reality,* if I may so call it, of his knowledge. He seems to have passed nothing that occurred in the course of his study unreflected on or unremembered. His conversation appeared like the elaboration of a mine of results: and if at any time a general observation of his became matter of question or ulterior disquisition it was found that he had ready his reasons at a moment's notice; so that it was clear that his opinions were the fruits of his own reflections on what had come before him, and had not been taken up from others.

Richard Woodhouse, 1821, "Notes of Conversations with
Thomas De Quincey," *De Quincey and his Friends,*
ed. Hogg, pp. 72, 73

You will doubtless read the last *Tait's Magazine.* It contains the first of a series of articles by DeQuincey on Wordsworth. Poor DeQuincey had a small fortune of eight or nine thousand pounds, which he has lost or spent; and now he lets his pen for hire. You know his articles on Coleridge: Wordsworth's turn has come now. At the close of his article, he alludes to a killing neglect which he once received from the poet, and which embittered his peace. I know the facts, which are not given. DeQuincey married some humble country-girl in the neighbordhood of Wordsworth; she was of good character, but not of that rank in which W. moved. The family of the latter never made her acquaintance nor showed her any civilities, though living comparatively in the same neighborhood. *Hinc illæ lacrimæ.* When you now read DeQuincey's lamentations you may thus better understand them.

Charles Sumner, 1839, *To George S. Hillard,* Jan. 23;
Memoir and Letters of Sumner, ed. Pierce, vol. II, p. 45

DeQuincey is a small old man of seventy years, with a very handsome face, and a face, too, expressing the highest refinement; a very gentle old man, speaking with the greatest deliberation and softness, and so refined in speech and manners as to make quite indifferent his extremely plain and poor dress. For the old man, summoned by message on Saturday by Mrs. Crowe to his dinner, had walked on this stormy, muddy Sunday ten miles, from Lass Wade, where his cottage is, and was not yet dry; and though Mrs. Crowe's hospitality is comprehensive and minute, yet she had no pantaloons in her house. Here DeQuincey is very serene and happy among just these friends where I found him; for he has suffered in all ways, and lived the life of a wretch for many years, but Samuel Brown and Mrs. C. and one or two more have saved him from himself, and defended him from bailiffs and a certain Fury of a Mrs. Macbold (I think it is), whom he yet shudders to remember, and from opium; and he is now clean, clothed, and in his right mind. . . . He talked of many matters, all easily and well, but chiefly social and literary; and did not venture into any voluminous music. When they first agreed at my request, to invite him to dine, I fancied some figure like the organ of York Minster would appear. In *tête-à-tête,* I am told, he sometimes soars and indulges himself, but not often in company. He invited me to dine with him on the following Saturday at Lass Wade, where he lives with his three daughters, and I accepted.

Ralph Waldo Emerson, 1848, *Letter,* Feb. 21; *A Memoir of*
Ralph Waldo Emerson, ed. Cabot, vol. II, p. 520

His sensitiveness was so extreme, in combination with the almost ultra-courtesy of a gentleman, that he hesitated to trouble a servant with any personal requests without a long prefatory apology. My family were in the country in the summer of 1825, when he was staying at my house in Pall Mall East. A friend or two had met him at dinner, and I had walked part of the way home with one of them. When I returned, I tapped at his chamber-door to bid him good night. He was sitting at the open window, habited as a prize-fighter when he enters the ring. "You will take cold," I exclaimed. "Where is your shirt?" "I have not a shirt—my shirts are unwashed." "But why not tell the servant to send them to the laundress?" "Ah! how could I presume to do that in Mrs. Knight's absence?"

Charles Knight, 1863, *Passages of a Working Life*
During Half a Century, p. 236

He was a pretty little creature, full of wire-drawn ingenuities; bankrupt enthusiasms, bankrupt pride; with the finest silver-toned low voice, and most elaborate gently-winding courtesies and ingenuities in conversation: "What wouldn't one give to have him in a Box, and take him out to talk! (That was *Her* criticism of him; and it was right good). A bright, ready and melodious talker; but in the end an inconclusive and long-winded. One of the smallest man-figures I ever saw; shaped like a pair of tongs; and hardly above five feet in all: when he sat, you would have taken him, by candle light, for the beautifullest little Child; blue-eyed, blondhaired, sparkling face,—had there not been a something too, which said, *"Eccovi,* this Child has been in Hell!"

Thomas Carlyle, 1866, "Edward Irving," *Reminiscences,*
ed. Norton, vol. II, p. 152

Opium cannot communicate to the brain any power or faculty of which it is not already possessed; although (as in DeQuincey's case), by subduing an enemy, which had by its painful assaults on a remote part of the nervous system temporarily paralyzed the central powers of the intellect, it could again restore harmony of action to these powers. It could in no way *create* moral affections, though it might resuscitate them, by removing from them an overpowering load of physical suffering. It could add no iota to the great light of the majestic intellect, although when this might be suffering a temporary eclipse, as was too frequently the case with this great writer, when his gnawing malady pervaded his entire consciousness with torments which dominated the power of thought—it might, under such circumstances, restore that great light, by dissipating the shadow that obscured it.

Surgeon-Major W. C. B. Eatwell, 1877, *A Medical View of
Mr. DeQuincey's Case,* in *Thomas DeQuincey: His Life and Writings,*
ed. Japp, Appendix, vol. II, p. 338

From childhood to old age, indeed, DeQuincey was a puzzle to all who knew him. In manners he was a courtly gentleman: in appearance, as Miss Mitford writes, he looked like a beggar. With knowledge that seemed boundless, he frequently acted like a child or a fool; always courteous in speech, he could be bitter, inconsiderate, and even malicious, in print; shy and reserved in society, he wrote of himself with a shamelessness that almost reminds us of Rousseau; regardless of money he scattered it among the most worthless of beggars, and was constantly in pecuniary difficulties. DeQuincey had the warmest affection for his wife and children, but he often left them to live, nobody knew how, in solitary lodgings. Throughout the night he would ramble for miles over the country, or write for the press, and the best part of the day was given to slumber, to be followed frequently by nervous suffering, and a wretchedness "not utterable to any human ear." With a mind of amazing versatility, and many a beautiful trait of character, it is impossible to read DeQuincey's life without seeing that it was, in great measure, a wreck, and that this failure was due, as in the case of Coleridge, to opium.

John Dennis, 1891, "DeQuincey," *Leisure Hour*, vol. 40, p. 241

Poverty is sometimes a noble and respectable thing, and when the issues have any sort of greatness there is a kind of excitement in the alternate downfalls and successes of the penniless but courageous struggle. But when the strife is for a few pounds, when the milkman's bill is the rock in the way, and shillings and pence the munitions of war, the echo of that dreary and hopeless fighting in the dark has nothing but misery in it. DeQuincey puts forth his privations, his wanderings about from one lodging to another, sometimes waylaid in his bed by a furious creditor, sometimes suffering torture for want of a box of Seidlitz powders, always with elaborate explanation of how in the extraordinary combination of fate it has come to be so, but can never by any calculation of human probabilities be so again —to the publisher who never seems to refuse the necessary dole, but inevitably is sometimes a little impatient and provoked by the perpetual messengers and the dole on the other side of a page or two at a time.

Margaret O. W. Oliphant, 1897, William Blackwood
and His Sons, vol. I, p. 423

Confessions of an English Opium-Eater (1821-22)

Have you heard anything of a book which every body (meaning every idle Athenian eager for novelty) is now reading? It is called *Confessions of an English Opium Eater.* Many strange things and persons have I encountered in my journey through life, and, among the rest, this same Opium Eater. I spent an idle half day talking with him fourteen years ago in London, when he was a student at Oxford, and met him once since. I directly recognized him through the thin disguise in his book: I am since assured that I have not been mistaken. Ask more about him, if you have any taste remaining for oddities.

Anne Grant, 1823, To Mrs. Brown, Feb. 13;
Memoir and Correspondence, ed. Grant, vol. II, p. 330

DeQuincey seems like a man bound on a journey to a certain place, the way to which is straight, but who prefers wandering out of the road, to which he occasionally returns—and immediately deviates off in another direction. It is not difficult to see that a long time must pass before he reaches his journey's end, or that, when he does reach it, the purpose for which he started may be rendered unavailable by the delay. This is the more unpardonable in DeQuincey, who, in *Confessions of an English Opium-Eater,* has produced one of the most charming books in the language, by making it simple in style and natural in expression.

R. Shelton Mackenzie, 1854, ed. Noctes Ambrosianæ,
vol. I, p. 5, note

DeQuincey himself, in descanting on the Dream-faculty, says, "Habitually to dream magnificently, a man must have a constitutional determination to reverie." In that sentence he announces the true law of all literature that comes under the order of pure phantasy. But in his case, in spite of the strength of the dream-element, we cannot proceed far till we discover that his determination to reverie was but the extreme projection of one phase of a phenomenal nature balancing its opposite. He was also shrewd, observant, master of a fine humour that demanded contact with life for its free exercise. From a nice examination of details he was under an inborn necessity to rise to the principle that relates them, linking the disparate together; deeply interested in the most practical and dry of studies—political economy. He was skilled in the exercises of the analytic understanding—a logician exacting and precise—else his dreaming had never gained for him the eminence it has gained. Surely it is calculated to strike the most casual reader on a perusal of that first edition of the "Confessions," that his powers of following up sensational effects and tracing with absolute exactness the most delicately varying shades of experience, and recording them with conscientious precision, were as noticeable as were the dreams to which they were served to give effect. No proper ground has been laid for a liberal and sympathetic appreciation of DeQuincey till these points have been clearly apprehended; and assuredly this is one of the cases where, as he himself has well said, "not to sympathise is not to understand."

Alexander H. Japp, 1877, Thomas DeQuincey;
His Life and Writings, vol. I, p. 1

While all controlled reasoning was suspended under the incantation of opium, his quick mind, without conscious intent, without prejudice or purpose, assembled such mysterious and wonderful sights and sounds as the naked soul might see and hear in the world of actual experience. For De Quincey's range of action and association was not as narrow as might seem. He had walked the streets of London friendless and starving, saved from death by a dram given by one even more wretched than he, only a few months after he had talked with the king. DeQuincey's talent images are therefore not grotesque, or mediæval, not conditioned by any philosophical theory, not of any Inferno or Paradise. The elements of his visions are the simple elements of all our striking experiences: the faces of the dead, the grieving child, the tired woman, the strange foreign face, the tramp of horses' feet. And opium merely magnified these simple elements, rendered them grand and beautiful without giving them any forced connection or relative meaning. We recognise the traces of our own transfigured experience, but we are relieved from the necessity of accepting it as having an inner meaning. DeQuincey's singular hold on our affection seems, therefore, to be his rare quality of presenting the unusual but typical dream or reverie as a beautiful object of interest, without endeavoring to give it the character of an allegory or a fable.

George R. Carpenter, 1897, *Library of the World's Best Literature,* ed. Warner, vol. VIII, p. 4558

GENERAL

This very clever work [*Logic of Political Economy*] is intended to unravel intricacies and to expose sundry errors in the application of the Ricardian theory of value. It would, however, have been more popular and successful had it been less scholastic. It is right to be logical, but not to be perpetually obtruding logical forms and technicalities on the reader's attention. This sort of affectation is little noticed in a brief essay like the Templars' Dialogues; but in a goodly-sized volume like the present it becomes tiresome and repulsive.

John Ramsay McCulloch, 1847, *Literature of Political Economy,* p. 20

The key-note of preparation, the claim which pre-eminently should be set forth in advance, is this: that DeQuincey was the prince of hierophants, or of pontifical hierarchs, as regards all those profound mysteries which from the beginning have swayed the human heart, sometimes through the light of angelic smiles lifting it upwards to an altitude just beneath the heavens, and sometimes shattering it, with a shock of quaking anguish, down to earth. As it was the function of the hierophant, in the Grecian mysteries, to show the sacred symbols as concrete incarnations of faith, so was it DeQuincey's to reveal in open light the everlasting symbols, universally intelligible when once disclosed, which are folded in the evolution of dreams and of those meditations which most resemble dreams; and as to the manner of those revelations, no Roman *pontifex maximus,* were it even Cæsar himself, could have rivalled their magisterial pomp.

Henry M. Alden, 1863, "Thomas DeQuincey," *Atlantic Monthly,* vol. 12, p. 345

If we take *Confessions of an English Opium-Eater* and follow it with, for an example, the essay on Shakespeare, then pursue the fortunes of the Spanish Nun, and wind up with a careful reading of the *Logic of Political Economy,* we shall come away with a dazzling impression of DeQuincey's range as a thinker, a student, and a writer. But this impression does not grow proportionately stronger on reviewing the whole bulk of his writings. We gradually lose faith in the comprehensiveness which at first seemed so positive and radical a characteristic. We observe also, that he repeats himself, that he covers large spaces with a very thin integument of thought, or with a sham, apparitional kind of humor, and that his monotony belonging to the styles of more creative writers. To acknowledge this is by no means to belittle DeQuincey's claims to our remembrance, but it enables us to define some things concerning him more clearly, perhaps, than they have usually been defined.

George Parsons Lathrop, 1877, "Some Aspects of DeQuincey,"
Atlantic Monthly, vol. 40, p. 569

DeQuincey's talent lay more in a narrative and imaginative writing than in literary criticism. He was too digestive and sensational, too much of a rhetorician, to rank with the greatest critics. His liveliness of fancy and the rapid play of his remarkable information, together with his verbal brilliancy, found their most congenial field in his extraordinary rambling sketches. But his knowledge of literature was so wide and sympathetic, and he had such genuine philosophical insight, that he stands well as a writer on literary topics. His best work in this field is to be found fragmentarily all through those numerous volumes which he composed after his late commencement as an author.

Edward T. McLaughlin, 1893, ed. *Literary Criticism
for Students*, p. 118

It is significant that most estimates of the value of DeQuincey's work concern themselves with his style. He was not a great thinker. Keen as were his powers of analysis, he was not always a logical thinker. Above all, he was not capable of sustained, systematic thinking. His writings are full of beginnings that end nowhere, and of promises that are never performed. His very habit of analysis led to a lack of proportion in his work. Little ideas get as much space as big ones. One is sometimes wearied by the feeling that it is not the thought that he is getting, but the author's power of saying things, irrespective of their worth, in a pleasing and original form.

Franklin T. Baker, 1896, ed. *Revolt of the Tartars*
by Thomas DeQuincey, p. 6

His writings are pre-eminently exegetical, lacking in the imperative mood. He analyzes, interprets, or expounds after his subtle, philosophic, though somewhat eccentric and paradoxical manner; taking nothing for granted, probing into everything he touches, and illuminating it by some flash of originality. Though not always a sound thinker, he marshals his arguments with an orderly precision, which is invaluable in a good cause. Exactness, carried to the verge of pedantry, is the conspicuous merit of his style; which is further strengthened by a scrupulous attention to the conditions of effective comparison, and by the explicitness with which his statements and clauses are connected. Even his grammar and punctuation are singularly clear and careful. Beneath this vigorous intellectuality lurks a curiously deliberate and "dæmonic" kind of humour, which largely consists in the sudden introduction of an unexpected point of view, and use of dignified language for the discussion of trivialities, and the application of artistic or professional terms to records of crime and passion. . . . His style is essentially decorative, and he aims consciously at sublimity of thought and diction. He does not shrink from daring appeals to the infinite, and risks bewildering his reader by dizzy flights to the uttermost limits of time and space. He builds up his sentences and his paragraphs with a sensitive ear for the music of words. One phrase seems like the echo of another, and even the impression of distance in sound is cunningly produced. His finest passages are distinguished by the crowded richness of fancy, the greater range and arbitrariness of combination, which are the peculiar attributes of poetry.

R. Brimley Johnson, 1896, *English Prose,*
ed. Craik, vol. V, pp. 260, 261

The interest of DeQuincey is that of an experimenter and pioneer in English prose. He may, in fact, be described as the inventor of that variety of prose —a questionable variety in the hands of many of his successors—which has been named the "poetic": a form in which to attain the ends of vivid description or of impassioned narrative, the restraints which the elder prose-masters deliberately imposed upon themselves in respect both of construction and vocabulary were as deliberately thrown off. In other words, the attempt was for the first time made to arouse emotions as vehement in the mind of a reader through the medium of prose as are or may be excited by the instrumentality of verse. In some of DeQuincey's most famous passages this exaltation of the *emotional* power of prose is overwhelmingly felt.

Henry Duff Traill, 1897, *Social England,* vol. VI, p. 29

He represents the reaction from the polish, reserve, and coldness of the eighteenth century to the warmth and glow of the seventeenth century,— the golden period of English prose. His masters are Milton, Jeremy Taylor, Fuller, and Browne, whose eloquence, rich coloring, and elaborate ornamentation he inherits. To these qualities he has added the finish and elegance of the eighteenth century writers, and the freedom, deep feeling, and lofty spiritual tone of our own age. In fineness of texture and in beauty of coloring he is unequalled save by Ruskin, whom he surpasses in form and general pictorial and sound effects. He is sometimes guilty of bad taste or bathos, but when at his best is a supreme master of the "grand style." With an imagination as great as Carlyle's, his style is more chastened, rhythmical, and exquisite, though not showing so much industry or moral earnestness. He has a finer rhetorical and critical faculty than Macaulay, and is more stately and vivacious than Landor. DeQuincey's unique power lies in his imagination, which is extraordinary. In his best passages there is a poetic loftiness, a phantasmagoric charm, and a spectacular gorgeousness which seizes and holds the mind of the reader with its subtile power. Even when we cannot accept the soundness of his conclusions on philosophical questions, or the accuracy of his statements in the historical and biographical essays, we delight in surrendering ourselves to his wonderful fancy. When he has on his magic robes, few can mount so high.

George Armstrong Wauchope, 1898, ed. *Confessions of an English Opium-Eater*, p. 18

A trait of DeQuincey closely allied to his habit of digression, and one which the general reader must always regard as a defect, is his tendency to overload his sentences with irrelevant particulars. He appends relative clause to relative clause in several degrees of subordination, and often adds to such a combination a parenthesis within a parenthesis. Obviously, this excessive qualification is generally due to DeQuincey's sometimes finical desire for exactness. . . . In one respect DeQuincey is far from a model writer, and that is in his ungovernable habit of digressing from his given theme. He not only digresses from his main theme, but he digresses from his first digression, and sometimes even from his third.

J. Scott Clarke, 1898, *A Study of English Prose Writers*, pp. 397, 399

WASHINGTON IRVING
1783-1859

Born, in New York, 3 April 1783. Educated at private schools, 1787-99. In a lawyer's office, 1801-04. Contrib. to *Morning Chronicle,* under pseud. of "Jonathan Oldstyle," 1802. Travelled in Europe, 1804-06. Edited *Salmagundi,* with his brother, William, and J. K. Paulding, Jan. to Oct., 1807. Partner with his brothers in a mercantile house, 1810-17. Assistant Editor of *Analectic Mag.,* 1813-14. In England, 1815-20. Travelled on Continent, 1820-25. Attaché to the U.S.A. Legation at Madrid, 1826-29. Sec. to U.S.A. Legation in London, 1829-32. Medal of Roy. Soc. of Lit., 1830. Hon. LL.D., Oxford, 1831. Returned to New York, 1832; settled at Sunnyside. Contrib. to *Knickerbocker Mag.,* 1839-40. U.S.A. Ambassador to Spain, 1842-46. Returned to America, April 1846. Unmarried. Died, at Sunnyside, 28 Nov. 1859. WORKS: *A History of New York* (under pseud. of "Diedrich Knickerbocker") 1809; *The Sketch-Book of Geoffrey Crayon,* 1819; *Bracebridge Hall* (by "Geoffrey Crayon," 2 vols.), 1822; *Letters of Jonathan Oldstyle,* 1824 (3rd edn. same year); *Tales of a*

Traveller (by "Geoffrey Crayon"), 1824; *A History of . . . Cristopher Columbus* (3 vols.), 1828; *A Chronicle of the Conquest of Granada,* 1829; *Voyages . . . of the Companions of Columbus,* 1831; *The Alhambra* (by "Geoffrey Crayon"), 1832; *Complete Works* (pubd. in Paris), 1834; *Abbotsford and Newstead Abbey* (anon.), 1835; *Tour on the Prairies,* 1835; *Legends of the Conquest of Spain* (anon.), 1835; *The Crayon Miscellany* (anon.), 1835; *Astoria* (3 vols.), 1836; *The Adventures of Captain Bonneville,* 1837; *Biography and Poetical Remains of M. M. Davidson,* 1841; *The Life of Oliver Goldsmith,* 1844; *A Book of the Hudson* (edited by "Geoffrey Crayon)",* 1849; *The Life of Mahomet,* 1850; *The Lives of Mahomet and his Successors,* 1850; *Chronicles of Wolfert's Roost,* 1855; *Life of Washington,* vols. I, II, 1855; vol. III, 1856; vol. IV, 1857; vol. V, 1859; *Wolfert Webber,* 1856; *Works* (15 vols.), 1857. POSTHUMOUS: *Spanish Papers,* ed. by P. M. Irving, 1866; *Biographies and Miscellaneous Papers,* ed. by P. M. Irving, 1867. He *translated:* Navarette's *Collection de los Viages, etc.,* 1825; and *edited:* Campbell's *Poems,* 1810; Bonneville's *Rocky Mountains,* 1843. COLLECTED WORKS: in 1 vol., 1834; in 27 vols., 1880-83. LIFE: *Life and Letters,* by P. M. Irving, 1862-63.

R. Farquharson Sharp, 1897, *A Dictionary of
English Authors,* p. 145

SEE: *Works,* 1882-84, 27 v. (Hudson Edition); *Works,* 1910, 40 v.; William R. Langfeld, *Poems,* 1931; William P. Trent and George S. Hellman, ed. *The Journals of Washington Irving, from July, 1815, to July, 1842,* 1921, 3 v.; Stanley T. Williams, *The Life of Washington Irving,* 1935, 2 v.

PERSONAL

Poor Washington is dead three months ago! I almost shed a tear when I heard it: it was a dream of mine that we two should be friends.

Thomas Carlyle, 1823, *To John A. Carlyle,* Nov. 11;
Early Letters, ed. Norton, p. 294

He is so sensible, sound, and straightforward in his way of seeing everything, and at the same time so full of hopefulness, so simple, unaffected, true, and good, that it is a privilege to converse with him, for which one is the wiser, the happier and the better.

Frances Ann Kemble, 1833, *Letter,* April 10;
Records of a Girlhood, p. 572

There is no man in the world who could have given me the heartfelt pleasure you have, by your kind note of the 13th of last month. There is no living writer, and there are very few among the dead, whose approbation I should feel so proud to earn. And with everything you have written upon my shelves, and in my thoughts, and in my heart of hearts, I may honestly and truly say so. If you could know how earnestly I write this, you would be glad to read it—as I hope you will be, faintly guessing at the warmth of the hand I autobiographically hold out to you over the broad Atlantic. . . . I have been so accustomed to associate you with my pleasantest and happiest thoughts and with my leisure hours, that I rush at once into full confidence with you, and fall, as it were naturally, and by the very laws of gravity, into your open arms.

Charles Dickens, 1841, To Irving; Life and Letters of
Washington Irving, ed. Irving, vol. III, pp. 164, 165

The mansion of this prosperous and valiant family, so often celebrated in his writings, is the residence of Washington Irving. It is approached by a sequestered road, which enhances the effect of its natural beauty. A more tranquil and protected abode, nestled in the lap of nature, never captivated a poet's eye. Rising from the bank of the river, which a strip of woodland alone intercepts, it unites every rural charm to the most complete seclusion. From this interesting domain is visible the broad surface of the Tappan Zee; the grounds slope to the water's edge, and are bordered by wooded ravines; a clear brook ripples near, and several neat paths lead to shadowy walks or fine points of river scenery. The house itself is a graceful combination of the English cottage and the Dutch farmhouse. The crow-stepped gables, and tiles in the hall, and the weather cocks, partake of the latter character; while the white walls gleaming through the trees, the smooth and verdant turf, and the mantling vines of ivy and clambering roses, suggest the former.

Henry Theodore Tuckerman, 1853-96, Homes of
American Authors, ed. Hubbard, p. 291

He was in the habit of rising in the night, between twelve and four o'clock, and reading, or even writing for half an hour or an hour. He did not get, on the average, more than four hours' sleep at night, but often took short naps in the afternoon and evening. This natural, or at least habitual, irregularity of sleep, became aggravated to extreme nervousness and restlessness after an attack of fever and ague in the autumn of 1858. He was still suffering from the effects of this when I saw him. But beneath all these disturbances lay a deeper difficulty, which was distinctly mentioned to me in his physician's letter as "enlargement of the heart," accompanied by "an obstructed circulation." Under these influences, with growing age to weaken the power of resistance, his health gradually declined, until the flame of life, which had been getting paler and feebler, was blown out, as it were, by a single breath: a gentle end of a sweet and lovely life,—such an end as Nature prepares by slow and measured approaches and consummates with swift kindness when she grants the blessing of euthanasia to her favorite children.

Oliver Wendell Holmes, 1859, *Remarks at a Meeting of the Massachusetts Historical Society,* Dec. 15; *Proceedings,* vol. 4, p. 421

Great and varied as was the genius of Mr. Irving, there was one thing he shrunk with a comical terror attempting; and that was a *dinner-speech.* A great dinner, however, was to be given to Mr. Dickens in New York, as one had already been given in Boston; and it was evident to all, that no man but Washington Irving could be thought of to preside. With all his dread of making a speech, he was obliged to obey the universal call, and to accept the painful pre-eminence. . . . Under the circumstances,—an invited guest, with no impending speech,—I sat calmly, and watched with interest the imposing scene. I had the honor to be placed next but one to Mr. Irving, and the great pleasure of sharing in his conversation. He had brought the manuscript of his speech, and laid it under his plate. "I shall certainly break down," he repeated over and over again. At last, the moment arrived. Mr. Irving rose, and was received with deafening and long-continued applause, which by no means lessened his apprehension. He began in his pleasant voice; got through two or three sentences pretty easily, but in the next hesitated; and, after one or two attempts to go on, gave it up, with a graceful allusion to the tournament, and the troops of knights all armed and eager for the fray; ended with the toast, "Charles Dickens, the guest of the nation." "There," said he, as he resumed his seat under a repetition of the applause which had saluted his rising,—"there I told you I should break down; and I've done it." There certainly never was made a shorter after-dinner speech: I doubt if there ever was a more successful one. The manuscript seemed to be a dozen or twenty pages long; but the printed speech was not as many lines.

Cornelius Conway Felton, 1859, *Remarks at a Meeting of the Massachusetts Historical Society,* Dec. 15; *Proceedings,* vol. 4, pp. 411, 412

William Irving, the father of the great author, was a native of Scotland— one of a race in which the instinct of veneration is strong—and a Scottish woman was employed as a nurse in his household. It is related that one day while she was walking in the street with her little charge, then five years old, she saw General Washington in a shop, and entering, led up the boy, whom she presented as one to whom his name had been given. The general turned, laid his hand on the child's head, and gave him his smile and his blessing, little thinking that they were bestowed upon his future biographer. The gentle pressure of that hand Irving always remembered, and that blessing, he believed, attended him through life. Who shall say what power that recollection may have had in keeping him true to high and generous aims? . . . From the time that he began the composition of his *Sketch Book,* his whole life was the life of an author. His habits of composition were, however, by no means regular. When he was in the vein, the periods would literally stream from his pen; at other times he would scarcely write anything. For two years after the failure of his brothers at Liverpool, he found it almost impossible to write a line. He was throughout life an early riser, and when in the mood, would write all the morning and till late in the day, wholly engrossed with his subject. In the evening he was ready for any cheerful pastime, in which he took part with an animation almost amounting to high spirits. These intervals of excitement and intense labor, sometimes lasting for weeks, were succeeded by languor, and at times by depression of spirits, and for months the pen would lie untouched; even to answer a letter at these times was an irksome task.

> William Cullen Bryant, 1860, "Washington Irving,"
> *Orations and Addresses,* pp. 98, 149

Mr. Irving was never a systematic collector of books, and his little library at Sunnyside might have disappointed those who would expect to see there rich shelves of choice editions, and a full array of all the favorite authors among whom such a writer would delight to revel. Some rather antiquated tomes in Spanish,—different sets of Calderon and Cervantes, and of some modern French and German authors,—a presentation-set of Cadell's "Waverley," as well as that more recent and elegant emanation from the classic press of Houghton,—a moderate amount of home-tools for the *Life of Washington,* (rare materials were consulted in the town-libraries and at Washington)—and the remainder of his books were evidently a haphazard collection, many coming from the authors, with their respects, and thus sometimes costing the recipient their full (intrinsic) value in writing a letter of acknowledgment.

> George P. Putnam, 1860, "Recollections of Irving,"
> *Atlantic Monthly,* vol. 6, pp. 603, 608, 609

When he died an old man, a lock to which he himself had always kept the key was found to guard a braid of hair and a beautiful miniature, with a slip of paper marked in his own handwriting, "Matilda Hoffman." No less faithfully had he kept her Bible and Prayer-Book throughout his life. Of the miniature his publisher George P. Putman, told the story of having once had it retouched and remounted for its possessor, forty years after Miss Hoffman's death. "When I returned it to him in a suitable velvet case," said

Mr. Putman, "he took it to a quiet corner and looked intently on the face for some minutes, apparently unobserved, his tears falling freely on the glass as he gazed." Who shall say that the cherishing of such a memory as this did not find its direct expression in the gentle chivalry with which he bore himself, as a writer and as a man, towards all women.

M. A. De Wolfe Howe, 1898, American Bookmen, p. 11

Salmagundi (1807)

We have no hesitation in saying at the outset, that we consider the good papers of *Salmagundi*, and the greater part of the Knickerbocker, superior to the *Sketch-Book.* . . . It [*Salmagundi*] was exceedingly pleasant morning, or after-dinner reading, never taking up too much of a gentleman's time from his business and pleasures, nor so exalted and spiritualized as to seem mystical to his far-seeing vision. . . . Though its wit is sometimes forced, and its serious style sometimes false, upon looking it over we have found it full of entertainment, with an infinite variety of characters and circumstances, and with that amiable, good-natured wit and pathos, which shows that the heart has not grown hard while making merry of the world.

Richard Henry Dana, 1819, "The Sketch Book,"
North American Review, vol. 9, pp. 323, 334, 344

The better pieces are written in Mr. Irving's best manner. Take it altogether, it was certainly a production of extraordinary merit, and was instantaneously and universally recognised as such by the public. It wants of course the graver merits of the modern British collections of Essays; but for spirit, effect, and actual literary value, we doubt whether any publication of the class since *The Spectator,* upon which it is directly modelled, can fairly be put in competition with it.

Alexander Hill Everett, 1829, "Irving's Life of Columbus,"
North American Review, vol. 28, p. 116

A History of New York by Diedrich Knickerbocker (1809)

I beg you to accept my best thanks for the uncommon degree of entertainment which I have received from the most excellent jocose of New York. I am sensible, that, as a stranger to American parties and politics, I must lose much of the concealed satire of the piece; but I must own, that, looking at the simple and obvious meaning only, I have never read anything so closely resembling the style of Dean Swift as the annals of Diedrich Knickerbocker. I have been employed these few evenings in reading them aloud to Mrs. S., and two ladies who are our guests; and our sides have been absolutely sore with laughing. I think, too, there are passages which indicate that the author possesses powers of a different kind, and has some touches which remind me much of Sterne.

Sir Walter Scott, 1813, *Letter to Carson Brevoort,* April 23

It is painful to see a mind as admirable for exquisite perception of the beautiful, as it is for its quick sense of the ridiculous, wasting the richness of its fancy on an ungrateful theme, and its exuberant humor in a coarse caricature.

Gulian C. Verplanck, 1818, *Address before the New York Historical Society,* Dec. 7

A work to be compared with anything of the kind in our language; a book of unwearying pleasantry, which, instead of flashing out, as English and American humour is wont, from time to time, with long and dull intervals, is kept up with a true French vivacity from beginning to end; a book which, if it have a fault, has only that of being too pleasant, too sustained a tissue of merriment and ridicule.

Edward Everett, 1822, *"Bracebridge Hall,"*
North American Review, vol. 15, p. 206

Conceived, matured, and brought forth, in a bold, original temper—unaided—and alone—by Irving: more entirely the natural thought, language, humour, and feeling of the man himself—without imitation or plagiarism—far more—than either of his late works: It was written, too, in the fervour and flush of his popularity, at home—after he had got a name, such as no other man had, among his countrymen; after *Salmagundi* had been read, with pleasure, all over North America: In it, however, there is a world of rich allusion—a vein of sober caricature—the merit of which is little understood here. . . . By nine readers out of ten, perhaps, *Knickerbocker* is read, as a piece of generous drollery—nothing more. Be it so. It will wear the better. The design of Irving himself is not always clear: nor was he always undeviating, in his course. Truth or fable, fact or falsehood—it was all the same to him, if a bit of material came in his way. In a word, we look upon this volume of *Knickerbocker,* though it *is* tiresome, though there *are* some wretched failures in it; a little overdoing of the humorous—and a little confusion of purpose, throughout—as a work, honourable to English literature —manly—bold—and so *altogether original,* without being extravagant, as to stand alone, among the labours of men.

John Neal, 1825, "American Writers," *Blackwood's Magazine,*
vol. 17, pp. 61, 62

At the first appearance of my work, its aim and drift were misapprehended by some of the descendants of the Dutch worthies; and I understand that now and then one may still be found to regard it with a captious eye. The far greater part, however, I have reason to flatter myself, receive my good-humoured picturings in the same temper in which they were executed; and when I find, after a lapse of forty years, the haphazard production of my youth still cherished among them,—when I find its very name become a "household word" and used to give the home stamp to everything recommended for popular acceptation, such as Knickerbocker societies, Knickerbocker insurance companies, Knickerbocker steamboats, Knickerbocker omnibuses, Knickerbocker bread, and Knickerbocker ice,—and when I find New Yorkers of Dutch descent priding themselves upon being "genuine Knickerbockers,"—I please myself with the persuasion that I have struck the right cord; that my dealings with the good old Dutch times, and the customs and usages derived from them, are in harmony with the feelings and humors of my townsmen; that I have opened a vein of pleasant associations and quaint characteristics peculiar to my native place, and which its inhabitants will not willingly suffer to pass away; and that, though other histories of New York may appear of higher claims to learned acceptation, and may take their dignified and appropriate rank in the family library, Knickerbocker's history will still be received with good-humored indulgence, and be thumbed and chuckled over by the family fireside.

Washington Irving, 1848, *A History of New York*, The Author's Apology

After some preliminary essays in humorous literature his genius arrived at the age of *in*discretion, and he produced at the age of twenty-six the most deliciously audacious work of humor in our literature, namely, *The History of New York by Diedrich Knickerbocker*. . . . It may be said of Irving that he not only caricatured, but had the courage of his caricatures. The persons whom he covered with ridicule were the ancestors of the leading families of New York, and these families prided themselves on their descent. After the publication of such a book he could hardly enter the "best society" of New York, to which he naturally belonged, without running the risk of being insulted, especially by the elderly women of fashion; but he conquered their prejudices by the same grace and geniality of manner, by the same unmistakable tokens that he was an inborn gentleman, through which he afterward won his way into the first society of England, France, Germany, Italy, and Spain.

Edwin Percy Whipple, 1876-86, *American Literature and Other Papers*, ed. Whittier, p. 43

We need not speak of him at great length, for his strictly historical works were few, and his fame was mainly achieved in other walks of literature. Nor did he have a great influence upon the development of historical writing among us, unless in the way of general influence upon American style. In fact, it is quite possible that no one of his mature and sober pieces of writing had as much real effect on the progress of American historiography as the admirable humorous composition with which he began, as far back as 1809,—the *History of New York by Diedrich Knickerbocker.* Aside from its striking success as a literary production, the book had a great effect in awakening interest in the early or Dutch period of New York history. Descendants rushed with sober indignation to the defense of ancestors at whom the genial humorist poked his fun, and very likely the great amount of work which the state government in the next generation did for the historical illustration of the Dutch period, through the researches of Mr. Brodhead in foreign archives, had this unhistorical little book for one of its principal causes. But, on the other hand, he made it permanently difficult for the American public to take a serious view of those early Dutch days. Oloffe the Dreamer and Walter the Doubter, Abraham with the ten breeches and Stuyvesant with the wooden leg, have become too thoroughly domesticated among us to admit of that.

> J. Franklin Jameson, 1891, *The History of Historical Writing*
> *in America*, p. 97

The Sketch-Book (1819)

Everything in it I find the marks of a mind of the utmost elegance and refinement, a thing as you know that I was not exactly prepared to look for in an American. . . . Each of the essays is entitled to its appropriate praise, and the whole is such as I scarcely know an Englishman that could have written it. The author powerfully conciliates to himself our kindness and affection. But the Essay on Rural Life in England is incomparably the best. It is, I believe, all true; and one wonders, while reading, that nobody ever said this before. There is wonderful sweetness in it.

> William Godwin, 1819, *Letter to James Ogilvie,* Sept. 15;
> *Life and Letters of Washington Irving,* ed. Irving, vol. I, p. 422

We believe that the public law of literature has entirely exempted periodical publications from the jurisdiction of the ordinary critical tribunals; and we therefore notice the first number of this work without any intention of formal criticism, but simply for the purpose of announcing its appearance, and of congratulating the American public that one of their choicest favorites has, after a long interval, again resumed his pen. It will be needless to inform any that have read the book, that it is from the pen of Mr. Irving. His rich, and sometimes extravagant humor, his gay and graceful fancy, his peculiar choice and felicity of original expression, as well as the pure and fine moral feeling which imperceptibly pervades every thought and image, without being anywhere ostentatious or dogmatic, betray the author in every page; even without the aid of those minor peculiarities of style, taste, and local allusions, which at once identify the travelled Geoffrey Crayon with the venerable Knickerbocker.

Gulian C. Verplanck, 1819, *Analectic Magazine,* July

Few recent publications have been so well received in England as *The Sketch-Book.* Several of the Waverley novels have passed through fewer editions than this agreeable work, and the journals of the most consequence have paid the highest compliments to its merit. We are nevertheless free to confess that we think *The Sketch-Book* as a whole, inferior to the author's earlier writings.

Edward Everett, 1822, *"Bracebridge Hall,"*
North American Review, vol. 15, p. 208

Of the merit of his *Knickerbocker* and New York stories, we cannot pretend to judge. But in his *Sketch-Book* and *Bracebridge Hall* he gives us very good American copies of our British Essayists and Novelists, which may be very well on the other side of the water, or as proofs of the capabilities of the national genius, but which might be dispensed with here, where we have to boast of the originals. Not only Mr. Irving's language is with great taste and felicity modelled on that of Addison, Goldsmith, Sterne, or Mackenzie; but the thoughts and sentiments are taken at the rebound, and as they are brought forward at the present period, want both freshness and probability. Mr. Irving's writings are literary *anachronisms.* He comes to England for the first [the second] time; and, being on the spot, fancies himself in the midst of those characters and manners which he had read in the Spectator and other approved authors, and which were the only idea he had hitherto formed of the parent-country. Instead of looking round to see what *we are,* he sets to work to describe us as *we were*—at second-hand.

William Hazlitt, 1825, *The Spirit of the Age*

Every reader has his first book: I mean to say, one book, among all others, which, in early youth, first fascinates his imagination, and at once excites and satisfies the desires of his mind. To me, this first book was the *Sketch-Book* of Washington Irving. I was a school-boy when it was published, and read each succeeding number with ever-increasing wonder and delight,—

spellbound by its pleasant humor, its melancholy tenderness, its atmosphere of revery; nay, even by its gray-brown covers, the shaded letters of the titles, and the fair, clear type,—which seemed an outward symbol of the style. How many delightful books the same author has given us, written before and since,—volumes of history and of fiction, most of which illustrate his native land, and some of which illuminate it, and make the Hudson, I will not say as classic, but as romantic as the Rhine! Yet still the charm of the *Sketch-Book* remains unbroken; the old fascination still lingers about it; and whenever I open its pages, I open also that mysterious door which leads back into the haunted chambers of youth.

> Henry Wadsworth Longfellow, 1859, *Remarks at a Meeting of the Massachusetts Historical Society*, Dec. 15; *Proceedings*, vol. 4, p. 393

The style of the sketches is everywhere his own—pure, chaste, easy, flowing; often elegant, and always appropriate to the theme in hand; rich, yet not extravagant with varied and pertinent imagery—pleasant flowers of speech intermingling themselves with his graceful and facile style, presenting themselves not in gorgeous superabundance as in some artificial garden of beauty, but constantly occurring in a sort of natural order and variety, like the floral adornments that greet us as we glance along some cultivated and beautiful landscape.

> Charles Adams, 1870, *Memoir of Washington Irving*, p. 93

Pathos is the great touchstone of humor, and Irving's pathos is always a lamentable failure. Is it not very significant, that he should have made so little of the story of Rip Van Winkle? In his sketch which has won so wide a fame and given a lasting association to the Kaatskills, there is not a suspicion of the immense pathos which the skill of an industrious playwright and the genius of that rare actor, Mr. Jefferson, have since developed from the tale. The Dame Van Winkle that we know now is the creation of Mr. Boucicault; to him it is we owe that vigorous character,—a scold, a tyrant to her husband, but nevertheless full of relentful womanliness, and by the justice of her cause exciting our sympathy almost as much as Rip himself does. . . . Certainly we should, as the case stands, have missed the whole immortal figment, had not Irving given it to us in germ; the fact that our playwright and our master comedian have made it so much greater and more beautiful does not annul that primary service; but, looking at the matter historically, we must admit that Irving's share in the credit is that of the first projector of a scientific improvement, and the latter sort of person always has to forego a great part of his fame in favor of the one who consummates the discovery. I am willing to believe that there was a peculiar advantage in Irving's treatment; namely, that he secured for his story a quicker and more general acceptance than might have been granted to something more profound; but this does not alter the critical judgment that we have to pass upon it. If Irving had grasped the tragic sphere at all, he would have shone more splendidly in the comic. But the literary part of him, at least, never passed into the shade: it somehow contrived to be always on that side of the earth which was towards the sun.

> George Parsons Lathrop, 1876, *A Study of Hawthorne*, pp. 304, 305, 306

One of those strokes of genius ["Rip Van Winkle"] that recreate the world and clothe it with unfading hues of romance; the theme was an old-world echo, transformed by genius into a primal story that will endure as long as the Hudson flows through its mountains to the sea. A great artist can paint a great picture on a small canvas.

> Charles Dudley Warner, 1881, *Washington Irving* (*American Men of Letters*), p. 119

It is in the *Sketch-Book* that Irving first appeals to us as a torch-bearer in the great procession of English prose-writers. In *Knickerbocker* he had been dancing or skipping in the lightness of his heart to a delicious measure of his own; in *Salmagundi* he had waked up to a sense of literary responsibility, without quite knowing in what direction his new-found sense of style would lead him. In the *Sketch-Book* he is a finished and classic writer, bowing to the great tradition of English prose, and knowing precisely what it is that he would do, and how to do it. . . . If the mark of any modern writer is to be found on the early style of Washington Irving, it appears to me to be rather that of Cobbett than of any other. . . . It has taken its place in literature, and there is hardly a page in it which does not appeal to us with the salutary lesson that "there was a noble way, in former times, of saying things simply, and yet saying them proudly."

> Edmund Gosse, 1883, "Irving's *Sketch-Book*," *The Critic*, vol. 3, pp. 140, 141

In ten minutes I had gone to the house and returned to the barn with *The Sketch-Book*. I had not read the story since I was a boy. I was disappointed in it; not as a story, of course, but the tale was purely a narrative. The theme was interesting, but not dramatic. The silver Hudson stretches out before you as you read; the quaint red roofs and queer gables of the old Dutch cottages stand out against the mist upon the mountains; but all this is descriptive. The character of Rip does not speak ten lines. What could be done dramatically with so simple a sketch? How could it be turned into an effective play? Three or four bad dramatisations of the story had already been acted, but without marked success. Yates, of London, had given one in which the hero dies; one had been acted by my father, one by Hackett, and another by Burke. Some of these versions I had remembered when I was a boy, and I should say that Burke's play and the performance were the best; but nothing that I remembered gave me the slightest encouragement that I could get a good play out of any of the existing materials. . . . I got together three old printed versions of the drama and the story itself. The plays were all in two acts. I thought it would be an improvement in the drama to arrange it in three, making the scene with the spectre crew an act by itself. This would separate the poetical from the domestic side of the story. But by far the most important alteration was in the interview with the spirits. In the old versions, they spoke and sang. I remember that the effects of this ghastly dialogue was dreadfully human, so I arranged that no voice but Rip's should be heard. This was entirely my own invention. . . . In the seclusion of the barn, I studied and rehearsed the part; and by the end of the summer, I was prepared to transplant it from the rustic realms of an old farm-house to a cosmopolitan audience, in the city of Washington, where I opened at Carusi's Hall, under the management of John T. Raymond. . . . To be brief, the play was acted with a result that was, to me, both satisfactory and disappointing. I was quite sure that the character was what I had been seeking, and I was equally satisfied that the play was not. The action had neither the body nor the strength to carry the hero; the spiritual quality was there, but the human interest was wanting. This defect was not remedied until five years later, when I met Dion Boucicault, in London. Then, he agreed to rewrite the drama for a consideration agreed upon between us. He never seemed to think much of his labour in this play; but I did, and do still, with good reason. His version was still cast in three acts. Later, I divided the first act into two, making the end of the dance the end of an act, rather than the end of a scene, and enlarged and strengthened it in various ways suggested by my experience. It will thus be seen that the play is by no means the work of one mind, but both as to its narrative and dramatic form, has been often moulded, and by many hands.

Joseph Jefferson, 1895, *Rip Van Winkle as played by*
Joseph Jefferson, Introduction, pp. xii, xiii, xiv, xv

Bracebridge Hall (1822)

The great charm and peculiarity of this work consist now, as on former occasions, in the singular sweetness of the composition, and the mildness of the sentiments,—sicklied over perhaps a little, now and then, with that cloying heaviness into which unvaried sweetness is too apt to subside. The rhythm and melody of the sentences are certainly excessive: As it not only gives an air of mannerism, from its uniformity, but raises too strong an impression of the labour that must have been bestowed, and the importance which must have been attached to that which is, after all, but a secondary attribute to good writing. It is very ill-natured in us, however, to object to what has given us so much pleasure; for we happen to be very intense and sensitive admirers of those soft harmonies of studied speech in which this author is so apt to indulge himself; and have caught ourselves, oftener than we shall confess, neglecting his excellent matter, to lap ourselves in the liquid music of his periods—and letting ourselves float passively down the mellow falls and windings of his soft-flowing sentences, with a delight not inferior to that which we derive from fine versification.

Francis, Lord Jeffrey, 1822-44, *"Bracebridge Hall," Contributions to the Edinburgh Review,* vol. IV, p. 214

As a genial chronicle of upper-class English life and character, nothing better could be asked for. Irving's mannerism had now become inveterate, but it was a mannerism in which well-balanced sentences, genuine humour, faithful descriptions, and hearty morality always had a place. His refinement of style was sometimes excessive, and his readers never completely lose sight of the rhetorician manipulating the printed words.

Charles F. Richardson, 1887, *American Literature,* 1607-1885, vol. I, p. 271

A History of Christopher Columbus (1828)

This is one of those works, which are at the same time the delight of readers and the despair of critics. It is as nearly perfect in its kind, as any work well can be; and there is therefore little or nothing left for the reviewer, but to write at the bottom of every page, as Voltaire said he should be obliged to do if he published a commentary on Racine, *Pulchre! bene! optime!*

Alexander Hill Everett, 1829, "Irving's Life of Columbus," *North American Review,* vol. 28, p. 103

Having access to original and fresh documents relating to the life of Christopher Columbus, he was encouraged and enabled to undertake and execute a great historical work, and on a subject the most rich in details, and the most magnificent in its results, of any that ever employed the pen of the historian. He brought to the task all his great and diversified powers. His materials were selected with judgment, studied with diligence, arranged with skill, exhibited with fidelity, polished with taste and recommended by finished specimens of a graceful, flowing, and dignified composition. The discovery of America was essentially a domestic theme. Though the enterprise was begun in Europe, it was consummated on this side of the Atlantic. The settlement of this New World seems to be a theme peculiarly appropriate to the pen of an American writer, who would naturally feel and appreciate, most deeply and justly, the inestimable value of the discovery, and the mighty consequences of the establishment of great nations on this continent, with their language and institutions, their freedom and religion, their arts and sciences spreading themselves over its surface. The choice was most propitious, and the "History of the Life and Voyages of Columbus" will probably become the standard work on that subject through all succeeding ages. It equals the most distinguished historical compositions, not only in the dignity of the subject, but in the judgment, skill, spirit, and felicity of its execution.

> James Kent, 1832, "Literature, Commerce and Fine Arts,"
> *Memoirs and Letters,* ed. Kent, p. 234

It is open to the charge of too much rhetorical color here and there, and it is at times too diffuse; but its substantial accuracy is not questioned, and the glow of the narrative springs legitimately from the romance of the theme. Irving understood, what our later historians have fully appreciated, the advantage of vivid individual portraiture in historical narrative. His conception of the character and mission of Columbus is largely outlined, but firmly and most carefully executed, and is one of the noblest in literature.

> Charles Dudley Warner, 1881, *Washington Irving*
> (*American Men of Letters*), p. 155

The Conquest of Granada (1829)

Mr. Irving has seldom selected a subject better suited to his peculiar powers than the conquest of Granada. Indeed, it would hardly have been possible for one of his warm sensibilities to linger so long among the remains of Moorish magnificence with which Spain is covered, without being interested in the fortunes of a people whose memory has almost passed into oblivion, but who once preserved the "sacred flame" when it had become extinct in every corner of Christendom, and whose influence is still visible on the intellectual culture of modern Europe.

> William Hickling Prescott, 1829, "Irving's *Conquest of Granada*,"
> *Biographical and Critical Miscellanies,* p. 109

It was long after my acquaintance with his work that I came to a due sense of Irving as an artist, and perhaps I have come to feel a full sense of it only now, when I perceive that he worked willingly only when he worked inventively. At last I can do justice to the exquisite conception of his *Conquest of Granada,* a study of history which, in unique measure, conveys not only the pathos, but the humor of one of the most splendid and impressive situations in the experience of the race. Very possibly something of the severer truth might have been sacrificed to the effect of the pleasing and touching tale, but I do not understand that this was really done.

William Dean Howells, 1895, *My Literary Passions,* p. 32

The Alhambra (1832)

On the whole, we consider the work before us as equal in literary value to any of the others of the same class, with the exception of *The Sketch-Book;* and we should not be surprised if it were read as extensively as even that very popular production. We hope to have it in our power, at no remote period, to announce a continuation of the series, which we are satisfied will bear, in the booksellers' phrase, several more volumes.

Edward Everett, 1832, "Irving's *Alhambra,*"
North American Review, vol. 35, p. 281

To speak of Granada is to speak of the Alhambra, but one falters at describing the vastness and the delicacy of that last effort of the Spanish Moor; one falters at treading in Irving's footsteps even in the humblest way, for he made the place and all its memories so thoroughly his own. The hotel beneath the walls bears his name; his *Tales* are sold by importunate venders; the guide shows the rooms in which he slept with an air of mysterious reverence, and wherever one turns one feels the presence of the American writer who, more than any man, has preserved the memory of the Moor.

H. C. Chatfield-Taylor, 1896, *The Land of the Castanet,* p. 161

Life of Oliver Goldsmith (1840)

Everything combines to make this one of the most fascinating pieces of biography in the English language. Enough is known of the personal history and character of Goldsmith, to tempt us to recur to the subject with fresh interest; but he has not been so bandied about by life-writers and reviewers as to satiate curiosity. The simplicity, and even the weaknesses of his nature, call forth feelings of affection; and the charm of his writings, so unaffected, so naïve, so transparent in their crystal purity of expression, attracts us to more intimate acquaintance with the author. Mr. Irving was in possession of abundant materials to do justice to the subject. He had only to insert his exquisite magnetic needle into the mass, to give a choice and shapely form to all that was valuable in the labors of previous biographers. He has done this in a manner which leaves nothing to be desired.

George Ripley, 1849, *New York Tribune*

For my part, I know of nothing like it. I have read no biographical memoir which carries forward the reader so delightfully and with so little tediousness of recital or reflection. I never take it up without being tempted to wish that Irving had written more works of the kind; but this could hardly be; for where could he have found another Goldsmith?

William Cullen Bryant, 1860, "Washington Irving," *Orations and Addresses*, p. 140

Life of George Washington (1855-59)

Candor, good judgment that knows no bias, the felicity of selections, these are yours in common with the best historians. But, in addition, you have the peculiarity of writing from the heart, enchaining sympathy as well as commanding confidence; the happy magic that makes scenes, events, and personal anecdotes present themselves to you at your bidding, and fall into their natural places and take color and warmth from your own nature. The style, too, is masterly, clear, easy, and graceful; picturesque without mannerism, and ornamented without losing simplicity. Among men of letters, who do well, you must above all take the name of Felix, which so few of the great Roman generals could claim. You do everything rightly, as if by grace; and I am in no fear of offending your modesty, for I think you were elected and foreordained to excel your contemporaries.

George Bancroft, 1855, *To Irving*, May 30; *Life and Letters of Washington Irving*, ed. Irving, vol. IV, p. 194

I referred to his last and chief work, the *Life of Washington* and asked if he felt on finishing it, any such sensation as Gibbon enjoyed over the last sheet of the *Decline and Fall*. He said that the work had engrossed his mind to such a degree that before he was aware, he had written himself into feeble health; that in the midst of his labor he feared he would break down before the end; that when at last the final pages were written, he gave the manuscript to his nephew to conduct it through the press, and threw himself back on his red-cushioned lounge with an indescribable feeling of relief. He explained that the chief fatigue of mind had resulted from care required in the construction and arrangement of materials, and not in the literary composition of the successive chapters.

Theodore Tilton, 1859-69, "A Visit to Washington Irving,"
Sanctum Sanctorum, p. 10

I confess, my admiration of this work becomes the greater the more I examine it. In the other writings of Irving are beauties which strike the reader at once. In this I recognize qualities which lie deeper, and which I was not sure of finding—a rare equity of judgment; a large grasp of the subject; a profound philosophy, independent of philosophical forms, and even instinctively rejecting them; the power of reducing an immense crowd of loose materials to clear and orderly arrangement; and forming them into one grand whole, as a skilful commander, from a rabble of raw recruits, forms a disciplined army, animated and moved by a single will.

William Cullen Bryant, 1860, *Washington Irving,
Orations and Addresses*, p. 145

There are passages in it that for incisiveness of characterization and for finish of form are the equal of anything that he produced in the days when his intellectual vigor was unimpaired; but the reader cannot escape the feeling that the author's grasp of the materials relating to the subject was feeble, and that his heart was not in his work.

Edwin W. Morse, 1897, *Library of the World's Best Literature*,
ed. Warner, vol. XIV, p. 7999

GENERAL

I know Washington Irving well, and when he was here two or three years ago, he promised to me to contribute regularly. The last time I saw him in London he repeated his promises; but he said, when he looked at our "audaciously original Magazine," he did not think he could give anything that could appear to advantage in it. These, of course, were mere phrases; but I do think he has perhaps been rather over-estimated. He is a man of an amiably elegant mind, and what he does do is well conceived and finely polished, but I rather think he is not a person of great originality or strength.

William Blackwood, 1820, *Letter to Maginn*, Oct. 18;
William Blackwood and His Sons, ed. Oliphant, vol. I, p. 378

Mr. Irving has travelled much, has seen many vicissitudes, and has been so thoroughly satiated with fame as to grow slovenly in the performance of his literary tasks. This slovenliness has affected his handwriting. . . . Irving's style is inimitable in its grace and delicacy, yet few of our practised writers are guilty of more frequent inadvertences of language. In what may be termed his mere English, he is surpassed by fifty whom we could name.

Edgar Allan Poe, 1841, *A Chapter on Autography, Works,* ed. Stedman and Woodberry, vol. IX, pp. 190, 229

I don't go up-stairs to bed two nights out of the seven—as a very creditable witness near at hand can testify—I say I do not go to bed two nights out of the seven without taking Washington Irving under my arm; and, when I don't take him, I take his own brother, Oliver Goldsmith.

Charles Dickens, 1842, *Speech at New York Dinner,* Feb. 18; *Speeches and Sayings,* p. 28

The books I have lately been reading are the works of Washington Irving. None of our present writers write such pure English; he reminds me of Addison, but has more genius and a richer invention. Perhaps on the whole he is more like Goldsmith.

Walter Savage Landor, 1863, *To Mrs. Graves-Sawle,* Jan. 19; *Letters,* ed. Wheeler, p. 228

Perhaps, of all American writers, in Washington Irving the polite air of the man of the European world is the most seen; but then, of all American writers, Washington Irving is the one who most sedulously imitated, and most happily caught the spirit of European writers, formed under aristocratic as well as popular influences;—of all American writers he is thus the least American.

Edward Bulwer-Lytton, Lord Lytton, 1863-68, *Caxtoniana, Miscellaneous Prose Works,* vol. III, p. 491

Irving might have walked arm-in-arm with Addison, and Addison would have run no risk of being discomposed by a trans-Atlantic twang in his companion's accent. Irving, if he betrays his origin at all, betrays it somewhat in the same way as Longfellow, by his tender, satisfied repose in the venerable, chiefly the venerable in English society and manners, by his quiet delight in the implicit tradition of English civility, the scarcely-felt yet everywhere influential presence of a beautiful and grave Past, and the company of unseen beneficent associations.

Edward Dowden, 1878, *Studies in Literature,* p. 470

The poet and romancer give back more than they borrow from the scenes which lend them their inspiration. What was this broad stream that runs by your walls before it was peopled by the creative touch of your story-teller's imagination? It is no longer Hudson's river,—it is Irving's. The trumpet of Anthony Van Corlear still rings over the wide expanse of the Tappan Zee. The rolling balls of the old nine-pin-players are still heard by the voyager, thundering in the far-off Kaatskills. There is not a brook that tumbles into the river which does not babble the name of Irving, not a wave which does not murmur its remembrance. I walk through thronged thoroughfares, and all at once my fancy carries me back to the days and scenes of Irving's New Amsterdam. The pavement becomes a great turf, a few scattered houses show their gables here and there. One stands apart, more lordly than the rest. What is this sound I hear from the stoop that stretches along its side? It is a strange sound to be heard through all this tumult, but I must be half dreaming. Hark! Abrupt, intermittent, rhythmical, resonant, emphatic; it must be,—it is,—the wooden leg of brave, peppery, pugnacious, irrepressible old Peter Stuyvesant,—Hard Koppig Piet,—the hard-headed, hot-hearted, one-legged but two-fisted Governor of this ancient Manhattan, already a flourishing settlement with burgarmeesters and schepens in place of aldermen and constables. Sagacious old Dutchmen, to fix on this tongue of land,—a tongue that laps up the cream of commerce of a continent.

Oliver Wendell Holmes, 1883, "Irving's Power of Idealization,"
The Critic, vol. 3, p. 138

If the Hudson is to us something more than a mere waterway and convenient natural agency for "moving the crops to tide-water"; if the Catskills are something more than a good place for establishing summer hotels, it is to Irving that the fact is due. If there is a touch of poetry, or romance, or human interest, about the background of New York, a mellow suggestion of myth and superstition, a legendary halo that soothes the sight tortured by the flaring, garish noon of our materialism, it is Irving who put it there.

A. G. Sedgwick, 1883, "Washington Irving,"
The Nation, vol. 36, p. 292

Unluckily, something more than extreme amiability, even when combined with the soundest sense, is necessary to the attainment of greatness in literature; and it is a fact that Washington Irving went far to blast the rich promise of his natural parts, and to render his admirable equipment of no avail by his blind and obstinate devotion to an obsolete and exploded convention. He did well to study Addison, Goldsmith, and Sterne with profound attention. He did very ill to imitate them with a fidelity as servile as it is ridiculous. No excellence was too great, no mannerism too trivial for him to mimic. Types of character and tricks of style, modes of thought and turns of phrase, all are appropriated and reproduced with the most painful exactitude. And they suffer sadly in the process. Pleasing and pertinent reflections become chilly and colourless platitudes; while exquisite humour is transformed into a laboured archness. . . . One crowded hour of Sir Walter Scott's careless and often slovenly prose is worth an age of Washington Irving's insipidities; and a single "tow-row" of Mr. Stevenson's thunder is infinitely more alarming than all the storms in which the clouds "roll in volumes over the mountain tops," the rain "begins to patter down in broad and scattered drops," the wind "freshens," the lightning "leaps from cloud to cloud," the peals "are echoed from mountain to mountain," and, in short, all the elements go through their appropriate and stereotyped evolutions with the punctuality, precision, and tameness of clock-work. The bones of the skeleton, to employ a familiar metaphor, are adjusted with the utmost nicety and correctness, but they have lost the potentiality of life. On the other hand, it is to be said, that the close study of such writers as Washington Irving selected for his models could scarce be barren of all good result; that if he never rises to animation he never sinks below a tolerably high standard of elegance; and that he everywhere preserves a spotless purity of idiom.

J. H. Millar, 1896, *English Prose*, ed. Craik, vol. V, pp. 233, 234

When a writer has won the title of the Father of American Literature—a name conventionally given to Washington Irving—it becomes plain that he is very important as a figure in our native development in letters. . . . Viewed in relation to current production in history or to what had already been done, he is seen to have possessed the instinct and habit of the true historian, the modern workman. I mean that he went to the sources and spared neither time nor labor in getting together his materials. Witness the years spent in the libraries and other repositories of Spain, when he was working on his *Columbus* and other main books. The result is that, in spite of the enormous amount of research since expended upon the Italian whose name is associated with our country's discovery, the Irving biography is confessedly a standard one to-day, and this quite aside from its literary merits. . . . His manner of writing as a whole, in its unobtrusive breeding and beauty, is admirable, and may well be put before us as a model of the kind of effect it aims for. It is especially valuable at the present time for its lack of strain, its avoidance of violence or bizarre effects, when our later writers incline to hunt for startling words and queer constructions; anything to excite and seem "original." Irving's style impresses one as a whole, rather than in particulars,—and that is the higher art.

Richard Burton, 1898, *Literary Likings*, pp. 249, 253, 266

JAMES HENRY LEIGH HUNT
1784-1859

Born, at Southgate, 19 Oct. 1784. At Christ's Hospital School, 1792-99. Contrib. to *Juvenile Library*, 1801; to *European Mag.*, 1801; to *Poetical Register*, 1801-11; to *The Traveller*, 1804-05. Clerk to his brother Stephen, 1803[?]-05. Dramatic critic to *The News* (started by his brother John), 1805. Clerkship in War Office, 1806[?]-08. Edited *The Examiner*, 1808-21; frequently contributed afterwards. Married Marianne Kent, 3 July 1809. Edited *The Reflector*, 1810. Imprisoned in Surrey gaol, for remarks in *Examiner* on Prince Regent, 3 Feb. 1813 to 3 Feb. 1815. Settled at Hampstead, 1816. Friendship with Shelley and Keats. Edited *The Indicator*, Oct. 1819 to March 1821. Edited, and wrote, *The Literary Pocket-Book*, 1819-22. Sailed for Italy, 15 Nov. 1821, but driven by storm to land at Dartmouth. Sailed again, May 1822; arrived at Leghorn, June. Contrib. to *New Monthly Mag.*, 1821-50. Edited *The Liberal* (with Shelley and Byron), 1822-23. To Genoa with Byron, Sept. 1822. In Florence, 1823-25. Edited *The Literary Examiner*, 1823. Returned to England, Sept. 1825. Lived at Highgate, 1825-28. Edited *The Companion*, Jan. to July, 1828. Contrib. to *The Keepsake*, 1828. Lived at Epsom, 1828-30[?]. Edited *The Chat of the Week*, June to Aug., 1830. Edited (and wrote) *The Tatler*, 4 Sept. 1830 to 13 Feb. 1832. Lived in Chelsea, 1833-40. Contrib. to *Tait's Mag.*, 1833; to *Monthly Chronicle*, Oct. 1838 to Feb. 1839. Edited *Leigh Hunt's London Journal*, 1834 to Dec. 1835; *The Monthly Repository*, July 1837 to April 1838. Contrib. to *Musical World*, Jan. to March, 1839. Lived in Kensington, 1840-53. Play, *A Legend of Florence*, produced at Covent Garden, 7 Feb. 1840. Contrib. to *Westminster Rev.*, 1837; to *Edinburgh Review*, 1841-44; to *Ainsworth's Mag.*, 1845; to *Atlas*, 1846; etc. Crown Pension of £200, Oct. 1847. Edited *Leigh Hunt's Journal*, 1850-51. Lived in Hammersmith, 1853-59. Contrib. to *Musical Times*, 1853-54; to *Household Words*, 1853-54; to *Fraser's Mag.*, 1858-59; to *Spectator*, Jan. to Aug. 1859. Died, at Putney, 28 Aug. 1859. Buried in Kensal Green Cemetery. WORKS: *Juvenilia*, 1801; *Classic Tales* (5 vols.), 1806-07; *Critical Essays on the Performers of the London Theatres* (from *The News*), 1807; *An Attempt to show the Folly . . . of Methodism* (anon., from *Examiner*), 1809; *Reformist's Reply to the Edinburgh Review*, 1810; *The Feast of the Poets* (anon.), 1814; *The Descent of Liberty*, 1815; *The Story of Rimini*, 1816; *The Round Table* (with Hazlitt, from *Examiner*, 2 vols.), 1817; *Foliage*, 1818; *Hero and Leander*, 1819; *Bacchus and Ariadne*, 1819; *Poetical Works*, 1819; *The Literary Pocket-Book* (4 vols.), 1819-22; *The Months* (selected from vol. I of preceding), 1821; *Ultra-Crepidarius*, 1823; *Lord Byron and some of his Contemporaries*, 1828; *The Companion*, 1828; *The Tatler*, 1830-32; *Christianism* (anon.; priv. ptd.), 1832 (enlarged edn. called: *The Religion of the Head*, 1853); *Poetical Works*, 1832; *Sir Ralph Esher*, 1832; *The Indicator and the Companion* (2 vols.), 1834; *Captain Sword and Captain Pen*, 1835; *The Seer*, 1840-41; *The Palfrey*, 1842; *One Hundred Romances of Real Life* (from *Leigh Hunt's London Journal*), 1843; *Poetical Works*, 1844; *Imagination and Fancy*, 1844; *Wit and Humour selected from the English Poets*, 1846; *Stories from the Italian Poets* (2 vols.), 1846; *A*

Saunter through the West-End (from *Atlas*), 1847; *Men, Women and Books* (2 vols.), 1847; *A Jar of Honey from Mount Hybla,* 1848; *The Town* (2 vols.), 1848; *A Book for a Corner,* 1849; *Readings for Railways,* 1849; *Autobiography* (3 vols.), 1850; (later edns., expanded 1859 and 1860); *Table-Talk,* 1851; *The Religion of the Heart,* 1853; *The Old Court Suburb,* 1855; *Stories in Verse,* 1855; *Poetical Works* (Boston, 2 vols.), 1857. POSTHUMOUS: *Poetical Works,* ed. by his son, 1860; *Correspondence,* 1862; *Tale for a Chimney Corner,* 1869; *Day by the Fire,* 1870; *Wishing Cap Papers* (from *Examiner*), 1873. He *translated:* Tasso's *Amyntas,* 1820; F. Redi's *Bacchus in Tuscany,* 1825; and *edited:* Shelley's *Masque of Anarchy,* 1832; Sheridan's Dramatic Works, 1840; The Dramatic Works of Wycherley, Congreve, Vanbrugh and Farquhar, 1840; Chaucer's Poems Modernized (with Horne and others), 1841; T. Hunt's *Foster Brother,* 1845; *Finest Scenes* from Beaumont and Fletcher, 1855; *The Book of the Sonnet* (with S. A. Lee, *posthumous*), 1867. LIFE: *Autobiography,* 1850, etc., *Life,* by Cosmo Monkhouse, 1893.

R. Farquharson Sharp, 1897, *A Dictionary of
English Authors,* p. 142

SEE: *Poetical Works,* ed. Humphrey S. Milford, 1923; *Essays and Poems,* ed. R. B. Johnson, 1891, 2 v.; [Selected] *Essays,* ed. J. B. Priestley, 1929; *Dramatic Criticism,* ed. L. H. and Carolyn W. Houtchens, 1949; *Autobiography,* ed. J. E. Morpurgo, 1949; Edmund Blunden, *Leigh Hunt and His Circle,* 1930.

PERSONAL

What though, for showing truth to flatter'd state,
Kind Hunt was shut in prison, yet has he,
In his immortal spirit, been as free
As the sky-searching lark, and as elate.
Minion of grandeur! think you he did wait?
Think you he nought but prison-walls did see,
Till, so unwilling, thou unturn'dst the key?
Ah, no! far happier, nobler was his fate!
In Spenser's halls he stray'd, and bowers fair,
Culling enchanted flowers; and he flew
With daring Milton through the fields of air:
To regions of his own his genius true
Took happy flights. Who shall his fame impair
When thou art dead, and all thy wretched crew?

John Keats, 1815, *Written on the Day that
Mr. Leigh Hunt left Prison*

Leigh Hunt's weather-cock estimation of you I cannot account for, nor is it worth while to attempt. He first attacks you when he had never read your works; then a friend, Barnes, brought him your "Excursion," pointed out your sonnets, and Leigh Hunt began to find that he really should have looked through a poet's works before he came to a conclusion on the genius displayed in them. . . . When first I knew Leigh Hunt, he was really a delightful fellow, ardent in virtue, and perceiving the right thing in everything but religion—he now finds "no end in wandering mazes lost," perplexes himself, and pains his friends. His great error is inordinate personal vanity, and he who pampers it not, is no longer received with affection. I am daily getting more estranged from him; and, indeed, all his old friends are dropping off.

Benjamin Robert Haydon, 1817, To Wordsworth, April 15;
Life, Letters and Table Talk, ed. Stoddard, pp. 196, 197

Leigh Hunt is a good man and a good father—see his Odes to all the Masters Hunt;—a good husband—see his sonnet to Mrs. Hunt;—a good friend—see his Epistles to different people;—and a great coxcomb and a very vulgar person in everything about him. But that is not his fault, but of circumstances.

Lord Byron, 1818, Letter to Mr. Moore, June 1

Had I known a person more highly endowed than yourself with all that it becomes a man to possess, I had solicited for this work the ornament of his name. One more gentle, honorable, innocent and brave; one of the most exalted toleration for all who do and think evil, and yet himself more free from evil; one who knows better how to receive and how to confer a benefit, though he must ever confer far more than he can receive; one of simpler, and, in the highest sense of the word, of purer life and manners, I never knew.

Percy Bysshe Shelley, 1819, The Cenci, Dedication to Leigh Hunt

In spite of *Rimini,* I must look upon its author as a man of taste and a poet. He is better than so; he is one of the most cordial-minded men I ever knew, and matchless as a fireside companion. I mean not to affront or wound your feelings when I say that in his more genial moods he has often reminded me of you. There is the same air of mild dogmatism—the same condescending to a boyish sportiveness—in both your conversations. His hand-writing is so much the same with your own, that I have opened more than one letter of his, hoping, nay, not doubting, but it was from you, and have been disappointed (he will bear with my saying so) at the discovery of my error. L. H. is unfortunate in holding some loose and not very definite speculations (for at times I think he hardly knows whither his premises would carry him) on marriage—the tenets, I conceive, of the *Political Justice* carried a little farther. For anything I could discover in his practice, they have reference, like those, to some future possible condition of society, and not to the present times. But neither for these obliquities of thinking (upon which my own conclusions are as distant as the poles asunder)—not for his political asperities and petulancies, which are wearing out with the heats and vanities of youth—did I select him for a friend; but for qualities which fitted him for that relation.

Charles Lamb, 1823, *The Tombs in the Abbey,*
in a Letter to Robert Southey, Esq.

He is a man of thoroughly London make, such as you could not find elsewhere, and I think about the *best* possible to be made of this sort: an airy, crotchety, most copious clever talker, with an honest undercurrent of reason too, but unfortunately not the deepest, not the most practical—or rather it is the most *un*practical ever man dealt in. His hair is grizzled, eyes black-hazel, complexion of the clearest dusky brown; a thin glimmer of a smile plays over a face of cast-iron gravity. He never laughs—can only titter, which I think indicates his worst deficiency. . . . His house excels all you have read of,—a poetical *Tinkerdom,* without parallel even in literature. In his family room, where are a sickly large wife and a whole shoal of well-conditioned wild children, you will find half a dozen old rickety chairs gathered from half a dozen different hucksters, and all seemingly engaged, and just pausing, in a violent hornpipe. On these and around them and over the dusty table and ragged carpet lie all kinds of litter,—books, papers, egg-shells, scissors, and last night when I was there the torn heart of a half-quarter loaf. His own room above stairs, into which alone I strive to enter, he keeps cleaner. It has only two chairs, a bookcase, and a writing-table; yet the noble Hunt receives you in his Tinkerdom in the spirit of a king, apologises for nothing, places you in the best seat, takes a window-sill himself if there is no other, and there folding closer his looseflowing "muslin cloud" of a printed nightgown, in which he always writes, commences the liveliest dialogue on philosophy and the prospects of man (who is to be beyond measure "happy" yet); which again he will courteously terminate the moment you are bound to go: a most interesting, pitiable, lovable man, to be used kindly but with discretion.

Thomas Carlyle, 1834, *To Alexander Carlyle,* June 27;
Thomas Carlyle, A History of the First Forty Years
of His Life, ed. Froude, vol. II, p. 354

One characteristic of Leigh Hunt, for which few gave him credit, was his great capacity for work. His writings were the result of immense labor and painstaking, of the most conscientious investigation of facts, where facts were needed; and of a complete devotion of his faculties towards the object to be accomplished. Notwithstanding his great experience, he was never a very rapid writer. He corrected, excised, reconsidered, and elaborated his productions (unless pressed for time), with the most minute attention to details.

Edmund Ollier, (?) 1859, Spectator, Sept. 3

Four or five years ago, the writer of these lines was much pained by accidentally encountering a printed statement, that Mr. Leigh Hunt was the original of Harold Skimpole in Bleak House. . . . The fact is this:—Exactly those graces and charms of manner which are remembered in the words we have quoted, were remembered by the author of the work of fiction in question, when he drew the character in question. Above all other things, that "sort of gay and ostentatious wilfulness" in the humoring of a subject, which had many a time delighted him, and impressed him as being unspeakably whimsical and attractive, was the airy quality he wanted for the man he invented. Partly for this reason, and partly (he has since often grieved to think) for the pleasure it afforded him to find that delightful manner reproducing itself under his hand, he yielded to the temptation of too often making the character speak like his old friend. He no more thought—God forgive him! that the admired original would ever be charged with the imaginary vices of the fictitious creature, than he has himself ever thought of charging the blood of Desdemona and Othello, on the innocent Academy model who sat for Iago's leg in the picture.

Charles Dickens, 1859, "Leigh Hunt," All the Year Round,
vol. 2, p. 207

He was held up to shame as an enemy of religion, whereas he was a man from whose heart there came a flowing pity spreading itself over all nature and in every channel in which it was possible to run. I remember a passage in one of his writings in which he says he never passed a church, of however unreformed a faith, without an instinctive wish to go in and worship for the good of mankind. And all this obloquy, all this injustice, all this social cruelty never for one moment soured the disposition or excited a revengeful feeling in the breast of this good man. He had as it were— I have no other phrase for it—a superstition of good. He did not believe in the existence of evil, and when it pressed against him, in the bitterest form against himself, he shut his eyes to it. . . . We know that through all the difficulties of a more than usually hard life he kept to the end a cheerfulness of temper which the most successful might have envied.

Richard Monckton Milnes (Lord Houghton), 1869, An Address

To be seated at the same table with Leigh Hunt was, I thought, like seeing Byron and Shelley by reflected light; and I could not but watch, with a curiosity amounting almost to awe, every movement of his face, and every word that fell from his lips. True, I soon discovered that, after all, he was but a mortal man, and that, despite the history of his past career, he talked and acted as a being of ordinary instincts rather than as one who might be supposed to have wings to fly with. Still I was constantly reminded of the indisputable fact that Leigh Hunt was "somebody," and that I was assuredly complimented in being brought into such close companionship with him. I hardly dare venture to describe his personal appearance, further than to say he *looked* the man of that refined intellectual power which had given him his place in the literature of his time; that his complexion seemed strangely to harmonize with his hair (for he wore no whiskers, and moustaches at that time had not found their way to this country), in one uniform tint of iron-gray; and that his shirt-collar ascended from his neck in a *négligé* manner, which might be considered slovenly, but which was picturesquely effective in its loose luxuriance. There was, moreover, a sort of valetudinarian air about him, and he appeared extremely particular as to what he ate and drank, preferring, he said, the mildest form of nutriment, such as he was accustomed to at home—"just the wing of a chicken," and "only a moderate quantity of sherry and water" being especially demanded. . . . At length our host prevailed upon his distinguished visitor himself to "favor us with a tune"—a knowledge of music being known to be one of Mr. Hunt's accomplishments. With this request he most readily complied, and good-humoredly observed, "I will give you a favorite *barcarolle* which I was in the habit of playing to Birron and Shelley in Italy" (he pronounced the first name as if it were spelt as I have written it—with two rr's and the "i" short). He executed the task with a spirit and delicacy which could hardly have been expected from an amateur who had passed the greater part of his days in the cultivation of literature.

George Hodder, 1870, *Memories of My Time*

As to Leigh Hunt's friendship for Keats, I think the points you mention loom equivocal, but Hunt was a many-laboured and much belaboured man, and as much allowance as may be made on this score is perhaps due to him—no more than that much. His own powers stand high in various ways—poetically higher perhaps than is at present admitted, despite his detestable flutter and airiness for the most part. But assuredly by no means could he have stood so high in the long run, as by a loud and earnest defence of Keats. Perhaps the best excuse for him is the remaining possibility of an idea on his part, that any defence coming from one who had himself so many powerful enemies might seem to Keats rather to damage than improve his position.

Dante Gabriel Rossetti, 1880, Letter; Recollections of Rossetti,
ed. Caine, p. 179

Though Leigh Hunt's character was simple and his gifts distinct, he is not easy to class either as an author or a man. His literary pretensions were well summed up by Charles Lamb in the couplet:—

> "Wit, poet, proseman, partyman, translator,
> Hunt, thy best title yet is 'Indicator.' "

With a nature filled with poetry, but yet most faulty as a poet; learned beyond the average, but hardly a scholar; full of sweet thoughts, but no thinker; vivacious and sportive to an extraordinary degree, yet falling short of supreme qualities as a humourist, Leigh Hunt scarcely attained to the first rank of writers, except as a sentimentalist, an anthologist, and a gossip, yet he so nearly touched it at so many points, and there is such a special quality in almost everything he wrote, that one hesitates to set him in a duller circle.

Cosmo Monkhouse, 1893, Life of Leigh Hunt
(Great Writers), p. 238

The Story of Rimini (1816)

This poem should be read twice to form a just opinion of its merits; the unusual, and in many places, the awkward versification will be apt to disgust the reader; we found more pleasure in the second perusal than the first. It contains some exquisite expressions of sentiment, and many passages that show an accurate and nice observation of the most delicate emotions of the human heart; the author also discovers a fine perception of harmony, in choosing the seasons and the picturesque circumstances of landscape, to accompany the joyous and painful feelings of the human breast. Many persons have judged that Lord Byron must possess a bad heart, because he delights in painting the bad and violent passions almost exclusively. By the same rule, Mr. Hunt should be presumed to have a most amiable character, since he so frequently describes frankness, openness, cheerfulness, &c. He does this almost to satiety; and there is a repetition of such description that becomes insipid.

W. Tudor, 1816, "Rimini," North American Review, vol. 3, p. 281

The poem has many pleasing, and some very sweet lines, but by endeavouring to be singular, or to exhibit somewhat of a novelty in his verse, he has introduced expressions and phrases that do not fall harmoniously upon the English ear. I mean they want that natural flow and those verbal combinations which are most pleasing. Some one, I remember, attacked his use of the word "swirl,"—

"—Swirl into the bay."

If this were the only objection to the structure and language of a poem that contains many fine lines, with what may be called here and there a concetto, it would be indeed hypercritical to notice them. Whoever has seen a vessel with a gentle breeze and strong tide in her favour run into a bay and anchor, will feel how very descriptive of the actual fact the word he thus used.

> Cyrus Redding, 1867, *Personal Reminiscences of Eminent Men,* vol. II, p. 202

He never realised the proper dignity of poetry, and in discarding monotony, became slipshod. Hard polish was replaced by limp jerkiness, and the couplet in his hands grew pert and garrulous. There are beautiful passages in the poem worthy of the great reform to be inaugurated, but they are few and far between. In the matter of language, again, he could not *maintain* a high standard. His very simplicity was in part artificial, and he had a singular taste for giving ordinary words an original significance which ruined his phrases, though it never made him obscure. The poem was considerably revised, but the changes related principally to the final development of the plot and are not all improvements. In old age Leigh Hunt referred to *Rimini* as the work of a "Tyro," but it does not contain any signs of youth from which he was afterwards exempt, and reaches as high a level as any of his longer pieces. It proves conclusively that he was not, in the highest sense, a poet.

> Reginald Brimley Johnson, 1896, *Leigh Hunt,* p. 95

Autobiography (1850-60)

Well, I call this an excellent good book, by far the best of the autobiographic kind I remember to have read in the English language; and, indeed, except it be Boswell's of Johnson, I do not know where we have such a picture drawn of human life as in these three volumes.

> Thomas Carlyle, 1850, *Letter to Leigh Hunt,* Jan. 17;
> *Thomas Carlyle* by Conway, p. 208

His *Autobiography* is brimming with expressions of good will to all mankind, and frank confession of youthful offences. His philanthropic sentiment was overflowing. Uncle Toby was his ideal—"divine Uncle Toby."

"He who created Uncle Toby was the wisest man since the days of Shakespeare." "As long as the character of Toby Shandy finds an echo in the heart of man, the heart of man is noble." In point of style, his model was Addison. In simplicity and felicitous grace of expression he may be contrasted with the more robust and careless vigour predominant in the early days of the *Edinburgh Review* and *Blackwood*. He particularly excels in the graceful touches of humorous caricature.

> William Minto, 1872-80, *A Manual of English
> Prose Literature*, p. 541

One of the most interesting books ever written is Leigh Hunt's biography of himself,—an autobiography almost unequaled. It is a book that ought to be read by all who wish to get authentic information of Hunt's contemporaries. It abounds in pen portraits of many writers who have long ago passed into fame.

> James T. Fields, 1885, "Recollections of Leigh Hunt," *Some Noted
> Princes, Authors, and Statesmen of Our Time*, ed. Parton, p. 140

POEMS

His self-delusions are very lamentable—they have enticed him into a Situation which I should be less eager after than that of a galley Slave. . . . There is no greater Sin after the seven deadly than to flatter oneself into an idea of being a great Poet.

> John Keats, 1817, *To Benjamin Robert Haydon*, May 11;
> *Letters of John Keats*, ed. Colvin, p. 15

One of Hunt's most apparent characteristics is his cheerfulness. His temperament is obviously mercurial. His fondness for the gayer class of Italian writers indicates a sympathy with southern buoyancy not often encountered in English poetry. His versification is easy and playful; too much so, indeed, for imposing effect. He seems to have written generally under the inspiration of high animal spirits. His sentiment is lively and tender, rather than serious and impressive. The reviewers have censured him with rather too much severity for occasional affectations. With a few exceptions on this score his *Story of Rimini* is a charming poem. *The Legend of Florence,* written at a later period, is one of the most original and captivating of modern plays. Many of his "Epistles" glow with a genial humour and spirit of fellowship which betray fine social qualities. He lives obviously in his affections, and cultivates literature with refined taste rather than with lukewarm assiduity.

> Rufus Wilmot Griswold, 1844, *The Poets and Poetry
> of England in the Nineteenth Century*, p. 194

Leigh Hunt's distinction as a poet is to be inspired by pleasure which never steals from his senses the freshness of boyhood, and never darkens his heart with the shadow of unsatisfied desire. . . . His poetry was not the poetry of thought and passion—which we have in Shakespeare; nor—to use Leigh Hunt's own words—that of "scholarship and rapt ambition," which we have in Milton. He would have passed his whole life writing eternal new stories in verse, part grave, part gay, of no great length, but "just sufficient," he says, "to vent the pleasure with which I am stung on meeting with some touching adventure, and which haunts me till I can speak of it somehow."

Edward Dowden, 1880, English Poets, ed. Ward,
vol. IV, pp. 340, 341

He wrote no great poems, to be sure; for here, as in his prose, he is earnestly bent on carving little baskets out of cherry-stones—little figures on cherry-stones—dainty hieroglyphics, but always on cherry-stones!

Donald G. Mitchell, 1897, English Lands, Letters and Kings.
The Later Georges to Victoria, p. 147

Hunt was the first who seriously set himself to tell a tale in Chaucer's manner, to imitate his sprightly familiarity, his genial unconstraint. He only succeeded in showing how rare and difficult a thing that Chaucerian grace of manner is. He is unconstrained enough, but his unconstraint, though not without moments of charm, is apt to recall the slovenly ease of an underbred man. He is at his best in describing scenery; for the human drama and its tragic climax he lacks sinew; the concentrated pathos of Dante dissolves away in his hands into a tender romantic dream. Nor did Hunt attempt to reproduce the dramatic element in the telling, which was Chaucer's final and most brilliant contribution to the Tale.

Charles Harold Herford, 1902, English Tales in Verse,
Introduction, p. liii

GENERAL

I was employed looking over law papers all the forenoon; I then walked in the rain to Clapton, reading by the way the *Indicator*. There is a spirit of enjoyment in this little work which gives a charm to it. Leigh Hunt seems the very opposite of Hazlitt. He loves everything, and, excepting that he has a few polemical antipathies, finds everything beautiful.

Henry Crabb Robinson, 1820, Diary, Oct. 29;
Diary, Reminiscences and Correspondence, ed. Sadler

A more amiable man in society I know not; nor (when he will allow his senses to prevail over his sectarian principles) a better writer.

Lord Byron, 1821, *A Second Letter on Bowles's Strictures on Pope*

Few men have effected so much by mere exquisiteness of taste in the absence of high creative power; fewer still, so richly endowed with taste, have so frequently and conspicuously betrayed the want of it. . . . This observation principally refers to his poetry, which, in spite of such vexatious flaws, nevertheless possesses a brightness, animation, artistic symmetry, and metrical harmony which lift the author out of the rank of minor poets, particularly when the influence of his example upon his contemporaries is taken into account. He excelled especially in narrative poetry. . . . As an appreciative critic, whether literary or dramatic, he is hardly equalled; his guidance is as safe as it is genial. The no less important vocation of a censor was uncongenial to his gentle nature, and was rarely essayed by him.

Richard Garnett, 1881, *Encyclopædia Britannica,*
Ninth Ed., vol. XII

His strength lies, as he himself suspected, in the brief narrative poems of which "Abou Ben Adhem" is the highest example. Here the impulse is from without, the lines are prompted by the enjoyment of a "tale that is told," and by the desire to express and impart that pleasure. The critical powers guide the creative, and lend them a vigour not their own. His manner at such times is simple and lucid, playful or tender according to circumstances, but always sincere and glowing. His ear, so keen for judgment, directs the rhythm, and makes the verse flowing and easy. His many admirable translations are composed in the same spirit. A loyal enthusiasm for the original prompts him to a rare fidelity in language and style, often achieved with marked success. Could Hunt have *maintained* these qualities of taste and self-control for any considerable period, he might have taken high rank as a poet. . . . He lacks passion, dignity, and restraint, his imagination is almost entirely fanciful; but by the winning charm of his own fresh and cultured personality he attracts and even occasionally subdues.

Reginald Brimley Johnson, 1896, *Leigh Hunt,* pp. 104, 105

When Leigh Hunt commenced to write essays, he was plainly under the spell of a past age, and the *Connoisseur* was admittedly his model. Nor did he ever wholly succeed in throwing off the faded garments of the eighteenth century, and there is always present in his style a touch of archaism which makes one rank him with the earlier essayists rather than with his own vigorous contemporaries. In 1812 he was known only as an unusually capable dramatic critic, and it was not till seven years later that he began in the *Indicator* to revive the essay on the lines of Addison and Goldsmith. He cannot, however, be placed in the first rank of English essayists. In all his work there is a lack of virility, and he had no special endowment of pathos or of humour. When it is said that he could write commonplace gracefully, his merits and defects are summarized. His essays bear nowhere the impress of a strong personality, they contain no fresh creations, and they scarcely ever deviate from one level of unemotional calm. Yet he had indubitable skill in writing on familiar subjects, and he wielded a simple style that on rare occasions became even eloquent.

J. H. Lobban, 1896, ed. *English Essays,* Introduction, p. liv

ELIZABETH BARRETT BROWNING
1806-1861

Born (Elizabeth Barrett Moulton-Barrett), at Coxhoe, co. Durham, 6 March 1806. Early life at Hope End, Herefordshire. Delicate health owing to accident to spine while at Hope End. Poem, *Battle of Marathon,* printed for her by her father, 1820. First publication, 1826. At Sidmouth, 1831-33. First contrib. to *Athenæum,* 1 July 1837. Contrib. to *Finden's Tableaux,* same year. To Torquay for health, 1838; brother drowned there, 11 July 1840. Returned to London, summer of 1841. Married to Robert Browning, 12 Sept. 1846. To Paris and Italy. Settled in Florence, winter of 1847. Son born, 9 March 1849. Visit to Rome, 1850; to England, 1851; winter and spring in Paris; to London summer of 1852; return to Florence in autumn. Winter of 1853-54 in Rome. Visit to Normandy, July 1858. To Rome, winter of 1859-60, and 1860-61. Died, at Florence, 29 June 1861. WORKS: *An Essay on Mind* (anon.), 1826; *Prometheus Bound,* 1833; *The Seraphim,* 1838; *Poems* (2 vols.), 1844 (reprinted at New York as *A Drama of Exile, etc.,* 1845); *The Runaway Slave at Pilgrim's Point,* 1849; *Casa Guidi Windows,* 1851; *Two Poems: by E. Barrett and R. Browning,* 1854; *Aurora Leigh,* 1857 [1856]; *Poems before Congress,* 1860. POST-HUMOUS: *Last Poems,* 1862; *The Greek Christian Poets and the English Poets,* 1863; *Selected Poems,* ed. by Robert Browning (2nd series), 1866, 1880; *Letters to R. H. Horne* (2 vols.), 1877 [1876]; *Earlier Poems, 1826-33,* 1877 [1878]; *The Battle of Marathon* (in type-facsimile, privately printed), 1891. She *edited:* Chaucer's Works (with R. H. Horne and others), 1841. COLLECTED WORKS: (2 vols.), New York, 1871; London, 1890. LIFE: by J. H. Ingram ("Eminent Women" series), 1888.

R. Farquharson Sharp, 1897, *A Dictionary of English Authors,* p. 34

SEE: *Complete Works,* ed. C. Porter and H. A. Clarke, 1900, 6 v.; *Complete Poetical Works,* ed. H. W. Preston, 1900 (Cambridge ed.); *New*

Poems of Robert Browning and Elizabeth Barrett Browning, ed. F. G. Kenyon, 1915; *Letters of Robert Browning and Elizabeth Barrett Browning, 1845-1846,* ed. R. W. B. Browning, 1926, 2 v.; *Letters To B. R. Haydon,* ed. M. H. Shackford, 1939; M. H. Shackford, *E. B. Browning; R. H. Horne: Two Studies,* 1935; Dorothy Hewlett, *Elizabeth Barrett Browning,* 1952; also see Rudolph Besier, *The Barretts of Wimpole Street* (drama), 1930, and Virginia Woolf, *Flush: A Biography,* 1933 (Flush was the name of Elizabeth's dog).

Personal

I read without principle. I have a sort of unity indeed, but it amalgamates instead of selecting—do you understand? When I had read the Hebrew Bible, from Genesis to Malachi, right through, and was never stopped by the Chaldee—and the Greek poets, and Plato, right through from end to end—I passed as thoroughly through the flood of all possible and impossible British and foreign novels and romances, with slices of metaphysics laid thick between the sorrows of the multitudinous Celestinas. It is only useful knowledge and the multiplication table I never tried hard at. And now—what now? Is this matter of exultation? Alas, no! Do I boast of my omnivorousness of reading, even apart from the romances? Certainly no!—never, except in joke. It's against my theories and ratiocinations, which take upon themselves to assert that we *all* generally err by *reading too much,* and out of proportion to what we *think.* I should be wiser, I am persuaded, if I had not read half as much—should have had stronger and better exercised faculties, and should stand higher in my own appreciation. The fact is, that the *ne plus ultra* of intellectual indolence is this reading of books. It comes next to what the Americans call "whittling."

Elizabeth Barrett Browning, 1843, *Letters of Elizabeth Barrett Browning addressed to Richard Hengist Horne,* Dec. 20; Letter lvii

Probably no living individual has a more extensive and diffuse acquaintance with literature—that of the present day inclusive—than Miss Barrett. Although she has read Plato, in the original, from beginning to end, and the Hebrew Bible from Genesis to Malachi (nor suffered her course to be stopped by the Chaldean), yet there is not probably a single good romance of the most romantic kind in whose marvellous and impossible scenes she has not delighted, over the fortunes of whose immaculate or incredible heroes and heroines she has not wept; nor a clever novel or fanciful sketch of our own day over the brightest pages of which she has not smiled inwardly, or laughed outright, just as their authors themselves would have desired.

Richard Hengist Horne, 1844, *A New Spirit of the Age*

I have also here a poet and poetess—two celebrities who have run away
and married under circumstances peculiarly interesting, and such as render
imprudence the height of prudence. Both excellent; but God help them!
for I know not how the two poet heads and poet hearts will get on through
this prosaic world. I think it possible I may go on to Italy with them.

> Anna Jameson, 1846, *Letter from Paris,* Sept.;
> *Memoirs,* ed. Macpherson, p. 228

She is little, hard-featured, with long, dark ringlets, a pale face, and
plaintive voice—something very impressive in her dark eyes and her brow.
Her general aspect puts me in mind of Mignon—what Mignon might be in
maturity and maternity.

> Sara Coleridge, 1851, *To Ellis Yarnall,* Aug. 28;
> *Memoir and Letters,* ed. her Daughter, p. 516

My first acquaintance with Elizabeth Barrett commenced about fifteen
years ago [1836]. She was certainly one of the most interesting persons
that I had ever seen. Everybody who then saw her said the same; so that
it is not merely the impression of my partiality or my enthusiasm. Of a
slight, delicate figure, with a shower of dark curls falling on either side of
a most expressive face, large tender eyes richly fringed by dark eye-lashes,
a smile like a sunbeam, and such a look of youthfulness that I had some
difficulty in persuading a friend, in whose carriage we went together to
Chiswick, that the translatress of the *Prometheus* of Æschylus, the authoress of the *Essays on Mind,* was old enough to be in company, in technical
language was *out*. Through the kindness of another invaluable friend, . . .
I saw much of her during my stay in town. We met so constantly and so
familiarly that in spite of the difference of age, intimacy ripened into
friendship, and after my return into the country, we corresponded freely
and frequently, her letters being just what they ought to be—her own talk
put upon paper.

> Mary Russell Mitford, 1851, *Recollections of a*
> *Literary Life,* p. 170

Mrs. Browning met us at the door of the drawing-room, and greeted us
most kindly,—a pale, small person, scarcely embodied at all; at any rate,
only substantial enough to put forth her slender fingers to be grasped, and
to speak with a shrill, yet sweet, tenuity of voice. Really, I do not see how
Mr. Browning can suppose that he has an earthly wife any more than an
earthly child; both are of the same elfin race, and will flit away from him
some day when he least thinks of it. She is a good and kind fairy, however,
and sweetly disposed towards the human race, although only remotely akin

to it. It is wonderful to see how small she is, how pale her cheeks, how bright and dark her eyes. There is not such another figure in the world; and her black ringlets cluster down into her neck, and make her face look the whiter by their sable profusion. I could not form any judgment about her age; it may range anywhere within the limits of human life or elfin life. When I met her in London at Lord Houghton's breakfast-table, she did not impress me so singularly; for the morning light is more prosaic than the dim illumination of their great tapestried drawing room; and, besides, sitting next to her, she did not have occasion to raise her voice in speaking, and I was not sensible what a slender voice she has. It is marvellous to me how so extraordinary, so acute, so sensitive a creature can impress us, as she does, with the certainty of her benevolence. It seems to me that there were a million chances to one that she would have been a miracle of acidity and bitterness.

Nathaniel Hawthorne, 1858, Passages from the French and
Italian Notebooks, June 9; p. 294

The main comfort is that she suffered very little pain, none besides that ordinarily attending the simple attacks of cold and cough she was subject to —had no presentiment of the result whatever, and was consequently spared the misery of knowing she was about to leave us: she was smilingly assuring me she was "better," "quite comfortable—if I would but come to bed," to within a few minutes of the last. . . . Through the night she slept heavily and brokenly—that was the bad sign; but then she would sit up, take her medicine, say unrepeatable things to me, and sleep again. At four o'clock there were symptoms that alarmed me; I called the maid and sent for the doctor. She smiled as I proposed to bathe her feet, "Well, you *are* determined to make an exaggerated case of it!" Then came what my heart will keep till I see her again and longer—the most perfect expression of her love to me within my whole knowledge of her. Always smilingly, happily, and with a face like a girl's, and in a few minutes she died in my arms, her head on my cheek. These incidents so sustain me that I tell them to her beloved ones as their right; there was no lingering, nor acute pain, nor consciousness of separation, but God took her to Himself, as you would lift a sleeping child from a dark, uneasy bed into your arms and the light. Thank God! Annunziata thought, by her earnest ways with me, happy and smiling as they were, that she must have been aware of our parting's approach, but she was quite conscious, had words at command, and yet did not even speak of Peni, who was in the next room. Her last word was, when I asked, "How do you feel?" "Beautiful."

Robert Browning, 1861, Letter to Miss Haworth, July 20;
Life and Letters of Robert Browning, ed. Orr, vol. II, p. 361

The date and place of Mrs. Browning's birth have been variously stated. For some years biographers wavered between London and Hope End, Herefordshire, as her natal place. Quite recently Mrs. Richmond Ritchie, authorized by Mr. Browning, declared Burn Hall, Durham, the place, and March 6, 1809, the date of Mrs. Browning's birth. My researches have enabled me to disprove these statements. In *The Tyne Mercury,* for March 14, 1809, is announced for March 4, "In London, the wife of Edward M. Barrett, Esq., of a daughter." Having published my data, their accuracy was challenged by Mr. Browning, who now asserted that his wife was "born on March 6, 1806, at Carlton Hall, Durham, the residence of her father's brother." Carlton Hall was not in Durham, but in Yorkshire, and, I am authoritatively informed, did not become the residence of Mr. S. Moulton Barrett until some time after 1810. Mr. Browning's latest suggestions cannot, therefore, be accepted.

John H. Ingram, 1888, *Elizabeth Barrett Browning,* p. 263

Aurora Leigh (1856)

The most successful book of the season has been Mrs. Browning's *Aurora Leigh.* I could wish some things altered, I confess; but as it is, it is by far (a hundred times over) the finest poem ever written by a woman. We know little or nothing of Sappho—nothing to induce comparison—and all other wearers of petticoats must courtesy to the ground.

Bryan Waller Procter, 1856, *Letter to James T. Fields,*
" 'Barry Cornwall' and Some of His Friends,"
Harper's Magazine, vol. 52, p. 63

Although . . . Mrs. Browning's *Aurora Leigh* is her finest work, there are many among her admirers whom her earlier poems will still move the most deeply. Comparatively few can follow, with full sympathy, her entire course. Perhaps most of those whose spiritual life has actually begun, stand yet upon the stage of sorrow and longing. While such gaze with admiration on the shining path of their poet, they will yet feel the deepest sympathy with her, as she is still walking among the shadows, and cheering them with her songs. It appears to us, also, that *Aurora Leigh* is not to be reckoned among the works destined for immortality. The universal element in it is too much mingled with the peculiarities of our time, to admit of its becoming naturalized in another age. This need not, however, lessen our enjoyment of it; as we should not find the blossom of the century-plant less beautiful for the thought that the entire age had been needed for its production, and that it yet would wither, very shortly, before our eyes.

Charles Carroll Everett, 1857, "Elizabeth Barrett Browning,"
North American Review, vol. 85, p. 441

It is a unique, wonderful and immortal poem; astonishing for its combination of masculine power with feminine tenderness; for its novelty, its facility, its incessant abundance of thought, and expression; its being an exponent of its age, and a prophetic teacher of it, its easy yet lofty triumph over every species of common place; and its noble and sweet avowal, after all, of a participation of error; its lovely willingness to be no loftier, or less earthly, than something on an equality with love.

> Leigh Hunt, 1857, *Letter to Robert Browning,* Jan. 1;
> *Cornhill Magazine,* vol. 76, p. 739

I am reading a poem full of thought and fascinating with fancy: Mrs. Browning's *Aurora Leigh.* In many pages, and particularly 126 and 127, there is the wild imagination of Shakespeare. I have not yet read much farther. I had no idea that any one in this age was capable of so much poetry. I am half drunk with it. Never did I think I should have a good hearty draught of poetry again; the distemper had got into the vineyard that produced it. Here are indeed, even here, some flies upon the surface, as there always will be upon what is sweet and strong. I know not yet what the story is. Few possess the power of construction.

> Walter Savage Landor, 1857, *Letter to John Forster,*
> in *Walter Savage Landor, a Biography* by John Forster, bk. ii, note

An extraordinary work, which is also a masterpiece; I repeat that space fails me in order that I may state, after having perused it twenty times, how beautiful I consider it to be. It contains the confession of a generous, heroic, and impassioned spirit, one superabounding in genius, of which the culture has been complete, of a philosopher and a poet dwelling amid the loftiest ideas, and surpassing the elevation of her ideas by the nobility of her instincts, wholly modern by her education, by her high-mindedness, by her daring, by the perpetual vibration of her strained sensibility, wound up to such a pitch that the slightest touch awakens in her a vast orchestra and a most wonderful symphony of concords. It is all soul, and the inward monologue, the sublime song of a young girl's and artist's great heart, attracted and irritated by an enthusiasm and a pride as strong as her own; the sustained contrast of the masculine and feminine utterance, which, amid the outbursts and the variations on the same theme, continually become separated and opposed in greater measure, till at last, suddenly combining, they unite in a prolonged, mournful and exquisite duo, of which the strain is so lofty and so penetrating as to be wholly unsurpassable.

> H. A. Taine, 1872, *Notes on England,* tr. Rae, p. 344

Concerning *Aurora Leigh* there will always be differences of opinion and feeling, for it exhibits the poet's weakness not less manifestly than her strength. Its form is defective, its inspiration intermittent, its style unequal; it is greater in parts than as a whole; but if we regard its finest details of description and characterisation, if we weigh the nuggets of imaginative thought which we turn over on nearly every page, we may fairly pronounce it, with all its faults, one of the fullest and most opulent poems produced in this century by any English poet.

James Ashcroft Noble, 1892, *The Poets and the Poetry of the Century, Joanna Baillie to Mathilde Blind*, ed. Miles, p. 163

Mrs. Browning herself considered *Aurora Leigh,* published in 1856, the most mature of her works, and the one into which her highest convictions upon Life and Art had entered. Her view was supported by its great popularity with the general public, but the critics have been more discriminating in their praise. They have been ready to acknowledge the abundance of poetical material, the moments of high suggestion, the many beautiful passages which this poem contains, but they have also pointed out its want of method, its ignorance of real life, its numerous digressions and frequent lapses into prose. Neither the situations nor the characters are dramatically conceived or well delineated.

Richard D. Graham, 1897, *Masters of Victorian Literature*, p. 325

SONNETS

I am disposed to consider the *Sonnets from the Portuguese* as, if not the finest, a portion of the finest subjective poetry in our literature. Their form reminds us of an English prototype, and it is no sacrilege to say that their music is showered from a higher and purer atmosphere than that of the Swan of Avon. . . . The most exquisite poetry hitherto written by a woman, and of themselves justify us in pronouncing their author the greatest of her sex,—on the ground that the highest mission of a female poet is the expression of love, and that no other woman approaching her in genius has essayed the ultimate form of that expression.

Edmund Clarence Stedman, 1875-87, *Victorian Poets*, pp. 137, 138

The poems which, from what may be called a technical point of view, may be counted irreproachable, may, if we except the Sonnets, almost be reckoned on the fingers. Her sonnets are among the very best work she has produced. Perhaps indeed her greatest poetic success is to be found in the *Sonnets from the Portuguese,*—sonnets, it need hardly be said, which are not "from the Portuguese" at all, but are the faintly disguised presentment of the writer's most intimate experience. Into the "sonnet's narrow room" she has poured the full flood of her profoundest thought, and yet the minuteness and exquisiteness of the mould has at the same time compelled a rigorous pruning alike of superabundant imagery and of harmonious verbosity, which has had the happiest results. She is one of the greatest sonnet writers in our language, worthy for this at all events to be ranked side by side with Milton and with Wordsworth.

William T. Arnold, 1880, *The English Poets*,
ed. Ward, vol. IV, p. 566

No more impassioned soul ever found expression in rhythmical speech than Elizabeth Barrett Browning, and there is nothing in her poetry which is finer than that famous love-record, the so-called *Sonnets from the Portuguese*. Impetuous as was her genius, hasty and frequently careless as she was in production, she never found the archetypal sonnet too circumscribed for her. The pathetic beauty, the fascinating personality, the pure poetry displayed in these sonnets, have touched many and many a heart since the tired singer was laid to rest under the cypresses not far from that beloved river whose flow she had so often followed in thought down the far-off Pisan sea. Only those who have thoroughly studied contemporary poetry, and not only the poetry which is familiar to many but that also which is quite unknown, and by minor writers of no reputation or likelihood of reputation, can realise the potency of Mrs. Browning's influence, especially among women.

William Sharp, 1886, *Sonnets of this Century*, Introduction, p. lxx

In these sonnets (which it is hardly necessary to say are not translations) she speaks the universal language; to her other graces had now been added that which she had somewhat lacked before, the grace of content; and for these probably she will be longest and most gratefully admired. Any one who steps for the first time through the door into which he has seen so many enter, and finds that poets and lovers and married folk, in their well-worn commonplaces, have exaggerated nothing, will love these sonnets as one of the sweetest and most natural records of a thing which will never lose its absorbing fascination for humanity. To those that are without, except for the sustained melody of expression, the poetess almost seems to have passed on to a lower level, to have lost originality—like the celebrated lady whose friends said that till she wrote to announce her engagement she had never written a commonplace letter.

Arthur Christopher Benson, 1896, *Essays*, p. 213

LETTERS

Her letters make Cowper's poor. In a hurried note, whose hurry is evident in the handwriting, she drops . . . incidental, but brilliant words—just as if the jewels in her rings, jarred by her rapid fingers, had been suddenly unset and fallen out on the paper. No other handwriting is like hers; it is strong, legible, singularly un-English and more like a man's than a woman's.

Theodore Tilton, 1862, *Last Poems of Mrs. Browning,*
Memorial Preface

These letters, familiarly written to her private friends, without the smallest idea of publication, treating of the thoughts that came uppermost in the ordinary language of conversation, can lay no claim to make a new revelation of her genius. On the other hand, perhaps because the circumstances of Mrs. Browning's life cut her off to an unusual extent from personal intercourse with her friends, and threw her back upon letter writing as her principal means of communication with them, they contain an unusually full revelation of her character. And this is not wholly unconnected with her literary genius, since her personal convictions, her moral character, entered more fully than is often the case into the composition of her poetry.

Frederic G. Kenyon, 1897, ed., *The Letters of
Elizabeth Barrett Browning,* Preface, vol. I, p. x

GENERAL

The principal poem in this volume is an "Essay on Mind," occupying some ninety pages. Viewing this as the production of a young lady of sixteen or seventeen, it is a remarkable, nay, extraordinary performance, to which the records of early genius can furnish very few parallels. It is a metaphysical and reflective poem, showing uncommon power of patient and discriminating thought, a wide range of reading, and a ripe judgment. The versification is easy and vigorous. It blends together, in a very happy combination, the forms of philosophic thought and the vivid hues of poetical fancy. It is especially remarkable for its freedom from any of those morbid elements, which are so apt to be attendant upon precocity of genius, especially in women. There is no exaggeration of personal feeling, no overwrought sensibility, no extravagance of thought and expression, and no sickly melancholy. It seems to be written by one whose mind had been healthy and naturally developed, and whose symmetry had not been impaired by rapid growth.

George S. Hillard, 1842, "Recent English Poetry,"
North American Review, vol. 55, p. 202

Poetry has been as serious a thing to me as life itself; and life has been a very serious thing; there has been no playing at skittles for me either. I never mistook pleasure for the final cause of poetry; nor leisure, for the hour of the poet. I have done my work, so far, as work,—not as mere hand and head work, apart from the personal being,—but as the completest expression of that being to which I could attain,—and as work I offer it to the public,—feeling its shortcomings more deeply than any of my readers, because measured from the height of my aspiration,—but feeling also that the reverence and sincerity with which the work was done should give it some protection with the reverent and sincere.

> Elizabeth Barrett Browning, 1844, *Poems,* Preface, p. xiv

That Miss Barrett has done more, in poetry, than any woman, living or dead, will scarcely be questioned:—that she has surpassed all her poetical contemporaries of either sex (with a single exception) is our deliberate opinion—not idly entertained, we think, nor founded on any visionary basis.

> Edgar Allan Poe, 1845, "Miss Barrett's *A Drama of Exile,*"
> *Works,* ed. Stedman and Woodberry, vol. VI, p. 316

Among my holiday gifts was Miss Barrett's poems. She is a woman of vigorous thought, but not very poetical thought, and throwing herself into verse involuntarily becomes honied and ornate, so that her verse cloys. It is not natural, quite. . . . Burrill did not see why I called Miss Barrett purple. It was because her highly colored robe was not harmonious with her native style of thought.

> George William Curtis, 1845, *To Dwight,* Jan. 12;
> *Early Letters to John S. Dwight,* p. 200

She has more poetic genius than any other woman living—perhaps more than any other woman ever showed before, except Sappho. Still there is an imperfectness in what she produces; in many passages the expressions are very faulty, the images forced and untrue, the sentiments exaggerated, and the situations unnatural and unpleasant. Another pervading fault of Mrs. Browning's poetry is rugged, harsh versification, with imperfect rhymes, and altogether that want of art in the department of metre which prevents the language from being an unobstructive medium for thought.

> Sara Coleridge, 1851, *To Ellis Yarnall,* Aug. 28;
> *Memoir and Letters,* ed. her Daughter, p. 516

Mrs. Browning's Death is rather a relief to me, I must say: no more Aurora Leighs, thank God! A woman of real Genius, I know: but what is the upshot of it all? She and her Sex had better mind the Kitchen and their Children; and perhaps the Poor: except in such things as little Novels, they only devote themselves to what Men do much better, leaving that which Men do worse or not at all.

> Edward FitzGerald, 1861, *To W. H. Thompson,* July 15;
> *Letters and Literary Remains,* ed. Wright, vol. I, p. 280

The long study of her sick-bed (and her constant chafing against the common estimate of the talents and genius of her sex) overcharged her works with allusions and thoughts relating to books, and made her style rugged with pedantry. She was often intoxicated, too, with her own vehemence. *Aurora Leigh* sets out determined to walk the world with the great Shakespearian stride, whence desperate entanglement of feminine draperies and blinding swirls of dust. The sonnets entitled *From the Portuguese* reveal better her inmost simple nature.

> James Thomson ("B. V."), 1864, "The Poems of William Blake,"
> *Biographical and Critical Sketches,* p. 267

The notes of Mrs. Browning's poetry are emotion, purity, pathos, intense earnestness, sympathy with every form of suffering, with everything great and good, hatred of everything evil, specially of all oppression. Her want of humour, a few rough and careless rhymes, and occasional forcing of sense and phrase, have made some critics of word and style complain; but students may rely on it, that to know Mrs. Browning as she reveals herself in her works is a liberal education, and to enter into her spirit one of the most ennobling pursuits that a man can undertake.

> Frederick James Furnivall, 1887, *Celebrities of the Century,* p. 181

Mrs. Browning's technique is uncertain, and she never freed herself from her characteristic faults of vagueness and unrestraint. But her sympathy with noble causes, the elevation and ardor of her moods of personal emotion, and the distinction of her utterances at its best, outbalance these negative considerations. She shares her husband's strenuousness and optimism, but she speaks always from the feminine vantage-ground.

> William Vaughn Moody and Robert Morss Lovett, 1902,
> *A History of English Literature,* p. 331

ARTHUR HUGH CLOUGH
1819-1861

Arthur Hugh Clough was born in Liverpool, England, January 1, 1819. When a small boy he accompanied his father on a business visit to the

United States. In 1828 he was sent to Rugby, where he soon excelled in scholarship and was a leading contributor to the *Rugby Magazine*. From Rugby he went to Oxford, where he gained a scholarship at Balliol, and afterward a fellowship at Oriel. While at Oxford he wrote a long poem entitled *The Bothie of Tober-na-Vuolich,* which was published in 1848. Clough gave up his fellowship in 1848, and travelled in France and Italy. On his return he was appointed principal of University Hall, and professor of English literature, in University College, London. In 1852 he resigned this chair, crossed the Atlantic, and became a private tutor in Cambridge, Massachusetts. In 1853 he returned to England to accept a place in the Education department of the Privy Council, married, and settled in London, devoting himself for several years to the hard work of his office, and giving his leisure hours to a revision of Dryden's translation of Plutarch, which was published in 1859. In 1861 his health gave way, and he went to travel on the Continent; but he died at Florence, Italy, November 13, and was buried there. His "Amours de Voyage," a story in verse, was published in *Atlantic Monthly* in 1858. His collected poems, with a memoir by Charles Eliot Norton, were published in Boston in 1862, and his complete works, with a life by his widow, in London, in 1869.

Rossiter Johnson, 1875, *Little Classics* (vol. XVI), *Authors,* p. 56

SEE: *Poems,* ed. Humphrey S. Milford, 1910; *Poems,* ed. H. F. Lowry, A. L. P. Norrington, F. L. Mulhauser, 1951; *Letters of Matthew Arnold to Arthur Hugh Clough,* ed. H. F. Lowry, 1932; *Emerson-Clough Letters,* ed. H. F. Lowry and R. L. Rusk, 1934; *The Correspondence*, ed. Frederick L. Mulhauser, 1957, 2 v.; J. I. Osborne, *Arthur Hugh Clough,* 1920; Katherine Chorley, *Arthur Hugh Clough: The Uncommitted Mind,* 1962; Walter E. Houghton, *The Poetry of Clough,* 1963.

PERSONAL

Here was a man who loved truth and justice, not coldly and afar off, as most, but with passion and intensely; . . . who walked the world's way as matter of duty, living a life, meanwhile, hidden with higher and holier things. . . . Plainer living and higher thinking were the texts on which he gave us many a humorous and admirable lesson. . . . His influence was always towards whatever should incline others to a liberal view of the questions of the day, of the claims of the feeble, and the feelings of the poor.

Francis Turner Palgrave, 1847, *Letter, Journals and Memories of his Life,* ed. Palgrave, p. 31

People seem very fond of Arthur, and to think a great deal of him; but Arthur does not seem to mind much about people here; they don't seem to suit him exactly, and he gets wearied and worn out with the continual talking about religious matters; and I think, too, the pomp and grandeur trouble him. He does not appear at all to fancy coming to live in London.

Anne Jemima Clough, 1849, *Journal, Memoir,* ed. Blanche Athena Clough, p. 73

I was glad to see Clough here, with whom I had established some kind of robust working-friendship, and who had some great permanent values for me. Had he not taken me by surprise and fled in a night, I should have done what I could to block his way. I am too sure he will not return. The first months comprise all the shocks of disappointment that are likely to disgust a newcomer. The sphere of opportunity opens slowly, but to a man of his abilities and culture—rare enough here—with the sureness of chemistry. The Giraffe entering Paris wore the label, "Eh bien, messieurs, il n'y a qu'une bête de plus!" And Oxonians are cheap in London; but here, the eternal economy of sending things where they are wanted makes a commanding claim. Do not suffer him to relapse into London. He had made himself already cordially welcome to many good people, and would have soon made his own place. He had just established his valise at my house, and was to come—the gay deceiver—once a fortnight for his Sunday; and his individualities and his nationalities are alike valuable to me.

Ralph Waldo Emerson, 1853, *To Carlyle,* Aug. 10;
Correspondence of Carlyle and Emerson, ed. Norton,
vol. II, p. 257a

Clough was five feet ten in height, well made, inclining to burliness; he had a handsome frank face, dark-eyed, full-chinned and ruddy complexioned, the nose being straight and rather short; his head, which was early bald, ran deep from front to back, and showed a graceful domed outline. In manner he was quiet, grave, and reticent; usually speaking little, by no means from want of sympathy, but in part, we should say, from a wish both to hear and reply with gravity and exactness, and also from a feeling of instinct of personal dignity and refinement which belonged to him in high degree. He carefully avoided all risk of intrusion, either on his own part or his interlocutor's, and kept in constant check every merely impulsive movement. It is probable that a more than commonly sensitive temperament was controlled and calmed into this habitual quietude of demeanour, which was not at all of the drowsy or thick-skinned sort, but living and palpitating. It would have been hard to find a readier friend, in little matters or great.

William Allingham, 1866, "Arthur Hugh Clough,"
Fraser's Magazine, vol. 74, p. 535

Apart from the gifts of imagination and mental analysis, Clough was of a noble, pure, and self-controlling nature. His friends felt certain that the temptations to excess which assail young men, at Universities and elsewhere, had by him been resolutely and victoriously resisted. His clear black eyes, under a broad, full, and lofty forehead, were often partly closed, as if through the pressure of thought; but when the problem occupying him was solved, a glorious flash would break from the eyes, expressive of an inner joy and sudden illumination, which fascinated any who were present. For though his sense of humour was keen, the spirit of satire was absent; benevolence in his kindly heart never finding a difficulty in quelling ill-nature. It will be said that there are many satirical strokes in "Dipsychus," and this is true; but they are aimed at classes—their follies and hyprocrisies —never at any individual, except himself. His mouth was beautifully formed, but both it and the chin were characterised by some lack of deter-mination and firmness. This deficiency, however, so far as it existed, was harmful only to himself; those who sought his counsel or help found in him the wisest of advisers, the steadiest and kindest of friends. . . . On the moral side he was firm as a rock.

Arnold Thomas, 1898, "Arthur Hugh Clough,"
Nineteenth Century, vol. 43. pp. 105, 115

He whom all his contemporaries counted certain to take a commanding place in the higher life of England sank into comparative insignificance. He began by failing of that First Class, which was the undoubted meed due to his knowledge and ability. He went on always hoping, longing to do some great thing, yet never doing it. For years he held his tutorship and fellow-ship, doubting whether he ought not to give them up since he no longer held the faith supposed to be their indispensable condition. At last he resigned them both, but not to give his splendid talents work to do for any high ends outside the circle of the university. One petty appointment after another he held—petty, that is, in comparison with what his intellectual endowments qualified him for—but always questioning whether this was or was not what he ought to be at. At last peace seems to have come to him only by giving up finally and forever all such noble ambitions for the bettering of the world as had inspired his early youth, quietly settling down into a useful, if somewhat narrow, government office, and taking all his joy from the homely love of wife and children. And yet this was a good man, a religious man, of whom I have been speaking, a man far better and more religious than many who have shone conspicuously as patriots and heroes, a man in the highest degree lovable, a man who inspired others to a strenu-ousness of which he himself failed, a man whose intellect was held in honor by the most intellectual.

Richard A. Armstrong, 1898, Faith and Doubt
in the Century's Poets

GENERAL

I quite agree in what you say of poor Clough. A man more vivid, ingenious, veracious, mildly radiant, I have seldom met with, and in a character so honest, modest, kindly. I expected very considerable things of him.

Thomas Carlyle, 1860, *Letter to Froude; Thomas Carlyle, A History of his Life in London,* ed. Froude, vol. II, p. 207

Of one metre, however,—the hexameter,—we believe the most accomplished judges, and also common readers, agree that Mr. Clough possesses a very peculiar mastery. . . . Whether any consummate poem of great length and sustained dignity can be written in this metre, and in our language, we do not know: until a great poet has written his poem, there are commonly no lack of plausible arguments that seem to prove he cannot write it; but Mr. Clough has certainly shown that in the hands of a skilful and animated artist, it is capable of adapting itself to varied descriptions of life and manners, to noble sentiments, and to changing thoughts. It is perhaps the most flexible of English metres. Better than any others, it changes from grave to gay without desecrating what should be solemn, or disenchanting that which should be graceful. And Mr. Clough was the first to prove this, by writing a noble poem in which it was done. . . . The sort of conversation for which he was most remarkable rises again in the *Amours de Voyage,* and gives them, to those who knew him in life, a very peculiar charm. It would not be exact to call the best lines a pleasant cynicism; for cynicism has a bad name, and the ill-nature and other offensive qualities which have given it that name were utterly out of Mr. Clough's way. Though without much fame, he had no envy.

Walter Bagehot, 1862, "Mr. Clough's Poems," *Works,* ed. Morgan, vol. I, pp. 196, 197

The oftener I return to Clough's unfinished but striking poems, the more I am struck by something in their fresh natural handling, and a certain lustre of sunlight on their surface, which suggests to me a modern and intellectualized Chaucer; and I think the same homely breadth and simplicity were strongly marked in his countenance. . . . I do not think that any competent judge who really studies Clough's Remains will doubt for a moment that he was one of the most original men of our age, and perhaps its most intellectual and buoyant, though very far, of course, from its richest, most musical and exquisite poet. There is a very peculiar and unique attraction about what I may call the physical and almost animal buoyancy of these subtly intellectual rhythms and verses, when once the mass of the poet's mind—by no means easy to get into motion—is fairly under way.

Richard Holt Hutton, 1869, "Arthur Hugh Clough,"
Essays in Literary Criticism, pp. 169, 178

There will always be a great charm, especially for Oxford men, in the "Long Vacation Pastoral," *The Bothie of Toberna-Vuolich.* Humour, pathos, clear character-drawing, real delight in nature and a power of rendering her beauties, above all a sense of life, of "the joy of eventful living"—it has all these, and over the whole is thrown, through the associations of the hexameter, a half-burlesque veil of academic illusion that produces the happiest effect. . . . Clough holds a high and permanent place among our poets, not only because, as Mr. Lowell says, he represents an epoch of thought, but because he represents it in a manner so rare, so individual. He is neither singer nor prophet; but he is a poet in virtue of the depth and sincerity with which he felt certain great emotions, and the absolute veracity with which he expressed them.

Thomas Humphry Ward, 1880, *The English Poets,* vol. IV, p. 591

Of *Dipsychus* in its intirety, we must confess that it is, when beheld in its present state, simply a *cul-de-sac;*—or if the reader prefer it, a suite of richly-adorned chambers, but not a perfect palace. If Clough had lived he might, like Goethe, have gradually, through a period of thirty years, developed his works, and at the age of sixty have delighted the world with the publication of another masterpiece,—another palace of art, or "lordly pleasure-house" for the soul.

Samuel Waddington, 1882, *Arthur Hugh Clough,* p. 241

There are few names in this century which have had, for young men especially, greater attractive power than that of Arthur Hugh Clough. This power has never been widely, but in many cases it has been deeply, felt. It has its source more in the nature of the man and in the conditions of his life than in his work, although the latter is full of the elevation, the aspiration, and the beauty of a very noble mind. But it is not as a finished artist, as a singer whose message is clear and whose note is resonant, that Clough attracts; it is rather as a child of his time, as one in whom the stir and change of the century were most distinctly reflected. There was an intense sympathy with his age in the heart of Clough, a sensitiveness to the tidal influences of thought and emotion, which made his impressionable nature, for a time at least, a prey to agitation and turmoil; and there is no more delicate registry of the tempestuous weather of the second quarter of the century than that which is found in his work.

Hamilton Wright Mabie, 1894, My Study Fire,
Second Series, p. 101

Far less polished than Arnold's, Clough's poetry yet shows in some respects a freer and broader power. His outlook on modern society is more manly, as more specific in severity; and his pungent gift of mockery is foreign to Arnold's pensive grace and musical despair. But the spiritual attitude of the two is wider apart than their artistic or social temper. We read Arnold's laments over the past, his intense longing for steadfastness and peace, and the conviction grows upon us that his keenest regret is not faith but assurance, less the truth which the world has forfeited than the tranquility which the truth produced. He craves with an almost querulous desire the unquestioning and serene spirit, which has fled never to return. Passing to the pages of his friend, we find pain of a different order—the agonized desire for a faith that is lost, and for a distant God. Tranquility is the supreme end of Arnold's ambition; the Truth alone could satisfy the soul of Clough.

Vida D. Scudder, 1895, The Life of the Spirit
in the Modern English Poets, p. 266

His poetry is the poetry of moods—moods of comparative hopefulness, moods of weariness and despair, moods of mere inquiry and deliberate reserve. To the superficial reader, turning over the pages of his collected works, there might even seem to be the strangest inconsistencies in the utterances of some of his shorter poems; for his sensitive nature catches up and repeats, though always in tempered tones, now the sad wail of some who mourn over the rapid dissolution of the world's great heritage of belief, and now again the glad shout of others who, boldly and trustfully, press forward to meet the coming day. But the wail and the shout—the song of sorrow and the song of promise—alike belong to the man himself, and, far from being discordant or incompatible, are in their own ways equally expressive of his relation to the great issues of the time.

William Henry Hudson, 1896, Studies in Interpretation, p. 117

There is perhaps no poet of the Victorian era in whom the Agnostic spirit has found more distinct and articulate utterance than in Arthur Hugh Clough. To him, the very essence of all religion worth having consists in the firm, resolute, unswerving conviction that nothing can be known of the Supreme. Providential schemes, creeds and certainties are all in his estimation a profane pretence of knowledge, and are to be strenuously resisted, as so many temptations to Baalism and idolatry. The only recipe he feels himself justified in prescribing, and he is never weary of recommending it, is "contentedness not to know."

S. Law Wilson, 1899, The Theology of Modern Literature,
Introduction, p. 17

HENRY DAVID THOREAU
1817-1862

> Born at Concord, Mass., July 12, 1817: died at Concord, May 6, 1862. An American writer. He graduated at Harvard in 1837, taught school, and afterward became a land-surveyor. He lived alone on the shore of Walden Pond, Concord, 1845-47. He was a transcendentalist, and a friend of Emerson, Alcott, etc.; stood out for the rights of the individual; and was at one time imprisoned for his refusal to pay taxes. Among his works are *A Week on the Concord and Merrimac Rivers* (1849), *Walden, or Life in the Woods* (1854), *Excursions in Field and Forest* (1863: with a memoir by Emerson), *The Maine Woods* (1864), *Cape Cod* (1865), *Letters to Various Persons* (1865: with a notice by Emerson), *A Yankee in Canada, etc.* (1866).
>
> Benjamin E. Smith, ed., 1894-97, The Century
Cyclopedia of Names, p. 993
>
> SEE: *Writings,* 1906, 20 v. (standard Walden Edition: Vol. VI is *Familiar Letters,* ed. Frank B. Sanborn; Vols. VII-XX include *Journals* (1837-61), ed. Bradford Torrey); *Complete Works,* ed. Harrison G. O. Blake, 1929, 5 v. (Concord Edition); *Collected Poems,* ed. Carl Bode. 1943; Odell Shepard, ed., *The Heart of Thoreau's Journals,* 1927; *Consciousness in Concord: Thoreau's Last Journal (1840-41),* ed. Perry Miller, 1958; Henry S. Canby, ed., *The Works of Thoreau, Selected and Edited,* 1937; H. S. Salt, *Life,* 1890; Henry S. Canby, *Thoreau,* 1939; in F. O. Matthiessen, *American Renaissance* (Book I), 1941; also see Walter C. Harding, *Thoreau: A Century of Criticism,* 1954; Walter C. Harding, *Thoreau Handbook,* 1959.

PERSONAL

He is a little under size, with a huge Emersonian nose, bluish gray eyes, brown hair, and a ruddy, weather-beaten face, which reminds me of some shrewd and honest animal's—some retired philosophical woodchuck or magnanimous fox. He dresses very plainly, wears his collar turned over like Mr. Emerson and often an old dress-coat, broad in the skirts, and by no means a fit. He walks about with a brisk, rustic air, and never seems tired.

Frank B. Sanborn, 1855, Diary, Henry D. Thoreau
(American Men of Letters), p. 199

There was somewhat military in his nature not to be subdued, always manly and able, but rarely tender, as if he did not feel himself except in opposition. He wanted a fallacy to expose, a blunder to pillory, I may say required a little sense of victory, a roll of the drum, to call his powers into full exercise. It cost him nothing to say No; indeed, he found it much easier than to say Yes. It seemed as if his first instinct on hearing a proposition was to controvert it, so impatient was he of the limitations of our daily thought. This habit, of course, is a little chilling to the social affections; and though the companion would in the end acquit him of any malice or untruth, yet it mars conversation. Hence, no equal companion stood in affectionate relations with one so pure and guileless. "I love Henry," said one of his friends, "but I cannot like him; and as for taking his arm, I should as soon think of taking the arm of an elm-tree." Yet, hermit and stoic as he was, he was really fond of sympathy, and threw himself heartily and childlike into the company of young people whom he loved, and whom he delighted to entertain, as he only could, with the varied and endless anecdotes of his experiences by field and river. And he was always ready to lead a huckleberry-party or a search for chestnuts or grapes. . . . There is a flower known to botanists, one of the same genus with our summer plant called "Life-Everlasting," a *Gnaphalium* like that which grows on the most inaccessible cliffs of the Tyrolese mountains, where the chamois dare hardly venture, and which the hunter, tempted by its beauty, and by his love, (for it is immensely valued by the Swiss maidens), climbs the cliffs to gather, and is sometimes found dead at the foot, with the flower in his hand. It is called by botanists the *Gnaphalium leontopodium,* but by the Swiss *Edelweiss,* which signifies *Noble Purity.* Thoreau seemed to me living in the hope to gather this plant, which belonged to him of right. The scale on which his studies proceeded was so large as to require longevity, and we were the less prepared for his sudden disappearance. The country knows not yet, or in the least part, how great a son it has lost.

Ralph Waldo Emerson, 1862, "Thoreau,"
Atlantic Monthly, vol. 10, pp. 240, 249

Thoreau was a stoic, but he was in no sense a cynic. His neighbors in the village thought him odd and whimsical, but his practical skill as a surveyor and in woodcraft was known to them. No man was his enemy, and some of the best men were his fastest friends. But his life was essentially solitary and reserved. Careless of appearances in later days, when his hair and beard were long, if you had seen him in the woods you might have fancied Orson passing by; but had you stopped to talk with him, you would have felt that you had seen the shepherd of Admetus's flock, or chatted with a wiser Jacques. For some time past he had been sinking under a consumption. He made a journey to the West a year ago, but in vain; and returned to die quietly at home.

George William Curtis, 1862, "The Easy Chair,"
Harper's Magazine, vol. 25, p. 270

> To him no vain regrets belong,
> Whose soul, that finer instrument,
> Gave to the world no poor lament,
> But wood-notes ever sweet and strong.
> O lonely friend! he still will be
> A potent presence, though unseen,—
> Steadfast, sagacious, and serene.
> Seek not for him,—he is with thee.

Louisa M. Alcott, 1863, "Thoreau's Flute,"
Atlantic Monthly, vol. 12, p. 281

His readers came many miles to see him, attracted by his writings. Those who could not come sent their letters. Those who came when they could no more see him, as strangers on a pilgrimage, seemed as if they had been his intimates, so warm and cordial was the sympathy they received from his letters. If he also did the duties that lay nearest and satisfied those in his immediate circle, certainly he did a good work; and whatever the impressions from the theoretical part of his writings, when the matter is probed to the bottom, good sense and good feeling will be detected in it. A great comfort in him, he was eminently reliable. No whim of coldness, no absorption of his time by public or private business, deprived those to whom he belonged of his kindness and affection. He was at the mercy of no caprice: of a reliable will and uncompromising sternness in his moral nature, he carried the same qualities into his relation with others, and gave them the best he had, without stint. He loved firmly, acted up to his love, was a believer in it, took pleasure and satisfaction in abiding by it. . . . In height, he was about the average; in his build, spare, with limbs that were rather longer than usual, or of which he made a longer use. His face, once seen, could not be forgotten. The features were quite marked: the nose aquiline or very Roman, like one of the portraits of Cæsar (more like a beak, as was said); large, overhanging brows above the deepest set blue eyes that could be seen, in certain lights, and in others gray,—eyes expressive of all shades of feeling, but never weak or near-sighted; the forehead not unusually broad or high, full of concentrated energy and purpose; the mouth with prominent lips, pursed up with meaning and thought when silent, and giving out when open a stream of the most varied and instructive sayings. His hair was a dark brown, exceedingly abundant, fine and soft; and for several years he wore a comely beard. His whole figure had an active earnestness, as if he had no moment to waste.

> William Ellery Channing, 1873, *Thoreau:*
> *The Poet-Naturalist,* pp. 18, 25

Both admirer and censor, both Channing in his memoir, and Lowell in his well-known criticism, have brought the eccentricities of Thoreau into undue prominence, and have placed too little stress on the vigor, the good sense, the clear perceptions, of the man. I have myself walked, talked, and corresponded with him, and can testify that the impression given by both these writers is far removed from that ordinarily made by Thoreau himself. While tinged here and there, like most New England thinkers of his time, with the manner of Emerson, he was yet, as a companion, essentially original, wholesome, and enjoyable. Though more or less of a humorist, nursing his own whims, and capable of being tiresome when they came uppermost, he was easily led away from them to the vast domains of literature and nature, and then poured forth endless streams of the most interesting talk. He taxed the patience of his companions, but not more so, on the whole, than is done by many other eminent talkers when launched upon their favorite themes. It is hard for one who thus knew him to be quite patient with Lowell in what seems almost wanton misrepresentation. Lowell applies to Thoreau the word "indolent": but you might as well speak of the indolence of a self-registering thermometer; it does not go about noisily, yet it never knows an idle moment. Lowell says that Thoreau "looked with utter contempt on the august drama of destiny, of which his country was the scene, and on which the curtain had already risen"; but was it Thoreau, or Lowell, who found a voice when the curtain fell, after the first act of that drama, upon the scaffold of John Brown? Lowell accuses him of a "seclusion which keeps him in the public eye," and finds something "delightfully absurd" in his addressing six volumes under such circumstances to the public, when the fact is that most of these volumes were made up by friends, after Thoreau's death, from his manuscripts, or from his stray papers in newspapers and magazines.

> Thomas Wentworth Higginson, 1879-88, *Short Studies*
> *of American Authors,* p. 22

Thoreau was, probably, the wildest civilized man this country has produced, adding to the shyness of the hermit and woodsman the wildness of the poet, and to the wildness of the poet the greater ferity and elusiveness of the mystic. An extreme product of civilization and of modern culture, he was yet as untouched by the worldly and commercial spirit of his age and country as any red man that ever haunted the shores of his native stream.

He put the whole of Nature between himself and his fellows. A man of the strongest local attachments—not the least nomadic, seldom wandering beyond his native township, yet his spirit was as restless and as impatient of restraint as any nomad or Tartar that ever lived. He cultivated an extreme wildness, not only in his pursuits and tastes, but in his hopes and imaginings.

> John Burroughs, 1882, "Henry D. Thoreau,"
> *The Century,* vol. 24, p. 371

Thoreau's thin, penetrating, big-nosed face, even in a bad woodcut, conveys some hint of the limitations of his mind and character. With his almost acid sharpness of insight, with his almost animal dexterity in act, there went none of that large, unconscious geniality of the world's heroes. He was not easy, not ample, not urbane, not even kind; his enjoyment was hardly smiling, or the smile was not broad enough to be convincing; he had no waste lands nor kitchen-midden in his nature, but was all improved and sharpened to a point.

> Robert Louis Stevenson, 1882, "Henry David Thoreau,"
> *Familiar Studies of Men and Books*

Walden (1854)

There is nothing of the mean or sordid in the economy of Mr. Thoreau, though to some his simplicity and abstemiousness may appear trivial and affected; he does not live cheaply for the sake of saving, nor idly to avoid labor; but, that he may live independently and enjoy his great thoughts; that he may read the Hindoo scriptures and commune with the visible forms of nature. We must do him the credit to admit that there is no mock sentiment, nor simulation of piety or philanthropy in his volume. He is not much of a cynic, and though we have called him a Yankee Diogenes, the only personage to whom he bears a decided resemblance is that good-humored creation of Dickens, Mark Tapley, whose delight was in being jolly under difficulties.

> Charles F. Briggs, 1854, "A Yankee Diogenes,"
> *Putnam's Magazine,* vol. 4, p. 445

In describing his hermitage and his forest life, he says so many pithy and brilliant things, and offers so many piquant, and, we may add, so many just comments on society as it is, that his book is well worth reading, both for its actual contents and its suggestive capacity.

> Andrew Preston Peabody, 1854, "Critical Notices,"
> *North American Review,* vol. 79, p. 536

The oddity of its record attracted universal attention. . . . As in the author's previous work, the immediate incident is frequently only the introduction to higher themes. The realities around him are occasionally veiled by a hazy atmosphere of transcendental speculation, through which the essayist sometimes stumbles into abysmal depths of the bathetic. We have more pleasures, however, in dwelling upon shrewd humors of the modern contemplative Jacques of the forest, and his fresh, nice observation of books and men, which has occasionally something of a poetic vein. He who would acquire a new sensation of the world about him, would do well to retire from cities to the banks of Walden pond, and he who would open his eyes to the opportunities of country life, in its associations of fields and men, may loiter with profit along the author's journey on the Merrimack, where natural history, local antiquities, records, and tradition, are exhausted in vitalizing the scene.

> Evert A. and George L. Duyckinck, 1855-65-75, *Cyclopædia of American Literature,* ed. Simons, vol. II, pp. 601, 602

Thoreau showed in a very marked degree the influence of Emerson. His biographer, who knew him personally, says that he imitated Emerson's tones and manners so that it was annoying to listen to him. Unconsciously he acquired Emerson's style of writing. He became a master of the short, epigrammatic sentence. Yet there is often a rudeness and an inartistic carelessness about Thoreau's style that is not at all like Emerson. No one has ever excelled him in the field of minute description. His acute powers of observation, his ability to keep for a long time his attention upon one thing, and his love of nature and of solitude, all lend a distinct individuality to his style.

> Fred Lewis Pattee, 1896, *A History of American Literature,* p. 226

Like every real book *Walden* is for its own hours and its own minds; a book for those who love books, for those who love nature, for those who love courageous thinking, courageous acting, and all sturdy, manly virtues; a book to be read through; a book, also, to be read in parts, as one uses a manual of devotion; a tonic book in the truest sense; a book against meanness, conformity, timidity, discouragement, unbelief; a book easily conceived of as marking an era in a reader's life; a book for the individual soul against the world.

> Bradford Torrey, 1897, *Walden,* Introduction, p. xxiii

GENERAL

A vigorous Mr. Thoreau,—who has formed himself a good deal upon one Emerson, but does not want abundant fire and stamina of his own;—recognizes us, and various other things, in a most admiring great-hearted manner; for which, as for *part* of the confused voice from the jury-box (not yet summed into a verdict, nor likely to be summed till Doomsday, nor needful to sum), the poor prisoner at the bar may justly express himself thankful! In plain prose I like Mr. Thoreau very well; and hope yet to hear good and better news of him.

> Thomas Carlyle, 1847, *To Emerson,* May 18; *Correspondence of*
> *Carlyle and Emerson,* ed. Norton, vol. II, p. 160

He was not a strong thinker, but a sensitive feeler. Yet his mind strikes us as cold and wintry in its purity. A light snow has fallen everywhere in which he seems to come on the track of the shier sensations that would elsewhere leave no trace. We think greater compression would have done more for his fame. A feeling of sameness comes over us as we read so much. Trifles are recorded with an overminute punctuality and conscientiousness of detail. He records the state of his personal thermometer thirteen times a day. . . . His better style as a writer is in keeping with the simplicity and purity of his life. We have said that his range was narrow, but to be a master is to be a master. He had caught his English at its living source, among the poets and prose-writers of its best days; his literature was extensive and recondite; his quotations are always nuggets of the purest ore; there are sentences of his as perfect as anything in the language, and thoughts as clearly crystal-lized; his metaphors and images are always fresh from the soil; he had watched Nature like a detective who is to go upon the stand; as we read him, it seems as if all-out-of-doors had kept a diary and become his own Montaigne; we look at the landscape as in a Claude Lorraine glass; com-pared with his, all other books of similar aim, even White's "Selborne," seem dry as a country clergyman's meteorological journal in an old almanac.

> James Russell Lowell, 1866-90, *Thoreau;*
> *Works,* Riverside Ed., pp. 378, 380

A scholar by birthright, and an author, his fame had not, at his decease, travelled far from the banks of the rivers he described in his books; but one hazards only the truth in affirming of his prose, that in substance and pith, it surpasses that of any naturalist of his time; and he is sure of large reading in the future. . . . More primitive and Homeric than any American, his style of thinking was robust, racy, as if Nature herself had built his sentences and seasoned the sense of his paragraphs with her own vigor and salubrity. Nothing can be spared from them; there is nothing superfluous; all is compact, concrete, as nature is.

> A. Bronson Alcott, 1869, *Concord Days,* pp. 14, 16

There are certain writers in American literature who charm by their eccentricity as well as by their genius, who are both original and originals. The most eminent, perhaps, of these was Henry D. Thoreau—a man who may be said to have penetrated nearer to the physical heart of Nature than any other American author. Indeed, he "experienced" nature as others are said to experience religion. . . . He was so completely a naturalist that the inhabitants of the woods in which he sojourned forgot their well-founded distrust of man, and voted him the freedom of their city. His descriptions excel even those of Wilson, Audubon, and Wilson Flagg, admirable as these are, for he was in closer relation with the birds than they, and carried no gun in his hand. In respect to human society, he pushed his individuality to individualism; he was never happier than when absent from the abodes of civilization, and the toleration he would not extend to a Webster or a Calhoun he extended freely to a robin or a wood-chuck. With all this peculiarity, he was a poet, a scholar, a humorist, also, in his way, a philosopher and philanthropist; and those who knew him best, and entered most thoroughly into the spirit of his character and writings, are the warmest of all the admirers of his genius.

Edwin Percy Whipple, 1876-86, *American Literature and Other Papers,* ed. Whittier, p. 111

"The man who goes alone can start today," was one of his sayings; "but he who travels with another must wait till that other is ready, and it may be a long time before they get off." It is this self-contained and self-sustaining temper which gives zest to all that Thoreau does and says, and makes him so thoroughly original.

Thomas Hughes, 1878, *The Academy*

Whatever question there may be of his talent, there can be none, I think, of his genius. It was a slim and crooked one, but it was eminently personal. He was imperfect, unfinished, inartistic; he was worse than provincial— he was parochial; it is only at his best that he is readable.

Henry James, 1880, *Nathaniel Hawthorne (English Men of Letters)*, p. 94

His English, we might judge, was acquired from the poets and prose-writers of its best days. His metaphors and images have the freshness of the soil. His range was narrow, but within his limits he was a master. He needed only a tender and pervading sentiment to have been a Homer. Pure and guileless, and fond of sympathy, he yet was cold and wintry. . . . His works are replete with fine observations, finely expressed. One cannot fail to see the resemblance of his style to Emerson's and Alcott's. Nothing that he wrote can be spared.

Alfred H. Welsh, 1883, *Development of English Literature and Language,* vol. II, p. 413

Thoreau's poetry is not of the kind that will lift the reader by any lyric sweep of prodigious exaltation, but it appeals rather to the inner spirit, like the lines of Wordsworth and Emerson. It brings with it no drum and fife; it expresses, instead, the rapture and fervor and ecstasy of the still, small voice. It carries with it the unconscious melody of the brook's ripple and the jocund spirit of the bird's song.

Joel Benton, 1886, "The Poetry of Thoreau," *Lippincott's Magazine,* vol. 37, p. 500

The interest in his books has steadily grown, and of late years many other writers have followed his footsteps in the woods and fields. But no one has rivalled Thoreau; the native power and fertility of his mind, his sturdy independence and originality, his keen perception of nature, and of the poetry of nature, the extent of his reading, and the delightful qualities of his style, combine to render him the ablest and most attractive of the writers of this century upon his chosen themes. He must be an author among ten thousand for whom so much has to be ignored or tolerated, and who yet is everywhere read with delight, in spite of passages on which some pitying angel should have dropped a tear.

Francis H. Underwood, 1888, "Henry David Thoreau," *Good Words,* vol. 29, p. 452

One of the most strongly-marked individualities of modern times. . . . Thoreau's fame will rest on *Walden,* the *Excursions,* and his *Letters,* though he wrote nothing which is not deserving of notice. Up till his thirtieth year he dabbled in verse, but he had little ear for metrical music, and he lacked the spiritual impulsiveness of the true poet. He had occasional flashes of insight and could record beautifully, notwithstanding: his little poem "Haze" is surcharged with concentrated loveliness. His weakness as a philosopher is his tendency to base the laws of the universe on the experience-born, thought-produced convictions of one man—himself. His weakness as a writer is the too frequent striving after antithesis and paradox. If he had all his own originality without the itch of appearing original, he would have made his fascination irresistible. As it is, Thoreau holds a unique place. He was a naturalist, but absolutely devoid of the pedantry of science; a keen observer, but no retailer of disjointed facts. He thus holds sway over two domains: he has the adherence of the lovers of fact and of

the children of fancy. He must always be read, whether lovingly or inter-
estedly, for he has all the variable charm, the strange saturninity, the contradictions, austerities, and delightful surprises, of Nature herself.

William Sharp, 1888, *Encyclopædia Britannica,*
Ninth Ed., vol. XXIII

In his moral and intellectual growth and experience, Thoreau seems to have
reacted strongly from a marked tendency to invalidism in his own body. He
would be well in spirit at all hazards. What was this neverending search of
his for the wild but a search for health, for something tonic and antiseptic
in nature? Health, health, give me health, is his cry. He went forth into
nature as the boys go to the fields and woods in spring after winter-greens,
black-birch, crinkle-root, and sweet-flag; he had an unappeasable hunger for
the pungent, the aromatic, the bitter-sweet, for the very rind and salt of the
globe. He fairly gnaws the ground and the trees in his walk, so craving is
his appetite for the wild. He went to Walden to study, but it was as a deer
goes to a deer-lick; the brine he was after did abound there. Any trait of
wildness and freedom suddenly breaking out in any of the domestic animals
as when your cow leaped your fence like a deer and ate up your corn, or
your horse forgot that he was not a mustang on the plains, and took the bit
in his mouth, and left your buggy and family behind high and dry, etc., was
eagerly snapped up by him. Ah, you have not tamed them, you have not
broken them yet! He makes a most charming entry in his journal about a
little boy he one day saw in the street, with a homemade cap on his head
made of a woodchuck's skin. He seized upon it as a horse with the crib-bite
seizes upon a post. It tasted good to him.

John Burroughs, 1889, *Indoor Studies,* p. 13

It has been claimed for Thoreau by some of his admirers, never by himself,
that he was a man of science, a naturalist. Certainly, in some respects, he
had in him the material for an almost ideal naturalist. His peculiar powers
of observation, and habits of noting and recording natural facts, his patience,
his taste for spending his days and nights in the open air, seem to furnish
everything that is required. Nor would his morbid dislike of dissection have
been any serious bar, for the least worked but by no means the least important portion of natural history is the study of living forms, and for this
Thoreau seems to have been peculiarly adapted; he had acquired one of the
rarest of arts, that of approaching birds, beasts and fishes, and exciting no
fear. There are all sorts of profoundly interesting investigations which only
such a man can profitably undertake. But that right question which is at
least the half of knowledge was hidden from Thoreau; he seems to have
been absolutely deficient in scientific sense. His bare, impersonal records

of observations are always dull and unprofitable reading; occasionally he stumbles on a good observation, but, not realizing its significance, he never verifies it or follows it up. His science is that of a fairly intelligent school-boy—a counting of birds' eggs and a running after squirrels. Of the vital and organic relationship of facts, or even of the existence of such relation-ships, he seems to have no perception. Compare any of his books with, for instance, Belt's *Naturalist in Nicaragua,* or any of Wallace's books: for the men of science, in their spirit of illuminating inquisitiveness, all facts are instructive; in Thoreau's hands they are all dead. He was not a naturalist: he was an artist and a moralist.

Henry Havelock Ellis, 1890-92, The New Spirit, p. 93

Thoreau's Mysticism, though born out of due time, is pure Darwinian. In that Walden wood he stands as the most wonderful and sensitive register of phenomena, finer and more exact than any cunningly devised measure. He is vision and learning, touch, smelling, and taste incarnate. Not only so, but he knows how to preserve the flashing forest colours in unfading light, to write down the wind's music in a score that all may read, to glean and garner every sensuous impression.

P. A. Graham, 1891, Nature in Books

He is self-conscious and splenetic, full of antipathies and whimsical fancies; and when he would be oracular he ruffles up his feathers after the manner of his beloved Walden owl. A strange embodiment of the cynical and the spiritual, of the cosmical and the translunary, together with a strain of the savage, existed in his character,—a certain element of the ghostly and un-canny, as of one who moved in a different sphere from that of his fellow-men, and whose soul was not actually human, but had absorbed some occult influence from the moon and the night.

George H. Ellwanger, 1895, Idyllists of the Country-Side, p. 186

Unlike many bookmaking folk, this swart, bumptious man has grown in literary stature since his death; his drawers have been searched, and cast-away papers brought to day. Why this renewed popularity and access of fame? Not by reason of newly detected graces of style; not for weight of his *dicta* about morals, manners, letters; there are safer guides than all these. But there is a new-kindled welcome for the independence, the tender partic-ularity, and the outspokenness of this journal-maker. If asked for a first-rate essayist, nobody would name Thoreau; if a poet, not Thoreau; if a scientist, not Thoreau; if a political sage, not Thoreau; if a historian of small socialities and of town affairs, again not Thoreau. Yet we read him—

with zest, though he is sometimes prosy, sometimes overlong and tedious; but always—Thoreau.

Donald G. Mitchell, 1899, *American Lands and Letters,
Leather-Stocking to Poe's "Raven,"* p. 278

Thoreau's individuality is often so assertive as to repel a sympathy which it happens not instantly to attract; but that sympathy must be unwholesomely sluggish which would willingly resist the appeal of his communion with Nature. If your lot be ever cast in some remote region of our simple country, he can do you, when you will, a rare service, stimulating your eye to see, and your ear to hear, in all the little commonplaces about you, those endlessly changing details which make life everywhere so unfathomably, immeasurably wonderous. . . . Nor is Thoreau's vitality in literature a matter only of his observation. Open his works almost anywhere,—there are ten volumes of them now,—and even in the philosophic passages you will find loving precision of touch. He was no immortal maker of phrases. Amid bewildering obscurities, Emerson now and again flashed out utterances which may last as long as our language. Thoreau had no such power; but he did possess in higher degree than Emerson himself the power of making sentences and paragraphs artistically beautiful. Read him aloud, and you will find in his work a trait like that which we remarked in the cadence of Brockden Brown and of Poe; the emphasis of your voice is bound to fall where meaning demands. An effect like this is attainable only through delicate sensitiveness to rhythm.

Barrett Wendell, 1900, *A Literary History of America,* pp. 334, 335

His writings cleave so closely to the man that they can hardly be studied wholly apart, nor is it necessary so to consider them at length here. What is most remarkable in them is their wild "tang," the subtlety and the penetrative quality of their imaginative sympathy with the things of field, forest, and stream. The minuteness, accuracy, and delicacy of the observation and feeling are remarkable; while mysticism, fancy, poetic beauty, and a vein of shrewd humor often combine with the other qualities to make a whole whose effect is unique. Thoreau's verse is much like Emerson's on a smaller scale and a lower plane, having the same technical faults and occasionally the same piercing felicity of phrase. On the whole, Thoreau must be classed with the minor American authors; but there is no one just like him, and the flavor of his best work is exceedingly fine.

Walter C. Bronson, 1900, *A Short History of
American Literature,* p. 213

The greatest by far of our writers on Nature, and the creator of a new sentiment in literature. . . . Much of his writing, perhaps the greater part, is the mere record of observation and classification, and has not the slightest claim on our remembrance,—unless, indeed, it possesses some scientific value, which I doubt. Certainly the parts of his work having permanent interest are just those chapters where he is less the minute observer, and more the contemplative philosopher. Despite the width and exactness of his information, he was far from having the truly scientific spirit; the acquisition of knowledge, with him, was in the end quite subordinate to his interest in the moral significance of Nature, and the words he read in her obscure roll were a language of strange mysteries, sometimes of awe. It is a constant reproach to the prying, self-satisfied habits of small minds to see the reverence of this great-hearted observer before the supreme goddess he so loved and studied.

Paul Elmer More, 1901, "A Hermit's Notes on Thoreau,"
Atlantic Monthly, vol. 87, p. 860

JAMES SHERIDAN KNOWLES
1784-1862

Born, at Cork, 12 May 1784. At his father's school there, 1790-93. Family removed to London, 1793. Left home on his father's second marriage, 1800. Served as ensign in Wilts Militia, 1804; in Tower Hamlets Militia, 1805-06. Studied medicine. M. D., Aberdeen, 1808. Resident Vaccinator to Jennerian Soc., 1808. First appeared on the stage, at Bath, 1809. Married Maria Charteris, 25 Oct. 1809. Play *Leo,* produced by Edmund Kean at Waterford, 1810. *Brian Boroihme* produced at Belfast, 1811 (at Covent Garden, 20 April 1837); *Caius Gracchus,* at Belfast, 13 Feb. 1815; at Covent Garden, 18 Nov. 1823. Kept a school at Belfast, 1812-16; at Glasgow, 1816-28. *Virginius* produced at Glasgow, 1820; at Covent Garden, 17 May 1820; *William Tell,* Covent Garden, 1825. On staff of Glasgow *Free Press,* Jan. 1823 to Dec. 1824. *The Beggar's Daughter of Bethnal Green* produced at Drury Lane, 28 May 1828. Removed from Glasgow to Newhaven, near Edinburgh, 1830. Contrib. to *Literary Souvenir, Keepsake,* and other periodicals. *Alfred the Great* produced at *Drury* Lane, 28 April 1831; *The Hunchback,* Covent Garden, 5 April 1832; *The Wife,* Covent Garden, 24 April 1833. Acted in America, 1834. *The Daughter,* Drury Lane, 29 Nov. 1836; *The Bridal,* Haymarket, 26 June 1837; *The Love Chase,* Haymarket, 10 Oct. 1837; *Woman's Wit,* Covent Garden, 23 May 1838; *Maid of Mariendorpt,* Haymarket, 9 Oct. 1838; *Love,* Covent Garden, 4 Nov. 1839; *John of Procida,* Covent Garden, 19 Sept. 1840; *Old Maids,* Covent Garden, 2 Oct. 1841. Wife died, Feb. 1841. Married Miss Elphinstone, 1842. *The Rose of Arragon,* Haymarket, 4 June 1842; *The Secretary,* Drury Lane, 24 April 1843. Retired from stage, 1843. Contrib. to various periodicals. Civil List Pension, 1848. One of committee for purchase of Shakespeare's Birthplace, 1848. Joined the Baptists about this time. Entertained at banquet in Cork, May 1862. Died, at Torquay, 30 Nov. 1862. Buried in Glasgow Necropolis. WORKS: *The Welch Harper,* 1796; *Fugitive Pieces,* 1810; *The Senate* (under pseud.

"Selim"), 1817; *Virginius,* 1820 (third edn. same year); *Caius Gracchus,* 1823; *The Elocutionist,* 1823; *William Tell,* 1825; *The Beggar's Daughter of Bethnal Green,* 1828 (second edn., called *The Beggar of Bethnal Green,* 1834); *Alfred the Great,* 1831; *The Hunchback,* 1832; *The Magdalen,* 1832; *A Masque* [on the death of Sir Walter Scott], 1832; *The Wife,* 1833; *The Daughter,* 1837 (second edn. same year); *The Love Chase,* 1837; *The Bridal* [from Beaumont and Fletcher], 1837, *Woman's Wit,* 1838; *Dramatic Works,* 1838; *The Maid of Mariendorpt,* 1838; *Love,* 1840; *John of Procida,* 1840; *Old Maids,* 1841; *The Rose of Arragon,* 1842; *The Secretary,* 1843; *Dramatic Works* (3 vols.), 1843; *George Lovell,* 1847; *Fortescue* (from *Sunday Times*) 1847 (priv. ptd., 1846); *The Rock of Rome,* 1849; *The Idol Demolished by its own Priest,* 1851; *The Gospel Attributed to Matthew is the Record of the Whole Original Apostlehood,* 1855; *Dramatic Works,* 1856. POSTHUMOUS: *True unto Death,* 1866 (another edn., called *Alexina,* same year); *Brian Boroihme,* 1872 (priv. ptd., 1871); *Lectures on Dramatic Literature* (2 vols.), 1873; *Various Dramatic Works* (priv. ptd.) 1874. He *edited:* J. A. Mason's *Treatise on the Climate,* 1850. LIFE: by R. B. Knowles. revised edn., 1872.

R. Farquharson Sharp, 1897, *A Dictionary of English Authors,* p. 159

SEE: L. H. Meeks, *Sheridan Knowles and the Theatre of his Time,* 1933.

PERSONAL

When Mr. James Sheridan Knowles shall die, the newspapers will mourn the loss of the best, most successful dramatist of the day; they will discourse pathetically of the many ills, which, during life, he suffered at the hands of a public. A goodly number of obituary notices will appear, and in the place of his burial, there will be erected, by the beneficently disposed, a monument, to perpetuate the memory of so popular a dramatist. No matter if the cost of this monument would, while he lived, have relieved his distress; no matter if even then his plays shall be acted, to thin houses, for the benefit of his widow and children.

Park Benjamin, 1835, "Sheridan Knowles,"
North American Review, vol. 40, p. 142

He lived a long life, and did not waste it. Up to a good old age he was healthy and hearty. Macready described to me their first interview, when the actor received the dramatist in the green-room. Sheridan Knowles presented himself—a jolly-looking fellow, with red cheeks, a man obviously full of buoyancy and good-humor—and read to the great manager his tragedy of *Virginius.* "What!" cried Macready, half-pleasantly, half-seriously, when the reading was over, "you the author of that tragedy— you? Why you look more like the captain of a Leith smack!" Nature had endowed Sheridan Knowles with a rare gift, but it was not improved by learning or study, and he owed little, if anything, to his great predecessors in dramatic art. In his later days, as I have remarked, the celebrated dramatist became a Baptist minister. I regret now that I never heard him preach, although I am told it was a performance that one might have been satisfied to witness only once. But I am sure that, whatever and wherever he was, in the pulpit or on the stage, Sheridan Knowles was in earnest—simple, honest, and hearty always. His was a nature that remained thoroughly unspoiled by extraordinary success.

Samuel Carter Hall, 1883, Retrospect of a Long Life, p. 388

Virginius (1820)

The only way in which Mr. Knowles personifies our age, is in his truly domestic feeling. The age is domestic, and so is he. Comfort—not passionate imaginings,—is the aim of everybody, and he seeks to aid and gratify this love of comfort. All his dramas are domestic, and strange to say, those that should be most classic, or most chivalric, most above and beyond it, are the most imbued with this spirit. In what consists the interest and force of this popular play of *Virginius?* The domestic feeling. The costume, the setting, the decorations are heroic. We have Roman tunics, but a modern English heart,—the scene is the Forum, but the sentiments those of the "Bedford Arms." The affection of the father for his daughter—the pride of the daughter in her father, are the main principles of the play.

Richard Hengist Horne, 1844, A New Spirit of the Age, p. 239

The Hunchback (1832)

A play made up of the rarest qualities of literary genius; a production which has shed a golden light on the cold and comfortless gloom of the modern theatre; a mental achievement that places its author in "the forehead of the times," that will embalm his memory with the higest dramatic genius of England, mighty and glorious as she is in that genius—*The Hunchback,* which has acted as a dream, a talisman, on the intellect of the vast metropolis.

Douglas Jerrold, 1832, The English Stage, The Life and Remains
of Douglas Jerrold, ed. Blanchard Jerrold, Appendix, p. 423

The Hunchback is the most original and the most successful of all the productions of Knowles. . . . The part of Julia in *The Hunchback* has always been a favorite part with our actresses, and we have had as many Julias on our stage as we have had leading ladies, or ladies who so considered themselves, to play it. In no other part, perhaps, have so many aspirants for dramatic fame tried their 'prentice hand as in Julia, and to no other do they seem to return so fondly. It is regarded as a sort of test part, and the rising star thinks if she can shine as Julia that she need fear no further eclipse.

Laurence Hutton, 1875, *Plays and Players,* pp. 146, 147

GENERAL

Ignorant alike of rules, regardless of models, he follows the steps of truth and simplicity, and strength, proportion, and delicacy are the infallible results. By thinking of nothing but his subject, he rivets the attention of the audience to it. All his dialogue tends to action, all his situations form classic groups. There is no doubt that *Virginius* is the best acting-tragedy that has been produced on the modern stage.

William Hazlitt, 1825, *The Spirit of the Age*

Knowles' plays were a great success upon a stage which could not hold the dramatic works of much greater poets. Setting aside the dramas written for the library, a long list might be made of the plays written by greater poets— from Coleridge to Tennyson—and meant to be acted, which cannot be credited with a tithe of the success that those of Sheridan Knowles achieved. That his dramatic instinct was far greater than his poetic gift is clear, and that his success was due rather to his dramatic skill than to his poetic force is doubtless true; and yet, taking his work as it stands, it can hardly be disputed that he demonstrated the possibility of making the poetic drama acceptable to nineteenth century audiences. . . . His dialogue, though sometimes marred by conceits and extravagances, is generally simple, direct and vigorous, and ever bright and rapid enough to excite and sustain interest. He had a wide range in his choice of subject, and a large command of dramatic situation. . . . His work, whether treating of classical or modern themes, always deals with men and women, and being instinct with human interest does not fail to interest the human. He worked simply, with simple means, and depended for his success upon the natural excitement of natural emotions.

Alfred H. Miles, 1892, *The Poets and the Poetry of the Century,*
Southey to Shelley, pp. 265, 266

WILLIAM MAKEPEACE THACKERAY
1811-1863

Born, at Calcutta, 18 July 1811. Brought to England at his father's death, 1816. At Charterhouse School, 1822-28. Matric., Trin. Coll., Camb., Feb. 1829. Left Cambridge, 1830; took no degree. Travelled on Continent, 1830-31. Lived in Hare Court, Temple, and studied Law, 1831-32. Edited *National Standard,* May to Dec. 1833. After severe monetary losses, removed to Paris, Dec. 1833. Contrib. to *Fraser's Mag.* from about 1833. Married Isabella Gethin Creagh Shawe, 20 Aug. 1836. Settled in London. Contrib. to *Fraser's Mag., New Monthly Mag., Ainsworth's Mag., Times, Westminster Rev.,* etc. Separation from his wife, 1840. Travelled in East, Aug. to Oct. 1844. Contrib. to *Punch,* 1842-50. Called to Bar at Middle Temple, 26 May 1848. First lectured in London, 1851. In America lecturing, Dec. 1852 to spring of 1853; again, Dec. 1855 to April 1856. Lectured in England and Scotland, 1856. Stood as M. P. for City of Oxford, 1857; was defeated. Edited *Cornhill Mag.,* Nov. 1859 to March 1862. Died, in London, 24 Dec. 1863. Buried at Kensal Green. WORKS: *The Yellowplush Correspondence* (anon.), 1838; *The Paris Sketch-Book* (under pseud. "Mr. Titmarsh"). 1840; *An Essay on the Genius of George Cruikshank* (anon.), 1840; *Comic Tales and Sketches* (under pseud. "Michael Angelo Titmarsh"), 1841; *The Second Funeral of Napoleon* (under pseud. "M. A. Titmarsh"), 1841; *The Irish Sketch-Book* (2 vols.), 1843; *The Luck of Barry Lyndon,* 1844; *Notes of a Journey from Cornhill to Cairo,* 1846; *Mrs. Perkin's Ball* (under pseud. "M. A. Titmarsh"), 1847; *The Book of Snobs,* 1848; *Vanity Fair,* 1848; *Our Street* (under pseud. "M. A. Titmarsh"), 1848; *Dr. Birch and his Young Friends* (under pseud. "M. A. Titmarsh"), 1849; *The History of Samuel Titmarsh; and the Great Hoggarty Diamond,* 1849; *An Interesting Event* (under pseud. "M. A. Titmarsh"), 1849; *The History of Pendennis* (2 vols.), 1849-1850; *Rebecca and Rowena* (under pseud. "M. A. Titmarsh"), 1850; Text to *Sketches after English Landscape Painters,* 1850; *The Kickleburys on the Rhine* (under pseud. "M. A. Titmarsh"), 1851; *The History of Henry Esmond,* 1852; *The English Humourists of the Eighteenth Century,* 1853; *Men's Wives,* 1853; *The Newcomes* (2 vols.), 1854-55; *Miscellanies* (4 vols.), 1854-57; *Ballads,* 1855; *The Rose and Ring* (under pseud. "M. A. Titmarsh"), 1855; *The Virginians* (2 vols.), 1858-59; *Lovel the Widower,* 1861; *The Four Georges,* 1861; *The Adventures of Philip,* 1862; *Roundabout Papers,* 1863 [1862]; POSTHUMOUS: *Dennis Duval,* 1867; *Ballads and Tales,* 1869; *The Orphan of Pimlico,* 1876; *Etchings while at Cambridge,* 1878; *The Chronicle of the Drum,* 1886; *A Collection of Letters . . . 1847-1855,* 1887; *Sultan Stork, etc.,* 1887. COLLECTED WORKS: in 26 vols., 1869-86.

R. Farquharson Sharp, 1897, *A Dictionary of English Authors,* p. 279

SEE: *Works,* ed. Anne Ritchie, 1898-99, 13 v., many repr.; *Works,* ed. George Saintsbury, 1908, 17 v.; *Thackeray and His Daughter: The Letters and Journals of Anne Thackeray Ritchie, with Many Letters of W. M. Thackeray,* ed. H. T. Ritchie, 1924; *Letters and Private Papers,* ed. Gordon N. Ray, 1945-46, 4 v.; Geoffrey Tillotson, *Thackeray the Novelist,* 1954; Gordon N. Ray, *Thackeray,* 1955-58, 2 v.; also see Geoffrey and Kathleen Tillotson, ed., *Vanity Fair: A Novel Without a Hero,* 1963.

PERSONAL

What a misfortune it is to have a broken nose, like poor dear Thackeray! He would have been positively handsome, and is positively ugly in consequence of it. John and his friend Venables broke the bridge of Thackeray's nose when they were schoolboys playing together. What a mishap to befall a young lad just beginning life.

Frances Ann Kemble, 1832, *Journal,* Jan. 17;
Records of a Girlhood, p. 490

We think there was no disappointment with his lectures. Those who knew his books found the author in the lecturer. Those who did not know his books were charmed in the lecturer by what is charming in the author—the unaffected humanity, the tenderness, the sweetness, the genial play of fancy, and the sad touch of truth, with that glancing stroke of satire which, lightning-like, illumines while it withers. The lectures were even more delightful than the books, because the tone of the voice and the appearance of the man, the general personal magnetism, explained and alleviated so much that would otherwise have seemed doubtful or unfair. For those who had long felt in the writings of Thackeray a reality quite inexpressible, there was a secret delight in finding it justified in his speaking; for he speaks as he writes—simply, directly, without flourish, without any cant of oratory, commending what he says by its intrinsic sense, and the sympathetic and humane way in which it was spoken. Thackeray is the kind of "stump orator" that would have pleased Carlyle. He never thrusts himself between you and his thought. If his conception of the time and his estimate of the men differ from your own, you have at least no doubt what his view is, nor how sincere and necessary it is to him.

George William Curtis, 1853-94, "Thackeray in America,"
Literary and Social Essays, p. 130

Thackeray has a dread of servants, insomuch that he hates to address them or to ask them for anything. His morbid sensibility, in this regard, has perhaps led him to study and muse upon them, so that he may be presumed to have a more intimate knowledge of this class than any other man.

Nathaniel Hawthorne, 1855, *English Note-Books,* vol. I, p. 240

The first drawback in his books, as in his manners, is the impression conveyed by both that he never can have known a good and sensible woman. I do not believe he has any idea whatever of such women as abound among the matronage of England,—women of excellent capacity and cultivation applied to the natural business of life. It is perhaps not changing the subject to say next what the other drawback is. Mr. Thackeray has said more, and more effectually, about snobs and snobism than any other man; and yet his frittered life, and his obedience to the call of the great are the observed of all observers. As it is so, so it must be; but "Oh! the pity of it! the pity of it!"

Harriet Martineau, 1855-77, Autobiography,
ed. Chapman, vol. II, p. 61

Mr. Thackeray is forty-six years old, though from the silvery whiteness of his hair he appears somewhat older. He is very tall, standing upwards of six feet two inches and as he walks erect, his height makes him conspicuous in every assembly. His face is bloodless, and not particularly expressive but remarkable for the fracture of the bridge of the nose, the result of an accident in youth. He wears a small grey whisker but otherwise is clean shaven. No one meeting him could fail to recognize in him a gentleman: his bearing is cold and uninviting, his style of conversation either openly cynical or affectedly good-natured and benevolent; his *bonhommie* is forced, his wit biting, his pride easily touched—but his appearance is invariably that of the cool, *suave,* well-bred gentleman, who, whatever may be rankling within, suffers no surface display of emotion.

Edmund Yates, 1858, Town Talk

I believe you have never seen Thackeray, he has the appearance of a colossal infant—smooth white shiny ringletty hair, flaxen, alas! with advancing years, a roundish face with a little dab of a nose, upon which it is a perpetual wonder how he keeps his spectacles, a sweet but rather piping voice, with something of the childish treble in it, and a very tall, slightly stooping figure—such are the characteristic of the great "snob" of England. His manner is like that of England—nothing original, all planed down into perfect uniformity with that of his fellow-creatures. There was not much more distinction in his talk than in his white choker, or black coat and waistcoat.

John Lothrop Motley, 1858, To his Wife, May 28;
Correspondence, ed. Curtis, vol I, p. 229

His medical attendants attributed his death to effusion on the brain. They added that he had a very large brain, weighing no less than 58½ oz. He thus died of the complaint which seemed to trouble him least.

John Camden Hotten (pseud. Theodore Taylor), 1864,
Thackeray the Humorist and the Man of Letters, p. 180

The last line he wrote, and the last proof he corrected, are among these papers through which I have so sorrowfully made my way. The condition of the little pages of manuscript where Death stopped his hand, shows that he had carried them about, and often taken them out of his pocket here and there, for patient revision and interlineation. The last words he corrected in print, were, "And my heart throbbed with an exquisite bliss." God grant that on that Christmas Eve when he laid his head back on his pillow and threw up his arms as he had been wont to do when very weary, some consciousness of duty done and Christian hope throughout life humbly cherished, may have caused his own heart so to throb, when he passed away to his Redeemer's rest! He was found peacefully lying as above described, composed, undisturbed, and to all appearance asleep, on the twenty-fourth of December, 1863. He was only in his fifty-third year; so young a man, that the mother who blessed him in his first sleep, blessed him in his last. . . . On the bright wintry day, the last but one of the old year, he was laid in his grave at Kensal Green, there to mingle the dust to which the mortal part of him had returned, with that of a third child, lost in her infancy years ago. The heads of a great concourse of his fellow-workers in the Arts, were bowed around his tomb.

Charles Dickens, 1864, "In Memoriam," *Cornhill Magazine,*
vol. 9, pp. 131, 132

I had the opportunity, both in England and America, of observing the literary habits of Thackeray, and it always seemed to me that he did his work with comparative ease, but was somewhat influenced by a custom of procrastination. Nearly all his stories were written in monthly instalments for magazines, with the press at his heels. He told me that when he began a novel he rarely knew how many people were to figure in it, and, to use his own words, he was always very shaky about their moral conduct. He said that sometimes, especially if he had been dining late and did not feel in remarkably good-humor next morning, he was inclined to make his characters villainously wicked; but if he arose serene with an unclouded brain, there was no end to the lovely actions he was willing to make his men and women perform. When he had written a passage that had pleased him very much he could not resist clapping on his hat and rushing forth to find an acquaintance to whom he might instantly read his successful composition. . . . The most finished and elegant of all *lecturers,* Thackeray often made a very poor appearance when he attempted to deliver a set speech to a public assembly. He frequently broke down after the first two or three sentences. He prepared what he intended to say with great exactness, and his favorite delusion was that he was about to astonish everybody with a remarkable effort. It never disturbed him that he commonly made a woeful failure when he attempted speech-making, but he sat down with such cool serenity if he found that he could not recall what he wished to say, that his audience could not help joining in and smiling with him when he came to a stand-still.

James T. Fields, 1871, *Yesterdays with Authors,* pp. 15, 18

His voice, as I recall it, was at once low and deep, with a peculiar and indescribable cadence; his elocution was matchless in its simplicity. His attitude was impressive and tranquil, the only movement of his hands being when he wiped his glasses as he turned over the leaves of his manuscript. He read poetry exquisitely.

Richard Henry Stoddard, 1874, "William Makepeace Thackeray," *Harper's Magazine*, vol. 49, p. 544

His remarks, with an occasional touch of satiric humor, were in their general spirit genial and benevolent; and it was easy to see that his disposition was charitable, however shrewd and even caustic his expressions may sometimes have been. I do not think he struck me as being what is technically called a *conversationist*—that is, one who would be invited to dinner for the purpose of keeping up the round of talk—and there was not the least shadow of attempt to show himself off; and though what he said was always sensible and to the point, it was the language of a well-bred and accomplished gentleman, who assumed no sort of superiority, but seemed naturally and simply at ease with his companions of the moment.

George Lamb, 1877, "Recollections of Thackeray," *Harper's Magazine*, vol. 54, p. 259

It was because Thackeray so desired the respect of others, was so anxious for the social consideration of the people he was meeting, that he thought so much about snobs and snobbishness. . . . He looked at the snobbish mind so closely and with such interest, because that mind had been directed upon himself. He examined it as a private soldier examines the cat-o'-nine-tails. It was the quickness of his sensibility to disrespect or unkindness, it was his keenly sympathetic consciousness of the hostile feelings of people toward himself, which awakened a rather indolent mind to such energetic perception of the snobbish moods. It was this which caused him to look with such power upon a snob. During his fifty years of life he had conned a vast number of snobbish thoughts, and must have accumulated a great quantity of snob lore. No doubt, he thought too much about snobs.

Ehrman Syme Nadal, 1881-82, *Thackeray's Relations to English Society, Essays at Home and Elsewhere*, pp. 93, 94

On Christmas Day, 1863, we were startled by the news of Thackeray's death. He had then for many months given up the editorship of the *Cornhill Magazine*—a position for which he was hardly fitted either by his habits or temperament—but was still employed in writing for its pages. I had known him only for four years, but had grown into much intimacy with him and his family. I regard him as one of the most tender-hearted human beings I ever knew, who, with an exaggerated contempt for the foibles of the world at large, would entertain an almost equally exaggerated sympathy with the joys and troubles of individuals around him. He had been unfortunate in early life—unfortunate in regard to money—unfortunate with an afflicted wife—unfortunate in having his home broken up before his children were fit to be his companions. This threw him too much upon clubs, and taught him to dislike general society. But it never affected his heart, or clouded his imagination. He could still revel in the pangs and joys of fictitious life, and could still feel—as he did to the very last—the duty of showing to his readers the evil consequences of evil conduct.

Anthony Trollope, 1882-83, *An Autobiography*

Thackeray, with all his good-nature, varied as it was by occasional bursts of the opposite quality, thought it fair to caricature other people, but very unfair for other people to caricature him. When Mr. Edmund Yates wrote and published a not particularly flattering, but not ill-natured description of him, derived solely from the knowledge he had acquired of him in the Garrick Club, of which they were both members, he forgot the similar case of Fowker, in which he was the offending party, and vowed such social vengeance against Mr. Yates as it was possible for him to take. The result was a literary *fiasco,* which led to the withwrawal of Mr. Yates from the Club, and threatened to lead to the withdrawal of Charles Dickens also. Happily for the Club, and perhaps for Thackeray also, this consummation of a dispute, which Mr. Thackeray ought never to have instigated, was averted.

Charles Mackay, 1887, *Through the Long Day*, vol. II, p. 63

The two key-secrets of Thackeray's great life, as I take it, were these— Disappointment, and Religion. The first was his poison; the second was his antidote. And, as always, the antidote won. No wonder that he was disappointed. First a man of fortune, then a ruined and a struggling artist, then a journalist, recognised to the full as such even by the brothers of the craft, but, like them, very little beyond it—then at last the novelist and the famous man.

Herman Merivale, 1891, *Life of W. M. Thackeray*
(*Great Writers*), p. 13

Thackeray's genius was the flowering of a century and a half of family culture; a culture of which the beautiful after-efflorescence still blooms in "Old Kensington," the "Story of Elizabeth," and the "Village on the Cliff." Thackeray's robustness of character, his hatred of shames, his scorn of all things base, had their roots deep down in the manly life of the old Yorkshire moorland. The power of producing high-class mental work to order, when work must needs be done, came to him from a century of later ancestors who had made their bread by their brains. . . . The clerical traditions of a family, with nineteen parsons among them, made Thackeray, quite apart from his intellectual convictions, the friend of true churchmen, and filled his imagination with the poetry of the rites of the Church. "How should he who knows you," he wrote," respect you or your calling? May this pen never write a pennyworth again if it ever cast ridicule upon either." . . . But the greatest single influence of Thackeray's life-work was still his mother. My earliest portrait of him is that of a little child clinging to his mother, her arm around his neck, and the father sitting close by. At any rate it is something that the best of Bengal civilian families in the last century furnished the mother of Thackeray. The lofty tenderness for women which he learned from that mother he lavished on his wife, until parted from her by her dark malady; it overflowed to his daughters, and breathes in his works.

Sir William Wilson Hunter, 1897, The Thackerays
in India and some Calcutta Graves, pp. 180, 181, 182

In May, his third child, Harriet Marion—afterwards Mrs. Leslie Stephen—was born, and his wife became very ill. The illness eventually affected her mind, and Thackeray, who regarded this as only a natural sequence of the illness, which would pass away in time, when her health was restored, threw all business aside, sent his children to their grandparents at Paris, and for many months travelled with his wife from watering-place to watering-place, as the doctors as a last resource had recommended, hoping against hope that the cloud on her intellect would dissolve. . . . At last Thackeray was compelled to realise the truth—that his poor wife would never recover sufficiently to undertake the duties of a mother and a wife. She was unable to manage her life, though she took interest in any pleasant things around her, especially in music; but it was essential that she should be properly cared for, and, with this object, she was placed with Mr. and Mrs. Thompson at Leigh, in Essex. She outlived her husband by so many years that it was with a shock, having already been dead to the world for nearly forty years, that the announcement of her death, in January, 1894, at the age of seventy-five, was read. She was interred in the same grave at Kensal Green cenmetery as her husband.

Lewis Melville, 1899, The Life of William Makepeace
Thackeray, vol. I, p. 129

Thackeray shocked Charlotte Brontë sadly by the fashion of his talk on literary subjects. The truth is, Charlotte Brontë's heroics roused Thackeray's antagonism. He declined to pose on a pedestal for her admiration, and with characteristic contrariety of nature he seemed to be tempted to say the very things that set Charlotte Brontë's teeth, so to speak, on edge, and affronted all her ideals. He insisted on discussing his books very much as a clerk in a bank would discuss the ledgers he had to keep for salary. But all this was, on Thackeray's part, an affectation; an affectation into which he was provoked by what he considered Charlotte Brontë's highfalutin'. Miss Brontë wanted to persuade him that he was a great man with a "mission"; and Thackeray, with many wicked jests, declined to recognise the "mission."

Sir George Murray Smith, 1901, "In the Early Forties,"
The Critic, vol. 38, p. 58

ART

We well remember, ten or twelve years ago, finding him day after day engaged in copying pictures in the Louvre, in order to qualify himself for his intended profession. It may be doubted, however, whether any degree of assiduity would have enabled him to excel in the money-making branches, for his talent was altogether of the Hogarth kind, and was principally remarkable in the pen-and-ink sketches of character and situation, which he dashed off for the amusement of his friends.

Abraham Hayward, 1848, *Thackeray's Writings,*
Edinburgh Review, vol. 87, p. 49

He had a genuine gift of drawing. The delicious *Book of Snobs* is poor without his own woodcuts; and he not only had the eye and the faculty of a draughtsman, he was one of the best of art critics. He had the true instinct and relish, and the nicety and directness, necessary for just as well as high criticism: the white light of the intellect found its way into this as into every region of his work.

John Brown, 1863-66, *Thackeray's Death, Spare Hours,*
Second Series, p. 232

Thackeray has been called a "lesser Hogarth," and, since he himself has included Hogarth among the humorists rather than among artists, we may admit, I think, the comparison so far; in their humor the two have a considerable amount in common. That Thackeray can in any true sense be called an artist—confining the term to pictorial art,—I do not for a moment believe. In drawing, as in writing, he had an inimitable gift of humorous conception; he had a wonderful power of catching a fit expression and fixing it in three or four strokes, and a fine capacity for humorous detail, but of *technique* he is absolutely innocent; "touching" as in Madame's hand in the last sketch, was ever anything so impossible? And we must remember, in this connection, that Thackeray could not claim to be an untaught genius, since he started his career by studying for an artist.

> Gerard Fiennes, 1894, "Some Notes upon Thackeray,"
> *New Review,* vol. 10, p. 339

How ill we could spare Thackeray's illustrations. Who can forget the sense of fitness which has recommended to him these drawings, weak and insufficient in themselves, but so evidently imbued with the living literary conception? That he could not satisfactorily illustrate the thoughts of others we have abundant evidence, but where have we ever seen book illustrations more helpful to the right understanding of the author's thought than those in *The Christmas Books, Dr. Birch, Our Street,* and *The Kickleburys on the Rhine?*

> George Somes Layard, 1899, "Our Graphic Humourists:
> W. M. Thackeray," *The Magazine of Art,* vol. 23, p. 260

Barry Lyndon (1844)

Barry Lyndon, the autobiography of the Irish adventurer, gambler, and scoundrel is a masterpiece. It is a worthy precursor of *Esmond* in the difficult piece of the historical novel. The hero is a scamp of the last century, not of ours. The world in which he moves is a world of long ago, a world as yet unshrivelled in the fire of the French Revolution. And it is a real world. We never feel doubt or hesitation about that. The characters, adventures, surroundings, all produce on us the impression of life. In the telling of the story, too, what witchery of style. How eloquent, for instance, the passage in which Barry Lyndon defends gambling—how admirable the long episode of the ill-fated love of the Princess Olivia, and of her terrible end! *Barry Lyndon* appeared in *Fraser* during the greater part of 1844, and one may legitimately wonder that the world did not then discover that a great novelist was writing for its amusement and edification. And perhaps an even greater work was to follow.

> Frank T. Marzials, 1891, *Life of W. M. Thackeray*
> (*Great Writers*), p. 131

I cannot tell how often I have read *The Scarlet Letter and Smoke, Henry Esmond* and *Pere Goriot, The Rise of Silas Lapham* and *Adventures of Huckleberry Finn.* To make a choice of them is frankly impossible, or even to say that these six are the favorite half dozen. But if a selection is imperative, I am ready for the moment at least, to declare that Thackeray is the novelist I would rather discuss here and now, well aware that no favourite has a right to expect a long continuance in grace. And the reason why I pick out Thackeray from among the other novelists I like as well as I like him (if not better) is that I may thus call attention to a book of his which I believe to be somewhat neglected. I hold this book to be his best artistically, the one most to be respected, if not the one to be regarded with the most warmth. It is perhaps the only story of Thackeray's which the majority of his readers have never taken up. It is the tale of his telling which most clearly reveals some of his best qualities and which most artfully masks some of his worst defects. It is the *Memoirs of Barry Lyndon, Esq., Written by Himself.* . . . *Barry Lyndon* is neither insipid nor dull; yet its secret history would be interesting enough. It was written when Thackeray was not yet thirty-five years of age—for he flowered late, like most of the greater novelists. . . . As Thackeray paints the portrait, it is worthy to hang in any rogues' gallery—as the original was worthy to be hanged on any scaffold. The villain double-dyed is very rare in modern fiction, and Barry Lydon is an altogether incomparable scoundrel, who believes in himself, tells us his own misdeeds, and ever proclaims himself a very fine fellow—and honestly expects us to take him at his own valuation, while all our knowledge of his evil doings is derived from his own self-laudatory statements!

Brander Matthews, 1897-1901, "On A Novel of Thackeray's,"
The Historical Novel and Other Essays, pp. 151, 152, 157

Book of Snobs (1848)

Never was satire so keen and unflinching. It is the boldest book ever written by a man who had no personal pique to gratify. We are not surprised that the author of it should have been blackballed at the clubs; the wonder rather is, that the doors of private mansions do not "grate harsh thunder" when he stands before them, and that "Jeames" does not positively refuse to take up his name.

John Foster Kirk, 1853, "Thackeray as a Novelist,"
North American Review, vol. 77, p. 218

I regard as a master-piece of humour. Its playfulness is, of course, of the satiric kind. The keen and vivacious satire of an accomplished man of the world is Thackeray's distinctive note as a humourist. . . . There is exaggeration, there is caricature, in the *Book of Snobs.* But its is substantially true. It is a very direct, a very amusing, and I will add, a very philosophical indictment of a specially English vice—a dominant vice, we may say, of the English mind, an unreasonable deference for artificial superiorities.

William Samuel Lilly, 1895, *Four English Humourists
of the Nineteenth Century,* p. 56

The "Snob Papers" had a very marked effect, and may be said to have made Thackeray famous. He had at last found out how to reach the public ear. The style was admirable, and the freshness and vigour of the portrait paint-ing undeniable. It has been stated (Spielmann, p. 319) that Thackeray got leave to examine the complaint books of several clubs in order to obtain material for his description of club snobs. He was speaking, in any case, upon a very familiar topic, and the vivacity of his sketches naturally sug-gested identification with particular individuals. These must be in any case doubtful, and the practice was against Thackeray's artistic principles.

Leslie Stephen, 1898, *Dictionary of National Biography,*
vol. LVI, p. 96

Vanity Fair (1848)

You mentioned Thackeray and the last number of *Vanity Fair.* The more I read Thackeray's works the more certain I am that he stands alone—alone in his sagacity, alone in his truth, alone in his feeling (his feeling, though he makes no noise about it, is about the most genuine that ever lived on a printed page), alone in his power, alone in his simplicity, alone in his self-control. Thackeray is a Titan, so strong that he can afford to perform with calm the most herculean feats; there is the charm and majesty of repose in his greatest efforts; *he* borrows nothing from fever, his is never the energy of delirium—his energy is sane energy, deliberate energy, thoughtful energy. The last number of *Vanity Fair* proves this peculiarly. Forcible, exciting in its force, still more impressive than exciting, carrying on the interest of the narrative in a flow, deep, full, resistless, it is still quiet—as quiet as reflection, as quiet as memory; and to me there are parts of it that sound as solemn as an oracle. Thackeray is never borne away by his own ardour—he has it under control. His genius obeys him—it is his servant, it works no fantastic changes at its own wild will, it must still achieve the task which reason and sense assign it, and none other. Thackeray is unique. I *can* say more, I *will* say no less.

Charlotte Brontë, 1848, *Letter to W. S. Williams,* March 29;
Charlotte Brontë and Her Circle, ed. Shorter, p. 411

I can read nothing but *Vanity Fair,* over and over again, which fills me with delight, wonder, and *humility.* I would sooner have drawn Rawdon Crawley than all the folks I ever drew.

Charles Kingsley, 1850, *Letter to his Wife;* in *Charles Kingsley,*
his Letters and Memoirs of his Life, ed. his Wife,
vol. II, p. 25, note

I confess to being unable to read *Vanity Fair,* from the moral disgust it occasions.

Harriet Martineau, 1855-77, *Autobiography,* ed. Chapman,
vol. II, p. 60

The tale may be said to have been in some degree deceptive, for the novel certainly had a heroine, Miss Rebecca, or, as she is profanely but more commonly called, Becky Sharp. No one, however, stopped to criticise the title; it was acknowledged at once to be a great work, not indeed of the very highest class, such as *Ivanhoe* or *Woodstock,* but rather of the school of Fielding, and worthy of the master, being indeed much such a work as he himself, if polished into decorum by the more refined civilization of the nineteenth century, would have written.

Charles Duke Yonge, 1872, *Three Centuries of
English Literature,* p. 631

How did Thackeray achieve his effects? Becky Sharp is a unique and permanent figure in literature, a subtle embodiment of duplicity, ambition, and selfishness. She is avaricious, hypocritical, specious, and crafty. Though not malignant nor to a certainty criminal, she is a conscienceless little malefactor, whose ill deeds are only limited by the ignoble dimensions of her passions. She lies with amazing glibness, is utterly faithless to her hulking husband, and utterly indifferent to her child. Her mendacity is superlative, and double-dealing enters into all her transactions. But she is so shrewd, so vivacious, so artful, so immensely clever and good-humoured, she has so much prettiness of manner and person, that, while we despise her, and have not the least pity for her when retribution falls heavily upon her, our indignation against her is not so great as we feel that it ought to be, principally because her sins have a certain feminine archness and irresponsibility in them, which keeps them well down to the level of comedy. When we close the book we know her through and through, and thoroughly understand all the complex workings of her strategic mind. How do we know her so well? Thackeray is not exegetical, and does not depend on elaborate analysis for his effects. The actions of the characters are themselves fully expository, and do not call for any outside comments or enlargement on the part of the author. This is the case to such an extent that, when we examine the completeness with which the characters are revealed to us, we are inclined to believe that Thackeray's art is of the very highest kind, and that, though in form it is undramatic, intrinsically it is powerfully dramatic.

William H. Rideing, 1885, *Thackeray's London,* p. 34

We have been to the show. What now are our reflections? What higher and braver thoughts have come to our minds when, wearied with toil and the witness of life's discordant realities, we turned aside to dream of the unreal? What encouragement have we gained for efforts at well-doing by the sight of honest work and patient endurance rewarded? Or what warning have we had from the contemplation of vice and intrigue overtaken by disaster, or at least by disappointment? Instead of these we have found—and to some extent been ashamed to find—ourselves admiring a creation that is as seductive as it is evil. Added to this we were conscious of a loss of some portion of that which it is most calamitous to lose. Woe to him who parts from his trust in mankind, who does not believe that in this world there is goodness beyond that which he has never found in his own being the capacity to practise! In this book the artist—and he was an eminently great artist—seemed to have endeavored to drive mankind to their own unaided struggles, taking away from them all good examples, and leaving them to conclude that nothing is real but folly and perfidy.

Richard Malcolm Johnston, 1886, "The Extremity of Satire,"
Catholic World, vol. 42, p. 688

George Osborn ought to be the hero of <i>Vanity Fair,</i> and in truth is handsome and outwardly attractive enough; but in almost all the higher qualities he is almost beneath contempt. What more can be said in his praise than that he won and retained the love of one of the sweetest and purest of women? Major Dobbin, with whom he is contrasted, is everything externally that the conventional hero of fiction ought not to be—uncouth and ridiculous, rough and forbidding. It is, however, within this ungainly casket that Thackeray places a truly beautiful soul, honest and brave, patient and unselfish, true and faithful. With the fortunes of these four persons the story is mainly concerned. But there are besides many others—Joseph Sedley, the older Osborne, and the Crawleys—all drawn to the life, and with a pencil that never falters. Whether we like his views of life and of society or not, we cannot help feeling that these pictures are as true in outline as they are faithful in detail. Thackeray never fails in his purpose to amuse, but in the exercise of his sterner functions as a moralist and censor, he may sometimes arouse a sentiment of pity for the puppets of his fancy on whom he has brought down with such terrible effect the lash of his retributory satire.

Richard D. Graham, 1897, The Masters of
Victorian Literature, p. 27

I cannot help thinking that although <i>Vanity Fair</i> was written in 1845 and the following years, it was really begun in 1817, when the little boy, so lately come from India, found himself shut in behind those filigree iron gates at Chiswick, of which he writes when he described Miss Pinkerton's establishment. Whether Miss Pinkerton was, or was not, own sister to the great Doctor at the head of the boarding-school for young gentlemen on Chiswick Mall, to which "Billy boy" (as the author of *Vanity Fair* used to be called in those early days) was sent, remains to be proved. There is certainly a very strong likeness between those two majestic beings, the awe-inspiring Doctor and the great Miss Pinkerton whose dignity and whose Johnsonian language marked an epoch in education. . . . My brother-in-law has some of the early MS. of *Vanity Fair*. It is curious to compare it with that of *Esmond,* for instance, which flows on straight and with scarcely an alteration. The early chapters of *Vanity Fair* are, on the contrary, altered and rewritten with many erasures and with sentences turned in many different ways.

Anna Isabella Thackeray Ritchie, 1898, ed. Vanity Fair,
Introduction, pp. xv, xxxvii

The story is none too engrossing, but the strength lies in the truth of the characters. It is indeed a novel "without a hero," devoid of thrilling occurrences or adventures, without a murder, or a forged will and with no lofty virtues or monstrous vices, for "Becky Sharp," Thackeray's most celebrated character, is no tigress, only a cat, or it may be a tiger-cat. The book is a thorough picture of English middle-class life. Thackeray is merciless in his treatment of this mediocrity, the spoilt child of the English novelist. The mean and ignoble standard of second-rate morality, too timid to be vicious, too indolent to be virtuous, is exposed in a number of characters that may be regarded as typical. *Vanity Fair* is the author's masterpiece; witness the delicacy and quiet reserve in the most touching scenes: the parting of George Osborne and Amelia, the battlefield of Waterloo and the death of Osborne—all depicted in a few brief memorable lines.

Edward Engel, 1902, A History of English Literature,
rev. Hamley Bent, p. 454

History of Pendennis (1849-50)

I can easily believe that a girl should be taught to wish to love by reading how Laura Bell loved Pendennis. Pendennis was not, in truth, a very worthy man, nor did he make a very good husband; but the girl's love was so beautiful, and the wife's love, when she became a wife, so woman-like, and at the same time so sweet, so unselfish, so wifely, so worshipful—in the sense in which wives are told that they ought to worship their husbands—

that I cannot believe that any girl can be injured, or even not benefited, by reading of Laura's love.

Anthony Trollope, 1882-83, An Autobiography

The *History of Pendennis*—more veracious than many a history of more pretension—is at once the delight and the despair of all young men who seek to lead the literary life. Indeed, one may often wonder how many men have taken to literature as the honest trade whereby they were to get their bread, after a youthful reading of those wonderful chapters which tell the entrancing tale of Pen's spending an evening in writing "The Church Porch" up to a plate in an annual, and which set forth the starting of the *Pall Mall Gazette,* written by a gentleman for gentlemen. And who is there to say that *Pendennis* is better or more beautiful or more captivating than *Henry Esmond* or *Vanity Fair* or *The Virginians.* When I recall certain pages of those books and of their fellows, *The Newcomes,* and the incomparable *Barry Lyndon,* I am ready to break out into dithyrambic rhapsodies of enthusiasm, and I know I had best be silent. The dithyrambic rhapsodist is not a fashionable critic, just now.

Brander Matthews, 1888, Books That Have Helped Me, p. 80

Here, as in *Vanity Fair,* the heroism has been found a little insipid; and there may be good ground for finding Laura Pendennis dull, though she has a spirit of her own. In later books she becomes, what Thackeray's people very seldom are, a tiresome as well as uninviting person. Costigan is unique, and so is Major Pendennis, a type which, allowing for differences of period and manners, will exist as long as society does, and which has been seized and depicted by Thackeray as by no other novelist. His two encounters, from both of which he comes out victorious, one with Costigan in the first, the other with Morgan in the second volume, are admirable touches of genius. In opposition to the worldliness of the Major, with which Pendennis does not escape being tainted, we have Warrington, whose nobility of nature has come unscathed through a severe trial, and who, a thorough gentleman if a rough one, is really the guardian of Pendennis's career. There is, it should be noted, a characteristic and acknowledged confusion in the plot of Pendennis, which will not spoil any intelligent reader's pleasure.

Walter H. Pollock, 1888, Encyclopædia Britannica,
Ninth Ed., vol. XXIII

In the same way perhaps that *Vanity Fair* was begun at Chiswick in the year 1818, some of the early chapters of *Pendennis* must have been written within the first quarter of the century, and Fairoaks and Charteris are certainly to be found between the folded sheets which travelled from Charterhouse and Cambridge to the mother at Larkbeare by Ottery St. Mary's. Some one very like Helen Pendennis was the mistress of Larkbeare, where my father spent his holidays as a boy; and there was a little orphan niece called Mary Graham, who also lived in the old house, with its seven straight windows and its background of shading trees. Major Pendennis, most assuredly, was *not* to be found there. I have heard my father describe the bitter journey in winter-time, when he drove from Charterhouse to Larkbeare upon the top of the snowy Exeter coach. On one occasion my grandmother told me he had to be lifted down, so benumbed was he with the cold. The journey from Cambridge must have been longer still, but he was older and better able to stand it, nor was it always winter-time then, any more than it is now. Between 1824 and 1825, after his fight with Mr. Venables and the accident which broke the bridge of his nose, my father left Penny's house and went to live in Charterhouse Square with Mrs. Boyes, who took in boys belonging to Charterhouse and Merchant Tailors. It was a low brick house with a tiled roof; he once pointed it out to us, and he took us across the playground and into the old chapel.

Anne Isabella Thackeray Ritchie, 1898, ed. *Pendennis,*
Introduction, p. xiii

In *Pendennis,* begun almost immediately after finishing *Vanity Fair,* Thackeray took his stand by Fielding, defending "the Natural in Art," and announcing that he was going to present the public with a new *Tom Jones.* His specific intent was an exact account of the doings of a young man, at school, at college, in the inns of court, and at the clubs, as he had observed them. But if *Pendennis* be compared with its prototype, certain points of difference are clear. Tom Jones yields to temptation. Arthur Pendennis and George Warrington, bundles of high manly qualities and very great weaknesses, are for a time led astray by passions which they afterward overcome. Thackeray admits frankly that there are some passages in the careers of his gentlemen that will not bear telling. Fielding concealed nothing; *Tom Jones* is a study in the nude. Thackeray reluctantly draped his figures, out of respect to conventions he was inclined from time to time to ridicule.

Wilbur L. Cross, 1899, *The Development of the
English Novel,* p. 204

Henry Esmond (1852)

There is abundance of incident in the book, but not much more plot than in one of Defoe's novels: neither is there, generally speaking, a plot in man's life, though there may be and often is in sections of it. Unity is given not by consecutive and self-developing story, but by the ordinary events of life blended with those peculiar to a stirring time acting on a family group, and bringing out and ripening their qualities; these again controlling the subsequent events, just as happens in life. The book has the great charm of reality.

George Brimley, 1852-58, *"Esmond," Essays,* ed. Clark, p. 254

For myself, I own that I regard *Esmond* as the first and finest novel in the English language. Taken as a whole, I think that it is without a peer. There is in it a completeness of historical plot, and an absence of that taint of unnatural life which blemishes, perhaps, all our other historical novels, which places it above its brethren. And, beyond this, it is replete with a tenderness which is almost divine,—a tenderness which no poetry has surpassed. Let those who doubt this go back and study again the life of Lady Castlewood. In *Esmond,* above all his works, Thackeray achieves the great triumph of touching the innermost core of his subject, without ever wounding the taste. We catch all the aroma, but the palpable body of the thing never stays with us till it palls us. Who ever wrote of love with more delicacy than Thackeray has written in Esmond?

Anthony Trollope, 1864, "W. M. Thackeray," *Cornhill Magazine,*
vol. 9, p. 136

Of Thackeray's works certainly the most remarkable and perhaps the best is *Esmond.* Many novelists following in the wake of Scott have attempted to reproduce for us past manners, scenes, and characters; but in *Esmond* Thackeray not only does this—he reproduces for us the style in which men wrote and talked in the days of Queen Anne. To produce the forgotten phraseology, to remember always not how his age would express an idea, but how Steele, or Swift, or Addison would have expressed it, might have been pronounced impossible of accomplishment. Yet in *Esmond* Thackeray did accomplish it, and with perfect success. The colouring throughout is exquisite and harmonious, never by a single false note is the melody broken.

Henry J. Nicoll, 1882, *Landmarks of English Literature,* p. 389

The greatest book in its own special kind ever written.

George Saintsbury, 1896, *A History of Nineteenth
Century Literature,* p. 152

The book shows even more than the lectures how thoroughly he had imbibed the spirit of the Queen Anne writers. His style had reached its highest perfection, and the tenderness of the feeling has won perhaps more admirers for this book than for the more powerful and sterner performances of the earlier period. The manuscript, now in the library of Trinity College, Cambridge, shows that it was written with very few corrections, and in great part dictated to his eldest daughter and Mr. Crowe. Earlier manuscripts show much more alteration, and he clearly obtained a completer mastery of his tools by long practice. He took, however, much pains to get correct statements of fact, and read for that purpose at the libraries of the British Museum and the Athenæum.

> Leslie Stephen, 1898, *Dictionary of National Biography,*
> vol. LVI, p. 99

English Humorists (1853)

Next to Macaulay and Hazlitt, he is the most entertaining of critics. You read his lectures with quite as much gusto as you do *Pendennis,* and with infinitely more than you do such dull mimicry of the past as is to be found in *Esmond*. Clever, too, of course, sagacious often, and sometimes powerful, are his criticisms, and a geniality not frequent in his fictions, is often here. Sympathy with his subject is also a quality he possesses and parades; indeed, he appears as one born out of his proper time, and seems, occasionally, to sigh for the age of big-wigs, bagnios, and sponging-houses.

> George Gilfillan, 1855, *A Third Gallery of Portraits,* p. 218

He gave his lectures on *The English Humourists* to large audiences in Carusi's saloon. The interest of these lectures was in their matter, and in their author, but not in their manner of delivery; for he was utterly wanting in those graces of oratory which add so much to the pleasure of listening to the reading of a genuinely literary performance. He was closely confined to his manuscript, which he read in a monotone; yet he was always audible, and he commanded the closest attention of his auditors.

> Charles H. Brainard, 1885, *Recollections of Thackeray;*
> *Some Noted Princes, Authors and Statesmen of Our Time,*
> ed. Parton, p. 54

By judicious selection, by innuendo, here a pitying aposiopesis, there an indignant outburst, the charges are heaped up. Swift was a toady at heart, and used Stella vilely for the sake of the hussy Vanessa. Congreve had captivating manners—of course he had, the dog! And we all know what that meant in those days. Dick Steele drank and failed to pay his creditors. Sterne —now really I know what Club life is, ladies and gentlemen, and I might tell you a thing or two if I would: but really, speaking as a gentleman before a polite audience, I warn you against Sterne.

> A. T. Quiller-Couch, 1891, *Adventures in Criticism,* p. 95

Thackeray knew not only the literature but the life of the eighteenth century as few have known it. In minute acquaintance with facts he has doubtless been surpassed by many professional historians; but there is no book to be compared to *Esmond* as a picture of life in the age of Queen Anne; and the lectures on the humourists are saturated, as *Esmond* is, with the eighteenth century spirit. The figures of the humourists live and move before our eyes. We may not always agree with the critic's opinion, but we can hardly fail to understand the subject better through his mode of treatment. Strong objection has been taken, perhaps in some respects with justice, to his handling of Swift. Yet, much as has been written about Swift, where does there exist a picture of him so vivid, so suggestive and so memorable? Who else has done such justice to Steele? Who has written better about Hogarth? Thackeray succeeded because he not only knew the work of these men but felt with them. He was at the bottom of the eighteenth century type. Much of Swift himself, softened and humanised, something of Fielding, whom he justly regarded as a model, and a great deal of Hogarth may be detected in Thackeray.

Hugh Walker, 1897, The Age of Tennyson, p. 92

The Newcomes (1854-55)

The Newcomes is perhaps the most genial of the author's works, and the one which best exhibits the maturity and the range of his powers. It seems written with a pen diamond-pointed, so glittering and incisive is its slightest touch.

Edwin Percy Whipple, 1866, "Thackeray," Character and
Characteristic Men, p. 214

Generally accounted his masterpiece; and which, if less sparkling than *Vanity Fair,* and less severely testing the artistic skill of the author than *Esmond,* yet deserves its fame by presenting us, in Colonel Newcome and Ethel, with the most beautiful pictures both of man and woman that he ever drew.

Charles Duke Yonge, 1872, Three Centuries of
English Literature, p. 632

One day, while the great novel of *The Newcomes* was in course of publication, Lowell, who was then in London, met Thackeray on the street. The novelist was serious in manner, and his looks and voice told of weariness and affliction. He saw the kindly inquiry in the poet's eyes, and said, "Come into Evans's, and I'll tell you all about it. *I have killed the Colonel.*" So they walked in and took a table in a remote corner, and then Thackeray, drawing the fresh sheets of MS. from his breast pocket, read through that exquisitely touching chapter which records the death of Colonel Newcome. When he came to the final *Adsum,* the tears which had been swelling his lids for some time trickled down his face, and the last word was almost an inarticulate sob.

Francis Henry Underwood, 1881, "James Russell Lowell,"
Harper's Magazine, vol. 62, p. 265

The Newcomes was written in the years that came between my father's first and second journey to America. He began the preface at Baden on the 7th of July 1853, he finished his book at Paris on the 28th of June 1855, and in the autumn of that year he returned to America. The story had been in his mind for a long time. While still writing *Esmond* he speaks of a new novel "opening with something like Fareham and the old people there," and of "a hero who will be born in India, and have a half-brother and sister." And there is also the description to be read of the little wood near to Berne, in Switzerland, into which he strayed one day, and where, as he tells us, "the story was actually revealed to him."

Anne Isabella Thackeray Ritchie, 1898, ed. *The Newcomes,*
Introduction, p. xxii

It is an epitome of human life in its manifold variety of social and individual phrases unmatched, I think, in fiction. Its range is extraordinary for the thread of a single story to follow. Yet all its parts are as interdependent as they are numerous and varied. It is Thackeray's largest canvas, and it is filled with the greatest ease and to the borders. It stands incontestably at the head of the novels of manners. And it illustrates manners with an un-exampled crowd of characters, the handling of which, without repetition or confusion, without digression or discord, exhibits the control of the artist equally with the imaginative and creative faculty of the poet—the "maker." The framework of *The Newcomes* would include three or four of Balzac's most elaborate books, which compared with it, indeed, seem like studies and episodes, lacking the large body and ample current of Thackeray's epic.

W. C. Brownell, 1899, "William Makepeace Thackeray,"
Scribner's Magazine, vol. 25, p. 245

The Virginians (1858-59)

The Virginians is the most carefully planned of his novels, and the most mature as regards his ideas, but the work has not been carried out so per-fectly as some others.

J. Scherr, 1874, *A History of English Literature,* tr. M. V., p. 277

The Virginians, Thackeray told Motley "was devilish stupid, but at the same time most admirable"; and the criticism, paradoxical as it may seem, possesses an element of truth. "Devilish stupid" the book, of course, is not. But it is thoroughly ill "composed," to borrow the art critic's term. The first half and the second half scarcely hang together; the interest is divided, somewhat clumsily, between the two brothers—and I, for one, confess to be very sorry when George comes to life again, and is installed as hero *vice* Henry deposed. But, with all drawbacks, the hand of the great master is there, in the matchless style, the admirable scenes, the excellent delineations of character, the exact reproduction of the life of the last century. All this is on the "most remarkable" side.

Frank T. Marzials, 1891, Life of W. M. Thackeray
(Great Writers), p. 194

I have never quite understood the common depreciation of *The Virginians* which contains things equal, if not superior, to the very finest of its author's other work, and includes the very ripest expression of his philosophy of life. For though indeed I do not approve a novel more because it contains the expression of a philosophy of life, others do. So, too, the irregularity and formlessness of plot which characterised most of Thackeray's work undoubtedly appear in it; but then, according to the views of our briskest and most modern critics, plot is a very subordinate requisite in a novel, and may be very well dispensed with. Here again I do not agree, and I should say that Thackeray's greatest fault was his extreme inattention to construction, which is all the more remarkable inasmuch as he was by no means a very rapid or an extremely prolific writer.

George Saintsbury, 1895, Corrected Impressions, p. 17

POEMS

Little has yet been said of Thackeray's performances in poetry. They formed a small but not the least significant part of his life's work. The grace and apparent spontaneity of his versification are beyond question. Some of the more serious efforts, such as *The Chronicle of the Drum* (1841), are full of power, and instinct with true poetic feeling. Both the half-humorous half-pathetic ballads and the wholly extravagant ones must be classed with the best work in that kind; and the translations from Béranger are as good as verse translations can be. He had the true poetic instinct, and proved it by writing poetry which equalled his prose in grace and feeling.

Walter H. Pollock, 1888, Encyclopædia Britannica,
Ninth Ed., vol. XXIII

His so-called ballads have the charm that belongs to the wholly or half-playful exercises, the recreations in rhyme, of a supreme literary craftsman. They are not verses of society; they are either too richly humorous, or too sharply satiric, or too deeply coloured by feeling. Through them, as all through his prose, mirth glides by the easiest transitions into sadness, mockery trembles into tenderness, to the strain of boon goodfellowship succeeds the irrepressible reminder that all below is vanity. Carelessly as they seem to have been penned, they abound in happy rhymes and turns of phrase, they show the hand of the writer born to work in metre no less than in prose. *The White Squall* is a really wonderful *tour de force* of vivid, rattling description and novel, dexterous rhyming; there is the true martial note in the rough swinging verses of *The Chronicle of the Drum;* and as for the Irish Ballads, they seem bound to amuse till the drying up of the fountain of laughter. Since Burns wrote the *Ordination,* no more telling, mirth-provoking bit of satire has been done in rhyme than the immortal *Battle of Limerick*; and where could there be found a more delicious revel of vocables, all honeyed by the Milesian usage, than in Mr. Maloney's account of the ball that was given to the Nepaulese ambassador?

Walter Whyte, 1894, *The Poets and the Poetry of the Century.*
Humour, Society, Parody, and Occasional Verse, ed. Miles, p. 321

GENERAL

There is a man in our own days whose words are not framed to tickle delicate ears; who, to my thinking, comes before the great ones of society much as the son of Imlah came before the throned kings of Judah and Israel; and who speaks truth as deep, with a power as prophet-like and as vital—a mien as dauntless and as daring. Is the satirist of *Vanity Fair* admired in high places? I cannot tell; but I think if some of those amongst whom he hurls the Greek fire of his sarcasm, and over whom he flashes the levin-branch of his denunciation, were to take his warnings in time, they or their seed might yet escape a fatal Ramoth-Gilead. Why have I alluded to this man? I have alluded to him, reader, because I think I see in him an intellect profounder and more unique than his contemporaries have yet recognized; because I regard him as the first social regenerator of the day—as the very master of that working corps who would restore to rectitude the warped system of things; because I think no commentator on his writings has yet found the comparison that suits him, the terms which rightly char-acterise his talent. They say he is like Fielding; they talk of his wit, humour, comic powers. He resembles Fielding as an eagle does a vulture; Fielding could stoop on carrion, but Thackeray never does. His wit is bright, his humour attractive, but both bear the same relation to his serious genius, that the mere lambent sheet-lightning, playing under the edge of the summer cloud, does to the electric deathspark hid in its womb.

Charlotte Brontë, 1847, Jane Eyre, Preface

Mr. Thackeray's humour does not mainly consist in the creation of oddities of manner, habit, or feeling, but in so representing actual men and women as to excite a sense of incongruity in the reader's mind—a feeling that the follies and vices described are deviations from an ideal of humanity always present to the writer. The real is described vividly, with that perception of individuality which constitutes the artist; but the description implies and suggests a standard higher than itself, not by any direct assertion of such a standard, but by an unmistakable irony. The moral antithesis of actual and ideal is the root from which springs the peculiar charm of Mr. Thackeray's writings; that mixture of gaiety and seriousness, of sarcasm and tenderness, of enjoyment and cynicism, which reflects so well the contradictory consciousness of man as a being with senses and passions and limited knowledge, yet with a conscience and a reason speaking to him of eternal laws and a moral order of the universe. It is this that makes Mr. Thackeray a profound moralist, just as Hogarth showed his knowledge of perspective by drawing a landscape throughout in violation of its rules. . . . No one could be simply amused with Mr. Thackeray's descriptions or his dialogues. A shame at one's own defects, at the defects of the world in which one was living, was irresistibly aroused along with the reception of the particular portraiture. But while he was dealing with his own age, his keen perceptive faculty prevailed, and the actual predominates in his pictures of modern society.

George Brimley, 1852-58, "Esmond," Essays,
ed. Clark, pp. 255, 256

Thackeray finds that God has made no allowance for the poor thing in his universe,—more's the pity, he thinks,—but 'tis not for us to be wiser; we must renounce ideals and accept London.

Ralph Waldo Emerson, 1856-84, English Traits;
Works, Riverside Ed., vol. V, p. 234

If it were asked what one aspect of life Mr. Thackeray has distinctively exhibited, the answer could be given in one word,—the trivial aspect. The characters he draws are neither the best of men nor the worst. But the atmosphere of triviality which envelopes them all was never before so plainly perceivable. He paints the world as a great Vanity Fair, and none has done that so well. The realism of Thackeray can hardly fail to have a good effect in fictitious literature. It represents the extreme point of reaction against the false idealism of the Minerva Press. It is a pre-Raphaelite school of novel writing. And as pre-Raphaelitism is not to be valued in itself, so much as in being the passage to a new and nobler ideal, the stern realism of Thackeray may lead the way to something better than itself.

Peter Bayne, 1857, Essays in Biography and Criticism,
First Series, p. 391

No one can read Mr. Thackeray's writings without feeling that he is perpetually treading as close as he dare to the border line that separates the world which may be described in books from the world which it is prohibited so to describe. No one knows better than this accomplished artist where that line is, and how curious are its windings and turns. The charge against him is that he knows it but too well; that with an anxious care and a wistful eye he is ever approximating to its edge, and hinting with subtle art how thoroughly he is familiar with and how interesting he could make the interdicted region on the other side. He never violates a single conventional rule, but at the same time, the shadow of the immorality that is not seen is scarcely ever wanting to his delineation of the society that is seen,—every one may perceive what is passing in his fancy.

Walter Bagehot, 1858, "Charles Dickens," Works,
ed. Morgan, vol. II, p. 266

Thackeray's range is limited. His genius is not opulent, but it is profuse. He does not create many types, but he endlessly illustrates what he does create. In this he reminds a traveler of Ruysdael and Wouvermann, the old painters. There are plenty of their pictures in the German galleries, and there is no mistaking them. This is a Ruysdael, how rich and tranquil! this is a Wouvermann, how open and smiling! are the instinctive words with which you greet them. The scope, the method, almost the figures and the composition are the same in each Ruysdael, in each Wouvermann, but you are not troubled. Ruysadel's heavy tree, Wouvermann's white horse, are not less agreeable in Dresden than in Berlin, or Munich, or Vienna. And shall we not be as tolerant in literature as in painting? Why should we expect simple pastoral nature in Victor Hugo, or electrical bursts of passion in Scott, or the "ideal" in Thackeray?

George William Curtis, 1862, "The Easy Chair,"
Harper's Magazine, vol. 25, p. 423

Unsteadfast, idle, changeable of purpose, aware of his own intellect but not trusting it, no man ever failed more generally than he to put his best foot foremost. Full as his works are of pathos, full of humour, full of love and charity, tending, as they always do, to truth and honor, and manly worth and womanly modesty, excelling, as they seem to me to do, most other written precepts that I know, they always seem to lack something that might have been there. There is a touch of vagueness which indicates that his pen was not firm while he was using it. He seems to me to have been dreaming ever of some high flight, and then to have told himself, with a half-broken heart, that it was beyond his power to soar up into those bright regions. I can fancy, as the sheets went from him every day, he told himself, in regard to every sheet, that it was a failure.

Anthony Trollope, 1879, Thackeray (English Men of Letters), p. 19

Thackeray's ideal of life is really childlike in its purity. In *Vanity Fair* he took, like Fielding whom he did not study in vain, a broad canvas on which to paint an image of the world. As Fielding, in Tom Jones, and Blifil, represented the two opposite poles about which our world turns, so Thackeray contrasted Becky Sharp and the Crawley side of the world with the side of Major Dobbin and Amelia. When it was said that his good people were innocent babies, that was his praise; for a childlike innocence, remote enough from the conception of the cynic, was Thackeray's ideal to the last. If Major Dobbin seemed too weak, Thackeray mended the fault in Colonel Newcome, to whom he gave the same feature of unworldly simplicity and innocence. Thackeray's sensibility made him, perhaps, a little too much afraid of the conscious idlers who consider themselves men of the world. Being himself tenderly framed, he took refuge like the hermit crab in a shell that was not his own but served well for protection. He certainly was, in his younger days, somewhat too much in awe of the conventions of sociey; for there is an implied bowing down before them in some of the Snob papers that is saved only by its honest origin from being not conventionally but essentially vulgar.

Henry Morley, 1881, Of English Literature in the Reign
of Victoria with a Glance at the Past, p. 380

Esmond apart, there is scarce a man or a woman in Thackeray whom it is possible to love unreservedly or thoroughly respect. That gives the measure of the man, and determines the quality of his influence. He was the average clubman *plus* genius and a style. And, if there is any truth in the theory that it is the function of art not to degrade but to ennoble—not to dishearten but to encourage—not to deal with things ugly and paltry and mean but with great things and beautiful and lofty—then, it is argued, his example is one to depreciate and to condemn. . . . He may not have been a great man but assuredly he was a great writer; he may have been a faulty novelist but assuredly he was a rare artist in words. Setting aside Cardinal Newman's, the style he wrote is certainly less open to criticism than that of any other modern Englishman. He was neither super-eloquent like Mr. Ruskin nor a Germanised Jeremy like Carlyle; he was not marmoreally emphatic as Landor was, nor was he slovenly and inexpressive as was the great Sir Walter; he neither dallied with antithesis like Macaulay nor rioted in verbal vulgarisms with Dickens; he abstained from technology and what may be called Lord Burleighism as carefully as George Eliot indulged in them, and he avoided conceits as sedulously as Mr. George Meredith goes out of his way to hunt for them. He is a better writer than any one of these, in that he is always a master of speech and of himself, and that he is always careful yet natural, and choice yet seemingly spontaneous.

William Ernest Henley, 1890, *Views and Reviews*, pp. 15, 16

It is precisely because Thackeray, discerning so well the abundant misery and hollowness in life, discerns also all that is not miserable and hollow, that he is so great. He has neither the somewhat bestial pessimism of M. Zola, nor the fatuous gaiety of M. Ohnet. Like any classic, he stands the test of experience, of psychology. We have mentioned together Swift, Addison, and Steele, we might take Lucretius, Virgil, and Horace. Each has left a picture of patrician life, glittering and tedious. Lucretius, contrasting the splendour without and the gloom within; Virgil, the restlessness and haste with the placid peace of the country; Horace, content to let it all go by, neither envying nor despising. Something of each, again, is in Thackeray: an English classic not less true and real than the classic Romans.

Lionel Johnson, 1891, *The Academy*, vol. 39, p. 227

One mark of Thackeray's realism is his refusal to take his art seriously. In his view an author is but the master of a set of puppets with which he can represent real life, if he please, but over whose movements it is absurd to pretend that he has not absolute control. Hence Thackeray jests at his art in a tone that was most unpleasant to minor craftsmen. This tone has done him a disservice with later readers, and belies the essential importance of his work; for though the world which he pictures is a bit antique in our eyes, its problems are ours, and granting the thirty years' difference in time, Thackeray treats them in a way as significant for us as that of Meredith or Ibsen.

William Vaughn Moody and Robert Morss Lovett, 1902,
A History of English Literature, p. 369

NATHANIEL HAWTHORNE

1804-1864

Born, in Salem, Mass., 4 July 1804. At school there. At Raymond, Maine, 1818-19. At Salem, 1819-21. Issued weekly paper, *The Spectator,* Aug. to Sept., 1820. To Bowdoin Coll., Brunswick, 1821; B. A., 1825. At Salem, engaged in literary pursuits, 1825-37. Contrib. to *The Token,* 1831-38; *New England Mag.,* 1834-35; *Knickerbocker,* 1837. Editor of *The American Mag. of Useful and Entertaining Knowledge,* 1836. Contrib. to the *Democratic Review,* 1838-46. Weigher and Gauger of Customs at Boston, 1839-41. Joined the *Arcadia* settlement at Brook Farm, April 1841. Married Sophia Amelia Peabody, July 9, 1842. Lived at the Old Manse, Concord, Mass., 1842-46. At Salem, as Surveyor of Customs, 1846-49. Removed to Lennox, Mass., 1850; to West Newton, near Boston, 1851; to Concord, 1852. American Consul at Liverpool, 1853-57; travelled on Continent, 1857-59; returned to America, 1860. Contrib. to *Atlantic Monthly,* 1860-64. Died, at Plymouth, N. H., 18 May, 1864. Buried at Concord. WORKS: *Fanshawe* (anon.), 1828; *Twice-Told Tales,* 1st series, 1837; 2nd series, 1842; *Grandfather's Chair,* (pt. i.), 1841; ("Famous Old People," 1841, and "Liberty Tree," 1842, extracted from preceding); *Biographical Stories for Children,* 1842; *Mosses from an Old Manse* (2 vols.), 1846; *The Scarlet Letter,* 1850; *The House of the Seven Gables,* 1851; *True Stories from History and Biography,* 1851; *The Wonder Book,* 1851; *The Snow Image, etc.,* 1851; *The Blithedale Romance,* 1852; *Life of Franklin Pierce,* 1852; *The Tanglewood Tales,* 1853; *A Rill from the Town Pump,* 1857; *The Marble Faun* (English edn. called *Transformation*), 1860; *Our Old Home,* 1863; *Pansie,* 1864. POSTHUMOUS WORKS: *Tales* (2 vols.), 1866; *Passages from the American Note-books of Hawthorne,* 1868; *Passages from the English Note-books of Hawthorne,* 1870; *Passages from the French and Italian Note-books of Hawthorne,* 1871; *Septimus Felton,* 1872; *The Dolliver Romance,* 1876; *Tales of the White Hills,* 1877; *A Virtuoso's Collection, etc.,* 1877; *Legends of New England,* 1877; *Legends of the Province House,* 1877; *Dr. Grimshawe's Secret,* 1883; *Sketches and Studies,* 1883. He edited: H. Bridge's *Journal of an African Cruiser,* 1865.

R. Farquharson Sharp, 1897, *A Dictionary of English Authors,* p. 127

SEE: *Complete Works,* ed. George P. Lathrop, 1883, 12 v.; *The Heart of Hawthorne's Journal,* ed. Newton Arvin, 1929; *American Notebooks,* ed. Randall Stewart, 1932; *English Notebooks,* ed. Randall Stewart, 1941; *Complete Novels and Selected Tales,* ed. Norman Holmes Pearson, 1939; *Short Stories,* ed. Newton Arvin, 1946; George E. Woodberry, *Nathaniel Hawthorne,* 1902; Newton Arvin, *Hawthorne,* 1929; Randall Stewart, *Nathaniel Hawthorne,* 1948; Roy R. Male, *Hawthorne's Tragic Vision,* 1957.

PERSONAL

I have not yet concluded what profession I shall have. The being a minister is of course out of the question. I should not think that even you could desire me to choose so dull a way of life. Oh, no, mother, I was not born to vegetate forever in one place and to live and die as calm and tranquil as—a puddle of water. As to lawyers, there are so many of them already that one half of them (upon a moderate calculation) are in a state of actual starvation. A physician, then, seems to be "Hobson's choice"; but yet I should not like to live by the diseases and infirmities of my fellow-creatures. And it would weigh very heavily on my conscience, in the course of my practice, if I should chance to send any unlucky patient "ad inferum," which being interpreted is, "to the realms below." Oh that I was rich enough to live without a profession! What do you think of my becoming a author, and relying for support upon my pen? Indeed, I think the illegibility of my hand-writing is very author-like. How proud you would feel to see my works praised by the reviewers, as equal to the proudest productions of the scribbling sons of John Bull. But authors are always poor devils, and therefore Satan may take them.

Nathaniel Hawthorne, 1821, *Letter to his Mother;*
Nathaniel Hathorne and his Wife, ed. Hawthorne, vol. I, p. 107

During Hawthorne's first year's residence in Concord I had driven up with some friends to an æsthetic tea at Mr. Emerson's. It was in the winter, and a great wood-fire blazed upon the hospitable hearth. There were various men and women of note assembled; and I, who listened attentively to all the fine things that was said, was for some time scarcely aware of a man who sat upon the edge of the circle, a little withdrawn, his head slightly thrown forward upon his breast, and his bright eyes clearly burning under his black brow. As I drifted down the stream of talk, this person, who sat silent as a shadow looked to me as Webster might have looked had he been a poet,—a kind of poetic Webster. He rose and walked to the window, and stood quietly there for a long time, watching the dead-white landscape. No appeal was made to him, nobody looked after him, the conversation flowed steadily on, as if everyone understood that his silence was to be respected. It was the same thing at table. In vain the silent man imbibed æsthetic tea. What-ever fancies it inspired did not flower at his lips. But there was a light in his eye which assured me that nothing was lost. So supreme was his silence, that it presently engrossed me, to the exclusion of everything else. There was very brilliant discourse, but this silence was much more poetic and fascinating. Fine things were said by the philosophers, but much finer things were implied by the dumbness of this gentleman with heavy brows and black hair. When he presently rose and went, Emerson, with the "slow, wise smile" that breaks over his face like day over the sky, said, "Hawthorne rides well his horse of the night."

George William Curtis, 1854-94, "Homes of American Authors,"
Literary and Social Essays, p. 43

> Do you ask me, "Tell me further
> Of this Consul, of this Hawthorne?"
> I would say, "He is a sinner,—
> Reprobate and churchless sinner,—
> Never goes inside a chapel,
> Only sees outsides of chapels,
> Says his prayers without a chapel!
> I would say that he is lazy,
> Very lazy, good-for-nothing;
> Hardly ever goes to dinners,
> Never goes to balls or soirees:
> Thinks one friend worth twenty friendly;
>
> Cares for love, but not for liking;
> Hardly knows a dozen people."

Henry Bright, 1855, *Song of Consul Hawthorne,* Dec. 25;
Nathaniel Hawthorne and his Wife, ed. Hawthorne, vol. II, p. 79

I sent my letter at once; from all that I had heard of Mr. Hawthorne's shyness, I thought it doubtful if he would call, and I was therefore very much pleased when his card was sent in this morning. Mr. Hawthorne was more chatty than I had expected, but not any more diffident. He remained about five minutes, during which time he took his hat from the table and put it back once a minute, brushing it each time. The engravings in the books are much like him. He is not handsome, but looks as the author of his books should look; a little strange and odd, as if not of this earth. He has large, bluish-gray eyes; his hair stands out on each side, so much so that one's thoughts naturally turn to combs and hair-brushes and toilet ceremonies as one looks at him.

Maria Mitchell, 1857, *Journal,* Aug. 5; *Life, Letters and
Journals,* ed. Kendall, p. 89

You will have seen, with profound sorrow the announcement of the death of the dearest and most cherished among our early friends. . . . He had been more or less infirm for more than a year. I had observed particularly within the last three or four months, evidences of diminished strength whenever we met. The journey, which was terminated by Mr. Ticknor's sudden death at Philadelphia, was commenced at the urgent solicitation of friends, who thought change essential for him. Mr. Ticknor's death would have been

a great loss and serious shock to H. at any time, but the effect was undoubtedly aggravated by the suddenness of the event and H.'s enfeebled condition.
About three weeks since I went to Concord (Mass.), and made arrangements to take a journey to the lakes, and thence up the Pemigewasset with
my carriage, leaving time and details of the trip to be settled by circumstances *en route*. . . . We arrived at Plymouth about six o'clock. After taking
a little tea and toast in his room, and sleeping for nearly an hour upon the
sofa, he retired. A door opened from my room to his, and our beds were not
more than five or six feet apart. I remained up an hour or two after he fell
asleep. He was apparently less restless than the night before. The light was
left burning in my room—the door open—and I could see him without
moving from my bed. I went, however, between one and two o'clock to his
bedside, and supposed him to be in a profound slumber. His eyes were
closed, his position and face perfectly natural. His face was towards my bed.
I awoke again between three and four o'clock, and was surprised—as he
had generally been restless—to notice that his position was unchanged—
exactly the same as it was two hours before. I went to his bedside, placed
my hand upon his forehead and temple, and found that he was dead. He
evidently had passed from natural sleep to sleep from which there is no
waking, without suffering, and without the slightest movement.

Franklin Pierce, 1864, *Letter to Horatio Bridge*, May 21;
Personal Recollections of Nathaniel Hawthorne, pp. 176, 178

Late in the afternoon of the day before he left Boston on his last journey
I called upon him at the hotel where he was staying. He had gone out but
a moment before. Looking along the street, I saw a form at some distance
in advance which could only be his,—but how changed from his former
port and figure! There was no mistaking the long iron-gray locks, the carriage of the head, and the general look of the natural outlines and movement; but he seemed to have shrunken in all his dimensions, and faltered
along with an uncertain, feeble step, as if every movement were an effort.
I joined him, and we walked together half an hour, during which time
I learned so much of his state of mind and body as could be got at without
worrying him with suggestive questions. . . . He spoke as if his work were
done, and he should write no more. With all his obvious depression, there
was no failing noticeable in his conversational powers. There was the same
backwardness and hesitancy which in his best days it was hard for him to
overcome, so that talking with him was almost like love-making, and his
shy, beautiful soul had to be wooed from its bashful prudency like an un-
schooled maiden. The calm despondency with which he spoke about himself
confirmed the unfavorable opinion suggested by his look and history.

Oliver Wendell Holmes, 1864, "Hawthorne,"
Atlantic Monthly, vol. 14, p. 99

Your father was lame a long time from an injury received while playing bat-and-ball. His foot pined away, and was considerably smaller than the other. He had every doctor that could be heard of; among the rest, your grandfather Peabody. But it was "Dr. Time" who at last cured him. I remember he used to lie upon the floor and read, and that he went upon two crutches. Everybody thought that, if he lived, he would be always lame. Mr. Joseph E. Worcester, the author of the *Dictionary*, who at one time taught a school, in Salem, to which your father went, was very kind to him; he came every evening to hear him repeat his lessons. It was during this long lameness that he acquired his habit of constant reading. Undoubtedly he would have wanted many of the qualities which distinguished him in after life, if his genius had not been thus shielded in childhood.

Elizabeth Hawthorne, 1865 (?), *Letter to Una Hawthorne,*
Nathaniel Hawthorne and his Wife, ed. Hawthorne, vol. I, p. 100

Hawthorne was of the darker temperament and tendencies. His sensitiveness and sadness were native, and he cultivated them apparently alike by solitude, the pursuits and studies in which he indulged, till he became almost fated to know gayer hours only by stealth. By disposition friendly, he seemed the victim of his temperament, as if he sought distance, if not his pen, to put himself in communication and possible sympathy with others, with his nearest friends even. His reserve and imprisonment were more distant and close, while the desire for conversation was livelier, than any one I have known. There was something of strangeness even in his cherished intimacies, as if he set himself afar from all and from himself with the rest. The most diffident of men, as coy as a maiden, he could only be won by some cunning artifice, his reserve was so habitual, his isolation so entire, the solitude so vast. How distant people were from him, they world they lived in, how he came to know so much about them, by what stratagem he got into his own house or left it, was a marvel. Fancy-fixed, he was not to be jostled from himself for a moment, his mood was so persistent. There he was in the twilight, there he stayed.

A. Bronson Alcott, 1869, *Concord Days,* p. 193

No man had more of the feminine element than he. He was feminine in his quick perceptions, his fine insight, his sensibility to beauty, his delicate reserve, his purity of feeling. No man comprehended woman more perfectly; none has painted woman with a more exquisite and ethereal pencil. And his face was as mobile and rapid in its changes of expression as is the face of a young girl. His lip and cheek heralded the word before it was spoken. His eyes would darken visibly under the touch of a passing emotion, like the waters of a fountain ruffled by the breeze of summer.

George S. Hillard, 1870, "The English Note-Books of
Nathaniel Hawthorne," *Atlantic Monthly,* vol. 26, p. 258

Hawthorne's superb head was by all odds the finest in the room. He looked genial, and, *mirabile dictu!* appeared at his ease. To me, who had not seen him since he lived at Lenox, in Massachusetts, this transformation appeared marvelous. I sat down by his side, and he talked brilliantly for half an hour, without exhibiting any of the shyness which for years had made him a perfect recluse. It was said that he was still unapproachable in his Consulate at Liverpool, but he appeared completely humanized at Mrs. Hall's.

Maunsell B. Field, 1873, *Memoirs of Many Men
and Some Women*, p. 145

A simple stone, with the single word "Hawthorne" cut upon it, was placed above him. He had wished that there should be no monument. He liked Wordsworth's grave at Grasmere, and had written: "It is pleasant to think and know that he did not care for a stately monument." Longfellow and Lowell and Holmes, Emerson and Louis Agassiz, and his friends Pierce, and Hillard, with Ellery Channing, and other famous men, assembled on that peaceful morning to take their places in the funeral train. . . . The orchards were blossoming; the roadside-banks were blue with violets, and the lilies of the valley, which were Hawthorne's favorites among the flowers, had come forth in quiet companies to look their last on his face, so white and quiet too. So, while the batteries that had murdered him roared sullenly in the distant South, the rites of burial were fulfilled over the dead poet. Like a clear voice beside the grave, as we look back and listen, Longfellow's simple penetrating chant returns upon the ear.

George Parsons Lathrop, 1876, *A Study of Hawthorne*, p. 325

The author's college life was prophetic of the after years, when he so dwelt apart from the mass of men, and yet stirred so deeply the world's sensibilities and delighted its fancy. His themes were written in the sustained, finished style that gives to his mature productions an inimitable charm. The late Professor Newman, his instructor in rhetoric, was so impressed with Hawthorne's powers as a writer, that he, not infrequently, summoned the family circle to share in the enjoyment of reading his compositions. The recollection is very distinct of Hawthorne's reluctant step and averted look, when he presented himself at the Professor's study, and with girlish diffidence submitted a composition which no man in his class could equal.

George Thomas Packard, 1876, "Bowdoin College,"
Scribner's Monthly, vol. 12, p. 52

The beauty of his countenance was remarkable. Crayon portraits and photographs preserve the fine outline of his head and face, but fail to give his vivid coloring and varying expression. His eyes, fringed with dark lashes, gleamed like tremulous sapphires. Whenever their look encountered mine, they seemed to say: "This sensitive soul prays the world not to be rough or rude."

Julia Ward Howe, 1881, Two Glimpses of Hawthorne,
The Critic, vol. 1, p. 158

She [Mrs. Nathaniel Hawthorne] believed in his inspiration; and her office was to promote, so far as in her lay, the favorableness of the conditions under which it should manifest itself. As food and repose nourish and refresh the body, so did she refresh and nourish her husband's mind and heart. Her feminine intuition corresponded to his masculine insight; she felt the truth that he saw; and his recognition of this pure faculty in her, and his reverence for it, endowed his perception with that tender humanity in which otherwise it might have been deficient. Her lofty and assured ideals kept him to a belief in the reality and veracity of his own. In the warmth and light of such companionship as hers, he could not fall into the coldness and gloom of a selfish intellectual habit. She revived his confidence and courage by the touch of her gentle humor and cheerfulness; before her unshakable hopefulness and serenity, his constitutional tendency to ill-foreboding and discouragement vanished away. Nor was she of less value to him on the merely intellectual side. Her mental faculties were finely balanced and of great capacity; her taste was by nature highly refined, and was rendered exquisitely so by cultivation. . . . Mr. Hawthorne never was a teetotaler, any more than he was an abolitionist or a thug; but he was invariably temperate. During his lifetime he smoked something like half a dozen boxes of cigars, and drank as much wine and spirits as would naturally accompany that amount of tobacco. Months and sometimes years would pass without his either drinking or smoking at all; but when he would resume those practices, it was not to "make up for lost time," his moderation was not influenced by his abstention. Though very tolerant of excesses in others, he never permitted them in himself; and his conduct in this respect was the result not more of moral prejudice than of temperamental aversion. He would have been sober if he had had no morality.

Julian Hawthorne, 1885, Nathaniel Hawthorne and His Wife,
vol. I, pp. 40, 87

Abutting upon the back yard of Hawthorne's birthplace is the old Manning homestead of his maternal ancestors, the home of his own youth and middle age and the theatre of his struggles and triumph. It is known as number twelve Herbert Street, and is a tall, unsightly, erratic fabric of wood, with nothing pleasing or gracious in its aspect or environment. The ugly and commonplace character of his surroundings here during half his life must have been peculiarly depressing to such a sensitive temperament as Hawthorne's, and doubtless accounts for his mental habits. That he had no joyous memories of this old house his letters and journals abundantly show. Its interior arrangement has been somewhat changed to accommodate the several families of laborers who have since inhabited it, and one front room seems to have been used as a shop; but it is not difficult to identify the haunted chamber which was Hawthorne's bed-room and study. This little, dark, dreary apartment under the eaves, with its multipaned window looking down into the room where he was born, is to us one of the most interesting of all the Hawthorne shrines. Here the magician kept his solitary vigil during the long period of his literary probation, shunning his family, declining all human sympathy and fellowship, for some time going abroad only after nightfall; here he studied, pondered, wrote, revised, destroyed, day after day as the slow months went by; and here, after ten years of working and waiting for the world to know him, he triumphantly recorded, "In this dismal chamber FAME was won." Here he wrote *Twice-Told Tales* and many others, which were published in various periodicals, and here, after his residence at the old Manse,—for it was to this Manning house that he "always came back, like the bad halfpenny," as he said,—he completed the *Mosses.* This old dwelling is one of the several which have been fixed upon as being the original *House of the Seven Gables,* despite the novelist's averment that the Pyncheon mansion was "of materials long in use for constructing castles in the air."

Theodore F. Wolfe, 1895, *Literary Shrines,* p. 131

If Thoreau was a recluse, Hawthorne was an anchorite. He brought up his children in such purity and simplicity as is scarcely credible,—not altogether a wise plan. It was said that he did not even take a daily paper. In the following year Martin F. Conway, the first United States representative from Kansas, went to Concord to call on Emerson, and Emerson invited Hawthorne to dine with them. Judge Conway afterwards remarked that Mr. Hawthorne said very little during the dinner, and whenever he spoke he blushed. Imagine a man five times as sensitive as a young lady in her first season, with the will of a Titan, and a mind like a crown-glass mirror, and you have Nathaniel Hawthorne. While he was in a state of observation, the expression of his face reflected everything that was going on about him; in his reflective moods, it was like looking in at the window of a dark room, or perhaps a picture-gallery; and if any accident disturbed him his look was something like a cracked pane of glass. Moreover there was something unearthly or superterrestrial about him, as if he had been born and brought up in the planet Saturn. Wherever he went he seemed to carry twilight with him. He walked in perfect silence, looking furtively about for fear he might meet some one that he knew. His large frame and strong physique ought to have lasted him till the year 1900. There would seem to be something strange and mysterious about his death, as there was in his life. His head was massive, and his face handsome without being attractive. The brow was finely chiseled, and the eyes beneath it were dark, luminous and fathomless. I never saw him smile, except slightly with his eyes.

Frank Preston Stearns, 1895, Sketches from Concord
and Appledore, p. 54

Fanshawe (1828)

Fanshawe is a work which derives its interest wholly from the author's later masterpieces. It has the slightest possible plot, and the characters are imperfectly presented, the descriptions are commonplace to the verge of tameness, yet one who reads the story carefully will easily detect the weak and timid presence of all Hawthorne's peculiar powers.

Bayard Taylor, 1876, "Nathaniel Hawthorne,"
Critical Essays and Literary Notes, p. 355

Fanshawe was published in 1828 by Marsh and Capen, at Boston, without the author's name but at his expense, one hundred dollars being the sum paid; it failed, and Hawthorne looked on it with so much subsequent displeasure that he called in all the copies he could find and destroyed them, and thus nearly succeeded in sinking the book in oblivion, but the few copies which survived secured its republication after his death. The novel is brief, with a melodramatic plot, well-marked scenes, and strongly contrasted character; the style flows on pleasantly; but the book is without distinction. . . . In fact, notwithstanding what Hawthorne had taken from his own observation and feelings, this provincial sketch, for it is no more, is a Scott story, done with a young man's clever mastery of the manner, but weak internally in plot, character, and dramatic reality. It is as destitute of any brilliant markings of his genius as his undergraduate life itself had been, and is important only as showing the serious care with which he undertook the task of authorship.

George E. Woodberry, 1902, Nathaniel Hawthorne
(American Men of Letters), pp. 31, 32

Twice-Told Tales (1837-42)

It is a singular fact that, of the few American writers by profession, one of the very best is a gentleman whose name has never yet been made public, though his writings are extensively and favorably known. We refer to Nathaniel Hawthorne, Esq., of Salem, the author of the "Gentle Boy," the

"Gray Champion," etc., etc., all productions of high merit, which have appeared in the annuals and magazines of the last three or four years. Liberally educated, but bred to no profession, he has devoted himself exclusively to literary pursuits, with an ardor and success which will, ere long, give him a high place among the scholars of this country. His style is classical and pure; his imagination exceedingly delicate and fanciful, and through all his writings there runs a vein of sweetest poetry. Perhaps we have no writer so deeply imbued with the early literature of America; or who can so well portray the times and manners of the Puritans.

> Horatio Bridge, 1836, *For Boston Post, Personal Recollections*
> *of Nathaniel Hawthorne,* p. 70

When a new star rises in the heavens, people gaze after it for a season with the naked eye, and with such telescopes as they may find. In the stream of thought, which flows so peacefully deep and clear, through the pages of this book, we see the bright reflection of a spiritual star, after which men will be fain to gaze "with the naked eye and with the spy-glasses of criticism." This star is but newly risen; and ere long the observations of numerous stargazers, perched up on arm-chairs and editors' tables, will inform the world of its magnitude and its place in the heaven of poetry, whether it be in the paw of the Great Bear, or on the forehead of Pegasus, or on the strings of the Lyre, or in the wing of the Eagle. Our own observations are as follows. To this little work we would say, "Live ever, sweet, sweet book." It comes from the hand of a man of genius. Everything about it has the freshness of morning and of May. These flowers and green leaves of poetry have not the dust of the highway upon them. They have been gathered fresh from the secret places of a peaceful and gentle heart. There flow deep waters, silent, calm, and cool; and the green trees look into them, and "God's blue heaven." The book, though in prose, is written nevertheless by a poet. He looks upon all things in the spirit of love, and with lively sympathies; for to him external form is but the representation of internal being, all things having a life, an end and aim.

> Henry Wadsworth Longfellow, 1837, "Hawthorne's Twice-Told
> Tales," *North American Review,* vol. 45, p. 59

From the press of Munroe & Co., Boston, in the year 1837, appeared *Twice-Told Tales.* Though not widely successful in their day and generation, they had the effect of making me known in my own immediate vicinity; insomuch that, however reluctantly, I was compelled to come out of my owl's nest and lionize in a small way. Thus I was gradually drawn somewhat into the world, and became pretty much like other people. My long seclusion had not made me melancholy or misanthropic, nor wholly unfitted for

the bustle of life; and perhaps it was the kind of discipline which my idiosyncrasy demanded, and chance and my own instincts, operating together,
had caused me to do what was fittest.

Nathaniel Hawthorne, 1853, *Letter to Richard Henry Stoddard;*
Nathaniel Hawthorne and His Wife, ed. Hawthorne, vol. I, p. 98

There is a propriety in Hawthorne's fantasy to which Poe could not attain.
Hawthorne's effects are moral where Poe's are merely physical. The situation and its logical development and the effects to be got out of it are all
Poe thinks of. In Hawthorne the situation, however strange and weird, is
only the outward and visible sign of an inward and spiritual struggle. Ethical
consequences are always worrying Hawthorne's soul; but Poe did not know
that there were any ethics.

Brander Matthews, 1888, *Pen and Ink,* p. 79

Mosses from an Old Manse (1846)

Hawthorne walked with me yesterday afternoon, and not until after our
return did I read his "Celestial Railroad," which has a serene strength
which we cannot afford not to praise, in this low life.

Ralph Waldo Emerson, 1843, *Letter to Thoreau;*
Familiar Letters of Thoreau, ed. Sanborn, p. 143

The truth of these sketches is their prime quality, for Hawthorne wrote them
with the familiar affection and home-attachment of one who had fleeted the
golden time of his youth amid these scenes of common day, and prolonged
it far into manhood, and should never quite lose its glow of mere existence,
its kindliness for humble things, its generous leisure for the perishable beauty
of nature dotted here and there with human life.

George E. Woodberry, 1902, *Nathaniel Hawthorne*
(American Men of Letters), p. 129

The Scarlet Letter (1850)

We are glad that *The Scarlet Letter* is, after all, little more than an experiment and need not be regarded as a step necessarily fatal. It is an attempt to
rise from the composition of petty tales, to the historical novel; and we use
the expression *an attempt,* with no disparaging significance, for it is confessedly a trial of strength only just beyond some former efforts, and was
designed as part of a series. It may properly be called a novel, because it
has all the ground-work, and might have been very easily elaborated into
the details, usually included in the term; and we call it *historical,* because

its scene-painting is in a great degree true to a period of our Colonial history, which ought to be more fully delineated. We wish Mr. Hawthorne would devote the powers which he only partly discloses in this book, to a large and truthful portraiture of that period, with the patriotic purpose of making us better acquainted with the stern old worthies, and all the *dramatis personæ* of those times, with their yet surviving habits, recollections, and yearnings, derived from maternal England.

Arthur Cleveland Coxe, 1851, "The Writings of Hawthorne,"
The Church Review, vol. 3, p. 503

The frivolous costume and brisk action of the story of fashionable life are easily depicted by the practised sketcher, but a work like *The Scarlet Letter* comes slowly upon the canvas, where passions are commingled and overlaid with the masterly elaboration with which the grandest effects are produced in pictorial composition and coloring. It is a distinction of such works that while they are acceptable to the many, they also surprise and delight the few who appreciate the nicest arrangement and the most high and careful finish. *The Scarlet Letter* will challenge consideration in the name of Art, in the best audience which in any age receives Cervantes, Le Sage, or Scott.

Rufus Wilmot Griswold, 1851, "Nathaniel Hawthorne,"
International Magazine, vol. 3, p. 157

With all the care in point of style and authenticity which mark his lighter sketches, this genuine and unique romance may be considered as an artistic exposition of Puritanism as modified by New England colonial life. In truth to costume, local manners, and scenic features, *The Scarlet Letter* is as reliable as the best of Scott's novels; in the anatomy of human passion and consciousness it resembles the most effective of Balzac's illustrations of Parisian or provincial life; while in developing bravely and justly the sentimental of the life it depicts, it is as true to humanity as Dickens.

Henry T. Tuckerman, 1853, "The Prose Poet;
Nathaniel Hawthorne," *Mental Portraits*

It may be said that it "captivated" nobody, but took everybody captive. Its power could neither be denied nor resisted. There were growls of disapprobation from novel-readers, that Hester Prynne and the Rev. Mr. Dimmesdale were subjected to cruel punishments unknown to the jurisprudence of fiction,—that the author was an inquisitor who put his victims on the rack,—and that neither amusement nor delight resulted from seeing the contortions and hearing the groans of these martyrs of sin; but the fact was no less plain that Hawthorne had for once compelled the most superficial lovers of romance to submit themselves to the magic of his genius.

Edwin Percy Whipple, 1860, "Nathaniel Hawthorne,"
Character and Characteristic Men, p. 227

The Scarlet Letter is, on the English side of the water, perhaps the best known. It is so terrible in its pictures of diseased human nature as to produce most questionable delight. The reader's interest never flags for a moment. There is nothing of episode or digression. The author is always telling his one story with a concentration of energy which, as we can understand, must have made it impossible for him to deviate. The reader will certainly go on with it to the end very quickly, entranced, excited, shuddering, and at times almost wretched.

Anthony Trollope, 1879, "The Genius of Nathaniel Hawthorne,"
North American Review, vol. 129, p. 208

It is densely dark, with a single spot of vivid color in it; and it will probably long remain the most consistently gloomy of English novels of the first order. But I just now called it the author's masterpiece, and I imagine it will continue to be, for other generations than ours, his most substantial title to fame. . . . The faults of the book are, to my sense, a want of reality and an abuse of the fanciful element—of a certain superficial symbolism. The people strike me not as characters, but as representatives, very picturesquely arranged, of a single state of mind; and the interest of the story lies, not in them, but in the situation, which is insistently kept before us, with little progression, though with a great deal, as I have said, of a certain stable variation; and to which they, out of their reality, contribute little that helps it to live and move.

Henry James, 1880, Hawthorne (English Men
of Letters),</i> pp. 106, 110</div>

Most perfect and finished as works of Art are the novels of the late Nathaniel Hawthorne, most finished of all *The Scarlet Letter,* an effusion of terrible and stupefying gloom, but wonderfully finely wrought. If Victor Hugo had been fettered by an art as rigid as that of Hawthorne, and had restricted his canvas accordingly, he would have escaped all those mad splashes of the brush which disfigure his best painting. Confined to the compass of *The Scarlet Letter, Les Travailleurs de la Mer* would have been double its present value.

Robert Buchanan, 1886, A Look Round Literature, p. 37

The novel of *The Scarlet Letter* is one of the links in the development of the novel from a means of portraying single phases of emotion to a vehicle of highest expressional power. It was written by a psychological student of the problems which harass the human soul. . . . It is a tragedy—a tragedy sombre, intense, unrelieved. It is almost a fatalistic tragedy; almost as stern as if it had been written by Æschylus. It is not a love story; it is not a story of youth; it is not a story of contemporaneous life; it is not a story of eager hope. . . . *The Scarlet Letter* is not alone an interpretation of personality. It is the first suggestion and forerunner of the Novel of Purpose and of the Novel of Problem. It is the convincing proof of the greatness of the art of Hawthorne that *The Scarlet Letter* is thus at once a presentation and a prophecy.

> Francis Hovey Stoddard, 1900, *The Evolution of the English Novel*, pp. 76, 77, 83

Consider for a moment *The Scarlet Letter;* the pathos of the subject, and the tragic scenes portrayed. All the world agrees that here is a masterpiece of mortal terror and remorse; we are lost in the admiration of the author's insight into the suffering human heart; yet has any one ever shed a tear over that inimitable romance? I think not. The book does not move us to tears; it awakens no sense of shuddering awe such as follows the perusal of the great tragedies of literature; it is not emotional, in the ordinary acceptance of the word, yet shallow or cold it certainly is not. . . . Why, then, we ask, should we have tears ready for *The Newcomes,* and none for *The Scarlet Letter,* although the pathos of the latter tale can so stir the depths of our nature as it did the author's? What curious trait in his writing, what strange attitude of the man toward the moral struggles and agony of human nature is this that sets him apart from other novelists?

> Paul Elmer More, 1901, "The Solitude of Nathaniel Hawthorne," *Atlantic Monthly,* vol. 88, pp. 588, 589

The Scarlet Letter is a great and unique romance, standing apart by itself in fiction; there is nothing else quite like it. Of all Hawthorne's works it is most identified with his genius in popular regard, and it has the peculiar power that is apt to invest the first work of an author in which his originality finds complete artistic expression. It is seldom that one can observe so plainly the different elements that are primary in a writer's endowment coalesce in the fully developed work of genius; yet in this romance there is nothing either in method or perception which is not to be found in the earlier tales; what distinguishes it is the union of art and intuition as they had grown up in Hawthorne's practice and had developed a power to penetrate more deeply into life.

> George E. Woodberry, 1902, *Nathaniel Hawthorne*, p. 189

The House of the Seven Gables (1851)

The House of the Seven Gables was finished yesterday. Mr. Hawthorne read me the close last evening. There is unspeakable grace and beauty in the conclusion, throwing back upon the sterner tragedy of the commencement an ethereal light, and a dear home-loveliness and satisfaction. How you will enjoy the book,—its depth of wisdom, its high tone, the flowers of Paradise scattered over all the dark places, the sweet wall-flower scent of Phœbe's character, the wonderful pathos and charm of old Uncle Venner. I only wish you could have heard the Poet sing his own song, as I did; but yet the book needs no adventitious aid,—it makes its own music, for I read it all over again to myself yesterday, except the last three chapters.

Sophia Hawthorne, 1851, Letter, Jan. 27; Nathaniel Hawthorne
and His Wife, ed. Hawthorne, vol. I, p. 383

The House of the Seven Gables, in my opinion, is better than *The Scarlet Letter;* but I should not wonder if I had refined upon the principal character a little too much for popular appreciation; nor if the romance of the book should be found somewhat at odds with the humble and familiar scenery in which I invest it. But I feel that portions of it are as good as anything I can hope to write, and the publisher speaks encouragingly of its success.

Nathaniel Hawthorne, 1851, Letter to Bridge, Mar. 15;
Personal Recollections of Nathaniel Hawthorne by
Horatio Bridge, p. 125

I think we have no romancer but yourself, nor have had any for this long time. I had become so set in this feeling, that but for your last two stories I should have given up hoping, and believed that all we were to look for in the way of spontaneous growth were such languid, lifeless, sexless creations as in the view of certain people constitute the chief triumphs of a sister art as manifested among us. But there is rich blood in Hester, and the flavor of the sweet-fern and the bayberry are not truer to the soil than the native sweetness of our little Phœbe! The Yankee mind has for the most part budded and flowered in pots of English earth, but you have fairly raised yours as a seedling in the natural soil.

Oliver Wendell Holmes, 1851, Letter to Hawthorne, April 9;
A Study of Hawthorne by G. P. Lathrop, p. 232

I have been so delighted with *The House of the Seven Gables* that I cannot help sitting down to tell you so. I thought I could not forgive you if you wrote anything better than *The Scarlet Letter;* but I cannot help believing it a great triumph that you should have been able to deepen and widen the impression made by such a book as that. It seems to me that the *House* is the most valuable contribution to New England history that has been made. It is with the highest art that you have typified (in the revived likeness of Judge Pyncheon to his ancestor the Colonel) that intimate relationship between the Present and the Past in the way of ancestry and descent, which historians so carefully overlook.

> James Russell Lowell, 1851, *Letter to Hawthorne*, April 24;
> *Nathaniel Hawthorne and His Wife*, ed. Hawthorne, vol. I, p. 390

The contents of this book do not belie its clustering romantic title. With great enjoyment we spent almost an hour in each separate gable. This book is like a fine old chamber, abundantly but still judiciously furnished with precisely that sort of furniture best fitted to furnish it. There are rich hangings, whereon are braided scenes from tragedies. There is old china with rare devices, set about on the carved beaufet; there are long and indolent lounges to throw yourself upon; there is an admirable sideboard, plentifully stored with good viands; there is a smell of old wine in the pantry; and finally, in one corner, there is a dark little black-letter volume in golden clasps, entitled "Hawthorne: A Problem."

> Herman Melville, 1851, *Letter to Hawthorne*,
> *A Study of Hawthorne* by G. P. Lathrop, p. 231

The scenery, tone, and personages of the story are imbued with a local authenticity which is not for an instant impaired by the imaginative charm of romance. We seem to breathe, as we read, the air, and be surrounded by familiar objects, of a New England town. . . . We may add that the same pure, even, unexaggerated, and perspicuous style of diction that we have recognised in his previous writings is maintained in this.

> Henry T. Tuckerman, 1853, "The Prose Poet;
> Nathaniel Hawthorne," *Mental Portraits*

No one should read *The House of The Seven Gables* for the sake of the story, or neglect to read it because of such faults as I have described. It is for the humor, the satire, and what I may perhaps call the philosophy which permeates it, that its pages should be turned. Its pages may be turned on any day and under any circumstances. To *The Scarlet Letter* you have got to adhere till you have done with it; but you take this volume by bits, here and there, now and again, just as you like it. There is a description of a few poultry, melancholy unproductive birds, running over four or five pages, and written as no one but Hawthorne could have written it. There are a dozen pages or more in which the author pretends to ask why the busy Judge does not move from his chair,—the Judge the while having dree'd his doom and died as he sat. There is a ghastly spirit of drollery about this which would put the reader into full communion with Hawthorne if he had not read a page before, and did not intend to read a page after. To those who can make literary food of such passages as these, *The House of the Seven Gables* may be recommended. To others it will be caviare.

Anthony Trollope, 1879, "The Genius of Nathaniel Hawthorne,"
North American Review, vol. 129, p. 216

If there are probably no four books of any author among which, for a favorite, readers hesitate longer than between Hawthorne's four longest stories, there are at any rate many for whom this remains distinctly his largest and fullest production. Suffused as it is with a pleasant autumnal haze, it yet brushes more closely than its companions the surface of American life, comes a trifle nearer to being a novel of manners. The manners it shows us indeed are all interfused with the author's special tone, seen in a slanting afternoon light; but detail and illustrations are sufficiently copious; and I am tempted for my own part to pronounce the book, taking subject and treatment together, and in spite of the position as a more concentrated classic enjoyed by *The Scarlet Letter,* the closest approach we are likely to have to the great work of fiction, so often called for, that is to do us nationally most honor and most good. . . . *The House of the Seven Gables,* I may add, contains in the rich portrait of Judge Pyncheon a character more solidly suggested than—with the possible exception of the Zenobia of *The Blithedale Romance*—any other figure in the author's list.

Henry James, 1897, *Library of the World's Best Literature,*
ed. Warner, vol. XII, pp. 7056, 7057

If not his best book (as the author thought it in his serener moods), it is certainly next best. If Dante had ever told a story of the crime and mysteries which saturated some old country house upon the Euganean hills, I think it would have had much of the color, and much of the high, fierce lights which blaze about the gables of the Pyncheons! Yet it is all his own;—change as his theme may, the author is redolent everywhere of his own clean and complete selfhood; he is not like the rare Stevenson of our day, on whose close-thumbed pages we encounter—now, Defoe with his delicious particularity and *naïveté*—now, find him egotizing, as does Montaigne, or lapsing into such placid humors as embalm the periods of Lamb; or, yet again, catching in smart grip the trumpet of some old glorified Romancer, and summoning his knights (who are more than toy-knights) to file down once more from their old mediævel heights upon the dusty plains of today. No such golden memorial-trail enwraps the books of the Master of Puritan Romance; but, always the severe, unshaken, individual note was uppermost.

Donald G. Mitchell, 1899, *American Lands and Letters,*
Leather-Stocking to Poe's "The Raven," p. 236

There is, of course, a choice in Hawthorne's romances, and I myself prefer *The Blithedale Romance* and *The Scarlet Letter* to *The Marble Faun,* and *The House of the Seven Gables.* The last, indeed, I have found as nearly tiresome as I could find anything of Hawthorne's. I do not think it is censuring it unjustly to say that it seems the expansion of a short story motive to the dimensions of a novel; and the slight narrative in which the concept is nursed with whimsical pathos to the limp end, appears sometimes to falter, and alarms the sympathetic reader at other times with the fear of an absolute lapse. The characters all lack the vitality which the author gives the people of his other books. . . . Hawthorne could not help giving form to his work, but as nearly as any work of his could be so *The House of the Seven Gables* is straggling. There is at any rate no great womanly presence to pull it powerfully together, and hold it in the beauitful unity characteristic of *The Blithedale Romance* and *The Scarlet Letter.*

William Dean Howells, 1901, Heroines of Fiction, vol. I, p. 163

The Blithedale Romance (1852)

It is enough for me that you have put another rose into your chaplet, and I will not ask whether it outblooms or outswells its sister flowers. Zenobia is a splendid creature, and I wish there were more such rich and ripe women about. I wish, too, you could have wound up your story without killing her, or that at least you had given her a drier and handsomer death. Priscilla is an exquisite sketch. I don't know whether you have quite explained Hollingsworth's power over two such diverse natures. Your views about reform and reformers and spiritual rappings are such as I heartily approve. Reformers need the enchantment of distance. Your sketches of things visible, detached observations, and style generally, are exquisite as ever. May you live a thousand years, and write a book every year!

George S. Hillard, 1852, Letter to Hawthorne, July 27;
Nathaniel Hawthorne and His Wife, ed. Hawthorne, vol. I, p. 448

The Blithedale Romance is a work of no ordinary power, and indicative of all its author's mental affluence. In character-painting, he has overtaken his highest previous skill in Hollingsworth, and exceeded it in Zenobia. Then, of lesser personages, who could fail to recognise, in Silas Foster, the agricultural foreman of the farm, a marvellously accurate type of the New England yeoman of the generation just now passing the meridian of manhood? The descriptions of the kitchen, the table, the style of dress, the manner of labor, and the Sunday habits of the Blithedale community, attractive as they are in themselves, are doubly so, as being beyond a question the portions in which observation and experience, rather than fancy, furnished the material for the narrative.

Andrew Preston Peabody, 1853, "Nathaniel Hawthorne,"
North American Review, vol. 76, p. 241

Contrary, perhaps, to the general verdict we are almost impelled to the conclusion that the most perfect work left by Hawthorne is *The Blithedale Romance.* . . . As regards composition alone, it may be pronounced a perfect work. The masterpiece of Oliver Goldsmith is brought to mind whilst reading it, though the two novels differ in most respects as widely as possible. In each, however, there is a charming style, whose easy flow has never been excelled, while in Hawthorne's story there is a poetic beauty which is not to be found in *The Vicar of Wakefield.* The drawing of character is also very satisfactory. The *dramatis personæ* are few in number, but all are realized with extraordinary vividness.

George Barnett Smith, 1875, "Nathaniel Hawthorne,"
Poets and Novelists, p. 181

The special characteristic of *The Blithedale Romance* seems to me to be its appearance of unlabored ease, and a consequent breeziness of effect distinguishing its atmosphere from that of any of the other romances. The style is admirably finished, and yet there is no part of the book that gives the same impression of almost unnecessary polish which occasionally intervenes between one's admiration and the *Seven Gables.* On this score, *Blithedale* is certainly the most consummate of the four completed romances.

George Parsons Lathrop, 1876, *A Study of Hawthorne,* p. 241

The book, indeed, is a mixture of elements, and it leaves in the memory an impression analogous to that of an April day—an alternation of brightness and shadow, of broken sun-patches and sprinkling clouds.

Henry James, 1880, *Hawthorne (English Men of Letters),* p. 128

The Marble Faun, or Transformation (1860)

I've finished *the* book, and am, I think, more angry at your tantalizing cruelty than either *Athenæum* or *Saturday Review.* I want to know a hundred things you do not tell me,—who Miriam was, what was the crime in which she was concerned and of which all Europe knew, what was in the packet, what became of Hilda, whether Miriam married Donatello, whether Donatello got his head cut off, etc. Of course you'll say I ought to *guess;* well, if I do guess, it is but a guess, and I want to *know.* Yesterday I wrote a review of you in the *Examiner,* and in spite of my natural indignation, I hope you will not altogether dislike what I have said. In other respects I admire *Monte Beni* more than I can tell you; and I suppose no one now will visit Rome without a copy of it in his hand. Nowhere are descriptions to be found so beautiful, so true, and so pathetic. And there are little bits of *you* in the book which are best of all,—half moralizing, half thinking aloud. There is a bit about *women sewing* which Harriet raves about. There are bits about Catholicism and love and sin, which are marvellously thought and gloriously written.

> Henry Bright, 1860, *Letter to Hawthorne; Nathaniel Hawthorne*
> *and His Wife,* ed. Hawthorne, vol. II, p. 240

Smith and Elder certainly do take strange liberties with the titles of books. I wanted to call it *The Marble Faun,* but they insisted upon *Transformation,* which will lead the reader to anticipate a sort of pantomime. They wrote some days ago that the edition was nearly all sold, and that they were going to print another; to which I mean to append a few pages, in the shape of a conversation between Kenyon, Hilda, and the author, throwing some further light on matters which seem to have been left too much in the dark. For my own part, however, I should prefer the book as it now stands.

> Nathaniel Hawthorne, 1860, *Letter to Henry Bright;*
> *Nathaniel Hawthorne and His Wife,* ed. Hawthorne, vol. II, p. 241

The minuteness and the closeness of his analysis of the secret workings of the human heart with guilt for a companion, and withal the extreme delicacy with which the subject is handled, is something marvelous, and has perhaps never been equalled by any writer.

> Samuel Smiles, 1860, *Brief Biographies,* p. 269

Everything that you have ever written, I believe, I have read many times, and I am particularly vain of having admired "Sights from a Steeple," when I first read it in the Boston *Token,* several hundred years ago, when we were both younger than we are now; of having detected and cherished, at a later day, an old Apple-Dealer, whom, I believe, you have unhandsomely thrust out of your presence, now that you are grown so great. But the *Romance of Monte Beni* has the additional charm for me that it is the first book of yours that I have read since I had the privilege of making your personal acquaintance. My memory goes back at once to those walks (alas, not too frequent) we used to take along the Tiber, or in the Campagna; . . . and it is delightful to get hold of the book now, and know that it is impossible for you any longer, after waving your wand as you occasionally did then, indicating where the treasure was hidden, to sink it again beyond plummet's sound. . . . With regard to the story, which has been somewhat criticised, I can only say that to me it is quite satisfactory. I like those shadowy, weird, fantastic, Hawthornesque shapes flitting through the golden gloom, which is the atmosphere of the book. I like the misty way in which the story is indicated rather than revealed; the outlines are quite definite enough from the beginning to the end to those who have imagination enough to follow you in your airy flights; and to those who complain, I suppose that nothing less than an illustrated edition, with a large gallows on the last page, with Donatello in the most pensile of attitudes,—his ears revealed through a white night-cap,—would be satisfactory.

John Lothrop Motley, 1860, Letter to Hawthorne, March 29;
A Study of Hawthorne by G. P. Lathrop, p. 261

His *Marble Faun,* whether consciously or not, illustrates that invasion of the æsthetic by the moral which has confused art by dividing its allegiance, and dethroned the old dynasty without as yet firmly establishing the new in an acknowledged legitimacy.

James Russell Lowell, 1866, Swinburne's Tragedies,
Prose Works, Riverside Ed., vol. II, p. 125

There are few books put so often into the hands of English and American visitors to Rome as Hawthorne's *Marble Faun,* or as it is more generally known here, *Transformation,* from the cheap and widely circulated Tauchnitz edition, which has followed the English style. Pilgrimages are made to what is now generally known as Hilda's Tower; and when young ladies go to the Capuchin church to see the picture of Guido, they almost dread to find a dead monk laid out and bleeding from the nostrils. The book gives a strong impression of local colour.

Eugene Schuyler, 1889-1901, "The Italy of Hawthorne,"
Italian Influences, p. 308

I cannot recall a writer more successful in this union of ornamental detail and organic structure. It is like the pediment end of the Doric order, whose beauty is not applied but wrought in. Whenever this is true, a style, whether in literature or architecture, painting or sculpture, gains immensely in dignity and unity. I do not say that it is not true of *The Marble Faun,* nor that its local color is less natural than that of Hawthorne's New England novels; but that mingled with what is strictly necessary to the scenic effect is a great deal of information which belongs to the guide-book rather than the work of art. Hawthorne's analysis of a painting or interpretation of a statue is often vital to the story, and has a value apart from its relation to it; but there is much of description and history which belongs rather to a work like Irving's *Alhambra* than to a romance.

Arthur Sherburne Hardy, 1889, "Hawthorne's Italian Romance,"
The Book Buyer, vol. 6, p. 428

Hawthorne's genius is expressed equally in other works, but it is in *Transformation* that his inner history is told,—and therein all the evolutionary years of New England, whereof he was the characteristic flower. Having come so far the book reaches far: it has the phenomenal success of becoming at once the tourist's guide and the scholar's interpreter.

Moncure Daniel Conway, 1890, *Life of Nathaniel Hawthorne*
(*Great Writers*), p. 162

One vital mistake has been made by many. They have taken *The Marble Faun* as a guide to Rome; almost as a picture of Italy. It gives neither Rome nor Italy. Read it by the light of those Note-Books and you will see that Hawthorne never fully appreciated Italy; therefore he could not portray that country "which most have considered the second in the world, thus really proving it the first." A man who could place Powers's Eve above the Venus di Milo, because its skin is smooth and its members sound; a man who gazed, again and again, upon the Venus di Medici,—which is no goddess, but a dainty Greek girl claiming love as her lawful right,—yet seldom visited the Medici Chapel whose giant forms writhe in a powerless passion as they give eternity limited by earth, could not really love Florence for her best, much less Rome for her grandest.

Jessie Kingsley Curtis, 1892, *"The Marble Faun,"*
Andover Review, vol. 18, p. 139

As for the plot, we may be wrong, ideally in demanding anything more than the ethereal or spiritual solution,—the completion of Donatello's education, but there is much truth in the complaint, that all imaginative literature heretofore, as Hawthorne's own stories, and even hints in the course of these scenes themselves, had led us to expect some final explanation as to Donatello's deed and his punishment, which would satisfy—I will not say our curiosity, for we know he is a creature of Hawthorne's, after all, but—our sense of artistic justice and finish. The reluctant final chapter of the second edition, we may all well agree with Hawthorne himself, is worthless. It only shows that in regard to these questions as to Miriam's earlier history as well, he had himself nothing to offer us.

William Cranston Lawton, 1898, *The New England Poets,* p. 92

Septimus Felton

There still remain little roughnesses, which the author's delicate revision would have swept away; as the enumeration of "beautiful flowers" under the head of "tender greenness" in the very third line of the story;—the ungrammatical "and which," at the bottom of the first page; the seeming to include Rose Garfield among her own progenitors, on the second; the awkward occurrence of "now" and "then," "before" and "floor," in ungraceful proximity on the third page;—and just below, the abrupt "so it was" and "passed through Cambridge" (college);—these trifles and such as these have interest because they prove, what I for one never doubted, that Hawthorne's pages owed something of their delicious smoothness to the use of the file.

> Thomas Wentworth Higginson, 1872, "Hawthorne's Last Bequest,"
> *Scribner's Monthly*, vol. 5, p. 105

It is plain to any reader that *Septimus Felton*, as it stands, with its roughness, its gaps, its mere allusiveness and slightness of treatment, gives us a very partial measure of Hawthorne's full intention; and it is equally easy to believe that this intention was much finer than anything we find in the book. Even if we possessed the novel in its complete form, however, I incline to think that we should regard it as very much the weakest of Hawthorne's productions.

> Henry James, 1880, *Hawthorne (English Men of Letters)*, p. 172

In the unfinished story of *Septimus,* we have an example of one of Hawthorne's stories in the making, and it seems to indicate how entirely Hawthorne always framed his work on facts. The Note-books show how precise an observer he was, and whatever he presented to the world was constructed on thes observations. The author says of *Septimus,* "our story is an internal one, dealing as little as possible with outward events, and taking hold of these only where it cannot be helped, in order, by means of them, to delineate the history of a mind." Yet it actually is, as it stands, far more full of action and incident than any of its predecessors. Here and there the narrative is broken; something was to have been filled in—something ghostly or speculative, perhaps. If Hawthorne had lived to complete this book, it is easy to believe the frame-work would have been so wrought upon that, in its final shape, the story would have ranked among the most weird of his romances.

> Walter Lewin, 1890, *The Academy*, vol. 38, p. 286

NOTEBOOKS

It is hard to conceive the existence of so much pettiness in a man so great and real; of such a resolution to brood over fancied slights and strange formalities, yet, withal, to generalize so widely on such narrow premises; of such vulgarity in one who had written for the public so exquisitely. It is difficult to accept such a writer's criticisms on "the steaks and sirloins" of English ladies. I still remember Hester Prynne and Pearl, in *The Scarlet Letter,* and Phœbe and Hepzibah, in *The House of the Seven Gables,* and ask myself how far the case in point proves the adage that there is nothing so essentially nasty as refinement. The tone of these English journals is as small and peevish as if their writer had been thwarted and overlooked, instead of waited on by hearty offers of service, which in most cases were declined almost as persistently as if they had been so many affronts. A more puzzling case of inconsistency and duality has never come before me.

Henry F. Chorley, 1870, Autobiography, Memoirs and Letters,
ed. Hewlett, vol. II, p. 248

The finish and deliberation of the style in these fragmentary chronicles, fitly known under the name of Notebooks, are very likely to mislead any one who does not constantly recall the fact that they were written *currente calamo,* and merely as superficial memoranda, beneath which lay the author's deeper meditation, always reserved in essence until he was ready to precipitate it in the plastic forms of fiction. Speaking of *Our Old Home,* which—charming though it be to the reader—was drawn almost wholly from the surface deposit of his *English Notebooks,* Hawthorne said: "It is neither a good nor a weighty book." And this, indirectly, shows that he did not regard the journals as concentrating the profounder substance of his genius.

George Parsons Lathrop, 1876, ed. Passages from the
American Notebooks

A very singular series of volumes; I doubt whether there is anything exactly corresponding to them in the whole body of literature. . . . I have just reread them carefully, I am still at a loss to perceive how they came to be written—what was Hawthorne's purpose in carrying on for so many years this minute and often trivial chronicle. . . . He rarely takes his Notebook into his confidence, or commits to its pages any reflections that might be adapted for publicity; the simplest way to describe the tone of these extremely objective journals is to say that they read like a series of very pleasant, though rather dullish and decidedly formal, letters, addressed to himself by a man who, having suspicions that they might be opened in the post, should have determined to insert nothing compromising. They contain much that is too futile for things intended for publicity; whereas, on the other hand, as a receptacle of private impressions and opinions, they are curiously cold and empty.

Henry James, 1880, Hawthorne (English Men
of Letters), pp. 39, 40

GENERAL

He has the purest style, the finest taste, the most available scholarship, the most delicate humor, the most touching pathos, the most radiant imagination, the most consummate ingenuity; and with these varied good qualities he has done *well* as a mystic. But is there any one of these qualities which should prevent his doing doubly as well in a career of honest, upright, sensible, prehensible, and comprehensible things? Let him mend his pen, get a bottle of visible ink, come out from the Old Manse, cut Mr. Alcott, hang (if possible) the editor of the *Dial,* and throw out of the window to the pigs all his odd numbers of the *North American Review.*

Edgar Allan Poe, 1847, Literary Criticism, Works,
ed. Stedman and Woodberry, vol. VII, p. 38

He is quiet, fanciful, quaint, and his humour is shaded by a meditativeness of spirit. Although a Yankee, he partakes of none of the characteristics of a Yankee. His thinking and his style have an antique air. His roots strike down through the visible mould of the present, and draw sustenance from the generations under ground. The ghosts that haunt that chamber of his mind are the ghosts of dead men and women. He has a strong smack of the Puritan; he wears around him, in the New England town, something of the darkness and mystery of the aboriginal forest. He is a shy, silent, sensitive, much ruminating man, with no special overflow of animal spirits. He loves solitude, and the things which age has made reverent. There is nothing modern about him. Emerson's writing has a cold, cheerless glitter, like the new furniture in a warehouse, which will come of use by and by; Hawthorne's, the rich, subdued color of furniture in a Tudor mansion house which has winked to long-extinguished fires, which has been toned by the usage of departed generations.

Alexander Smith, 1863, Dreamthorp, p. 190

Hawthorne has been called a mystic, which he was not,—and a psychological dreamer, which he was in very slight degree. He was really the ghost of New England,—I do not mean the "spirit," nor the "phantom," but the ghost in the older sense in which that term is used, the thin, rarified essence which is to be found somewhere behind the physical organization: embodied, indeed, and not by any means in a shadowy or diminutive earthly tabernacle, but yet only half embodied in it, endowed with a certain painful sense of the gulf between his nature and its organization, always recognising the gulf, always trying to bridge it over, and always more or less unsuccessful in the attempt. His writings are not exactly spiritual writings, for there is no dominating spirit in them. They are ghostly writings. Hawthorne was, to my mind, a sort of sign to New England of the divorce that has been going on there (and not less perhaps in old England) between its people's spiritual and earthly nature, and of the difficulty which they will soon feel, if they are to be absorbed more and more in that shrewd, hard earthly sense which is one of their most striking characteristics, in even *communicating* with their former self.

Richard Holt Hutton, 1871, *Nathaniel Hawthorne,*
Essays in Literary Criticism, p. 98

Hawthorne was melancholy, laborious, reflective—one of the greatest of modern novelists. His works are so richly adorned with all the vivid ornaments of fancy that they seem poems truly epic; he wrote them with intense feeling, lost in his own fine visions. When he had finished *The Scarlet Letter,* and read it to his wife, he was racked by an intense excitement, he relates, and at its close burst into tears. Writing, to him, was no holiday recreation, but a violent labor that stirred the very sources of his life. We may imagine Homer weeping as he described the sorrows of Priam; it was thus that Hawthorne felt with his own characters. His disposition was too sad to resemble altogether that of the manly Greek poet; he might have stood almost for Milton's *Il Penseroso.* He was fond of the dark, mysterious, gloomy, he was a conservative who seemed to care little for the future; he studied spiritualism, and examined the old and forgotten; he is never very cheerful.

Eugene Lawrence, 1880, *A Primer of American Literature,* p. 110

There is a propriety in Hawthorne's fantasy to which Poe could not attain. Hawthorne's effects are moral, where Poe's are merely physical. The situation and its logical development, and the effects to be got out of it, are all Poe thinks of. In Hawthorne the situation, however strange and weird, is only the outward and visible sign of an inward and spiritual struggle. Ethical consequences are always worrying Hawthorne's soul; but Poe did not know that there were any ethics. . . As to which of the two was the greater, discussion is idle; but that Hawthorne was the finer genius, few would deny. . . . In all his most daring fantasies Hawthorne is natural; and, though he may project his vision far beyond the boundaries of fact, nowhere does he violate the laws of nature. He had at all times a wholesome simplicity, and he never showed any trace of the morbid taint which characterises nearly all Poe's work. Hawthorne, one may venture to say, had the broad sanity of genius, while we should understand any one who might declare that Poe had mental disease raised to the nth.

Brander Matthews, 1885-1901, *The Philosophy of the Short-story*, pp. 39, 41, 43

To men of our time, beyond doubt, his work seems generally not fantastic but imaginative, and surely not meretricious but in its own way beautiful. Nor is this the whole story: almost alone among our writers, we may say, Hawthorne has a lasting native significance. For this there are surely two good reasons. In the first place, he is almost the solitary American artist who has phrased his meaning in words of which the beauty seems sure to grow with the years. In the second place, what marks him as most impregnably American is this: when we look close to see what his meaning really was, we find it a thing that in the old days, at last finally dead and gone, had been the great motive power of his race. What Hawthorne really voices is that strange, morbid, haunting sense of other things that we see or hear, which underlay the intense idealism of the emigrant Puritans, and which remains perhaps the most inalienable emotional heritage of their children. It is Hawthorne, in brief, who finally phrases the meaning of such a life as Theophilus Eaton lived and Cotton Mather recorded.

Barrett Wendell, 1893, *Stelligeri and other Essays Concerning America*, p. 139

In truth, for many persons his great, his most touching sign will have been his aloofness wherever he is. He is outside of everything, and an alien everywhere. He is an æsthetic solitary. His beautiful, light imagination is the wing that on the autumn evening just brushes the dusky window. It was a faculty that gave him much more a terrible sense of human abysses than a desire rashly to sound them and rise to the surface with his report. On the surface —the surface of the soul and the edge of the tragedy—he preferred to remain. He lingered to weave his web, in the thin exterior air. This is a partial expression of his characteristic habit of dipping, of diving just for sport, into the moral world without being in the least a moralist. He had none of the heat nor of the dogmatism of that character; none of the impertinence, as we feel he would almost have held it, of any intermeddling. He never intermeddled; he was divertedly and discreetly contemplative. pausing oftenest wherever, amid prosaic aspects, there seemed most of an appeal to a sense for subtleties. But of all cynics he was the brightest and kindest, and the subtleties he spun are mere silken threads for stringing polished beads. His collection of moral mysteries is the cabinet of a dilettante.

Henry James, 1897, *Library of the World's Best Literature,* ed. Warner, vol. XII, p. 7061

WALTER SAVAGE LANDOR
1775-1864

Born, at Warwick, 30 Jan. 1775. At school at Knowle, 1779-85; at Rugby, 1785-91. With private tutor, 1791-93. Matric. Trin. Coll., Oxford, 13 Nov. 1792; rusticated, 1794; did not return to Oxford. Visit to Paris, 1802. Settled at Bath, 1805; intimacy with Southey begun, 1808. In Spain, Aug. to Nov., 1808. Settled at Llanthony Abbey, Monmouthshire, 1809. Married Julia Thuillier, May 1811. Removed to Jersey, and thence to Tours, 1814. To Italy, Sept. 1815. Lived at Como. 1815-18. At Pisa, 1818-21. At Florence, 1821-35. Visit to England, 1832. Quarrelled with his wife and went to England, 1835. Returned to Florence, 1858. Died there, 17 Sept. 1864. WORKS: *Poems,* 1795; *Moral Epistle respectfully dedicated to Earl Stanhope,* 1795; *Gebir* (anon.), 1798 (Latin version, by Landor, 1803); *Poems from the Arabic and Persian* (anon.), 1800; *Poetry* (anon.), 1802; *Simonidea* (anon.), 1806; *Three Letters to D. Francisco Riqueline,* 1809; *Count Julian* (anon.), 1812; *Commentary on the Memoirs of Mr. Fox* (anon.), 1812; *Idyllia Heroica,* 1814 (enlarged edn.. 1820); *Poche Osservazioni sullo stato attuale di que' popoli che vogliono governarsi per mezzo delle Rappresentanze,* 1821; *Imaginary Conversations,* vols. i, ii, 1824; vols. iii, iv, 1828; vol. v, 1829; *Gebir, Count Julian, and other Poems,* 1831; *Citation and Examination of William Shakespeare* (anon.), 1834; *The Letters of a Conservative,* 1836; *Terry Hogan* (anon., attrib. to Landor), 1836; *Pericles and Aspasia,* 1836; *A Satire on Satirists,* 1836; *The Pentameron and Pentalogia* (anon.), 1837; *Andrea of Hungary and Giovanna of Naples,* 1839; *Fra Rupert,* 1840; *Works* (collected 2 vols.), 1846; *Hellenics,* 1847; *Poemata et Inscriptiones,* 1847; *Imaginary Conversation of King Carlo Alberto and the Duchess Belgoioiso,* 1848; *Italics,* 1848; *Popery, British and Foreign,* 1851; *Imaginary Conversations of Greeks and Romans,* 1853; *The Last Fruit off an Old Tree,* 1853; *Letters of an American,* 1854; *Letter . . . to R. W. Emerson,* 1856; *Antony and Octavius,* 1856; *Dry Sticks,* 1858; *Hebrew Lyrics* (anon.), 1859; *Savonarola e il Priore di San Marco,* 1860; *Heroic Idyls, with Additional Poems,* 1863. COLLECTED WORKS: in 8 vols., 1876. LIFE: by J. Forster, 1869; by Sidney Colvin, 1881.

R. Farquharson Sharp, 1897, *A Dictionary of English Authors,* p. 162

SEE: *Complete Works,* ed. T .Earle Welby and Stephen Wheeler, 1927-36, 16 v.; *Imaginary Conversations,* ed. Ernest de Selincourt, 1915; R. H. Super, *Walter Savage Landor: A Biography,* 1954; Matthew Elwin, *Landor: A Replevin,* 1958.

PERSONAL

Mr. Landor, who has long been known to scholars as a Latin poet beyond the elegance of centos, and has lately shown himself one of our most powerful writers of prose, is a man of a vehement nature, with great delicacy of imagination. He is like a stormy mountain pine, that should produce lilies.

After indulging the partialities of his friendships and enmities, and trampling on Kings and ministers, he shall cool himself, like a Spartan worshipping a moon-beam, in the patient meekness of Lady Jane Grey. . . . Mr. Landor's conversation is lively and unaffected, as full of scholarship or otherwise as you may desire, and dashed now and then with a little superfluous will and vehemence, when he speaks of his likings and dislikes. His laugh is in peals, and climbing: he seems to fetch every one from a higher story.

> Leigh Hunt, 1828, *Lord Byron and Some of His Contemporaries,* vol. II, pp. 377, 380

Met today [1830] the one man living in Florence whom I was anxious to know. This was Walter Savage Landor, a man of unquestionable genius, but very questionable good sense; or rather, one of those unmanageable men,—

> "Blest with huge stores of wit,
> Who want as much again to manage it."

He was a man of florid complexion, with large, full eyes, and altogether a *leonine* man, and with a fierceness of tone well suited to his name; his decisions being confident, and on all subjects, whether of taste or life, unqualified; each standing for itself, not caring whether it was in harmony with what had gone before or would follow from the same oracular lips. But why should I trouble myself to describe him? He is painted by a master hand in Dickens' novel, *Bleak House,* now in course of publication, where he figures as Mr. Boythorn. The combination of superficial ferocity and inherent tenderness, so admirably portrayed in *Bleak House,* still at first strikes every stranger—for twenty-two years have not materially changed him—no less than his perfect frankness and reckless indifference to what he says.

> Henry Crabb Robinson, 1830-52, *Diary, Reminiscences and Correspondence,* ed. Sadler

The high breeding and urbanity of his manners, which are very striking, I had not been taught to expect. . . . His avoidance of general society, though courted to enter it, his dignified reserve when brought in contact with those he disapproves, and his fearless courage in following the dictates of a lofty mind, had somehow or other given the erroneous impression that his manners were, if not somewhat abrupt, at least singular. This is not the case, or, if it be, the only singularity I can discern is a more than ordinary politeness towards women. . . . The politeness of Landor has nothing of the troublesome officiousness of a *petit-maître,* nor the oppressive ceremoniousness of a fine gentleman of *l'ancien régime;* it is grave and respectful, without his ever losing sight of what is due to himself, when most assiduously practising the urbanity due to others. There is a natural dignity which appertains to him that suits perfectly with a style of his conversation and his general appearance.

Marguerite Countess Blessington, 1839, Idler in Italy, p. 283

A tall, broad, burly man, with gray hair, and large fierce-rolling eyes; of the most restless, impetuous vivacity, not to be held in by the most perfect breeding,—expressing itself in high-colored superlatives, indeed in reckless exaggeration, now and then in a dry, sharp laugh not of sport but of mockery; a wild man, whom no extent of culture had been able to tame! His intellectual faculty seemed to me to be weak in proportion to his violence of temper; the judgment he gives about anything is more apt to be wrong than right,—as the inward whirlwind shows him this side or the other of the object; and *sides* of an object are all he sees. He is not an original man; in most cases one but sighs over the spectacle of common-place torn to rags.

Thomas Carlyle, 1840, To Emerson, April 1; Correspondence
of Carlyle and Emerson, ed. Norton, vol. I, p. 303

Mr. Landor carried to its height the love of freak which the English delight to indulge, as if to signalize their commanding freedom. He has a wonderful brain, despotic, violent and inexhaustible, meant for a soldier, by what chance converted to letters; in which there is not a style or a tint not known to him, yet with an English appetite for action and heroes. The thing done avails, and not what is said about it. An original sentence, a step forward, is worth more than all the censures. Landor is strangely undervalued in England; usually ignored and sometimes savagely attacked in the Reviews. The criticism may be right or wrong, and is quickly forgotten; but year after year the scholar must still go back to Landor for a multitude of elegant sentences; for wisdom, wit and indignation that are unforgettable.

Ralph Waldo Emerson, 1856, English Traits,
Riverside Ed., vol. V, p. 13

He who is within two paces of his ninetieth year may sit down and make no excuses; he must be unpopular, he never tried to be much otherwise; he never contended with a contemporary, but walked alone on the far eastern uplands, meditating and remembering.

Walter Savage Landor, 1863, Heroic Idyls with
Additional Poems, Preface; Works, vol. VIII, p. 305

For a moment I recall the well-remembered figure and face, as they first became known to me nearly thirty years ago. Landor was then upwards of sixty, and looked that age to the full. He was not above the middle stature, but had a stout stalwart presence, walked without a stoop, and in his general aspect, particularly the set and carriage of his head, was decidedly of what is called a distinguished bearing. His hair was already silvered gray, and had retired far upward from his forehead, which, wide and full but retreating, could never in the earlier time have been seen to such advantage. What at first was noticeable, however, in the broad white massive head, were the full yet strangely-lifted eyebrows; and they were not immediately attractive. They might have meant only pride or self-will in its most arrogant form, but for what was visible in the rest of the face. In the large gray eyes there was a depth of composed expression that even startled by its contrast to the eager restlessness looking out from the surface of them; and in the same variety and quickness of transition the mouth was extremely striking. The lips that seemed compressed with unalterable will would in a moment relax to a softness more than feminine; and a sweeter smile it was impossible to conceive. What was best in his character, whether for strength or gentleness, had left its traces there. It was altogether a face on which power was visibly impressed, but without the resolution and purpose that generally accompany it. . . . The eye is fine; but black hair covers all the forehead, and you recognize the face of the later time quite without its fulness, power and animation. The stubbornness is there, without the softness; the self-will, untamed by any experience; plenty of energy, but a want of emotion. The nose was never particularly good; and the lifted brow, flatness of cheek and jaw, wide upper lip, retreating mouth and chin, and heavy neck, peculiarities necessarily prominent in youth, in age contributed only to a certain lion-look, he liked to be reminded of, and would confirm with a loud, long laugh hardly less than lionine. Higher and higher went peal after peal, in continuous and increasing volleys, until regions of sound were reached very far beyond ordinary human lungs.

John Forster, 1865-69, Walter Savage Landor,
A Biography, bk. i

The arms were very peculiar. They were rather short, and were curiously restrained and checked in their action at the elbows; in the action of the hands, even when separately clenched, there was the same kind of pause, and a noticeable tendency to relaxation on the part of the thumb. Let the face be never so intense or fierce, there was a commentary of gentleness in the hands, essential to be taken along with it. . . . In the expression of his hands, though angrily closed, there was always gentleness and tenderness; just as when they were open, and the handsome old gentleman would wave them, with a ltitle courtly flourish that sat well upon him, as he recalled some classic compliment that he had rendered to some reigning Beauty, there was a chivalrous grace about them such as pervades his softer verses

Charles Dickens, 1869, "Landor's Life," All the Year Round,
vol. 22, p. 182

Dashed by his volcanic temperament and his blinding imagination into collision with facts, he suffered shipwreck once and again. But if we apply to his character and career the measure not of results, but of intention, we shall acknowledge in Landor a model on the heroic scale of many noble and manly virtues. He had a heart infinitely kind and tender. His generosity was royal, delicate, never hesitating. In his pride there was no moroseness, in his independence not a shadow of jealousy. From spite, meanness or uncharitableness he was utterly exempt. He was loyal and devoted in friendship, and, what is rare, at least as prone to idealize the virtues of his friends as the vices of his enemies. Quick as was his resentment of a slight, his fiercest indignations were never those which he conceived on personal grounds, but those with which he pursued an injustice or an act of cruelty; nor is there wanting an element of nobleness and chivalry in even the wildest of his breaches with social custom. He was no less a worshipper of true greatness than he was a despiser of false. He hated nothing but tyranny and fraud, and for those his hatred was implacable. His bearing under the consequences of his own impracticability was of an admirable courage and equanimity.

Sidney Colvin, 1881, Landor (English Men of Letters), p. 217

In 1811 he married a very pretty girl aged seventeen, Miss Julia Thuillier. She was a moneyless damsel, of noble Swiss family, and was remarkable for the rich abundance of her curls; her tone of mind, romantic and self-indulgent; her charms of person, coupled with much youthful amiability. Landor married her for her good looks, and perhaps little true sympathy existed between them. There were quarrels and reconciliations, and the poet, in the earlier years of his marriage, showed as much forebearance as was consistent with one of the least forebearing and intolerant, imperious, liberty-loving characters on record. At last, after they had had four children, Landor left his wife behind in Fiesole, near Florence, returned to England, and would never see her again; the motive was probably nothing more unbearable than what he would now at length no longer bear, incompatibility of temper. He relinquished to her his Italian villa and almost the whole of his fortune. In advanced age, towards 1855, he returned to Florence; but he lived in lodgings, and there he died in 1864, aged eighty-nine. His wife outlived him till the spring of 1879, dying at the age of eighty-five.

William M. Rossetti, 1881, "The Wives of Poets,"
Atlantic Monthly, vol. 47, p. 521

In the north Park Cemetery of Calcutta there is a black marble slab containing the inscription:

IN MEMORY OF

THE HONOURABLE

ROSE WHITWORTH AYLMER,

WHO DEPARTED THIS LIFE MARCH 2D, A. D.

1800.

AGED 20 YEARS

This name calls to mind the most romantic period of the life of Walter Savage Landor. Landor left Oxford in 1797. He spent some time on the Welsh coast, where he made the acquaintance of Lord Aylmer's family. An attachment sprang up between Rose, the daughter of Lord Aylmer, and young Landor. One day she loaned him a book from the Swansea Circulating Library. It was a romance by Clara Reeve. Here he found an Arabic tale which so profoundly impressed him that it suggested his first great work, *Gebir*. . . . Landor, in his poem, "Abertawy," indicates both her unwillingness to go and his own sorrow at her departure.

> John Fletcher Hurst, 1891, "English Writers in India,"
> *Harper's Magazine,* vol. 82, p. 358

Landor's face put me in mind of the portraits of Hogarth. He had a diabolical laugh—a prolonged mockery, with apparently no heart or happiness in it, and when you thought he had done he went on and on; perhaps his extreme age was the cause of his prolongation, but not of its *timbre*. He gave me *an apercu* of his views on art, politics and literature. I suppose he was a very wrong-headed man, and that his fierce individuality (Welsh choler) made his acquaintance as uncomfortable as his friendship was perilous. Every now and then the Tuscan States rang with his 'larum, and at one time he made Florence too hot to hold him. A parodoxical old Jacobin, it seemed to me that there was nothing really genial about the man Landor. Alfred Tennyson tells me he used to meet him at Mr. John Forster's chambers in Lincoln's Inn Fields; that one day, while Landor was reciting some poetry, a member of the company tumbled down stairs and broke his leg, and that Landor the while went on spouting without showing any special concern.

> Frederick Locker-Lampson, 1895, *My Confidences,* p. 162

We cannot wonder that the Italians failed to understand this imperious and eccentric Englishman. Strange stories about him were current among the people. He was believed to have challenged the Secretary of Legation for whistling in the street when Mrs. Landor passed; to have walked up to the judges in a court of justice, with a bag of dollars in his hand, asking how much was necessary to obtain him a favourable verdict; to have thrown his cook out of the window, for neglect of a dinner, and while the man lay groaning on the ground with a broken limb, thrust his head out with the exclamation "Good God, I forgot the violets!"

John Fyvie, 1895, "Walter Savage Landor," *The Temple Bar*,
vol. 105, p. 256

My mother's near relationship to the Rose Aylmer of his boyish romance was the first link in the chain of this long friendship, for he remembered her as a little girl running by her sister, Rose Alymer's side. They never met after that until 1835 at Florence, and the intimacy continued which ceased only with their lives. It must have been to the charm of that inherited name that I am indebted for the many lovely verses—then so carelessly appreciated, now so deeply valued—with which he honoured a young and ignorant girl. . . . He was as full of fun as a boy; but if sometimes his boisterous spirits outran his discretion a reproving look would instantly restore his balance. These letters may not add one laurel to his brow, but their tenderness and grace will cling round his memory like the perfume of the gracious cyclamen, the flower he loved so well.

Rose C. Graves-Sawle, 1898, *Letter to Mr. Wheeler*, Feb.;
Letters of Walter Savage Landor, Private and Public,
ed. Wheeler, Introduction, p. x

POEMS

What is it that Mr. Landor wants, to make him a poet? His powers are certainly very considerable, but he seems to be totally deficient in that modifying faculty, which compresses several units into one whole. The truth is he does not possess imagination in its highest form,—that of stamping *il più nell' uno*. Hence his poems, taken as wholes, are unintelligible; you have eminences excessively bright, and all the ground around and between them in darkness. Besides which, he has never learned with all his energy, how to write simple and lucid English.

Samuel Taylor Coleridge, 1834, *Table Talk*,
ed. Ashe, Jan. 1, p. 268

Walter Savage Landor is of all English modern poets the one least read by the public, and the one whom the fewest impostors care even to pretend they have read. The reasons for this are twain: he achieved a literary position so many years ago, that the new generation have never known him; and his poetry has not at any time been the fashion, its austere simplicity rendering it unintelligible to the mass of men. He himself has aptly compared it to the wood of the olive-tree, which is known when it burns by the purity of its flame and the paucity of its ashes.

Mortimer Collins, 1871, "Landor's Country," *Belgravia*,
vol. 13, p. 435

We place Landor, who was greater, even, as a prose-writer, among the foremost poets, because it was the poetry within the man that made him great; his poetry belongs to a high order of that art, while his prose, though strictly prosaic in form—he was too fine an artist to have it otherwise—is more imaginative than other men's verses. Radically a poet, he ranks among the best essayists of his time; and he shares this distinction in common with Milton, Coleridge, Emerson, and other poets, in various eras, who have been intellectual students and thinkers. None but sentimentalists and dilettanti confuse their prose and verse,—tricking out the former with a cheap gloss of rhetoric, or the false and effeminate jingle of a bastard rhythm. . . . Landor belonged, in spite of himself, to the Parnassian aristocracy; was, as he has said, a poet for poets, and one who personally impressed the finest organizations. Consider the names of those who, having met him and known his works, perceive in him something great and worshipful.

Edmund Clarence Stedman, 1875-78, Victorian Poets, p. 37

Landor was the earliest of our modern poets specially characterised by their devotion to ideal beauty and to classical associations. With classical literature his name has long been intimately joined, not only by many an "Imaginary Conversation," in which the heroes, poets, and philosophers of antiquity are invoked from the shades, but yet more by his poetry, formed as that was, after a classical model,—his English poetry, not less than that written with such signal merit in the Latin language. . . . Landor's poetry has sometimes been charged with a deficiency of pathos. It is true that in general he loves rather to exhibit human life in the exhilarating and equable light of day, than tinged with the lights of a low horizon, and clouded with the shadows of eve. His pathos has, notwithstanding, a peculiar depth and tenderness; and though unostentatious, is very far from being infrequent. The "Death of Artemidora" may serve as a specimen.

Aubrey De Vere, 1887, "Landor's Poetry," Essays Chiefly
on Poetry, vol. II, pp. 143, 156

Imaginary Conversations (1824-28)

Now for twenty years we have still found the *Imaginary Conversations* a sure resource in solitude, and it seems to us as original in its form as in its matter. Nay, when we remember his rich and ample page wherein we are always sure to find free and sustained thought, a keen and precise understanding, an affluent and ready memory familiar with all his chosen books, an industrious observation in every department of life, an experience to which nothing has occurred in vain, honor for every just and generous sentiment and a scourge like that of furies for every oppressor, whether public or private,—we feel how dignified is the perpetual censor in his curule chair, and we wish to thank a benefactor of the reading world.

Ralph Waldo Emerson, 1843, Walter Savage Landor;
Papers from the Dial; Works, Riverside Ed., vol. XII, p. 204

There is, doubtless, something of labor in reading Landor's *Conversations* if one is not conversant with high thinking, and if one is but slenderly endowed with the historic imagination, but the labor is not in the writing. The very form of conversation permits a quickness of transition and sudden shifting of subject and scene which enliven the art and give an inexhaustible variety of light and shade. One returns to passages again and again for their exceeding beauty of expression and their exquisite setting. To one accustomed to the glitter of current epigrammatic writing, the brilliancy of some of Landor's sentences may not at first be counted for its real worth, but to go from Landor to smart writers is to exchange jewels for paste. What I have said may serve partly to explain the limited audience which Landor has had and must continue to have. If it is a liberal education to read his writings, it requires one to receive them freely. The appeal which Landor makes to the literary class is very strong, and apart from a course of study in the Greek and Latin classics, I doubt if any single study would serve an author so well as the study of Landor. Indeed, there is perhaps no modern work which gives to the reader not familiar with Greek or Latin so good an idea of what we call classical literature. Better than a translation is the original writing of Landor for conveying the aroma which a translation so easily loses. The dignity of the classics, the formality, the fine use of sarcasm, the consciousness of an art in literature,—all these are to be found in the *Imaginary Conversations;* and if a reader used to the highly seasoned literature of recent times complains that there is rather an absence of humor, and that he finds Landor sometimes dull, why, Heaven knows we do not often get hilarious over our ancient authors, and Landor, for his contemporaries, is an ancient author with a very fiery soul. . . . Landor is sometimes characterized as arrogant and conceited; stray words and acts might easily be cited in support of this, but no one can read his *Conversations* intelligently and not perceive how noble was his scorn of mean men, how steadfast his admiration of great men.

Horace E. Scudder, 1887, Men of Letters, pp. 102, 104

One of the great charms of the *Conversations* is their unexpectedness, and want of visible sequence; one never knows whither the writer's quickly changing moods will take him, or what surprises are not in store for the reader. . . . When Landor leaves the domain of what he has himself witnessed and experienced, he becomes wild, absurd and too often trivial. The conversations between ancient Greeks and Romans should be excepted, because of the fitness and propriety of these the judgment of the reader must be guided by a great familiarity with the classics, which Landor had, and by a large experience of humanity, in which he was notably deficient. What I particularly refer to are the *Conversations,* the scene of which is laid in Russia, Poland, or the East, on which his authorities were imperfect, and the spirit of which he by his nature could not understand.

Eugene Schuyler, 1888-1901, Italian Influences, pp. 69, 71

Pentameron (1837)

Petrarch and Boccaccio were highly esteemed by Landor, who did not sympathize with Lord Chesterfield in his opinion that the former deserved his *Laura* better than his *lauro*. The best evidence of this predilection is Landor's great work, *The Pentameron,* second only to his greatest, *Pericles and Aspasia.* Its *coleur locale* is marvellous. On every page there is a glimpse of cloudless blue sky, a breath of warm sunny air, a sketch of Italian manner. The masterly *gusto* with which the author enters into the spirit of Italy would make us believe him to be "the noblest Roman of them all," had he not proved himself a better Grecian. Margaret Fuller realized this when, after comparing *The Pentameron* and *Petrarca* together, she wrote: "I find the prose of the Englishman worthy of the verse of the Italian. It is a happiness to see such marble beauty in the halls of a contemporary."

Kate Field, 1866, "Last Days of Walter Savage Landor,"
Atlantic Monthly, vol. 17, p. 550

A hundred volumes of travels and a thousand biographical and antiquarian dissertations would not place so vividly or graphically before the reader, with their appropriate framing of local scenery, the Tuscan peasant and the Tuscan priest as they were, and with small changes are still, and the Tuscan man of letters as he was in the middle ages. It is impossible to doubt that Landor had made himself thoroughly acquainted with the locality. But he has erred, or more probably has chosen to modify the real facts in his treatment of his fiction, in representing Boccaccio's house to have been a *"villetta* hard by Certaldo," and in that delicious account of Ser Francisco's ride to his Sunday's morning mass at the church of Certaldo. For the house is, as has been said, in the main street of the town, and within a hundred yards of the church. If, however, a more accurate accordance with the particulars of the locality had been the means of depriving us of the "crowned martyr's" ride, and of the saddling of the canonico's nag by the joint efforts of himself and Assuntina, we should have lost infinitely more than we could have gained in minuteness of matter of fact information.

Thomas Adolphus Trollope, 1874, "Some Recollections of Walter Savage Landor," *Lippincott's Magazine,* vol. 13, p. 447

GENERAL

There is little moral courage in our literary world. Few will speak what they think; and they gather what they think from conduits and common sewers rather than from springs and fountains. They do not guide the mass, but are moved along and soon confounded with it. In all other countries the literary part of the community is the best; in England, I am sorry to say, it is guided by spleen, fashion, and interest.

Walter Savage Landor, 1838, *To Leigh Hunt,* Feb. 6; *Correspondence of Leigh Hunt,* ed. his Son, vol. I, p. 319

Few men have ever impressed their peers so much, or the general public so little, as Walter Savage Landor. Of all celebrated authors, he has hitherto been one of the least popular. Nevertheless he is among the most striking figures in the history of English literature; striking alike by his character and his powers. . . . The place occupied by Landor among English men of letters is a place apart. He wrote on many subjects and in many forms, and was strong both in imagination and criticism. He was equally master of Latin and English, and equally at home in prose and verse. He cannot properly be associated with any given school, or, indeed, with any given epoch of our literature, as epochs are usually counted, but stands alone, alike by the character of his mind and by the tenour and circumstances of his life. . . . Everything he says must be his own, and nothing but his own. On the other hand, it is no part of Landor's originality to provoke attention, as many even of illustrious writers have done, by emphasis or singularity of style. Arbitrary and vehement beyond other men in many of his thoughts, in their utterance he is always sober and decorous. He delivers himself of whatever is in his mind with an air, to borrow an expression of his own, "majestically sedate."

Sidney Colvin, 1881, *Landor (English Men of Letters)*, pp. 1, 2

To some of us Landor's imagination is not only inferior in kind but poverty-stricken in degree; his creative faculty is limited by the reflection that its one achievement is Landor's; his claim to consideration as a dramatic writer is negatived by the fact that, poignant as are the situations with which he loved to deal, he was apparently incapable of perceiving their capacities: inasmuch as he has failed completely and logically to develop a single one of them; inasmuch, too, as he has never once succeeded in conceiving, much less in picturing, such a train of conflicting emotions as any one of the complications from which he starts might be supposed to generate. To many there is nothing Greek about his dramatic work except the absence of stage directions; and to these that quality of "Landorian abruptness" which seems to Mr. Sidney Colvin to excuse so many of its shortcomings is identical with a certain sort of what in men of lesser mould is called stupidity.

William Ernest Henley, 1890, Views and Reviews, p. 164

In Landor's eight volumes there are more fine thoughts, more wise apothegms, than in any other discursive author's works in English literature; but they do not tell on the mind. They bloom like flowers in their gardens, but they crown no achievement. At the end, no cause is advanced, no goal is won. . . . His prose is rather the monologue of a seer. In reading his works one feels somewhat as if sitting at the feet of Coleridge. Landor has the presence that abashes companions. His manner of speech is more dignified, more ceremonial, his enunciation is more resonant, his accent more exquisite, than belong to the man of the world. He silences his readers by the mere impossibility of interrupting with a question so noble and smooth-sliding a current of words. The style is a sort of modern Miltonic; it has the suggestion of the pulpit divine in Hooker, the touch of formal artificiality that characterizes the first good English prose.

George Edward Woodberry, 1890-1900, Makers of
Literature, pp. 73, 85

Born in the decade which gave us Wordsworth, Coleridge, Southey, and Scott, at his maturity, when the fervid generation of Keats, Shelley and Byron were in full tide of song, Landor was as secluded and solitary as a mountain tarn. His long life of well-nigh ninety years included the entire Romantic movement of modern times. He stood in relations of personal friendship with the English poets who gave a new impulse and direction to the national imagination; he was a young man when the Schlegels, Novalis, and Tieck were recalling the enchantments of the Middle Ages in Germany; he was at the full maturity of his power when Lamartine published the *Meditations* and Victor Hugo routed the French Classicists on the stage of the Theatre Français with his drama of *Hernani.* Through this tumultuous age, so intensely modern in spirit that for the moment the antique seemed wholly obliterated, Landor preserved a calmness, a moderation, a self-possession that were born of hourly companionship with a world of classical repose and strength. To study him is to get in clear perspective the proportions of his contemporaries, and to feel what is easily apprehended but not so easily described—the difference between the Classical and the Romantic manner.

Hamilton Wright Mabie, 1893, Short Studies in Literature, p. 139

ELIZABETH CLEGHORN GASKELL
1810-1865

Born [Elizabeth Cleghorn Stevenson], in Chelsea, 29 Sept. 1810. Mother died Oct. 1810. Lived with her aunt in youth. At school at Stratford-on-Avon, 1825-27. Married to Rev. William Gaskell, 30 Aug. 1832. Lived in Manchester. Intimacy with William and Mary Howitt, and Dickens. Contrib. to *Household Words* from first no., March 1850. Friendship with Charlotte Brontë begun, 1850. Active literary life. Died suddenly, at Holybourne, Hampshire, 12 Nov. 1865. Buried at Knutsford. WORKS: *Clopton Hall*, in Howitt's *Visits to Remarkable Places*, 1840; *Mary Barton* (anon.), 1848; *The Mooreland Cottage* (anon.), 1850; *Ruth* (anon.), 1853; *Cranford* (anon.), 1853; *North and South* (anon.), 1855; *Lizzie Leigh* (anon.), 1855; *Life of Charlotte Brontë*, 1857 (2nd and 3rd edns. same year); *Round the Sofa*, 1859; *My Lady Ludlow*, 1859; *Right at Last* (anon.), 1860; *Lois the Witch*, 1861; *A Dark Night's Work*, 1863; *Sylvia's Lovers*, 1863 (2nd and 3rd edns. same year); *The Grey Woman*, 1865; *Hand and Heart*, 1865; *Cousin Phyllis*, 1865. POSTHUMOUS: *Wives and Daughters*, 1866. She *edited: Mabel Vaughan*, 1857; C. A. Vecchi's *Garibaldi at Caprera*, 1862. COLLECTED WORKS: in 7 vols., 1873.

R. Farquharson Sharp, 1897, *A Dictionary of
English Authors*, p. 110

SEE: *Novels and Tales*, ed. Clement Shorter, 1906-19, 11 v.; Annette B. Hopkins, *Elizabeth Gaskell: Her Life and Work*, 1952.

PERSONAL

Report says that she was most beautiful to behold [1829]. There are, however, I believe, no portraits of her at that time of life. The friends who knew her intimately in later years describe her face as possessing extreme interest rather than rare beauty. In a photograph taken shortly before her death, which one of her old pupils had the goodness to show me, she is seated at a table with a lace shawl thrown lightly over the figure. Rare refinement and delicacy of feature are the points which strike one at the first glance. One sees at once that she was a cultivated and high-souled woman. Her mouth is most delicately curved, and the eyes are of an exquisite shape. The same lady favoured me with the following detailed verbal description of Mrs. Gaskell from memory: "Her face was most interesting, with very delicately-cut features, and a specially fine brow. Her hair was dark, and her hazel eyes had an unusual brightness and animation when their owner was engaged in conversation. Her mouth was firm but kind, and almost always playing into a smile. She was of the medium height, graceful and dignified in her bearing." This description, given by one who frequently saw her at the head of her own table, and also while she was engaged in teaching at the Sunday School, may, I think, be accepted, and justifies the idea entertained of her early beauty.

Mat Hompes, 1895, "Mrs. Gaskell," *Gentleman's Magazine,*
vol. 279, p. 127

Mary Barton (1848)

Although pre-eminently a moralist in the sense of being a writer whose works touch the heart rather than the imagination or the philosophical intellect, Mrs. Gaskell is not to be numbered among the preachers. No one, however impatient of reproof and correction, need be frightened away from her novels by the fear of having to listen to didactic homilies. She prefixed a little sermon, pithy and well-timed, by way of preface to *Mary Barton,* extracting from it a lesson for the day; but the lesson is not formulated and expounded in the novel, which is, what it professes to be, a tale—a representation of life. It is shaped and coloured by the author's good-natured wisdom but it is not stiffened and distorted as a work of art by any hard specific moral purpose. Mrs. Gaskell was, indeed, a born story-teller, charged through and through with the story-teller's peculiar element, a something which may be called suppressed gipsiness, a restless instinct which impelled her to be constantly making trial in imagination of various modes of life.

William Minto, 1878, "Mrs. Gaskell's Novels,"
Fortnightly Review, vol. 30, p. 366

Of all Mrs. Gaskell's books her earliest has enjoyed the most widespread reputation. It has been translated into French and German and many other languages, including Finnish; while at home the author became an established favourite. Some of the chief employers of labour in the Manchester district, however, complained that they were unjustly treated, and that she spoke rashly of some "burning questions of social economy." She was accused in the Manchester *Guardian* (28 Feb. and 7 Mar. 1849) of "maligning" the manufacturers. Much of the same position was taken in W. R. Greg's "Essay on Mary Barton" (1849), which he thought worth reprinting many years afterward (1876), in his volume entitled *Mistaken Aims and Attainable Ideals of the Artisan Class.* Without discussing the point here, it may be observed, as Prof. Minto has done, that John Barton must not be taken too hastily as a type of his whole class; that the book refers to the period of distress (1842) which suggested Disraeli's *Sybil;* and that it has unquestionably contributed to the growth of sentiments which have helped to make the manufacturing world and Manchester very different from what they were forty years ago. The sincerity of its pathos and insight into the very hearts of the poor are of enduring value. Its humour is marked by the rather patriarchal flavour characteristic of Lancashire humour in general; nothing is more striking in Mrs. Gaskell's literary life than the ease and rapidity with which, in this respect, her genius contrived to emancipate itself.

Adolphus William Ward, 1890, Dictionary of
National Biography, vol. XXI, p. 50

Cranford (1853)

No short tale could be more delightful; the early chapters describe the quiet, aristocratic country life of the female population of the little town, and are full of the richest humour. All is so telling and yet so good-natured, for Mrs. Gaskell is telling us about the worthy people among whom she passed the happy days of her girlhood.

Mat Hompes, 1895, Mrs. Gaskell, Gentlemen's Magazine,
vol. 279, p. 133

In *Cranford* (1853) Mrs. Gaskell passed into a more serene atmosphere, in which, describing under this name the Knutsford of her early acquaintance, she lovingly sets forth the genteel poverty, the innocent self-respecting pride, the quaint humours, and the gentle charities of a society of elderly spinsters and widows without children. Nothing could be done more simply, exquisitely, or with a higher air of truth. To have read *Cranford* is to have personally known the sleepy old place, to have come forever under the power of its charm, to have taken part in its innumerable tea-drinkings and games of Preference, to have trembled at the uncanny feats of Signor Brunoni, and to have fallen irrevocably in love with dear, old, pathetic Miss Matty.

Richard D. Graham, 1897, The Masters of
Victorian Literature, p. 84

One province she discovered and made her own—feminine society in out-of-the-way towns and villages before the encroachment of railroads and penny postage. Of this life Cranford is the classic. Here is described the old-style etiquette, the genteel poverty, the formal calls, and evening parties, of a village wholly in the possession of the Amazons—widows and spinsters —where no men are tolerated, except the country doctor, who is allowed to stay there occasionally over-night when on his long circuit. Old maids spent their time in tea-drinking and stale gossip, and in chasing sunbeams from their carpets. Before going to bed they peep beneath the white dimity valance or roll a ball under it, to be sure no Iachimo with "great fierce face" lies concealed there. So ends the day of trivialities and Gothic fears.

Wilbur L. Cross, 1899, The Development of the
English Novel, p. 234

It was discovered long ago that the place "Cranford," described in Mrs. Gaskell's famous story, was Knutsford—in England, of course. To the old house on the heath in Knutsford, the baby, Elizabeth Cleghorn Stevenson, came when only a few weeks old to be brought up by her aunt; and there she lived till she grew to womanhood. In the parish church she was married, and in the quiet graveyard on the sloping bankside by Brook Street her ashes rest. Thus it is that Knutsford is identified with the personality of Mrs. Gaskell and, besides, she has put it into many of her books. It is *Cranford* most of all.

Howard M. Jenkins, 1901, *The Real "Cranford,"*
Ladies' Home Journal, vol. 18, No. 11, p. 9

The Life of Charlotte Brontë (1857)

Patrick Branwell Brontë was no domestic demon—he was just a man moving in a mist, who lost his way. More sinned against, mayhap, than sinning, *at least* he proved the reality of his sorrows. They killed him, and it needed not that his memory should have been tarnished, much, as I think, to the detriment of the *Biography* of his sister. I am desirous to be anything rather than a hostile critic of the memoir. Mrs. Gaskell was an intimate friend of my family, and her husband at one time my father's colleague in the ministry. I admire *Mary Barton* and her other Novels greatly. Towards her memory I have the kindest feeling; but *Fiat justitia!* and I must say what I can in favour of my old friend.

Francis H. Grundy, 1879, *Pictures of the Past*, p. 92

The substantial accuracy of the picture drawn by Mrs. Gaskell of her heroine's life and character, and of the influences exercised upon them by her personal and local surroundings, has not been successfully impugned. As to her literary skill and power and absolute uprightness of intention as a biographer there cannot be two opinions. She expressly disclaimed having made any attempt at psychological analysis; but she was exceptionally successful in her endeavor to bring before her readers the picture of a very peculiar character and altogether original mind.

Adolphus William Ward, 1890, *Dictionary of*
National Biography, vol. XXI, p. 52

In the whole of English biographical literature there is no book that can compare in wide-spread interest with the *Life of Charlotte Brontë* by Mrs. Gaskell. It has held a position of singular popularity for forty years; and while biography after biography has come and gone, it still commands a place side by side with Boswell's *Johnson,* and Lockhart's *Scott.* As far as mere readers are concerned, it may indeed claim its hundreds as against the tens of intrinsically more important rivals. There are obvious reasons for this success. Mrs. Gaskell was herself a popular novelist, who commanded a very wide audience, and *Cranford,* at least, has taken a place among the classics of our literature. She brought to bear upon the biography of Charlotte Brontë all those literary gifts which had made the charm of her seven volumes of romance. And these gifts were employed upon a romance of real life, not less fascinating than anything which imagination could have furnished. . . . It is quite certain that Charlotte Brontë would not stand on so splendid a pedestal today but for the single-minded devotion of her accomplished biographer.

> Clement K. Shorter, 1896, *Charlotte Brontë and*
> *her Circle,* pp. 1, 20

Mrs. Gaskell's book was avowedly incomplete in so far as she was unable to give the names of many persons and places, indeed, in some cases she cannot have known them, as Miss Nussey eliminated many of them from the letters she lent Mrs. Gaskell. But when these are filled in, and, apart from what Mary Taylor called the declamation, which is practically confined to the Branwell-Robinson episode, it is difficult to conceive a biography of Charlotte Brontë, which, even with all the new facts before the writer, would be an improvement on Mrs. Gaskell's. A few minor details might be added, but her main facts and conclusions have in no instance been proved wrong, and they are presented in such a way as to give a true and vivid picture of the life and character of the subject of her memoir which is hardly surpassed by any biography in the English language.

> B. W. Willett, 1901, ed. *The Life of Charlotte Brontë*
> *by E. C. Gaskell,* Introduction, p. XV

GENERAL

The authoress was a prose Crabbe—earnest, faithful, and often spirited in her delineations of humble life. By confining herself chiefly to the manufacturing population, she threw light on conditions of life, habits, and feelings comparatively new and original in our fictitious literature.

> Robert Chambers, 1876, *Cyclopædia of English Literature,*
> ed. Carruthers

Mrs. Gaskell saw everything in the light of a sympathetic humour. It is this quality that has served hitherto as salt to her books and has preserved their flavour while that of a great deal of more ambitious literature has been lost. If her humour is not equal to the best specimens of that of George Eliot, it is more diffused; if less powerful, it is gentler and quite as subtle. In style she is easy and flowing; and her later books show more freedom than her first attempt. At the same time, her writing rarely rises to eloquence. She had more talent than genius. She has created many good, but no great characters; and she stands midway between Thackeray and Dickens, who are emphatically men of genius, and writers like Trollope who, with abundant talent and exhaustless industry, have no genius whatever.

Hugh Walker, 1897, The Age of Tennyson, p. 108

Hardly aspiring to the title of novelist, she frequently reminded her public that she was writing only tales. These tales were told in the first person, and for the moral edification of her own sex. In form and aim they were accordingly of the Edgeworth type. Indeed Mrs. Gaskell may be said, in a general way, to have performed in them the same noble service to her contemporaries that Maria Edgeworth did to hers. She entered into the thoughts and wayward moods of children with true insight; she gave us the first English nurses and housekeepers of hard common sense and racy wit, the Nancys and the Sallys.

Wilbur L. Cross, 1890, The Development of the
English Novel, p. 234

THOMAS LOVE PEACOCK
1785-1866

Born, at Weymouth, 18 Oct. 1785. At a school at Englefield Green, 1793-98. To London, 1801, Sec. to Sir Home Riggs Popham, winter of 1808-09. Friendship with Shelley begun, 1812; visit to Edinburgh with him, 1813. Appointed to post in East India House, 1819; Chief Examiner, 1836. Married Jane Gryffydh, 20 March 1820. Settled at Lower Halliford, 1823. Retired from East India House, March 1856. Died, at Halliford, 23 Jan. 1866. Buried in Shepperton Cemetery. WORKS: *The Monks of St. Mark,* 1804; *Palmyra,* 1806; *The Genius of the Thames,* 1810; *The Philosophy of Melancholy,* 1812; *Sir Proteus* (under pseudonym: "P. M. O'Donovan, Esq."), 1814; *Headlong Hall* (anon.), 1816; *Melincourt* (anon.), 1817; *Nightmare Abbey* (anon.), 1818; *Sir Hornbrook* (anon.), 1818; *Rhododaphne* (anon.), 1818; *Maid Marian* (anon.), 1822; *The Misfortunes of Elphin* (anon.), 1829; *Crotchet Castle* (anon.), 1831; *Paper Money Lyrics,* 1837; *Gryll Grange* (anon.), 1861. He *translated: Gli Ingannat;* and *Ælia Lælia Crispis,* 1862.

R. Farquharson Sharp, 1897, A Dictionary of
English Authors, p. 224

SEE: *Works: Halliford Edition,* ed. H. F. B. Brett-Smith and Claude E. Jones, 1924-34, 10 v. (Volume I contains the standard life by Brett-Smith); Carl Van Doren, *The Life of Thomas Love Peacock,* 1911. J. B. Priestley, *Thomas Love Peacock,* 1927.

PERSONAL

Did you ever read *Headlong Hall* and *Maid Marian*?—a charming lyrical poet and Horatian satirist he was when a writer; now he is a white-headed jolly old worldling, and secretary to the E. India House, full of information about India and everything else in the world.

> William Makepeace Thackeray, 1850, *Collection of Letters,* p. 100

I met Peacock; a clever fellow, and a good scholar. I am glad to have an opportunity of being better acquainted with him. We had out Aristophanes, Æschylus, Sophocles and several other old fellows, and tried each other's quality pretty well. We are both strong enough in these matters for gentlemen. But he is editing the Supplices. Æschylus is not to be edited by a man whose Greek is only a secondary pursuit.

> Thomas Babington Macaulay, 1851, *Journal,* Dec. 31;
> *Life and Letters,* ed. Trevelyan, ch. xii

The portrait prefixed to the collected edition of his works conveys a very good idea of the man as I first saw him—a stately old gentleman with hair as white as snow, a keen, merry eye, and a characteristic chin. His dress was plain black, with white neckcloth, and low shoes, and on his head he wore a plaited straw hat. One glance at him was enough to reveal his delightful character, that of his own Dr. Opimian. "His tastes in fact were four: a good library, a good dinner, a pleasant garden, and rural walks." This was the man who, as a beautiful boy, had been caught up and kissed by Queen Caroline; who, when he grew up to manhood, had been christened "Greeky Peeky," on account of his acquirement in Greek. . . . Age had mellowed and subdued the "cameo leopard," but the "fine wit," as I very speedily discovered, was as keen as ever. His life had been passed in comparative peace and retirement. . . . He had his "good library," and it *was* a good one—full of books it was a luxury to handle, editions to make a scholar's mouth water, bound completely in the old style in suits as tough as George Fox's suit of leather. . . . Knowing Peacock only from his books, I was not prepared to find in him that delightful *bonhomie* which was in reality his most personal characteristic, in old age at least; and when we became acquainted, and read and talked together, I was as much astonished at the sweetness of his disposition as amused and captivated by his quaint erudition. In that green garden, in the lanes of Halliford, on the bright river, in walks and talks such as "brightened the sunshine," I learned to know him, and although he was so much my senior he took pleasure (I am glad to say) in my society, partly because I never worried him with "acrimonious dispute," which he hated above all things.

> Robert Buchanan, 1886, *A Look Round Literature,*
> pp. 165, 166, 167, 168

Peacock's literary style was elaborately polished, and he disliked writing letters, lest he should fall into any fault in hasty composition. . . . If, in conclusion, I may supplement these imperfect memories and family traditions from the sources of Peacock's books and the memoirs of his granddaughter, I should say that he was a kind-hearted, genial, friendly man, who loved to share his enjoyment of life with all around him; and he was self-indulgent without being selfish. His ideals of life were noble and generous, and in *Melincourt* they temper with seriousness, even sadness, the boyish love of fun and caricature which never fail him. And if we see in *The Misfortunes of Elphin* and *Crotchet Castle* increased intellectual power accompanied by a more worldly tone of thought, the natural consequence of prosperous enjoyment of life as he found it, it is pleasant to recognise signs in *Gryll Grange,* the child of his old age, a softer and better morality than that which characterises the two last-named books.

Sir Edward Strachey, 1891, Recollections of Thomas Love Peacock

POETRY

The poetry of Peacock is neither the poetry of sentimental namby-pambyism nor of burning passion. If he does not glow with the fire of Shelley, he does not pall with the sickly maunderings of later nerveless versifiers, whose genius has had some difficulty in crawling through its long clothes. While our author's verse is liquid and musical, it is never weak and faltering. He is able to endow his creations with some amount of life-breathing power. It can scarcely be said that he was happier in his poetry than his prose; rather, indeed, must the reverse be admitted. His intellectual and dissecting strength was greater than his emotional. He knew, probably, that the general reader would take no delight in his verse; but that mattered little to him; he could give him none other—consequently all his work in this direction betrays rather the thinking than the feeling man.

George Barnett Smith, 1875, "Thomas Love Peacock,"
Poets and Novelists, p. 144

The fame of Peacock as a prose humorist of incomparable vivacity has tended to overshadow and stunt his reputation as a poet. It is time, however, that his claims in verse should be vindicated, and a place demanded for him as an independent figure in the crowded Parnassus of his age,—a place a little below the highest, and somewhat isolated, at the extreme right of the composition. He has certain relations, not wholly accidental, with Shelley, who stands above him, and with such minor figures as Horace Smith and Thomas Haynes Bayly, who stand no less obviously below him; but in the main he is chiefly notable for his isolation. His ironical and caustic songs are unique in our literature, illuminated by too much fancy to be savage, but crackling with a kind of ghastly merriment that inspires quite as much terror as amusement. In parody he has produced at least one specimen, "There is a fever of the spirit," which does not possess its equal for combined sympathy and malice. When we pass to his serious and sentimental lyrics, our praise cannot be so unmeasured.

Edmund Gosse, 1880, *The English Poets*, ed. Ward, vol. IV, p. 417

Thomas Love Peacock wrote for respectable and sentimental England five of the very best drinking-songs ever given to an ungrateful world. No thought of possible disapprobation vexed his soul's serenity. He lived in the nineteenth century, as completely uncontaminated by nineteenth-century ideals as though Robinson Crusoe's desert island had been his resting place. The shafts of his good-tempered ridicule were leveled at all that his countrymen were striving to prove sacred and beneficial. His easy laugh rang out just when everybody was most strenuous in the cause of progress. His wit was admirably calculated to make people uncomfortable and dissatisfied. And in addition to these disastrous qualities, he apparently thought it natural and reasonable and right that English gentlemen—sensible, educated, *married* English gentlemen—should sit around their dinner-tables until the midnight hour, drinking wine and singing songs with boyish and scandalous joviality.

Agnes Repplier, 1897, *Varia*, p. 146

GENERAL

A new generation rose around him, to many of whose name—the name of one who had written novels when Bulwer and Disraeli were children—was unknown. His vigorous and versatile mind employed itself in new directions. He planned vessels which weathered the Cape, as he had produced books which will weather the century; but so far was he from abandoning letters, that his genius had an Indian summer not a whit less full of life and colour than the summer of its prime. *Gryll Grange,* published in *Fraser* some six or seven years ago, when Peacock was more than seventy years of age, is quite as fresh as any book of the *Headlong Hall* series, and even more remarkable than the best of them, for ingenuity, liveliness of humor, genial vigour of wit, and wide reading in literature. What is no less interesting about *Gryll Grange* is its similarity in tone and character to the author's novels of half a century before. His favorite views are not altered, only strengthened and confirmed.

James Hannay, 1866, "Recent Humourists,"
North British Review, vol. 45, p. 92

It would, perhaps, be too much to aver that without his classicism, without his constant resort to the rich bank of ancient authors for the loan of thoughts and images, his novels would have been devoid of a residuary charm; for Peacock had a strong vein, a rare lyrical faculty, some invention, and a large and decided bent for satire: but the grace which harmonized these, and lent a spirit of "long, long ago" to the quaint modern figures, with which he loved to people his halls and granges, abbeys, castles, and green woods, was derived from those intellectual repasts of Greek and Latin authors which furnished to him a perpetual banquet.

James Davies, 1875, Thomas Love Peacock,
Contemporary Review, vol. 25, p. 736

Smile as we may at the formality and pedantry of the eighteenth century, there were giants in those days; and Peacock resembled them in intellectual stature. His books will live, if only for their touches of quaint erudition; but they abound in delicious little pictures, such as that of Mr. Falconer and his seven Vestal attendants in *Gryll Grange,* or those of Coleridge and Shelley in *Nightmare Abbey.* Sir Oran Haut-ton is perfect, a masterpiece of characterisation, and as for Dr. Opimian, he is as sure of immortality as "my Uncle Toby" himself.

Robert Buchanan, 1886, A Look Round Literature, p. 183

Peacock's novels are unlike those of other men: they are the genuine expressions of an original and independent mind. His reading and his thinking ran together; there is free quotation, free play of wit and satire, grace of invention, too, but always unconventional. The story is always pleasant, although always secondary to the play of thought for which it gives occasion.

Henry Morley, 1887, ed. Crotchet Castle, Introduction, p. 6

When his robust independence is associated with a congenial subject, the effect is very agreeable,—it is like being made thoroughly at home by one who is thoroughly at home himself. Peacock seldom responded to the mere call of a publisher or editor, for such a call was seldom addressed to him. He was neither popular enough nor needy enough to be frequently diverted from his own bent, and thus exempt from taskwork, he could always be fresh and vigorous.

Richard Garnett, 1891, ed. Calidore and Miscellanea,
Introduction, p. 7

There is no obscurity in Peacock; there is no gush; and there is a great deal of very active and poignant ridicule of gush, of obscurity, and of affection.

. . . He began by making fun of the times of our grandfathers, he ended by making fun of the times which are almost, if not quite our own; and if, as perhaps he did, he showed himself rather obstinately blind to many of the higher aspects of life in general, he saw what he did see with an unmatched clearness of vision, and expressed the ironic results of his sight with powerful distinction and scholarship. . . . Peacock had a more poetical, a more ironic, and a less popular temperament than Macaulay's: but there was a good deal in him which might be called Macaulayish, on the negative side. He was nearly as knock-down in his depreciation as Macaulay was in his eulogism of progress and reform; he was, also like Macaulay, an omnivorous reader, and he had to a great extent the same clear, emphatic, unshadowed and unclouded caste of thought. Being, as has been said, an unpopular Macaulay, he never pushes his positiveness even in the negative direction to the extent of Philistinism; but he is open to the charge of being as hard if not as hollow as Macaulay at his worst. His special merits, however, will always, while they indispose towards him those whom Macaulay fully satisfies, enchant those who, while they fully admit the merits of Macaulay, are half disgusted by his demerits.

George Saintsbury, 1896, *English Prose*, ed. Craik,
vol. V, pp. 286, 287

CHARLES DICKENS
1812-1870

Born, at Landport, Portsea, 7 Feb. 1812. (Christened "Charles John Huffham," but never used last two names). Family moved to Chatham, 1816. To school under Mr. Giles, Baptist minister. Family moved to Camden Town. Neglected education. Father arrested for debt, 1822 [?]. Dickens obtained situation as packer in a blacking warehouse. At Mr. Jones's school in Hampstead Road, 1824-26. Employed as solicitor's clerk, May 1827 to Nov. 1828. Taught himself shorthand. Parliamentary reporter to *The True Sun*, 1831-32; for *The Mirror of Parliament;* for *The Morning Chronicle,* from 1835. Contributed papers, afterwards pub. as *Sketches by Boz,* to *Monthly Magazine, Morning Chronicle, Evening Chronicle, Bell's Life,* and *Library of Fiction,* 1833-35. Married Catherine Hogarth, 2 April 1836. *The Strange Gentleman* produced at St. James's Theatre, 29 Sept. 1836; *Is she his Wife?* same theatre, 6 March 1837. Edited *Bentley's Miscellany,* 1837-39. Growing popularity. Freedom of City of Edinburgh, summer of 1841. Severe illness, autumn of same year. Visit to America and Canada, Jan. to June 1842. Visits to Italy, July to Nov. 1844, and Jan. to June 1845. First editor of *Daily News,* 21 Jan. to 9 Feb. 1846; subsequently an occasional contributor. Started General Theatrical Fund. Visit to Switzerland, June to Nov. 1846, in Paris, Nov. 1846 to Feb. 1847 (with visit to

London, Dec. 1846). Active part in various amateur theatrical performances for charities, 1847-52. *Household Words* started 30 March 1849;
edited it till 1859. Testimonial at Birmingham, 1853. At Boulogne, sum-
mers of 1853, 54, 56. In Switzerland and Italy, autumn of 1853; in Paris,
Nov. 1855 to May 1856. Bought Gadshill Place, 1856; settled there, 1860.
First public "Reading" from his works, 29 April 1858. Separation from
his wife, May 1858. On cessation of *Household Words,* started *All the
Year Round,* 30 April 1859. Four series of public Readings, 1858-59,
1861-63, 1866-67, 1868-70, in London, provinces and Scotland. Readings
in Paris, 1863. Severe illness in 1865. Readings in America, Dec. 1867 to
April 1868. Breakdown of health. Last Reading, in London, 1 March
1869. Died, at Gadshill, 9 June 1870. Buried in Westminster Abbey.
WORKS: *Sketches by Boz,* 1st series, 1835; 2nd, 1836; *Sunday under Three
Heads . . . By Timothy Sparks,* 1836; *The Strange Gentleman . . . By Boz,*
1837; *The Village Coquettes,* 1836; *Posthumous Papers of the Pickwick
Club,* 1837 (in monthly nos., April 1836 to Nov. 1837); *Memoirs of
Joseph Grimaldi, edited by Boz,* 1838; *Oliver Twist . . . By Boz,* (from
Bentley's Miscellany, 2 vols.), 1838; *Sketches of Young Gentlemen*
(anon.), 1838; *Life and Adventures of Nicholas Nickleby,* 1839 (in
monthly nos., April 1838 to Oct. 1839); *Sketches of Young Couples*
(anon.), 1840; *Master Humphrey's Clock,* vol. i., 1840; vols. ii. and iii.,
1841 (in weekly nos., April 1840 to Nov. 1841); *Barnaby Rudge,* 1841;
The Old Curiosity Shop, 1841; *American Notes,* 1842; *A Christmas
Carol,* 1843; *The Life and Adventures of Martin Chuzzlewit,* 1844 (in
monthly nos., Jan. 1843 to July 1844), *The Chimes,* 1844; *The Cricket on
the Hearth,* 1845; *Pictures from Italy* (from *Daily News*), 1846; *The
Battle of Life,* 1846; *Dealings with the firm of Dombey and Son,* 1848 (in
monthly nos., Oct. 1846 to April 1848); *The Haunted Man,* 1848; *The
Personal History of David Copperfield,* 1850 (in monthly nos., May 1849
to Nov. 1850); *Bleak House,* 1853 (in monthly nos., March 1852 to Sept.
1853); *A Child's History of England* (from *Household Words*), 1854;
Hard Times for these Times (from *Household Words*), 1854; *Little
Dorrit,* 1857 (in monthly nos., Dec. 1855 to June 1857); *A Tale of Two
Cities* (from *All the Year Round*), 1859; *The Uncommercial Traveler,*
1861 [1860] (originally in weekly parts, Jan. to Oct., 1860; 2nd edn.
enlarged, 1868; 3rd edn. enlarged, 1869); *Great Expectations* (from *All
the Year Round*), 1861; *Our Mutual Friend,* 1865 (in monthly nos., May
1864 to Nov. 1865); *The Mystery of Edwin Drood* (unfinished) six nos.,
April to Sept., 1870. POSTHUMOUS: *Speeches,* 1870; *Mr. Nightingale's
Diary,* 1877; *Is she his Wife?* 1877; *The Lamplighter,* 1879; *The Mudfog
Papers* (from *Bentley's Miscellany*), 1880; *Letters* (3 vols.), 1880-82. He
edited: *The Pic-Nic Papers,* 1841; J. Overs' *Evenings of a Working Man,*
1844; *Method of Employment,* 1852; A. A. Procter's *Legends and Lyrics,*
1866; *Religious Opinions of the late C. H. Townshend,* 1869. COLLECTED
WORKS in 22 vols., 1858-59; in 21 vols., 1867-74. LIFE: by Forster, 1872;
by Marzials, 1887.

R. Farquharson Sharp, 1897, *A Dictionary of
English Authors,* p. 79

SEE: *The Nonesuch Dickens,* ed. Arthur Waugh, Walter Dexter, and
others, 1937-38, 23 v.; *Speeches,* ed. K. J. Fielding, 1960; *Letters,* ed.
Madeleine House and Graham Storey, 1965- (edition in progress):

Selected Letters, ed. F. W. Dupee, 1960; John Forster, Life, 1872-74, 3 v.; Edgar Johnson, Charles Dickens: His Tragedy and Triumph, 1952, 2 v.

PERSONAL

I admire and love the man exceedingly, for he has a deep warm heart, a noble sympathy with and respect for human nature, and great intellectual gifts wherewith to make these fine moral ones fruitful for the delight and consolation and improvement of his fellow-beings.

Frances Ann Kemble, 1842, Letter, April 22;
Records of Later Life, p. 318

Called on Dickens at 10.30 A.M. by appointment, as he leaves at one. He was at breakfast. Sat down with him. He was very agreeable and full of life. He is the *cleverest* man I ever met. I mean he impresses you more with the alertness of his various powers. His forces are all light infantry and light cavalry, and always in marching order. There are not many heavy pieces, but few *sappers and miners,* the scientific corps is deficient, and I fear there is no chaplain in the garrison.

Richard Henry Dana, 1842, Journal, Feb. 5;
Richard Henry Dana, ed. C. F. Adams, vol. I, p. 33

Among the passengers in the *Britannia* are Mr. Charles Dickens and his wife. This gentleman is the celebrated "Boz," whose name "rings through the world with loud applause,"—the fascinating writer whose fertile imagination and ready pen conceived and sketched the immortal Pickwick, his prince of valets, and his bodyguard of choice cronies; who has made us laugh with "Mantilini," and cry with poor "little Nell;" caused us to shrink with horror from the effects of lynch law, as administered by the misguided Lord George Gordon, and to listen with unmitigated delight to the ticking of "Master Humphrey's Clock." The visit of this popular writer has been heralded in advance. He was expected by this packet, and I signed, three or four days ago, with a number of other persons, a letter to be presented to him on his arrival in this city, giving him a hearty welcome and inviting him to a public dinner, which, from the spirit which appears to prevail on the subject, will be no common affair. . . . The great dinner to Dickens was given yesterday, at the City Hotel, and came off with flying colours. Two hundred and thirty persons sat down to dinner at seven o'clock. The large room was ornamented with two illuminated scenes from the works of "Boz," busts of celebrated persons and classical devices, all in good taste; and the eating and drinking part of the affair was excellent. The president was

Washington Irving (I beg pardon, "His Excellency"). "Non Nobis" was sung by Mr. Horn and his little band of vocalists, who gave several glees during the evening. After the unintellectual operation of eating and drinking was concluded, the president rose and began a prepared speech, in which he broke down flat (as he promised us beforehand he would), and concluded with this toast: "Charles Dickens, the literary guest of the nation." To this the guest made his acknowledgment in an excellent speech, delivered with great animation, and characterized by good taste and warm feeling.

Philip Hone, 1842, *Diary,* Jan. 24, Feb. 19, vol. II, pp. 109, 118

You ask about Mr. Boz. I am quite delighted with him. He is a thorough good fellow, with nothing of the author about him but the reputation, and goes through his task as Lion with exemplary grace, patience, and good-nature. He has the brilliant face of a man of genius, and a pretty Scottish lassie for a wife, with roses on her cheeks, and "een sae bonny blue." His writings you know. I wish you had listened to his eloquence at the dinner here. It was the only specimen of eloquence I have ever witnessed. Its charm was not in its words, but in the manner of saying them.

Fitz-Greene Halleck, 1842, *To Mrs. Rush,* March 8;
Life and Letters, ed. Wilson, p. 434

At a dinner-party at Mr. Holland's last evening, a gentleman, in instance of Charles Dickens's unweariability, said that during some theatrical performances in Liverpool he acted in play and farce, spent the rest of the night making speeches, feasting, and drinking at table, and ended at seven o'clock in the morning by jumping leapfrog over the backs of the whole company.

Nathanal Hawthorne, 1853, *English Notebooks,* vol. I, p. 59

He looks about the age of Longfellow. His hair is not much grizzled and is thick, although the crown of his head is getting bald. His features are good, and the nose rather high, the eyes largish, greyish and very expressive. He wears a moustache and beard, and dresses at dinner in exactly the same uniform which every man in London or the civilised world is bound to wear, as much as the inmates of a penitentiary are restricted to theirs. I mention this because I had heard that he was odd and extravagant in his costume. I liked him exceedingly. We sat next each other at table, and I found him genial, sympathetic, agreeable, unaffected, with plenty of light easy talk and touch-and-go fun without any effort or humbug of any kind.

John Lothrop Motley, 1861, *To His Mother,* March 15;
Correspondence, ed. Curtis, vol. I, p. 365

I emphatically direct that I be buried in an inexpensive, unostentatious, and strictly private manner, that no public announcement be made of the time or place of my burial, that at the utmost not more than three plain mourning coaches be employed, and that those who attend my funeral wear no scarf, cloak, black bow, long hatband, or other such revolting absurdity. I direct that my name be inscribed in plain English letters on my tomb, without the addition of "Mr." or "Esquire." I conjure my friends on no account to make me the subject of any monument, memorial, or testimonial whatever. I rest my claims to the remembrance of my country upon my published works, and to the remembrance of my friends upon their experience of me; in addition thereto, I commit my soul to the mercy of God, through our Lord and Saviour Jesus Christ, and I exhort my dear children to try to guide themselves by the teaching of the New Testament in its broad spirit, and to put no faith in any man's narrow construction of its letter here or there.

Charles Dickens, 1869, *Will,* May 11

No man ever kept himself more aloof than Dickens from the ordinary honours of life. No titles were written after his name. He was not C. B., or D. C. L., or F. R. S.; nor did he ever attempt to become M. P. What titles of honour may ever have been offered to him I cannot say; but that titles were offered I do not doubt. Lord Russell, a year or two ago, proposed a measure by which, if carried, certain men of high character and great capacity would have been selected as peers for life; but Charles Dickens would never have been made a lord. He probably fully appreciated his own position; and had a noble confidence in himself, which made him feel that nothing Queen, Parliament, or Minister, could do for him would make him greater than he was. No title to his ear could have been higher than that name which he made familiar to the ears of all reading men and women.

Anthony Trollope, 1870, "Charles Dickens,"
Saint Paul's Magazine, vol. 6, p. 374

I had the honor of being Mr. Dickens's school-fellow for about two years (1824-1826), both being day-scholars at Mr. Jones's "Classical and Commercial Academy." . . . My recollection of Dickens whilst at school . . . is that of a healthy looking boy, small but well built, with a more than usual flow of spirits, inducing to harmless fun, seldom or never I think to mischief, to which so many lads at that age are prone. I cannot recall any thing that then indicated he would hereafter become a literary celebrity; but perhaps he was too young then. He usually held his head more erect than lads ordinarily do, and there was a general smartness about him. His week-day dress of jacket and trousers, I can clearly remember, was what is called pepper-and-salt; and, instead of the frill that most boys of his age wore then, he had a turn-down collar, so that he looked less youthful in consequence. He invented what he termed a "lingo," produced by the addition of a few letters of the same sound to every word; and it was our ambition, walking and talking thus along the street, to be considered foreigners.

Owen P. Thomas, 1871, *Letter to John Forster,* Feb.; Forster's *The Life of Charles Dickens,* vol. I, ch. III

Of his attractive points in society and conversation I have particularized little, because in truth they were himself. Such as they were, they were never absent from him. His acute sense of enjoyment gave such relish to his social qualities that probably no man, not a great wit or a professed talker, ever left, in leaving any social gathering, a blank so impossible to fill up. In quick and varied sympathy, in ready adaptation to every whim or humour, in help to any mirth or game, he stood for a dozen men. If one may say such a thing, he semed to be always the more himself for being somebody else, for continually putting off his personality. His versatility made him unique.

John Forster, 1874, *The Life of Charles Dickens,* vol. III, ch. xix

Close under the bust of Thackeray lies Charles Dickens, not, it may be, his equal in humour, but more than his equal in his hold on the popular mind, as was shown in the intense and general enthusiasm evinced over his grave. The funeral, according to Dickens's urgent and express desire in his will, was strictly private. It took place at an early hour in the summer morning, the grave having been dug in secret the night before, and the vast solitary space of the Abbey was occupied only by the small hand of mourners, and the Abbey Clergy, who, without any music except the occasional peal of the organ, read the funeral service. For days the spot was visited by thousands; many were the flowers strewn upon it by unknown hands; many tears shed by the poorer visitors. He rests beside Sheridan, Garrick, and Henderson.

Arthur Penrhyn Stanley, 1876-82, *Historical Memorials of Westminster Abbey,* p. 283

It is idle to speculate whether he went into the state of matrimony from the heat and impulse of youth, or after long and sober reflection. He laid some store by his exact and practical wisdom, and probably in that he was superior to most authors. Nor was he one to plunge into the ocean of wedded possibility without retiring to some remote and tranquil inlet where he might adjust compasses before setting sail. Yet his incongruous incapability in erotic affairs in general must, we think, have given an oblique turn to any calculations he had formed on this subject; at all events, his romance, so far as his wife was concerned, does not seem to have extended much beyond the honeymoon. He never speaks of her with fondness; there was no ethereal mixing of souls, such as we find in the biographies of other equally gifted and ecstatic pairs. We are left in the dark as to the causes of the estrangement; there are only occasional murmurs of extravagant house-keeping on the one side and nervous irritability on the other. The former was of course a risk he faced, and a burden from which, however vexatious it might be, he should not have flinched. On the other hand, it does not say a great deal for the sympathy or patience of any wife, especially an intellectual one, that she did not understand or, failing to understand, that she did not bear with, a failing which many great thinkers and writers have found inseparable from the indulgence of fanciful or philosophic thought.

James Crabb Watt, 1880, *Great Novelists: Scott, Thackeray, Dickens, Lytton*

The blacking-warehouse at Old Hungerford Stairs, Strand, opposite Old Hungerford Market, in which he tied up the pots of blacking in company with Bob Fagin . . . has long since been torn down. That "crazy old house, with a wharf of its own, abutting on the water when the tide was in and on the mud when the tide was out, and literally overrun with rats," is now replaced by a row of stone buildings; the embankment has risen over the mud; and the vast Charing Cross Station stands opposite on the site of the old Hungerford Market and of "The Swan, or The Swan and something else"—the miserable old "public" where he used to get his bread and cheese and glass of beer. The very name of the street is gone, and Villiers street has sponged out the memory of Hungerford Stairs. . . . Indeed, it is no longer possible to find any of the places he makes mention of in his narrative to Forster. . . . Bayham street, where he lived, is entirely rebuilt.

B. E. Martin, 1881, "In London with Dickens," *Scribner's Monthly,* vol. 21, p. 650

I have heard Dickens described by those who knew him as aggressive, imperious, and intolerant, and I can comprehend the accusation; but to me his temper was always of the sweetest and kindest. He would, I doubt not, have been easily bored, and would not have scrupled to show it; but he never ran the risk. He was imperious in the sense that his life was conducted in the *Sic volo sic jubeo* principle, and that everything gave way before him. The society in which he mixed, the hours which he kept, the opinions which he held, his likes and dislikes, his ideas of what should or should not be, were all settled by himself, not merely for himself, but for all those brought into connection with him, and it was never imagined they could be called in question. Yet he was never regarded as a tyrant: he had immense power of will, absolute mesmeric force, as he proved beneficially more than once; and that he should lead and govern seemed perfectly natural to us. . . . Dickens was not only a genius, but he had the volcanic activity, the perturbed restlessness, the feverish excitability of genius. What he created, that he was. His personages were, as readers of his letters know, an integral part of his life. . . . In regard to the friendship which Dickens vouchsafed me, I have been frequently asked, "Did he come up to the expectations you had formed of him? Was Dickens the man as lovable as Dickens the author?" and I have always replied, "Yes; wholly."

Edmund Yates, 1884, *Recollections and Experiences*

In bringing up his children, Charles Dickens was always most anxious to impress upon them that as long as they were honest and truthful, so would they always be sure of having justice done to them. . . . Notwithstanding his constant and arduous work, he was never too busy to be unmindful of the comfort and welfare of those about him, and there was not a corner in any of his homes, from kitchen to garret, which was not constantly inspected by him, and which did not boast of some of his neat and orderly contrivances. We used to laugh at him sometimes and say we believed that he was personally acquainted with every nail in the house. . . . He loved all flowers, but especially bright flowers, and scarlet geraniums were his favourite of all. . . . Charles Dickens was very fond of music, and not only of classical music. He loved national airs, old tunes, songs, and ballads, and was easily moved by anything pathetic in a song or tune, and was never tired of hearing his special favourites sung or played. He used to like to have music of an evening, and duets used to be played for hours together, while he would read or walk up and down the room. . . . Among his many attributes, that of a doctor must not be forgotten. He was invaluable in a sick room, or in any sudden emergency; always quiet, always cheerful, always useful, and skillful, always doing the right thing, so that his very presence seemed to bring comfort and help. From his children's earliest days his visits, during any time of sickness, were eagerly longed for and believed in, as doing more good than those even of the doctor himself. He had a curiously magnetic and sympathetic hand, and his touch was wonderfully soothing and quieting. As a mesmerist he possessed great power, which he used, most successfully, in many cases of great pain and distress.

Mamie Dickens, 1885, "Charles Dickens at Home,"
Cornhill Magazine, vol. 51, pp. 37, 39, 43, 47, 49

We were at first disappointed, and disposed to imagine there must be some mistake. No! *that* is not the man who wrote *Pickwick*! What we saw was a dandified, pretty-boy-looking sort of figure; singularly young-looking, I thought, with a slight flavor of the whipper-snapper genius of humanity. . . . Dickens' eyes were not blue, but of a very distinct and brilliant hazel—the color traditionally assigned to Shakespeare's eyes. . . . Dickens was only thirty-three when I first saw him, being just two years my junior. I have said what he appeared to me then. As I knew him afterwards, and to the end of his days, he was a strikingly manly man, not only in appearance, but in bearing. The lustrous brilliancy of his eyes was very striking. And I do not think that I have ever seen it noticed that those wonderful eyes which saw so much and so keenly were appreciably, though to a very slight degree, near-sighted eyes. Very few persons, even among those who knew him well, were aware of this, for Dickens never used a glass. But he continually exercised his vision by looking at distant objects, and making them out as well as he could without any artificial assistance. It was an instance of that force of will in him which compelled a naturally somewhat delicate frame to comport itself like that of an athlete. Mr. Forster somewhere says of him, "Dickens' habits were robust, but his health was not." This is entirely true as far as my observation extends.

Thomas Adolphus Trollope, 1888, *What I Remember*,
pp. 315, 352, 353

My first experience, I think, of my father's extraordinary energy and of the thoroughness—the even alarming thoroughness—with which he always threw himself into everything he had occasion to take up, was in connection with a toy theatre of which I was the proud possessor somewhere about the middle forties. Toy theatres with scenery and sheets of the characters only requiring painting and cutting out—one Skelt was the principal artist for such things—were very popular indeed in my very early youth, and it was the aim of every self-respecting boy to be the manager of one or more of them. . . . This extraordinary, eager, restless energy, which first showed itself to me in this small matter, was never absent from my father all through his life. Whatever he did he put his whole heart into, and did as well as ever he could. Whether it was for work or for play, he was always in earnest. Painting the scenes for a toy theatre, dancing Sir Roger de Coverley at a children's party, gravely learning the polka from his little daughters for a similar entertainment, walking, riding, picnicing, amateur acting, public reading, or the every-day hard work of his literary life—it was all one to him. Whatever lay nearest to his hand at the moment had to be done thoroughly.

Charles Dickens, Jr., 1895, "Glimpses of Charles Dickens,"
North American Review, vol. 160, pp. 526, 527

Mr. Dickens's visit was measurably disappointing; we did too much for him and his lady; they did not appreciate the honor bestowed on them, and overrated their importance. When in Washington they were charged with a neglect of etiquette amounting to incivility. It must be added that on the subsequent visit of Mr. Dickens, at the Press Dinner given to him in April, 1868, just before his departure, he made a graceful and feeling statement in the nature of an apology, or even a recantation, which he engaged to have appended to every copy of the offending works so long as he or his representatives should retain control of their publication.

Charles H. Haswell, 1896, Reminiscences of an
Octogenarian, p. 384

One fails to see that he ever thought for a moment about the title of gentleman. Commercial by instinct, he wished his genius to receive the material reward which was its due; he wanted to live largely, liberally, and generously. His tastes and his beneficence needed money, and the making of money by labour in his art probably tended to become, unconsciously, an end in itself. He never could bear to yield to age, to resign his endeavour, to leave his portentous energy unoccupied. Like Scott, he might have said, "No rest for me but in the woolen"; he could not withdraw, like Shakespeare, to country quiet. His native bent was as much towards the stage as to fiction, and he wore himself out untimely in working the theatrical side of his nature, in his Readings. The desire to be conspicuously before the world which idolised him, may have been as potent as the need of money in spurring the energy of Dickens to its fatal goal. It is to these circumstances, extraordinary energy, craving for employment, a half-suppressed genius for the stage, need of money, and need of publicity, that we trace these defects of Dickens's work which are due to surplusage. He did too much, with the inevitable consequences. He read too little. His nature was all for literary action; not for study, criticism, and reflection. The results were these blemishes with which he is reproached in that age of reaction which ever succeeds to a career of vast popular success. Criticism, indeed, was not lacking, even when he was best accepted. It is quite an error to think that Dickens's literary contemporaries did not see the motes where a younger generation is apt to see the beams.

Andrew Lang, 1898, "Charles Dickens,"
Fortnightly Review, vol. 70, p. 945

READINGS AND THEATRICALS

I had to go yesterday to Dickens's Reading, 8 p.m., Hanover Rooms, to the complete upsetting of my evening habitudes and spiritual composure. Dickens does do it capitally, such as *it* is; acts better than any Macready in the world; a whole tragic, comic, heroic *theatre* visible, performing under one *hat,* and keeping us laughing—in a sorry way, some of us thought, the whole night. He is a good creature, too, and makes fifty or sixty pounds by each of these readings.

Thomas Carlyle, 1863, *Letter, Thomas Carlyle, A History of His Life in London,* ed. Froude, vol. II, p. 229

Every character was individualized by the voice and by a slight change of expression. But the reader stood perfectly still, and the instant transition of the voice from the dramatic to the descriptive tone was unfailing and extraordinary. This was perfection of art. Nor was the evenness of the variety less striking. Every character was indicated with the same felicity. Of course the previous image in the hearer's mind must be considered in estimating the effect. The reader does not create the character, the writer has done that; and now he refreshes it into unwonted vividness, as when a wet sponge is passed over an old picture. Scrooge, and Tiny Tim, and Sam Weller and his wonderful father, and Sergeant Buzfuz, and Justice Stareleigh have an intenser reality and vitality than before. As the reading advances the spell becomes more entrancing. The mind and heart answer instantly to every tone and look of the reader. In a passionate outburst, as in Bob Cratchit's wail for his lost little boy, or in Scrooge's prayer to be allowed to repent, the whole scene lives and throbs before you. And when, in the great trial of Bardell against Pickwick, the thick, fat voice of the elder Weller wheezes from the gallery, "Put it down with a wee, me Lerd, put it down with a wee," you turn to look for the gallery and behold the benevolent parent.

George William Curtis, 1867, "Dickens Reading," *From the Easy Chair,* p. 47

Unlike most professional rehearsals, where waiting about, dawdling, and losing time, seem to be the order of the day, the rehearsals under Charles Dickens' stage-managership were strictly devoted to work—serious, earnest work; the consequence was, that when the evening of performance came, the pieces went off with a smoothness and polish that belong only to finished stage-business and practised performers. He was always there among the first arrivers at rehearsals, and remained in a conspicuous position during their progress till the very last moment of conclusion. He had a small table placed rather to one side of the stage, at which he generally sat, as the scenes went on in which he himself took no part. On this table rested a moderate-sized box; its interior divided into convenient compartments for holding papers, letters, etc., and this interior was always the very pink of neatness and orderly arrangement. Occasionally he would leave his seat at the managerial table, and stand with his back to the foot-lights, in the very centre of the front of the stage, and view the whole effect of the re-hearsed performance as it proceeded, observing the attitudes and positions of those engaged in the dialogue, their mode of entrance, exit, etc. He never seemed to overlook anything; but to note the very slightest point that con-duced to the "going well" of the whole performance. With all this super-vision, however, it was pleasant to remark the utter absence of dictatorial-ness or arrogation of superiority that distinguished his mode of ruling his troop; he exerted his authority firmly and perpetually; but in such a manner as to make it universally felt to be for no purpose of self-assertion or self-importance; on the contrary, to be for the sole purpose of ensuring general success to their united efforts.

Mary Cowden Clarke, 1878, Recollections of Writers, p. 300

In taking leave of Mr. Dickens in this capacity, it may be interesting to set down the total number of public Readings he gave. Putting aside those given for charitable or friendly purposes between the years 1854 and 1858, in which latter year, at St. Martin's Hall, April 29, 1858, he commenced reading for his own especial benefit, up to the time of his retirement from the platform, at St. James's Hall, March 15, 1870, the full number of Readings was 423. Of these 111 were given under the management of Mr. Arthur Smith; 70 under the management of Mr. Headland (who suc-ceeded to the post of manager on the death of Mr. Smith), and 242 under my management. These latter were delivered in England, Ireland, Scotland, and America, between April 10, 1866, and March 15, 1870. Mr. Dickens kept no particular account of the amount of money he netted from the Readings under the management of Messrs. Arthur Smith and Headland, but he always computed it at about £12,000. Out of the 242 Readings given under my management (which included the three engagements of Messrs. Chappell and Co.), he cleared nearly £33,000. Handsome as these results were, and of course highly satisfactory to Mr. Dickens, they were purchased at the dear cost of the sacrifice of his health. But his career as a public reader was his own choice, and setting aside his pecuniary profits, the pleasure he derived from it is not to be told in words. For my part, at this distance of time, I think less of the dark than of the bright side of those never-to-be-forgotten days.

George Dolby, 1885, Charles Dickens as I Knew Him, p. 45

Pickwick Papers (1837)

The most cursory reference to preceding English writers of the comic order will show, that, in his own peculiar walk, Mr. Dickens is not simply the most distinguished, but the first. Admirers and detractors will be equally ready to admit that he has little, if anything, in common with the novelists and essayists of the last century. Of Fielding's intuitive perception of the springs of action, and skill in the construction of the prose epic—or Smollett's dash, vivacity, wild spirit of adventure and rich poetic imagination— he has none: still less can he make pretensions to the exquisite delicacy, fine finish, and perfect keeping of Steele's and Addison's pet characters,— Sir Roger de Coverley, Will Wimble, Will Honeycombe, Sir Andrew Freeport, and the rest; though we know few things better in conception than Sam Weller, with his chivalrous attachment to his master, his gallantry to the fair sex, his imperturbable self-possession, and singularly acquired knowledge of the world.

John Wilson Croker, 1837, "The Pickwick Papers,"
Quarterly Review, vol. 59, p. 484

By most people *Pickwick* is accepted as Dickens's *Magnum Opus.* It certainly is a typical one, but while the whole book is farcical in the extreme, while character degenerates to caricature, and fun to pantomimic romp and "rally," there are now and then touches of very clever shrewd observation, most admirable sketches of character—Sergeant Buzfuz and the trial scene are evidently quite true to nature, and pathos of the genial easy and ordinary kind in which the author delighted. But as a novel of nature and of plot and character compared to Fielding, *Pickwick* is very small. Who ever met with man, woman, or child, who could sit down by a winter fire and tell the "plot" of *Pickwick?* Had it come out as a whole book, it would have failed to find readers, it would, like Hudibras, have palled on the taste; it is too full of incident, scene succeeds scene, and adventure adventure. The novel is crowded with persons, and each person is—how different from real life and Mr. Trollope—not cut to pattern, but a character.

James Hain Friswell, 1870, *Modern Men of Letters
Honestly Criticised,* p. 8

It would be vain to praise or to disparage the immortal *Pickwick.* Everything about it is remarkable. No modern work of the century has engendered so many other books, commentaries, illustrations, &c., and been so Protean in its developments. Drama, opera, music, translations, pictures, topography, philology, almanacs, songsters, advertisements, pens, cigars, all exhibit this generative influence. There is a little library of writers on Pickwick. Grave professors, men of law, politicians, schoolmasters, all have been drawn to it. Neither Scott, nor Thackeray, nor Byron, nor Macaulay, nor Tennyson can show anything like it. The commentary on the Waverleys is quite meagre by comparison. The oddity, too, is that no other work of

"Boz" has had this fruitfulness. The reason would seem to be the tone of perfect conviction and reality in which it is conceived and carried out. The characters are treated almost biographically, and move forward according to its dates.

Percy Fitzgerald, 1898, "Among My Books,"
Literature, vol. 2, p. 384

There are three official accounts variously explaining the veracious story, each materially differing in dates and details, and respectively emanating from the three principal personages most likely to be fully informed upon the actual facts of the case. The artist Seymour undoubtedly originated the initial scheme of illustrating various unconnected adventures of Cockney sportsmen, to be graphically portrayed under the convenient if trite expedient of a "Nimrod Club"—all three accounts are agreed to this extent. The vivacious author of *Pickwick* from the first start, turned, twisted, shaped, and made the crude materials his very own by the absolute force of his genius, and fiery Pegasus-like, immediately dashing away with the lead, from ingredients, perhaps a trifle uncongenial to himself, produced the most popularly appreciated book of the century—possibly of any century; and, at one lucky bound, on the strength of his parts, became the most famous of novelists. The "third party" was the connecting link, the useful, necessary publishers, upon whose business-like conduct of the affair the commercial responsibilities depended.

Joseph Grego, 1899, ed. *Pictorial Pickwickiana,* vol. I, p. 6

Pickwick has always been a fascinating book for the artist. At one time everybody who could draw attempted to illustrate it. Indeed, the number of artists who indulged in such attempts are legion, *Pickwick Papers* being more favored in this respect than the others. At the time of its issue in 1836 and 1837, more than one artist produced sets of etchings to be used as "extras" for the monthly parts as they appeared. The best of these were by Onwhyn, who used the pseudnoym of "Sam Weller" on some of his engravings, William Heath, Alfred Crowquill (A. H. Forrester), and T. Gibson. We recall a characteristic one by Heath and also one by Sir John Gilbert, whose series on wood appeared later.

B. W. Matz, 1902, "Dickens and his Illustrators,"
The Critic, vol. 40 p. 44

Oliver Twist (1838)

The work which is most full of crimes and atrocities and the lowest characters, of all its author's productions, in which these things are by no means scarce—there are some of the deepest touches of pathos, and of the purest tenderness, not exceeded by any author who ever lived—simply because they grow out of the very ground of our common humanity, and being Nature at her best, are in themselves perfect, by universal laws.

Richard Hengist Horne, 1844, *A New Spirit of the Age,* p. 17

When Dickens wrote *Oliver Twist* he desired, as he says, to paint vice in its true characters, without the fascinations of highway adventure, or snug robbers' caves, or anything approaching the attractions that too often pervaded the literature of profligacy. He wishes to answer those who

> Proved, by cool discriminating sight,
> Black's not so black, nor white so very white.

The dens and stews of London are painted from life, and the picture is not inviting. In the character of Nancy there is some redeeming quality— she might have been different under different circumstances; in the characters of Fagin or Bill Sikes there is none; they are simply bad, as bad as they can be, without one silver thread lining the edge of the cloud. Unfortunately for the artist, but fortunately for the rest of the world, the haunts of vice that were standing when this work was written are demolished; and whatever remains of the Bill Sikes or the Fagin element is left in the cold; but if we read the police summaries we are sadly reminded that they are hardly extinct.

Alfred Rimmer, 1883, *About England with Dickens,* p. 133

Here and there appeared glimpses of the humor which had marked his earlier work, but on the whole, the tale was cast in the mold of the horrible, and depended for its strength on the debased characters and the criminal life of which Fagin is the central figure. It was eighteen years since Ivanhoe had appeared, and what a contrast between its Jewish personage and the character in this, the next work of a great English writer, in which a Jew plays a prominent rôle! In the one the charm, in the other the disgrace of the work; in the one the possessor of all human virtues, in the other of all human vices; in the one fair in body and fairer in soul, in the other distorted in body and black in soul; the one a plea for kindness toward a community at that time still unrecognized as worthy of the rights of men and women, the other calculated to re-awaken all the old thoughts, if ever they had died out, of the baseness and wickedness of the Jews. . . . All that interests us here is the character of Fagin, who is continually intruded upon our notice as "the Jew." Were the miscreant, whenever introduced upon the scene, merely spoken of as Fagin, we would look upon him as an example of London's criminal class, and there would be nothing further to arrest our special attention. . . . The author presented this character as a Jew, and hence has laid himself open to the charge of gross wrong and injustice. The fact of Fagin being a Jew does not make him what he is; but when the novel was written such an idea was far from being deemed impossible. The Jew was still an unknown quantity; people thought him *sui generis;* it was not known, according to popular opinion, what he was likely to do. . . . Strange it is, at best, that Charles Dickens, who, of all fictionists, contributed the most toward reforming social abuses, should, in this one instance, have joined the vulgar cry, and marked his worst character as a Jew. Knowing what we do of his works, we should rather have looked for the opposite.

David Philipson, 1889, *The Jew in English Fiction,* pp. 89, 90, 93

When we pass from the subjects of Dickens's stories to the mechanism of their plots we find little to admire and much to condemn. The most serious fault from the artistic stand-point is their lack of probability. In *Oliver Twist* the series of remarkable coincidences is perfectly absurd. When Oliver goes up to London and falls in with the pickpockets, the first person he comes across is the old gentleman whom he is suspected of robbing and who afterwards befriends him. This turns out to be his father's oldest friend. By a curious chance Oliver is captured by the thieves again and forced to take part in the robbery of a house in the country. He is caught, and the young lady of the house, who befriends him, turns out to be his aunt! Really this is too childish. We allow a novelist a good deal of freedom in arranging his incidents to suit his purposes, but if he cannot manage them in a more convincing fashion than that, the whole illusion is gone.

James Oliphant, 1899, *Victorian Novelists,* p. 38

Nicholas Nickleby (1839)

Nickleby is very good. I stood out against Mr. Dickens as long as I could, but he has conquered me.

Sydney Smith, 1838, *To Sir George Philips,* Sept.;
Letters of Sydney Smith, ed. Mrs. Austin

The town of Barnard Castle is most picturesque, with a ruined castle of the Baliols. Dickens, in early life, used frequently to come down and stay there with some young artist friends of his. The idea of *Humphrey's Clock* first sprung from Humphrey, the watchmaker in the town, and the picture in the beginning of the book is of the clock over the door of his shop. While at Barnard Castle, Dickens heard of the school at Bowes which he afterwards worked up as Dotheboys Hall. Many of these schools, at £15 and

£20 a year, existed at that time in the neighbourhood, and were principally used for the sons of London tradesmen, who, provided their sons got a moderate education, cared little or nothing what became of them in the meantime. Dickens went over to see the school at Bowes, and was carefully shown over it, for they mistook him for a parent coming to survey it with a view of sending his son there. Afterwards the school was totally ruined. At one of Mr. Bowes's elections, the Nicholas Nickleby or former usher of the school, who was then in want of a place, wrote to him to say in what poverty he was. He "had formerly been living with Mr. Shawe at Bowes, and they had been happy and prosperous, when Mr. Dickens's misguided volume, sweeping like a whirlwind over the schools of the North, caused Mr. Shawe to become a victim to paralysis, and brought Mrs. Shawe to an untimely grave."

Augustus J. C. Hare, 1861, The Story of My Life,
Sept. 27, vol. II, p. 275

Nicholas Nickleby combined the comic and the sensational elements for the first time, and is still the type of Dickens's longer books, in which the strain of violent pathos or sinister mystery is incessantly relieved by farce, either of incident or description. In this novel, too, the easy-going, old-fashioned air of *Pickwick* is abandoned in favour of a humanitarian attitude more in keeping with the access of puritanism which the new reign had brought with it, and from this time forth a certain squeamishness in dealing with moral problems and a certain "gush" of unreal sentiment obscured the finer qualities of the novelist's genius.

Edmund Gosse, 1897, A Short History of Modern
English Literature, p. 341

Barnaby Rudge (1841)

That this fiction, or indeed that any fiction written by Mr. Dickens, should be based in the excitement and maintenance of curiosity, we look upon as a misconception, on the part of the writer, of his own very great yet very peculiar powers. He has done this thing well, to be sure—he would do anything well in comparison with the herd of his contemporaries; but he has not done it so thoroughly well as his high and just reputation would demand.

Edgar Allan Poe, 1842, Literary Criticism, Works.
ed. Stedman and Woodberry, vol. VII, p. 64

This was Dickens's first attempt at what is called the historical novel, and it must be confessed that it contained slight promise of the conspicuous success which he afterwards achieved in this field with *The Tale of Two Cities*. Though constructed with much care, and exceptionally well written, it seems to lack both reality and interest; and, though the management of the Raven is a masterpiece of humorous fancy, *Barnaby Rudge* has afforded fewer than any other of Dickens's novels of those types of character, and racy sayings, which fasten themselves upon the memory of the reader.

Charles H. Jones, 1880, *A Short Life of Charles Dickens*, p. 95

What the author of *The Pupil of Pleasure* assayed to do in the last century, the author of *Barnaby Rudge* has assayed to do in our own time. On the unspeakable vulgarity and absurdity of Dickens's caricature and travesty—with pain do we say a disrespectful word of one to whom we in common with half the world are so much indebted—it would be superfluous to comment. But what is certain is that in the imagination of millions Chesterfield will exist, and exist only, in association with a character combining all that is worst, all that is most vile, most contemptible, most repulsive, in the traditionary portrait of him.

John Churton Collins, 1895, *Essays and Studies*, p. 200

In any just sense there is no heroine in *Barnaby Rudge,* which is a book of more skill and power than any that Dickens had yet written. We may dismiss without self-reproach such a ladylike lay-figure as Emma Haredale, and a goblin effigy like Miss Miggs, and come without delay to Dolly Varden, who, in turn, need hardly delay us longer. She is a cheap little coquette, imagined upon the commonest lines, with abundant assertion as to her good looks and graces, but without evidence of the charm that the silliest flirt has in reality. She is nothing and she does nothing; and she cannot be petted and patted by her inventor, with all his fondness, into any semblance of personality.

William Dean Howells, 1901, *Heroines of Fiction*, vol. I, p. 136

The Old Curiosity Shop (1841)

Extravagance and want of fidelity to nature and the possibilities of life are what everywhere mar Dickens to me, and these faults are fatal, because the *modes* of life amongst which these extravagances intrude are always the absolute realities of vulgarized life as it exists in plebeian ranks amongst our countrymen at this moment. Were the mode of life one more idealized or removed from our own, I might be less sensible of the insupportable extravagances.

Thomas DeQuincey, 1847, *Letter to his Daughter,
Life,* ed. Japp, vol. I, p. 349

In *The Old Curiosity Shop* was created the character of "Little Nell," the most famous of all the author's pathetic children, and perhaps as famous as any in literature—even as the Mignon of Goethe, a being as pure and good as Nell, though as impassioned as the little English girl is snow-cold.

F. B. Perkins, 1870, *Charles Dickens*, p. 62

A whole generation, on either side of the Atlantic, used to fall sobbing at the name of Little Nell, which will hardly bring tears to the eyes of any one now, though it is still apparent that the child was imagined with real feelings, and her sad little melodrama was staged with sympathetic skill. When all is said against the lapses of taste and truth, the notion of the young girl wandering up and down the country with her demented grandfather, and meeting good and evil fortune with the same devotion, till death overtakes her, is something that must always touch the heart. It is preposterously overdone, yes, and the author himself falls into pages of hysterical rhythm, which once moved people, when he ought to have been writing plain, straight prose; yet there is in all a sense of the divinity in common and humble lives, which is the most precious quality of literature, as it is almost the rarest, and it is this which moves and consoles. It is this quality in Dickens which Tolstoy prizes and accepts as proof of his great art, and which the true critic must always set above any effect of literary mastery.

William Dean Howells, 1901, *Heroines of Fiction,* vol. I, p. 131

I believe that the first book—the first real, substantial book—I read through was *The Old Curiosity Shop.* At all events, it was the first volume of Dickens which I made my own. . . . *The Old Curiosity Shop* makes strong appeal to a youthful imagination, and contains little that is beyond its scope. Dickens's sentiment, however it may distress the mature mind of our later day, is not unwholesome, and, at all events in this story, addresses itself naturally enough to feelings unsubdued by criticism. His quality of picturesqueness is here seen at its best, with little or nothing of that melodrama which makes the alloy of *Nicholas Nickleby* and *Oliver Twist* —to speak only of the early books. The opening scene, that dim-lighted storehouse of things old and grotesque, is the best approach to Dickens's world, where sights of every day are transfigured in the service of remance. The kindliness of the author's spirit, his overflowing sympathy with poor and humble folk, set one's mind to a sort of music which it is good to live with; and no writer of moralities ever showed triumphant virtue in so cheery a light as that which falls upon these honest people when rascality has got its deserts.

George Gissing, 1902, *Dickens in Memory,*
The Critic, vol. 40, p. 48

American Notes (1842)

I have read Dickens's book. It is jovial and good-natured, and at times very severe. You will read it with delight and, for the most part, approbation. He has a grand chapter on Slavery. *Spitting* and *politics at Washington* are the other topics of censure. Both you and I would censure them with equal severity, to say the least.

> Henry Wadsworth Longfellow, 1842, *Letter to Charles Sumner*,
> Oct. 16; *Life*, ed. Longfellow, vol. I, p. 440

His *Notes* upon America come out, I believe, immediately; and I shall be extremely curious to see them, and sorry if they are unfavorable, because his popularity as a writer is immense, and whatever he publishes will be sure of a wide circulation. Moreover, as it is very well known that, before going to America, he was strongly prepossessed in favor of its institutions, manners, and people, any disparaging remarks he may make upon them will naturally have proportionate weight, as the deliberate result of experience and observation. M— told me, after dining with Dickens immediately on his return, that one thing that had disgusted him was the almost universal want of conscience upon money matters in America; and the levity, occasionally approaching to something like self-satisfaction, for their "sharpness," which he had repeated occasions of observing, in your people when speaking of the present disgraceful condition of their finances and deservedly degraded state of their national credit. . . . But I do hope (because I have a friend's and not a "foe's" heart towards your country) that Dickens will not write unfavorably about it, for his opinion will influence public opinion in England, and deserves to do so.

> Frances Ann Kemble, 1842, *Letter*, Oct. 2;
> *Records of Later Life*, p. 359

Dear Napier,—This morning I received Dickens's book. I have now read it. It is impossible for me to review it; nor do I think that you would wish me to do so. I cannot praise it, and I will not cut it up. I cannot praise it, though it contains a few lively dialogues and descriptions; for it seems to me to be on the whole a failure. It is written like the worst part of *Humphrey's Clock*. What is meant to be easy and sprightly is vulgar and flippant, as in the first two pages. What is meant to be fine is a great deal too fine for me, as the description of the Fall of Niagara. A reader who wants an amusing account of the United States had better go to Mrs. Trollope, coarse and malignant as she is. A reader who wants information about American politics, manners, and literature, had better go even to so poor a creature as Buckingham. In short, I pronounce the book, in spite of some

gleams of genius, at once frivolous and dull. Therefore I will not praise
it. Neither will I attack it; first, because I have eaten salt with Dickens;
secondly, because he is a good man, and a man of real talent; thirdly, because he hates slavery as heartily as I do; and, fourthly, because I wish
to see him enrolled in our blue and yellow corps, where he may do excellent service as a skirmisher and sharp-shooter.

Thomas Babington Macaulay, 1842, *Letter,* Oct. 19;
Life and Letters, ed. Trevelyan, ch. ix

The little information to be gleaned from these two volumes, with few exceptions, might be gained much more advantageously from the map and
gazetteer. The perusal of them has served chiefly to lower our estimate of
the man, and to fill us with contempt for such a compound of egotism, cox-
combry, and cockneyism. . . . We have never read a book, professing to
give an account of any country, which, in respect to its natural features,
its towns and cities, its manners and customs, its social, civil, and religious
institutions—in short, in respect to everything about which the reader
wishes to receive information, or at least to ascertain the opinions of the
author, is so profoundly silent as the book before us.

J. P. Thompson, 1843, "Dickens' Notes on America,"
The New Englander, vol. I, pp. 67, 76

Though the book is said to have given great offence on the other side of
the Atlantic, we cannot see any sufficient reason for it. To us it appears
that Mr. Dickens deserves great praise for the care with which he has
avoided all offensive topics, and abstained from amusing his readers at the
expense of his entertainers; and if we had an account of the temptations
in this kind which he has resisted, we do not doubt that the reserve and
self-control which he has exercised would appear scarcely less than heroical. But, on the other hand, we cannot say that his book throws any new
light on his subject. He has done little more than confide to the public what
should have been a series of letters for the entertainment of his private
friends. Very agreeable and amusing letters they would have been; and
as such, had they been posthumously published, would have been read
with interest and pleasure. As it is, in the middle of our amusement at
the graphic sketches of life and manners, the ludicrous incidents, the way-
side conversations about nothing, so happily told, and the lively remarks,
with which these *Notes* abound—in the middle of our respect for the tone
of good sense and good humour which runs through them.

James Spedding, 1843, "Dickens's American Notes,"
Reviews and Discussions, p. 247

The debt which American owed to this man was hardly less than that which England owed him. The insane fury with which his *American Notes* was received in our country was simply an outburst of the same rage that afterward was visited on Mrs. Stowe for her *Uncle Tom's Cabin.* The outcries about "exaggerated and distorted statements" heard in England from poor-house authorities, when *Oliver Twist* was published, were counterparts of the angry denunciations of slavery when Dickens published the advertisements about negroes which he read daily. I remember that the Southerners were also furious at his description of the roads and the driver in Northern Virginia, declaring it all a caricature. But I happened to have been born and reared close to that old Acquis road, and have often seen the stage and the driver which figure in the *American Notes;* and it was known to me, as to others dwelling in the same region, that the descriptions were all not only graphic, but photographic in their accuracy.

Moncure Daniel Conway, 1870, "Footprints of Charles Dickens," *Harper's Magazine,* vol. 41, p. 612

A Christmas Carol (1843)

It is the work of the master of all the English humourists now alive; the young man who came and took his place calmly at the head of the whole tribe, and who has kept it. . . . Who can listen to objections regarding such a book as this? It seems to me a national benefit, and to every man or woman who reads it a personal kindness. The last two people I heard speak of it were women; neither knew the other, or the author, and both said, by way of criticism, "God bless him!" . . . As for Tiny Tim, there is a certain passage in the book regarding that young gentleman about which a man should hardly venture to speak in print or in public, any more than he would of any other affections of his private heart. There is not a reader in England but that little creature will be a bond of union between the author and him; and he will say of Charles Dickens, as the woman just now, "God bless him!" What a feeling is this for a writer to be able to inspire, and what a reward to reap!

William Makepeace Thackeray, 1844, "*A Christmas Carol* by Dickens," *Fraser's Magazine,* vol. 29, pp. 167, 169

There was indeed nobody that had not some interest in the message of the *Christmas Carol.* It told the selfish man to rid himself of selfishness; the just man to make himself generous; and the good-natured man to enlarge the sphere of his good nature. Its cheery voice of faith and hope, ringing from one end of the island to the other, carried pleasant warning alike to all, that if the duties of Christmas were wanting no good could come out of its outward observances; that it must shine upon the cold hearth and

warm it, and into the sorrowful heart and comfort it; that it must be kindness, benevolence, charity, mercy, and forbearance, or its plum pudding
would turn to bile, and its roast beef be indigestible. Nor could any man
have said it with the same appropriateness as Dickens.

> John Forster, 1873, *The Life of Charles Dickens,* vol. II, p. 89

Simple in its romantic design like one of Andersen's little tales, the *Christmas Carol* has never lost its hold upon a public in whom it has called forth
Christmas thoughts which do not all center on "holly, mistletoe, red ber-
ries, ivy, turkeys, geese, game, poultry, brawn, meat, pigs, sausages, oy-
sters, pies, puddings, fruit and punch;" and the Cratchit household, with
Tiny Tim, who did NOT die, are living realities even to those who have not
seen Mr. Toole—an actor after Dickens's own heart—as the father of the
family, shivering in his half-yard of comforter.

> Adolphus William Ward, 1882, *Dickens*
> (*English Men of Letters*), p. 60

Martin Chuzzlewitt (1844)

Dickens has just published, as one of the chapters of *Martin Chuzzlewit,* an
account of the arrival of his hero in New York, and what he saw, and
heard, and did, and suffered, in this land of pagans, brutes, and infidels. I
am sorry to see it. Thinking that Mr. Dickens has been ungenerously treated
by my countrymen, I have taken his part on most occasions; but he has
now written an exceedingly foolish libel upon us, from which he will not
obtain credit as an author, nor as a man of wit, any more than as a man
of good taste, good nature, or good manners. It is difficult to believe that
such unmitigated trash should have flown from the same pen that drew
the portrait of the immortal Pickwick and his expressive gaiters, the honest locksmith and his pretty Dolly of Clerkenwell, and poor little Nell, who
has caused so many tears to flow. Shame, Mr. Dickens! Considering all
that we did for you, if, as some folks say, I and others made fools of ourselves to make much of you, you should not afford them the triumph of
saying, "There! we told you so!" "It serves you right!" and other such
consolatory phrases. If we were fools, you were the cause of it, and should
have stood by us. *"Et tu, Brute!"*

> Philip Hone, 1843, *Diary,* July 29, vol. II, p. 189

This novel is one of the finest of his compositions—not the American
scenes, perhaps, for these have generally an air of exaggeration which in-
jures them; but the adventures which occur before and after the hero
makes his unfortunate and unsuccessful voyage across the Atlantic.

> Thomas B. Shaw, 1847, *Outlines of English Literature,* p. 394

I liked Martin Chuzzlewit, too, and the other day I read a great part of it again, and found it roughly true in the passages that referred to America, though it was surcharged in the serious moods, and caricatured in the comic. The English are always inadequate observers; they seem too full of themselves to have eyes and ears for any alien people; but as far as an Englishman could, Dickens had caught the look of our life in certain aspects. His report of it was clumsy and farcical; it wanted nicety of accent and movement, but in a large, loose way it was like enough; at least he had caught the note of our self-satisfied, intolerant and hypocritical provinciality, and this was not altogether lost in his mocking horseplay.

William Dean Howells, 1895, My Literary Passions, p. 100

Dombey and Son (1848)

Oh, my dear, dear Dickens! what a No. 5 you have now given us! I have so cried and sobbed over it last night, and again this morning; and felt my heart purified by those tears, and blessed and loved you for making me shed them; and I never can bless and love you enough. Since the divine Nelly was found dead on her humble couch, beneath the snow and the ivy, there has been nothing like the actual dying of that sweet Paul, in the summer sunshine of that lofty room. And the long vista that leads us so gently and sadly, and yet so gracefully and winningly, to the plain consummation! Every trait so true and so touching—and yet lightened by the fearless innocence which goes playfully to the brink of the grave, and that pure affection which bears the unstained spirit, on its soft and lambent flash, at once to its source in eternity.

Francis, Lord Jeffrey, 1847, Letter to Dickens, Jan. 31;
The Life of Charles Dickens, ed. Forster, vol. II, p. 361

It was Thackeray's delight to read each number of Dombey and Son with eagerness as it issued from the press. He had often been heard to speak of the work in terms of the highest praise, and when it had reached its fifth number, wherein Dickens describes the end of little Paul with a depth of pathos which produced a vibrating emotion in the hearts of all who read it, Thackeray seemed electrified at the thought that there was one man living who could exercise so complete a control over him. Putting No. 5 of Dombey and Son in his pocket, he hastened down to the printing-office of Punch, and entering the editor's room, he dashed it on the table with startling vehemence, and exclaimed, "There's no writing against such power as this—one has no chance! Read that chapter describing young Paul's death: it is unsurpassed—it is stupendous!"

George Hodder, 1870, Memories of My Time

It is, perhaps, not generally known that Dickens's pen-picture of Paul Dombey was inspired by the pathetic personality of a favourite nephew, Master Harry Burnett. This poor lad, who unfortunately became a cripple and died in his tenth year, resembled in many respects the little Paul of fiction; notwithstanding his affliction, he was one of the happiest and brightest of children, with a mind always marvellously active, and especially during the last months of his short life, was full of religious sentiment, for he insisted upon having his much-thumbed Bible placed ready to his hand.

Frederic G. Kitton, 1897, *The Novels of Charles Dickens,* p. 106

David Copperfield (1850)

I do not find it easy to get sufficiently far away from this Book, in the first sensations of having finished it, to refer to it with the composure which this formal heading would seem to require. My interest in it, is so recent and strong; and my mind is so divided between pleasure and regret—pleasure in the achievement of a long design, regret in the separation from many companions—that I am in danger of wearying the reader whom I love, with personal confidences, and private emotions. Besides which, all that I could say of the Story, to any purpose, I have endeavoured to say in it. It would concern the reader little, perhaps, to know, how sorrowfully the pen is laid down at the close of a two years' imaginative task; or how an Author feels as if he were dismissing some portion of himself into the shadowy world, when a crowd of the creatures of his brain are going from him for ever. Yet, I have nothing else to tell; unless, indeed, I were to confess (which might be of less moment still) that no one can ever believe this Narrative, in the reading, more than I have believed it in the writing. Instead of looking back, therefore, I will look forward. I cannot close this Volume more agreeably to myself, than with a hopeful glance towards the time when I shall again put forth my two green leaves once a month, and with a faithful remembrance of the genial sun and showers that have fallen on these leaves of David Copperfield, and made me happy.

Charles Dickens, 1850, *The Personal History and Experience of David Copperfield the Younger,* Preface

Have you read *David Copperfield,* by the way? How beautiful it is—how charmingly fresh and simple! In those admirable touches of tender humour —and I should call humour, Bob, a mixture of love and wit—who can equal this great genius? There are little words and phrases in his books which are like personal benefits to the reader. What a place it is to hold in the affections of man! What an awful responsibility hanging over a writer! What man holding such a place, and knowing that his words go forth to vast congregations of mankind,—to grown folks—to their children, and perhaps to their children's children,—but must think of his calling with a solemn and humble heart! May love and truth guide such a man always! It is an awful prayer, may heaven further its fulfilment! And then, . . . let the *Record* revile him.

William Makepeace Thackeray, 1856, "Brown the Younger
at a Club," *Sketches and Travels in London*

It is a great pleasure to find in an author's innermost circle the types of those characters that have delighted one in his works. I had previously heard many people remark that Agnes in *David Copperfield* was like Dickens's own wife; and although he may not have chosen her deliberately as a model for Agnes, yet still I can think of no one else in his books so near akin to her in all that is graceful and amiable. Mrs. Dickens had a certain soft, womanly repose and reserve about her; but whenever she spoke there came such a light into her large eyes, and such a smile upon her lips, and there was such a charm in the tones of her voice, that henceforth I shall always connect her and Agnes together.

Hans Christian Andersen, 1870, "A Visit to Charles Dickens,"
The Temple Bar, vol. 31, p. 29

The imagination of Dickens's is like that of monomaniacs. To plunge oneself into an idea, to be absorbed by it, to see nothing else, to repeat it under a hundred forms, to enlarge it, to carry it thus enlarged to the eye of the spectator, to dazzle and overwhelm him with it, to stamp it upon him so tenacious and impressive that he can never again tear it from his memory,—these are the great features of this imagination and style. In this *David Copperfield* is a masterpiece. Never did objects remain more visible and present to the memory of a reader than those which he describes.

H. A. Taine, 1871, *History of English Literature*,
tr. Van Laun, vol. II, bk. v, p. 344

I have said that in *David Copperfield* Dickens is freer from defect than in any other of his works. It is rarely that public opinion has ratified an author's judgment so completely as it has here. As we all know, this was Dickens's favourite, and the reason we all know. It may be noted in passing how characteristic of the two men is their choice. To Dickens *David Copperfield* was, to use his own words, his favourite child, because in its pages he saw the reflection of his own youth. . . . It is not only Dickens's most attractive work, but it is his best work. And it is his best for this reason, that whereas in all his others he is continually striving to realise the conception of his fancy, in this alone his business is to idealise the reality; in this alone, as it seems to me, his imagination prevails over his fancy. In this alone he is never grotesque, or for him so rarely that we hardly care to qualify the adverb. Nowhere else is his pathos so tender and so sure; nowhere else is his humour, though often more boisterous and more abundant, so easy and so fine; nowhere else is his observation so vivid and so deep; nowhere else has he held with so sure a hand the balance between the classes.

Mowbray Morris, 1882, "Charles Dickens,"
The Fortnightly Review, vol. 38, p. 776

Copperfield's first meeting with Dora is Dickens's meeting (when little more than a boy) with a lady by no means so young as Dora is there represented. The courtship is derived from his youthful love for the original of Flora. The married life with Dora, so far as her household ways are concerned, presents Dickens's own experience, so that Dora there represents a third person, and that person his wife. And lastly the death of Dora, and Copperfield's sorrow during the following years, are drawn from the death of his wife's younger sister, Mary, and the sorrow Dickens felt for years thereafter. Yet, though the real Flora furnished only one of these four copies from which the Dora of fiction was combined, we find her forming part of two distinct and very unlike characters, the characteristics of her later years being in part reproduced in Flora—but only in part, for some of Dora's ways were derived from other sources. Nor can it be said that, after all, Dickens so artistically combines and distributes what he had observed that they become effective as if they were real creations. For no one possessing any power of critical discrimination had failed to recognise the incongruity of many—one may almost say all—of Dickens's characters long before it became known that he had constructed them of heterogeneous materials and applied his materials to heterogeneous purposes.

Richard A. Proctor, 1885, "Dickens and Thackeray,"
Knowledge, vol. 7, p. 537

Here was a man and an artist, the most strenuous, one of the most endowed; and for how many years he laboured in vain to create a gentleman! With all his watchfulness of men and manners, with all his fiery industry, with all his exquisite native gift of characterisation, with his clear knowledge of what he meant to do, there was yet something lacking. In part after part, novel after novel, a whole menagerie of characters, the good, the bad, the droll and the tragic, came at his beck like slaves about an oriental despot; there was only one who stayed away; the gentleman. If this ill fortune had persisted it might have shaken man's belief in art and industry. But years were given and courage was continued to the indefatigable artist; and at length, after so many and such lamentable failures, success began to attend upon his arms. David Copperfield scrambled through on hands and knees; it was at least a negative success; and Dickens, keenly alive to all he did, must have heaved a sigh of infinite relief.

Robert Louis Stevenson, 1888, "Some Gentlemen in Fiction,"
Miscellaneous Papers, p. 368

The popular instinct is not astray in selecting *David Copperfield* out of the long list of Dickens's stories and giving it the foremost place. It is not so powerful a story as *A Tale of Two Cities,* the most dramatic and soundly constructed of all the stories that Dickens gave the world, but it is far more characteristic, sweeter in sentiment, and as fresh in feeling and touch. It is the personal note which gives this beautiful tale its victorious appeal for the suffrages of the greatest number of readers. It is significant of a sound taste, also, that *The Old Curiosity Shop* and *Dombey and Son,* in which, to recall Mr. Lang's phrase, Dickens wallowed in a sea of sentimentalism, appear well down on the list, and that *Barnaby Rudge* does not appear.

Hamilton W. Mabie, 1893, "The Most Popular Novels
in America," *The Forum*, vol. 16, p. 512

Bleak House (1853)

Bleak House is, even more than any of its predecessors, chargeable with not simply faults, but absolute want of construction. . . . In *Bleak House,* the series of incidents which form the outward life of the actors and talkers has no close and necessary connexion; nor have they that higher interest that attaches to circumstances which powerfully aid in modifying and developing the original elements of human character. The great Chancery suit of Jarndyce and Jarndyce, which serves to introduce a crowd of persons as suitors, lawyers, law-writers, law-stationers, and general spectators of Chancery business, has positively not the smallest influence on the character of any one person concerned; nor has it any interest of itself.

George Brimley, 1853-58, *"Bleak House,"*
Essays, ed. Clark, pp. 282, 283

Whoever wishes to get a good look at Landor will not seek for it alone in John Forster's interesting life of the old man, admirable as it is, but will turn to Dickens's *Bleak House* for side-glances at the great author. In that vivid story Dickens has made his friend Landor sit for the portrait of

Lawrence Boythorn. The very laugh that made the whole house vibrate, the roundness and fulness of voice, the fury of superlatives, are all given in Dickens's best manner, and no one who has ever seen Landor for half an hour could possibly mistake Boythorn for any body else. Talking the matter over once with Dickens, he said, "Landor always took that presentation of himself in hearty good humor, and seemed rather proud of the picture."

James T. Fields, 1875, " 'Barry Cornwall' and Some of His Friends," *Harper's Magazine,* vol. 51, p. 785

Bleak House (1853) is constructed only too well. Here Dickens applied himself laboriously to the perfecting of that kind of story he had always had in view, and produced a fine example of theatrical plot. One cannot say, in this case, that the intrigue refuses to be remembered; it is a puzzle, yet ingeniously simple; the parts fitting together very neatly indeed. So neatly, that poor untidy Life disclaims all connection with these doings, however willingly she may recognize for her children a score or so of the actors. To be sure there are oversights. How could Dickens expect one to believe that Lady Dedlock recognized her lover's handwriting in a piece of work done by him *as law-writer*—she not even knowing that he was so employed? What fate pursued him that he could not, in all the resources of his brain, hit upon a device for such a simple end more convincing than this? Still, with an aim not worth pursuing, the author here wrought successfully. The story is child's play compared with many invented, for instance by Wilkie Collins; but in combination with Dickens's genuine powers, it produces its designed effect; we move in a world of choking fog and squalid pitfalls, amid plot and counterplot, cold self-interest and passion overwrought, and can never refuse attention to the magician who shows it all.

George Gissing, 1898, *Charles Dickens,* p. 67

In *Bleak House* the prominence accorded to the sensational is somewhat repellent, though this is artistically the best constructed of Dickens' novels, as it is also the most exciting.

Edward Engel, 1902, *A History of English Literature,* rev. Hamley Bent, p. 452

Hard Times (1854)

The essential value and truth of Dickens' writings have been unwisely lost sight of by many thoughtful persons, merely because he presents his truths with some colour of caricature. Unwisely, because Dickens's caricature, though often gross, is never mistaken. Allowing for his manner of telling them, the things he tells us are always true. I wish that he could think it right to limit his brilliant exaggeration to works written only for public amusement; and when he takes up a subject of high national importance, such as that which he handled in *Hard Times,* that he would use severer and more accurate analysis. The usefulness of that work (to my mind, in several respects, the greatest he has written) is with many persons seriously diminished because Mr. Bounderby is a dramatic monster, instead of a characteristic example of a worldly master; and Stephen Blackpool a dramatic perfection, instead of a characteristic example of an honest workman. But let us not lose the use of Dickens's wit and insight, because he chooses to speak in a circle of stage fire. He is entirely right in his main drift and purpose in every book he has written; and all of them, but especially *Hard Times,* should be studied with close and earnest care by persons interested in social questions. They will find much that is partial, and, because partial, apparently unjust; but if they examine all the evidence on the other side, which Dickens seems to overlook, it will appear, after all their trouble, that his view was the finally right one, grossly and sharply told.

John Ruskin, 1862, "The Roots of Honour," Unto this Last, Note

In comparison with most of Dickens's novels, *Hard Times* is contained within a narrow compass; and this, with the further necessity of securing to each successive small portion of the story a certain immediate degree of effectiveness, accounts, in some measure, for the peculiarity of the impression left by this story upon many of its readers. Short as the story relatively is, few of Dickens's fictions were elaborated with so much care.

Adolphus William Ward, 1882, Dickens
(English Men of Letters), p. 126

Little Dorrit (1857)

About four months after Dickens's death, an incident happened that would have more than counteracted the effects upon the author's mind of the most unfavourable comments upon *Little Dorrit*. The scene was the meeting of Bismarck and Jules Favre under the walls of Paris; as the Prussian was waiting to open fire on the city, the Frenchman was engaged in the arduous task of showing the wisdom of not doing it, and "while the two eminent statesmen were trying to find a basis of negotiation, Von Moltke was seated in a corner reading *Little Dorrit*." One is inclined to ask, with

Mr. Forster, "Who will doubt that the chapter on 'How to do it' was then absorbing the old soldier's attention?"

Frederic G. Kitton, 1897, *The Novels of Charles Dickens*, p. 170

Of *Little Dorrit,* as of *Martin Chuzzlewit,* who can pretend to bear the story in mind? There is again a moral theme; the evils of greed and vulgar ambition. As a rule, we find this book dismissed rather contemptuously; it is held to be tedious, and unlike Dickens in its prevalent air of gloom. For all that, I believe it to contain some of his finest work, some passages in which he attains an artistic finish hardly found elsewhere; and to these I shall return. . . . As a narrative, *Little Dorrit* is far from successful; it is cumbered with mysteries which prove futile, and has no proportion in its contrasting parts. Here and there the hand of the master is plainly weary.

George Gissing, 1898, *Charles Dickens*, pp. 70, 71

The conception of *Little Dorrit* was far happier and more promising than that of *Dombey and Son;* which indeed is not much to say for it. Mr. Dombey is a doll; Mr. Dorrit is an everlasting figure of comedy in its most tragic aspect and tragedy in its most comic phase. Little Dorrit herself might be less untruly than unkindly described as Little Nell grown big, or, in Milton's phrase, "writ large." But on that very account she is a more credible and therefore a more really and rationally pathetic figure.

Algernon Charles Swinburne, 1902, "Charles Dickens,"
Quarterly Review, vol. 196, p. 29

A Tale of Two Cities (1859)

It is a story of human passions, of misery, crime, guilt, revenge, heroism, love, and happiness. And if the lack of the properly historical element does not so strongly appear in this novel as in *Barnaby Rudge,* the reason is clear: it is, that the period was one that, beyond any other in history, boiled and burned with passion; so that in fact, the novelist who writes a romance of the French Revolution must, if his story is to seem truthful, write a story of psychology.

F. B. Perkins, 1870, *Charles Dickens*, p. 63

Mr. Dickens, however, wrote one book so noble in its spirit, so grand and graphic in its style, and filled with a pathos so profound and simple, that it deserves, and will surely take, a place among the great serious works of imagination. *A Tale of Two Cities,* his shortest story, and the one least thought of by the public of his own day, is the work that will secure him an enduring fame. It has little humor, and that is not of its author's best; but its picture of the fierce passion of the first French Revolution, of the hideous oppression which provoked that outbreak of ruthless revenge on the part of a whole people, and above all its portrayal of the noble-natured castaway Sidney Carton, make it almost a peerless book in modern literature, and give it a place among the highest examples of all literary art.

Richard Grant White, 1870, "The Styles of Disraeli and Dickens,"
The Galaxy, vol. 10, p. 259

It is a profitable experience for one who read Dickens forty years ago to try to read him now. Last winter I forced myself through his *Tale of Two Cities*. It was a sheer dead pull from start to finish. It all seemed so insincere, such a transparent make-believe, a mere piece of acting. My sympathies were hardly once touched. I was not insensible to the marvelous genius displayed in the story, but it left me cold and unmoved. A feeling of unreality haunted me on every page.

John Burroughs, 1897, "On the Re-reading of Books,"
Century Magazine, vol. 55, p. 149

To Dickens as an historical novelist imperfect justice has been done. The *Tale of Two Cities* is said to be most admired by those who admire Dickens the least. A similar remark has been made of *Esmond*. The *Tale of Two Cities* is founded upon Carlyle's *French Revolution*. It has no humour, or next to none. But it is a marvelous piece of writing; the plot, though simple, is excellent, and, whatever may be thought about the genuineness of the pathos in *Dombey and Son,* or the *Old Curiosity Shop,* the tragedy of Sidney Carton is a tragedy indeed.

Herbert Paul, 1897, "The Apotheosis of the Novel,"
The Nineteenth Century, vol. 41, p. 771

A Tale of Two Cities presents an interesting field for study of Dickens's varying literary style. From the first remarkably "balanced" paragraph to the supposed prophesies of Carton at the foot of the guillotine, are constant and conscious mannerisms. Of the use of balance, another passage may be instanced, where Madame Defarge seeks vengeance on Charles Darnay. . . . Dickens's narrative style appears at its best, not in the melodramatic scene at the guillotine, but in the flight from Paris and the thrilling narrative of Dr. Manette.

George Henry Nettleton, 1901, ed. *Specimens of the Short Story,* p. 138

Great Expectations (1861)

I am now reading *Great Expectations* and like it much. The characters, though, seem to me unreal somehow. Dickens appears to make his characters as the Chinese do those distorted wooden images. He picks out the crookedest and knottiest roots of temperament or accidental distortion and then cuts a figure to match. But this book is full of fine touches of nature, though I can't help dreading something melodramatic to come.

> James Russell Lowell, 1861, *To C. E. Norton,* Aug. 7;
> *Letters,* ed. Norton, vol. I, p. 312

Last night I made my Reader begin Dickens's wonderful *Great Expectations*: not considered one of his best, you know, but full of wonderful things, and even with a Plot which, I think, only needed less intricacy to be admirable. I had only just read the Book myself: but I wanted to see what my Reader would make of it; and he was so interested that he re-interested me too.

> Edward Fitzgerald, 1877, *Letter,* May 5;
> *Letters to Fanny Kemble,* ed. Wright, p. 122

Notwithstanding the fact that the first edition of *Great Expectations* contains no illustrations, the price demanded for a clean copy is from £7 to £10. This high figure is accounted for by the great scarcity of the three consecutive volumes in their original form, purchasers having sometimes to be content with making up the set with volumes of varying editions. The book, when first issued, was sold out immediately, the greater part of the impression going to the libraries; it was therefore looked upon with comparative disrespect, and, being immensely popular, became popularly thumbed, torn, and marked; whereas the weekly instalments in *All the Year Round* were preferred by private purchasers and collectors, who preserved them for binding. Mr. Wilkie Collins's copy of *Great Expectations* realised £9, 5s in the auction-room, at the sale of his library in 1890.

> Frederic G. Kitton, 1897. *The Novels of Charles Dickens,* p. 195

Our Mutual Friend (1865)

We are justified in concluding that Dickens's opinion of the Jews underwent a complete change, as we may learn from this novel, which may be regarded in a manner as his literary last will and testament. . . . Riah is as little the picture of the Jew as Fagin is; he gives utterance to some words about the Jews which are true enough, but he can not stand as a representative of the Jews. If they are to be characters in fiction, they wish but justice, and no more. An advocate who gives a rose-colored account of his client will not be believed. The Jew has his faults as all men have. There is as much harm in overestimating as in undervaluing. A constant flow of praise loses all strength for an impartial mind, as does also a constant flow of abuse. We have in fiction demonically bad Jews, and ideally good ones. Barabbas and Fagin on the one hand, Sheva, Rebecca, and Riah on the other. In the works we have treated thus far, the true picture has not yet been given; it will only be drawn by such a one who has made a searching and psychological study of the religious and hereditary traits of the descendants of this most remarkable stock.

David Philipson, 1889, *The Jew in English Fiction*, pp. 97, 101

It is very easy to select from the army of characters which Dickens has given us, those which were the truly beloved children of his brain. Sometimes he seemed to adopt a hero or a heroine, generally the latter, and to make himself believe that she was really his own offspring. Such a character occurs in one of Dickens' poorest novels, *Our Mutual Friend*. This is Bella, and in regard to her, Dickens writes in the notes to the manuscript of *Our Mutual Friend,* in which he frequently calls upon himself to do his duty by his characters, these words: "Make Bella as attractive as I can." Now he would never have written, in relation to Mr. Pickwick, "Make him as jolly, as funny, and as good hearted as I can." It would not have been necessary. Pickwick, in the mind of Dickens, was a real man; Bella Wilfer was not a real person, and, do his best, he could not make her the lovely woman he wanted her to be.

Frank R. Stockton, 1897, "My Favorite Novelist and His Best Books," *Munsey's Magazine,* vol. 17, p. 354

In *Our Mutual Friend* he relapsed into his outworn satire, the stage diction out of place, the needless and *voulu* phantastic.

Andrew Lang, 1898, "Charles Dickens," *Fortnightly Review,* vol. 70, p. 957

The Mystery of Edwin Drood (1870)

Of Mr. Fildes's work for Charles Dickens's book, our own opinion is that it is the best illustrative interpretation which has ever been made of the author, albeit old and fine reputations belong to the former associations of artists' names with the great series of the Dickens novels.

Alice Meynell, 1884, "How Edwin Drood was Illustrated," *The Century,* vol. 27, p. 527

Edwin Drood would probably have been his best constructed book: as far as it goes, the story hangs well together, showing a care in the contrivance of detail which is more than commonly justified by the result. One cannot help wishing that Dickens had chosen another subject—one in which there was neither mystery nor murder, both so irresistibly attractive to him, yet so far from being the true material of his art. Surely it is unfortunate that the last work of a great writer should have for its theme nothing more human than a trivial mystery woven about a vulgar deed of blood. . . . His selection of scene was happy and promising—the old city of his childhood, Rochester. The tone, too, of his descriptive passages is much more appropriate than the subject. But Dickens had made his choice in life, and therefrom inevitably resulted his course in literature.

George Gissing, 1898, *Charles Dickens*, pp. 76, 77

LETTERS

Ten years are nearly enough to show that in Dickens himself the future admirers of his works will take almost no interest at all. In reading through these letters one's irresistible feeling is that it is at least well that their publication was not delayed longer, if, indeed, it has not been delayed too long already. They present the man very adequately, we imagine, and, in presenting him, inevitably betray how slight was the real foundation for the quick personal interest taken in him during the last thirty or forty years. . . . But, though the lapse of time is slow, it is also certain, and, unless we are mistaken about the fact, popular interest in the man has already appreciably declined, if it has not subsided. There are probably few who will read these two volumes from cover to cover.

W. C. Brownell, 1879, "The Letters of Dickens,"
The Nation, vol. 29, p. 388

Charles Dickens was an excellent correspondent—punctual, regular—and when he had said all that was necessary, he stopped. His letters are easy, simple, and unaffected, and show him to have been a frank, genial, vain, generous, egotistical fellow. His spirits were high, his enjoyment of life keen, and he was an industrious and indefatigable literary worker: in the latter respect he was like Scott. But he differed from the author of *Waverly* in being a very painstaking and laborious writer. These letters open to us glimpses of Dickens's domestic life which are calculated to increase our interest in their author. He was essentially a domestic man; his children ever occupied the first place in his thoughts; and, when absent from them, his letters were very frequent, and evinced the deepest interest in all that concerned them.

Eugene L. Didier, 1880, "Recent Biography, etc.,
North American Review, vol. 130, p. 303

GENERAL

Mr. Dickens' characters, numerous as they are, have each the roundness of individual reality combined with generalization—most of them representing a class. The method by which he accomplishes this, is worth observing, and easily observed, as the process is always the same. He never developes a character from within, but commences by showing how the nature of the individual has *been* developed externally by his whole life in the world. To this effect, he first paints his portrait at full-length; sometimes his dress before his face, and most commonly his dress and demeanor. When he has done this to his satisfaction, he *feels in* the man, and the first words that man utters are the key-note of the character, and of all that he subsequently says and does. The author's hand never wavers, never becomes untrue to his creations.

Richard Hengist Horne, 1844, A New Spirit of the Age, p. 21

We have one great novelist who is gifted with the utmost power of rendering the external traits of our town population; and if he could give us their psychological character—their conceptions of life, and their emotions—with the same truth as their idiom and manners, his books would be the greatest contribution Art has ever made to the awakening of social sympathies. But while he can copy Mrs. Plornish's colloquial style with the delicate accuracy of a sun-picture, while there is the same startling inspiration in his description of the gestures and phrases of "Boots," as in the speeches of Shakespeare's mobs or numskulls, he scarcely ever passes from the humorous and external to the emotional and tragic without becoming as transcendent in his unreality as he was a moment before in his artistic truthfulness. But for the precious salt of his humour, which compels him to reproduce external traits that serve in some degree as a corrective to his frequently false psychology, his preternaturally virtuous poor children and artisans, his melo-dramatic boatmen and courtesans, would be as obnoxious as Eugène Sue's idealized proletaires in encouraging the miserable fallacy that high morality and refined sentiment can grow out of harsh social relations, ignorance, and want; or that the working-classes are in a condition to enter at once into a millennial state of *altruism,* wherein everyone is caring for everyone else, and no one for himself.

George Eliot, 1856, The Natural History of German Life

If we glance over the wit and satire of the popular writers of the day, we shall find that the *manner* of it, so far as it is distinctive is always owing to Dickens; and that out of his first exquisite ironies branch innumerable other forms of wit, varying with the dispositions of the writers; original in the matter and substance of them, yet never to have been expressed as they now are, but for Dickens.

John Ruskin, 1856, *Modern Painters,* vol. III, Appendix

From the incessant repetition by Mr. Dickens of this inventive process openly and without variation, except in the results, the public have caught what is called his mannerism or trick; and hence a certain recoil from his later writings among the cultivated and fastidious. But let any one observe our current table-talk or our current literature, and despite this profession of dissatisfaction, and in the very circles where it most abounds, let him note how gladly Dickens is used, and how frequently his phrases, his fancies and the names of his characters come in, as illustration, embellishment, proverb, and seasoning. Take any periodical in which there is a severe criticism of Dicken's last publication; and, ten to one, in the same period-cal, and perhaps by the same hand, there will be a leading article, setting out with a quotation from Dickens that flashes on the mind of the reader the thought which the whole article is meant to convey, or containing some allusion to one of Dickens's characters which enriches the text in the middle and floods it an inch round with colour and humour.

David Masson, 1859, *British Novelists and Their Styles,* p. 252

Dickens sees and feels, but the logic of feeling seems the only logic he can manage. Thought is strangely absent from his works. I do not suppose a single thoughtful remark on life or character could be found throughout the twenty volumes. Not only is there a marked absence of the reflective tendency, but one sees no indication of the past life of humanity having ever occupied him; keenly as he observes the objects before him, he never connects his observations into a general expression, never seems interested in general relations of things. Compared with that of Fielding or Thackeray, his was merely an *animal* intelligence, *i. e.,* restricted to perceptions. On this ground his early education was more fruitful and less injurious than it would have been to a nature constructed on a more reflective and intel-lectual type. It furnished him with rare and valuable experience, early de-veloped his sympathies with the lowly and struggling and did not starve any intellectual ambition. He never was and never would have been a student.

George Henry Lewes, 1872, "Dickens in Relation to Criticism," *Fortnightly Review,* vol. 17, p. 151

The mirror held up by him to Nature was certainly not provided with a properly even surface, and consequently all the images he saw in it, and drew from it, were apt to be distorted and out of proportion. . . . In this respect Dickens strikingly contrasts, to his disadvantage, with Chaucer, whose fidelity to nature is far too sincere to permit him to take such liberties with her fair works, or to select her monstrosities as her types. Both writers are pre-eminently realistic; no Englishmen, perhaps, exhibit more clearly that intense realism which it may be lies at the basis of the Low German mind, and which produced that school of painting amongst our own nearest kinsmen on the Continent which may compete with photography in the minute accuracy and exactness of its representations. Chaucer and Dickens are as precise in their delineations of external life and manners as are Hooge or Teniers. We know the outside look of the Miller and the Reeve just as we know that of Mr. Pickwick and Sam Weller. But even in wardrobe matters the modern is not seldom fantastic and grotesque, which Chaucer never is. To some extent the difference between these two great writers is one of culture. Chaucer was of the highest culture to be reached in his age, and all his works are fragrant with evidence of it. Dickens could have drawn certain of the Pilgrims with excellent success, but he could not have drawn the Knight or the Prioress. But the difference is not only of culture; it is also of soil.

John W. Hales, 1873-84, Notes and Essays on Shakespeare, p. 73

Dickens's want of perfect sympathy with the cultured society of his time incapacitated him for that kind of novel which answers to comedy in dramatic composition, although it left him free for work of a greater and more enduring kind. What may be called the comedy novel, the novel of Thackeray in Dickens's generation, is much less sure of enduring fame, because the sentiments on which it rests, being the product of a particular knot of circumstances, are more fugitive, and pass sooner into the province of the historian. The novels of Dickens will live longer because they take hold of the permanent and universal sentiments of the race,—sentiments which pervade all classes, and which no culture can ever eradicate. His fun may be too boisterous for the refined tastes of his own time, or, for the matter of that, of posterity; his pathos may appear maudlin; but they carried everything before them when they first burst upon our literature, because, however much exaggerated, they were exaggerations of what our race feels in its inner heart; and unless culture in the future works a miracle, and carries its changes beneath the surface, we may be certain that Dickens will keep his hold.

William Minto, 1878, Encyclopædia Britannica,
Ninth Ed., vol. VII, p. 154

It is very noticeable that Dickens seemed incapable of intellectual growth. The greatest expansion to which he ever attained he arrived at very early. Thereafter history, literature, even contemporanous events, added little to his store of thought and knowledge. Endless fun, inimitable drollery, were the gifts which he had to bestow upon his fellow-men; these, indeed, he bestowed lavishly, gloriously, so that the English-reading world would doubtless much more readily part with any three of its profoundest thinkers than with this most witty and laughter-moving of all its writers. But this was all he had to give; and from the very nature of the gift it was nearer perfection in his earlier years than as he advanced in life. This is apparent enough in his letters.

John T. Morse, 1880, "Charles Dickens's Letters," *The International Review*, vol. 8, p. 273

His faults were many and grave. He wrote some nonsense; he sinned repeatedly against taste; he could be both noisy and vulgar; he was apt to be a caricaturist where he should have been a painter; he was often mawkish and often extravagant; and he was sometimes more inept than a great writer has ever been. But his work, whether bad or good, has in full measure the quality of sincerity. He meant what he did; and he meant it with his whole heart. He looked upon himself as representative and national—as indeed he was; he regarded his work as a universal possession; and he determined to do nothing that for lack of pains should prove unworthy of his function. If he sinned it was unadvisedly and unconsciously; if he failed it was because he knew no better. . . . I love to remember that I come into the world contemporaneously with some of his bravest work, and to reflect that even as he was the inspiration of my boyhood so is he a delight of my middle age. I love to think that while English literature endures he will be remembered as one that loved his fellow-men, and did more to make them happy and amiable than any other writer of his time.

William Ernest Henley, 1890, *Views and Reviews*, pp. 5, 7

A critical autocrat recently informed me that "Charles Dickens was going out of fashion;" whereupon I inquired as one profoundly impressed and gasping for more information, "whether he thought that Shakespeare would be *à la mode* this season, and what he considered the newest and sweetest thing in the *beau monde* of intellect?" *Pickwick, Nicholas Nickleby, Oliver Twist, The Old Curiosity Shop, David Copperfield, A Tale of Two Cities, A Christmas Carol,* out of fashion! Not while the English language remains as now, and they who speak it have brains to appreciate humour, and hearts to sympathize with woe.

Samuel Reynolds Hole, 1893, *Memories*, p. 84

Dickens was a humorist and nothing else; but Dickens took himself so seriously that he broke with *Punch* because that journal refused to publish his account of his quarrel with the wife he had promised to love, cherish, and protect. Probably, also, if the sense-of-humor had been more acutely developed in Dickens he would have spared us the blank-verse pathos of his dying children; he might even have refrained from out-heroding Herod in his massacre of the innocents.

Brander Matthews, 1894-1902, Aspects of Fiction, p. 47

It is the language of a compliment and not of detraction to call him the Cockney's Shakespeare. In Shakespeare he was steeped. His favorite novelist was Smollett. But his art was all his own. He was the Hogarth of literature, painting with a broad brush, never ashamed of caricature, but always an artist, and not a dauber. There is little or no resemblance between Falstaff and Sam Weller. But they are the two comic figures which have most thoroughly seized upon the English mind. Touchstone and Mr. Micawber may be each a finer specimen of his creator's powers. They are not, however, quite so much to the taste of all readers. They require a little more fineness of palate.

Herbert Paul, 1897, "The Apotheosis of the Novel,"
The Nineteenth Century, vol. 41, p. 770

The characters of Dickens, then, are personified humours, his method is the method not of Shakespeare, but of Ben Jonson. Pecksniff is just another name for hypocrisy, Jonas Chuzzlewit for avarice, Quilp for cruelty. The result is excellent of its kind. The repetitions and catch-words are, within limits, highly effective. Sometimes they are genuinely illuminative; but sometimes, on the other hand, they reveal nothing and are used to weariness.

Hugh Walker, 1897, The Age of Tennyson, p. 87

Dickens was England's greatest educational reformer. . . . Was Dickens consciously and intentionally an educator? The prefaces to his novels; the preface to his *Household Words;* the educational articles he wrote; the prominence given in his books to child training in homes, institutions, and schools; the statements of the highest educational philosophy found in his writings; and especially the clearness of his insight and the profoundness of his educational thought, as shown by his condemnation of the wrong and his appreciation of the right in teaching and training the child, prove beyond question that he was not only broad and true in his sympathy with childhood, but that he was a careful and progressive student of the fundamental principles of education.

James L. Hughes, 1900, Dickens as an Educator, p. 1

CHARLES JAMES LEVER
1806-1872

Born, in Dublin, 31 Aug. 1806. Educated at private schools. To Trinity College, Dublin, 14 Oct. 1822; B. A., 1827. Visit to Holland and Germany, 1828; to Canada, 1829. Returned to Dublin, 1830; studied medicine. M. D., Trinity College, Dublin, 1831. Held various Board of Health appointments, 1831-33. Married Catherine Baker, 1832 or 1833. Contrib. fiction to *Dublin Univ. Mag.,* from May 1836. In Brussels, 1840-42; returned to Dublin, 1842. Editor of *Dublin Univ. Mag.,* 1842-45. In Belgium and Germany, 1845-47. In Florence, 1847-57. British Consul at Spezzia, 1857-67; at Trieste, 1867-72. Visit to Ireland, 1871. LL.D., Dublin, 1871. Died suddenly, at Trieste, 1 June 1872. WORKS: *The Confessions of Harry Lorrequer* (anon.), 1839; *Horace Templeton,* 1840 [?]; *Charles O'Malley* (anon.), 1841; *Our Mess* (vol. i., *Jack Hinton, the Guardsman;* vols. ii., iii., *Tom Burke of Ours*), 1843; *Arthur O'Leary* (anon.), 1844; *St. Patrick's Eve,* 1845; *Tales of the Trains* (under pseud.: "Tilbury Tramp"), 1845; *The O'Donoghue,* 1845; *The Knight of Gwynne,* 1847; *Diary and Notes of Horace Templeton* (anon.), 1848; *Confessions of Con Cregan* (anon.), 1849-50; *Roland Cashel,* 1850; *The Daltons,* 1852; *The Dodd Family Abroad,* 1854; *Sir Jasper Carew* (anon.), 1855; *The Fortunes of Glencore,* 1857; *The Martins of Cro' Martin,* 1856; *Davenport Dunn* 1857-59; *One of Them,* 1860; *Maurice Tiernay* (anon.), 1861; *Barrington,* 1862; *A Day's Ride,* 1864; *Cornelius O'Dowd upon Men and Women* (anon.), 1864-65; *Luttrell of Arran,* 1865; *Tony Butler* (anon.), 1865; *Sir Brook Fossbrooke,* 1866; *The Bramleighs of Bishop's Folly,* 1868; *Paul Gosslett's Confessions,* 1868; *That Boy of Norcott's,* 1869; *A Rent in a Cloud, and St. Patrick's Eve,* 1871; *Lord Kilgobbin,* 1872. COLLECTED NOVELS: ed. by his daughter, Julia Kate Neville, 1897-99, 37 v. LIFE: by W. F. Fitzpatrick, 1879, 2 v.

R. Farquharson Sharp, 1897, *A Dictionary of English Authors,* p. 167

SEE: *Letters,* ed. E. Downey, 1906, 2 v.; Lionel Stevenson, *Dr. Quicksilver: The Life of Charles Lever,* 1939.

PERSONAL

In his character were many different elements combined. He had the fearlessness of manhood, softened by woman's sensibility and purity, with the exuberance of life belonging to a boy. He possessed marvellous powers of fascination, attracting to him and straightway converting into friends for a lifetime, men of different stations and moulds. The peer, the fellow of college, the judge, the country squire, the parson, the doctor, the statesman, the lawyer, the *littérateur,* the lowly peasant both in Italy and at home, alike appreciated him.

W. J. Fitzpatrick, 1879, *The Life of Charles Lever,*
vol. II, p. 339

With regard to the famous accusation of "lordolatry" which Thackeray is said to have brought against him, I think that the passage in the *Book of Snobs* has been somewhat misinterpreted. But nobody can read either his novels or his life without seeing that from the last infirmity of British minds he was not free. He gained plenty of money, but he got rid of it in all sorts of ways, to which it is difficult to apply any milder description than that which was applied to the extravagance of his greater countryman Goldsmith. If he did not exactly fling it away and hide it in holes and corners, like Lamb's eccentric friend, he did what amounted to nearly the same thing. He was an inveterate gambler. He kept absurd numbers of horses, and gave unreasonable prices for them. To his lavish hospitality one feels less inclined to object, were it not that "wax candles and some of the best wine in Europe" are not wholly indispensable to literary fellowship. Like many other men of letters in our country, he could not be satisfied without meddling with politics, and endeavouring, though with no great success, to mingle in political society. His wild oats were not of a very atrocious wildness, but he never ceased sowing them. The consequence was that his literary work was not only an indispensable *gagne-pain* to him, but was also never anything else than a *gagne-pain*. It was always written in hot haste, and with hardly any attention to style, to arrangement, or even to such ordinary matters as the avoidance of repetitions, anachronisms, and such-like slovenliness.

> George Saintsbury, 1879, "Two Men of Letters,"
> *Fortnightly Review*, vol. 32, p. 386

Dr. Lever was at that time (1840) the only English physician in Brussels, and never perhaps was a physician less fitted for his calling. Although (possibly "pressed by hunger and request of friends") he "practised," he could not and did not inspire much confidence in his patients, for he made no secret of being a *médecin malgré lui,* loudly proclaiming, even among his *clientèle,* his hatred of the occupation, and taking every opportunity of practically proving his words. He used to come into his consulting-room in the most literary style of costume, wearing a black velvet dressing-gown, confined at the waist by a scarlet silk cord and tassels, and with the inevitable pen behind his ear, not for the convenience of inditing prescriptions, but to lose no time in getting back to his magazine articles as soon as he should have dispatched his patient.

> Mrs. William Pitt Byrne, 1898, *Social Hours
> with Celebrities,* vol. I, p. 204

GENERAL

He has a large circle of readers, and many of them would say they prefer him to anybody else; but if you tried to elicit from them one good reason,

they would have no better answer to give than "Oh! he's a capital fellow!"
What the French call *material life,* is the whole life he recognizes; and *that*
life is a jest, and a very loud one, in his philosophy. The sense of beauty
and love he does not recognize at all, except in our modern condition of
social animals. To read him is like sitting in the next room to an orgie of
gentlemen topers, with their noisy gentility and "hip! hip! hurras!" and the
rattling din of plates and glasses. In his way, he is a very clever writer,
nobody can deny; but he is contracted and conventional, and unrefined in
his line of conventionality. His best descriptions are of military life. He is
most at home in the mess-room. He has undoubted humour and a quick
talent of invention of comic scenes, which generally end in broad farce.
He does not represent fairly even the social and jovial side of men of much
refinement, or, if he does he should not represent them as he does, on *all*
sides thus social and jovial.

> Richard Hengist Horne, 1844, *A New Spirit of the Age*

O'Dowd's anecdotes constitute his greatest charm; and his sketches of national character show minute and delicate portraiture.

> William Spalding, 1852, *A History of English Literature,* p. 417

As a delineator of the droll side of Irish life and character, and of army
life in general, Lever is unequalled. The plot of his novels is usually weak,
and the professed heroines are tame and conventional. But the other characters are all highly marked, and reveal a wealth of humor and fun that
borders on the incredible. They are all excellent, and some of them, like
Mickey Free and Major Monsoon, may be safely classed among the greatest literary creations. Lever's later works are not so good as his early ones,
because they treat of the same general themes, and are consequently lacking in freshness. . . . Of all care-dispelling, mirth-provoking books,
Charles O'Malley is the most genial. It is one carnival of wit, humor, and
revelry from end to end, with just enough of the shady side of life to temper the merriment, and prevent it from becoming monotonous, as is the
case in *Verdant Green.*

> John S. Hart, 1872, *A Manual of English Literature,* pp. 533, 534

The works of Charles Lever, while possessing considerable interest for
most mature minds, are much more popular with the young. . . . The style
is bold, dashing and careless. There is no attempt at close analysis of motives or balancing of probabilities. The hero relates his own adventures,
and leaves his audience to guess at the motives which actuated those with
whom he came in contact. Incidents follow each other in rapid succession.

When one danger is escaped by the hero, he immediately gets into another scrape of some kind. We are kept in a state of constant concern for him. Either his liberty is threatened by the machinations of enemies, his life endangered by duels, or his hope of winning the one woman who can make him happy on the point of being changed to despair by his temporary yielding to the fascinations of pretty women, with whom he is brought into contact. He is no monster of perfection, like many heroes who are popular with the young, but endowed with a fair share of human weaknesses.

> J. L. Stewart, 1878, "Lever's Military Tales,"
> *Canadian Monthly,* vol. I, p. 199

Although it is only a few years since Lever died, his popularity as a novelist had been at the time so long waning that his death had not the effect, as in the case of Thackeray and Dickens, of bringing to an abrupt termination a brilliant career; but rather of reviving for a brief time a reputation already almost extinct. And yet there was a time when instalments of a new novel by the author of *Harry Lorrequer* were almost as eagerly awaited as those of the authors of *Vanity Fair* or *Oliver Twist,* and there was never a period during his long literary activity when Lever's ready wit and fertile imagination were not equal to the task of producing fiction far more deserving of attention than nine-tenths of the successful novels of the present time.

> A. G. Sedgwick, 1879, "Charles Lever," *The Nation,* vol. 29, p. 368

The latter part of his life Lever spent chiefly on the continent as a consul at Spezza, Trieste, etc., and his later works were more elaborate, full of diplomacy and intrigue, full, too, of the speculations and devices of that special figure, the Irishman abroad, but failing considerably in the racy wit and fun of his earlier works. His plots become too intricate, and the various threads of his story so irretrievably mixed that the author himself often seemed to forget what his original intention had been, and merely sought the quickest way out of the labyrinth in which he had involved himself.

> Margaret O. W. Oliphant, 1892, *The Victorian Age*
> *of English Literature*

SIR EDWARD GEORGE BULWER-LYTTON
Lord Lytton

1803-1873

Born [Edward George Earle Lytton Bulwer], in London, 25 May 1803. Educated privately. Matric. Trin. Coll., Camb., Easter, 1822; removed to

Trin. Hall, Oct. 1822; Chancellor's Medal for Prize Poem, 1825; B. A., 1826; M. A., 1835. First visit to Paris, autumn of 1825. Married Rosina Doyle Wheeler, 29 Aug. 1827. Settled near Pangbourne. Prolific contributor to periodicals. Removed to London, Sept. 1829. Active literary life. Edited *New Monthly Mag.,* Nov. 1831 to Aug. 1833. M. P. for St. Ives, 1831-32. Legal separation from his wife, April 1836. Play, *The Duchess de la Vallière,* produced at Drury Lane, 1836; *The Lady of Lyons,* Drury Lane, 1838; *Richelieu,* Drury Lane, 1839; *The Sea-Captain* (afterwards called *The Rightful Heir*), Haymarket, 1839; *Money,* Haymarket, 1840. M. P. for Lincoln, 1833-41. Baronet, July 1838. Joint editor (with Brewster and Lardner) of *Monthly Chronicle,* 1841. Play, *Not so Bad as we Seem,* acted at Devonshire House, 1851. Succeeded to estate of Knebworth at his mother's death, Dec. 1843; assumed surname of Lytton, Feb. 1844. M. P. for Hertfordshire, 1852-66. Hon. D. C. L., Oxford, 9 June 1853. Lord Rector of Glasgow Univ., 1856 and 1858. Sec. of State for Colonies, 1858-59. Privy Councillor, June 1858. Hon. LL.D., Cambridge, 1864. Created Baron Lytton at Knebworth, 14 July 1866. G. C. M. G. 15 Jan. 1870. Died, at Torquay, 18 Jan. 1873. Buried in Westminster Abbey. WORKS: *Ismael,* 1820; *Delmour* (anon.), 1823; *A Letter to a late Cabinet Minister,* 1824; *Sculpture,* 1825; *Weeds and Wild Flowers* (anon.; priv. ptd.), 1825; *O'Neill* (anon.), 1827; *Falkland* (anon.), 1827; *Pelham* (anon.), 1828; *The Disowned* (anon.), 1829; *Devereux* (anon.), 1829; *Paul Clifford* (under initials: E. B. L.), 1830; *The Siamese Twins,* 1831; *Eugene Aram* (anon.), 1832; *Asmodeus at large* (anon.), 1833; *Godolphin* (anon.), 1833; *England and the English,* 1833 (2nd edn. same year); *Pilgrims of the Rhine* (anon.), 1834; *The Last Days of Pompeii* (anon.), 1834; *Letter to a Cabinet Minister,* 1834; *The Student* (from *New Monthly Mag.*), 1835; *Rienzi,* 1835; *The Duchesse de la Vallière* (under initials: E. B. L.), 1836; *Athens, its rise and fall* (2 vols.), 1837; *Ernest Maltravers* (anon.), 1837; *Alice* (anon.), 1838; *Leila,* 1838; *Calderon the Courtier* (anon.), 1838; *The Lady of Lyons* (under initials: E. B. L.), 1838; *Richelieu* (anon.), 1838; *The Sea-Captain* (anon.), 1839; *Money* (anon.), 1840; *Works* (10 vols.), 1840; *Night and Morning* (anon.), 1841; *Dramatic Works,* 1841; *Zanoni* (anon.), 1842; *Eva,* 1842 (2nd edn. same year); *The Last of the Barons* (under initials: E. L. B.), 1843; *Confession of a Water Patient,* 1845; *The Crisis* (anon.), 1845; *The New Timon* (anon.), 1846; *Lucretia* (anon.), 1846; *A Word to the Public* (anon.), 1847; *Harold* (anon.), 1848; *King Arthur,* 1848-49 (2nd edn., 1849); *The Caxtons* (from *Blackwood's Mag.*), 1849; *Night and Morning,* 1851; *Letter to John Bull, Esq.,* 1851 (11th edn. same year); *Not so Bad as we Seem,* 1851; *Outlines of the early history of the East,* 1852; *Poetical and Dramatic Works* (5 vols.), 1852-54; *My Novel* (from *Blackwood;* under pseud.: "Pisistratus Caxton"), 1853; *Address to the Associated Societies of the University of Edinburgh,* 1854; *Clytemnestra* (anon.), 1855; *Speech at the Leeds Mechanics' Institution,* 1854; *What will he do with it?* (under pseud.: Pisistratus Caxton), 1859; *Novels* (43 vols.), 1859-63; *St. Stephen's* (anon.), 1860; *A Strange Story* (anon.; from *All the Year Round*), 1862; *Caxtoniana,* 1863; *The Boatman* (from *Blackwood;* under pseud.: Pisistratus Caxton), 1864; *The Lost Tales of Miletus,* 1866; *The Rightful Heir* (anon.), 1868; *Miscellaneous Prose Works,* 1868; *Walpole,* 1869; *The Coming Race* (from *Blackwood;* anon.), 1871; *Kenelm Chill-*

ingly (anon.), 1873; *The Parisians* (from *Blackwood*), 1873. POST-
HUMOUS: *Speeches,* and other political writings, ed. by his son, 1874;
Pausanias the Spartan, ed. by his son, 1876; *Life, Letters and Literary
Remains* (autobiog.), ed. by his son, 1883. He *translated: Poems and
Ballads* from Schiller, 1844; Horace's *Odes and Epodes,* 1869. COLLECTED
WORKS: in 37 vols., 1873-75.

R. Farquharson Sharp, 1897, A Dictionary of
English Authors, p. 176

SEE: V. A. G. R. Bulwer-Lytton, *Life,* 1913, 2 v.

PERSONAL

Pelham is writ by a Mr. Bulwer, a Norfolk squire, and horrid puppy. I
have not read the book, from disliking the author, but shall do so since
you approve it.

John Gibson Lockhart, 1828, To Sir Walter Scott, Nov.;
The Life and Letters, ed. Lang, vol. II, p. 37

After the debate I walked about the streets with Bulwer till near three
o'clock. I spoke to him about his novels with perfect sincerity, praising
warmly, and criticising freely. He took the praise as a greedy boy takes
apple pie, and the criticism as a good dutiful boy takes senna-tea. He has
one eminent merit, that of being a most enthusiastic admirer of mine; so
that I may be the hero of a novel yet, under the name of Delamere or
Mortimer. Only think what an honor!

Thomas Babington Macaulay, 1831, To Hannah M. Macaulay;
Life and Letters, ed. Trevelyan, ch. iv

Intrinsically a poor creature this Bulwer; has a bustling whisking agility
and restlessness which may support him in a certain degree of significance
with some, but which partakes much of the nature of *levity.* Nothing truly
notable can come of him or of it.

Thomas Carlyle, 1834, Journal, Feb. 13; Early Life of
Thomas Carlyle, ed. Froude, vol. II, p. 327

The author of *Pelham* is a younger son and depends on his writings for a
livelihood, and truly, measuring works of fancy by what they will bring
(not an unfair standard perhaps), a glance around his luxurious and elegant rooms is worth reams of puff in the quarterlies. He lives in the heart
of the fashionable quarter of London, where rents are ruinously extravagant, entertains a great deal, and is expensive in all his habits, and for this
pay Messrs. Clifford, Pelham, and Aram—(it would seem) most excellent

good bankers. As I looked at the beautiful woman [Mrs. Bulwer] seated on the costly ottoman before me, waiting to receive the rank and fashion of London, I thought that old close-fisted literature never had better reason for his partial largess. I half forgave the miser for starving a wilderness of poets.

Nathaniel Parker Willis, 1835, *Pencillings by the Way,*
Letter CXIX

Yes, he is a thoroughly *satin* character; but then it is the *richest* satin. Whether it will wear as well as other less glossy materials remains to be seen. There was something inconceivably strange to me in his dwelling, with a sort of hankering, upon the Count d'Orsay's physical advantages; something beneath the dignity of an author, my fastidiousness fancied, in the manner in which he spoke of his own works, saying that the new ones only interested him as far as they were *experiments*. It is a fine, energetic, inquisitive, romantic mind, if I mistake not, that has been blighted and opened too soon. There wants the repose "the peace that passeth all understanding," which I must believe (and if it be a delusion, I hope I shall never cease to believe) is the accompaniment of the *highest* mind.

Henry Fothergill Chorley, 1836, *Autobiography,*
Memoirs and Letters, ed. Hewlett, vol. I, p. 194

His friendly temper, his generous heart, his excellent conversation (at his best) and his simple manners (when he forgot himself) have many a time "left me mourning" that such a being should allow himself to sport with perdition. Perhaps my interest in him was deepened by the evident growth of his deafness, and by seeing that he was not, as yet, equal to cope with the misfortune of personal infirmity. He could not bring himself practically to acknowledge it; and his ignoring of it occasioned scenes which, painful to others, must have been exquisitely so to a vain man like himself. I longed to speak, or get spoken, to him a word of warning and encouragement out of my own experience: but I never met with any who dared mention the subject to him; and I had no fair opportunity after the infirmity became conspicuous. From the time when, in contradicting in newspapers a report of his having lost his hearing altogether, he professed to think conversation not worth hearing, I had no hope for his fortitude: for it is the last resource of weakness to give out that grapes are sour.

Harriet Martineau, 1855-77, *Autobiography,*
ed. Chapman, vol. I, p. 266

The most pleasing thing about Lord Lytton is his humanity. He goes into the cottages of the poor people, and they seem to adore him. They have known him ever since he was a boy, and called him Sir and Mr. instead of My Lord, and when they correct themselves and beg pardon he says, "O never mind that."

> Matthew Arnold, 1869, *To his Mother,* May 12;
> *Letters,* ed. Russell, vol. II, p. 8

So Lytton is gone to Westminster Abbey. It was, on the whole, a noble life, for its untiring industry, energy, and many-sidedness both of genius and scholarship and practical business. He died pen in hand, and they say his novel soon to appear is among his best. His play of "Money," which I have read, is running hundreds of nights now at one of the chief theatres in London. He was a good Grecian, Latinist, German. He was a respectable Cabinet Minister. He achieved a peerage for his declining years, and a tomb in Westminster Abbey. I knew him very well, and once spent a few days with him at Knebworth, and always thought him delightful company.

> John Lothrop Motley, 1873, *Letter to Oliver Wendell Holmes,*
> Jan. 26; *Correspondence,* ed. Curtis, vol. II, p. 360

LADY LYTTON

I have now given, from the only authentic record of them, all the particulars relative to the circumstances of my father's marriage. Their multiplied evidence of his early affection for my mother is, I think, no unworthy tribute to her character and conduct at a time when, a young unmarried girl, she was placed in a very difficult and unhappy position. And on my father's side the history illustrates with great force that depth and strength of character which it is my object to portray with the utmost fidelity in my power. The facts which have here been related without reserve will, I trust, greatly abbreviate my task in dealing with the painful sequel of the story, into which it would be impossible for me to enter minutely without the appearance of sitting in judgment on my parents. I might have spared a part of what I have printed already if their ill-omened union had not produced a multiplicity of published extravagances which would not permit me to dismiss the subject with the simple statement that at an early age, my father married for love, contrary to the wishes of his mother, and that his marriage was imprudent and unhappy. His own letters will now enable all candid persons to judge for themselves whether the writer of them could have been capable of the brutality, the cruelty, the meanness and selfishness, attributed to him in the numerous libels which he himself scorned to notice, and which cannot be repeated by his son, even for the purpose of refuting them.

> Edward Robert Bulwer-Lytton, Earl of Lytton (Owen Meredith), 1883,
> *The Life, Letters, and Literary Remains of Edward Bulwer*
> *Lord Lytton,* vol. II, bk. VII, ch. III

His wife was beautiful, witty, and accomplished. Mr. Willis is entirely truthful when he speaks of her as the object of universal admiration in London. She was Irish by birth, and her maiden name was Rosina Wheeler. From early youth she had moved in a circle of some brilliancy in London, and had borne a distinguished place in it. In conjunction with Miss Elizabeth Spence she had written a novel called "Dame Rebecca Berry," which had met with a certain measure of success. Miss Spence was a clever, kindly, and eccentric old maid, who affected literature and the society of eminent people. At her weekly reunions many of the rising celebrities were occasionally to be seen. It was here that Bulwer first met the lady who was to be his wife. Miss Wheeler was not then quite eighteen years of age, and Bulwer had only recently attained his majority. An attachment sprang up at once which soon developed into a passion, and when the young couple were married, it seemed as cordial a love-match as London society had ever known. And for a time perhaps it was. But a few years passed, and then it began to be known among Bulwer's intimate friends that he had caught a Tartar. Mrs. Bulwer had a furious temper, and she was insanely jealous of her husband. She quarrelled with all his female friends, without respect to their age. She accused Lady Blessington of alienating his affections, though Lady Blessington was almost old enough to be his mother. She had a fight with Lady Caroline Lamb, who was even older. She resented Bulwer's affection for Letitia Landon, the lively little woman who seemed so much his junior that his relations to her were almost paternal in their character. Nor did she vent her ill-humors on the ladies alone. She turned her husband's home into a small domestic hell.

William Shepard Walsh, 1884, *Pen Pictures of
Earlier Victorian Authors,* p. 50

For the last seven years of her life Lady Lytton resided at a small house, "Glenómera," at Upper Sydenham, latterly with only one servant. She rarely left her room, and the house once only during the last five years. Naturally of a too generous disposition, wholly unselfish, and frequently left to the care of a servant who was equally unable to comprehend or to supply her requirements, she could hardly have lived so long had it not been for friends who commiserated her neglected and desolate condition, and tried to alleviate her sorrows and to supply what were really necessities by assisting her to the utmost extent of their ability. Although in her eightieth year, she possessed to the last the remains of a beauty that had been so noted in her youth. Neither her general tone nor manners had deteriorated through adversity, but remained to the last as distinguished as they were polished and winning. She was full of anecdote and wit, and though not reticent on the subject of her wrongs, she never failed to impress upon her hearers a feeling of sadness and regret that so much capacity for all that was loving and affectionate had been so ruthlessly destroyed by neglect, wrong, and persecution. No one can defend some of her published extravagances, but our blame should more justly be laid upon those who abused her highly sensitive nature, and induced those feelings of exasperation under the infliction of wrong which she had no other opportunity to express.

Louisa Devey, 1887, Life of Rosina, Lady Lytton, p. 388

Pelham (1828)

Pray who writes *Pelham?* I read it only yesterday and found it very interesting: the light is easy and gentleman-like, the dark very grand and sombrous. There are great improbabilities, but what can a poor devil do? There is, I am sorry to say, a *slang* tone of morality which is immoral, and of policy void of everything like sound wisdom. I am sorry if these should be the serious opinions of so powerful an author.

Sir Walter Scott, 1828, Letter to Lockhart, Nov. 20;
The Life and Letters of John Gibson Lockhart,
ed. Lang, vol. II, p. 35

Read sections 6-10 of the eleventh *Philippic,* and a very few chapters of *Pelham.* The notes are changed to tragic. The chapter giving the account of the murder of Sir John Tyrrell is written with great powers of description, both of the scenes of nature and of the dark passions of the soul. Walter Scott is the founder of this school of writing, and the author of *Pelham* is an imitator not inferior to his original. There is more of nature in the characters, more of variety in the dialogue, less of pedantry in the discourses, and more frequent transitions in the narrative, than in Scott. There is also more invention, the basis of Scott's novels being historical, and this being altogether fictitious. All writing for the public should have some moral purpose. This indeed is the intended purpose of most, if not of all the novels of the present age. There is a refinement of delicacy in them which renders them more suitable for youth, but which takes from their merit as pictures of manners. Pelham goes to Paris, but he paints only Duchesses and gamblers, salons and boudoirs. In England it is the same —high life in London, and palaces in the country—Almacks or Newmarket. Notwithstanding this, he gives great interest to the story, and abounds with wit, though he has very little humor.

John Quincy Adams, 1829, Diary, April 2;
Memoirs, ed. C. F. Adams, vol. VIII, p. 126

The publication of *Pelham* heralded a new intellectual dynasty of fops and puppies. Bulwer's original idea of a hero was the greatest satire ever written by a man of talent on his own lack of mental elevation. He attempted to realize in a fictitious character his notion of what a man should be, and accordingly produced an agglomeration of qualities, called Pelham, in which the dandy, the scholar, the sentimentalist, the statesman, the *roué,* and the blackguard, were all to be included in one "many-sided" man, whose merits would win equal applause from the hearty and the heartless, the lover and the libertine. Among these, however, the dandy stood preëminent; and scholarship, sentiment, politics, licentiousness, and ruffianism, were all bedizened in the frippery of Almacks.

Edwin Percy Whipple, 1844, "Literature and Life,"
Novels and Novelists, p. 54

Falkland was succeeded by *Pelham,* which was published with his name, and which was the first, perhaps the most successful, and by far the most brilliant, of the novels in which authors have endeavoured to secure the rank of man of the world even more than that of man of letters, taking the method chiefly of fashionable, and therefore somewhat ephemeral, epigram.

George Saintsbury, 1896, *A History of Nineteenth
Century Literature,* p. 142

Pelham, written at twenty-five years of age, is a creditable boy's book; it aims to portray character as well as to develop incidents, and in spite of the dreadful silliness of its melodramatic passages it has merit. Conventionally it is more nearly a work of art than that other famous boy's book, Disraeli's *Vivian Grey.*

Julian Hawthorne, 1897, *Library of the World's
Best Literature,* ed. Warner, vol. V, p. 2071

The Last Days of Pompeii (1834)

We feel throughout his book all the inspiration of the poetic and sublime creations of ancient genius, and share in the scholar-like fervor which evidently swells the author's mind.

G. H. Devereux, 1835, "*The Last Days of Pompeii,*"
North American Review, vol. 40, p. 449

There is great talent, much learning, and vigorous conception in *The Last Days of Pompeii,* by Bulwer; and the catastrophe with which it concludes is drawn with his very highest powers; but still it is felt by every class of readers to be uninteresting. We have no acquaintance or association with Roman manners; we know little of their habits; scarce anything of their conversation in private; they stand forth to us in history in a sort of shadowy grandeur totally distinct from the interest of novelist composition. No amount of learning or talent can make the dialogues of Titus and Lucius, or Gallius and Vespasia, interesting to a modern reader.

Sir Archibald Alison, 1845, "The Historical Romance,"
Blackwood's Magazine, vol. 58, p. 350

Probably no historical romance has had more readers than *The Last Days of Pompeii*.

Wilbur L. Cross, 1899, *The Development of
the English Novel*, p. 144

I read all his books at that most impressionable time of life when but to name a woman's name is to conjure up a phantom of delight in the young fancy; but nothing remains to me now from the multitude of his inventions in the figure of women but the vague image of the blind girl Nydia in *The Last Days of Pompeii*. I think this sort of general remembrance or oblivion no bad test in such matters, and I feel pretty sure that if Bulwer had imagined any other heroine of equal authenticity I should find some trace of her charm in my memory. But I find none from the books of an author whom I once thought so brilliant and profound, and whom I now think so solemnly empty, so imposingly unimportant. . . . Nydia fairly operates the whole action, in which the machinery creaks more audibly than it once did; but she is imagined upon old-fashioned lines of girlhood which have their charm. Like Milton's ideal of poetry, she is "simple, sensuous, passionate," and from her first meeting with Glaucus, the young Athenian swell who goes about snubbing the Latin civilization at Pompeii, she loves him. He saves her from the scourge of the savage virago who owns her, but when he has bought her he sends her to bear the declaration of his love to the beautiful Ione; and Nydia has to hear, if not to see, the tenderness of the lovers. . . . It may seem hard that a novelist whose fiction afterwards went so far and wide in the great English world of society and politics, should have lodged no other heroine so securely in the memory of his public as she of his early romance; but this appears to have been the fate of Bulwer. Yet, after all, it is no mean achievement. She was so well imagined, in a time when her type was fresher than now, that one's regret is rather for the heroine than the author; one wishes that she had been the creature of a talent able to do her full justice in the realization.

William Dean Howells, 1901, *Heroines of Fiction*,
vol. I, pp. 118, 120, 124

Richelieu (1838)

In one peculiarity, at least, Bulwer-Lytton the novelist surpassed all his rivals and contemporaries. His range was so wide as to take in all circles and classes of English readers. He wrote fashionable novels, historical novels, political novels, metaphysical novels, psychological novels, moral-purpose novels, immoral-purpose novels. *Wilhelm Meister* was not too heavy nor *Tristram Shandy* too light for him. He tried to rival Scott in the historical romance; he strove hard to be another Goethe in his *Ernest Maltravers*; he quite surpassed Ainsworth's *Jack Sheppard,* and the general run of what we in England call "thieves' literature," in his *Paul Clifford*; he became a sort of pinch-beck Sterne in *The Caxtons,* and was severely classical in *The Last Days of Pompeii.* One might divide his novels into at least half a dozen classes, each class quite distinct and different from all the rest, and yet the one author, the one Bulwer-Lytton, showing and shining through them all. Bulwer is always there. He is masquerading now in the garb of a mediæval baron, and now in that of an old Roman dandy; anon he is disguised as a thief from St. Giles's, and again as a full-blooded aristocrat from the region of St. James's. But he is the same man always, and you can hardly fail to recognize him even in his cleverest disguise. It may be questioned whether there is one spark of true and original genius in Bulwer.

Justin McCarthy, 1872, "Edward Bulwer-Lytton, Lord Lytton,"
Modern Leaders, p. 160

The Coming Race (1871)

The class of composition to which *The Coming Race* belongs is one peculiarly adapted to Bulwer's genius. Bulwer possessed in a high degree the rich fancy of the romanticist and the keen perception of the satirist. If he had been less of a romanticist he would have been more effective as a novelist. In *The Coming Race* he was free to let his imagination run romantic riot without weakening the effect of his satire.

T. H. S. Escott, 1874, "Bulwer's Last Three Books,"
Fraser's Magazine, vol. 89, p. 767

My two favourite novels are Dickens's *Tale of Two Cities* and Lytton's *Coming Race.* Both these books I can read again and again, and with an added pleasure. Only my delight in the last is always marred afresh by disgust at the behaviour of the hero, who, in order to return to this dull earth, put away the queenly Zoe's love.

H. Rider Haggard, 1887, *Books which Have Influenced Me,* p. 67

The Coming Race, published anonymously and never acknowledged during his life, was an unexpected product of his mind, but is useful to mark his limitations. It is a forecast of the future, and proves, as nothing else could so well do, the utter absence in Bulwer of the creative imagination. It is an invention, cleverly conceived, mechanically and rather tediously worked out, and written in a style astonishingly commonplace. The man who wrote that book (one would say) had no heaven in his soul, nor any pinions whereon to soar heavenward. Yet it is full of thought and ingenuity, and the central conception of "vril" has been much commended. But the whole concoction is tainted with the deadness of stark materialism.

Julian Hawthorne, 1897, Library of the World's Best Literature,
ed. Warner, vol. V, p. 2703

GENERAL

The brilliant fame of Sir Edward Lytton Bulwer as a novelist, and as a dramatic writer, has tended much to eclipse and disparage his appearances as a poet. In the two former departments he ranks deservedly as a magnate; in the last, his status is more questionable, although, I confess, this is a thing rather to be felt than explained. He constantly touches the confines of success, and stands before the gate—but the "Open Sesame!" comes not to his lips. Perhaps it is that, in his themes, we have rather able and eloquent treatment than that colouring glow of imagination which has been termed an inspiration. With fine descriptive powers, and with boundless range of illustration, there is a want of reliance on simple nature—of that fusion of the poet in his subject, which can alone give that subject consecration—the poetic art, without the poetic vision; and this defect is apparent in all his verse, from his early *Weeds and Wildflowers, O'Neil the Rebel, Ismael,* and *The Siamese Twins,* down to his *Eva, or the Ill-omened Marriage,* his *Modern Timon,* and his more elaborate and ambitious *King Arthur.* His translations of the poems and ballads of Schiller are, however, justly held in estimation among scholars for their spirit and fidelity.

D. M. Moir, 1851-52, Sketches of the Political Literature
of the Past Half Century

The author is an orator, and has tried to be a poet. Dickens' John the Carrier was perpetually on the verge of a joke, but never made one: Bulwer's relation to poetry is of the same provoking kind. The lips twitch, the face glows, the eyes light; but the joke is not there. An exquisite *savoir faire* has led him within sight of the intuitions of poetic instinct. Laborious calculation has almost stood for sight, but his maps and charts are not the earth and the heavens. His vision is not a dream, but a nightmare; you have Parnassus before you, but the light that never was on sea or shore is wanting. The whole reminds you of a lunar landscape, rocks and caves to spare, but *no atmosphere*. It is fairy-land travelled by dark. How you sigh even for the chaos, the *discordia semina* of genius, while toiling through the impotent waste of this sterile maturity.

> Sydney Dobell, 1855, *Letter to George Gilfillan,*
> *A Third Gallery of Portraits,* p. 341

I am well aware of the modern tendency to belittle Bulwer, as a slight creature; but with the fresh recollection of his books as they fell upon my own boyhood, I cannot recall a single one which did not leave as a last residuum the picture in some sort of the chivalrous gentleman impressed upon my heart. I cheerfully admit that he sometimes came dangerously near snobbery, and that he was uncivil and undignified and many other bad things in the *New Timon* and the Tennyson quarrel; and I concede that it must be difficult for us—you and me, who are so superior and who have no faults of our own—to look upon these failings with patience; and yet I cannot help remembering that every novel of Bulwer's is skillfully written and entertaining, and that there is not an ignoble thought or impure stimulus in the whole range of his works.

> Sidney Lanier, 1881, *The English Novel,* p. 195

Lytton is one of the authors upon whose merits the critics have never agreed with the public. He won immense popularity in the face of generally hostile criticism, and even his success failed to obtain a reversal of the judgment. Some of his qualities, however, are incontestable. No English author has displayed more industry, energy, versatility, or less disposition to lapse into slovenliness. His last works are among his best.

> Leslie Stephen, 1893, *Dictionary of National Biography,*
> vol. XXXIV, p. 385

For style he cared nothing: his own manner remained the same, explosive, and undisciplined, except in the very rare cases where he was interested in his own productions. But as for the matter, there is no subject capable of romantic treatment which this astonishingly versatile man did not make his own. So long as cheap cynicism, paltry witticisms, and little stories about "success in society" paid, Lytton wrote them, and wrote them as well as stories of this kind can be written. When taste grew ultra-Byronic —perhaps under the stimulus of Lytton's writing—Lytton followed it as far as was safe, and then commenced writing for the more domestic public. Thieves' patter was in the fashion for some time, and Lytton promptly showed his admiring public that he knew more about the patter than the

thieves themselves. Then came the turn of the historical novel, and *Rienzi,*
The Last of the Barons, and *Devereux* showed that Lytton could write
about any country and any period, and could write quite well enough for
his works to sell. His ghost stories scared his readers literally into fits. . . .
His commercial instincts were admirable, but his works have very little
relation to literature. Had he lived now, he would have written English, as
he could very well have done in his own time if he had cared to take the
trouble. He did not care to take the trouble because it did not pay.

Walter Frewen Lord, 1901, "Lord Lytton's Novels,"
Nineteenth Century, vol. 50, p. 457

JOHN STUART MILL
1806-1873

Born, in London, 20 May 1806. Educated by his father. In France, May
1820 to July 1821. On return studied for Bar for short time, till appointment as Junior Clerk in Examiner's Office, India House, May 1823; Assist-
ant Examiner, 1828; First Assistant, 1836; Head of Office, 1856. Founded
Utilitarian Soc., winter of 1822. Contrib. to *Traveller,* 1822; to *Morning
Chronicle,* 1823; to *Westminster Rev.,* 1824-28, 1835-38, 1864; to *Parliamentary Hist. and Rev.,* 1826-28. Founded Speculative Soc., 1825. In
Paris, 1830. Contrib. to *Examiner* and *Monthly Rev.,* 1831-34; to *Tait's
Mag.,* 1832; to *Monthly Repository,* 1834; and to *Jurist.* Editor *London
Rev.,* afterwards *Westminster Rev.,* 1834-40. Friendship with Mrs. Taylor
begun, 1831; married her, April 1851. [Editor] of *Westminster Rev.,*
1837-40. Severe illness, 1839. Correspondence with Comte, 1841-46.
Contrib. to *Edinburgh Rev.,* 1845-46, 1863. Severe illness, 1854. Retired
from India House, 1857. In south of France, winter of 1858-59; wife died,
at Avignon. For remainder of life spent half the year at Blackheath, half
at Avignon. Contrib. articles on "Utilitarianism" to *Fraser's Mag.,* 1861.
M. P. for Westminster, 1865-68. Lord Rector of St. Andrews Univ., 1866.
Died, at Avignon, 8 May 1873; buried there. WORKS: *A System of Logic*
(2 vols.), 1843; *Essays on some unsettled Questions of Political-Economy,*
1844; *Principles of Political Economy* (2 vols.), 1848; *Memorandum on
the Improvements in the Administration of India during the last Thirty
Years* (anon.), 1858; *On Liberty,* 1859; *Thoughts on Parliamentary Reform,* 1859 (2nd edn. same year); *Dissertations and Discussions* (4 vols.),
1859-75; *Considerations on Representative Government,* 1861 (2nd edn.
same year); *Utilitarianism* (from *Fraser's Mag.*), 1863; *Examination of
Sir William Hamilton's Philosophy,* 1865 (2nd edn. same year); *Auguste
Comte and Positivism* (from *Westminster Rev.*), 1865; *Inaugural Address*
at Univ. of St. Andrews, 1867; *Speech on the Admission of Women to the
Electoral Franchise,* 1867; *England and Ireland,* 1868; *On the Subjection of
Women,* 1869 (2nd edn. same year); *Chapters and Speeches on the Irish
Land Question,* 1870; *Speech in favour of Woman's Suffrage,* 1871. POST-
HUMOUS: *Autobiography,* ed. by Helen Taylor, 1873-74; *Nature; the Utility*

of Religion; and *Theism,* ed. by Helen Taylor, 1874 (2nd edn. same year); *Views . . . on England's Danger through the Suppression of her Maritime Power,* 1874; *Early Essays,* ed. by J. W. M. Gibbs, 1897. He *edited:* Bentham's *Rationale of Judicial Evidence,* 1827; and the 1869 edn. of James Mill's *Analysis of the Phenomena of the Human Mind.* LIFE: *Autobiography,* 1873; *Criticism, with Personal Recollections,* by Prof. Bain, 1882; *Life,* by W. L. Courtney, 1889.

R. Farquharson Sharp, 1897, *A Dictionary of*
English Authors, p. 197

SEE: *Collected Works,* ed. Friedrich A. Hayek, 1963-   (edition in progress); *Letters,* ed. Hugh S. R. Elliott, 1910; *Mill and Harriet Taylor: Their Correspondence,* ed. Friedrich A. Hayek, 1951; Michael St. John Packe, *Life,* 1954.

PERSONAL

This young Mill, I fancy and hope, is "a *baying* you can love." A slender, rather tall and elegant youth, with small clear Roman-nosed face, two small earnestly-smiling eyes; modest, remarkably gifted with precision of utterance, enthusiastic, yet lucid, calm; not a great, yet distinctly a gifted and amiable youth.

Thomas Carlyle, 1831, *Letter to Mrs. Carlyle,* Sept. 4;
Thomas Carlye, A History of the First Forty Years
of his Life, ed. Froude, vol. II, p. 153

John Mill is summoned to town, and goes to-night; the rest leave to-morrow. They feel leaving Falmouth deeply, and say that no place out of London will be so dear to them. Now for some glimpses at Truth through those wonderfully keen, quiet eyes. . . . His father made him study ecclesiastical history before he was ten. This method of early intense application he would not recommend to others; in most cases it would not answer, and where it does, the buoyancy of youth is entirely superseded by the maturity of manhood, and action is very likely to be merged in reffection. "I never was a boy," he said; "never played at cricket: it is better to let Nature have her own way." In his essays on French affairs he has infused more of himself than into any of his other writings, the whole subject of that country so deeply interests him.

Caroline Fox, 1840, *Memories of Old Friends,*
ed. Pym, *Journal,* April 10, p. 94

Mr. Mill is of a light complexion—is long and thin; his clear blue eye is deep sunk, as if its gaze had been rather internal than external. He has a brisk, genial appearance, and is always neatly and scrupulously dressed in black. His appearance is different from that of any other member. His is not the horsey look of some, nor has he the business air of others, still less does he affect the style of a man of fashion. Altogether, he seems out of his element on his seat on the third row below the gangway on the Opposition side. The men around seem of a coarser and less refined nature. There is a *genus loci* connected with the House, of hard drinkers, mighty sportsmen, big blusterers, eager partisans. You would never expect to find a philosopher there, yet there is Mr. Mill; and there is not a more constant attendant, or one more able or willing to take his part in the debates when the opportunity occurs.

J. Ewing Ritchie, 1869, *British Senators: or, Political Sketches
Past and Present,* p. 300

I found that Mill, although possessed of much learning, and thoroughly acquainted with the state of the political world, was, as might have been expected, the mere exponent of other men's ideas, those men being his father and Bentham; and that he was utterly ignorant of what is called society; that of the world, as it worked around him, he knew nothing; and, above all, of *woman,* he was as a child. He had never played with boys; in his life he had never known any, and we, in fact, who were now his associates, were the first companions he had ever mixed with. His father took occasion to remark to myself especially, that he had no great liking for his son's new friends. I, on the other hand, let him know that I had no fear of him who was looked upon as a sort of Jupiter Tonans. James Mill looked down upon us because we were poor, and not greatly allied, for while in words he was a severe democrat, in fact and in conduct he bowed down to wealth and position. To the young men of wealth and position who came to see him, he was gracious and instructive, while to us he was rude and curt, gave us no advice, but seemed pleased to hurt and offend us. This led to remonstrance and complaint on the part of John Mill, but the result was that we soon ceased to see John Mill at his home.

John Arthur Roebuck, 1879(?), 1897, *Autobiography,
Life and Letters,* ed. Leader, p. 28

In the year 1851 occurred Mill's marriage to Mrs. Taylor, the "almost infallible counsellor," whose friendship and assistance he had previously enjoyed for many years, and whose memory, after their brief married life of seven and a half years, had been terminated by her death, remained to him a "religion." More remarkable and touching devotion to the memory of a woman has rarely been shown than that paid by Mill to the memory of his wife, in his Autobiography, and in the introductory page of his (or, as he says, their joint) work, *On Liberty.* It is not only in marked contrast with his father's unchivalrous, not to say brutally unkind, treatment of his own wife (J. S. Mill, too, has nothing to say, in his Autobiography, of his mother), but is also another passionate manifestation of that potentiality of essential human life which was wholly ignored in his training.

George S. Morris, 1880, *British Thought and Thinkers*, p. 326

John Stuart Mill always seemed to me to grow suddenly aged when Carlyle was spoken of. The nearest to painful emotion in him which I ever saw was when he made that remark, "Carlyle turned against all his friends." I did not and do not think the remark correct. When Carlyle came out with his reactionary opinions, as they were deemed, his friends became afraid of him, and nearly all stopped going to see him at the very time when they should have insisted on coming to a right understanding.

Moncure Daniel Conway, 1881, *Thomas Carlyle*, p. 90

He was the natural leader of Liberal thought; not in the House, but out of it. "Saint of Rationalism," however, in Mr. Gladstone's happy phrase, he remained. He had been declared to be Adam Smith and Petrarch rolled into one; and if he thus combined sentimentalism with the doctrines of political economy, he equally exhibited the cold clearness of the Rationalistic thinker, tempered by the emotional warmth of high moral ideas.

William L. Courtney, 1888, *Life of John Stuart Mill*
(*Great Writers*), p. 142

When Mill made her [Mrs. Taylor] acquaintance, his father remonstrated, but he replied that he had no other feeling towards her than he would have towards an equally able man. The equivocal friendship, which was the talk of all Mill's circle of acquaintances, lasted for twenty years, when Mr. Taylor died, and Mill married his widow. It is impossible to regard the enthusiasm of Mill for this lady without feeling how much there was in it of the humorous, how much also of the pathetic. That Mill had a most exaggerated opinion of her intellectual attainments there can be no doubt. . . . His language with regard to her was always extravagant, and Grote said that "only John Mill's reputation could survive such displays." Mill's brother George declared that she was "nothing like what John thought her," and there is much evidence to show that she was but a weak reflection of her husband. Still, it is impossible not to sympathize with such an illusion.

Clement Shorter, 1897, *Victorian Literature,* p. 139

On Liberty (1859)

I am reading that terrible book of John Mill's *On Liberty,* so clear and calm and cold; he lays it on one as a tremendous duty to get oneself well contradicted, and admit always a devil's advocate into the presence of your dearest, most sacred truths, as they are apt to grow windy and worthless without such tests, if, indeed, they can stand the shock of argument at all. He looks you through like a basilisk, relentless as Fate. We knew him well at one time, and owe him very much. I fear his remorseless logic has led him far since then. No, my dear, I don't agree with Mill, though I, too, should be very glad to have some of my "ugly opinions" corrected, however painful the process; but Mill makes me shiver, his blade is so keen and so unhesitating.

Caroline Fox, 1859, *Letter to E. T. Carne; Life of John Stuart Mill* by Courtney, p. 125

Nowhere is there to be read a more eloquent defence of the rights of individualism, a more generous protest against the tyranny of governments, and still more against that of custom and opinion. It is still in this religious respect for the liberty of all, this tolerance for every idea, this confidence in the final results of the struggle, that we recognize true Liberalism. The author's notions have not always equal solidity, but his instincts are always lofty. We see on every page the man whose own independence has set him at odds with prejudice.

Edmund Scherer, 1862-91, "John Stuart Mill," *Essays on English Literature,* tr. Saintsbury, p. 22

So far as it confuses character with eccentricity, so far as it belongs to the combative, negative spirit of revolt, rather than to the positive, constructive spirit of organised reform; so far it shares the fate of the old *laisser-faire* doctrine of political economy, and is out of harmony with the tendencies and the ideas of the modern age. We have advanced fast and far in the last thirty years, and organism and synthesis are our mottoes rather than atomism and individuality.

William L. Courtney, 1888, *Life of John Stuart Mill (Great Writers)*, p. 126

The book *On Liberty,* from beginning to end, is an invaluable text-book for the legislator, for the politician, for the social reformer; and its powerful protest against all forms of over-legislation, intolerance, and the tyranny of majorities, is rich with perennial wisdom and noble manliness. But as a piece of social philosophy it is based upon a sophism as radical as that of Rousseau himself, with his assumption of a primordial Contract. And, if these absolute dogmas as to "the sovereignty of the individual" against even the moral coercion of his fellow-citizens were literally enforced, there would be a bar put to the moral and religious development of civilised communities.

Frederic Harrison, 1896, "John Stuart Mill," *Nineteenth Century,* vol. 40, p. 496

On The Subjection of Women (1869)

The highest encomium which John Stuart Mill now receives—that which he would most value—is that every noble woman's heart in Europe is this day comfortless beside his grave. I remember to have been present once in a company composed chiefly of ladies of the higher class in Moscow, when a friend, introducing me, said, "He is a friend of John Stuart Mill," when instantly I was surrounded by all of that sex in the room, begging to be told of his look, his manner, and every word I had ever heard him speak. Each declared that she kept his work on *The Subjection of Women* by her side, and read it as her gospel. Throughout Russia I found it the same, and heard the sentiments of that work quoted on the stage amidst applause in which every woman made her hands attest the homage of her heart. In France the best women proudly claimed him as their adopted fellow-citizen, and the tribute he had written on his wife's grave made them forget the romances of Hugo and About.

Moncure Daniel Conway, 1873, "John Stuart Mill,"
Harper's Magazine, vol. 47, p. 529

In many ways the most eloquent of his works, the most characteristic, and perhaps that which has had the most direct and immediate effect. Like the *Liberty,* it was written many years before it was published, and was to a great degree a joint production. His biographer, Professor Bain, very justly calls it "the most sustained exposition of Mill's life-long theme—the abuses of power." And Mr. John Morley calls it "the best illustration of all the best and richest qualities of its author's mind." "It is fortunate," he adds, "that a subject of such incomparable importance should have been first effectively presented for discussion in so worthy and pregnant a form."

Frederic Harrison, 1896, "John Stuart Mill,"
Nineteenth Century, vol. 40, p. 500

Autobiography (1873-74)

You have lost nothing by missing the autobiography of Mill. I have never read a more uninteresting book, nor should I say a sillier, by a man of sense, integrity, and seriousness of mind. The penny-a-liners were very busy with it, I believe, for a week or two, but were evidently pausing in doubt and difficulty by the time the second edition came out. It is wholly the life of a logic-chopping engine, little more of human in it than if it had been done by a thing of mechanized iron. Autobiography of a steam-engine, perhaps, you may sometimes read it. As a mournful psychical curiosity, but in no other point of view, can it interest anybody. I suppose it will deliver us henceforth from the cock-a-leerie crow about "the Great Thinker of his Age." Welcome, though inconsiderable! The thought of poor

Mill altogether, and of his life and history in this poor muddy world, gives me real pain and sorrow.

Thomas Carlyle, 1873, *To John Carlyle,* Nov. 5; *Thomas Carlyle, History of his Life in London,* ed. Froude, vol. II, p. 358

As an autobiography, the book has but little merit; though this should not be insisted on, since success in writing of this kind is extremely rare. . . . Mill seems to have been incapable of a healthful sentiment of any kind. The same quality in his stunted and warped moral nature which caused him to have a false and exaggerated sense of the evil that is in the world, leading him to atheism, made him a blind and superstitious worshipper of the imaginary endowments of his wife. . . . We have never read a sadder book, nor one which to our mind contains stronger proof that the soul longs with an infinite craving for God, and, not finding him, will worship anything—a woman, a stone, a memory.

J. L. Spaulding, 1874, "John Stuart Mill," *Catholic World,* vol. 18, pp. 721, 733

Mill's life is an autobiography with a vengeance! It is his life of himself, and of nobody else! Account for this as you please. He seems to have regarded his father's life and his own as one; that it was his duty and work to continue his father's work and duty with such added light as time gave. His wife's life and his own he seems to consider as one life. There are no more profound and interesting passages in the book than those which describe their perfect communion. These two lives, therefore, are alluded to in the autobiography. Miss Taylor gets mentioned in a postscript, as if for the same reason. But, for the rest, people are mentioned as Westminster Bridge might be mentioned, or the penny-post, if they served to carry out Mill's wishes and plans, and only so. You would not know that he had a mother, or brothers, or sisters. There are associates spoken of sometimes; but the same plan of the book, or the temperament of the author, or both, hinder him from pausing one moment to give us any view of them. This book is simply and wholly given to the life of John Stuart Mill. . . . A fascinating book it is from beginning to end.

Edward Everett Hale, 1874, "John Stuart Mill," *Old and New,* vol. 9, p. 128

GENERAL

No writer, it is probable, was ever more read between the lines: his authoritative force of intellect, his perfect mastery of his materials, his singular neatness of exposition, marked him as a great power in the speculative world: but, as usual, the real interest felt was not less scientific than moral

—as to the direction in which that power would work. A certain air of suppression occasionally assumed by Mr. Mill himself, with hints for a revision of the existing narrow-minded morals, has increased this tendency. This suppressive air is the greatest fault we find in him; it is his only illegitimate instrument of power, for it weighs chiefly on the weak; and the shade which it passes across his face is sometimes so strong as almost to darken the philosopher into the mystagogue.

James Martineau, 1859, *Essays, Philosophical and Theological,* vol. I, p. 118

As a whole, I should say that Mill was wanting in strength, energy, or momentum. His happiest strokes were of the nature of a corruscation—a lightning flash, rather than effects of impetus or mass of motion. His sentences and paragraphs are apt to diffuse; not because of unnecessary circumstances, but from a want of steady endeavour after emphasis by good collocation and condensation. Every now and then, one of his pithy sentences comes across us, with inexpressible welcome. He is himself conscious when he is becoming too involved, and usually endeavours to relieve us by a terse summary at the close of the paragraph.

Alexander Bain, 1882, *John Stuart Mill, A Criticism; with Personal Recollections,* p. 177

In all his writings he is clear in expression and abundant in illustration. This abundance, in truth, appears to the reader not wholly ignorant of the subject to be cognate to verbosity. It was however part of the secret of Mill's great influence. He forced people to understand him. He talked round and round the subject, looked at it from every point of view and piled example upon example, until it was impossible to miss his meaning. When we add wide knowledge, patient study, keen intelligence and a considerable, if not exactly a great talent for original speculation, Mill's influence as a philosopher is explained. He wielded, from the publication of his *Logic* till his death, a greater power than any other English thinker, unless Sir William Hamilton is to be excepted for the earlier part of the period.

Hugh Walker, 1897, *The Age of Tennyson,* p. 163

CHARLES KINGSLEY
1819-1875

Born, at Holne Vicarage, Devonshire, 12 June 1819. At school at Clifton, 1831-32; at Helston, Cornwall, 1832-36. Family removed to London,

1836. Student at King's Coll., London, 1836-38. Matric. Magdalene Coll., Camb., Oct. 1838; Scholar, 1839; B. A., 1842; M. A., 1860. Ordained Curate of Eversley, Hampshire, July 1842. Married Fanny Grenfell, 10 Jan. 1844; Rector of Eversley, same year. Clerk in Orders, St. Luke's, Chelsea, 1844-49. Canon of Middleham, 1845. Prof. of English Lit., Queen's Coll., London, 1848. Contrib. (under pseud. of "Parson Lot") to *Politics for the People*, 1848; and to *The Christian Socialist*, 1850-51. Contrib. to *Fraser's Mag.*, 1848, etc. Ill-health, winter 1848-49. First visit to Continent, 1851. At Torquay, winter 1853-54. Chaplain in Ordinary to the Queen, 1859. Prof. of Modern History, Cambridge, 1860-69. Increasing ill-health from 1864. Pres. of Social Science Congress, 1869. Canon of Chester, 1869. Visit to West Indies, winter 1869-70. Resided at Chester, May 1870 to 1873. Pres. of Midland Institute, 1872. Canon of Westminster, 1873. Visit to America, 1874. Died, at Eversley, 23 Jan. 1875. Buried there. WORKS: *The Saint's Tragedy*, 1848; *Twenty-five Village Sermons*, 1849; *Alton Locke* (anon.), 1850; *Cheap Clothes and Nasty* (under pseud. "Parson Lot"), 1850; *The Application of Associative . . . Principles to Agriculture*, 1851; *Yeast* (anon.), (from *Fraser's Mag.*), 1851; *The Message of the Church to Labouring Men*, 1851; *Phaethon*, 1852; *Sermons on National Subjects* (2 ser.), 1852-54; *Hypatia* (from *Fraser's Mag.*), 1853; *Alexandria and her Schools*, 1854; *Who causes Pestilence?* 1854; *Sermons for the Times*, 1855; *Westward Ho!* 1855; *Glaucus*, 1855; *The Heroes*, 1856 [1855]; *Two Years Ago*, 1857; *Andromeda*, 1858; *The Good News of God*, 1859; *Miscellanies*, 1859; *The Limits of Exact Sciences as applied to History*, 1860; *Why should we pray for Fair Weather?* 1860; *Town and Country Sermons*, 1861; *A Sermon on the death of . . . the Prince Consort*, 1862 [1861]; *Speech of Lord Dundreary . . . on the great Hippocampus question* (anon.), 1862; *The Gospel of the Pentateuch*, 1863; *The Water Babies*, 1863; *What, then, does Dr. Newman mean?* 1864; *The Roman and the Teuton*, 1864; *Hints to Stammerers* (anon.), 1864; *David*, 1865; *Hereward the Wake*, 1866; *The Temple of Wisdom*, 1866; *Three Lectures on the Ancient Régime*, 1867; *The Water of Life*, 1867; *The Hermits*, 1868; *Discipline*, 1868; *God's Feast*, 1869; *Madame How and Lady Why*, 1870 [1869]; *At Last*, 1871; *Poems*, 1872 [1871]; *Town Geology*, 1872; *Prose Idylls*, 1873; *Plays and Puritans*, 1873; *Health and Education*, 1874; *Westminster Sermons*, 1874; *Lectures delivered in America*, 1875. POSTHUMOUS: *Letters to Young Men*, 1877; *True Words for Brave Men*, ed. by his wife, 1878; *All Saints' Day, and other Sermons*, ed. by W. Harrison, 1878; *From Death to Life*, ed. by his wife, 1887. He *edited:* Mansfield's *Paraguay*, 1856; Tauler's *History and Life*, 1857; Brooke's *The Fool of Quality*, 1859; Bunyan's *Pilgrim's Progress*, 1860 [1859]; *South by West*, 1874. COLLECTED WORKS: in 28 vols., 1880-85. LIFE: *Letters and Memories*, by his wife, 1877.

R. Farquharson Sharp, 1897, *A Dictionary of English Authors*, p. 157

SEE: *Life and Works*, 1901-3, 19 v.; *Charles Kingsley: His Letters and Memoirs of His Life*, ed. by his wife, 1901, 2 v.; U. B. Pope-Hennessy, *Canon Charles Kingsley*, 1948.

PERSONAL

He is tall, slender, with blue eyes, brown hair, and a hale, well-browned face, and somewhat loose-jointed withal. His wife is a real Spanish beauty. How we did talk and go on for three days! I guess he is tired. I'm sure we were. He is a nervous, excitable being, and talks with head, shoulders, arms, and hands, while his hesitance makes it the harder. Of his theology, I will say more some other time. He, also, has been through the great distress, the "Conflict of Ages," but has come out at a different end from Edward, and stands with John Forster, though with more positiveness than he.

> Harriet Beecher Stowe, 1856, *To Mr. Stowe,* Nov. 7;
> *Life and Letters,* ed. Fields, p. 227

A high noble forehead, large, earnest, deep-set eyes (which the lithograph had made hollow as if with thought and work) a firm, close-shut mouth, and large and powerful jaw; here was a poet as well as a parson, a fighter as well as a writer, a leader as well as a priest. Waving black hair, now thinned by time, adorned the head, and earnest, glowing, lustrous, and true-hearted eyes shone out from beneath the forehead, and seemed to speak openly to whomsoever listened, "Come, let us work togther for the good of mankind. Love me, for I love you; or if I can't convince you, then——" Such was Charles Kingsley, as good and as free-natured a soul as one would care to see.

> James Hain Friswell, 1870, *Modern Men of Letters*
> *Honestly Criticised,* p. 315

Charles and Herbert Kingsley were brought to Helston Grammar School, in Cornwall, in the year 1832. . . . Charles was a tall, slight boy, of keen visage, and of great bodily activity, high-spirited, earnest, and energetic, giving full promise of the intellectual powers, and moral qualities, by which he was afterwards distinguished. Though not a close student, he was an eager reader and enquirer, sometimes in very out of the way quarters. I once found him busily engaged with an old copy of *Porphyry and Iamblichus,* which he had ferreted out of my library. Truly a remarkable boy, original to the verge of eccentricity, and yet a thorough boy, fond of sport, and up to any enterprise—a genuine out-of-doors English boy.

> Derwent Coleridge, 1875, *Letter to Mrs. Kingsley,* Oct. 7;
> *Charles Kingsley, his Letters and Memories of his Life,*
> ed. his Wife, vol. I, p. 23

Kingsley's conversational powers [1849] were very remarkable. In the first place he had, as may be easily understood by the readers of his books, a rare command of racy and correct English, while he was so many sided that he could take keen interest in almost any subject which attracted those about him. He had read, and read much, not only in matters which every one ought to know, but had gone deeply into many out-of-the-way and unexpected studies. Old medicine, magic, the occult properties of plants, folklore, mesmerism, nooks and bye-ways of history, old legends; on all these he was at home. On the habits and dispositions of animals he would talk as though he were that king in the Arabian Nights who understood the language of beasts, or at least had lived among the gypsies who loved him so well. The stammer, which in those days was so much more marked than in later years, and which was a serious discomfort to himself, was no drawback to the charm of his conversation. . . . No man loved a good story better than he, but there was always in what he told or what he suffered himself to hear, a good and pure moral underlying what might be coarse in expression. While he would laugh with the keenest sense of amusement at what might be simply broad, he had the most utter scorn and loathing for all that could debase and degrade. And he was the most reverent of men, though he would say things which seemed daring because people were unaccustomed to hear sacred things named without a pious snuffle. This great reverence led him to be even unjust to some of the greatest humourists.

C. Kegan Paul, 1876, *Letter to Mrs. Kingsley;*
Charles Kingsley, his Letters and Memories of his Life,
ed. his Wife, vol. I, pp. 225, 227

I have read every word of Canon Kingsley's *Life and Letters,* and thought better of him for reading it. He was very decided in his opinions, but very modest in his notion of his own merits; and, though conservative in regard to the Anglican Church, tolerant and kind to those who did not agree with him. He was a friend to the humbler classes, and a most faithful and sympathetic pastor, wearing out his life for his flock; yet I cannot see that he contemplated doing them any good, save by personal effort and kind attentions. I do not find in any part of the memoir that he sought to improve the institutions under which the working class in England had been kept poor and degraded. But his personal attentions with respect to their comfort, their health, their spiritual condition, and their mental improvement, were constant, and these, along with his literary labors, undermined his health and broke it down once in two or three years. He was a worn-out man when he came to America. But read the book, if you can get it. If you skip anything, skip the letters in which he tries to be jocular and runs into slang—mere slang, which he seems to take for fun.

William Cullen Bryant, 1877, *To Miss J. Dewey,* June 2;
in Parke Godwin, *William Cullen Bryant; A Biography,*
vol. II, p. 383

Charles Kingsley has been one of the Forces of the present generation. He literally pitched heart-foremost, if not head-foremost, into all the social, scientific, and political problems, thoughtfully discussed by the more careful thinkers of the time, as a kind of "free lance," committed from the start to a championship of the emotional side of every question which his calmer contemporaries were inclined to consider from its reasonable side. If the difficulties which trouble all thinking-men in their endeavors to advance the human race could be overcome by gushes of philanthropic sentiment, Kingsley would have rapidly risen to be the first man of his time. . . . The real lesson taught by Charles Kingsley's life is this: that he was the most impulsive, the most inconsistent, the most passionate, and, at heart, the most conscientious, of human beings. . . . Kingsley never arrived at intellectual and moral manhood. He was a boy,—a grand, a glorious boy, when he first appeared as a dogmatic man, assuming to direct English thought; and a boy, a splendid boy, he remained to the last year of his life. All his vagaries of opinion and sentiment, all the strange inconsistencies of his career, all the sense and all the nonsense which alternately shocked or attracted his contemporaries, were properly to be referred to the plain fact that he never became a mature man. All the learning he acquired, all the experience of life he accumulated through long years, all his contacts and collisions with the minds of friends who represented the most advanced intellect of the age, never could cure him of the boyish defect of substituting impulse for intelligence, even in the consideration of those complicated problems in which intelligence should manifestly be the supreme guide and arbiter.

Edwin Percy Whipple, 1885, Some Noted Princes, Authors,
and Statesmen of Our Time, ed. Parton, pp. 230, 231

His keen interest in country sport, and in country pursuits generally, enabled him to sympathize with country gentlemen and sportsmen of all grades, and with agriculturists, farmers, and labourers alike; and his soldierly instincts, which he never lost, drew to him the soldier class, both officers and men, whom the neighbourhood of Eversley to Aldershot gave him rare opportunities of influencing. Hence, men were affected by him as they had not been affected by clergymen before; and he was regarded as the apostle of "muscular Christianity," a term which he thought most offensive, but which was understood at any rate by many, in a complimentary, not an offensive sense.

John Henry Overton, 1897, The Church in England, vol. II, p. 391

Alton Locke (1850)

Nowhere can you find any proof that the author is able to think about anything. An idea strikes him; he seizes it, and, to use Hawthorne's expression, "wields it like a flail." Then he throws it down and takes up something else, to employ it in the same wild and incoherent fashion. This is Kingsley all out, and always. He is not content with developing his one only gift of any literary value—the capacity to paint big, striking pictures with a strong glare or glow on them. He firmly believes himself a profound philosopher and social reformer, and he will insist on obtruding before the world on all occasions his absolute incapacity for any manner of reasoning on any subject whatsoever. Wild with intellectual egotism, and blind to all teaching from without, Kingsley rushes at great and difficult subjects head downwards like a bull.

Justin McCarthy, 1872, "The Reverend Charles Kingsley,"
Modern Leaders, p. 216

Alton Locke may be fairly regarded as his best piece of work. . . . With all the genuine force of *Alton Locke*—and no living novelist has excelled the vividness of certain passages—there is an unsatisfactory side to the whole performance. It is marred by the feverishness which inspires most of his work. There is an attempt to crowd too much into the space, and the emphasis sometimes remains when the power is flagging. Greater reserve of power and more attention to unity of effect would have been required to make it a really great book.

Leslie Stephen, 1877-92, Hours in a Library, vol. III, pp. 47, 52

As a novel it is almost a failure, but not so as a propagandist work of fiction. In its presentation of fact it is a complete success. In the description of fetid and filthy workshops and fever dens of the sweaters, in its exposure of the causes which turned honest and peaceable workmen into conspirators, the author of *Alton Locke* did the work of half a dozen labour commissions, and did it much more effectually by appealing in fervid tones of passionate sympathy to the well-to-do people of his day, calling upon them to rescue their fellow-men from destruction of soul and body, and stimulating private and public philanthropy to set about and face the social problem with honesty of purpose.

Moritz Kaufmann, 1892, Charles Kingsley, Christian Socialist
and Social Reformer, p. 130

Hypatia (1853)

It is difficult to believe that, either in *Hypatia* or in *Two Years Ago,* he had laid his plot beforehand: in *Yeast* there does not pretend to be any plot at all. *Hypatia* especially might have been so grand, and is so disappointing. There is a consummate mastery of the costume and character of the epoch; there are magnificent materials of character and fancy brought together to the workshop; there are gorgeous descriptions of external beauty; there are individual scenes of thrilling interest; there are wonderful glimpses both of thought and passion. . . . The inconsiderate confusion in which the incidents of the story jostle and stumble over one another, and the indistinctness with which many of them are told, compel us to reserve our admiration for particular scenes and portions, and render it impossible to praise the work as a whole. . . . Still, with all its faults, it is unquestionably a work of genius; but of genius in a hurry,—of genius, as it were, shut up without fire or candle, like an inharmonious jury, and compelled to complete its task before it can regain its liberty.

William Rathbone Greg, 1860-73, "Kingsley and Carlyle,"
Literary and Social Judgments, p. 139

The summer of 1863 added a third contest, which was provoked by the same theological bitterness. Stanley and Dr. Liddell had proposed that the University should confer the honorary degree of D. C. L. on the Rev. Charles Kingsley. The proposal was resisted by Dr. Pusey, partly on the ground of Kingsley's universalism, but more particularly on the ground that *Hypatia* was a work not fit to be read by our "wives and sisters." To Stanley the attack on *Hypatia* seemed the more unjustifiable and offensive because the book had been recommended to him by Mrs. Augustus Hare, and because he had himself urged his mother to read it. He carefully prepared a speech for the Council, in which he demanded "that the aspersions cast upon the moral character of the book, in the gross language which I have copied out from Pusey's lips, be withdrawn."

Rowland E. Prothero, 1893, *The Life and Correspondence
of Arthur Penrhyn Stanley*, vol. II, p. 135

Hypatia still remains the sublimest subject that historical fiction has appropriated to its use—the death struggle between Greek and Christian civilization in the fifth century. . . . A second purpose is unmistakably conveyed in his sub-title to *Hypatia*: *New Foes with an Old Face*. Kingsley was bitterly anti-Roman, and wished to arrest the movement toward Rome that Newman had given the Church of England. These ulterior aims lent to *Hypatia* a modern tone, making out of it a novel of aggressive purpose. But they stood in the way of real history. What purports to be historical facts in *Hypatia* Leslie Stephen has pronounced a bubble that bursts on the most delicate touch; the Church of Rome as therein represented is not the church of the fifth century, and the Goths are mythical.

Wilbur L. Cross, 1899, *The Development of the
English Novel*, p. 145

Westward Ho! (1855)

The construction of the romance we think, bears the marks of haste, and may perhaps be pronounced clumsy. . . . In beauties of detail no work of the author is more rich. Mr. Kingsley rarely constructs a character. But in the honest Jack Brimblecombe, that strange compound of imperfect literature and genuine feeling, of skin-deep valor and heart-sound faith, he has drawn a living man, less adequately developed indeed, but as fresh and original, as the inimitable Saunders Mackey of Alton Locke. . . . We hail it as a strong and a suggestive work.

W. H. Hurlbut, 1855, "Kingsley's Sir Amyas Leigh,"
Christian Examiner, vol. 59, pp. 289, 290, 295

Westward Ho! partakes much more of the character of biography and history than of the ordinary sentimental novel. Love plays a great part in the progress of the story, as it does in the lives of most men; but it is as motive influencing character and determining action that it exhibited, not as itself the sole interest of life, the single feeling which redeems human existence from dulness and inward death. The love which acts on the career and character of Amyas Leigh does not spend itself in moonlight monologues or in passionate discourses with its object; nor does the story depend for its interest upon the easily roused sympathy of even the stupidest readers with the ups and downs, the fortunes and emotions, of a passion common in certain degrees and certain kinds to all the race. It is no such narrow view of life that is presented here, but rather that broad sympathy with human action and human feeling in its manifold completeness which gives to art a range as wide as life itself, and throws a consecrating beauty over existence from the cradle to the grave, wherever human affections act, wherever human energies find their object and their field, wherever the battle between right and wrong, between sense and spirit, is waged—wherever and by whatever means characters are trained, principles strengthened, and humanity developed.

George Brimley, 1855-58, *"Westward Ho!", Essays,*
ed. Clark, p. 300

It is just the author's sympathy with the times, and with the men of the times, even down to their prejudices and fierce dislikes, that has given to *Westward Ho!* its unique success as a romance of that age of young and energetic enthusiasms. It is a manly book, and therefore pre-eminently a book for boys. From cover to cover there is nothing maudlin or weakly sentimental in it. Its verve and energy are infectious. All through [the book,] the reader is conscious of that tingling of the blood that accompanies the excitement of a succession of high adventures.

Richard D. Graham, 1897, *The Master of*
Victorian Literature, p. 91

Andromeda (1858)

His *Andromeda* is an admirable composition,—a poem laden with the Greek sensuousness, yet pure as crystal, and the best-sustained example of English hexameters produced up to the date of its composition. It is a matter of indifference whether the measure bearing that name is akin to the antique model, for it became, in the hands of Kingsley, Hawtrey, Long-fellow, and Howells, an effective form of English verse. The author of *Andromeda* repeated the error of ignoring such quantities as do obtain in our prosody, and relying upon accent alone; but his fine ear and command of words kept him musical, interfluent, swift.

> Edmund Clarence Stedman, 1875-87, *Victorian Poets*, p. 251

In *Andromeda* Kingsley has shown a measure of power with which those who know him only through his lyrics would scarcely credit him. Many a canvas has gleamed with the statuesque figure of that old-world princess, but in none has it stood out more clearly than in the word-pictures of this fine poem. It is presented to us steeped in the clear golden air of the southern day; and the pure Pagan joy of existence, with its refusal to "look before and after," its absolute satisfaction with the present, and its shrinking even from the shadow of death, characterise most strikingly this late version of the oft-told tale.

> Horace G. Groser, 1892, *The Poets and the Poetry of the Century, Kingsley to Thomson,* ed. Milnes, p. 4

POEMS

His work abounds in charming phrases and in those verbal inspirations that catch the ear and linger long about the memory:—as witness the notes that are audible in the opening verses of "The Sands of Dee," the "pleasant Isle of Avès" of "The Last Buccaneer," and the whole first stanza of the song of the Old Schoolmistress in *The Water-Babies*. But as it is with his music, so is it with his craftmanship as well. He would begin brilliantly and suggestively and end feebly and ill, so that of perfect work he has left little or none. It is also to be noted of him that his originality was decidedly eclectic—an originality informed with many memories and showing sign of many influences; and that his work, even when its purpose is most dramatic, is always very personal, and has always a strong dash in it of the sentimental manliness, the combination of muscularity and morality, peculiar to its author.

> William Ernest Henley, 1880, *The English Poets,* ed. Ward, vol. IV, p. 608

Simple, brave, resolute, manly, a little given to "robustiousness," Kingsley transfigured all these qualities by possessing the soul and the heart of a poet. He was not a very great poet indeed, but a true poet—one of the very small band who are cut off, by a gulf that can never be passed, from mere writers of verse, however clever, educated, melodious, ingenious, amiable, and refined. He had the real spark of fire, the true note; though the spark might seldom break into flame, and the note was not always clear. Never let us confuse true poets with writers of verse, still less with writers of "poetic prose." Kingsley wrote a great deal of that—perhaps too much: his descriptions of scenes are not always as good as in Hereward's ride round the Fens, or when the tall, Spanish galleon staggers from the revenge of man to the vengeance of God, to her doom through the mist, to her rest in the sea. Perhaps only a poet could have written that prose; it is certain no writer of "poetic prose" could have written Kingsley's poems.

Andrew Lang, 1891, Essays in Little, p. 156

If Kingsley, with all his literary gifts, was never quite in the first rank in anything, he came nearest to being a poet of mark. Some of his ballads almost touch the high-water mark of true ballad poetry, with its abrupt fierce blows of tragedy and pathos, its simple touches of primitive rude speech, its reserve of force, its unspoken mysteries. At any rate, Kingsley's best ballads have no superior in the ballads of the Victorian era in lilt, in massiveness of stroke, in strange unexpected turns. "The Weird Lady" is an astonishing piece for a lad of twenty-one.

Frederic Harrison, 1895, Studies in Early Victorian
Literature, p. 166

GENERAL

He reminds of nothing so much as of a war-horse panting for the battle; his usual style is marvellously like a neigh,—a "ha! ha! among the trumpets!" the dust of the combat is to him the breath of life; and when once, in the plenitude of grace and faith, fairly let loose upon his prey—human, moral, or material—all the Red Indian within him comes to the surface, and he wields his tomahawk with an unbaptized heartiness, slightly heathenish, no doubt, but withal unspeakably refreshing. It is amazing how hard one who is a gladiator by nature strikes when convinced that he is doing God service.

William Rathbone Greg, 1860-73, "Kingsley and Carlyle,"
Literary and Social Judgments, p. 117

His novels have fine artistic qualities, but they are really parables rather than novels, pure and simple, and they can only be adequately valued by people who are in sympathy with the ethical thought and sentiment which they hold in solution. Enthusiasm for Kingsley as a novelist is hardly ever found uncombined with enthusiasm for him as a theologian, a politician, and a social reformer; nor would Kingsley have valued the most ardent appreciation of the body of his work unaccompanied by sympathy with its indwelling soul.

James Ashcroft Noble, 1886, Morality in English Fiction, p. 44

In the beginning of 1864 Kingsley had an unfortunate controversy with John Henry Newman. He had asserted in a review of Mr. Froude's <i>History</i> in <i>Macmillan's Magazine</i> for January 1860 that "Truth, for its own sake, had never been a virtue with the Roman catholic clergy," and attributed this opinon to Newman in particular. Upon Newman's protest, a correspondence followed, which was published by Newman (dated 31 Jan. 1864), with a brief, but cutting, comment. Kingsley replied in a pamphlet called "What, then, does Dr. Newman mean?" which produced Newman's famous <i>Apologia.</i> Kingsley was clearly both rash in his first statement and unsatisfactory in the apology which he published in <i>Macmillan's Magazine</i> (this is given in the correspondence). That Newman triumphantly vindicated his personal character is also beyond doubt. The best that can be said for Kingsley is that he was aiming at a real blot on the philosophical system of his opponent; but, if so, it must also be allowed that he contrived to confuse the issue, and by obvious misunderstandings to give a complete victory to a powerful antagonist. With all his merits as an imaginative writer, Kingsley never showed any genuine dialectical ability.

Leslie Stephen, 1892, Dictionary of National Biography,
vol. XXXI, p. 178

To put it plainly, I cannot like Charles Kingsley. Those who have had opportunity to study the deportment of a certain class of Anglican divines at a foreign <i>table d'hôte</i> may perhaps understand the antipathy. There was almost always a certain sleek offensiveness about Charles Kingsley when he sat down to write. He had a knack of using the most insolent language, and attributing the vilest motives to all poor foreigners and Roman Catholics and other extra-parochial folk, and would exhibit a pained and completely ludicrous surprise on finding that he had hurt the feelings of these unhappy inferiors—a kind of indignant wonder that Providence should have given them any feelings to hurt. At length, encouraged by popular applause, this very second-rate man attacked a very first-rate man. He attacked with every advantage and with utter unscrupulousness; and the first-rate man handled him; handled him gently, scrupulously, decisively; returned him to his parish; and left him there, a trifle dazed, feeling his muscles.

A. T. Quiller-Couch, 1895, Adventures in Criticism, p. 139

The merits of Kingsley as a writer, and especially as a writer of fiction, are so vivid, so various, and so unquestionable by any sound and dispassionate criticism, that while cynics may almost wonder at his immediate and lasting popularity with readers, serious judges may feel real surprise at his occasional disrepute with critics. The reasons of this latter, however, are not really very hard to fiind. He was himself a passionate partisan, and exceedingly heedless as to the when, where, and how of obtruding his partisanship. He had that unlucky foible of inaccuracy in fact which sometimes, though by no means always, attends the faculty of brilliant description and declamation, and which especially characterised his own set or coterie. Although possessed of the keenest sense both of beauty and of humour, he was a little uncritical in expressing himself in both these departments, and sometimes laid himself open in reality, while he did so much oftener in appearance, to the charge of lapses in taste. Although fond of arguing he was not the closest or most guarded of logicians. And lastly, the wonderful force and spontaneity of his eloquence, flowing (like the pool of Bourne, that he describes at the opening of his last novel) a river all at once from the spring, was a little apt to carry him away with it.

George Saintsbury, 1896, *English Prose,* ed. Craik,
vol. V, p. 647

HARRIET MARTINEAU
1802-1876

Born, at Norwich, 12 June 1802. Early education at home. At a school at Norwich, 1813-15. At Bristol, 1818-19. Returned to Norwich, April 1819. Contrib. to *Monthly Repository,* from 1821. Severe illness, 1827, followed by financial difficulties. Wrote three prize essays for Central Unitarian Association, 1830-31. Visit to her brother James at Dublin, 1831. Engaged on *Illustrations of Political Economy,* Feb. 1832 to Feb. 1834. Settled in London. Visit to America, Aug. 1834 to Aug. 1836. Travelled on Continent, 1839. Refused Crown Pensions, 1834, 1841, and 1873. Testimonial raised to her by her friends, 1843. Lived at Tynemouth, 1839-45; at Ambleside, Westmoreland, 1845 till her death. Friendship with Wordsworth. Visit to Egypt and Palestine, Aug. 1846 to July 1847. Contrib. to *Daily News,* 1852-66; to *Edinburgh Review,* from 1859. Died, at Ambleside, 27 June 1876. WORKS: *Devotional Exercises* (anon.), 1823; *Addresses, with Prayers* (anon.), 1826; *Traditions of Palestine,* 1830; *Five Years of Youth,* 1831; *Essential Faith of the Universal Church,* 1831; *The Faith as unfolded by many Prophets,* 1832; *Providence as manifested through Israel,* 1832; *Illustrations of Political Economy* (9 vols.), 1832-34; *Poor Laws and Paupers Illustrated,* 1833-34; *Illustrations of Taxation,* 1834; *Miscellanies* (2 vols., Boston), 1836; *Society in America,* 1837; *Retrospect of Western Travel,* 1838; *How to Observe,* 1838; *Addresses,* 1838; *Deerbrook,* 1839; *The Martyr Age of the United States* (under initials: H. M.), 1840; *The Playfellow* (4 pts.: "The Settlers at Home";

"The Peasant and the Prince"; "Feats on the Fiord"; "The Crofton Boys"),
1841; *The Hour and the Man,"* 1841; *Life in the Sick Room* (anon.),
1844; *Letters on Mesmerism,* 1845 (2nd edn. same year); *Forest and
Game-Law Tales* (3 vols.), 1845-46; *Dawn Island,* 1845; *The Billow and
the Rock,* 1846; contribution to *The Land we Live In* (with C. Knight and
others), 1847, etc.; *Eastern Life,* 1848; *History of England during the
Thirty Years' Peace* (with C. Knight), 1849; *Household Education,* 1849;
Introduction to the History of the Peace, 1851; *Letters on the Laws of
Man's Nature* (with H. G. Atkinson), 1851; *Half a Century of the British
Empire* (only 1 pt. pubd.), 1851; *Sickness and Health of the people of
Bleaburn* (anon.), 1853; *Letters from Ireland* (from *Daily News*), 1853;
Guide to Windermere, 1854; *A Complete Guide to the English Lakes,*
1855; *The Factory Controversy,* 1855; *History of the American Com-
promises* (from *Daily News*), 1856; *Sketches from Life,* 1856; *Corporate
Traditions and National Rights,* 1857; *British Rule in India,* 1857; *Guide
to Keswick,* 1857; *Suggestions towards the Future Government of India,*
1858; *England and her Soldiers,* 1859; *Endowed Schools of Ireland* (from
Daily News), 1859; *Health, Husbandry, and Handicraft,* 1861; *Biographical Sketches* (from *Daily News*), 1869; [1868]. POSTHUMOUS: *Autobiography,* ed. by M. W. Chapman, 1877 (3rd edn., same year); *The
Hampdens,* 1880 [1879]. She *translated:* Comte's *Positive Philosophy,*
1853. LIFE: by Mrs. Fenwick Miller, 1884.

R. Farquharson Sharp, 1897, *A Dictionary of
English Authors,* p. 188

SEE: *Harriet Martineau's Autobiography,* with Memorials by M. W.
Chapman, 1877, 3 v.; R. K. Webb, *Harriet Martineau: A Radical
Victorian,* 1960.

PERSONAL

Two or three days ago there came to call on us a Miss Martineau, whom
you have perhaps often heard of in the *Examiner.* A hideous portrait was
given of her in the *Fraser* one month. She is a notable literary woman of her
day, has been traveling in America these two years, and is now come home
to write a book about it. She pleased us far beyond expectation. She is very
intelligent-looking, really of pleasant countenance, was full of talk, though
unhappily deaf almost as a post, so that you have to speak to her through
an ear-trumpet. She must be some five-and-thirty. As she possesses very
"favourable sentiments" towards this side of the street, I mean to cultivate
the acquaintance a little.

Thomas Carlyle, 1836, *Letter to His Mother,* Nov.;
Thomas Carlyle, A History of His Life in London,
ed. Froude, vol. I, p. 83

She is a very admirable woman—and the most logical intellect of the age,
for a woman. On this account it is that the men throw stones at her, and
that many of her own sex throw dirt; but if I begin on this subject I shall

end by gnashing my teeth. A righteous indignation fastens on me. I had a note from her the other day, written in a noble spirit, and saying, in reference to the insults lavished on her, that she was prepared from the first for *publicity,* and ventured it all for the sake of what she considered the truth— she was sustained, she said, by the recollection of Godiva.

> Elizabeth Barrett Browning, 1844, *To H. S. Boyd,* Dec. 24;
> *Letters,* ed., Kenyon, vol. I, p. 225

She became at length almost another estate in the realm. Cabinet Ministers consulted her upon the gravest questions of policy. She interposed to settle disputes between leaders which were embarrassing the reform movements of the time. She brought about a reconciliation between Sir Robert Peel, when Prime Minister, and Cobden. She was full of diplomatic skill and social address. We cannot be surprised that without vanity, she felt herself a power, and became dogmatic and dictatorial. No man or woman ever lived who guarded more jealously a personal self-respect. The noble family of Lansdowne wished an introduction to her at a London party, at which her mother was present; but as they did not ask that her mother be presented to them, she rejected every overture for further acquaintance. She refused an introduction to the poet Tom Moore, because he published a poem of raillery in the *Times.* It wounded her and she never forgave it. Different administrations urged a government pension upon her, which she refused. This great, proud, toilsome, self-contained character, wrought her work until she attained the age of seventy-four years, and, measured either by the powers developed in her life, or by its results upon the thought and policy of her time, she appears a peerless woman. Indeed we almost forget she was a woman, and think of her as a human force thrown upon our century when great revolutions were demanding great leaders.

> James O. Putnam, 1877-80, "Harriet Martineau's *Autobiography,*"
> *Addresses, Speeches and Miscellanies,* p. 226

Autobiography

Deeply interesting as the work is, it is impossible to deny that it has given more pain than pleasure to large numbers of those friends who knew her best and valued her most truly. Her own autobiography does her so much less than justice, and the needless, tasteless, and ill-conditioned memorials of the lady to whom she injudiciously entrusted the duties of editor, have managed to convey such an unsound and disfiguring impression of her friend, that the testimony of one who enjoyed her intimacy for many years, and entertained a sincere regard for her throughout, seems wanting to rectify the picture.

> William Rathbone Greg, 1877, "Harriet Martineau,"
> *Miscellaneous Essays,* p. 176

You must read Harriet Martineau's *Autobiography*. The account of her childhood and early youth is most pathetic and interesting; but as in all books of the kind, the charm departs as the life advances, and the writer has to tell of her own triumphs. One regrets continually that she felt it necessary not only to tell of her intercourse with many more or less distinguished persons—which would have been quite pleasant to everybody—but also to pronounce upon their entire merits and demerits, especially when, if she had died as soon as she expected, these persons would nearly all have been living to read her gratuitous rudeness. Still I hope the book will do more good than harm.

> George Eliot, 1877, *To Mrs. Bray*, March 20; *George Eliot's Life as related in her Letters and Journals*, ed. Cross, vol. III, p. 219

GENERAL

Know that a great new light has arisen among English women. In the words of Lord Brougham, "There is a deaf girl at Norwich doing more good than any man in the country." You may have seen the name and some of the productions of Harriet Martineau in the *Monthly Repository*, but what she is gaining glory by are *Illustrations of Political Economy*, in a series of tales published periodically, of which nine or ten have appeared. It is impossible not to wonder at the skill with which, in the happiest of these pieces, for they are unequal, she has exemplified some of the deepest principles of her science, so as to make them plain to very ordinary capacities, and demonstrated their practical influence on the well-being, moral and physical, of the working classes first, and ultimately on the whole community. And with all this, she has given to her narratives a grace, an animation, and often a powerful pathos, rare even in the works of pure amusement.

> Lucy Aikin, 1832, *To Dr. Channing*, Oct. 15; *Correspondence of William Ellery Channing and Lucy Aikin*, ed. LeBreton, p. 148

I have no great faith in some of her doctrines, but I delight in her stories. The *Garveloch Tales* are particularly good. What a noble creature Ella is! To give us in a fishing-woman an example of magnanimity and the most touching affection, and still keep her in her sphere; to make all the manifestations of this glorious virtue appropriate to her condition and consistent with her nature,—this seems to me to indicate a very high order of mind, and to place Miss Martineau among the first moral teachers as well as first writers of her time. Perhaps I may be partial. I feel so grateful to her for doing such justice to the poor and to human nature, and I am strongly tempted to raise her to the highest rank.

William Ellery Channing, 1833, To Miss Aikin, May 30;
Correspondence of William Ellery Channing and Lucy Aikin,
ed. LeBreton, p. 172

Hard work and high courage were, to our thinking, her most noteworthy characteristics. Even those most familiar with her life and work will have been startled at the list of her writings drawn up by herself, "to the best of my recollection," which appeared in the *Daily News* as an appendix to the autobiographical sketch left by her for publication with the editor of that journal, to which alone in her later years she had contributed no less than 1642 articles. From this list it appears that her first book, *My Servant Rachel,* was published in 1827, her last, *Biographical Sketches,* in 1869. In those fifty-two years more than 100 volumes (103 we believe to be the exact number) appeared from her pen, besides which she was a constant contributor to quarterlies, and monthly magazines, and newspapers, and carried on a correspondence which would of itself have been enough to use up the energy of most women. Apart from all the questions of its contents, the mere feat of getting such a mass of matter fairly printed and published could not easily be matched, and the more the matter is examined the more our wonder will grow. In all that long list there is not a volume, so far as we are aware, which bears marks of having been put together carelessly, or for mere book-making purposes, and her fugitive articles are as a rule upon burning topics, the questions by which men's minds were most exercised at the time. Indeed, though she lived by the pen, no writer ever wielded it with greater independence and singlemindedness.

Thomas Hughes, 1876, "Harriet Martineau," The Academy, p. 367

Opinions may differ as to what constitutes Harriet Martineau's best work, but my view is that her translation and condensation of Auguste Comte's six volumes into two will live when all her other work is forgotten. Comte's own writings were filled with many repetitions and rhetorical flounderings. He was more of a philosopher than a writer. He had an idea too big for him to express, but he expressed at it right bravely. Miss Martineau, trained writer and thinker, did not translate verbally; she caught the idea, and translated the thought rather than the language. And so it has come about that her work has been translated literally back into French and is accepted as a text-book of Positivism, while the original books of the philosopher are merely collected by museums and bibliophiles as curiosities.

Elbert Hubbard, 1897, *Little Journeys to the Homes of Famous Women,* p. 106

WILLIAM   CULLEN   BRYANT
1794-1878

William Cullen Bryant born Nov. 3, 1794. First poems printed, March 18, 1807. "The Embargo" printed, 1808. "The Genius of Columbia," 1810. Enters Williams College, Oct., 1810. Leaves Williams College, May, 1811. "Thanatopsis" written, 1812. Begins the Study of Law, 1812. Admitted to the Bar, 1815. "Thanatopsis" printed, 1817. Marries Miss Fanny Fairchild, 1821. Delivers "The Ages" at Harvard, 1821. Removes to New-York City, 1825. Union of *The New-York Review* and *The New-York Literary Gazette,* March 17, 1826. Becomes Assistant Editor of *The Evening Post,* 1826. Edits *The Talisman* with Verplanck and Sands, 1827-1830. Becomes chief Editor of *The Evening Post,* 1829. First European Tour, 1834-1836. *The Fountain, and other Poems,* published, 1842. First Tour in the South, March-May, 1843. *The White-Footed Deer, and other Poems,* published, 1844. Purchases the Estate at Roslyn, 1845. Second European Tour, April-Dec., 1845. Delivers the Oration on Thomas Cole, 1848. Second Tour in the South, and First Visit to Cuba, March-May, 1849. Third European Tour, June-Oct., 1849. *Letters of a Traveller* published, 1850. Presides at the Banquet to Kossuth, Dec. 9, 1851. Delivers the Oration on J. Fennimore Cooper, Feb. 25, 1852. Fourth European Tour, visit to the Holy Land, and Second Visit to Cuba, 1852. A Complete Edition of Poems published, 1854. Fifth European Tour, and First Visit to Spain, 1857-1858. Baptized at Naples, April, 1858. Dangerous Illness of Mrs. Bryant at Naples, May, 1858. *Letters from Spain and other Countries,* published, 1859. Address at the Schiller Festival, Nov. 11, 1859. Delivers the Oration on Washington Irving, 1860. Made Presidential Elector, 1860. *Thirty Poems* published, 1863. Seventieth Birthday Celebrated by the Century Club, Nov. 3, 1864. Death of Mrs. Bryant, June, 1866. Last European Tour, 1867. The Free-Trade Banquet to Bryant, Jan. 30, 1868. *Letters from the East* published, 1869. Delivers the Oration on Fitz-Greene Halleck, Feb. 3, 1869. Translation of *The Iliad* published, 1870. Delivers the Oration on Gulian C. Verplanck, May 17, 1870. Translation of *The Odyssey* published, 1871. Address on Italian Unity, Jan., 1871. Address on the Unveiling of the Morse Statue, June 10, 1871. Tour in Mexico, Winter of 1871-72. Address on the Unveiling of the Shakespeare Statue, May 22, 1872. Address on Reform, Sept. 23, 1872. Address on the Scott Statue, Nov. 4, 1872. Visited by the Commemorative Committee, Nov. 3, 1874. *The Flood of Years* published, 1876. Presentation of the Commemorative Vase, June 20, 1876. Delivers the Oration on Mazzini, May 29, 1878. Death of Bryant, June 12, 1878. Burial, June 14, 1878.

David J. Hill, 1879, *William Cullen Bryant,* p. 13

SEE: *Poetical Works,* ed. Parke Godwin, 1883-84, 6·v.; *Poetical Works,* ed. H. C. Sturges and R. H. Stoddard, 1903 (Roslyn Edition); William Cullen Bryant, *Representative Selections,* ed. Tremaine McDowell, 1935; Parke Godwin, *A Biography of William Cullen Bryant, with Extracts from His Private Correspondence,* 1883; William A. Bradley, *William Cullen Bryant,* 1905; H. H. Peckham, *Gotham Yankee,* 1950; also see Allan Nevins, *The Evening Post: A Century of Journalism,* 1922.

PERSONAL

With one exception (and that's Irving) you are the man I most wanted to see in America. You have been here twice, and I have not seen you. The fault was not mine; for on the evening of my arrival committee-gentlemen were coming in and out until long after I had your card put into my hands. As I lost what I most eagerly longed for, I ask you for your sympathy, and not for your forgiveness. Now, I want to know when you will come and breakfast with me: and I don't call to leave a card at your door before asking you, because I love you too well to be ceremonious with you. I have a thumbed book at home, so well worn that it has nothing upon the back but one gilt "B," and the remotest possible traces of a "y." My credentials are in my earnest admiration of its beautiful contents.

Charles Dickens, 1842, Letter to Bryant, Feb. 14; in
Parke Godwin, William Cullen Bryant, A Biography, vol. I, p. 395

In height, he is, perhaps, five feet nine. His frame is rather robust. His features are large but thin. His countenance is sallow, nearly bloodless. His eyes are piercing gray, deep set, with large projecting eyebrows. His mouth is wide and massive, the expression of the smile hard, cold—even sardonic. The forehead is broad, with prominent organs of ideality; a good deal bald; the hair thin and grayish, as are also the whiskers, which he wears in a simple style. His bearing is quite distinguished, full of the aristocracy of intellect. . . . His dress is plain to the extreme of simplicity, although of late there is a certain degree of Anglicism about it. In character no man stands more loftily than Bryant. The peculiarly melancholy expression of his countenance has caused him to be accused of harshness, or coldness of heart. Never was there a greater mistake. His soul is charity itself, in all respects generous and noble. His manners are undoubtedly reserved.

Edgar Allan Poe, 1846, William Cullen Bryant, Works,
ed. Stedman and Woodberry, vol. VI, pp. 118, 119

His manners and whole aspect are very particularly plain, though not affectedly so; but it seems as if in the decline of life, and the security of his position, he had put off whatever artificial polish he may have heretofore had, and resumed the simpler habits and deportment of his early New England breeding. Not but what you discover, nevertheless, that he is a man of refinement, who has seen the world, and is well aware of his own place in it. . . . He uttered neither passion nor poetry, but excellent good sense, and accurate information, on whatever subject transpired; a very pleasant man to associate with, but rather cold, I should imagine, if one should seek to touch his heart with one's own. He shook hands kindly all around, but not with any warmth of grip, although the ease of his deportment had put us all on sociable terms with him.

Nathaniel Hawthorne, 1858, *Passages from French and*
Italian Notebooks, May 22, pp. 210, 211, 212

From his childhood and through all his eighty-four years his habits of life were temperate and careful. . . . He rose early, took active exercise, walked far and easily, spared work at night, yet had time for every duty of a fully occupied life, and at seventy-one sat down in the shadow of the great sorrow of his life to seek a wise distraction in translating the *Iliad* and the *Odyssey*. His sobriety was effortless; it was that of a sound man, not of an ascetic. He was not a vegetarian nor a total abstainer from wine; but of tobacco, he said, playfully, that he did not meddle with it except to quarrel with its use. No man ever bore the burden of years more lightly, and men of younger generations saw with admiration and amazement an agility that shamed their own. At four-score his eyes were undimmed, and his ears had a boy's acuteness.

George William Curtis, 1878, *William Cullen Bryant,*
A Commemorative Address, p. 61

There was a mournful propriety in the circumstances of the death of Bryant. He was stricken just as he had discharged a characteristic duty with all the felicity for which he was noted, and he was probably never wholly conscious from that moment. Happily we may believe that he was sensible of no decay, and his intimate friends had noted little. He was hale, erect, and strong to the last. All his life a lover of nature and an advocate of liberty, he stood under the trees in the beautiful park on a bright June day, and paid an eloquent tribute to a devoted servant of liberty in another land. And while his words yet lingered in the ears of those who heard him, he passed from human sight. There is probably no eminent man in the country upon whose life and genius and career the verdict of his fellow-citizens would be more immediate and unanimous. His character and life had a simplicity and austerity of outline that had become universally familiar, like a neighbouring mountain or the sea. His convictions were very strong, and his temper uncompromising; he was independent beyond most Americans.

He was an editor and a partisan; but he held politics and all other things subordinate to the truth and the common welfare, and his earnestness and sincerity and freedom from selfish ends took the sting of personality from his opposition, and constantly placated all who, like him, sought lofty and virtuous objects.

William Swinton, 1880, *Studies in English Literature,* p. 408

Probably the title of the Great American could be as fittingly applied to Bryant as to any man our nation has produced. He has been happily called the Puritan Greek; and this epithet applies equally well to his life as to his writings. If he was a Stoic in his earlier years, he was as unmistakably a Christian in later life. During both periods he was pure as ice, lofty in thought, noble in deed, an inspiration toward the True Life to all who watched his course. No errors of passion or of over-heated blood did he have to mourn over, even in youth; yet he was not cold or unimpassioned, as his deep devotion throughout life to the woman of his choice proved. He led emphatically the intellectual life, with as little admixture of the flesh as possible; yet the warm currents of feeling were never dried up in his nature, but bubbled up freshly to the end. He lived largely on the heights of life, yet he was not uncharitable to the weaknesses and follies he saw everywhere about him, but rather looked upon them with a half-pitying tenderness; and he dropped a tear occasionally where the integrity of his own nature counselled a stern reproof.

Hattie Tyng Griswold, 1886, *Home Life of Great Authors,* p. 132

Bryant's office desk was his newspaper Egeria. It was also a curiosity. Except for a space immediately in front of him about two feet long and eighteen inches deep, his desk was usually covered to the depth of from twelve to twenty inches with opened letters, manuscript, pamphlets, and books, the accumulation of years. During his absence in Europe in 1859-60, his associate thought to do Bryant a good turn by getting rid of this rubbish and clearing his table so that he should have room for at least one of his elbows on the table. When he returned and saw what had been done, it was manifest from his expression—he said nothing—that what had been so kindly intended was regarded as anything but a kindness. He had also one habit in common with Pope, of always writing his "copy" for the paper on the backs of these old letters and rejected MSS. One who was associated with him for many years in the management of the *Evening Post* affirms that he never knew Bryant to write an article for its columns on a fresh sheet of paper. He also used a quill pen, which he was in the habit of mending with a knife nearly as old as himself, and which might originally have cost him fifty cents. He has been heard to speak of this knife with affection, and to resent the suggestion that he should replace it with a better one. Every year had added a value to it which no new knife could possibly have in his eyes. The same attachment to old servants made him hold on to a blue cotton umbrella which had very little to commend it either in fair weather or foul but its age. The ladies of his household at last, and when he was about setting out for Mexico, conspired against the umbrella, hid it away, and in its place packed a nice new silk one. He discovered the fraud that had been practised upon him, turned his back upon the *parvenu,* and insisted upon the restoration of his old and injured friend to its accustomed post of honor by his side. To him age made everything sacred but abuses. He petted the old brutes of his barnyard and stables, and held to his old friends with hooks of steel, closing his eyes resolutely to everything about them which he could not admire.

John Bigelow, 1890, *William Cullen Bryant*
(*American Men of Letters*), p. 109

EDITOR

During Mr. Bryant's editorial career of more than fifty years, have been waged the most important political conflicts in the history of the Republic, and in these he has manfully participated. On questions of national policy concerning the old United States Bank, the war with Mexico, the admission of slavery into the territories and its abolition, the tariff, the Ashburton treaty, the war of the rebellion, amnesty, the Alabama claims, the San Domingo muddle, civil service, resumption of specie payments, and other subjects of vital importance, his utterances have been prompt, unequivocal, and just; and he has maintained his principles with an unshaken constancy. He has never waited to catch the breath of popular opinion before flinging abroad his standard. The question with him has always been, "What is right? What subserves human interests best? What is the province and duty of government?" And so he has been the uncompromising enemy of political rings, class legislation, and jobbery, and corruption of all sorts, and the friend and ally of humane and liberal institutions, righteous reform, and the administration of impartial justice. Indeed, there is no species of political iniquity that he has not vigorously assailed, and no doctrines of permanent advantage to the commonwealth that he has not judiciously advocated and set firmer in the minds and hearts of men. He is a statesman of the best type and, as has been said by a distinguished senator, "he is a teacher of statesmen." He has asked nothing of his country but the privilege to serve her interests. Not even his bitterest political opponents have ever accused him of a desire for public office. It is one of the marvels of his great career that, amid the engrossing labors and cares of editorial life, he has kept a sweet temper for scholastic pursuits.

Horatio N. Powers, 1878, "William Cullen Bryant,"
Scribner's Monthly, vol. 16, p. 484

But although as a journalist Bryant took high ground and defended it firmly, he was never carried away by the fury of partisan discussion. In his editorial writings, as in his poetry, the tone is full of dignity. Calm in his strength, he was both temperate in expressing his opinions and good-tempered. He fought fairly and he respected his adversary. He was never a snarling critic either of men or of measures. He elevated the level of the American newspaper, but it was by his practice, not by his preaching. He was choice in his own use of words, and there was in the office of the *Evening Post* a list of words and phrases not allowed in its pages. But he was not a stickler for trifles, and he had no fondness for petty pedantries.

Brander Matthews, 1896, An Introduction to the
Study of American Literature, p. 77

The Embargo (1808)

Among instances of literary precocity, there are few recorded more remarkable than that of Bryant. Tasso, when nine years old, wrote some lines to his mother, which have been praised; Cowley, at ten, finished his *Tragical History of Pyramus and Thisbe*; Pope, when twelve, the *Ode to Solitude*; and the "wondrous boy Chatterton," at the same, some verses entitled *A Hymn for Christmas Day*, but one of these pieces evidence the possession of more genius than is displayed in Bryant's *Embargo* and *Spanish Revolution*, written in his thirteenth year.

Anon, 1809, The Embargo, Second Ed., Advertisement

It was just as good and just as bad as most American imitations of Pope; but the boy indicated a facility in using the accredited verse of the time which excited the wonder and admiration of his elders. Vigor, compactness, ringing emphasis in the constantly recurring rhymes,—all seemed to show that a new Pope had been born in Massachusetts.

Edwin Percy Whipple, 1876-86, American Literature and
Other Papers, ed. Whittier, p. 36

Thanatopsis (1812-17)

Thanatopsis is the poem by which its author is best known, but is by no means his best poem. It owes the extent of its celebrity to its nearly absolute freedom from defect, in the ordinary understanding of the term. I mean to say that its negative merit recommends it to the public attention. It is a thoughtful, well-phrased, well-constructed, well-versified poem. The concluding thought is exceedingly noble, and has done wonders for the success of the whole composition.

Edgar Allan Poe, 1846, William Cullen Bryant, Works,
ed. Stedman and Woodberry, vol. VI, p. 113

There is not, probably, an educated man now living among our English race in whose mind this solemn and beautiful meditation is not associated with "the last bitter hour." Its pictured phrases occur at every coming up of the grisly thought that haunts us all. Its serene philosophy has touched thousands who could never reason calmly for themselves upon the inevitable order of nature. It leaves a clear impression upon the memory that defies the blur of misquotation, for its well chosen words are united by the cohesive power of genius, like the cemented blocks of Old World temples, into imperishable forms.

Francis H. Underwood, 1872, A Hand-Book of
English Literature, American Authors, p. 136

Thanatopsis is a Saxon and New England poem. Its view of death reflects the race characteristics of ten centuries. It shows "no trace of age, no fear to die." Its morality and its trust are ethnic rather than Christian. It nowhere expresses that belief in personal immortality which the author possessed and elsewhere stated. It is a piece of verse of which any language or age might be proud. Yet, as I have just said, this strong and serene utterance of philosophy and of poetry, expressed in the best blank verse of the period, came from a mere boy, who but a few years before had been writing political poems, dashed with fire and vitriol, on *The Embargo* and *The Spanish Revolution*. In its earliest publication *Thanatopsis* was much less than perfect, and was manifestly inferior to the final version. But even then it was, as it is now, a microcosm of the author's mind and powers.

Charles F. Richardson, 1888, American Literature,
1607-1885, vol. II, p. 37

Iliad and *Odyssey* (1870-77)

Mr. Bryant has long been known, by his original poems, as resembling the old epic poets, in his language, more than other living writer of English. It may be said that contemporary poets have excelled his verse, one in splendor, another in suggestiveness, another in fulness of knowledge and in reach of thought, and more than one in nearness to the great mental conflicts of the age; but he has certainly not been surpassed, perhaps not approached by any writer since Wordsworth, in that majestic repose and that self-reliant simplicity which characterized the morning stars of song. He has adhered to the permanent element in our language; and the common perversions in the meaning of good old words, which make it so nearly impossible even for most men of culture to write a sentence that Chaucer could have understood, seem to be unknown to him. No qualification for a translator of Homer could be more essential than this; and the reader who has duly considered its importance will find that it has given Mr. Bryant's translation a vast superiority over all others. The simplicity of Professor Newman's ballad verse is gained only by the sacrifice of dignity; that of the writers of English hexameters is mere baldness; even that of Lord Derby is habitually weak, forced and halting; but that of Mr. Bryant is at once majestic and direct, at once noble, rapid, and vigorous; it is, in a large degree, the simplicity of Homer.

Charlton T. Lewis, 1871, "Mr. Bryant's Translation of the Iliad,"
North American Review, vol. 112, p. 360

He worked only in the mornings, after his usual exercise, when both mind and body were fresh. With a copy of Homer open on his desk, and a lexicon near by, he wrote for three or four hours, and then laid his papers aside for the day. There were other translations on his bookshelves, Chapman, Pope, and Cowper, of course; Voss's German version, and one in Spanish and another in Italian; later on he procured Professor Blackie's; but these he consulted only at intervals, to settle some point of construction of which he had doubts. It confused and fettered him, he said, to know how others had done a passage before him. Besides, he intended his version for popular, not learned, use, and he could give it a more popular cast, he thought, with the original text alone for his guide. The fluency with which he commonly wrote is apparent from the manuscript, where page follows page without inconsiderable erasures. Yet, at times, there are pages almost illegible from the number of the interlineations and changes. In original composition his habit was to fix his verses in his head while he was walking the fields, and to commit them to paper afterward; and, as his verbal memory was a retentive one, it is probable he pursued the same method in translating the old Greek.

Parke Godwin, 1883, *William Cullen Bryant,
A Biography*, vol. II, p. 271

The best characteristics of Bryant's *The Iliad* and *The Odyssey* are: (1), general, though not invariable, fidelity to the text, as compared with former versions by poets of equal rank; (2), simplicity of phrase and style;

(3), approximate transfusion of the heroic spirit; (4), a purity of language that pleases a sensible reader. It is not likely that Bryant possessed a scholar's mastery of even the familiar Ionic Greek, but the text of Homer long has been substantially agreed upon by European editors, there are special lexicons devoted to it, and it is faithfully rendered in German and English translations: so that the poet could have little trouble in adjusting it to his metrical needs. His choice of words is meagre, and so—in a modern sense—was that of Homer; there is no lack of minstrels, nowadays, who ransack their vocabularies to fill our jaded ears with "words, words, words." As a presentment of standard English the value of these translations is beyond serious cavil. When they are compared with the most faithful and poetic blank-verse rendering which proceded them, the work of Cowper, they show an advance in both accuracy and poetic quality. Lord Derby's contemporaneous version is dull and inferior. Bryant naturally handled to best advantage his descriptive passages,—the verses in the Fifth Odyssey, which narrate the visit of Hermes to Calypso, furnishing a case in point. His rendering of these is more literal than the favorite transcript by Leigh Hunt, and excels all others in ease and choice of language.

Edmund Clarence Stedman, 1885, *Poets of America,* p. 84

GENERAL

As a poet, he is entitled to rank with the most eminent among us for originality, and finished, chaste execution. He does not offend us by abruptness and inequality. He presents us with here and there a bold image, but the tenor of his poetry is even and sustained. He shows good judgment, and a careful study of the materials of his verse. He does not aim with an over-daring attempt at those lofty and bewildering flights which too often fill the poet's pages with cloudy and confused representations. His delineations are clear and distinct, and without any indications of an endeavor to be startling and brilliant by strange metaphors, or unlicensed boldness of phraseology. His writings are marked by correct sentiment and propriety of diction.

Samuel Kettell, 1829, *Specimens of American Poetry,*
vol. III, p. 133

No poet has described with more fidelity the beauties of the creation, nor sung in nobler song the greatness of the Creator. He is the translator of the silent language of the universe to the world. His poetry is pervaded by a pure and genial philosophy, a solemn, religious tone, that influence the fancy, the understanding, and the heart. He is a national poet. His works are not only American in their subjects and their imagery, but in their spirit. They breathe a love of liberty, a hatred of wrong, and a sympathy with mankind. His genius is not versatile; he has related no history; he has not sung of the passion of love; he has not described artificial life. Still, the tenderness and feeling in the "Death of the Flowers," "Rizpah," "The Indian Girl's Lament," and other pieces, show that he might have excelled in delineations of the gentler passions, had he made them his study. The melodious flow of his verse, and the rigour and compactness of his language, prove him a perfect master of his art. But the loftiness of his imagination, the delicacy of his fancy, the dignity and truth of his thoughts, constitute a higher claim to our admiration than mastery of the intricacies of rhythm, and of the force and graces of expression.

Rufus Wilmot Griswold, 1842, The Poets and
Poetry of America, p. 126

> There is Bryant, as quiet, as cool, and as dignified,
> As a smooth, silent iceberg, that never is ignified,
> Save when by reflection 'tis kindled o' nights
> With a semblance of flame by the chill Northern Lights,
> He may rank (Griswold says so) first bard of your nation
> (There's no doubt that he stands in supreme ice-olation),
> Your topmost Parnassus he may set his heel on,
> But no warm applauses come, peal following peal on,—
> He's too smooth and too polished to hang any zeal on:
> Unqualified merits, I'll grant, if you choose, he has 'em,
> But he lacks the one merit of kindling enthusiasm;
> If he stir you at all, it is just, on my soul,
> Like being stirred up by the very North Pole.

James Russell Lowell, 1848, A Fable for Critics

The qualities by which Mr. Bryant's poetry are chiefly distinguished are serenity and gravity of thought; an intense though repressed recognition of the morality of mankind; an ardent love for human freedom; an unrivalled skill in painting the scenery of his native land. He had no superior in his walk of poetic art—it might almost be said no equal, for his descriptions of nature are never inaccurate or redundant. *The Excursion* is a tiresome poem, which contains several exquisite episodes. Mr. Bryant knew how to write exquisite episodes, and to omit the platitudes through which we reach them in other poets.

Richard Henry Stoddard, 1878, Poetical Works of
William Cullen Bryant, Household Ed., p. xxii

Bryant's poems inevitably bring Wordsworth to our minds, yet it seems unfair to Bryant's talents to measure their increase by comparison with the fruits of Wordsworth's genius. Bryant's lot took him to the city, to news-papers and daily cares, while Wordsworth sauntered contemplative over Helvellyn and along the margin of Windermere. Great poetry has never been written by a man who was not able to give to it his concentrated thought and his whole heart. Chaucer, Shakespeare, Spenser, Pope, Words-worth, Shelley, Byron, all the great poets of England have given undivided allegiance to poetry. Bryant could not do so, and his poems bear the marks of his involuntary disloyalty. A poet must be judged by his achievement alone. Bryant's verses, except at their best, show a lack of art. They are a little undisciplined; they betray truancy to the classics.

Henry D. Sedgwick, Jr., 1897, "Bryant's Permanent Contribution
to Literature, Atlantic Monthly, vol. 79, p. 541

GEORGE ELIOT

Mary Ann Cross

1819-1880

1819.—Mary Ann Evans, "George Eliot," born November 22 at South Farm, Arbury, in Warwickshire. 1820-1841.—Lived at Griff House, Nun-eaton in the midst of farmhouses, and scenery described in *Adam Bede* and *The Mill on the Floss*. 1824-1827.—Attended Miss Lathom's boarding school. 1827-1831.—Attended Miss Wallington's school and read Bunyan, Defoe, Johnson, Scott, Lamb, etc. 1831-1834.—At the Misses Franklin's school at Coventry, under strong Calvinistic influences. 1836.—Death of her brother; domestic cares; learns Italian and German; studies music, science, metaphysics, mathematics, and the great English poets. 1841.—March, removed to Coventry with her father; friendship with the Brays, resulting in a change in her religious views to Unitarianism; domestic dis-turbances. 1846.—Translated Strauss's *Leben Jesu*. 1849.—May 31, death of her father, Robert Evans. 1849-1850.—Visited France and Italy; re-sided eight months in Geneva. 1851-1857.—Wrote for the *Westminster Review,* of which she became assistant editor; met Lewes, Chapman, Spencer, and the Martineaus. 1953.—Removed to Hyde Park, London. 1854.—Translated Feuerbach's *Essence of Christianity*. 1854-1858.—Union with George Lewes, journalist and philosopher; spent eight months in Weimar and Berlin; wrote for the *Leader* and *Westminster*. 1856-1858.—Publication of *Scenes of Clerical Life;* end of her incognito. 1859.—Publication of *Adam Bede,* her first long novel. 1860.—Publication of *The Mill on the Floss;* visited Italy. 1861.—Publication of *Silas Marner;* visited Florence in May. 1863.—Publication of her great Italian novel *Romola,* begun in the *Cornhill Magazine* for July, 1862. 1866.—Publication of *Felix Holt,* a socialistic novel. 1867.—Visited Spain. 1868.—Publication of *The Spanish Gypsy,* a dramatic poem, and other poems, "Agatha," "How Liza Loved the King," "Brother and Sister," etc. 1870.—Journey to Berlin and Vienna. 1871-1872.—Publication of *Middlemarch*. 1872-1873.—Visited Hamburg and Cambridge. 1874.—Publication of *Legend of*

Jubal, and other poems. 1876.—Publication of *Daniel Deronda,* a Jewish novel. 1877.—Removed to "The Heights," her country home in Surrey. 1878.—Met Turgenev and the Crown Prince and Princess of Germany; death of Lewes, November 28. 1879.—Publication of *Theophrastus Such.* 1880.—May 6, marriage with John Walter Cross; death December 22.

George Armstrong Wauchope, 1899, ed. *George Eliot's*
Silas Marner, p. 15

SEE: *Works,* 1901-3, 12 v. (Warwick Edition); *Complete Poems,* ed. E. Wood, 1901; *Essays,* ed. Thomas Pinney, 1963; *The George Eliot Letters,* ed. Gordon S. Haight, 1954-55, 7 v.; John W. Cross, *George Eliot's Life as Related in Her Letters and Journals,* 1885, 3 v.; Lawrence and Elisabeth Hanson, *Marian Evans and George Eliot: a Biography,* 1952; W. J. Harvey, *The Art of George Eliot,* 1961.

PERSONAL

Miss Evans (who wrote *Adam Bede*) was the daughter of a steward, and gained her exact knowledge of English rural life by the connection with which this origin brought her with the farmers. She was entirely self-educated, and has made herself an admirable scholar in classical as well as in modern languages. Those who knew her had always recognized her wonderful endowments, and only watched to see in what way they would develop themselves. She is a person of the simplest manners and character, amiable and unpretending, and Mrs. B— spoke of her with great affection and respect.

Nathaniel Hawthorne, 1860, *French and Italian Notebooks,* p. 555

July 14th.—A. travelled down from London with G. H. Lewes, who took him to his home at Witley and introduced him to Mrs. Lewes (George Eliot). A. thought her "like the picture of Savonarola." . . . *July 22nd*—. . . A. and Hallam called on Mr. and Mrs. Lewes. She is delightful in a *tête-à-tête,* and speaks in a soft soprano voice, which almost sounds like a fine falsetto with her strong masculine face.

Hallam Tennyson, 1871, *Journal; Alfred Lord Tennyson,*
A Memoir by his Son, vol. II, p. 107

She is an accomplished linguist, a brilliant talker, a musician of extraordinary skill. She has a musical sense so delicate and exquisite that there are tender, simple, true ballad melodies which fill her with a pathetic pain almost too keen to bear; and yet she has the firm, strong command of tone and touch, without which a really scientific musician cannot be made. I do not think this exceeding sensibility of nature is often to be found in combination with a genuine mastery of the practical science of music. But Mrs.

Lewes has mastered many sciences as well as literatures. Probably no other novel writer, since novel writing became a business, ever possessed one tithe of her scientific knowledge. . . . Mrs. Lewes is all genius and culture. Had she never written a page of fiction, nay, had she never written a line of poetry or prose, she must have been regarded with wonder and admiration by all who knew her as a woman of vast and varied knowledge; a woman who could think deeply and talk brilliantly, who could play high and severe classical music like a professional performer, and could bring forth the most delicate and tender aroma of nature and poetry lying deep in the heart of some simple, old-fashioned Scotch or English ballad. Nature, indeed, seemed to have given to this extraordinary woman all the gifts a woman could ask or have—save one. It will not, I hope, be considered a piece of gossiping personality if I allude to a fact which must, some day or other, be part of literary history. Mrs. Lewes is not beautiful. In her appearance there is nothing whatever to attract admiration.

Justin McCarthy, 1872, " 'George Eliot' and George Lewes,"
Modern Leaders, p. 137

However I may lament the circumstances, Westminster Abbey is a Christian church and not a Pantheon, and the Dean thereof is officially a Christian priest, and we ask him to bestow exceptional Christian honours by this burial in the Abbey. George Eliot is known not only as a great writer, but as a person whose life and opinions were in notorious antagonism to Christian practice in regard to marriage, and Christian theory in regard to dogma. How am I to tell the Dean that I think he ought to read over the body of a person who did not repent of what the Church considers mortal sin, a service not one solitary proposition in which she would have accepted for truth while she was alive? How am I to urge him to do that which, if I were in his place, I should most emphatically refuse to do? You tell me that Mrs. Cross wished for the funeral in the Abbey. While I desire to entertain the greatest respect for her wishes, I am very sorry to hear it. I do not understand the feeling which would create such a desire on any personal grounds, save those of affection, and the natural yearning to be near even in death to those whom we have loved. And on public grounds the wish is still less intelligible to me. One cannot eat one's cake and have it too. Those who elect to be free in thought and deed must not hanker after the rewards, if they are to be so called, which the world offers to those who put up with its fetters. Thus, however I look at the proposal it seems to me to be a profound mistake, and I can have nothing to do with it.

Thomas Henry Huxley, 1880, *Letter to Herbert Spencer,* Dec. 27;
Life and Letters, ed. his Son, vol. II, p. 19

George Eliot, when you saw her in repose, had a forbidding countenance. People who did not like her used to say she looked like a horse; a remark which has also been made about a celebrated living actor. It was true so far as this: that the portion of the face below the eyes was disproportionately long and narrow. She had that square fullness of brow over the eyes which Blake had, and which led Blake to affirm that the shape of his head made him a Republican. George Eliot's radicalism went much farther than mere republicanism. She never can have been a beautiful woman, either in face or figure. She was tall, gaunt, angular, without any flowing ease of motion, though with a self-possession and firmness of muscle and fibre which saved her from the shambling awkwardness often the characteristic of long and loose-jointed people. . . . Her eyes were, when she talked, luminous and beautiful, dark in colour and of that unfathomable depth and swift changefulness which are seldom to be seen in the same orbs, except in persons whose force of character and force of intellect are both remarkable. They could be very soft, and she smiled with her eyes as well as with that large mouth of hers; and the smile was full of loveliness when it did not turn to mocking or mark that contemptuous mood which was not, I gather, very infrequent with her. In conversation which did not wake this demon of scornfulness, born of conscious intellectual superiority, the face was full of vivacity and light, whether illuminated by a smile or not.

> George W. Smalley, 1880-91, *George Eliot,* Dec. 25;
> *London Letters and Some Others,* vol. I, pp. 246, 247

The life of Marian Evans had much I never knew—a doom of fruit without the bloom, like the Niger fig:—

> Her losses make our gains ashamed—
> She bore life's empty pack
> As gallantly as if the East
> Were swinging at her back.
> Life's empty pack is heaviest,
> As every porter knows—
> In vain to punish honey,
> It only sweeter grows.

> Emily Dickinson, 1885, *To Thomas Niles, Letters,* vol. II, p. 418

Her speaking voice was, I think, one of the most beautiful I ever heard, and she used it *conscientiously,* if I may say so. I mean that she availed herself of its modulations to give thrilling emphasis to what was profound in her utterances, and sweetness to what was gentle or playful. She bestowed great care, too, on her enunciation, disliking the slipshod mode of pronouncing which is so common. I have several times heard her declare with enthusiasm that ours is a beautiful language, a noble language even to the ear, when properly spoken; and imitate with disgust the short, *snappy*, inarticulate way in which many people utter it.

Thomas Adolphus Trollope, 1888, What I Remember, pp. 470, 471

Her marriage with Mr. John Cross took place on May 6, 1880. It would be wrong to attempt to present any other account of this than that which Mr. Cross has himself given in the life of his wife. The marriage was severely criticized at the time by her best friends. This was due to various causes. Second marriages are absolutely forbidden by the Positivist creed, and her breach of this rule would be sure to alienate all who were of this persuasion. The world, which has forgiven her relations with Lewes on the ground that they arose from an overmastering devotion, was shocked when it found that the affection which had caused such an act of sacrifice was capable of being succeeded by another equally strong. The difference of nearly twenty years between the age of the bride and bridegroom also gave occasion for remark. On the other hand, no one can have studied the character of George Eliot, even superficially, without being convinced how necessary it was for her to have some one to depend upon, and how much her nature yearned for sympathy and support. No better companion could certainly have been found than Mr. Cross, with his strong vigorous sense, manly character, and business habits.

Oscar Browning, 1890, Life of George Eliot
(Great Writers), p. 134

Only her intimate friends knew the exhausting labour which she bestowed on her books, and the untiring patience with which she strove to answer every call made on her attention by friendship, or her own household, or any incident of her literary life. Everything she did was carefully planned and studiously worked out; and whether it was a letter, the visit of a friend, a foreign tour, or the plot of a novel, she put into it the best she had, and the utmost pains to make it perfect. Where she failed at all, I think, was in spontaneity, verve, and *abandon*. This extreme conscientiousness to do everything as well as she could do it gave a certain air of stiffness to her letters, made some of her books overcharged and *langweilig* (this is especially true of *Romola*), and it certainly ruined her poetry.

Frederic Harrison, 1901, George Washington and other
American Addresses, p. 210

MARRIAGE

If there is any one action or relation of my life which is, and always has been profoundly serious, it is my relation to Mr. Lewes. It is, however, natural enough that you should mistake me in many ways for not only are you unacquainted with Mr. Lewes's real character and the course of his actions, but also it is several years now since you and I were much together, and it is possible that the modifications my mind has undergone may be quite in the opposite direction of what you imagine. No one can be better aware than yourself that it is possible for two people to hold different opinions on momentous subjects with equal sincerity, and an equally earnest conviction that their respective opinions are alone the truly moral ones. If we differ on the subject of the marriage laws, I at least can believe of you that you cleave to what you believe to be good; and I don't know of anything in the nature of your views that should prevent you from believing the same of me. *How far* we differ I think we neither of us know, for I am ignorant of your precise views; and, apparently, you attribute to me both feelings and opinions which are not mine. We cannot set each other quite right in this matter in letters, but one thing I can tell you in few words. Light and easily broken ties are what I neither desire theoretically nor could live for practically. Women who are satisfied with such ties do *not* act as I have done. That any unworldly, unsuperstitious person who is sufficiently acquainted with the realities of life can pronounce my relation to Mr. Lewes immoral, I can only understand by remembering how subtile and complex are the influences that mould opinion. But I *do* remember this: and I indulge in no arrogant or uncharitable thoughts about those who condemn us, even though we might have expected a somewhat different verdict. From the majority of persons, of course, we never looked for anything but condemnation. We are leading no life of self-indulgence, except, indeed, that, being happy in each other, we find everything easy. We are working hard to provide for others better than we provide for ourselves, and to fulfil every responsibility that lies upon us. Levity and pride would not be a sufficient basis for that.

George Eliot, 1855, *To Mrs. Bray,* Sept. 4;
George Eliot's Life as related in her Letters and Journals,
ed. Cross, vol. I, p. 235

Of her relations to Lewes it seems to me discussion is not now possible. It is known that Lewes's wife had once left him, that he had generously condoned the offence and received her again, and that in a year she again eloped; the laws of England make such a condonation preclude divorce; Lewes was thus prevented from legally marrying again by a technicality of the law which converted his own generosity into a penalty; under these circumstances George Eliot, moved surely by pure love, took up her residence with him, and according to universal account, not only was a faithful wife to him for twenty years until his death, but was a devoted mother to his children. That her failure to go through the form of marriage was not due to any contempt for that form, as has sometimes been absurdly alleged, is conclusively shown by the fact that when she married Mr. Cross a year and a half after Lewes's death, the ceremony was performed according to the regular rites of the Church of England.

Sidney Lanier, 1881, The English Novel, p. 298

Society was at first as stern to George Eliot after her domestic intimacy with Lewes as Mrs. Carlyle had been. I remember hearing an instance of this some years after that connection was formed. Lewes and George Eliot once thought of establishing a domicile in Kent, and a south-eastern semi-suburb of London, much tenanted by wealthy city-people. When news of the intention of the distinguished pair reached the denizens of the region a council of male and female heads of families was held to consider whether George Eliot should be "received." It was decided that she should not. As is well known, public opinion altered in course of time, and ultimately, the lady rejected by London citizens was courted and caressed by daughters of Queen Victoria herself.

Francis Espinasse, 1893, Literary Recollections and
Sketches, p. 300

George Eliot's more transcendental friends never forgave her for marrying. In a morally immoral manner they washed their virtuous hands of her. I could not help thinking it was the most natural thing for the poor woman to do. She was a heavily laden but interesting derelict, tossing among the breakers, without oars or rudder, and all at once the brave Cross arrives, throws her a rope, and gallantly tows her into harbour. I am sure that she was very sensitive, and must have had many a painful half-hour as the help-mate of Mr. Lewes. By accepting the position, she had placed herself in opposition to the moral instincts of most of those whom she held most dear. Though intellectually self-contained, I believe she was singularly dependent on the emotional side of her nature. With her, as with nearly all women, she needed a something to lean upon. Though her conduct was socially indefensible, it would have been cruel, it would be stupid, to judge her exactly as one would judge an ordinary offender. What a genius she must have had to have been able to draw so many high-minded people to her! I have an impression that she felt her position acutely, and was unhappy. George Eliot was much to be pitied. I think she knew that I felt for her. . . for more than once, when I was taking leave, she said, "Come and see me soon, Mr. Locker; don't lose sight of us." And this to an outsider, a nobody, and not in her set!

Frederick Locker-Lampson, 1895, My Confidences, p. 316

Scenes of Clerical Life (1857-58)

I trouble you with a MS. of *Sketches of Clerical Life* which was submitted to me by a friend who desired my good offices with you. It goes by this post. I confess that before reading the MS. I had considerable doubts of my friend's powers as a writer of fiction; but, after reading it, these doubts were changed into very high admiration. I don't know what you will think of the story, but, according to my judgment, such humor, pathos, vivid presentation, and nice observation have not been exhibited (in this style) since the *Vicar of Wakefield;* and, in consequence of that opinion, I feel quite pleased in negotiating the matter with you.

> George Henry Lewes, 1856, *Letter to John Blackwood,* Nov. 6;
> *George Eliot's Life as related in her Letters and Journals,*
> ed. Cross, vol. I, p. 300

My Dear Sir,—I have been so strongly affected by the two first tales in the book you have had the kindness to send me, through Messrs. Blackwood, that I hope you will excuse my writing to you to express my admiration of their extraordinary merit. The exquisite truth and delicacy both of the humor and the pathos of these stories, I have never seen the like of; and they have impressed me in a manner that I should find it very difficult to describe to you, if I had the impertinence to try. In addressing these few words of thankfulness to the creator of the Sad Fortunes of the Rev. Amos Barton, and the sad love-story of Mr. Gilfil, I am (I presume) bound to adopt the name that it pleases that excellent writer to assume. I can suggest no better one: but I should have been strongly disposed, if I had been left to my own devices, to address the said writer as a woman. I have observed what seemed to me such womanly touches in those moving fictions, that the assurance on the title-page is insufficient to satisfy me even now. If they originated with no woman, I believe that no man ever before had the art of making himself mentally so like a woman since the world began.

> Charles Dickens, 1858, *To George Eliot,* Jan. 17;
> *George Eliot's Life as related in her Letters and Journals,*
> ed. Cross, vol. II, p. 2

You would not, I imagine, care much for flattering speeches, and to go into detail about the books would carry me farther than at present there is occasion to go. I can only thank you most sincerely for the delight which it has given me; and both I myself, and my wife, trust that the acquaintance which we seem to have made with you through your writings may improve into something more tangible. I do not know whether I am addressing a young man or an old—clergyman or a layman. Perhaps, if you answer this note, you may give us some information about yourself. But at any rate, should business or pleasure bring you into this part of the world, pray believe that you will find a warm welcome if you will accept our hospitality.

James Anthony Froude, 1858, To George Eliot, Jan. 17;
George Eliot's Life as related in her Letters and Journals,
ed. Cross, vol. II, p. 4

The *Scenes of Clerical Life* were to George Eliot's future works what a bold, spirited sketch is to a carefully elaborated picture. All the qualities that distinguished her genius may be discovered in this, her first essay in fiction. With all Miss Austen's matchless faculty for painting commonplace characters, George Eliot has that other nobler faculty of showing what tragedy, pathos, and humor may be lying in the experience of a human soul "that looks out through dull gray eyes and that speaks in a voice of quite ordinary tones."

Mathilde Blind, 1883, George Eliot (Famous Women), p. 130

A piece of work which in all her after life, George Eliot never surpassed. It was probably only the humourous *mise en scène,* the delightful picture of the village and the surrounding farms and their inhabitants, Mrs. Hackett, and her neighbours, which he (Mr. Lewes) read in that tremendous moment while the author stood by, not the least aware that her faltering essay was in fact, in its brevity and humility, as perfect a work of genius as ever was given to the world.

Margaret O. W. Oliphant, 1892, The Victorian Age
of English Literature, p. 465

Adam Bede (1859)

When on October 29, I had written to the end of the love-scene at the Farm between Adam and Dinah, I sent the MS. to Blackwood, since the remainder of the third volume could not affect the judgment passed on what had gone before. He wrote back in warm admiration, and offered me, on the part of the firm, £800 for four years' copyright. I accepted the offer. The last words of the third volume were written and despatched on their way to Edinburgh, November the 16th, and now on the last day of the same month I have written this slight history of my book. I love it very much, and am deeply thankful to have written it, whatever the public may say to it—a result which is still in darkness, for I have at present had only four sheets of the proof.

George Eliot, 1858, Journal, Nov. 16; George Eliot's Life
as related in her Letters and Journals, ed. Cross, vol. II, p. 51

That beautiful Dinah Morris you will remember in *Adam Bede,*—solemn, fragile, strong, Dinah Morris, the woman-preacher whom I find haunting my imagination in strange but entrancing unions of the most diverse forms, as if, for instance, a snowdrop could also be St. Paul, as if a kiss could be a gospel, as if a lovely phrase of Chopin's most inward music should become suddenly an Apocalypse revealing us Christ in the flesh,—that rare, pure and marvelous Dinah Morris who would alone consecrate English literature if it had yielded no other gift to man. . . . This publication of *Adam Bede* placed George Eliot decisively at the head of English novel-writers, with only Dickens for second, even.

> Sidney Lanier, 1881, *The English Novel*, pp. 165, 203

Whether, in Dinah Morris, George Eliot intended to represent Mrs. Evans or not, she did represent her faithfully and fully. . . . The only point at which the writer has deviated from fact is the marriage of Dinah and Adam. As a matter of fact the real Dinah married Seth Bede (Samuel Evans). Adam was George Eliot's father, Robert Evans.

> L. Buckley, 1882, "Dinah Morris and Mrs. Elizabeth Evans," *Century Magazine*, vol. 24, p. 552

The first and last master-piece of George Eliot. *Adam Bede* breaks upon the reader with all the freshness and truth of nature. Every element influencing character is expressed in the workings of the very souls of the rural, half-educated folk acting out their lives according to their conscience, their early training and their personal character. Their beliefs are there, and their lives are colored by their beliefs.

> Patrick Francis Mullany (Brother Azarias), 1889, *Books and Reading*, p. 39

It is of all her books the heartiest, the wittiest, the most cheerful, or rather the least desponding. In that book it may be that she exhausted herself and her own resources of observation as an eye-witness. She wrote fine things in other veins, in different scenes, and she conceived other characters and new situations. But, for all practical purposes *Adam Bede* was the typical romance which everything she had thought or known impelled her to write, in which she told the best of what she had seen and the most important of what she had to say. Had she never written anything but *Adam Bede,* she would have had a special place of her own in English romance: —and I am not sure that anything else which she produced very materially raised, enlarged, or qualified that place.

> Frederic Harrison, 1895, *Studies in Early Victorian Literature*, p. 213

No one of George Eliot's novels has given to the world a larger number of clear and memorable portraits. The weakness and vanity of Hetty, the thoughtless profligacy of the not wholly evil Donnithrone, the genial common sense and humor of Parson Irwine, the rapt and mystic yet most practical piety of Dinah Morris, and the shrewd wit and caustic proverbs of Mrs. Poyser. All these are household words. Of the picture of the hero, Adam Bede himself, the present Bishop Wilkinson once said in his pulpit that it seemed to him the best presentment in modern guise and colour of the earthly circumstances which surrounded the life of the divine Founder of Christianity, as he toiled in the carpenter's shop, to supply His own, His mother's wants. That surely is no commonplace effort of fiction which throws any illustrative light, however faint or broken, on the sacred narrative of human redemption.

> George W. E. Russell, 1896, "George Eliot Revisited,"
> *The Contemporary Review,* vol. 65

The Mill on the Floss (1860)

It is a masterly fragment of fictitious biography in two volumes, followed by a second-rate one-volume novel,—the three connected into a single whole by very inadequate links. . . . Yet, *The Mill on the Floss* is a book of great genius. Its overflowing humor would alone class its author high among the humorists, and there are some sketches in it of English country life which have all the vivacity and not a little of the power of Sir Walter Scott's best works.

> Richard Holt Hutton, 1871, "George Eliot,"
> *Essays in Literary Criticism*

Few or none, I should suppose, of the most passionate and intelligent admirers would refuse to accept *The Mill on the Floss* as on the whole at once the highest and the purest and the fullest example of her magnificent and matchless powers—for matchless altogether, as I have already insisted, they undoubtedly are in their own wide and fruitful field of work. The first two-thirds of the book suffice to compose perhaps the very noblest of tragic as well as of humorous prose idyls in the language; comprising, as they likewise do, one of the sweetest as well as saddest and tenderest as well as subtlest examples of dramatic analysis—a study in that kind as soft and true as Rousseau's, as keen and true as Browning's, as full as either of the fine and bitter sweetness of a pungent and fiery fidelity. But who can forget the horror of inward collapse, the sickness of spiritual reaction, the reluctant incredulous rage of disenchantment and disgust, with which the first came upon the thrice unhappy third part?

> Algernon Charles Swinburne, 1877, *A Note on*
> *Charlotte Brontë,* p. 28

I suppose it is her best book, though it may not contain her best scenes. The objection which is often made and still oftener felt to the repulsiveness of Maggie's worship of a counter-jumping cad like Stephen, is somewhat uncritical. I suspect that most women resent it, because they feel the imputation to be true: and most men out of a not wholly dissimilar feeling which acts a little differently.

George Saintsbury, 1895, Corrected Impressions, p. 165

A work in which passion and the tumult of the soul are not objectively analyzed but sympathetically portrayed with unsurpassed vividness and elemental power, a work which is undisputably one of the great literary epitomes of the pathos and tragedy of human existence—it is hard to reconcile one's self to the evolution in which temperament disappeared so completely in devotion to the intellect alone as to result in the jejune artificiality of *Daniel Deronda.*

W. C. Brownell, 1900, "George Eliot," Scribner's Magazine,
vol. 28, p. 273

Silas Marner (1861)

To a certain extent, I think *Silas Marner* holds a higher place than any of the author's works. It is more nearly a masterpiece; it has more of that simple, rounded, consummate aspect, that absence of loose ends and gaping issues, which marks a classical work.

Henry James, 1866, "The Novels of George Eliot,"
Atlantic Monthly, vol. 18, p. 482

Men of letters, I believe, give the palm to *Silas Marner.* They are attracted by the exquisite workmanship of the story. The plot was constructed by George Eliot out of the merest hint. The story was written in haste, at one gush. It is a perfect gem—a pure work of art, in which the demands of art have alone to be considered.

Oscar Browning, 1888, "The Art of George Eliot,"
Fortnightly Review, vol. 49, p. 538

In Silas Marner George Eliot is a little tempted to fall into the error of the amiable novelists who are given to playing the part of Providence to their character. It is true that the story begins by a painful case of apparent injustice. . . . A modern "realist" would, I suppose, complain that she had omitted, or touched too slightly for his taste, a great many repulsive and brutal elements in the rustic world. The portraits, indeed, are so vivid as to convince us of their fidelity, but she has selected the less ugly, and taken the point of view from which we see mainly what was wholesome and kindly in the little village community. Silas Marner is a masterpiece in that way, and scarcely equalled in English literature, unless by Mr. Hardy's rustics in *Far From the Madding Crowd* and other early works.

Leslie Stephen, 1902, *George Eliot*
(*English Men of Letters*), pp. 107, 110

Romola (1863)

George Eliot first went astray in *Romola*. All her previous works had been living products of the imagination,—*Romola was manufactured*. A very great piece of work, unquestionably: a piece of work that perhaps produces a higher sense of the writer's immense and diversified *force* than any of her other works; but bearing the same relation to art, when compared with Hetty or Janet, that an elaborate imitation of one of the great Italian masters does when compared with a bit of true rainy sky by Turner or one of Wilkie's dirty boy-faces.

John Skelton, 1868, "Poetry and George Eliot,"
Fraser's Magazine, vol. 78, p. 470

Her *Romola* is one of the finest historical novels in our language, yet it was a publisher's failure. Its style was too pure, its art too refined, its pictures too clearly and faithfully drawn, for the readers of her former works. But the book lifted her instantly into a new importance in the estimate of the small class whose verdict is but another term for fame.

Bayard Taylor, 1876, *Essays and Notes,* p. 339

I have just read through the cheap edition of *Romola,* and though I have only made a few alterations of an important kind—the printing being unusually correct—it would be well for me to send this copy to be printed from. I think it must be nearly ten years since I read the book before, but there is no book of mine about which I more thoroughly feel that I could swear by every sentence as having been written with my best blood, such as it is, and with the most ardent care for veracity of which my nature is capable. It has made me often sob with a sort of painful joy as I have read the sentences which had faded from my memory. This helps one to bear false representations with patience; for I really don't love any Gentleman who undertakes to state my opinions well enough to desire that I should find myself all wrong in order to justify this statement.

George Eliot, 1877, *To John Blackwood,* Jan. 30;
George Eliot's Life as related in her Letters and Journals,
ed. Cross, vol. III, p. 217

In *Silas Marner,* beautiful and complete in itself as it is, we have only the preface, to which *Romola* is the accomplished fact. While *Silas Marner* is perfect in its simplicity, *Romola* is great in its complexity. We must remember the stupendous historic background of the story—Florence with all her ancient grandeur, her teeming inhabitants with their cries of joy, of pain, of hope, of revenge; and above all is heard the clarion voice of Savonarola rushing through the Florentine soul like a mad river. All this gigantic background is conjured up to show—what? The evolution of one beautiful life! Great and good people always leave their souls behind them, whether it be in statuary, or books, or deeds. George Eliot has left her living soul with Romola.

> Thomas Dawson, 1895, "Character Development in *Romola,*"
> *Four Years of Novel-Reading,* ed. Moulton, p. 93

Romola is unique in its way, and has hosts of admirers. There are readers to whom it introduced the Italian Renaissance, who, in its pages first read of Florence, Savonarola, the Medici. There are scholars who shared George Eliot's enthusiasm for "The City by the Arno" and "the wonderful fifteenth century," so cordially as to credit *Romola* with having successfully reproduced a moment and a *milieu* which they were only too grateful to have recalled. Besides, there is that master-piece of evolution, the character of Tito Melema.

> W. C. Brownell, 1900, "George Eliot," *Scribner's Magazine,*
> vol. 28, p. 724

It would be absurd to speak without profound respect of a book which represents the application of an exceptionally powerful intellect carrying out a great scheme with so serious and sustained a purpose. . . . Romola is to me one of the most provoking of books. I am alternately seduced into admiration and repelled by what seems to me a most lamentable misapplication of first rate powers. . . . If we can put aside the historical paraphernalia, forget the dates and the historical Savonarola and Machiavelli, there remains a singularly powerful representation of an interesting spiritual history; of the ordeal through which a lofty nature has to pass when brought into collision with characters of baser composition; throw into despair by the successive collapses of each of the supports to which it clings; and finding some solution in spite of its bewilderment amidst conflicting gospels, in each of which truth and falsehood are strangely mixed. There is hardly any novel, except *The Mill on the Floss,* in which the stages in the inner life of a thoughtful and tender nature are set forth with so much tenderness and sympathy.

> Leslie Stephen, 1902, *George Eliot*
> (*English Men of Letters*), pp. 125, 126, 141

Felix Holt contains at least the lovable Mr. Lyon, and though the weari-some wordiness of the book is a handicap from which it will always suffer, it will always remain a highly interpretative picture of a momentous epoch in English political and social history—the birth, in fact, of the modern English world engendered by the Reform Bill.

> W. C. Brownell, 1900, "George Eliot," *Scribner's Magazine,*
> vol. 28, p. 724

Mr. Felix Holt would have been quite in his place at Toynbee Hall; but is much too cold-blooded for the time when revolution and confiscation were really in the air. Perhaps this indicates the want of masculine fiber in George Eliot and the deficient sympathy with rough popular passions which makes us feel that he represents the afterthought of the judicious sociologist and not the man of flesh and blood who was the product of the actual conditions. Anyhow, the novel appears to be regarded as her least interesting.

> Leslie Stephen, 1902, *George Eliot*
> (*English Men of Letters*), p. 155

Middlemarch (1871-72)

I suppose you cannot have read *Middlemarch,* as you say nothing about it. It stands quite alone. As one only just moistens one's lips with an ex-quisite liqueur, to keep the taste as long as possible in one's mouth, I never read more than a single chapter of *Middlemarch* in the evening, dreading to come to the last, when I must wait two months for a renewal of the pleasure. The depth of humour has certainly never been surpassed in English literature. If there is ever a shade too much learning, that is Lewes' fault.

> Connop Thirlwall, 1872, *Letters to a Friend,*
> ed. Stanley, June 4, p. 278

The book has all the multifariousness of life; the author has, as it were, created a world in which we see the diverse feelings, passions, and interests of complicated characters without the veils of self adulation or of exag-gerated distrust with which we view our own lives, or the prejudice with which we regard those of our neighbors. Ordinary terms of praise sound insipid before the excellence with which this task is done. The very truth which this writer possesses seems so like simplicity that we feel inclined to take it for granted as a *sine qua non,* which we ought to accept with as little emotion as we do the air we breathe. . . . One of the most remarkable books of one of the greatest living writers. . . . From its wonderful accuracy in depicting life, from the morality of its lesson, from the originality, keenness, and fate-like sternness of the author, we may draw the conclusion that it is a book which every one should read for a wide knowledge of the world.

S. S. Perry, 1873, "George Eliot's *Middlemarch*,"
North American Review, vol. 116, pp. 433, 440

Despite the vigorous bloom, the inconsistent life of *Middlemarch,* do we not feel that there is an overwrought completion about it? The persons of the story are elaborated almost to exhaustion; there appears to be a lack of proportion in the prominence so fully accorded to each individual in his or her turn, for minor characters are dwelt upon too much in detail; and there is little or no mystery of distance about any of the figures, at any time. . . . As an effort of clear intellectual penetration into life, we could hardly demand anything better than *Middlemarch.* But it is still too much an effort, and not enough an accomplished insight; it remains, as the author has called it, a study, rather than a finished dramatic representation.

George Parsons Lathrop, 1874, "Growth of the Novel,"
Atlantic Monthly, vol. 33, pp. 688, 689

It is a great prose epic, large in size, commanding in structure, affording an ample space for a great artist to work upon. Perhaps even more than *Adam Bede* has it become part of the ordinary furniture of our minds, of the current coin of our thoughts. Casaubon, Will Laidlaw, Mr. Brooks are types which are ever present with us, like Becky Sharp and Colonel Newcome; and if Dorothea and Lydgate are more remote, it is because they are rarer characters, not because they are less truly drawn. *Middlemarch* gives George Eliot the chiefest claim to stand by the side of Shakespere. Both drew their inspiration from the same sources, the villages and the country houses which we know so well.

Oscar Browning, 1890, *Life of George Eliot*
(*Great Writers*), p. 142

In truth, *Middlemarch* is to me as a landscape seen in the twilight; *au teint grisâtre.* It is from first to last the plaint of a lost ideal. I do not think it even a true rendering of life as it was lived in England sixty years ago. It would be easy to account for this by saying that the writer had lost "the wider hope." I prefer not to do it. Such an explanation is, indeed, so far obviously true as that in a country town the most strenuous belief, the most unflagging work, is religious. But the scepticism of *Middlemarch* also extends to things social and human.

Bessie Rayner Belloc, 1894, *In A Walled Garden,* pp. 6, 12

It is, indeed, a half dozen novels in one. Its scale is cyclopædic, as I said, and it is the microcosm of a community rather than a story concerned with a unified plot and set of characters. And it is perhaps the writer's fullest expression of her philosophy of life.

> W. C. Brownell, 1900, "George Eliot," *Scribner's Magazine*,
> vol. 28, p. 724

Daniel Deronda (1876)

Here we have what goes a considerable way towards filling an intellectual void—faithful pictures of modern Anglo-Jewish domestic life. But the author in some respects proceeds further, and evidently possesses loftier and wider aims than the mere exercise of the romance-writer's skill among new scenes. George Eliot has thrown no hasty or superficial glance over the externals of Judaism. She has acquired an extended and profound knowledge of the rites, aspirations, hopes, fears, and desires of the Israelites of the day. She had read their books, inquired into their modes of thought, searched their traditions, accompanied them to the synagogue; nay, she had taken their very words from their lips, and, like Asmodeus, has unroofed their houses. To say that some slight errors have crept into *Daniel Deronda* is to say that no human work is perfect; and these inaccuracies are singularly few and unimportant. . . . Curiously enough the Jewish episodes in *Daniel Deronda* have been barely adverted to by the reviewers. Most of these gentlemen have slurred over some of the finest and most characteristic passages in the book, with the remark that they possessed no general interest. Possibly the critics were unable to appreciate the beauty of the scenes they deemed unworthy of attention, or perhaps they consider the Jewish body too insignificant to be worth much discussion. . . . The book is a romance. Artistic truth in literature, as in painting, is always sought for by great workmen in preference to mere realistic truth. In Daniel Deronda, George Eliot has created a type which, though scarcely likely to appeal to the masses, ought to teach more than one lesson to serious thinkers. Here is a man who lays aside entirely all purely personal considerations, all feelings of ambition or aggrandisement, to devote the best years of his existence to the loftiest national aims.

> James Picciotto, 1876, "Deronda the Jew,"
> *Gentleman's Magazine*, N. S., vol. 17, pp. 594, 595, 597

Daniel Deronda alone (the book, not the man) is proof enough that its author has the courage to enter upon the surest road to the highest kind of popularity—that which apparently leads above it. There is not a sentence, scarcely a character, in *Daniel Deronda* that reads or looks as if she were thinking of her critics before her readers at large, or of her readers at large before the best she could give them. She has often marred a stronger or more telling effect for the sake of a truer and deeper—and this belongs to a kind of courage which most artists will be inclined to envy her. But her processes of construction open another question, too long to speak of in a few words. Apart from all considerations of such processes in detail, *Daniel Deronda* is a probably unique example of the application of the forms of romance to a rare and difficult problem in human nature, by first stating the problem—(the transformation of Gwendolen)—in its extremest form, and then, with something like scientific precision as well as a philosophic insight, arranging circumstances so as to throw upon it the fullest light possible.

R. E. Francillon, 1876, "George Eliot's First Romance,"
Gentleman's Magazine, N. S., vol. 17, p. 427

It seems to us that none of George Eliot's former novels so distinctly present the quality of her intellect, as *Daniel Deronda*. In it she has reached both her clearest height of achievement and the barriers of art which she is unable to scale. It is no disparagement to recognize the latter, for they equally mark the extent of her development and the intensity of her aspiration. In reviewing the first volume of the work we noticed her tendency to analyze, as well as present, her characters. She explains, and comments upon them, their words, movements, and changes of countenance: sometimes a chapter seems to open in some realm of abstract philosophical speculation, out of which the author slowly descends to take up the thread of her story. Sometimes these disquisitions are so sound and admirably stated that we are glad to come upon them: frequently they strike us as unnecessary and not particularly important; and occasionally they are mere high-sounding platitudes.

Bayard Taylor, 1876, *Essays and Notes,* p. 340

The first thing that it is natural for a Jew to say about *Daniel Deronda* is some expression of gratitude for the wonderful completeness and accuracy with which George Eliot has portrayed the Jewish nature. Hitherto the Jew in English fiction has fared unhappily; being always represented as a monstrosity, most frequently on the side of malevolence and greed, as in Marlowe's Barabbas and Dickens's Fagin, or sometimes as in Dicken's Riah, still more exasperatingly on the side of impossible benevolence. What we want is truth, not exaggeration, and truth George Eliot has given us with the large justice of the great artist. The gallery of Jewish portraits contained in *Daniel Deronda* gives in a marvelously full and accurate way all the many sides of our complex national character. . . . Perhaps the most successful of the minor portraits is that of the black sheep Lapidoth, the Jew with no redeeming love for family, race or country to preserve him from the sordid egotism (the new name for wickedness) into which he has sunk. His utter unconsciousness of good and evil is powerfully depicted in the masterly analysis of his state of mind before purloining Deronda's ring. . . . Criticism on the Mordecai part of *Daniel Deronda* has been due to lack of sympathy and want of knowledge on the part of the critics, and hence its failure is not (if we must use the word) objective. If a young lady refuses to see any pathos in Othello's fate because she dislikes dark complexions, we blame the young lady, not Shakspeare; and if the critics have refused to see the pathos of Mordecai's fate because he is a Jew of the present day—so much the worse for the critics!

Joseph Jacobs, 1877, "Mordecai: a Protest against the Critics,"
Jewish Ideals, pp. 61, 64, 82

Beside the clever critics some readers of *Daniel Deronda* ought perhaps to put on record their experience, and confess what have been the dealings of this book with their spirits. Those who have heard in it "the right voice," which one follows "as the water follows the moon, silently," will have been conscious of a quickening and exaltation of their entire spiritual life. The moral atmosphere they breathed became charged with a finer and more vivifying element; the face of the world seemed to glow for them with richer tint, "a more vivid gravity of expression"; moods of *ennui* or rebellion appeared more futile and unworthy than formerly; it became natural to believe high things of man; and a certain difficulty and peril attended the necessary return to duller or at least humbler tempers of heart (as it is difficult to pass from a sonata of Beethoven to the common household sounds) until these too were touched and received a consecration. The book has done something to prevent our highest movements from making our everyday experience seem vulgar and incoherent, and something to prevent our every-day experience from making our highest moments seem spectral and unreal. To discover the central motive of *Daniel Deronda* it should be studied in connection with its immediate predecessor, *Middlemarch*.

Edward Dowden, 1877-78, *Studies in Literature*, p. 277

I repeat that the story of Gwendolen and Grandcourt takes its place beside the author's best work: and that, if the character-drawing is not stronger, it is at any rate subtler and more scientific. Gwendolen's conversation with Klesmer on her vocation as an actress, her interview with Mirah when she wishes to ascertain the truth of the rumors she has heard about Deronda, the tragedy on board the boat in the Gulf of Genoa, the good-byes and the confessions at the moment of final separation, are among the scenes, hard to manage, or even unmanageable, where the genius of George Eliot, compact at once of tact and power, breaks out in all its supremacy.

Edmond Scherer, 1877-91, *"Daniel Deronda," Essays on English Literature,* tr. Saintsbury, p. 62

The story of Gwendolen in *Deronda,* up to the moment of her marriage, is one of the most masterly of impersonations. When, however, a female perfection comes in the shape of Dorothea, and still more a male perfection in the form of Daniel Deronda, this admirable genius fails and sinks into morasses of fictitious imagination, and laboured utterance. Her true inspiration had nothing to do with these artificial and fantastic embodiments of new philosophy and a conventional ideal.

Margaret O. W. Oliphant, 1892, *The Victorian Age of English Literature,* p. 469

One day she told me that in order to write *Daniel Deronda,* she had read through two hundred books. I longed to tell her that she had better have learned Yiddish and talked with two hundred Jews, and been taught, as I was by my friend Solomon the Sadducee, the art of distinguishing Fraülein Löwenthal of the Ashkenazim from Senorita Aguado of the Sephardim *by the corners of their eyes!*

Charles Godfrey Leland, 1893, *Memoirs,* p. 390

The chief sign of decline in George Eliot's last novel, *Daniel Deronda,* is the attempt to replace these vigorous living beings with badly imagined puppets like the Meyricks. She had used up the material of her youth, and found nothing in her brilliant life of culture and travel to take its place.

William Vaughn Moody and Robert Morss Lovett, 1902, *A History of English Literature,* p. 377

Impressions of Theophrastus Such (1879)

A great authoress of our time was urged by a friend to fill up a gap in our literature by composing a volume of Thoughts: the result was that least felicitous of performances, *Theophrastus Such.*

John Morley, 1887, "Aphorisms," *Studies in Literature,* p. 71

The summer of 1878 was partly occupied by George Eliot in writing *Theophrastus Such*—perhaps the only one of her books which was not a success. I have a guilty conscience as to this book, as I may have contributed to induce her to write it. I pointed out to her that our English literature, so rich and splendid in almost every field of poetry and prose, was deficient in those collections of Thoughts which the French call *Pensées*—pregnant apothegms embedded in terse and memorable phrase which would be remembered like fine lines of poetry, and be cited as readily as a familiar proverb. It seemed to me—it seems to me still—that she was eminently fitted to produce such a book, and indeed the *Wit and Wisdom of George Eliot* was a volume culled from her writings. But *Theophrastus Such*—where the queer title came from I know not—was not an adequate expression of her powers. She was in very poor health all the time, and George Lewes was then stricken with his last illness. His death delayed publication, and when she read *Theophrastus* in revise, she had serious thoughts of suppressing it. . . . Would she had done so! Her life was ebbing away when it was actually published.

> Frederic Harrison, 1901, "Reminiscences of George Eliot,"
> *Harper's Magazine,* vol. 103, p. 582

POEMS

We imagine George Eliot is quite philosopher enough, having produced her poems mainly as a kind of experimental entertainment for her own mind, to let them commend themselves to the public on any grounds whatever which will help to illustrate the workings of versatile intelligence,—as interesting failures, if nothing better. She must feel they are interesting; an exaggerated modesty cannot deny that. . . . In whatever George Eliot writes, you have the comfortable certainty, infrequent in other quarters, of finding an idea, and you get the substance of her thought in the short poems, without the somewhat rigid envelope of her poetic diction. If we may say, broadly, that the supreme merit of a poem is in having warmth, and that it is less valuable in proportion as it cools by too long waiting upon either fastidious skill or inefficient skill, the little group of verses entitled "Brother and Sister" deserve our preference.

> Henry James, 1874, "George Eliot's Legend of Jubal,"
> *North American Review,* vol. 119, p. 485

George Eliot's metrical work has special interest, coming from a woman acknowledged to be, in her realistic yet imaginative prose, at the head of living female writers. She has brought all her energies to bear, first upon the construction of a drama, which was only a *succes d'estime,* and recently upon a new volume containing "The Legend of Jubal" and other poems. The result shows plainly that Mrs. Lewes, though possessed of great intellect and sensibility, is not, in respect to metrical expression, a poet. Nor has she a full conception of the simple strength and melody of English verse, her polysyllable language, noticeable in the moralizing passages of *Middle-*

march, being very ineffective in her poems. That wealth of thought which atones for all her deficiencies in prose does not seem to be at her command in poetry. *The Spanish Gypsy* reads like a second-rate production of the Byronic school. "The Legend of Jubal" and "How Lisa Loved the King" suffer by comparison with the narrative poems, in rhymed pentameter, of Morris, Longfellow, or Stoddard. A little poem in blank-verse, entitled "O may I join the choir invisible!" and setting forth her conception of the "religion of humanity," is worth all the rest of her poetry, for it is the outburst of an exalted soul foregoing personal immortality and compensated by a vision of the growth and happiness of the human race.

Edmund Clarence Stedman, 1875-87, Victorian Poets, p. 254

The fatal objection to *The Spanish Gypsy,* and to all George Eliot's poems, is that, save for a few lines here and there, they might as well, or better, have been written in prose.

Herbert Paul, 1901, "George Eliot," The Nineteenth Century,
vol. 51, p. 938

GENERAL

It is one of the greatest merits of the greatest living writer of fiction,—of the authoress of *Adam Bede,*—that she never brings you to anything without preparing you for it; she has no loose lumps of beauty, she puts in nothing at random: after her greatest scenes, too, a natural sequence of subordinate realities again tones down the mind to this sublunary world. Her logical style—the most logical, probably, which a woman ever wrote—aids in this matter her natural sense of due proportion; there is not a space of incoherency, not a gap. It is not natural to begin with the point of a story, and she does not begin with it; when some great marvel has been told, we all wish to know what came of it, and she tells us. Her natural way—as it seems to those who do not know its rarity—of telling what happened, produces the consummate effect of gradual enchantment and as gradual disenchantment.

Walter Bagehot, 1864, Sterne and Thackeray, Works,
ed. Morgan, vol. II, p. 167

From the time when the interesting *Scenes of a Clerical Life* were published, down to the issue of *Felix Holt,* George Eliot has the great merit of being true to herself. . . . The corruption which a life of fiction-writing, like a life of politics, is apt to produce, has not been able to dull her moral sense, nor to rust the keenness of her sympathy for the sorrows and joys of men and women. Even the wearing effects of time she shows but little.

She has neither become a cynic, nor a humorist, nor coarse, but still keeps in the path of realistic art, studying the roadside nature, and satisfied with it. She continues to receive the great reward which every true realist longs for, that she is true to nature without degenerating to the commonplace, and the old blame, that they have not enough of the ideal, which they covet too.   •

Arthur G. Sedgwick, 1866, "Felix Holt the Radical,"
North American Review, vol. 103, p. 557

To exalt the social and abase the selfish principle, to show the futility of merely personal claims, cares and cravings, to purify the passions by exhibiting their fatal or miserable issues when they are centered in the individual alone—such are the moral purposes which we feel at work beneath all her artistic purposes. . . . The flow of George Eliot's writing, we have felt, is apt to be impeded with excess of thought; while of writing which does flow, and in flowing carry the reader delightfully along, George Sand is an incomparable mistress. But this is only the sign of deeper differences. George Sand excels in the poetical part of her art. George Eliot excels in the philosophical. Each is equally mistress of human nature and its secrets, but the one more by instinct, the other more by reflection. In everything which is properly matter of the intellect, the English writer is the superior of the French by far.

Sidney Colvin, 1876, "Daniel Deronda," Fortnightly Review,
vol. 26, pp. 602, 614

At the present moment George Eliot is the first of English novelists, and I am disposed to place her second of those of my time. She is best known to the literary world as a writer of prose fiction, and not improbably whatever of permanent fame she may acquire will come from her novels. But the nature of her intellect is very far removed indeed from that which is common to the tellers of stories. Her imagination is, no doubt, strong, but it acts in analyzing rather than in creating. Everything that comes before her is pulled to pieces so that the inside of it shall be seen, and be seen, if possible, by her readers as clearly as by herself. This searching analysis is carried so far that in studying her later writings, one feels one's self to be in company with some philosopher rather than with a novelist. I doubt whether any young person can read with pleasure either <i>Felix Holt, Middlemarch,</i> or <i>Daniel Deronda.</i> I know that they are very difficult to many that are not young. Her personifications of character have been singularly terse and graphic and from them has come her great hold on the public, though by no means the greatest effect which she has produced. The lessons which she teaches remain, though it is not for the sake of the lessons that her pages are read. Seth Bede, Adam Bede, Maggie and Tom Tulliver, old Silas Marner, and, much above all, Tito, in *Romola,* are characters, which when once known, can never be forgotten. I cannot say quite so much for any of those in her later works, because in them the philosopher so greatly overtops the portrait-painter, that, in the dissection of the mind, the outward signs seem to have been forgotten. In her, as yet, there is no symptom whatever of that weariness of mind which, when felt by the reader, induces him to declare that the author has written himself out. It is not from decadence that we do not have another Mrs. Poyser, but because the author soars to things which seem to her to be higher than Mrs. Poyser.

Anthony Trollope, 1882-83, Autobiography, p. 178

That she did teach positivism is unfortunately true, so far as her literary touch and expression is concerned. That philosophy affects all her books with its subtly insinuating flavor, and it gives meaning and bias to most of them. They thus gain in definiteness of purpose, in moral vigor, in minutely faithful study of some phases of human experience, and in a massive impression of thoughtfulness which her work creates. At the same time, they undoubtedly lose in value as studies of life; in free range of expression for her genius, her poetry and her art; and in that spiritual vision which looks forward with keen gazing eyes of hope and confident inquiry. Her teaching, like most teaching, is a mingled good and evil.

George Willis Cooke, 1883, George Eliot: A Critical Study
of Her Life, Writings and Philosophy, pp. 413, 414, 418

In George Eliot, a reader with a conscience may be reminded of the saying that when a man opens Tacitus he puts himself into the confessional. She was no vague dreamer over the folly and the weakness of men, and the cruelty and blindness of destiny. Hers is not the dejection of the poet who "could lie down like a tired child, and weep away this life of care," as Shelley at Naples; nor is it the despairing misery that moved Cowper in the awful verses of the "Castaway." It was not such self-pity as wrung from Burns the cry of life "Thou art a galling load, along, a rough, a weary road, to wretches such as I;" nor such general sense of the woes of the race as made Keats think of the world as a place where men sit and hear each other groan, "Where but to think is to be full of sorrow, and leaden-eyed despairs." She was as far removed from the plangent reverie of Rousseau as from the savage truculence of Swift. Intellectual training had given her the spirit of order and proportion, of definiteness and measure, and this marks her alike from the great sentimentalists and the sweeping satirists.

John Morley, 1885, "The Life of George Eliot,"
Macmillan's Magazine, vol. 51, p. 250

Religion even to George Eliot is not an inner power of Divine mystery awakening the conscience. It is at best an intellectual exercise, or a scenic picture, or a beautiful memory. Her early Evangelicalism peeled off her like an outer garment, leaving behind only a rich vein of dramatic experience which she afterwards worked into her novels. There is no evidence of her great change having produced in her any spiritual anxiety. There is nothing indeed in autobiography more wonderful than the facility with which this remarkable woman parted first with her faith and then with the moral sanctions which do so much to consecrate life, while yet constantly idealizing life in her letters, and taking such a large grasp of many of its moral realities. Her scepticism and then her eclectic Humanitarianism had a certain benignancy and elevation unlike vulgar infidelity of any kind. There are gleams of a higher life everywhere in her thought. There is much self-distrust, but no self-abasement. There is a strange externality—as if the Divine had never come near to her save by outward form or picture— never pierced to any dividing asunder of soul and spirit. Amid all her sadness—and her life upon the whole is a very sad one—there are no depths of spiritual dread (of which dramatically—as in *Romola*—she had yet a vivid conception), or even of spiritual tenderness.

John Tulloch, 1885, *Movements of Religious Thought
in Britain During the Nineteenth Century*, p .162

Her style is everywhere pure and strong, of the best and most vigorous English, not only broad in its power, but often intense in its description of character and situation, and always singularly adequate to the thought. Probably no novelist knew the English character—especially in the Midlands— so well as she, or could analyze it with so much subtlety and truth. She is entirely mistress of the country dialects. In humour, pathos, knowledge of character, power of putting a portrait firmly upon the canvas, no writer surpasses her, and few come near her.

J. M. D. Meiklejohn, 1887, *The English Language:
Its Grammar, History and Literature*, p. 365

In *The Mill on the Floss* and *Silas Marner* a curious phenomenon appeared —George Eliot divided into two personages. The close observer of nature, mistress of laughter and tears, exquisite in the intensity of cumulative emotion, was present still, but she receded; the mechanician, overloading her page with pretentious matter, working out her scheme as if she were building a steam-engine, came more and more to the front. In *Felix Holt* and on to *Daniel Deronda* the second personage preponderated, and our ears were deafened by the hum of the philosophical machine, the balance of scenes and sentences, the intolerable artificiality of the whole construction. George Eliot is a very curious instance of the danger of self-cultivation. No writer was ever more anxious to improve herself and conquer an absolute mastery over her material. But she did not observe, as she entertained the laborious process, that she was losing those natural accomplishments which infinitely outshone the philosophy and science which she so painfully acquired. She was born to please, but unhappily she persuaded herself, or was persuaded, that her mission was to teach the world, to lift its moral tone, and, in consequence, an agreeable rustic writer, with a charming humour and very fine sympathetic nature, found herself gradually uplifted until, about 1875, she sat enthroned on an educational tripod, an almost ludicrous pythoness. From the very first she had been weak in that quality which more than any other is needed by a novelist, imaginative invention. So long as she was humble, and was content to reproduce, with the skillful subtlety of her art, what she had personally heard and seen, her work had delightful merit. But it was an unhappy day, when she concluded that strenuous effort, references to a hundred abstruse writers, and a whole technical system of rhetoric would do the wild-wood business of native imagination. The intellectual self-sufficiency of George Eliot has suffered severe chastisement. At the present day scant justice is done to her unquestionable distinction of intellect or to the emotional intensity of much of her early work.

Edmund Gosse, 1897, *A Short History of Modern
English Literature*, p. 369

Notwithstanding all these differences between her earlier and her later work, George Eliot was from first to last a philosopher and moralist. All her novels and tales are constructed on the ethical formula of Mrs. Gaskell's *Ruth*. For the way in which she thought out and applied this doctrine of the act and its train of good and ill, the only appropriate epithet is magnificent. She explained chance and circumstance, giving to these words a new content. All happenings, she showed, are but the meeting and the intermingling of courses of events that have their source in the inner history of mankind. This invisible medium in which we move is outside of time. The past is here in what was done yesterday; the future is here in what is done to-day; and "our finest hope is finest memory." Whatever may be her method of telling a story,—whether she begins at the beginning or breaks into the midst of her plot and in due time gathers up its threads,— George Eliot always comes quickly to an incident which discovers somewhat the moral quality of her characters; and then she proceeds slowly with their self-revelation.

Wilbur L. Cross, 1899, *The Development of the
English Novel*, p. 244

JONES VERY
1813-1880

Born in Salem, Mass., 28 Aug., 1813; died there, 8 May, 1880. He made voyages with his father, a cultivated sea-captain, and had schooling in Salem and New Orleans. A graduate of Harvard in 1836, he taught Greek there for two years. His first volume of essays and poems appeared in 1839. In 1843 the Cambridge Association licensed him to preach, but he was never ordained. He was the intimate friend of Emerson and Channing, and a frequent contributor to *The Christian Register* and other Unitarian journals. His friend James Freeman Clarke edited a complete posthumous edition of his poems and essays. In 1883 Very's *Poems* were reëdited by William P. Andrews, with a memoir. The sonnet, somewhat on the Shakespearean model, was the form of expression most natural to him.

Edmund Clarence Stedman, ed., 1900, *An American Anthology, Biographical Notes*, p. 829

SEE: William I. Bartlett, *Jones Very: Emerson's "Brave Saint,"* 1942.

PERSONAL

Jones Very came hither two days since. His position accuses society as much as society names that false and morbid. And much of his discourse concerning society, church and college was absolutely just. He says it is with him a day of hate: that he discerns the bad element in every person whom he meets, which repels him: he even shrinks a little to give the hand, that sign of receiving. The institutions, the cities which men have built the world over, look to him like a huge ink-blot. His only guard in going to see men is, that he goes to do them good, else they would injure him spiritually. He lives in the sight that He who made him, made the things he sees. He would as soon embrace a black Egyptian mummy as Socrates. He would obey,—obey. He is not disposed to attack religions or charities, though false. The bruisëd reed he would not break, smoking flax not quench. . . . He had the manners of a man,—one, that is, to whom life was more than meat. He felt it, he said, an honour to wash his face, being, as it was, the temple of the spirit. I ought not to omit to record the astonishment which seized all the company when our brave Saint the other day fronted the presiding Preacher. The preacher began to tower and dogmatise with many words. Then I foresaw that his doom was fixed; and, as soon as he had ceased speaking, the Saint set him right, and blew away all his words in an instant,—unhorsed him, I may say, and tumbled him along the ground in utter dismay, like my angel of Heliodorus; never was discomfiture more complete. In tones of genuine pathos, he bid him wonder at the Love which suffered him to speak there in his chair of things he knew nothing of; one might expect to see the book taken from his hands and him thrust out of the room, and yet he was allowed to sit and talk, whilst every word he spoke was a step of departure from the truth; and of this he commanded himself to bear witness.

Ralph Waldo Emerson, 1838, Journal, Oct. 26

In college, as in school, he was too sedate to be widely and generally popular, but all who knew him reverenced the lofty purity of his character, and he soon gathered around him a small circle of warmly attached friends. He was sensitive and reserved, but the cordiality of his tone and the sweet naturalness of his smile of welcome at once attracted whoever made his acquaintance, though the uniform gravity of his daily walk and conversation prevented the many from approaching him as an intimate. . . . "Men in General," said Dr. Channing, "have lost or never found this higher mind, their insanity is profound, Mr. Very's is only superficial. To hear him talk was like looking into the purely spiritual world, into truth itself. He had nothing of self-exaggeration, but seemed to have attained self-annihilation and become an oracle of God." Dr. Channing repeated that he had "not lost his reason," and quoted some of his sayings, identical with many parts of his sonnets, as proofs of the "iron sequence of his thoughts."

William P. Andrews, 1883, ed. Poems by Jones Very,
Memoir, pp. 7, 10

GENERAL

His essays entitled "Epic Poetry," "Shakespere," and "Hamlet," are fine specimens of learned and sympathetic criticism; and his sonnets, and other pieces of verse, are chaste, simple, and poetical, though they have little range of subjects and illusion. They are religious, and some of them are mystical, but they will be recognised by the true poet as the overflowings of a brother's soul.

Rufus Wilmot Griswold, 1842, The Poets and Poetry
of America, p. 392

Jones Very, a sort of Unitarian monk and mystic, packed into many a sonnet or meditative hymn rich and weighty words of reverence and consecration, which he deemed inspired by ghostly power from above, and which he wrote in implicit obedience to the spiritual voice within. Some of these poems are harmed by a semi-Buddhistic Christian Quietism, as though Molinos had been incarnated anew in the Salem streets; others display the serene sure beauty of church-yard lilies.

Charles F. Richardson, 1888, American Literature,
1607-1885, vol. II, p. 233

Very has received a rarer and nobler recognition than popularity; men of genius have concurred in praising him. In respect to his poems and the voice that speaks in them, Bryant, Emerson, and Hawthorne have each paid positive tribute. The mind from which Very's poetry came was of an unusual order, and one that cannot be judged without special study, though the poetry of that mind may be enjoyed. He was one of those few Americans (perhaps the only American) for whom religious contemplation is everything; and one of those mortals to whom above others is, in spiritual things, granted the clearest vision. Such a man, as we know with regard to oriental mystics, with whom conditions are more favorable for solitary, rapt meditation than in America, naturally and rightly regards himself as a teacher of divine truth, and an exposer of worldly pretension and sin; in America less naturally but not less rightly, this was the case with Very.

Arthur B. Simonds, 1894, American Song, p. 57

His sympathy with nature is profound, but his methods of expression not varied. This and the frequent repetition of his subject give his writings an impression of monotony fatal to an extended reading. He is seldom trite, though his reflections are often drawn from the commonest objects. Close to ourselves lie the wonders of nature, is the keynote of his poetry. The wind-flower, the columbine, and the snowdrop were to him as eloquent as a forest, a mountain, or an ocean. He was one of the most original as well as most unreadable of our poets. All his poems are infused with the sweetness of his anemones and columbines, of too subtle an essence to suit the general taste.

James L. Onderdonk, 1899-1901, History of
American Verse, p. 185

THOMAS CARLYLE
1795-1881

1795, Born at Ecclefechan, Annandale, Dumfriesshire. 1800, at the Village School. 1806-1809, at the Grammar School, Annan. 1809, enters Edinburgh University. 1814-1815, Teacher of Mathematics at Annan. 1816-1818, Master at Kirkcaldy; friendship with Edward Irving. 1818-1820, at Edinburgh; divinity and law; writes first articles for Brewster's *Encyclopædia;* begins the study of German literature. 1821, his *New Birth;* visits Haddington with Irving; meets Miss Jane Welsh. 1822, tutor to the Bullers; writes *Life of Schiller* for the *London Magazine.* 1824, translates *Wilhelm Meister;* first visit to London with the Bullers; meets Coleridge at Highgate; visits Paris; correspondence with Goethe begun. 1825, at home, Hoddam Hill. 1826, marries Jane Welsh, and settles at Comely Bank,

Edinburgh; meets Jeffrey; writes *Jean Paul* for the *Edinburgh Review.* 1827-1831, removes to the Welshs' Manor, Craigenputtock; "Essay on Burns" in the *Edinburgh Review;* contributes magazine articles now published under *Miscellanies;* writes *Sartor Resartus.* 1831, removes to London; his father's death. 1832-1833, returns to Craigenputtock; visit from Emerson; *Sartor Resartus* published in *Fraser's Magazine;* winter in Edinburgh. 1834, settles at Cheyne Row (Chelsea), London. 1837, lectures in London on German Literature; *The French Revolution.* 1839, *Chartism.* 1841, lectures in London on heroes; *Heroes and Hero Worship* published. 1843, *Past and Present.* 1845, *Cromwell.* 1850, *Latter-Day Pamphlets.* 1851, *Life of Sterling.* 1858-1865, *History of Frederick the Second.* 1866, elected Lord Rector of Edinburgh University; address on the Choice of Books; death of Mrs. Carlyle. 1874, order of merit from the German Emperor. 1875, *The Early Kings of Norway.* 1881, death; *Reminiscences,* J. A. Froude, Ed. 1882, *Thomas Carlyle,* J. A. Froude, Ed. 1883, *Letters and Memorials of Jane Welsh Carlyle,* J. A. Froude, Ed. 1883. *Correspondence of Carlyle and Emerson,* C. E. Norton, Ed. 1886, *Early Letters of Thomas Carlyle,* C. E. Norton, Ed. 1887, *Correspondence between Goethe and Carlyle,* C. E. Norton, Ed.

> Andrew J. George, 1897, ed. *Carlyle's Essay*
> *on Burns,* p. 80

SEE: *Works,* ed. and with Introduction by H. D. Traill, 1896-99, 30 v. (Centenary Edition); *Carlyle: An Anthology,* ed. G. M. Trevelyan, 1953; *Love Letters of Thomas Carlyle and Jane Welsh,* ed. A. Carlyle, 1909, 2 v.; D. A. Wilson, *The Life of Thomas Carlyle,* 1923-34, 6 v.

PERSONAL

Carlyle breakfasted with me, and I had an interesting morning with him. He is a deep-thinking German scholar, a character, and a singular compound. His voice and manner, and even the style of his conversation, are those of a religious zealot, and he keeps up that character in his declamations against the anti-religious. And yet, if not the god of his idolatry, at least he has a priest and prophet of his church in Goethe, of whose profound wisdom he speaks like an enthusiast. But for him, Carlyle says, he should not now be alive. He owes everything to him! But in strange union with such idolatry is his admiration of Bonaparte. Another object of his eulogy is—Cobbett, whom he praises for his humanity and love of the poor! Singular, and even whimsical, combinations of love and reverence these.

> Henry Crabb Robinson, 1832, *Diary,* Feb. 12;
> *Reminiscences,* ed. Sadler, vol. II, p. 168

I found him one of the most simple and frank of men, and became acquainted with him at once. We walked over several miles of hills, and talked upon all the great questions that interested us most. The comfort of meeting a man is that he speaks sincerely; that he feels himself to be so rich, that he is above the meanness of pretending to knowledge which he has not, and Carlyle does not pretend to have solved the great problems, but rather to be an observer of their solution as it goes forward in the world. I asked him at what religious development the concluding passage in his piece in the *Edinburgh Review* upon German literature (say five years ago), and some passages in the piece called "Characteristics," pointed? He replied that he was not competent to state even to himself,— he waited rather to see. My own feeling was that I had met men of far less power who had got greater insight into religious truth. He is, as you might guess from his papers, the most catholic of philosophers; he forgives and loves everybody, and wishes each to struggle on in his own place and arrive at his own ends. . . . He talks finely, seems to love the broad Scotch, and I loved him very much at once. I am afraid he finds his entire solitude tedious, but I could not help congratulating him upon the treasure in his wife, and I hope he will not leave the moors; 'tis so much better for a man of letters to nurse himself in seclusion than to be filed down to the common level by the compliance and imitations of city society.

Ralph Waldo Emerson, 1833, *Letter to Alexander Ireland,*
Aug. 31; *Ralph Waldo Emerson: Recollections of his Visits
to England,* ed. Ireland, p. 53

I found time to make a visit to Carlyle, and to hear one of his lectures. He is rather a small, spare, ugly Scotchman, with a strong accent, which I should think he takes no pains to mitigate. His manners are plain and simple, but not polished, and his conversation much of the same sort. He is now lecturing for subsistence, to about a hundred persons, who pay him, I believe, two guineas each. . . . To-day he spoke—as I think he commonly does—without notes, and therefore as nearly extempore as a man can who prepares himself carefully, as it was plain he had done. His course is on Modern Literature, and his subject to-day was that of the eighteenth century; in which he contrasted Johnson and Voltaire very well, and gave a good character of Swift. He was impressive, I think, though such lecturing could not well be very popular; and in some parts, if he were not poetical, he was picturesque. He was nowhere obscure, nor were his sentences artificially constructed, though some of them, no doubt, savored of his peculiar manner.

George Ticknor, 1838, *Journal,* June 1;
Life, Letters and Journals, vol. II, p. 180

Carlyle's conversation and general views are curiously dyspeptic, his indigestion coloring everything. There was something particularly engaging in his approbation of a heartless caricature of the execution of poor Louis XVI, which he desired us not to look at, but introduced a beautiful one of himself smoking in his tub, which John Sterling compares to one of Michael Angelo's prophets. He stood at the window with his pipe to help us draw a comparison.

Caroline Fox, 1842, *Memories of Old Friends,* ed. Pym;
Journal, June 6, p. 179

Accustomed to the infinite wit and exuberant richness of his writings, his talk is still an amazement and a splendor scarcely to be faced with steady eyes. He does not converse: only harangues. . . . Carlyle allows no one a chance, but bears down all opposition, not only by his wit and onset of words, resistless in their sharpness as so many bayonets, but by actual, physical superiority—raising his voice, and rushing on his opponent with a torrent of sound. This is not in the least from unwillingness to allow freedom to others. On the contrary, no man would more enjoy a manly resistance to his thought. But it is the habit of a mind accustomed to follow out its own impulse, as the hawk its prey, and which knows not how to stop in the chase. Carlyle, indeed, is arrogant and over-bearing; but in his arrogance there is no littleness—no self-love. It is the heroic arrogance of some old Scandinavian conqueror, it is his nature and the untameable energy that has given him power to crush the dragons. You do not love him, perhaps, nor revere; and perhaps, also, he would only laugh at you if you did; but you like him heartily, and like to see him the powerful smith, the Siegfried, melting all the old iron in his furnace till it glows to a sunset red, and burns you, if you senselessly go too near. He seems, to me, quite isolated,—lonely as the desert,—yet never was a man more fitted to prize a man, could he find one to match his mood. He finds them, but only in the past. He sings rather than talks. He pours upon you a kind of satirical, heroical, critical poem, with regular cadences, and generally, near the beginning, hits upon some singular epithet, which serves as a *refrain* when his song is full, or with which, as with a knitting needle, he catches up the stitches, if he has chanced, now and then, to let fall a row. For the higher kind of poetry he has no sense, and his talk on that subject is delightfully and gorgeously absurd. He sometimes stops a minute to laugh at it himself, then begins anew with fresh vigour.

Margaret Fuller Ossoli, 1846, *Letters from Paris,* Dec.;
Memoirs, vol. II, p. 188

I believe that what Mr. Carlyle loves better than his fault-finding, with all its eloquence, is the face of any human creature that looks suffering, and loving, and sincere; and I believe further, that if the fellow-creature were suffering only, and neither loving nor sincere, but had come to a pass of agony in this life, which put him at the mercies of some good man for some last help and consolation toward his grave, even at the risk of loss to repute, and a sure amount of pain and vexation, that man, if the groan reached him in its forlornness, would be Thomas Carlyle.

Leigh Hunt, 1850, *Autobiography,* ed. Ingpen, vol. II, pp. 209, 211

Carlyle dresses so badly, and wears such a rough outside, that the flunkies are rude to him at gentlemen's doors.

Nathaniel Hawthorne, 1855, *English Note-Books,* vol. I, p. 241

Yellow as a guinea, with downcast eyes, broken speech at the beginning, and fingers which nervously picked at the desk before him, he could not for a moment be supposed to enjoy his own effort; and the lecturer's own enjoyment is a prime element of success. The merits of Carlyle's discourses were however so great that he might probably have gone on year after year till this time, with improving success, and perhaps ease: but the struggle was too severe. From the time that his course was announced till it was finished, he scarcely slept, and he grew more dyspeptic and nervous every day; and we were at length entreated to say no more about his lecturing, as no fame and no money or other advantage could counterbalance the misery which the engagement caused him.

Harriet Martineau, 1855-77, *Autobiography,* ed. Chapman,
vol. I, p. 289

I have no doubt he would have played a Brave Man's Part if called on; but, meanwhile, he has only sat pretty comfortably at Chelsea, scolding all the world for not being Heroic, and not always very precise in telling them how. He has, however, been so far heroic, as to be always independent, whether of Wealth, Rank, and Coteries of all sorts: nay, apt to fly in the face of some who courted him. I suppose he is changed, or subdued, at eighty; but up to the last ten years he seemed to me just the same as when I first knew him five and thirty years ago. What a Fortune he might have made by showing himself about as a Lecturer, as Thackeray and Dickens did; I don't mean they did it for Vanity: but to make money: and that spend generously. Carylye did indeed lecture near forty years ago before he was a Lion to be shown, and when he had but few readers. I heard his *Heroes* which now seems to me one of his best Books. He looked very handsome then, with his black hair, fine Eyes, and a sort of crucified Expression.

Edward FitzGerald, 1876, *To C. E. Norton,* Jan. 23;
Letters, ed. Wright, vol. I, p. 378

A residence of more than forty years in London has not modified the strong Scottish enunciation which Carlyle brought with him from his native Dumfriesshire. The vowels come out broad and full; the gutturals—which are so sadly clipped in modern English speech, depriving it of all masculine vigor—have their due prominence. His manner in talking is striking and peculiar; now bursting into Titanic laughter at some odd conceit; now swelling into fierce wrath at some meanness or wrong; now sinking into low tones of the tenderest pathos; but running through all is a rhythmic flow, a sustained recitative, like that in which we may imagine old Homer to have chanted his long-resounding hexameters.

Alfred H. Guernsey, 1879, Thomas Carlyle:
His Life—His Books—His Theories, p. 20

In the grave matters of the law he walked for eighty-five years unblemished by a single moral spot. There are no "sins of youth" to be apologised for. In no instance did he ever deviate even for a moment from the strictest lines of integrity. He had his own way to make in life, and when he had chosen his profession, he had to depend on popularity for the bread which he was to eat. But although more than once he was within sight of starvation he would never do less than his very best. He never wrote an idle word, he never wrote or spoke any single sentence which he did not with his whole heart believe to be true. Conscious though he was that he had talents above those of common men, he sought neither rank nor fortune for himself. When he became famous and moved as an equal among the best of the land, he was content to earn the wages of an artisan, and kept to the simple habits in which he had been bred in his father's house. He might have had a pension had he stooped to ask for it; but he chose to maintain himself by his own industry, and when a pension was offered him it was declined. He despised luxury; he was thrifty and even severe in the economy of his own household; but in the times of his greatest poverty he had always something to spare for those who were dear to him. When money came at last, and it came only when he was old and infirm, he added nothing to his own comforts, but was lavishly generous with it to others. Tenderhearted and affectionate he was beyond all men whom I have ever known. His faults, which in his late remorse he exaggerated, as men of noblest natures are most apt to do, his impatience, his irritability, his singular melancholy, which made him at times distressing as a companion, were the effects of temperament first, and of a peculiarly sensitive organisation; and secondly of absorption in his work and of his determination to do that work as well as it could possibly be done. Such faults as these were but as the vapours which hang about a mountain, inseparable from the nature of the man. They have to be told because without them his character cannot be understood, and because they affected others as well as himself. But they do not blemish the essential greatness of his character, and when he is fully known he will not be loved or admired the less because he had infirmities like the rest of us.

James Anthony Froude, 1884, Thomas Carlyle,
A History of his Life in London, vol. I, p. 4

He was not constitutionally arrogant; he was a man of real modesty; he was even, I think, constitutionally diffident. He was a man, in short, whom you could summer and winter with, without ever having your self-respect wantonly affronted as it habitually is by mere conventional men and women. He was, to be sure, a very sturdy son of earth, and capable at times of exhibiting the most helpless natural infirmity. But he would never ignore nor slight your human fellowship because your life or opinions exposed you to the reproach of the vain, the frivolous, the self-seeking. He would of course curse your gods ever and anon in a manful way, and scoff without mercy at your tenderest intellectual hopes and aspirations; but upon yourself personally, all the while,—especially if you should drink strong tea and pass sleepless nights, or suffer from tobacco, or be menaced with insanity, or have a gnawing cancer under your jacket,—he would have bestowed the finest of his wheat. He might not easily have forgiven you if you used a vegetable diet, especially if you did so on principle; and he would surely have gnashed his teeth upon you if you should have claimed any scientific knowledge or philosophic insight into the social problem,— the problem of man's coming destiny upon the earth. But within these limits you would have felt how truly human was the tie that bound you to this roaring, riotous, most benighted, yet not unbenignant brother.

Henry James, Sr., 1884, "Some Personal Recollections of Carlyle,"
Literary Remains, ed. James, p. 430

It has been a personal pain to me in recent times to find among honourable and cultivated people a conviction that Carylye was hard, selfish, and arrogant. I knew him intimately for more than an entire generation—as intimately as one who was twenty years his junior, and who regarded him with unaffected reverence as the man of most undoubted genius of his age, probably ever did. I saw him in all moods and under the most varied conditions, and often tried his impatient spirit by dissent from his cherished convictions, and I found him habitually serene and considerate, never, as so many have come to believe of his ordinary mood, arrogant or impatient of contradiction. I was engaged for nearly half the period in the conflict of Irish politics, which from his published writings one might suppose to be utterly intolerable to him; but the readers of these letters will find him taking a keen interest in every honest attempt to raise Ireland from her misery, reading constantly, and having sent after him, wherever he went, the journal which embodied the most determined resistance to misgovernment from Westminister, and throwing out friendly suggestions from time to time how the work, so far as he approved of it, might be more effectually done. This is the real Carlyle; a man of generous nature, sometimes disturbed on the surface by trifling troubles, but never diverted at heart from what he believed to be right and true.

Sir Charles Gavan Duffy, 1892, *Conversations with Carlyle*, p. 6

JANE WELSH CARLYLE

I suppose you have read by this time Mrs. Carlyle's *Correspondence*. A very painful book in more ways than one. There are disclosures there that never should have been made, as if they had been caught up from the babblings of discharged housemaids. One blushes in reading, and feels like a person caught listening at the keyhole.

James Russell Lowell, 1883, *To C. E. Norton*, April 22;
Letters, ed. Norton, vol. II, p. 273

Had she even shared to the full, the literary interest of the man of genius whose overwhelming personality left her so lonely, she would doubtless have entered the lists as a brilliant and successful authoress. But her share seemed, for the most part, limited to the listening to Carlyle's tremendous denunciations of all people, things, and systems, since the creation of the world. On her sofa she lay, night after night, exhausted, with nerves "all shattered to pieces," and gave her word of sympathy when she could. To the casual visitor these fierce and powerful monologues of Carlyle's were fascinating—to her, they must have been almost intolerable at times. Had she been placed in a congenial companionship, with a man many degrees less intellectual than Thomas Carlyle—a man with whom the deeper sympathies of a woman's heart had met full response—we cannot doubt that the world would have known Jane Welsh Carlyle as a writer. But that career was closed to her, and all connected with literature seemed interwoven with the loneliness and disappointment of her own lot.

Annie E. Ireland, 1891, *Life of Jane Welsh Carlyle*, p. 307

Mr. Froude has been severely censured as painting in too dark colors Carlyle's grim, savage humour, his thoughtless cruelty to his wife, and her unhappiness; but the documentary evidence he has presented fully justifies him. Mrs. Carlyle said herself, not long before her death: "I married for ambition. Carlyle has exceeded all that my wildest hopes ever imagined of him; and I am miserable." Her husband, indeed, appreciated her talents and found pleasure in her society but he never seems to have experienced for her the passion of love as it is commonly understood. The pair had no children, and, as Mr. Froude tells us, when Carlyle was busy his wife rarely so much as saw him save when she would steal into his dressing-room in the morning while he was shaving. . . . Whether Mrs. Carlyle would have been happier with Irving for a husband instead of Carlyle is doubtful. That Irving would have been to her most tender, loving and considerate, his treatment of the woman he married, not from love, but from a sense of duly, compels us to believe; but whether his failure in his career, and the want of that gratification of her pride and satisfaction of her ambition which she got with Carlyle, would not have been as sore a trial to her as Carlyle's harshness is not so sure.

Thomas Hitchcock, 1891, *Unhappy Loves of Men of Genius,* pp. 209, 211

Essay on Burns (1828)

It is one of the very best of his essays, and was composed with an evidently peculiar interest, because the outward circumstances of Burn's life, his origin, his early surroundings, his situation as a man of genius born in a farmhouse not many miles distant, among the same people and the same associations as were so familiar to himself, could not fail to make him think often of himself while he was writing about his countryman.

James Anthony Froude, 1882, *Thomas Carlyle; A History of the First Forty Years of his Life,* vol. II, p. 25

The essay on Burns is the very voice of Scotland, expressive of all her passionate love and tragic sorrow for her darling son. It has paragraphs of massy gold, capable of being beaten out into volumes, as indeed they have been. Unlike some of Carlyle's essays, it is by no means open to the charge of mysticism, but is distinguished by the soundest good sense.

Richard Garnett, 1887, *Thomas Carlyle (Great Writers),* p. 48

Sartor Resartus (1834)

The work before us is a sort of philosophical romance in which the author undertakes to give, in the form of a review of a German treatise on dress, and a notice of the life of the writer, his own opinions upon Matters and Things in General. The hero, Professor Teufelsdröckh, seems to be intended for a portrait of human nature as affected by the moral influences to which, in the present state of society, a cultivated mind is naturally exposed.

Alexander H. Everett, 1835, "Thomas Carlyle,"
North American Review, vol. 41, pp. 459, 481, 482

This consists of two intertwisted threads, though both spun off the same distaff, and of the same crimson wool. There is a fragmentary, though, when closely examined, a complete biography of a supposed German professor, and, along with it, portions of a supposed treatise of his on the philosophy of clothes. Of the three books, the first is preparatory, and gives a portrait of the hero and his circumstances. The second is the biographical account of him. The third under the rubric of extracts from his work, presents us with his picture of human life in the nineteenth century. How so unexampled a topic as the philosophy of clothes can be made the vehicle for a philosophy of man, those will see who read the book. But they must read with the faith that, in spite of all appearances to the contrary, it is the jest which is a pretence, and that the real purport of the whole is serious, yea, serious as any religion that ever was preached, far more serious than most battles that have ever been fought since Agamemnon declared war against Priam. . . . In this book that strange style appears again before us in its highest oddity. Thunder peals, flute-music, the laugh of Pan and the nymphs, the clear disdainful whisper of cold stoicism, and the hurly-burly of a country fair, succeed and melt into each other. Again the clamour sinks into quiet, and we hear at last the grave, mild hymn of devotion, sounding from a far sanctuary, though only in faint and dying vibrations. So from high and low, from the sublime to the most merely trival, fluctuates the feeling of the poet.

John Sterling, 1839, "Carlyle's Works," London and
Westminster Review,</i> vol. 33, pp. 52, 53</div>

When Carlyle's <i>Sartor Resartus</i> first appeared, as a serial in Fraser's Magazine, the publisher would have discontinued it, in despair, but for the letters of earnest appreciation received from two men, one of whom was Ralph Waldo Emerson. This was in 1835; and in 1870 the same work, in a cheap popular edition, reached a sale of 40,000 copies.

Bayard Taylor, 1879, Studies in German Literature, p. 395

A work which, with all its affectations, obscurities (I do not hesitate to add, insincerities), has taken a strong hold on the imaginations of that large section of the public which does not go to the poets for its edification, but prefers the fashioners of "mystical" prose. . . . In <i>Sartor Resartus</i> the traces of literary conventionalism were kicked over altogether. The work might be called a wild hotch-potch of German mysticism, Lowland Scotch, broad caricature, and literal autobiography. In its long-windedness, in the zeal with which the one solitary idea, or "Clothes" theory, was worked to death, it was certainly very German. But with all its defects,—or rather perhaps, in consequence of its defects,—it was a work of genius.

Robert Buchanan, 1881, "Wylie's Life of Carlyle,"
Contemporary Review, vol. 39, pp. 797, 798

A very large part of the book owes nothing at all to Swift. In the second portion, the story of Teufelsdröckh's life, his clothes philosophy sinks out of sight altogether; and such chapters as the fifth and eighth of the third book are too weighty and earnest to be really part and parcel of what was in the first instance a jest. The influence of Swift's thought is strongest in the first or original portion. The rest is really made up of Carlyle's own experience of life and his brooding over all problems that can engage the active brain, from the reality of the universe and the existence of God to the condition of the poor and the phenomenon of the man of fashion. The book is to be regarded as the epitome of all that Carlyle thought and felt in the course of the first thirty-five years of his residence on this planet. Many things which he wishes to say that cannot be ranged under any rubric of the philosophy of clothes, such as his criticism of duelling, are, notwithstanding, given room. This position I hope to make good.

Archibald MacMechan, 1895, ed. *Sartor Resartus,*
Introduction, p. xxi

It is to *Sartor Resartus* we must turn for the fullest disclosure of Carlyle's religious history and beliefs. In that book, written among the solitudes of Craiggenputtock, we have a revelation of his own interior life, though to some extent veiled and symbolical. Herr Teufelsdröckh is the spiritual counterpart of Carlyle himself, and the work partakes of the nature of an autobiography. Through its pages we get a vivid insight into the mental struggles, heart sorrows, and soul-conflicts of an earnest and thoughtful man, groping his way through the thick darkness of scepticism out into the daylight of faith and liberty. Autobiographies are a species of literature in whose favour we are not much prepossessed, they are so often stilted and artificial, and so manifestly got up for effect. But no such suspicions can possibly attach to *Sartor,* which is undoubtedly the product of a sincere and unaffected soul, and enjoys the reputation of being "one of the truest self-revelations ever penned."

S. Law Wilson, 1899, *The Theology of Modern Literature,* p. 158

The French Revolution (1837)

He left us [John Stuart Mill] in a relapsed state, one of the pitiablest. My dear wife has been very kind, and has become dearer to me. The night has been full of emotion, occasionally of sharp pain (something cutting or hard grasping me round the heart) occasionally of sweet consolation. I dreamt of my father and sister Margaret alive; yet all defaced with the sleepy stagnancy, swollen hebetude of the grave, and again dying as in some strange rude country: a horrid dream, the painfullest too when you wake first. But on the whole should I not thank the Unseen? For I was not driven out of composure, hardly for moments: "Walk humbly with thy God." How I longed for some psalm or prayer that I could have uttered, that my loved ones could have joined me in! But there was none. Silence had to be my language. This morning I have determined so far that I *can* still write *a* book on the French Revolution, and will do it. Nay, our money will still suffice. It was my last throw, my *whole* staked in the monstrosity of this life—for too monstrous, incomprehensible, it has been to me. I will not *quit* the game while faculty is given me to try playing. I have written to Fraser to buy me a "Biographie Universelle" (a kind of increasing the stake) and fresh paper: mean to huddle up the *Fête des Piques* and look farther what can be attempted.

Thomas Carlyle, 1835, *Journal,* March 6; *Thomas Carlyle:*
A History of his Life in London, ed. Froude, vol. I, p. 24

This is not so much a history, as an epic poem; and notwithstanding, or even in consequence of this, the truest of histories. It is the history of the French Revolution, and the poetry of it, both in one; and on the whole no work of greater genius, either historical or poetical, has been produced in the country for many years. . . . We need not fear to prophesy that the suffrages of a large class of the very best qualified judges will be given, even enthusiastically, in favor of the volumes before us; but we will not affect to deny that the sentiment of another large class of readers (among whom are many entitled to the most respectful attention on other subjects) will be far different; a class comprehending all who are repelled by quaintness of manner. For a style more peculiar than that of Mr. Carlyle, more unlike the jog-trot characterless uniformity which distinguishes the English style of this age of periodicals, does not exist. Nor indeed can this style be wholly defended even by its admirers. Some of its peculiarities are mere mannerisms, arising from some casual association of ideas, or some habit accidentally picked up; and what is worse, many sterling thoughts are so disguised in phraseology borrowed from the spiritualist school of German poets and metaphysicians, as not only to obscure the meaning, but to raise, in the minds of most English readers, a not unnatural or inexcusable presumption of there being no meaning at all. Nevertheless, the presumption fails in this instance (as in many other instances); there is not only a meaning, but generally a true, and even a profound meaning, and, although a few dicta about the "mystery" and the "infinitude" which are in the universe and in man, and such like topics, are repeated in varied phrases greatly too often for our taste, this must be borne with, proceeding as one cannot but see, from feelings the most solemn, and the most deeply rooted which can lie in the heart of a human being. These transcendentalisms, and the accidental mannerisms excepted, we pronounce the style of this book to be not only good, but of surpassing excellence; excelled, in its kind, only by the great masters of epic poetry; and a most suitable and glorious vesture for a work which is itself, as we have said, an epic poem.

> John Stuart Mill, 1837, "The French Revolution,"
> *Early Essays,* ed. Gibbs, pp. 271, 272

By the way, have you read Carlyle's extraordinary History of that wonderful period? Does it offend your classical taste? It finds great favour with many intelligent people here. They seem to think that the muses of History and Poetry have struck up a truce, and are henceforth to go on lovingly together. I must confess myself much interested. Carlyle seems to be an example of the old proverb of "the prophet without honour in his own country."

> William Ellery Channing, 1838, *To Miss Aikin,* Feb. 7;
> *Correspondence of William Ellery Channing and Miss Aikin,*
> ed. Le Breton, p. 304

He has done no more than give us *tableaux,* wonderful in execution, but nothing in conception, without connection, without a bearing. His book is the French Revolution *illustrated*—illustrated by the hand of a master, we know, but one from whom we expected a different labour. . . . The eternal *cursus et recursus* inexorably devours ideas, creeds, daring, and devotedness. The Infinite takes, to him, the form of Nihilation. It has a glance of pity for every set of enthusiasms, a smile, stamped with scepticism for every act of great devotedness to ideas. Generalities are odious to it; detail is its favorite occupation, and it there amuses itself as if seeking to lay at rest its inconsolable cares.

> Joseph Mazzini, 1840, *Monthly Chronicle,* No. 23

In these times there have appeared in Europe few works so worthy of attention; few so notable at once for their repulsive and attractive qualities.

If your glance stops at the surface, and external singularities repel you, do not read this strange book. The mystic and obscure form chosen by Carlyle will soon fatigue you, and you will chafe at so many disguises which are not even transparent. If you are charmed by purity of diction, if you are accustomed to the Anglo-Gallic style of Addison, to the brief, incisive, altogether British sentences of Bacon, to the energetic and robust periods of Southey, Carlyle will displease you. . . . If you are an historian of fact, and pride yourself above all on a practical study of events and circumstances, you will be still more annoyed; for facts are badly told by him, sometimes magnified as to their importance, sometimes heaped together or scattered apart, always without that clear arrangement which constitutes history. But if you are a philosopher, that is to say a sincere observer of mankind, you will re-read his work more than once. It will specially charm you, if you dare lift yourself above parties, and the prejudices of the day. It is neither a well-written book, nor an exact history of the French Revolution. It is not an eloquent dissertation,—still less a transmutation of events and men into romantic narrative. It is a philosophic study, mingled with irony and drama, nothing more. . . . In writing it, the author concerned himself much more with the thought than the expression; he has thought more of the work than he has elaborated it. He has almost always seen clearly; he has often spoken badly. His narrative has all the glow of a present and actual scene. He has found himself profoundly isolated in England. This misfortune for his life is auspicious for his glory. He has sacrificed nothing to party. He has been the man of his own thought, and the expression of his own character.

Victor Euphémion Philarète Chasles, 1840, *Revue des Deux Mondes,* 4th S. vol. 24

He saw nothing but evil in the French Revolution. He judges it as unjustly as he judges Voltaire, and for the same reasons. He understands our manner of acting no better than our manner of thinking. He looks for Puritan sentiment; and, as he does not find it, he condemns us. The idea of duty, the religious spirit, self-government, the authority of an austere conscience, can alone, in his opinion, reform a corrupt society; and none of all these are to be met with in French society.

H. A. Taine, 1871, *History of English Literature,* tr. Van Laun, vol. II, bk. v, ch. IV, p. 472

So overmastering is the interest of the story, that it is only by an effort that the supreme intellectual feat implied in the creation of such a work can be realised. To consult all authorities, however insignificant, which could throw light on the events, to keep the thread of narrative and chain of circumstances distinct in the mind, and weld all into one well-balanced piece of artistic work, nowhere marred by undue insistence on trivial points, or insufficient examination of important ones—this could be accomplished only by the possessor of an unexampled historic imagination. It is small wonder that such a history as this was hailed by the leading minds of England and America as the production of a great man of genius.

Richard Herne Shepherd, 1881, Memoirs of the Life and
Writings of Thomas Carlyle, vol. I, p. 166

Mr. Carlyle's *Revolution* is more and more felt to be a literary picture, and less and less a historical examination. It is based on an idea now recognised to be thoroughly inadequate; it is saturated with doctrines for which the author himself no longer retained any trust or hope; and it leads us to a conclusion which all that is manly and true in our generation rejects with indignation.

Frederic Harrison, 1883, "Histories of the French Revolution,"
The Choice of Books and Other Literary Pieces, p. 410

Carlyle wrote the last word of *The French Revolution* as the clock was striking ten and the supper of oatmeal porridge was coming up. He naturally felt the house was too narrow, and went forth into the night. Before departing he said to his wife, "I know not whether this book is worth anything, nor what the world will do with it, or misdo, or entirely forbear to do, as is likeliest: but this I could tell the world: You have not had for a hundred years any book that comes more direct and flamingly from the heart of a living man. Do what you like with it, you." After which oration, the hall-door closed upon the most angry and desperate man of genius then in the flesh; with cause, had he known it, to have been the most thankful and hopeful.

Richard Garnett, 1887, Thomas Carlyle,
(Great Writers), pp. 81, 86

Chartism (1840)

I will tell you some good things to read—though not sure they are quite in your way: viz., Carlyle's *Chartism*. . . . Carlyle is a very striking writer; full of a sort of grim humour:—the grin-horribly-a-ghastly-smile kind of style; the subject, too, being one which develops such a power well. This is not an inviting or flowery description to give of an author; but for a variety he is wonderfully impressive.

James Bowling Mozley, 1840, To his Sisters, March 7;
Letters, ed. his Sister, p. 101

Chartism, Carylye's next book, is the briefest, and also the most simple, direct, and business-like of any of his works. The splendours of diction which characterised his previous efforts were now, as in his account of Luther, rigorously laid aside, as if he had resolved that he would have practical belief or nothing. No one could read this little book with any intelligence, and think of it as a mere literary performance: it is his first distinct effort as a Social Reformer. German Transcendentalism retires into the Divine Silences, and English practically comes to the front. It must be understood that *Chartism* was published long before the Corn Laws were repealed, and that it made a very deep impression at the time of its appearance. How much of the subsequent practical legislation may have been directly or indirectly influenced by it, it is perhaps impossible now to determine. All we can say is, that from this time legislation did begin, in various directions, to take the practical tone Carlyle here strove to initiate.

Henry Larkin, 1886, Carlyle and the Open Secret of his Life, p. 96

Heroes and Hero Worship (1841)

Have you read poor Carlyle's raving book about heroes? Of course you have, or I would ask you to buy my copy. I don't like to live with it in the house. It smoulders. He ought to be laughed at a little. But it is pleasant to retire to the Tale of a Tub, Tristram Shandy, and Horace Walpole, after being tossed on his canvas waves. This is blasphemy. Dibdin Pitt of the Coburg could enact one of his heroes.

Edward FitzGerald, 1841, To W. H. Thompson, March 26;
Letters, ed. Wright, vol. I, p. 71

Carlyle's *Hero Worship* trembled in my hand like a culprit before a judge; and as the book is very full of paradoxes, and has some questionable matter in it; this shaking seemed rather symbolical. But, oh! it is a book fit rather to shake (take it all in all) than to be shaken. It is very full of noble sentiments and wise reflections, and throws out many a suggestion which will not waste itself like a blast blown in a wilderness, but will surely rouse many a heart and mind to a right, Christian-like way of acting and of dealing with the gifted and godlike in man and of men.

Sara Coleridge, 1843, To Mrs. Farrer, Sept. 5;
Memoir and Letters, ed. her Daughter, p. 204

However the matter may have stood in 1841, in 1887 *Hero Worship* is likely to be read with great admiration but little astonishment. The stars in their courses have fought for Carlyle. The influence of great or reputed great men upon politics and thought has been so enormous, the impotence of the most respectable causes without powerful representatives has been so notorious, that the personal element in history has regained all the importance of which it has been deprived by the study of general laws. The problem of harmonizing it with the truth of general laws remains without solution from Carlyle. He simply ignores these laws, and assumes that the hero appears when God pleases, and acts as pleases himself. It is also difficult to square the truth of *Hero Worship* with the truth of *Sartor Resartus*.

Richard Garnett, 1887, *Thomas Carlyle*
(*Great Writers*), p. 101

He was more alive than any man since Swift to the dark side of human nature. The dullness of mankind weighed upon him like a nightmare. "Mostly fools" is his pithy verdict upon the race at large. Nothing then could be more idle than the dream of the revolutionists that the voice of the people could be itself the voice of God. From millions of fools you can by no constitutional machinery extract anything but folly. Where then is the escape? The millions, he says (essay on Johnson), "roll hither and thither, whithersoever they are led"; they seem "all sightless and slavish," with little but "animal instincts." The hope is that, here and there, are scattered the men of power and of insight, the heaven-sent leaders; and it is upon loyalty to them and capacity for recognizing and obeying them that the future of the race really depends. This was the moral of the lectures on *Hero Worship*. Odin, Mahomet, Dante, Shakespeare, Luther, Cromwell, and Napoleon, are types of the great men who now and then visit the earth as prophets or rulers. They are the brilliant centers of light in the midst of the surrounding darkness; and in loyal recognition of their claims lies our security for all external progress. By what signs, do you ask, can they be recognized? There can be no sign. You can see the light if you have eyes; but no other faculty can supply the want of eyesight. And hence arise some remarkable points both of difference from and coincidence with popular beliefs.

Leslie Stephen, 1897, *Library of the World's Best Literature,*
ed. Warner, vol. VI, p. 3238

Past and Present (1843)

Past and Present is at once a monument of the keen practical spirit of the man and of what may be called his literary *flair*, or scent. Ecclesiological mediævalism was at its very height, and in itself Mr. Carlyle hated it, or regarded it with a partly unutterable sense of sarcastic astonishment. Yet he managed, out of a book published to interest readers who read in this spirit, to make something quite different,—to expound his own views, preach his own gospel, and illustrate his own fancies. . . . A unique book, which no one, perhaps, but its author could have written, neither the like of it will any other man write.

> George Saintsbury, 1881, "The Literary Work of Thomas Carlyle," *Scribner's Monthly,* vol. 22, pp. 100, 101

With my memory of the Preston riots still vivid, I procured *Past and Present,* and read it perseveringly. It was far from easy reading, but I found in it strokes of descriptive power unequalled in my experience, and thrills of electric splendour which carried me enthusiastically on. I found in it, moreover, in political matters, a morality so righteous, a radicalism so high, reasonable, and humane, as to make it clear to me that without truckling to the ape and tiger of the mob, a man might hold the views of a radical.

> John Tyndall, 1890, "Personal Recollections of Thomas Carlyle," *New Fragments,* p. 349

He has left us in *Past and Present* our truest and most sympathetic picture of mediæval monasticism at its high water mark, a picture which no Catholic writer can hope to rival. He understood what those monks of St. Edmundsbury felt and thought, with perfect comprehension. Yet was he a student of the Middle Ages? Far from it, but he was a student of man.

> G. M. Trevelyan, 1899, "Carlyle as a Historian," *The Nineteenth Century,* vol. 46, p. 500

Life and Letters of Oliver Cromwell (1845)

We do not quarrel with Mr. Carlyle for his enthusiasm, if he feels it; but he really must not call people "flunkeys" and "canting persons" if they do not share it with him. He has thrown himself for the present on Oliver's own account of himself, and is content to stand by in the humble posture of direction post, or, at the highest, of showman. He shows us Oliver; an engraving of his portrait, very characteristic and striking; his letters and his speeches, equally full of character. We are left alone with the great man, to form our own judgment of him. Mr. Carlyle ought not to complain if his own interjectional bursts of rapture, and orders to love Oliver, produce less effect than the sight he presents to us. We do not grudge Puritanism its great man any more than its temporary triumph. It earned what it won by good means as well as bad. . . . His book labours and struggles, and leaves only impressions which counteract one another. Its parts do not adjust themselves naturally; fact pulls against commentary; elucidation falls dead upon the latter; and between them the living image of Cromwell drops through. Mr. Carlyle's own idea does not rise of itself out of his documents; he has to protect and foster it. There is a painful effort, a monotonous, impatient bluster, to keep up the reader's heroic mood. . . . We believe that he meant to bring out a genuinely English idea of excellence, to portray a man of rude exterior and speech, doing great things in a commonplace and unromantic way. But he must match his ideal with something better than Cromwell's distorted and unreal character, his repulsive energy, his dreary and ferocious faith, his thinly veiled and mastering selfishness.

Richard William Church, 1846-97, "Carlyle's Cromwell,"
Occasional Papers, pp. 15, 26, 52

Many will find Carlyle presumptuous, coarse; they will suspect from his theories, and also from his way of speaking, that he looks upon himself as a great man, neglected, of the race of heroes; that, in his opinion, the human race ought to put themselves in his hands, and trust him with their business. Certainly he lectures us, and with contempt. He despises his epoch; he has a sulky, sour tone; he keeps purposely on stilts. He disdains objections. In his eyes, opponents are not up to his form. He bullies his predecessors; when he speaks of Cromwell's biographers, he takes the tone of a man of genius astray amongst pedants. He has the superior smile, the resigned condescension of a hero who feels himself a martyr, and he only quits it, to shout at the top of his voice, like an ill-taught plebian. . . . Carlyle's masterpiece is but a collection of letters and speeches, commented on and united by a continuous narrative. The impression which they leave is extraordinary. Grave constitutional histories hang heavy after this compilation. The author wishes to make us comprehend a soul, the soul of Cromwell, the greatest of the Puritans, their chief, their abstract, their hero, and their model.

H. A. Taine, 1871, *History of English Literature,*
tr. Van Laun, vol. II, bk. V, ch. IV, pp. 451, 470

This book is, in my opinion, by far the most important contribution to English history, which has been made in the present century. Carlyle was the first to break the crust which has overlaid the subject of Cromwell since the Restoration, and to make Cromwell and Cromwell's age again intelligible to mankind. Anyone who will read what was written about him before Carlyle's work appeared, and what has been written since, will perceive how great was the achievement. The enthusiast, led away by ambition, and degenerating into the hypocrite, the received figure of the established legend, is gone for ever. We may retain each our own opinion about Cromwell, we may think that he did well or that he did ill, that he was wise or unwise; but we see the real man. We can entertain no shadow of doubt about the genuineness of the portrait; and, with the clear insight of Oliver himself, we have a new conception of the Civil War and of its consequences.

> James Anthony Froude, 1884, *Thomas Carlyle,*
> *A History of his Life in London,* vol. I, p. 305

Life of John Sterling (1851)

Well, the book has come at last, and, notwithstanding the evil animus of parts of it, a milder, more tender, and more pleasant gossiping little volume we have not read for many a day. The mountain has been in labor, and lo! a nice lively field-mouse, quite frisky and good-humored, has been brought forth. It is purely ridiculous and contemptible to speak, with some of our contemporaries, of this volume as Mr. Carlyle's best, or as, in any sense, a great work. The subject, as *he* has viewed it, was not great, and his treatment of it, while exceedingly graceful and pleasant, is by no means very powerful or very profound.

> George Gilfillan, 1855, *A Third Gallery of Portraits,* p. 267

I have always felt, notwithstanding a great affection and admiration for Carlyle, that his *Life of Sterling* has in it a breath of Mephistopheles, something of the mocking scornful spirit, satirically superior to all a young man's hereditary beliefs, and with a careless pleasure in pursuing and stripping him of these but weakly founded non-individual religious views which had built up the outer fabric of his life, such as hurts the moral sense, wonderful as is the almost lyrical strain of its lament and praise.

> Margaret O. W. Oliphant, 1897, *William Blackwood*
> *and his Sons,* vol. II, p. 186

One winter night I tried to re-read Carlyle's *Past and Present* and certain of his *Latter-Day Pamphlets;* but I found I could not, and thanked my stars that I did not have to. It was like riding a spirited but bony horse bareback. There was tremendous go in the beast; but oh, the bruises from those knotty and knuckle-like sentences! But the *Life of Sterling* I have found I can re-read with delight; it has a noble music.

> John Burroughs, 1897, "On the Re-reading of Books,"
> *Century Magazine,* vol. 55, p. 148

History of Friedrich II (1857-65)

Infinitely the wittiest book that ever was written,—a book that one would think the English people would rise up in mass and thank the author for, by cordial acclamation, and signify, by crowning him with oak-leaves, their joy that such a head existed among them, and sympathizing and much-reading America would make a new treaty or send a Minister Extraordinary to offer congratulation of honoring delight to England, in acknowledgment of this donation,—a book holding so many memorable and heroic facts, working directly on practice; with new heroes, things unvoiced before;—the German Plutarch (now that we have exhausted the Greek and Roman and British Plutarchs), with a range, too, of thought and wisdom so large and so elastic, not so much applying as inosculating to every need and sensibility of man, that we do not read a stereotype page, rather we see the eyes of the writer looking into ours, mark his behavior, humming, chuckling, with under-tones and trumpet-tones and shrugs, and long-commanding glances, stereoscoping every figure that passes, and every hill, river, road, hummock, and pebble in the long perspective. With its wonderful new system of mnemonics, whereby great and insignificant men are ineffaceably ticketed and marked and modelled in memory by what they were, had, and did; and withal a book that is a Judgment Day, for its moral verdict on the men and nations and manners of modern times. And this book makes no noise; I have hardly seen a notice of it in any newspaper or journal, and you would think there was no such book. I am not aware that Mr. Buchanan has sent a special messenger to Great Cheyne Row, Chelsea, or that Mr. Dallas has been instructed to assure Mr. Carlyle of his distinguished consideration. But the secret wits and hearts of men take note of it, not the less surely. They have said nothing lately in praise of the air, or of fire, or of the blessing of love, and yet, I suppose, they are sensible of these, and not less of this book, which is like these.

> Ralph Waldo Emerson, 1859, *Diary, Correspondence of Carlyle and Emerson*, ed. Norton, vol. II, p. 305

In conclusion, after saying, as honest critics must, that *The History of Friedrich II, called Frederick the Great* is a book to be read in with more satisfaction than to be read through, after declaring that it is open to all manner of criticism, especially in point of moral purpose and tendency, we must admit with thankfulness, that it has the one prime merit of being the work of a man who has every quality of a great poet except that supreme one of rhythm which shapes both matter and manner to harmonious proportion, and that where it is good, it is good as only genius knows how to be. With the gift of song, Carlyle would have been the greatest of epic poets since Homer. Without it, to modulate and harmonize and bring parts into their proper relation, he is the most amorphous of humorists, the most shining avatar of whim the world has ever seen. . . . The figures of most historians seem like dolls stuffed with bran, whose whole substance runs out through any hole that criticism may tear in them, but Carlyle's are so real in comparison, that, if you pick them, they bleed. He seems a little wearied, here and there, in his Friedrich, with the multiplicity of detail, and does his filling-in rather shabbily; but he still remains in his own way, like his hero, the Only, and such episodes as that of Voltaire would make the fortune of any other writer. Though not the safest of guides in politics or practical philosophy, his value as an inspirer and awakener cannot be overestimated.

James Russell Lowell, 1866-71, "Carlyle,"
My Study Windows, pp. 147, 148, 149

The first effect of the book in England was to weaken its author's moral influence, for the Christian conscience of the country revolted against its teaching, and was shocked by the pictures of Frederick and his father. It was only as the book receded from view, and its author's previous writings were reverted to, that the painful impression wore off. That feeling was only too well founded. Though he did not magnify Frederick, in whom Force without Righteousness was incarnate, as he had magnified Cromwell, it cannot be denied that he treats this unspeakable monster with a deference to which he was in no way entitled; and at times it would almost appear as if he loved him for his unendurable brutality, while he has actually the hardihood to charge other historians with injustice in not recognising the candour with which Frederick owned that his seizure of Silesia was one of the greatest crimes ever perpetrated.

William Howie Wylie, 1881, Thomas Carlyle,
The Man and his Books, p. 269

A work of superlative genius, which defies every canon of criticism and sets at nought every rule of historical composition. It is a succession of startling flashes and detonations. In no one of Carlyle's works do the peculiar qualities of his genius show themselves with more intensity. There is scarcely a paragraph that does not contain in itself either a poem or a picture. The book is founded on the most exhaustive study and the most careful observation. The author even visited the more important of Frederick's battle-fields, and had surveys made in the interests of absolute accuracy. Every scrap of German writing that would throw light upon the reign appears to have been examined and weighed. The result is one of the most remarkable books in the English language, and one which, all things considered, is unquestionably the best history of Frederick the Great in any language.

Charles Kendall Adams, 1882, *A Manual of Historical Literature*, p. 272

Just at the time when the first instalment of Carlyle's *Life of Frederick* was published, I found him [Macaulay] engaged in the perusal of the opening chapters. His wrath—I can use no milder word—against Carlyle's style was boundless. He read aloud to me four or five of the most Carlylean sentences, and then, throwing the book on the library table, exclaimed, "I hold that no Englishman has the right to treat his mother-tongue after so unfilial a fashion." . . . Before a week had elapsed I was again at Holly Lodge, and he at once recurred to Carlyle's history. "Pray read it," he said, "as soon as you can find time. Of course I have not got, and never shall get, reconciled to his distortions and contortions of language; but there are, notwithstanding, passages of truly wonderful interest and power, and in the infinite variety of new historical facts, and in the delight and instruction they afford, if my first feeling has been that of annoyance at the strange way of telling the story, my second and permanent feeling is one of gratitude that—even in such a way—the story has been told."

James Montgomery Stuart, 1885, *Reminiscences and Essays*

By this later work Carlyle outstripped, in the judgment of serious critics, his only possible rival, Macaulay, and took his place as the first scientific historian of the early Victorian period. His method in this class of work is characteristic of him as an individualist; he endeavours, in all conjunctions, to see the man moving, breathing, burning in the glow and flutter of adventure. This gives an extraordinary vitality to portions of Carlyle's narrative, if it also tends to disturb the reader's conception of the general progress of events.

Edmund Gosse, 1897, *A Short History of Modern English Literature*, p. 346

Correspondence and Reminiscences (1881)

The hasty and ill-advised publication of the *Reminiscences,* abounding in unfortunate matter, given to the world with feminine zeal but without even the pretence of clear-headed editorial supervision, has certainly let loose the full tongue of detraction.

Robert Buchanan, 1881, "Wylie's Life of Carlyle," *Contemporary Review*, vol. 39, p. 793

It was the lot of the present writer to read nearly all the obituary notices of him which appeared in the leading journals after his death. With not an exception they were extremely eulogistic, praising his works and applauding in the highest terms the dignity and stern conscientiousness of his life. But when, about three weeks later, the *Reminiscences* were published by Mr. Froude, the tide took a turn. They were found to be full of harsh, and, as in the case of Charles Lamb, even cruel and heartless judgments; and Carlyle's faults of temper, his malice, and his uncharitableness began to be sharply commented on. A few of the more sturdy admirers of the Seer of Chelsea protested that the *Reminiscences* did not give any idea of the real Carlyle at all; that nothing could be more unjust than to form an estimate of his character from angry passages written in his old age, when weak health and agonising sorrow had rendered him scarcely responsible for his utterances. This defence proved to be but a refuge of lies.

Henry J. Nicoll, 1882, Landmarks of English Literature, p. 424

Reluctantly, and only when he found that his wishes would not and could not be respected, Carlyle requested me to undertake the task which he had thus described as hopeless; and placed materials in my hands which would make the creation of a true likeness of him, if still difficult, yet no longer as impossible as he had declared it to be. Higher confidence was never placed by any man in another. I had not sought it, but I did not refuse to accept it. I felt myself only more strictly bound than men in such circumstances usually are, to discharge the duty which I was undertaking with the fidelity which I knew to be expected from me. Had I considered my own comfort or my own interest, I should have sifted out or passed lightly over the delicate features in the story. It would have been as easy as it would have been agreeable for me to construct a picture, with every detail strictly accurate, of an almost perfect character. An account so written would have been read with immediate pleasure. Carlyle would have been admired and applauded, and the biographer, if he had not shared in the praise, would at least have escaped censure. He would have followed in the track marked out for him by a custom which is all but universal. . . . Had I taken the course which the "natural man" would have recommended, I should have given no faithful account of Carlyle. I should have created a "delusion and a hallucination" of the precise kind which he who was the truest of men most deprecated and dreaded; and I should have done it not innocently and in ignorance, but with deliberate insincerity, after my attention had been specially directed by his own generous openness to the points which I should have left unnoticed. I should have been unjust first to myself—for I should have failed in what I knew to be my duty as a biographer. I should have been unjust secondly to the public.

James Anthony Froude, 1884, Thomas Carlyle,
A History of his Life in London, vol. I, pp. 2, 3

Every one agrees with you as to Froude and Carlyle, but there is no doubt that one of the bad effects of Froude's extraordinary proceedings has been to tire people of Carlyle, and discipline them from occupying themselves any more with him, for the present at any rate.

Matthew Arnold, 1887, To C. E. Norton, Aug. 31;
Letters, ed. Russell, vol. II, p. 430

Mr. Froude has done his worst or his best, and it cannot be undone. Even Mr. Eliot Norton's brilliant re-editing cannot undo it. And what is the result? Simply that we must thank either Mr. Froude or his blunder for enabling us to understand how great Carlyle really was. . . . Carlyle, as we know him now, is more real, and immeasurably more impressive than the Carlyle we knew before. The literary small-talkers may say the idol is shattered; but those to whom Carlyle was never an idol, but an instructor and inspirer, must be glad and not sorry that he has become so real to them.

Walter Lewin, 1887, "Garnett's Life of Carlyle,"
The Academy, vol. 32, p. 128

The indiscretions of a biographer who thought it his duty to let "the many-headed beast know" everything, even the most private details of the life of one of the most whimsical and dyspeptic of men,—a biographer, I may add, who misjudged his hero, as a man without humour was sure to misjudge one who was full of it, by taking all his extravagant statements *au pied de la lettre.* Perhaps too much has been made of the indiscretion of a writer, who, so far as indiscreet publication was concerned, seems not to have gone much beyond what he was commissioned or allowed to do by Carlyle himself. But it is worth while to remark that there are many details of a man's life, which gain an undue importance by being revived after the lapse of years, and when it is no longer possible to supply the necessary explanation of the words and action that express only the feelings of the passing hour.

Edward Caird, 1892, "The Genius of Carlyle,"
Essays on Literature and Philosophy, vol. I, p. 237

The *Reminiscences* and the volumes that succeeded them gave, in many quarters apparently, the *coup de grâce* to Carlyle's vogue. Vogue of their own they notoriously had in a true *succès de scandale,* and Carlyle's friends could only denounce his chosen executor and biographer. But this was of course extremely transient, and the result was an immense weariness with the whole subject. Carlyle's own writings fell speedily into a neglect as complete probably as has ever happened to a writer of anything like his power.

W. C. Brownell, 1901, Victorian Prose Masters, p. 50

GENERAL

When I recollect how the "Edinburgh Reviewers" treated my works not many years since, and when I now consider Carlyle's merits with respect to German literature, I am astonished at the important step for the better. . . . The temper in which he works is always admirable. What an earnest man he is! and how he has studied us Germans! He is almost more at home in our literature than ourselves. At any rate, we cannot vie with him in our researches in English literature.

> Johann Wolfgang Goethe, by Eckermann, 1828,
> *Conversations,* tr. Oxenford, vol. II, p. 86

Not one obscure line, or half-line did he ever write. His meaning lies plain as the daylight, and he who runs may read; indeed, only he who runs *can* read, and keep up with the meaning. It has the distinctness of a picture to his mind, and he tells us only what he sees printed in largest English type upon the face of things. He utters substantial English thoughts in plainest English dialects; for it must be confessed, he speaks more than one of these. . . . His felicity and power of expression surpass even his special merit as historian and critic. Therein his experience has not failed him, but furnished him with such a store of winged, ay and legged words, as only a London life, perchance, could give account of. We had not understood the wealth of the language before. Nature is ransacked, and all the resorts and purlieus of humanity are taxed, to furnish the fittest symbol for his thought. He does not go to the dictionary, the word-book, but to the word-manufactory itself, and has made endless work for the lexicographers.

> Henry David Thoreau, 1847-66, *Thomas Carlyle
> and His Works, A Yankee in Canada,* pp. 218, 219

Mr. Carlyle seems to be in the condition of a man who uses stimulants, and one must increase his dose from day to day as the senses become dulled under the spur. He began by admiring strength of character and purpose, and the manly self-denial which makes a humble fortune great by steadfast loyalty to duty. He has gone on till mere strength has become such washy weakness that there is no longer any titillation in it; and nothing short of downright violence will rouse his nerves now to the needed excitement. . . . Since *Sartor Resartus* Mr. Carlyle has done little but repeat himself with increasing emphasis and heightened shrillness. Warning has steadily heated toward denunciation, and remonstrance soured toward scolding.

> James Russell Lowell, 1866-71, "Carlyle," *My Study Windows,*
> pp. 130, 131

His books opened anywhere show him berating the wrong he sees, but seldom the means of removing. There is ever the same melancholy advocacy of work to be done under the dread master: force of strokes, the right to rule and be ruled, the dismal burden. He rides his Leviathan as fiercely as did his countryman,—Hobbes; can be as truculent and abusive. Were he not thus fatally in earnest, we should take him for the harlequin he often seems, not seeing the sorrowing sadness thus playing off its load in this grotesque mirth, this scornful irony of his; he painting in spite of himself his portraits in the warmth of admiration, the blaze of wrath, giving us mythology for history mostly.

A. Bronson Alcott, 1869, *Concord Days,* p. 161

When you ask Englishmen, especially those under forty, who amongst them are the thinking men, they first mention Carlyle; but at the same time they advise you not to read him, warning you that you will not understand him at all. Then, of course, we hasten to get the twenty volumes of Carlyle—criticism, history, pamphlets, fantasies, philosophy; we read them with very strange emotions, contradicting every morning our opinion of the night before. We discover at last that we are in presence of an extraordinary animal, a relic of a lost family, a sort of mastodon, lost in a world not made for him. We rejoice in this zoological good luck, and dissect him with minute curiosity, telling ourselves that we shall probably never find another animal like him. . . . We are at first put out. All is new here—ideas, style, tone, the shape of the phrases, and the very vocabulary. He takes everything in a contrary meaning, does violence to everything, expressions and things. With him paradoxes are set down for principles; common sense takes the form of absurdity. We are, as it were, carried unto an unknown world, whose inhabitants walk head downwards, feet in the air, dressed in motley, as great lords and maniacs, with contortions, jerks, and cries; we are grievously stunned by these extravagant and discordant sounds; we want to stop our ears, we have a headache, we are obliged to decipher a new language. . . . Carlyle is a Puritan seer, before whose eyes pass scaffolds, orgies, massacres, battles, and who, besieged by furious or bloody phantoms, prophesies, encourages, or curses. If you do not throw down the book from anger or weariness, you will lose your judgment; your ideas depart, nightmare seizes you, a medley of contracted and ferocious figures whirl about in your head; you hear the howls of insurrection, cries of war; you are sick; you are like those listeners to the Covenanters, whom the preaching filled with disgust or enthusiasm, and who broke the head of their prophet, if they did not take him for their leader. . . . From the sublime to the ignoble, from the pathetic to the grotesque, is but a step with Carlyle. With the same stroke he touches the two extremes. His adorations end in sarcasms. . . . He leaps in unimpeded jerks from one end of the field of ideas to the other; he confounds all styles, jumbles all forms, heaps together pagan allusions, Bible reminiscences, German abstractions, technical terms, poetry, slang, mathematics, physiology, archaic words, neologies. . . . Carlyle takes religion in the German manner, after a symbolical fashion. This is why he is called a Pantheist, which in plain language means a madman or a rogue.

H. A. Taine, 1871, *History of English Literature,* tr. Van Laun, vol. II, bk. V, ch. IV, pp. 436, 437, 438, 440, 463

I have already mentioned Carlyle's earlier writings as one of the channels through which I received the influences which enlarged my early narrow creed; but I do not think that those writings, by themselves, would ever have had any effect on my opinions. What truths they contained, though of the very kind which I was already receiving from other quarters, were presented in a form and vesture less suited than any other to give them access to a mind trained as mine had been. They seemed a haze of poetry and German metaphysics, in which almost the only clear thing was a strong animosity to most of the opinions which were the basis of my mode of thought; religious scepticism; utilitarianism, the doctrine of circumstances, and the attaching any importance to democracy, logic, or political economy. Instead of my having been taught anything, in the first instance, by Carlyle, it was only in proportion as I came to see the same truths through media more suited to my mental constitution, that I recognised them in his writings. Then, indeed, the wonderful power with which he put them forth made a deep impression upon me, and I was during a long period one of his most fervent admirers; but the good his writings did me, was not as philosophy to instruct, but as poetry to animate. . . . I did not, however, deem myself a competent judge of Carlyle. I felt that he was a poet, and that I was not; that he was a man of intuition, which I was not; and that as such, he not only saw things long before me, which I could only when they were pointed out to me, hobble after and prove, but that it was highly probable he could see many things which were not visible to me even after they were pointed out. I knew that I could not see round him, and could never be certain that I saw over him; and I never presumed to judge him with any definiteness, until he was interpreted to me by one greatly the superior of us both—who was more a poet than he, and more a thinker than I—whose own mind and nature included his, and infinitely more.

John Stuart Mill, 1873, *Autobiography,* pp. 174, 176

The way to test how much he has left his country were to consider, or try to consider, for a moment, the array of British thought, the resultant *ensemble* of the last fifty years, as existing to-day, *but with Carlyle left out.* It would be like an army with no artillery. The show were still a gay rich one—Byron, Scott, Tennyson, and many more—horsemen and rapid infantry, and banners flying—but the last heavy roar so dear to the ear of the train'd soldier, and that settles fate and victory, would be lacking.

Walt Whitman, 1881, "Death of Thomas Carlyle,"
Specimen Days and Collect, p. 169

Anything that I can do to help in raising a memorial to Carlyle shall be most willingly done. Few men can have dissented more strongly from his way of looking at things than I; but I should not yield to the most devoted of his followers in gratitude for the bracing wholesome influence of his writings when, as a very young man, I was essaying without rudder or compass to strike out a course for myself.

Thomas Henry Huxley, 1881, *To Lord Stanley,* March 9;
Life and Letters, ed. Huxley, vol. II, p. 36

To sum up, if I had to characterize the moral and intellectual influence exercised by Carlyle, I should say that he seems to me to have, above all things, helped to loosen the fetters of positive creed in which thought was imprisoned among his countrymen. Carlyle was a mystic, and mysticism here, as elsewhere, discharged the function which belongs to it in the chain of systems; to wit, that of dissolving dogma under pretence of spiritualizing it, of shattering faith under pretence of enlarging it. When men heard Carlyle speak so much of divinity and eternity, of mystery and adoration, they hailed him as the preacher of a religion higher and wider than current belief. In vain did orthodoxy, more keen-sighted, point out the negations which lay hid under the writer's formulas. It is so pleasant to free oneself without appearing to break too sharply with consecrated words and institutions. Since then speculation has made much way in England. The universal mysteries of our author have been exchanged for exact research, precise definitions, rigorous ascertainments. I do not know whether Carlyle was aware of it, but he lived long enough to see his influence exhausted, his teaching out of date. It is true that, as consolation, he could take himself to witness that he had served as the transition between the past and the present, and that this is in the long run the best glory to which a thinker can pretend here below.

Edmond Scherer, 1881-91, *Thomas Carlyle,*
Essays on English Literature, tr. Saintsbury, p. 235

To me, profoundly averse to autocracy, Carlyle's political doctrines had ever been repugnant. Much as I did, and still do, admire his marvellous style and the vigour, if not the truth, of his thought—so much so that I always enjoy any writing of his, however much I disagree with it—intercourse with him soon proved impracticable. Twice or thrice, in 1851-2, I was taken to see him by Mr. G. H. Lewes; but I soon found that the alternatives were—listening in silence to his dogmas, sometimes absurd, or getting into a hot argument with him, which ended in our glaring at one another; and as I did not like either alternative I ceased to go.

> Herbert Spencer, 1894, "The Late Professor Tyndall,"
> *Fortnightly Review,* vol. 61, p. 144

Carlyle was probably never at his best when he gave himself to the study of a particular author. His genius rather lay in the more general aspects of his work, and in the force with which he gave an entirely new turn to the currents of English criticism.

> C. E. Vaughan, 1896, ed. *English Literary Criticism,* p. 200

I have said all that is to be said against Carlyle's work almost designedly; for he is one of those who are so great that we rather need to blame them for the sake of our own independence than praise them for the sake of their fame. He came and spoke a word, and the chatter of rationalism stopped, and the sums would no longer work out and be ended. He was a breath of Nature turning in her sleep under the load of civilisation, a stir in the very stillness of God to tell us he was still there.

> G. K. Chesterton, 1903, *Thomas Carlyle*

BENJAMIN DISRAELI
Earl of Beaconsfield
1804-1881

Born, in London, 21 Dec. 1804. Educated at school at Blackheath. Articled to solicitor 18 Nov. 1821. Entered at Lincoln's Inn, 1824. Visit to Spain, Italy, and Levant, 1828-31. Worked at literature for five years. M. P. for Maidstone, July 1837. Married Mrs. Wyndham Lewis, 23 Aug. 1839. M. P. for Shrewsbury, 1841. Visit to Germany and France, autumn of 1845. Leader of Opposition in House of Commons, Sept. 1848. Chancellor of Exchequer, Feb. 1852. Contrib. to *The Press* newspaper, 1853-58. Chancellor of Exchequer second time, 1865. Prime Minister, March to Nov., 1868. Active political life. Wife died, 15 Dec. 1872. Prime Minister second time, Jan. 1874 to March 1880. Last speech in House of Commons, 11 Aug. 1876. Created Earl of Beaconsfield, 12 Aug. 1876. Died, 19 April

1881. Buried at Hughenden. WORKS: *Vivian Grey* (anon.), pt. i., 1826; pt. ii., 1827; *The Star Chamber* (anon.; suppressed), 1826; *The Voyage of Captain Popanilla* (anon.), 1828; *The Young Duke* (anon.), 1831; *Contarini Fleming* (anon.), 1832; *England and France* (anon.), 1832; *What is he?* (anon.), 1833; *The Wondrous Tale of Alroy* (anon.), 1833; *The Present Crisis Examined*, 1834; *The Rise of Iskander*, 1834; *The Revolutionary Epic*, 1834; *Vindication of the British Constitution*, 1835; *Letters of Runnymede* (anon.), 1836; *The Spirit of Whigism*, 1836; *Venetia* (anon.), 1837; *Henrietta Temple* (anon.), 1837; *The Tragedy of Count Alarcos* (anon.), 1839; *Coningsby*, 1844; *Sybil*, 1845; *Tancred*, 1847; *Mr. Gladstone's Finance*, 1862; *Lothair*, 1870; *Novels and Tales* (collected), 1870-71; *Endymion* (anon.), 1880. POSTHUMOUS: *Home Letters*, 1885; *Correspondence with his Sister*, 1886. He *edited* the following editions of works by his father: *Curiosities of Literature*, 1849; *Charles I.*, 1851; *Works*, 1858-59; *Amenities of Literature*, 1881; *Literary Character*, 1881; *Calamities of Authors*, 1881. LIFE: by Kebbel, 1888; by Froude, 1890.

R. Farquharson Sharp, 1897, *A Dictionary of English Authors*, p. 81

SEE: *Tales and Sketches*, ed. J. Logie Robertson, 1891; W. F. Monypenny and G. E. Buckle, *The Life of Disraeli*, 1910-20, 6 v., rev. 1929, 2 v.; Muriel Masefield, *Peacocks and Primroses: A Study of Disraeli's Novels*, 1953.

PERSONAL

Disraeli has one of the most remarkable faces I ever saw. He is lividly pale, and but for the energy of his action and the strength of his lungs, would seem to be a victim to consumption. His eye is as black as Erebus, and has the most mocking, lying-in-wait sort of expression conceivable. His mouth is alive with a kind of working and impatient nervousness, and when he has burst forth, as he does constantly, with a particularly successful cataract of expression, it assumes a curl of triumphant scorn that would be worthy of a Mephistopheles. His hair is as extraordinary as his taste in waistcoats. A thick heavy mass of jet-black ringlets falls over his left cheek almost to his collarless stock, while on the right temple it is parted and put away with the smooth carefulness of a girl's, and shines most unctuously—

"With thy incomparable oil, Macassar!"

Nathaniel Parker Willis, 1835, *Pencillings by the Way*

By and by came a rather tall, slender person, in a black frock-coat, buttoned up, and black pantaloons, taking long steps, but I thought rather feebly or listlessly. His shoulders were round, or else he had a habitual stoop in them. He had a prominent nose, a thin face, and a sallow, very sallow complexion; . . . and had I seen him in America I should have taken him for a hard-worked editor of a newspaper, weary and worn with night-labor and want of exercise,—aged before his time. It was Disraeli, and I never saw any other Englishman look in the least like him; though, in America, his appearance would not attract notice as being unusual.

Nathaniel Hawthorne, 1856, English Notebooks, vol. II, p. 20

If Mr. Disraeli had, as he once said, the "best of wives," he, on his part, proved the best of husbands. Till the last day of her life he paid to his wife those attentions which are too often associated rather with the romance of youthful intercourse than with the routine of married life. When he rose to the highest point of his ambition, the only favor he would accept of the Queen was a coronet for his wife. He was scarcely ever absent from her side until the dark day when the fast friends were to be parted. She knew that she was dying, but refrained from telling him so, in order that he might be spared the pain of bidding her farewell. He also knew that her last hour was at hand but kept silence lest he should distress her. Thus they parted, each anxious to avoid striking a blow at the other's heart. The domestic lives of public men are properly held to be beyond the range of public comment; but in an age when marriage is the theme of ridicule from "leaders of progress" it may be that this passage in Mr. Disraeli's career may be pondered with some profit by the young.

L. J. Jennings, 1873, "Benjamin Disraeli,"
Atlantic Monthly, vol. 32, p. 642

The enclosed letter and copy of my answer ought to go to you as a family curiosity and secret. Nobody whatever knows of it beyond our two selves here, except Lady Derby,whom I believe to have been the contriver of the whole affair. You would have been surprised, all of you, to have found unexpectedly your poor old brother converted into Sir Tom; but alas! there was no danger at any moment of such a catastrophe. I do, however, truly admire the magnanimity of Dizzy in regard to me. He is the only man I almost never spoke of except with contempt; and if there is anything of scurrility anywhere chargeable against me, he is the subject of it; and yet see, here he comes with a pan of hot coals for my guilty head. I am, on the whole, gratified a little within my own dark heart at this mark of the goodwill of high people—Dizzy by no means the chief of them—which has come to me now at the very end, when I can have the additional pleasure of answering, "Alas friends! it is of no use to me, and I will not have it." Enough, enough! Return me the official letter, and say nothing about it beyond the walls of your own house.

Thomas Carlyle, 1875, Letter to John Carlyle, Jan. 1;
Thomas Carlyle, A History of his Life in London,
ed. Froude, vol. II, p. 369

With Lord Beaconsfield everything is in keeping; the novelist is part of the man, and the Prime Minister of the novelist. I can never read his books or see him at work on the world's stage without recalling the Mr. Disraeli of fifty years ago, as a contemporary depicts him, dressed in velvet and satin, his wrists encircled by ruffles, his hair cunningly curled, his fingers loaded with rings, an ivory cane in his hand; with all the exterior of a dandy—a dandy of genius; a bundle of contradictions, ambition allied to scepticism, determination hiding itself under sallies and paradoxes. So much for his person: his life has followed suit. A foreigner, a Jew, he raised himself from an attorney's office to the peerage of England, and the headship of his country's government. The character of his policy—full of theatrical strokes, of new departures, whimsical or bold as the case may be—is well known. In everything that he has done, you feel the Oriental's taste for the brilliant, the adventurer's taste for the turns of Fortune's wheel, the parvenu's taste for pomp. But it is in his writings more than anywhere else that he shows himself as he is: because Lord Beaconsfield is at bottom an artist first of all. His old dandyism was already literary; and his modern policy is still romantic.

Edmond Scherer, 1880-91, *Essays on English Literature,*
tr. Saintsbury, p. 240

Those who had observed his course from the beginning gave him no credit for settled convictions upon any subject, except the honour and interest of the race from which he had sprung; and his books, in which there was much glitter and tinsel, but little solid or genuine matter, confirmed that impression. He seemed to be an actor, in a mask which he never took off. He had courage, audacity, temper, patience, and an indomitable will; and by these qualities, and a study of men, too cynical to be deep, but useful for party management, he established his position. He had also a certain magnanimity, which made him generally impassive and unruffled, even when successfully attacked, and free from all appearance of ill-will or resentment against those who attacked him; a hard hitter himself whenever it suited his purpose, he could take hard blows, as nothing more than the regular practice of the game. He seems to have drawn his own portrait, when he said of Sidonia: "It was impossible to penetrate him. Though unreserved in his manner, his frankness was strictly limited to the surface. He observed everything, thought ever, but avoided serious discussion. If you pressed him for an opinion, he took refuge in raillery, or threw out some grave paradox, with which it was not easy to cope." Lord Beaconsfield was a man of genius, certainly; those of his writings which have most the appearance of seriousness leave the impression that he was more Radical than Conservative, with a strong sense of the hollowness of the politics of his time. As an orator, he was greatest when least serious; no man excelled him in the satirical vein. But his graver efforts were turgid and artificial; wrapping up the absence of much definite meaning in ponderous words. Even in private he did not seem (to observers like myself, who seldom met him) to talk naturally. The one really great work of his life was to raise his own race to a footing of fuller social and political equality in this country with their fellow-citizens; obliterating the last remnants of a state of feeling towards them, which had formerly been productive of much wrong.

Roundell Palmer (Earl of Selborne), 1898, *Memorials, Part II., Personal and Political,* vol. I, p. 478

Vivian Grey (1826-27)

Murray was much pleased with the philip [*sic*] at young D'Israeli in the "Noctes" a month or two ago. This fellow has humbugged him most completely. After the tricks of which he has been guilty, he will scarcely dare show his face in London again for some time. You are aware, I dare say, that *Vivian Grey* was palmed off upon Colburn by Mrs. Austin, the wife of the Honourable Mr. Warde's [*sic*] lawyer, as the production of the author of *Tremaine!* and upon this understanding Colburn gave three times as much as he would otherwise have done.

Alaric A. Watts, 1826, *Letter to Blackwood,* Oct. 7; *William Blackwood and his Sons,* ed. Oliphant, vol. I, p. 507

This is a piquant and amusing novel, though its merits are not of a very high order. . . . The foundation of the story is extravagant. The powers, purposes, and influence of a mature man are attributed to a boy of twenty; and the work is rather a series of sketches than a regularly built story. The hero has no mistress but politics, and no adventures but political adventures. The other prominent characters are all fools or knaves, and all are more or less forced and unnatural. Their aggregate makes a strong picture, which dazzles, but does not satisfy. The style of writing is dashing and careless, occasionally rising into hasty extravagance, and at times sinking into mawkish sentimentality. The morality of the book is loose. It is, in fact, little more than a picture of the vices and follies of the great, with an active spirit in the midst of them, making their vices and follies the stepping-stones to his ambition.

William Cullen Bryant, 1827, *New York Review,* Dec.

One day, suddenly, *Vivian Grey* burst upon astonished society, and took it by storm. It found its way at once to every drawing-room table. It was the town talk at ministerial *soirées,* in the lobbies of the House of Commons, at the Pall Mall clubs. Great ladies asked each other if they had read it; wondered who wrote it; guessed whom the author meant to represent by the Marquis of Carabas, and Lord Courtown, and Mr. Cleveland; and who was Vivian Grey himself.

George Makepeace Towle, 1878, *Beaconsfield,* p. 21

Coningsby (1844)

Ben Disraeli, the Jew scamp, has published a very blackguard novel, in which the Pusey and Young England doctrines are relieved by a full and malignant but clever enough detail of all the abominations of Lord Hertford, and Croker figures in full fig. I should not wonder if there were some row—the abuse of Crokey is so very horrid, ditto of Lord Lowther. Peel is flattered, but the Government lashed. Awful vanity of the Hebrew.

John Gibson Lockhart, 1844, *To Walter Scott Lockhart,*
May 13; *Life and Letters,* ed. Lang, vol. II, p. 199

Did you read *Coningsby,* that very able book, without character, story, or specific teaching? It is well worth reading, and worth wondering over. D'Israeli, who is a man of genius, has written, nevertheless, books which will live longer, and move deeper. But everybody should read *Coningsby.* It is a sign of the times.

Elizabeth Barrett Browning, 1844, *To Mrs. Martin,* Oct. 5;
Letters, ed. Kenyon, vol. I, p. 203

As a tale, *Coningsby* is nothing; but it is put together with extreme skill to give opportunities for typical sketches of character, and for the expression of opinions on social and political subjects. We have pictures of fashionable society, gay and giddy, such as no writer ever described better; peers, young, middle-aged, and old, good, bad, and indifferent, the central figure a profligate old noble of immense fortune, whose person was equally recognised, and whose portrait was also preserved by Thackeray. Besides these, intriguing or fascinating ladies, political hacks, country gentlemen, mill-owners, and occasional wise outsiders, looking upon the chaos and delivering oracular interpretations or prophecies. Into the middle of such a world the hero is launched, being the grandson and possible heir of the wicked peer.

James Anthony Froude, 1890, *Lord Beaconsfield*
(*Prime Ministers of Queen Victoria*), p. 109

On no subject is he more prone to give the reins to his imagination than that of the intellectual and artistic superiority of the Jewish race, as in *Coningsby,* his finest story.

Richard D. Graham, 1897, The Masters of
Victorian Literature, p. 69

Sybil (1845)

Sybil is not an improvement upon *Coningsby.* The former novel was received with marked approbation, from the apparent sympathy which it displayed with a suffering and neglected class. *Sybil* will meet with far inferior success; its pictures only show how strongly and coarsely the author can paint, and are obviously not the result of any genuine regard for the poor and afflicted. It is not as a mere work of fiction that we intend to criticise *Sybil,* or the *Two Nations,* though even in this point of view we think it very faulty,—abrupt in its transitions—incorrect in costume—extravagant in delineation—and fantastic, and sometimes absurd in its philosophy—and far from high-minded in its conception and its plot.

W. R. Greg, 1845, "Sybil," The Westminster Review,
vol. 44, p. 141

Lothair (1870)

Lothair is certainly free from the prevailing vice of the present age of novels. It is in no degree tinted with *sensationalism.* It has as distinct a purpose as a Parliamentary Blue Book, and is about as exciting as one. Its object is to expose the arts and wiles of the Catholics, clergy and laity to entice into the fold of Rome young noblemen and gentlemen of great estates. If our indistinct recollection of Mr. Disraeli's former novels does not much mislead us, their fundamental errors as works of art, lay in their being virtually pamphlets in the disguise of stories, to prove this or that theory of politics or morals. . . . It is hard to see how a man capable of those caustic, bitter, cruel diatribes of twenty years since against Sir Robert Peel could be capable of the platitudinous dulness of *Lothair.* It shows at least how very absurd a novel a very clever man can write—which is consolatory to the average stupidity of mankind.

Edmund Quincy, 1870, "Lothair," The Nation, vol. 10, pp. 372, 373

Lothair is not a mere novel, and its appearance is not simply a fact for Mr. Mudie. It is a political event. When a man whose life has been passed in Parliament, who for a generation has been the real head of a great party, sits down, as he approaches the age of seventy, to embody his view of modern life, it is a matter of interest to the politician, the historian, nay, almost the philosopher. The literary qualities of the book need detain no man. Premiers not uncommonly do write sad stuff; and we should be thankful if the stuff be amusing. But the mature thoughts on life of one who has governed an empire on which the sun never sets, have an inner meaning to the thoughtful mind. Marcus Aurelius, amidst his imperial eagles, thought right to give us his Reflections. The sayings of Napoleon at St. Helena have strange interest to all men. And Solomon in all his glory was induced to publish some amazing rhapsodies on human nature and the society of his own time.

Frederic Harrison, 1870-86, *The Choice of Books and Other Literary Pieces*, p. 148

What makes *Lothair* psychologically interesting arises from the same position of affairs that has made the style official, namely, that the author stands at the summit of his wishes, and has realized his schemes, so that he no longer needs to take various circumstances into consideration. *Lothair* is a more straightforward book than the *Trilogy,* so called, which preceded it. It is not only without false mysticism, but in a religious point of view, it is the most openly free-thinking work that Disraeli has written, so opposed to miracles that it might be taken for the work of a Rationalist if the fantastic author had not signed it with his fantastic doctrine, never renounced, of the sole victorious Semitic principle.

Georg Brandes, 1880, *Lord Beaconsfield,* tr. Mrs. George Sturge, p. 347

GENERAL

We pass to analyse, in a general way, Disraeli's intellectual powers. These are exceedingly varied. He has one of the sharpest and clearest of intellects, not, perhaps, of the most philosophical order, but exceedingly penetrating and acute. He has a fine fancy, soaring up at intervals into high imagination, and marking him a genuine child of that nation from whom came forth the loftiest, richest and most impassioned song which earth has ever witnessed—the nation of Isaiah, Ezekiel, Solomon and Job. He has little humor, but a vast deal of diamond-pointed wit. The whole world knows his powers of sarcasm. They have never been surpassed in the combination of savage force, and, shall we say, Satanic coolness, of energy and of point, of the fiercest *animus* within, and the utmost elegance of outward expression. He wields for his weapon a polar icicle—gigantic as a club—glittering as a star—deadly as a scimitar—and cool as eternal frost. His style and languge are the faithful index of these varied and bril-

liant powers. His sentences are almost always short, epigrammatic, conclu-
sive—pointed with wit and starred with imagery—and so rapid in their
bickering, sparkling progress! One, while reading the better parts of his
novels, seems reading a record of the conversations of Napoleon.

George Gilfillan, 1855, *A Third Gallery of Portraits,* p. 360

It is easy to detect faults, which stand out on the very surface of his work,
and are, indeed, an essential part of the methods by which he produced
his effect. The imagination is often fantastic, the ornament is unduly lavish, the gilding is sometimes tawdry and overdone, the sentiment often in-
flated. Mediocrity will satisfy itself by calling this vulgarity and preten-
tiousness. But in truth it was only the natural result of an imagination
singularly luxuriant, combined with a far-reaching sarcasm, and an undercurrent of deep thought and brooding melancholy.

Henry Craik, 1896, *English Prose,* vol. V, p. 486

GEORGE HENRY BORROW
1803-1881

Born, at East Dereham, 5 July 1803. Educated at Norwich Grammar
School, 1815-18. Family changed place of residence constantly, 1803-20.
Articled to Solicitor in Norwich, 1818-23. First literary publication, 1825.
To London at father's death. Assisted in compilation of *Newgate Calendar.*
Tour through England; through France, Germany, Russia and the East,
as agent for British and Foreign Bible Society, 1833-39. Contrib. letters on
his travels to *Morning Post,* 1837-39. Married Mary Clarke, 1840. Tour in
S. E. Europe, 1844. Bought estate on Oulton Broad. Lived there till about
1865. Removed to Brompton. Wife died there, 1869. Died, at Oulton, 26
July, 1881. WORKS: *Romantic Ballads* (from the Danish), 1826; *Targum,*
1835; *The Bible in Spain* (3 vols.), 1843; *The Zincali* (2 vols.), 1841;
Lavengro, 1851; *The Romany Rye,* 1857; *Wild Wales,* 1862; *Romano
Lavo-Lil,* 1874. He *translated:* F. M. von Klinger's *Faustus,* 1825; Push-
kin's *The Talisman,* 1835; St. Luke's Gospel into Gitano dialect, *Embéo e
Majoró Lucas,* 1837; *Crixote e Majoró Lucas,* 1872; Ellis Wynn's *Sleeping
Bard* from the Cambrian-British, 1860; Nasr Al-Dín's *Turkish Jester*
(posthumous), 1884; Ewald's *Death of Balder* (posthumous), 1889. He
edited: Evangelisa San Lucusan Guissan (Basque translation of St. Luke's
Gospel), 1838.

R. Farquharson Sharp, 1897, *A Dictionary of
English Authors,* p. 29

SEE: *Works,* ed. Clement Shorter, 1923-4, 16 v. (Norwich Edition);
William I. Knapp, *Life, Writings and Correspondence of Borrow,* 1899,
2 v.; Martin Armstrong, *George Borrow,* 1950.

He must have been, I should say, full six feet four inches in height—a very well-built man, with somewhat of a military carriage; snow-white hair; dark, strongly marked eyebrows; his countenance pleasing, betokening calm firmness, self-confidence, and a mind under control, though capable of passion. His frame was without heaviness, but evidently very powerful. His hands were small for his size, beautifully formed, and very white. He was very vain of his hands, which he used to say he derived from his mother, who was of Huguenot extraction. He was, when in the vein, a delightful talker. It will give some idea of the effect of his appearance, if I recount a circumstance which occurred on his first visit at the Vicarage. My eldest son, then between ten and eleven years of age, having been introduced, stood with eyes fixed on him for some moments, and then without speaking left the apartment. He passed into the room where his mother was engaged with some ladies, and cried out, "Well, mother, that *is* a man." He could find no other words to express his admiration. The child's enthusiasm evidently delighted Borrow, who, from all I saw of him, I should judge to have been singularly alive to, and grateful for, tokens of affection. We soon came to delight in his society. He often dropped in of an evening, when he would, after tea, sit in the centre of a group before the fire with his hands on his knees—his favourite position—pouring forth tales of the scenes he had witnessed in his wanderings—sometimes among the gypsies of Spain, sometimes among those of England. Then he would suddenly spring from his seat and walk to and fro the room in silence; anon he would clap his hands and sing a Gypsy song, or perchance would chant forth a translation of some Viking poem; after which he would sit down again and chat about his father, whose memory he revered as he did his mother's; and finally he would recount some tale of suffering or sorrow with deep pathos—his voice being capable of expressing triumphant joy or the profoundest sadness.

John R. P. Berkeley, 1887, Reminiscences of Borrow in 1854,
Writings and Correspondence of George Borrow,
ed. Knapp, vol. II, p. 95

From early youth he had a passion, and an extraordinary capacity for languages, and on reaching manhood he was appointed agent to the Bible Society, and was sent to Russia to translate and introduce the Scriptures. While there he mastered the language, and learnt besides the Sclavonian and the Gypsie dialects. He translated the Testament into the Tartar Mantchow, and published versions from English into thirty languages. He made successive visits into Russia, Norway, Turkey, Bohemia, Spain and Barbary. In fact, the sole of his foot never rested. While an agent for the Bible Society in Spain, he translated the Testament into Spanish, Portuguese,

Romany, and Basque—which language, it is said, the Devil himself never could learn—and when he had learnt the Basque he acquired the name of Lavengro, or word-master. . . . He had a splendid physique, standing six-feet two in his stockings, and he had brains as well as muscles, as his works sufficiently show.

Samuel Smiles, 1891, Memoir and Correspondence of
John Murray, vol. II, pp. 484, 485

I never remember to have seen him dressed in anything but black broadcloth, and white cotton socks were generally distinctly visible above his low shoes. I think that with Borrow the desire to attract attention to himself, to inspire a feeling of awe and mystery, must have been a ruling passion. No one will ever unravel the true from the fictitious in his charming writings; it is possible that the incidents and characters connected with his extraordinary life and adventures had become so intermingled in his own mind, that he himself could hardly have unraveled them.

John Murray, 1895, Some Authors I Have Known,
Good Words, vol. 36, p. 91

The Bible in Spain (1842)

Its literary merits were considerable—but balanced by equal demerits. Nothing more vivid and picturesque than many of its descriptions of scenery and sketches of adventure: nothing more weak and confused than every attempt either at a chain of reasoning, or even a consecutive narrative of events that it included. It was evidently the work of a man of uncommon and highly interesting character and endowments; but as clearly he was quite raw as an original author. The glimpses of a most curious and novel subject that he opened were, however, so very striking, that on the whole, that book deserved well to make a powerful impression, and could not but excite great hopes that his more practised pen would hereafter produce many things of higher consequence. The present volumes will, we apprehend, go far to justify such anticipations. In point of composition, generally, Mr. Borrow has made a signal advance; but the grand point is, that he seems to have considered and studied himself in the interval; wisely resolved on steadily avoiding in future the species of efforts in which he had been felt to fail; and on sedulously cultivating and improving the peculiar talents which were as universally acknowledged to be brilliantly displayed in numerous detached passages of his *Gipsies.*

John Gibson Lockhart, 1842, "The Bible in Spain,"
Quarterly Review, vol. 71, p. 169

Having real merit and universal interest, being wholly popular in its style, and yet exceedingly curious in its information, crowded with anecdote and adventure, dialogue and incident, throwing a flood of light over Spain from a wholly new point of view, carrying us into the huts of the miserable peasants, giving us the gipsey-talk by the way-side, laying open the inner heart of the land, leading into the reality or prospect of danger every step of the way—although thousands and tens of thousands have been sold already, it has not yet taken its true place in general esteem. We have passed over the peninsula with many travellers, sometimes with great pleasure; but never so agreeably or profitably before: never with one who made us so familiar with national character, or gave us such a home-bred feeling for the people at large. Others have described the cities and works of art of this famous old land; many others have acquainted us sufficiently with the life of a single class in the cities—still, a large field remained unoccupied which Mr. Borrow has tilled with great patience and success. No one has ever trodden that ill-fated soil under more manifest advantages. To say nothing of his unwearied perseverance, his heroic daring, his calmness in peril, his presence of mind in disaster, and his love of adventure—several languages, the keys to the people's heart, were at his command.

F. W. Holland, 1843, "The Bible in Spain,"
The Christian Examiner, vol. 34, p. 170

Lavengro (1851)

He has written a book called *Lavengro,* in which he proposes to satisfy the public curiosity about himself, and to illustrate his biography as "Scholar, Gypsy, and Priest." The book, however, is not all fact; it is fact mixed liberally with fiction,—a kind of poetic rhapsody; and yet it contains many graphic pictures of real life,—life little known of, such as exists to this day among the by-lanes and on the moors of England. One thing is obvious, the book is thoroughly original, like all Mr. Borrow has written. It smells of the green lanes and breezy downs,—of the field and the tent; and his characters bear the tan of the sun and the marks of the weather upon their faces. The book is not written as a practised bookmaker would write it; it is not pruned down to suit current tastes. Borrow throws into it whatever he has picked up on the highways and by-ways, garnishing it up with his own imaginative spicery *ad libitum,* and there you have it,— "Lavengro; the Scholar, the Gypsy, the Priest!" But the work is not yet completed, seeing that he has only as yet treated us to the two former parts of the character; "The Priest" is yet to come, and then we shall see how it happened that Exeter Hall was enabled to secure the services of this gifted missionary.

Samuel Smiles, 1860, Brief Biographies, p. 158

Circumstantial as Defoe, rich in combinations as Lesage, and with such an instinct of the picturesque, both personal and local, as none of these possessed, this strange wild man holds on his strange wild way, and leads you captive to the end. His dialogue is copious and appropriate; you feel that like Ben Jonson he is dictating rather than reporting, that he is less faithful and exact than imaginative and determined; but you are none the less pleased with it, and suspicious though you be that the voice is Lavengro's and the hands are the hands of some one else, you are glad to surrender to the illusion, and you regret when it is dispelled.

William Ernest Henley, 1890, *Views and Reviews*, p. 136

GENERAL

The *Gypsies of Spain,* Mr. Borrow's former work, was a Spanish olla—a hotch-potch of the jockey tramper, philologist, and missionary. It was a thing of shreds and patches—a true book of Spain; the chapters, like her bundle of unamalgamating provinces, were just held together, and no more, by the common tie of religion, yet it was strange, and richly flavoured with genuine *borracha.* It was the first work of a diffident unexperienced man, who, mistrusting his own powers, hoped to conciliate critics by leaning on Spanish historians and gypsie poets. These corks, if such a term can be applied to the ponderous levities by which he was swamped, are now cast aside; he dashes boldly into the tide, and swims gallantly over the breakers. The Gypsies were, properly speaking, his pilot balloon. The Bible and its distribution have been *the* business of his existence; wherever moral darkness brooded, there, the Bible in his hand, he forced his way. . . . Mr. Borrow, although no tourist "in search of the picturesque," has a true perception of nature. His out-of-door existence has brought him in close contact with her, in all her changes, in all her fits of sunshine, or of storm; and well can he portray her, whatever be the expression. Always bearing in mind the solemn object of his mission, he colours like Rembrandt, and draws like Spagnoletto, rather than with the voluptuous sunniness of Claude Lorraine and Albano. His chief study is man; and therefore, as among the classics, landscape becomes an accessory.

Richard Ford, 1843, *"The Bible in Spain,"*
Edinburgh Review, vol. 77, pp. 105, 114

It was by his publication of the *Gipsies in Spain,* but more especially by the *Bible in Spain,* that Borrow won a high place in literature. The romantic interest of these two works drew the public towards the man as much as towards the writer, and he was the wonder of a few years. But in the writings which followed he went too far. *Lavengro,* which followed his first successes in 1850, and which, besides being a personal narrative, was a protest against the "kidglove" literature introduced by Bulwer and Disraeli, made him many enemies and lost him not a few friends. The book, which has been called an "epic of ale," glorified boxing, spoke up for an open-air life, and assailed the "gentility nonsense of the time." Such things were unpardonable, and Borrow, the hero of a season before, was tabooed as the high-priest of vulgar tastes. In the sequel to the book which had caused so much disfavour he chastised those who had dared to ridicule him and his work. But it was of no avail. He was passing into another age, and the critics could now afford to ignore his onslaught. *Wild Wales,* published in 1862, though a desultory work, contained much of the old vigorous stuff which characterised previous writings, but it attracted small attention, and *Romano Lavo-Lil,* when it appeared in 1872, was known only to the specially interested and the curious. Still Borrow remained unchanged. His strong individuality asserted itself in his narrowed circle. His love for the roadside, the heath, the gipsies' dingle, was as true as in other days. He was the same lover of strange books, the same passionate wanderer among strange people, the same champion of English manliness, and the same hater of genteel humbug and philistinism. Few men have put forth so many high qualities and maintained them untarnished throughout so long a career as did this striking figure of the nineteenth century.

A. Egmont Hake, 1886, *Dictionary of National Biography,*
vol. V, p. 407

Lavengro is like nothing else in either biography or fiction—and it is both fictitious and biographical. It is the gradual revelation of a strange, unique being. But the revelation does not proceed in an orderly and chronological fashion; it is not begun in the first chapter, and still less is it completed in the last. After a careful perusal of the book, you will admit that though it has fascinated and impressed you, you have quite failed to understand it. . . . *Romany Rye* is the continuation of *Lavengro,* but scarcely repeats its charm; its most remarkable feature is an "Appendix," in which Borrow expounds his views upon things in general, including critics and politics. It is a marvellous trenchant piece of writing, and from the literary point of view delightful; but it must have hurt a good many people's feelings at the time it was published, and even now shows the author on his harsh side only. We may agree with all he says, and yet wish he had uttered it in a less rasping tone.

Julian Hawthorne, 1897, *Library of the World's Best Literature,*
ed. Warner, vol. IV, pp. 2178, 2179

Capricious as was Borrows' social satire, there was in it salutary truth. The public needed to be addressed with a frankness that Thackeray was unwilling to venture upon, before it could free itself from the slough of sentiment and sham. . . . Borrow carried his readers back over the romantic revivals to the adventures of Defoe. But hanging over his books is a dreamy, poetic glamour wanting in the old picaresque novel.

Wilbur L. Cross, 1899, *The Development of the English Novel*, p. 211

SIDNEY LANIER

1842-1881

An American poet; born at Macon, Ga., Feb. 3, 1842; died at Lynn, N. C., Sept. 7, 1881. He served in the Confederate Army as a private soldier; after the war studied law, and for a while practiced it at Macon; but abandoned that profession and devoted himself to music and poetry. From 1879 till his death he was lecturer on English literature in Johns Hopkins University. The poem "Corn," one of his earliest pieces (1874), and "Clover," "The Bee," "The Dove," etc., show insight into nature. His poetic works were collected and published (1884) after his death. He wrote also several works in prose, mostly pertaining to literary criticism and to mediæval history: among the former are: *The Science of English Verse* (1880); *The English Novel and the Principles of its Development* (1883). He edited or compiled *The Boys Froissart* (1878); *The Boy's King Arthur* (1880); *The Boy's Percy* (1882).

Charles Dudley Warner, ed., 1897, *Library of the World's Best Literature, Biographical Dictionary*, vol. XXIX, p. 326

SEE: *Centennial Edition*, ed. Charles R. Anderson, 1945, 10 v.; Henry W. Lanier, *Selections from Sidney Lanier: Prose and Verse*, 1916; *Letters, 1866-1881*, ed. Henry Lanier, 1899; Edwin Mims, *Sidney Lanier*, 1905; Aubrey H. Starke, *Sidney Lanier: A Biographical and Critical Study*, 1933; Lincoln Lorenz, *Life*, 1935.

PERSONAL

For six months past, a ghastly fever has been taking possession of me every day about 12 M., and holding my head under the surface of indescribable distress for the *next twenty hours,* subsiding only enough each morning to let me get on my working-harness, but *never intermitting*. A number of tests show it to be *not* the hectic, so well known in consumption, and to this day it has baffled all the skill I could find in N. York, Philadelphia and here. I have myself been disposed to think it arose wholly from the bitterness of having to spend my time in making academic lectures and boy's books—pot-boilers—all *when a thousand songs are singing in my heart, that will certainly kill me, if I do not utter them soon.* But I don't think *this* diagnosis has found favor with my practical physicians; and meanwhile, I work day after day in such suffering as is piteous to see. I hope this does not sound like a Jeremiad. I mention these matters only in the strong rebellion against what I fear might be your thought —namely, forgetfulness of you—if you did not know the causes which keep me from sending you more frequent messages.

Sidney Lanier, 1880, *Letter to Paul Hamilton Hayne,* Nov. 19;
The Critic, No. 112

His earliest passion was for music. As a child he learned to play, almost without instruction, on every kind of instrument he could find; and while yet a boy he played the flute, organ, piano, violin, guitar, and banjo, especially devoting himself to the flute in deference to his father, who feared for him the powerful fascination of the violin. For it was the violin-voice, that above all others commanded his soul. He has related that during his college days it would sometimes so exalt him in rapture, that presently he would sink from his solitary music-worship into a deep trance, thence to awake alone, on the floor of his room, sorely shaken in nerve. In after years more than one listener remarked the strange violin effects which he conquered from the flute. His devotion to music rather alarmed than pleased his friends, and while it was here that he first discovered that he possessed decided genius, he for some time shared that early notion of his parents, that it was an unworthy pursuit, and he rather repressed his taste. He did not then know by what inheritance it had come to him, nor how worthy is the art.

William Hayes Ward, 1884, *Poems of Sidney Lanier,*
ed. his Wife, Memorial, p. 12

He gloried in antiquarian lore and antiquarian literature. Hardly "Old Monkbarns" himself could have pored over a black-letter volume with greater enthusiasm. Especially he loved the tales of chivalry, and thus, when the opportunity came, was fully equipped as an interpreter of Froissart and King Arthur for the benefit of our younger generation of students. With the great Elizabethans Lanier was equally familiar. Instead of skimming Skakspeare, he went down into his depths. Few have written so subtly of Shakspeare's mysterious sonnets. Through all Lanier's productions we trace the influence of his early literary loves; but nowhere do the pithy quaintnesses of the old bards and chroniclers display themselves more effectively —not only in the illustrations, but through the innermost warp and woof of the texture of his ideas and his style—than in some of his familiar epistles.

Paul Hamilton Hayne, 1886, *A Poet's Letters to a Friend,*
Letters of Sidney Lanier, p. 220

From childhood the others of us felt an impression of his distinction: this may be a reflection from a light now shining, but I do not think so. It was a distinct feeling that here was not only an elder but an original personality. . . . His imperishable work is done in seven years. He *planned* enough, in addition to that which he wrought, to require seventeen or twenty-seven. As she still lives, it may not be delicate to more than speak of her, who from the troth-plight of 1867 has been a perfect help-meet, and who since the dark September day of 1881, when he died, has kept alight the sacred flame upon the hearth-stone of his memory: four sons have been nurtured and educated in the best tradition of his teaching and of his name,—a fourfold chaplet worthy of any woman's wearing.

Clifford Lanier, 1895, "Reminiscences of Sidney Lanier,"
The Chautauquan, vol. 21, pp. 403, 409

Lanier fought a battle with death (technically, consumption) to which Keats's classic consumption was child's play. It is so easy to fight anything, even consumption, if you have nothing else to do; but if you have a home to keep going as well, and only a pen to keep it going with—well, you look upon John Keats as one of the sybarites of immortality. Fortunately, Lanier had a flute, too, and thereby hangs much of his history, as well as the explanation of his temperament and gift.

Richard LeGallienne, 1900, "Sidney Lanier,"
The Academy, vol. 58, p. 147

GENERAL

[*Tiger Lillies*] is a spirited story of Southern life beginning just before the war, and closing with the war. The earlier scenes are among the mountains of Tennessee; later shifting with the Southern army to Virginia; and having an echo or two of European adventure. The author disclaims making the bloody sensational his style; and yet we have a little murder and some pretty melodramatic touches. . . . The story is entertaining, and the style lively. The latter is paragraphical and exclamationary; and in a remote way—in its mingling pedantry and raillery, grotesquely together sometimes—it reminds the reader, remotely and just a little, of the *Sketch-Book of Meister Karl.* Italian, French and German words and phrases abound throughout the work.

James Wood Davidson, 1869, *Living Writers of the South,* p. 321

Perhaps the most remarkable feature of his gifts was their complete symmetry. It is hard to tell what register of perception, or sensibility or wit, or will was lacking. The constructive and the critical faculties, the imaginative and the practical, balanced each other. His wit and humour played upon the soberer background of his more recognized qualities. . . . But how short was his span, and how slender his opportunity! From the time he was of age he waged a constant, courageous, hopeless fight against adverse circumstance for room to live and write. Much very dear, and sweet, and most sympathetic helpfulness he met in the city of his adoption, and from friends elsewhere, but he could not command the time and leisure which might have lengthened his life and given him opportunity to write the music and the verse with which his soul was teeming. Yet short as was his literary life, and hindered though it were, its fruits will fill a large space in the garnering of the poetic art of our country.

> William Hayes Ward, 1884, *Poems of Sidney Lanier,*
> ed. his Wife, Memorial, pp. xi, xli

To an age assailed by the dangerous doctrines of the fleshy school in poetry, and by that unhealthy "æstheticism" and that debauching "realism" which see in vice and uncleanness only new fields for the artist's powers of description, and no call for the artist's divine powers of denunciation—to save young men into whose ears is dinned the maxim, "art for art's sake only," "a moral purpose ruins art," Lanier came, noble-souled as Milton in youthful consciousness of power, yet humble before the august conception of a moral purity higher than he could hope to utter or attain, discerning with the true poet's insight the "beauty of holiness" and the "holiness of beauty." Had he lived and died in England, how he would have been embalmed in living odes, his sepulchre how perpetually draped with insignia of national appreciation! He is *ours*. He was an American to the centre of his great, loving heart. Shall we cherish his memory any the less lovingly because his works are the first-fruits of a reunited people— the richest contribution to our national fame in letters yet made by our brothers of the South?

> Merrill Edwards Gates, 1887, "Sidney Lanier,"
> *Presbyterian Review,* vol. 8, p. 701

Lanier's death was a loss to American literature, relatively almost equal to that which England sustained in the death of Keats. With a matchless gift of cadence, intensest humanity and sincerity, rich creative imagination, and intellectual powers of the highest order, he was advancing, I believe, to the chief place in American song, when death stayed him. As it is, he will always be among poets a stimulating force.

> Charles G. D. Roberts, 1888, ed. *Poems of Wild Life,* p. 233, Note

His were a larger mind and a stronger hand than Timrod's or even Hayne's, yet his was a fatal fault: he lacked that spontaneity which is the chief pleasure in the verse of Hayne and Timrod. In the midst of the products of a genius that certainly at times seemed large, and that was bold to the extent of eccentricity, are the too-conspicuous signs of mere intellectual experiment and metrical or verbal extravaganza. Lanier theorizes in verse; the practice-hand seeks to strike chords that can only come from the impassioned and self-forgetful singer of nature and the soul. His analytical and exhaustive musical studies—applied to literature in *The Science of English Verse*—greatly harmed his creative work.

Charles F. Richardson, 1888, *American Literature,*
1607-1885, vol. II, p. 232

What are really the characteristics of this amazing and unparalleled poetry of Lanier? Reading it again, and with every possible inclination to be pleased, I find a painful effort, a strain and rage, the most prominent qualities in everything he wrote. Never simple, never easy, never in one single lyric natural and spontaneous for more than one stanza, always forcing the note, always concealing his barrenness and tameness by grotesque violence of image and preposterous storm of sound, Lanier appears to me to be as conclusively not a poet of genius as any ambitious man who ever lived, labored, and failed.

Edmund Gosse, 1888, "Has America Produced a Poet?"
The Forum, vol. 6, p. 180

Lanier was indubitably a lyrical poet of quite exceptional faculty, though affectation and strained effect spoilt much of his verse; but here we have to do with him simply as a sonneteer. Why he wrote sonnets at all is a mystery, for he had no inevitable bias that way; on the contrary, his mannerisms became more and more obvious and distracting. Yet his sonnets have many admirers, and undoubtedly even when most obviously "manipulated" have still a certain quality of saving grace. For this reason I have represented him by several examples, though personally I admit that their lack of rhythmic strength is a vital drawback to enjoyment. "The Harlequin Dreams," the series entitled "In Absence," and the two comprised in "Acknowledgment," are his best; in the latter there is an exuberance, an exaggeration of address which is strongly suggestive of the diction of the lesser Elizabethans. "Laus Mariae" is accepted by many as his best sonnet. Yet, interesting as it is in some respects, one cannot but wonder at the critical blindness of those who called Lanier the American Keats.

William Sharp, 1889, ed., *American Sonnets,* Introductory Note

Sidney Lanier, in nervous crises, would seem to hear rich music. It was an inherited gift. Thus equipped with rhythmical sense beyond that of other poets, he turned to poetry as to the supreme art. Now, the finer and more complex the gift, the longer exercise is needful for its full mastery. He strove to make poetry do what painting has done better, and to make it do what only music hitherto has done. If he could have lived three lives, he would have adjusted the relations of these arts as far as possible to his one satisfaction. I regard his work, striking as it is, as merely tentative from his own point of view. It was as if a discoverer should sail far enough to meet the floating rockweed, the strayed birds, the changed skies, that betoken land ahead; should even catch a breath of fragrance wafted from outlying isles, and then find his bark sinking in the waves before he could have sight of the promised continent.

> Edmund Clarence Stedman, 1892, "The Nature and Elements
> of Poetry," *Century Magazine,* vol. 44, p. 865

A poet of rare promise, whose original genius was somewhat hampered by his hesitation between two arts of expression, music and verse, and by his effort to co-ördinate them. His *Science of English Verse,* 1880, was a most suggestive, though hardly convincing, statement of that theory of their relation which he was working out in his practice. Some of his pieces, like "The Mocking Bird" and the "Song of the Chattahoochee," are the most characteristically southern poetry that has been written in America.

> Henry A. Beers, 1895, *Initial Studies in American Letters,* p. 212

Lanier's theory of verse is in accord with Poe's. Beauty and music are poetry's all in all.
"Music is Love in search of a word,"
and lyricism is hardly more articulate. But Lanier longed for the completest intellectual equipment for his work. Poe, he said, "did not know enough." The Baltimore flute-player was a born musician, walking in an enveloping cloud of harmonies, having only to turn aside from the noises of the world and listen to become aware of an unceasing "holy song." He purposed the creation of great symphonies written in a new musical notation as eagerly as he planned for the creation of great poems framed in accordance with new laws of verse. What with his intricate endeavor to bring his two arts into close technical relation, and his thirst to compass all knowledge and acquire all skill, he put away the day of actual performance even farther than the struggle for bread had already thrust it. The most liberal span of life would have been too short for Sidney Lanier, and the life that he wrested from disease and death was but a splendid

fragment. Yet his poems as they stand, in their swift surprises of beauty, their secrets of sweet sound, their "Faith that smiles immortally," rank close upon the best achievements of American song.

Katharine Lee Bates, 1897, *American Literature*, p. 189

Is second only to Poe among Southern poets. His versification sometimes falls into excessive intricacy and mere caprice, and his thought occasionally fades away into inarticulate dreamery. But these errors are only the defects of his virtues. A man of the finest sensitiveness without effeminacy, and a skilled musician, he has produced dreamy, floating, mist-like, musical effects that are new in English verse; and his feeling for nature, especially for wood and marsh life as seen in parts of the South, is thoroughly modern in its union of exact observation with imaginative subtlety. Lanier had also a keen intellect, as appears from his original and suggestive books on versification and the novel. Had he lived to develop his gifts fully, he might have come to be numbered with the foremost American poets; as it is he stands only a little lower and in a secure place of his own.

Walter C. Bronson, 1900, *A Short History of American Literature*, p. 287